PATHWORK FOR POWER

HIS THEN IS *your quest." He stands and looks hard at you. "You must travel to the Otherworld and retrieve for yourself an amulet of your personal power. In doing this, you will face many choices, and you will be asked to overcome many of your deepest anxieties and fears. This amulet will forevermore be yours and will aid you in time of need. It is a powerful amulet and a powerful quest—one which few can complete."*

You tell him you wish to go anyway.

Merlin studies you carefully for a moment. "Very well. To begin your journey, you must start where all those who leave this life start…."

from "Chapter Twelve—A Lesson from Merlin"

PATHWORKING IS ONE of the most potent tools we have for aligning ourselves with the energies of deities and mythic figures. This magickal practice will allow you to stretch your personal power to the limit as it stimulates your deep mind and forges a link between the conscious and sub-conscious. The pathworking process—also known as astral travel or vision questing—has benefits beyond the performance of magick and ritual, reaching far beyond the working itself into the everyday life of the journeyer to fuel personal transformation.

Human and divine energies complement each other; when joined, they become a potent catalyst for magick and change. *Celtic Myth & Magick* shows you how forming a working partnership with the archetypal energies of the Celtic pantheon can aid you in achieving your goals. These energies represent universal powers which exist in the deepest part of you, laying in wait for you to discover them anew so they can shine through the darkness and light your path. Through the pathworking journeys and the many exercises provided in this well-researched book, Pagans seeking to expand the boundaries of their practice have a one-of-a-kind guide to evoking the Celtic deities and mythic powers to supercharge every ritual and magickal working.

ABOUT THE AUTHOR

EDAIN McCOY WAS born to parents from diverse backgrounds who always encouraged her to explore the history of religious thought and to draw her own conclusions from those studies. As a teenager she began seeking the roots of her birth religion. Eventually that search, and her increasing feminist outlook, brought her back to the Old Religion. A chance meeting with a hereditary witch at a *ceilidh* (Irish Dance) in Houston led her to study the Irish tradition of the craft. She has been part of several covens and is always anxious to meet and work with like-minded persons. Edain was born August 11, 1957, a Leo with Pisces rising. She numbers among her colorful ancestors Sir Roger Williams, the 17th century religious dissenter who laid down the principles of separation of church and state which govern the United States, and the infamous feuding McCoy family of Kentucky. A graduate of The University of Texas, she now lives in the Midwest where she is continuing her formal graduate studies in Cultural History. She is a member of the Indiana Historical Society, the Authors Guild, the Wiccan/Pagan Press Alliance, and is active in her local Irish Arts Association.

TO WRITE TO THE AUTHOR

If you wish to contact the author, please write to her in care of Llewellyn Worldwide, and we will forward your request. Both the author and the publisher appreciate hearing from you and learning of your enjoyment of this book and how it has helped you. Llewellyn Worldwide cannot guarantee that every letter written to the author can be answered, but all will be forwarded. Please write to:

Edain McCoy
c/o Llewellyn Worldwide
P.O. Box 64383, Dept. K661-0, St. Paul, MN 55164-0383, U.S.A.

Please enclose a self-addressed, stamped envelope or $1.00 to cover costs.
If outside the U.S.A., enclose international postal reply coupon.

LLEWELLYN'S WORLD RELIGION AND MAGIC SERIES

CELTIC MYTH & MAGICK

*Harness the Power
of the
Gods and Goddesses*

 EDAIN McCOY

2000
Llewellyn Publications
St. Paul, Minnesota 55164-0383, U.S.A.

FIRST EDITION, 1995
Eighth printing, 2000

Cover design by Tom Grewe
Cover painting by Lisa Hunt
Book design and layout by Susan Van Sant

Library of Congress Cataloging-in-Publication Data
McCoy, Edain, 1957–
    Celtic myth & magick : harness the power of the gods and goddesses
  / Edain McCoy. — 1st ed.
    p.   cm. — (Llewellyn's world religion and magic series.)
    Includes bibliographical references and index.
    ISBN 1-56718-661-0
    1. Magic, Celtic. 2. Mythology, Celtic. 3. Gods, Celtic.
  I. Title. II. Title: Celtic myth and magick.   III. Series:
Llewellyn's world religion & magic series.
BF1622.C2M33 1995
299'.16—dc20   95-1369
                                                        CIP

Llewellyn Publications
A Division of Llewellyn Worldwide, Ltd.
P.O. 64383, St. Paul, MN 55164-0383
www.llewellyn.com

Printed in United States of America

LLEWELLYN'S WORLD RELIGION AND MAGIC SERIES

AT THE CORE of every religion, at the foundation of every culture, there is Magick.

Magick sees the world as alive, as the home which humanity shares with beings and powers both visible and invisible with whom and which we can interface to either our advantage or disadvantage—depending upon our awareness and intention.

Religious worship and communion is one kind of magick, and just as there are many religions in the world, so are there many magickal systems. Religion, and magick, are ways of seeing and relating to the creative powers, the living energies, the all-pervading spirit, the underlying intelligence that is the universe within which we and all else exist.

Neither religion nor magick conflict with science. All share the same goals and the same limitations: always seeking truth, forever haunted by human limitations in perceiving that truth. Magick is "technology" based upon experience and extrasensory insight, providing its practitioners with methods of greater influence and control over the world of the invisible before it impinges on the world of the visible.

The study of world magick not only enhances your understanding of the world in which you live, and hence your ability to live better, but brings you into touch with the inner essence of your long evolutionary heritage and most particularly—as in the case of the magickal system identified most closely with your genetic inheritance—with the archetypal images and forces most alive in your whole consciousness.

OTHER BOOKS BY EDAIN McCOY

DEDICATION

The harp that once through Tara's halls
The soul of music shed,
Now hangs as mute on Tara's walls
As if that soul were fled.
So sleeps the pride of former days,
So glory's thrill is o'er,
And hearts that once beat high with praise,
Now feel that pulse no more.

No more to chiefs and ladies bright
The harp of Tara swells;
The chord alone that breaks at night,
Its tale of ruin tells.
Thus Freedom now so seldom wakes,
The only throb she gives
Is when some heart indignant breaks,
To show that still she lives.

—Thomas Moore

THIS BOOK IS lovingly dedicated to all Pagans on the many Celtic paths who are determined that the ancient magick, lore, and majesty of Tara shall not be forgotten. May the mystic music of her golden harp play sweetly within your soul forever. And…

…for Granny McCoy

May your adventures in *Tir-na-nOg* be joyous and deeply fulfilling,
but not so grand that you tarry over-long in returning
to those of us left behind
who love and miss you so very much.

CONTENTS

Part I: Understanding the Celts and Their Pantheon

Part II: Practical Ritual and the Celtic Pantheon

Part III: The Power of Pathworking

Part IV: Gods and Goddesses, Heroes and Heroines

Part V: References and Resources

ACKNOWLEDGEMENTS

THANKS AS ALWAYS to Mark, my partner and proofreader, who always turns down the television when I need to work. Likewise to Avigail who, though her views of Celtic life and religion occasionally differ from mine, nonetheless provides knowledgeable and stimulating insights for me to ponder. I thank her, too, for keeping me balanced and helping me maintain my much-needed sense of humor.

A special thank you to Niamh for helping me sort through the confusing maze of Gaelic regional dialects and variant spellings. Also to Ben for the crash course in Welsh, especially when I proved to be a less than gifted student.

To Vanessa, a fellow seeker, goes a big thank you for not only being supportive, but for actually comprehending what it is that I try to impart when I take on the monumental task of writing about spiritual matters.

A special heart-felt thanks to Molly, my teacher and friend now in spirit; and to Sandra and Dr. Morgan for their unique guidance; and, of course, to Oghma, Celtic God of writing and communication for his magickal support and inspiration.

And finally, thanks to Anne Marie Garrison, Tom Grewe, Nancy Mostad, Susan Van Sant, and all the other hardworking people at Llewellyn for turning my simple word-processor pages into works of art.

A decorative letter from The Book of Kells, *probably the world's most famous illuminated manuscript. This ninth-century monastic writing of the Christian Gospels is on display at Trinity University, Dublin.*

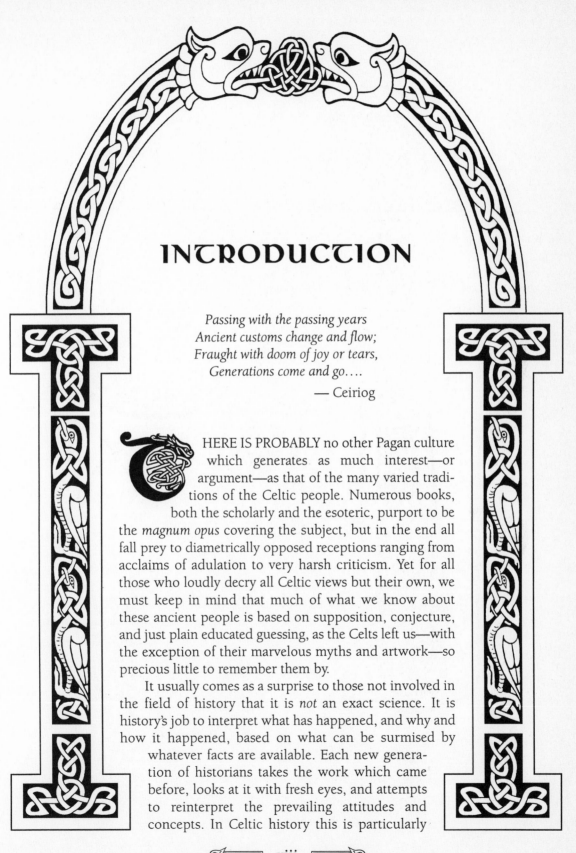

INTRODUCTION

Passing with the passing years
Ancient customs change and flow;
Fraught with doom of joy or tears,
Generations come and go....
— Ceiriog

HERE IS PROBABLY no other Pagan culture which generates as much interest—or argument—as that of the many varied traditions of the Celtic people. Numerous books, both the scholarly and the esoteric, purport to be the *magnum opus* covering the subject, but in the end all fall prey to diametrically opposed receptions ranging from acclaims of adulation to very harsh criticism. Yet for all those who loudly decry all Celtic views but their own, we must keep in mind that much of what we know about these ancient people is based on supposition, conjecture, and just plain educated guessing, as the Celts left us—with the exception of their marvelous myths and artwork—so precious little to remember them by.

It usually comes as a surprise to those not involved in the field of history that it is *not* an exact science. It is history's job to interpret what has happened, and why and how it happened, based on what can be surmised by whatever facts are available. Each new generation of historians takes the work which came before, looks at it with fresh eyes, and attempts to reinterpret the prevailing attitudes and concepts. In Celtic history this is particularly true, and is most clearly evidenced in the disagreement between scholars on exactly when the leading fringe of the Celtic invasion reached Britain. The most generally accepted date is around 800 B.C.E., though a new revisionist school of thought believes the Celts began arriving as early as 1500–1200 B.C.E., and a more conservative viewpoint says they did not show up until around 600–500 B.C.E. (The revisionist date is based on, among other things, the earlier arrival of the Milesians [also known as the Gaels], a cousin-race of the Celts, who were previously living in Spain.)

It also used to be widely believed that the Celts came mostly in one large group and essentially "conquered" their island home in one blow, but now archaeological and anthropological evidence shows us that the Celts most likely came over in small waves, one after the other, hitting the shores of Britain and Ireland over a period of several hundred years. In other words, Celtic culture slowly inundated the island, and in that way conquered the land just as surely as did those warriors and warrioresses who drew their swords in combat.

While I was an undergraduate at The University of Texas, I knew a young woman who had trouble understanding these subtle distinctions in historical interpretation. She would often complain bitterly about a book "lying" to her, she raged about how much she hated to be "lied to" and questioned how was she supposed to know what was "true" and what was not. All this angst was due to the fact that not all historians wrote about the Celts from her own narrow point of view, and she failed to see that, in some way, all the viewpoints were "true."

Rest assured that no historian who values his or her credibility or future career deliberately sets out to lie about anything, but the conclusions they each draw from the same sources can vary greatly. The best way to assess history—or anything else for that matter—is to read all you can get your hands on, and include in that study many points of view, and then decide for yourself, based on knowledge, what you believe to be right.

Among the hard facts that we do know about the Celts is that they lived in a highly organized society, but one which allowed for some latitude in the interpretation of regional law. They held in high esteem their Brehon judges and laws.

We know they were a large and fearless people who valued a good fight, their warrior class was the most privileged caste in their culture, and both males and females were trained as warriors. It was from the warrior class that they chose their leaders, and many women also became rulers, though no known High King was ever female. Rulers were selected for their skills in battle as much as for their sense of fairness and good judgment.

The Celts also made war on each other, and these disagreements and separations, exacerbated by differences in language, regional dialect, individual clan customs, and variations in local oral traditions, created for us numerous versions of what we erroneously call *"The* Celtic Pagan Tradition." The petty wars which arose from these differences created divisions in their society which helped open the door to the invasions from the Vikings and the Church.

The Celts were excellent and gifted artisans, particularly in metalcraft, and they lived in clans (extended families) based on blood ties to a clan matriarch, though they took their family names from a clan patriarch.

From the second century B.C.E. to the second century C.E. the Celts had a highly stratified priestly class, known as the Druids, which was male-dominated. They valued knowledge and education and were well-represented in the prestigious schools of Europe even into the eighteenth century.

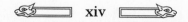

We know that the Celtic religion, like those of other Pagan peoples, was a nature or earth religion with the holy days calculated by the change of seasons and the phases of the moon. The central feature of this spirituality was a sovereign Goddess, a symbol of the bountiful mother earth from which all other life flowed. Her consort was a God who had to be sacrificed every so many years in order that his blood would spill on the earth, fertilizing it so that life could continue. He would then be reborn to this Goddess as her son, and the cycle would begin again.

The Celts loved to play rough games which highlighted and honed their physical prowess, and their children were initiated into these at an early age. Celtic children were most often raised by foster parents, usually maternal aunts and uncles, who trained the children in the special skills they would need as adults depending upon their rank in society. Around the time of puberty they were returned to their parents' homes and ritually recognized as "adults" of the clan or community. Children destined to become warriors were sent off for further training at special battle schools. An ancient belief about the transfer of power by gender made sure that boy warriors were taught by women, and girl warriors by men.

While we believe the Celts had their tribal origins in the Caucasus or the upper Middle East, we do know they heavily settled and dominated the southern Germanic regions and Gaul as early as 1800 B.C.E., from whence they waged war on neighboring countries. We also know where they ultimately settled. They populated and ruled the modern day regions we know as England (the place where they arrived first), Ireland, Scotland, Cornwall, Brittany, the Isle of Man, and Wales (the place where it is believed they arrived last). Though England, under the influence of the Romans and the Saxons, later developed its own semi-separate Pagan tradition popularly called Wicca, the other Celtic lands fought, and in most cases succeeded, against the tide to retain more of their own ethnic identities. The Celtic languages, cultures, political ideology, and most importantly, the attitudes, religion, and cosmology of these invaders are still inherently a part of the modern expression of the lives of their Celtic progeny who live there still.

The Celts also left us their surnames, names which densely populate not only the old Celtic countries, but are found in copious numbers in the lands to which these people have migrated for centuries. The oldest of the Milesian-Celtic names are the ones we usually think of today as being inherently Scottish or Irish. These are the names preceded by the patronymics *Mc* or *Mac* (pronounced "mawk"), meaning "son of," or *O'*, meaning "from," also denoting the name of the father's clan. (The modern Irish word for son is *mhac* and is pronounced "wok.") An older variation of these family names was *Ni* (Nee), meaning "daughter of" (in modern Irish the word is *inion,* and *ni* has other meanings), but this designation did not survive in common usage very long into the Druidic period. For example, my own name, McCoy, means "son of Coy," but NiCoy would have meant "daughter of Coy." The Welsh appellation for "son of" is *Ap,* and is used in the names of many of the Welsh Gods. Some of the world's oldest cultures still use patronymics as part of their names; of particular note are the Russian, Icelandic, and Jewish cultures.

Most important to this study of the Celtic people, especially to us Pagans, is the fact that they left us their rich body of mythology. *Celtic Myth & Magic* is not really about Celtic history, but rather Celtic mythology and the deities and heroic figures which populate it. However, the mythology of any people is altered, affected, and influenced by history's impact on its culture, and, in turn, it can be a valuable study tool for decoding the long hidden past.

J. Kent Calder, managing editor of *Traces,* the official publication of the Indiana Historical

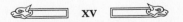

Viking figure carved into a Celtic Cross in the tenth century. The Norse began invading large parts of Britain and Ireland in the 900s, and had a profound influence on the Pagan cultures of these countries.

Society, writes, "the two [myth and history] are so thoroughly intermingled that only the most skeptical and diligent can keep them separated for long." Fortunately, we Pagans need not separate them—we just need to understand them enough to use them.

Myths are defined as a body of lore about any land or people which makes up their mythology and cosmology. These are deeply linked to a people's religious and spiritual viewpoints. Contrary to popular usage, the word "myth" does not mean something which is false or from an unsound source. Dictionaries often define a myth first as a theme, motif, or traditional story. Nor is a myth something which is written in eternal stone, static and unyielding. People who have studied myths in depth, such as the world-renowned mythologist Joseph Campbell, even came to view them as living things in and of themselves. Many of the Celtic myths tell true stories about real people, a good number of others impart made-up stories about fictional characters, and most of them are a happy mixture falling somewhere in between.

When these myths as we know them today—and there are actually many versions of each to be found—were committed to paper for the first time, mostly by Christian monks (from 600–900 C.E.), Britain and Ireland had already undergone profound internal changes due to the cultures by whom they had been conquered and with whom they had inter-related. These people included Danes/Vikings, Pagan Romans, Christian clerics, Normans, and Saxons. In the future there would be others, all of them leaving their indelible stamp on the culture of the Celts. Depending on where in the Celtic kingdom one lived, the impact of these invaders would be very different, and, as a result, the Celts were not as much of a united people as many modern Pagans like to believe. For example, Celtic England was heavily influenced by Rome, while Ireland felt Roman presence only peripherally. In turn, Ireland was most profoundly influenced by the Norse, a culture which made much less of a mark on Celtic England.

While it is possible to assume alterations might have been made in the content of the old oral myths by those who transcribed them, especially those with a vested interest in changing the religious world-view of the Celts, they were probably written down very much as they were heard *at the time of the writing,* which means they had already endured several hundred years of slow erosion and alteration with each telling. The major changes we most surely know of that were made were within the divine family trees, particularly in making Goddesses the subordinate daughters of Gods, and in outcomes being influenced by the Judeo-Christian God rather than by the local deities.

Though the monks probably left the essence intact, if not the details, of the folktales they collected, this does not mean that any one single form of the myth existed even back then. The monks could only transcribe the particular version they were told, no matter how many others which were more like the older Pagan versions might have been floating around the islands.

These oral traditions, such as the Celts lived with for many generations, were not only very ancient, but also very malleable occurrences, subject to great flexibility, and would change and bend with the growth or stagnation of the culture of which they were a part. Sir John Rhys, a mythologist writing at the turn of the century, said, "A mythology must always be far older than the oldest verses and stories that celebrate it."

A Celtic design from The Book of Durrow, *an eleventh-century monastic work.*

For example, we can see in the myths and remaining fragments of knowledge we have about the Celts, that human and animal sacrifice was undoubtedly a part of the culture's religious ethos. As modern Pagans we read these passages, understand the reasons behind them, and find constructive new ways to adopt them into our practices. None of us would want to see blood sacrifice revived. We have moved past this, and, if we were still relying on oral tradition, our myths would reflect this change. On the other hand, we also see how the deities are presented as being very human, and, therefore, we are taught that the people had—and still should have— a very personal relationship with them.

Mythology, much more so than straight academic history, preserves for us the attitudes, religious practices, and cosmology of the Celts. Those of us who wish to reconstruct as much of the Old Religion as possible often read through these myths with a critical eye, ever in search of clues and insights into a world long gone. Through mythology we can learn a lot about the way they looked at the world, how they believed life began, how they viewed the roles of the sexes, who was in charge of child-rearing, who constituted a privileged class, and who the deities were and how the people related with them. By understanding which deities were important to the Celts, we can learn what aspects of life were most important to them. For example, we see the prominence and high status of cattle deities and we know that the health and safety of livestock was highly valued by this predominately herding culture. Through these myths we can also find clues toward practical ways of harnessing the energy of the deities for our own needs. We can call them to our circle-side and ask their guidance, and we can bring their energy into our own being and direct it outward at will. We also see that we can go on lavish inner-journeys, called pathworkings, to gain further insights into our spiritual lives and to forge more intimate relationships with the colorful characters who populate them.

As is true with the study of history, one should never accept wholesale anyone else's view of mythology. If you do, you cheat yourself out of a mind-expanding experience, one which will directly impact upon your spiritual development. Read mythological accounts from several viewpoints. This will not only broaden your scope of general Celtic knowledge, but help you to get a feel for the stories and the way they have been perceived for thousands of years. These perceptions are part of the great "collective unconscious" and the better we understand them, the better we can work with them. The writings of mythologist Joseph Campbell will provide a broad context for you and a rich spectrum of comparative mythology. Padriac Colum is a Celtic traditionalist, relying heavily on both the monastic writings and on the few remaining oral traditions. Jean Markale is a studious revisionist, and Myles Dillon is a noted scholar in Celtic literature who manages to brilliantly merge the traditional with the esoteric. These are good places to start your personal venture into the world of Celtic myth. Check the Bibliography for more ideas, or go to your local library (university libraries are especially helpful) for more information.

All these interpretations are based on the old writings of the Celts, and upon the aforementioned oral sources, taken down by traveling mythographers over the past hundred years. Parts of these myths are truly ancient, with perhaps the oldest threadbare strings within them reaching as far back as 4000 B.C.E. when the Celts were still an unformed tribe living near the Caucasus. However, it was not until the first known collection of some of these old stories was compiled in Ireland in a seventh-century manuscript known as *The Book of the Dun Cow*, also sometimes called *The Cattle Raid of Cooley* (*Tain Bo Cuailagne*), that any of them were committed to writing.

Another important Irish manuscript is *The Irish Book of Invasions* (*Lebor Gabala Erenn*), which contains the five-fold invasion myth cycle. Also of note are *The Book of Ballymote*, *The Book of Lecan*, *The Book of Lismore*, *Leabhor Laigneach* (*The Book of Leinster*), *Acallamh na Senorach* (*The Colloquy of the Ancients* which contains the Fennian Cycle of myths), and *The Cattle Drive of Fraich* (also known as the *Tain Bo Fraich*, which contains one of the few written references to Cernunnos, the Horned God), all of which date from about the twelfth century.

Charles Squire, an early twentieth-century mythologist, feels the Welsh stories suffered more alterations "from the sophistications of the euhemerist [sic]" than did the better-preserved Irish ones. In Wales the writing down of the ancient myths came much later, between the twelfth and sixteenth centuries, and are not so well fleshed-out. The earliest of these was *The Black Book of Caermarthen*. Among the most important of the others are *The Book of Aneurin*, *The Book of Taliesin* (a collection of poetic works associated with the famous bard), *The Red Book of Hergest*, and *The Book of Barddas*, a Druidic tract. The *Red Book* was the last of these to be compiled, and is probably the most beautiful, poetically speaking. It contains the famous poetic *Welsh Triads* and also the famous and romantic *Mabinogion* stories, including the medieval version of what many believe are references to the King Arthur legends. The greatest and oldest body of stories about King Arthur come from the *Annales Cambriae* (*The Annals of Wales*), a Latin text dating to the tenth century.

Another collection of antiquarian manuscripts which elaborate on the Irish myths is housed in the Advocate's Library at Edinburgh, Scotland, and a similar collection of works known as the *Dinnshenchas*, a set of very old recorded legends based on famous places, is housed in Dublin, Ireland.

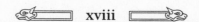

Many dozens of other smaller books and collections complete the cherished body of extant Celtic myths, many of which are available in reprints through specialty publishers in London, Dublin, or Edinburgh.

Unlike written traditions, no culture's oral traditions have ever been committed to paper as a whole and, sadly, many have been lost and forgotten. Other parts of them have fortunately been snatched up by diligent scholars and placed on paper but, like a photograph, they can only catch a fleeting glimpse of a single moment in an ever-evolving, ever-changing life. It is from these rich oral sources that many variations in the modern incarnations of myths and folktales arise, all of them valid in their own right, and all of them claiming to be able to trace their roots to much older sources. Most of the folktales from Cornwall and Brittany which have survived until today were collected from oral sources in the 1880s when an interest in regional Celtic mythology peaked. For example, the Breton stories of Marie de France and Villemarque preserve much for us today which might otherwise be lost.

It is important to remember several different versions of some of the myths survive, and haggling over which is truest or more true, or which is older, younger, purer, adulterated, etc., wastes our time and devalues the inherent power of the myth. The Irish historian Seamas MacManus said, "The evidential points taken from tales are not set down as facts—but as probable or possible echoes of facts." It is these echoes which reverberate within us still, and the power and energy they generate is what makes them work for us as potently today as two thousand years ago.

Carl Jung, the psychologist who first dealt with the deeper meanings of myths, saw, as did Campbell, many universal themes—or archetypes—in world mythology. He suggested that myths were based on human dreams and fantasies which expressed in concrete terms our unconscious thought processes, and from there became powerful tools for profound inner change and growth.

How is that possible? This pantheon of mythic images spans the vast continuum of all human desires and fears, and through them we can vicariously live out our wildest fantasies, create our greatest dreams, or be allowed to fail at any effort in a safe setting in which we can eventually work out a victory. Our deities and heroic figures are vibrant and real, living archetypes which are imprinted on our brains, images made real through our thought projections and imaginations. Famed occultist William G. Gray in his self-proclaimed "swan song" book, *Evoking the Primal Goddess,* explains it best when he says:

> *"By mentally making such images and handing them down to their children…they [early Pagan people] were focusing actual forces of nature into convenient forms of consciousness that could provide future power."*

Celtic Myth & Magic attempts to teach how to harness these "convenient forms of consciousness" in workable, usable, highly powerful ways by constructing rituals around the Celtic Goddesses and Gods, heroes and heroines who populate our mythic stories. They are a part of each of us and, with practice, we can draw these consciousnesses into ourselves where they can shine forth, becoming a beacon which lights our way. These are very potent archetypes with

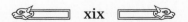

which we can align ourselves or which we can call upon to aid us when we need their special powers.

This feat is accomplished through the use of rituals designed to help us merge our energy and essence of being with that of the Celtic deities and heroic figures. The Celtic deities are some of the easiest to access in our inner worlds because, unlike many other cultures, the Celts did not view their deities as being supreme beings, or even as being separate from each other or from humanity. This is made clear in the way the Celtic myths are written, and points out clearly that pantheism (many deities all in one entity) was the ruling force of Celtic religious life rather than polytheism (many separate deities).

The mental baggage we have brought to Paganism from the teachings of our mainstream religions has, sadly, clouded much of our judgment when it comes to how we view our Pagan ancestors and their deities. Some Pagans—and some scholars—try to refute the idea that the Celts had anthropomorphic deities by claiming this was merely a ploy of the clerics who transcribed the myths to devalue the power of the Celtic pantheon. While this may be true in some small way, on the whole it is an idea rooted in the sanctimonious smugness of our modern culture which always feels—often wrongly so—that ancient peoples were no more than sniveling dishrags when confronted with the power of raw nature from which the power of most of the deities arose.

Trust that the large-bodied, war-like Celts did not fall to their knees trembling in fear and prostrating themselves in supplication every time a whirlwind blew across their islands or lightning flashed brightly in the night sky. Their powers of observation told them from whence these natural phenomena came. For instance, they knew that the dry winds came from the directions of large land masses and brought them sunshine, and they knew the wet winds came from over the western sea and brought rain, and they understood that when the cool winds and the warm came together that the sky was likely to turn violent. But they didn't fear this as some arbitrary display of a displeased deity, but as the natural power which comes from two halves of a whole joined. Unlike modern humans, if cyclonic winds occasionally destroyed their meager homes, there was no cause for bitter tears. What little was destroyed could be easily replaced, and was quickly done with the help of the clan—not with insurance companies! There was little sense of wanting to control nature through religious means, other than the basic needs of water and sun to ensure the successful harvest, and these were addressed during the solar festivals or Sabbats. When the rain or warmth did fail them, it simply proved out their belief that the deities, like their human children, were neither omnipotent nor perfect.

In other words, the deities and mythic figures were powerful in the sense that they could, usually, produce phenomena which most humans could not (though today we know we all have the power to do these things, even though that power may go unrealized or be slow in revealing itself), but they were not the infallible gods conceived of by the later patriarchal religions. They were heroes and heroines because of their bravery and daring accomplishments, not necessarily by virtue of their divinity. They were eternal, but not ageless. As the seasons turned and all things died and were reborn, so it was the same with the deities. They were powerful because they, as nature personified, represented both the macrocosm and microcosm of existence just as humans did. But humans, as a macrocosm, watched these cycles come and go many times in their lives, but, as microcosms, would grow old and die and the cycle would continue on.

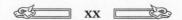

Celtic deities did not come in well-ordered hierarchies as so many other pantheons conveniently did, and this remained true even with regional deities. We can, however, loosely order them into one of seven categories, denoted by their functions or spheres of influence:

◆ Otherworld Deities

◆ Stellar or Planetary Deities

◆ Creative or Destructive Deities

◆ Nature and Earth Deities

◆ Warriors and Warrioresses

◆ Kings and Queens

◆ Human Mythic Heroes or Heroines

How each of these is restricted, and how they function and interrelate with figures from the other categories, will be made clear later on.

The Celtic world-view included many complex and subtle ideas whose conceptualizations are often difficult even for today's scholars to fully grasp. However, it takes no great intellectual leap to see how winter became a time of the deity's old age and/or death. With no refrigeration or international commerce, fresh produce with all its necessary nutrients was absent during the cold Celtic winter. It is also no wonder that, in the midst of all this hibernation, the Winter Solstice was celebrated enthusiastically as the return of the Sun God (a Celtic conceptualization, not a factual belief) who would eventually warm their lives again and bring back the game and fertilize the next harvest as personified in the Goddess.

Because of these beliefs, a few Celtic scholars also put forth the notion that, while the Celts used magick and ritual for contacting and working with the deities, they did not worship them in the sense that we think of worship today. Again, this is a misconception. All people with deities have sought to honor them in some way. The difference with the Celts was in the way they approached the worshipping process. The Celtic deities were honored for being what they were—one great mass of primal power in which there was no differentiation of individuals except in how the human mind divided this power and drew from it. They saw the deities as being a part of themselves, especially if one particular deity, like a mascot, was regularly called upon to merge his or her energy for a specific purpose. This is borne out in the many myths in which a heroic figure is called the "son" or "daughter" of a God or Goddess. The relationship was not really intended to be thought of as genetic, but was a metaphor for a spiritual kinship. For example, the warrior hero Cuchulain is said to be the son of the God Lugh (after whom the Lughnasadh Sabbat is named), a warrior God who battled his rival, Balor, to the death. Cuchulain was always identified with Lugh's powers and abilities as would be a son. Since we have to look at the message behind myths rather than just the superficial story, we can glean that the relationship was a magickal one, one in which Cuchulain deliberately sought to draw into himself the powers of the deity he most identified with, the one whose powers he most needed to do his warrior's tasks.

There is an old Celtic blessing which asks "the blessings of the Gods and the not-Gods upon thee." This ambiguous line has been interpreted by both scholars and Pagans to mean that Celtic Gods were any persons of exceptional power, and the not-Gods were everyone else who has only

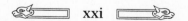

yet to realize their potential by choosing to align themselves with the powers of the divine which are there, within and without, for all of us to find.

Through carefully crafted ritual we can still align ourselves with the potent mythic figures of the Celtic pantheon with the same powerful results as were obtained by those long ago mythic heroes and heroines.

The role of ritual in religion is as old as humankind's first inkling of a belief in a creative power, a concept born nearly 40,000 years ago. Ritual is defined as a systematic, formal or informal, prescribed set of rites whose purpose is to imprint a lasting change on the life and psyche of the participant. Ritual does not have to be stagnant and repetitious to the point of boredom, but it can evolve with us as we grow and develop spiritually. Through such ceremonies we can, like our Celtic ancestors, harness the power of the deities which is, after all, power which lies dormant within each of us waiting only to be tapped.

In the rituals given herein no attempt is made to force anyone to conform to any single practice. There are just too many varied traditions within the Celtic framework for that to be possible. All of these variations are valid and have many unique expressions within Celtic Paganism. Though the rituals presented here are complete and whole unto themselves, they are meant to be used as a framework on which to hang your own ideas and through which to manifest your own expressions of God/dess-hood. The ritual tools you use, the directional orientations you adopt, the elemental symbols you prefer, all are unique and special and should never be discarded simply for the purpose of conforming to anyone else's theology. Ideas will be presented for those who have not made up their minds yet about these things, but no one standard will be pushed.

The most effective rituals are those you construct by yourself, for yourself, and to facilitate this, this book addresses itself almost exclusively to solitary practice. While by its very nature, ritual involves a certain amount of repetition, when you are on your own, working as a solitary, you have great latitude to make meaningful changes in your ritual content and form as you evolve with your magick and spirituality. The deities are most certainly best experienced when working alone, and it is from solitary ritual that you will gain the most from the contact.

The reason(s) you embark on a ritual is more important than the content. Don't make the mistake of sacrificing that all-important emotional connection with your ritual act for fear of making some nearly-impossible-to-make mistake. If any of you have seen the powerful Canadian-made telefilm, *Lost in the Barrens* (shown periodically in the United States on The Disney Channel), you may recall the scene where the two stranded teenage boys, one Native American and one Anglo, have finally stopped quarreling over their predicament and have begun to work together for their mutual survival. The Amerindian boy is bothered by the fact that, though he has killed a deer to provide them with food, he is not with his people who would have ritually initiated him into manhood for this act. His Anglo companion offers to help him do the ritual which the young Amerindian says he does not know. With wisdom beyond his years the Anglo boy tells his new friend, "It's not what you do, it's why you do it."

Why you do it *is* your ritual!

It's that simple. If you keep the ultimate goal of your ritual always in sight, you will never go wrong. If you are new to ritual, Appendix A will provide you with an outline for constructing your own. Reading about ritual construction and psychology, and studying already written rituals can help too. Two books which devote themselves wholly to discussing the nature and

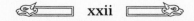

practice of ritual, and which would make valuable additions to any Pagan library, are Donald Tyson's *Ritual Magic,* and Lady Sabrina's *Reclaiming the Power.* Both of these works discuss ritual in detail, breaking down its components, showing how it works, and how to construct and work with it effectively.

Various other topics and concepts related to ritual use of mythic figures are made as clear as possible, but the space afforded the scope of this book does not allow for excessive and elaborate detail of all peripheral subjects. Therefore, along the way, you will find numerous references to other works which can give you more details about many of the subjects being discussed such as the Sabbats or Esbats. Some of these present ideas from a strictly Celtic point of view, while others are broader in focus. (Any unfamiliar terms which are not fully explained within the text can be clarified in the Glossary of Terms found in Appendix H.)

Celtic Myth & Magick includes, after the ritual and pathworking sections, a vast dictionary of Celtic deities and heroic figures along with a brief encapsulation of their mythic stories (usually taken from the most popular single version), as well as ideas for using the energy they represent and a list of any correspondences associated with them. These, too, are only meant to be used as a framework. For example, if Lugh is to you more a grain God than a sun God, then he should be approached by you from that perspective. To do anything else would lessen the potency of any ritual you undertake with him because your psyche is aligned differently as regards his energy.

Forming working partnerships with the divine fulfills the laws of balance which enable us to more easily create. In modern lingo the process is called *synergism,* the joining of two different energies to create one whole in which each complements what the other lacks. This is an ancient magickal principle still seen today in the joining of psychic forces such as above and below, in and out, astral and earth, and male and female. Each of these can stand alone but, when joined, become a potent catalyst for magick and transformation. Each of these pairs need the other for completeness. The same is true of the human and divine energies. We complement and need each other.

The divine energy of the Celtic pantheon holds untold treasures for all of us whether we boast Celtic blood in our veins or not. The archetypal power they represent and hold within themselves is universal, powers which are deeply part of us. They lie anxiously in wait for us to discover them anew, to shine through the darkness and light our path.

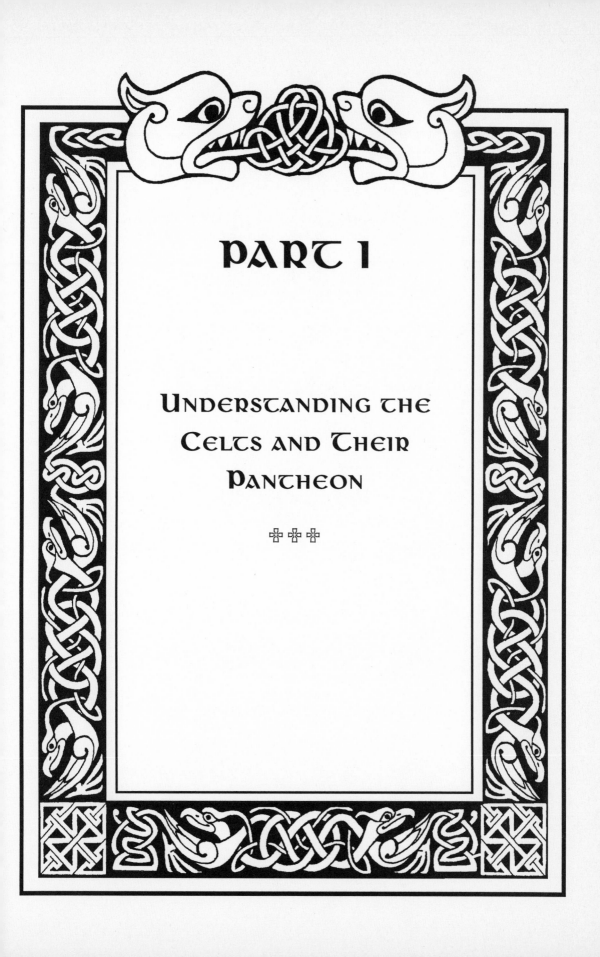

PART 1

UNDERSTANDING THE CELTS AND THEIR PANTHEON

✠ ✠ ✠

CHAPTER ONE

CELTIC TRADITIONS AND CREATING A CELTIC SETTING

*Should auld acquaintance be forgot
And never brought to mind?
Should auld acquaintance be forgot,
And days of auld lang syne?*
—Robert Burns

F YOU ARE new to Paganism, or to any of the Celtic traditions of the craft, you may wish to know a little more about the Celts and their lives and discover ways to make your ritual environment as evocative of Celtic ways as is possible. This chapter outlines some of the ways in which this can be done.

For many of us, one of the most attractive things about Paganism is that it does not require enslavement to a dogma, elaborate clothing, tools, or settings. Over the years many ideas about these things have been taken from other sources or from scant evidence, but none are required. Paganism of almost any tradition can be practiced simply, alone, and without lots of accoutrements; though there are many things we can do, some inexpensive and others not, which can add to the ambience of our ritual experiences.

Few of us have the land and monetary resources to recreate a Celtic kingdom complete with hearth-centered homes, streams, and cairns (though this type of residence can be created astrally, the methods lie outside the scope of this work), but most of us can afford to make or buy certain items for ritual use which offer us a touch of Celtic atmosphere.

The Triskele   *The Pentagram*

The two principal symbols of Celtic Paganism.

It matters little exactly what tools, directional orientations, garb, jewelry, instruments, music, dances, or settings were used in the proverbial "once upon a time." Celtic religion has evolved, as all religions do, to what it has become today—a multi-faceted, multi-traditional Pagan religion appealing to a great number of neo-Pagans. However, without trying to interpolate one person's or group's interpretation of Celtic spiritual practice, we can look at the Celtic past and find ways to add a Celtic flavor to our workings, creating an atmosphere in which Celtic magic, myth, and ritual can not only survive, but flourish.

SORTING OUT THE CELTIC TRADITIONS

Many altars are in Banba,
Many chancels hung in white,
Many schools and many abbeys....
—Thomas D'Arcy McGee

AMONG TODAY'S ECLECTIC Pagans, it is perfectly acceptable to work and worship outside the confines of a specific tradition, especially if one elects to be a solitary Pagan (one with no ties to a larger coven or group). In either case, most of us still prefer to align our practices with one distinct tradition with its pre-determined set of beliefs and ritual exercises whether or not we are solitary in our practice or whether or not we accept all of that tradition's teachings.

Polls taken at Pagan festivals throughout the United States show Celtic Paganism is the most popular choice, followed very closely by the various Teutonic traditions, many of which strongly influenced the Celts. But it is misleading to accept this fact at face value. Celtic Paganism has many different expressions, and each of these constitutes a tradition in itself. Some are eclectic amalgamations of various Celtic pathways, and others have well-ordered hierarchies of practice and politics. If you wish to fully understand Celtic Paganism, it would be wise to explore several of these traditions and to try to glean an understanding of what each stands for, how it works, and how it views this world and all others, and how it interprets magickal and ritual practice.

The following is a list of some—but by no means all—of the traditions which are in some way Celtic. It will hopefully clear up any terminology and labels related to Celtic magickal traditions which may be confusing. Information on most of them can be found in occult books, Pagan periodicals, or through diligent networking. Others are highly secretive and it may take some time to begin to unravel their secrets. (See Appendix D for information on ordering any of the books or periodicals mentioned in this listing.)

ALEXANDRIAN TRADITION

Although not exactly a Celtic tradition, many Celtic paths today use words and expressions which reflect the Kabbalistic influence of this Pagan tradition. Its founder, Alexander Saunders, was a Pagan leader who successfully blended Kabbalistic practice with Anglo-Celtic Pagan practice. Many people believe that this blending first began in the late 1400s when Moors, Jews, Pagans, and other non-Catholics fled the Spanish Inquisition. Many of these people came to the west of Ireland, then the end of the known world, to hide and begin a new life. The book, *Secrets of a Witches' Coven,* by Morwyn, outlines the basic teachings of this tradition.

ANGLO-ROMANY TRADITION

A tradition based upon the beliefs of the itinerant Gypsy people of Britain and Ireland, commonly called "Tinkers." This tradition often is blended with the more mystical aspects of European Catholicism.

ANGLO-SAXON TRADITION

An English path combining the practices of the Celts with those of the southern Teutons, whose Pagans are also sometimes called "witches." Though the popular word "Wicca" is Anglo-Saxon in origin, the followers of this path discard it as a label for themselves. There are many followers of this tradition, and many varied expressions of its teachings.

ARTHURIAN TRADITION

A tradition from Wales and Cornwall based upon the Arthurian myths which sees each of the figures in his stories as individual divine images. Books on the Arthurian legends can give you a basic idea of the practices of this pathway. Look to the writings of Geoffrey Ashe and John Matthews for the best and broadest presentations.

BREZONEK TRADITION (Bray-zone-AY'K)

This is the little-known Celtic tradition of Brittany. It has most likely been influenced by both Roman and Celtic Gaul, and by the Celts of the British Isles, though its followers think of themselves first and foremost as Celtic.

BRITTANIC TRADITION

An Anglo-Celtic tradition which encompasses the beliefs brought to England by the invading Romans, as well as those of the Celts.

BRYTHONIC TRADITIONS

A generic label often applied to traditions of Wales, Cornwall, and England. Though the Bretons also speak a Brythonic language, this name is usually not applied to their spiritual practices.

CALEDONII TRADITION

This Scottish tradition receives little publicity in the Pagan press. The name Caledonii is Roman in origin and may indicate that it, like the Hibernian tradition of Ireland, has strong Roman influences. The now defunct *Samildanach* was the quarterly newsletter of this tradition.

CELTIC TRADITION

A broad and eclectic branch of Paganism originating in Celtic Gaul, western and northern England, Ireland, Wales, Scotland, Brittany, and the Isle of Man. Generally they share much in common, but, specifically, they have many differences. A basic overview of shared Celtic Pagan beliefs can be found in D.J. Conway's book, *Celtic Magic.*

CREABH RUADH TRADITION (Crahv ROO-ah)

The "Red Branch" tradition is a highly secretive, initiatory, male mysteries Irish path based upon

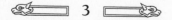

the myths and exploits of the Red Branch warriors of Ulster. It is highly stratified in character, much like Celtic society.

CYMRI TRADITION (KIM-ree or KEEM-ree)
The principal Pagan tradition of Wales. It claims to be a pre-Celtic path which may antedate many of the Arthurian legends, though Arthur and his legions figure heavily in the teachings and mythology of this tradition.

DEBOREAN TRADITION (Deb-OR-ee-awn)
This American eclectic tradition has Celtic ties in the sense that they use names from the Anglo-Celtic myths to designate their leaders. They are an initiatory tradition which attempts to reconstruct Wicca as it was before the witch persecutions, known in the Craft as "The Burning Times." They view their principal purpose as being to help all humans find their inner spiritual home.

DRUIDIACTOS
A Druidic path, as much cultural as it is magickal and religious, which devotes itself to Celtic study and as accurate as possible a reconstruction of past practices. The teachings and beliefs of the Druidiactos are outlined in *The Sacred Cauldron,* by Tadhg MacCrossan.

DRUIDIC TRADITIONS
The pathways based on the practices, rituals, and magick of the Celtic priestly class known as the Druids. Many expressions of this tradition exist, and their differences have often been cause for dissension in the Pagan community. Two of the best books published in recent years on Druidism are *Book of Druidry,* by Ross Nicols, and *The 21 Lessons of Merlin,* by Douglas Monroe.

DRYAD TRADITION
A feminist tradition of female Druidesses who were given their name by the tree faeries of the Celtic lands, who are also known as Dryads. Faery lore plays a strong role in their practices, and the majority of their other teachings are Druidic with a modern feminist slant.

EIREANNACH TRADITION (AIR-un-n'yock)
Several distinct traditions claiming this label seem to be operating in North America. The name simply means "Irish." Eireannach is probably best described as a catch-all term for the various Irish paths rather than the name of any one single expression.

FAERY TRADITION
An environmentally-minded path which claims its origins in the oral teaching of the Tuatha De Dannan of Ireland, the deities who became the faery folk. Once a secretive, California-based group, their beliefs and practices have been made public in the *Faery Wicca* series of books by Kisma K. Stepanich.

FAMILY TRADITIONS
Various traditions passed down through individual families are usually tossed together under this label. Some of these are secretive for reasons of personal security, others openly combine their Celtic Pagan beliefs with those of mainstream religions. A Family Tradition can be a part of any culture's indigenous religion, not just Celtic.

FENNIAN TRADITION
An initiatory Irish path which takes its name from Fionn MacCumhal's warriors, the Fianna.

GAELIC TRADITION
A generic label sometimes applied to the traditions of Ireland and Scotland.

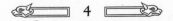

GARDNERIAN CRADITION

This is not exactly a Celtic tradition, but many of Gerald Gardner's ideas have had so much impact on modern Paganism since he first begin writing about his vision of witchcraft in the 1950s that many Celtic groups have adopted them. His tenets include ritual nudity, hierarchies of leadership, and an organized, graduated training system for new converts. A very stratified, initiatory tradition. The many books of Janet and Stewart Farrar best present Gardnerian ways.

HEBRIDEAN CRADITION

A secretive Scottish tradition which is based on the Irish myths, but to which local legends associated with them are applied.

HIBERNIAN CRADITION

This Irish tradition probably developed during the Middle Ages and shows Roman influence.

IRISH CRADITION

A generic term used to identify traditions native to Ireland and her people. Many individual traditions come under this broad heading, though some believe the only true Irish tradition is one which is pre-Celtic.

KINGSTONE CRADITION

An English tradition with Celtic roots. Look in Appendix D for the *International Red Garters,* a publication and umbrella organization for followers of English ways.

MAIDENHILL CRADITION

This initiatory path was founded in England in the late 1970s and worships a generic Mother Goddess, sometimes called Rhiannon, and the Horned God. Maidenhill does not have a significant number of followers in North America.

MAJESTIC CRADITION

An English tradition which views the long succession of ruling monarchs as sacrificial kings and fertility queens. Look in Appendix D for the *International Red Garters,* a publication and umbrella organization for followers of English ways.

MANX CRADITION

An Irish tradition which traces its roots to the mystical Isle of Man. Lots of faery lore-based beliefs and ritual workings are part of this path. Manann Mac Llyr, God of the Sea, and Fand, a Faery Queen, are its principal deities.

NORTH COUNTRY CRADITION

The Pagan tradition of the Yorkshire region of England. The principal influences on it were from England (which was heavily influenced by Pagan Rome) and from the Scottish lowlands.

NORTH ISLES CRADITION

The tradition from the Orkney and Shetland Islands of Scotland. This path was heavily influenced by the Norse, and many Nordic festivals are still celebrated here. Some of the regional names of the deities, faeries, and other Pagan beliefs are still identified by Old Norse words.

NORTHERN CRADITION

A combined path which follows the old Norse and Celtic ways—sometimes labeled *Asatru.* A Pagan group which calls itself "Northern Way" incorporated in Chicago in 1982. Their beliefs are broadly outlined in *Northern Magic,* by Edred Thorsson.

OBOD

The anacronym for the Order of Bard, Ovates and Druids, a tradition of Celtic Druidry based in

England. As of this writing, the OBOD offers correspondence courses, a newsletter, and networking. See Appendix D for more information.

PECTI-WITA

This is the solitary path of the pre-Celtic people known as the Picts. They inhabited northern Scotland and warred frequently with the Celts before being absorbed by them. The beliefs and practices of this path are recorded by Raymond Buckland in his 1991 book, *Scottish Witchcraft*.

REFORMED DRUIDS

This flourishing tradition was organized at Carleton College in Minnesota in 1963 in protest against a school rule which required Sunday chapel attendance. The original group rituals were based on the Episcopal form of worship, but its splinter groups have since tried to revise their rituals in line with the old Celtic ways.

ROMANO-GAULISH TRADITION

This tradition combines Celtic and Roman Pagan practices in the same way that they merged and blended in Gaul many centuries ago.

SACRED WHEEL TRADITION

An eclectic neo-Pagan path which was organized in Delaware within the past decade. Calling themselves Wiccan, they focus on balance and learning. Celtic beliefs are a part of their teachings. Still concentrated in the eastern states, covens are formed from study groups which include both old-timers and novices. Notices about the formation of Sacred Wheel study groups can be found in Pagan periodicals, especially those based in the northeastern United States.

SCOTIA TRADITION

A tradition for which little public information exists. It is a path which attempts to reconstruct the early Milesian faith as practiced about the time the Celts came to Britain. This would of necessity seek to include old Iberian (Spanish) Pagan beliefs which are now virtually extinct thanks to the gross efficiency of the Spanish Inquisition.

SCOTTISH TRADITION

A generic term used to identify traditions native to Scotland and her people. Many individual traditions come under this broad heading, though some believe that the only true Scottish tradition is one which is pre-Celtic.

SHAMANIC TRADITIONS

While most people do not at first think of Shamanism when they think of the Celts, this spiritual practice has been noted in all ancient cultures. John Matthews book, *The Celtic Shaman,* is an excellent text on this largely forgotten path.

TUATHA DE DANANN (TOO-ah Day THAY-nan or DAWN-an)

An Irish tradition based upon the mythic tales of the Tuatha De Danann, the last race to hold power in Ireland before the Milesian (human) invasion. The mythic figures of the Tuatha constitute most of the Irish pantheon and serve as a divine foundation for virtually all of the Irish traditions. Llewellyn Publications will soon be releasing a book on this tradition by long-time Danann, Katharine Clark.

UELEDA TRADITION (WEE-lay-dah)

Ueleda was a name sometimes broadly applied to female Druids, and today it is the name for an all-female, initiatory Druidic tradition.

WELSH TRADITION
A catch-all term for the several different Pagan traditions which came out of Wales.

WEST COUNTRY TRADITION
The principal Pagan tradition of Cornwall and Devonshire in southwestern England. *West Country Wicca,* by Rhiannon Ryall, discusses the Anglo-Celtic practices of the West Country Pagans before the influence of Gerald Gardner.

WICCA (WICK-AH, WEECH-AH, OR WEEK-AH)
The Anglo-Saxon term for witchcraft popularized by Pagan writers since the 1950s. The term usually refers to an Anglo-Celtic practice, particularly as interpreted by Wiccan leader Gerald Gardner. Wicca is an Anglo-Saxon word meaning "wise one," a term which came to label the craft as it was practiced in England, Wales, and the continental region once known as Saxony. Many good books have been written about Wicca and are easily found. Look for authors such as Raymond Buckland, Scott Cunningham, Dion Fortune, Diane Stein, and Doreen Valiente for solid, ethical presentations.

WICCE
The Olde English word for Wicca. It is sometimes used to refer to an English Tradition where the Saxon influences, but not Celtic ones, have been eliminated wherever possible.

WITAN TRADITION
An eclectic Scottish path which combines the Scottish, Celtic, Pictish, and Norse traditions. Like the Irish Witta, it values the many influences upon itself as an asset to be cherished rather than eliminated. Modern Wita has done away with much of the stratification of Celtic society and accepts self-initiation as valid.

WITCHCRAFT
This is another broad term which encompasses several, rather than any single, Pagan tradition. All witches are Pagans, but not all Pagans are witches. The term "witch" seems to have become a term exclusively reserved for practitioners of any of the Celtic or Anglo traditions, or, less often, for the Teutonic paths (this latter is probably because the Saxons and the Norse had such a great impact on Celtic Paganism). You will find witch used occasionally in this book in place of the word Pagan.

WITTAN TRADITION (WEED-an)
An eclectic Irish path which keeps very old Irish traditions and combines them with the influences of the Norse. Witta values Irish Pagan history and recognizes that at each stage in its development, over many centuries, each generation has been able to add something of value. Until recent times Wittan covens were characterized by strict stratification and one-on-one teaching for its apprentices. Today most Wittan covens operate on a consensus basis and will accept self-initiation and the solitary life as valid. The precepts of the Wittan tradition are outlined in my own book, *Witta: An Irish Pagan Tradition.*

Y TYLWYTH TEG TRADITION (Ee TEE-Loo-eeth Tay'g)
A Welsh-based tradition named for the faery folk of that land, a people who roughly correspond to the Tuatha De Danann in Ireland. Though the tradition was officially founded in the United States, it maintains deeply Celtic roots and very humanistic philosophy. Students of this path are asked to place heavy emphasis on the study of Welsh myth, folklore, and faery lore.

All of the previously mentioned traditions have the right to call themselves Celtic, as well as Irish, or Welsh, etc. Each falls within a Celtic or semi-Celtic framework, but has different outward expressions of those basic ideals.

Some of these differences have to do with the inner-structure of the tradition itself. It is no secret that by the time Celtic civilization crumbled under the Normans and the church, that it had become an extremely stratified society with the warrior and priestly classes possessing the bulk of power and wealth. This upper strata had taken their love of war and rank to a dangerous extreme, even to the point of enslaving their own people to fight in their petty wars. The growing discontent of the subjugated populace created a fundamental weakness in their society which made it possible for their conquerors to play a game of divide, conquer, and win.

Taking a valuable lesson from that experience, we see that more and more Celtic traditions are moving away from hierarchical models of coven leadership towards a more egalitarian structure. Even within traditions which are very stratified it is not unusual to find the occasional coven operating on a consensus or rotating leadership basis rather than on a hierarchical one. This trend also reflects the belief that we all have some skill which we can teach, and something lacking which we can learn from others regardless of our "rank." While these beliefs are certainly not a part of all Celtic Pagan groups (those following Druidic teachings do not share this viewpoint), there does seem to be an increasing interest in working without "leaders."

Whether you choose to be a part of any large Pagan group at any time in the future is up to you alone. Please keep in mind that the most often cited single reason for the failure of covens is the internal structure rather than the spiritual practices. Examine your own feelings about coven hierarchies before getting involved, deciding not only if this is what you want, but also why it is you want it that way. If your goal is to dominate, or to be dominated by, others, you don't have to go to all the trouble of seeking out a coven. Your local corporate complex or fundamentalist church will be glad to provide this atmosphere for you.

The rest of this chapter deals with ways to help you set a Celtic mood and form for your spiritual workings *without* prescribing any practice and without attempting to contradict the teachings of any single Celtic tradition or expression.

THE SACRED THREE-TIMES-THREE

Three things that foster high spirits:
self-esteem, courting, drunkenness.
—From *The 33 Triads*, ninth century

ALL CULTURES HAVE a number they believe to be sacred. For the Celts that number was three, and all multiples of three. Throughout Celtic myth we find the theme of three and its multiples over and over again, from the faces of the Triple Goddess to the number of magickal objects owned by wizards and Druids.

In Celtic Paganism there are two primary configurations which symbolize the sacred three, though there are others. These are the trefoil, shaped like the Irish shamrock; and the inverted triangle, often referred to as the Triangle of Manifestation.

The most important of the multiples of three was nine—the natural manifestation of three-times-three. When the science of mathematics began to be commonplace in the 1600s, the Celts

The Triquerta *The Nonegram* *The Trefoil*

Three expressions of the Celtic sacred numbers.

found they were justified in their choice of nine as the magickal number manifestation. Nine was not only the natural multiple of three, but it was a number which could always magickally come back to itself, and as such it became a symbol of creative power and energy. Nine was also associated in many cultures with the mysteries of the moon, and like the moon, the number nine returns to itself no matter how it is manipulated.

Test it for yourself. Multiply any number by nine, add the digits of the resulting sum, and you will get nine again. It never fails. For example, take 9 X 5. The resulting sum is 45. Break apart the 4 and 5, add them together, and you again get 9.

In each of the exercises, spells, and rituals in the upcoming chapters, you will see the number three, or some multiple thereof, prominently featured. In any Celtic rituals you design for yourself, you should always add things in threes and multiples of three whenever possible. For instance, you can do this through the number of items you place on your altar, the number of candles you light, the repetition of your gestures, the number of times the circle is walked, the number of times a chant is repeated, etc.

Some Celtic traditions believe that you won't even get your desired results unless three is utilized at some point in the ritual or magickal working.

RITUAL TOOLS AND ELEMENTAL ATTRIBUTES

I am the winde which breathes upon the sea,
I am the wave of the ocean…
I am a beam of the sun,
I am the fairest of plants….

—Amergin

IT IS ARGUABLE that before the fifteenth century, when Spaniards began their infamous Inquisition, elaborate ritual tools were not a part of Celtic Paganism. It is believed that when Kabbalists, Gnostics, and High Magicians from the Moorish lands began to flee to Celtic ports (notably to Galway in western Ireland), the various magickal traditions blended, creating a more codified system of Celtic Pagan practice.

Today most Pagans use some sort of ritual tools, sometimes called elemental weapons, to represent the four directions (also called "quarters") and their corresponding attributes. These vary not only by Celtic region, but also within each interpretation of those regional traditions.

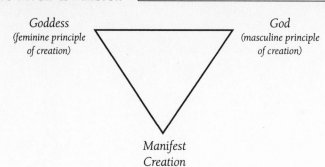

Goddess
(feminine principle
of creation)

God
(masculine principle
of creation)

Manifest
Creation

The triangle of manifestation.

For the rituals given here you can make do with only a chalice or cup for directing feminine power, and a wand, athame (ritual knife), or fingertip for directing masculine power. For the spellwork you will need a variety of items depending upon your wish or goal, and with which element you personally feel the greatest affinity. Tools are only a catalyst to help the Pagan magician focus on his goal by helping to direct the powers of the four elements, the building blocks of all creation, to manifest the desired outcome.

The elements, though they are often assigned different symbols and directions, all have approximately the same general meanings and attributes throughout Celtic Paganism. Some of the many items which have been used to represent each element are listed twice because various Celtic traditions classify them differently. The direction which represents each element varies so greatly by tradition that no attempt will be made here to give those attributes which are decided upon by various means, particularly weather patterns, mythological associations, and astrological phenomena.

WATER (FEMININE)

Water is the realm of the psychic, the dream world. It is related to children and/or childbirth, pregnancy, inner transformation, purification, emotional healing, romantic love, manifesting, most spellwork, death and rebirth, past-lives and new beginnings.

Associated Items: Cup, Chalice, Cauldron, Hollow Horn (*Buabhaill*), Bowl, Pitcher, Drinking Tumbler, Wine Goblet, Water, Wine, Meade, Ale, Ring, Wine Cask, Barrel, Silver, Shield.

EARTH (FEMININE)

Earth is the realm of stability, growth, and of the eternal Mother Goddess. It is related to fertility, prosperity, grounding and centering, money, dance, motherly love, planting and harvesting, the home, and herds and pets.

Associated Items: Disk, Carved Wood Block (Pentacle), Stone, Clay, Bowl of Earth, Salt, Gems, Tree Branch, Plants, Double-Headed Axe (*Gall-o Glach*), Shield, Wheel, Pentagram, Necklace, Club, Tree Bark, Roots, Bodhran, Shamrock, Bronze, Bow.

AIR (MASCULINE)

Air is the unpredictable realm of the mind. It is related to the intellect, study, astral travel, communication, music and sound, weather magick, and power raising.

Associated Items: Staff, Shillelagh, Slat, Trident (*Craebh Ciuil*), Stang, Athame, Wand, Sword, Feather, Incense, Sling, Claymore, Pike, Axe, Pick-Axe, Dirk, Dagger, Spear, Javelin (*Gaesum*), Earrings, *Pen-Bas,* Club, Falchion, Leaves, Besom (Witch's Broom), Bagpipes, Tin Whistle, Thistle, Smoking Pipe, Copper, Bow, Arrow, Cromach.

FIRE (MASCULINE)

Fire is the realm of transformation and passion. It is related to protection, exorcism and banishing, sex and sex magick, work, purification, divination, masculine power, personal energy and strength, the God, and candle magick.

Associated Items: Candle, Balefire (Bonfire), All Blades Forged in Fire, Wand, Red or Orange Stones, Pike, Claymore, Matches, Flint, Ashes, Wheel, Torch, Bracelet, Solar Disk, Besom, Gold, Spear, Cromach.

SPIRIT (NO GENDER ASSOCIATION)

A fifth element is Spirit, usually called by its Vedic Indian name, *Akasha*. Spirit is in and of all the elements, and it transcends them. In Native American traditions spirit is honored in the direction of "above." The Celts also knew of and honored Spirit, not so much as a fifth element, but rather as the unifying force which animates all the other elements. Spirit is often represented in Celtic traditions by a cord. The Germanic equivalent of Akasha is *aether,* and is more and more often becoming the preferred usage by Celtic Pagans.

The Celts also associated each element with a specific time of day, a time they thought of as magickal. The Celts believed there was great power in the times which were "not times," or the "times in between." These were the natural turning points of time such as dusk, dawn, midnight, new moon, full moon, seasonal changes, etc. All these points were a turning or blending time, a time when one was not really sure if the moon was dark or new, or whether it was still night or now day. They believed that time, for a brief moment, actually stood still, that the doors to the spirit world were opened, and that there were potent divine forces at work which made up two halves of a whole. In other words, night/day, new/old, today/yesterday, summer/winter—all these meeting points were times when the polarities, like the Goddess and God, came together and creation could easily take place.

These are the traditional Celtic time associations for the four elements:

Air	Dawn
Fire	Midday
Water	Dusk
Earth	Midnight

Some eclectic Celtic groups choose to switch the associations for water and earth. If you care to do this, the choice is yours to make. The rationale for the change is that midnight is always associated in the popular mind with death as is the Celtic element of water.

The Celts also gave each element a principal active property which can further help you when selecting an element for magick and ritual, especially if you are new to magick:

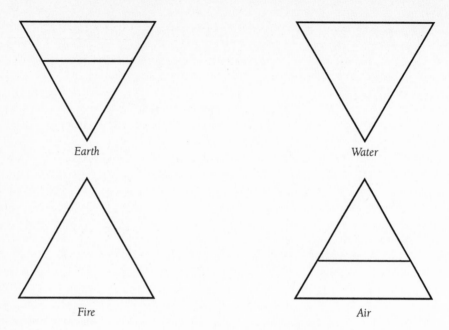

The alchemical symbols for the four elements date to at least the early medieval period. Today they are used not only by those involved in the esoteric science of alchemy, but also by ceremonial magicians and Pagans of all traditions.

Air	Mobility
Fire	Transformation
Water	Purification
Earth	Stability

Altars within your circle, or ones set up loosely around your home, should be set up and oriented toward whichever direction you or your tradition see fit. In the many Celtic paths this is usually any direction except south. You can make an altar out of a dresser, desk, occasional table, block of wood, flat stone, a piece of cloth, or a roomy box covered with a piece of fabric. Having a sturdy place to rest your tools and be the center of your circle is what is most important. Some opt to use their entire circle for an altar and place their tools against the perimeter at the various quarters. All of these are workable, valid options.

Upon the altar you will place your chosen tools—all aligned to the proper direction according to your choice—and any magickal items, personal icons, statuary, or other talismans you choose to have present during a ritual or magickal rite.

An altar cloth on which to set out and arrange all your tools can also add a touch of Celtic art to your rituals. Instead of using a plain, solid-colored cloth, you can embroider the border with colorful Celtic designs. (See the section on "Celtic Art" for the address of a company which can supply you with a book of charted Celtic designs.)

BEING SKYCLAD OR CLOTHED?

What is title, what is treasure, What is reputation's care?
If we lead a life of pleasure, 'Tis no matter how or where!
—Robert Burns

SOME PAGANS IMMEDIATELY dismiss the idea of adopting special dress for ritual occasions, preferring instead to not dress at all. Going skyclad, or ritual nudity, is a concept that was probably not part of the ancient Celtic ritual experience, though no one can actually prove it either way. The concept came into modern Wicca via Italy where the words "you shall be naked in your rites" was found in a fifteenth century "confession" by a witch and said to be part of the "Charge of the Goddess," a commission usually attributed to the Greco-Roman Goddess, Aradia. Whether this was truly a part of Italian Paganism or not is still open for debate, but the climate was certainly better suited to it than in the Celtic lands.

We do have extant references to Celtic warriors stripping naked for battle, which seems linked to their cosmological and religious beliefs. In C.E. 225, Polybius, a Roman general in the British Isles, wrote that the Celts believed that to disrobe would expand their personal "life force" (what we today think of as an aura or astral body), and that with this expansion, they became one with nature and the divine. They would also better be able to attune to each other, allowing them to move as one in battle. Certainly this is also a valid reason to adopt ritual nudity, as are the other commonly cited ideas: the belief that nudity expresses freedom and equality, or that it enables you to view the other members of your coven as God or Goddess incarnate. (Keep in mind that a study taken in the late 1980s showed that more than 95% of Westerners mentally view their deity as a robed figure.)

Regardless of this history, if you choose to go skyclad, either alone or with a group, you should be aware of the reasons you choose this option. I have found that many Pagans who embrace skyclad rites as a *must* come from families who followed a strictly orthodox version of their mainstream faith which frowned upon sexuality and viewed the body as dirty and shameful. These poor souls lived very repressed lives under those tenets, and now, under the liberalizing tenets of Paganism, feel free to coerce others into nude rituals which make them uncomfortable. In order to do this they use the same manipulative tactics that they were coerced by as children. This constitutes ritual abuse and, if recognized, should be immediately stopped for the health and well-being of all concerned.

Worse yet, many of these people see the coven as little more than an endless supply of bodies for engaging in promiscuous sexual activities, which puts both the individuals and the group as a whole at risk. Sex used this way is not a sacred act, but one which degrades both the experience and the spirituality of the participants. It also grossly violates the Pagan Rede which requires us to "harm none," and only provides ample fuel for the witch-burning fires of the anti-Pagan fundamentalists.

Certainly not all Pagans who opt to go skyclad have these emotional problems, and ritual nudity can, in the right setting with the right people, be a powerful and meaningful experience. You should be aware, however, that problem people are out there and be cautious when approaching other groups you might wish to be a part of. I know of several sad cases where irresponsible individuals carried their sexual problems into group dynamics and wreaked havoc in the lives of everyone present.

Being skyclad should be a choice everyone is free to adopt or dismiss at will. Neither way is inherently right or wrong, just a different interpretation of Paganism, as is choosing a wand instead of a knife to represent the element of air. To choose to be robed or clothed does not mean someone is ashamed of their body, but that they view it as sacred and holy and not to be put on display for just everyone.

In the past when we humans had less psychological baggage to tote around in our heads, we mentally viewed our deities as nude and equated that with their primal power. Hence, being skyclad does not indicate freedom or an expression of fertility, as some Pagans mistakenly are taught. Rather, those who go skyclad are expected to view not only themselves, but all unclothed human beings as deity incarnate, a hard leap of thought to make in a society which fetishizes body parts as ours does. Those who would not or cannot see you in this light have no business being allowed to invade your privacy.

Since the rites and rituals given here are solitary in nature, the issue of how one dresses will affect only the practitioner, but they should still be thought out so that the solitary Pagan is knowledgeable about, and comfortable with, the choices made.

Paganism is a choice of conscience, and all decisions made within should be viewed as sacred ones. Be nude or robed as you will, but offer neither ridicule nor harm to others for remaining true to their choices.

CELTIC DRESS: THE MEDIEVAL FANTASY

I bought thee petticoats of the best,
The cloth so fine as fine might be;
I gave thee jewels for thy chest,
And all this cost I spent on thee.
—*Greensleeves*
(Elizabethan Folk Song)

THOSE FOLLOWING THE Celtic tradition known as the "Arthurian Tradition" take their mythology, deities, etc., from the legends of King Arthur, Queen Guinevere, Merlin, and the Knights of the Round Table. Though the mythic images involved pre-date Arthur—a sixth century King of the Britons—the stories of his life best known to us come from Thomas Malory and the other writers who flourished in the late Middle Ages, and poetically place the legendary King in the medieval kingdom of Cornwall.

Hence, when we think of Arthurian times, what naturally comes to mind is medieval costumes, men with heraldic tunics and leggings, polished swords at their side, women with long diaphanous gowns, pointed hats trailing voile, and wide draping sleeves. Many Pagan robes which are purchased or made by the wearer have these wide sleeves. These appeal to our sense of the dramatic, but they are not Celtic, nor are they particularly practical. These sleeves are hard to control in a darkened ritual setting and have been known to knock things about at best and, at worst, catch fire when they are inadvertently dragged through a candle's flame.

If you follow the traditions of Arthur, or of Wales and Cornwall which claim him, you may opt to dress yourself in medieval garb. The clothing of this period is well documented and even has a national following in the Society for Creative Anachronism, which holds medieval festivals for its members. Just be aware of the drawbacks of this style of dress and remember that it was not Celtic, but Anglo-Frankish in origin.

VARIATIONS ON ETHNIC CELTIC DRESS

Three excellent qualities in dress:
style, comfort, durability.
—From *The 33 Triads,* ninth century

CELTIC COSTUMES VARY by century and by region, with each country having a slightly differing variation on its so-dubbed "National Costume." Many of these traditional outfits as we know them today were developed in the Elizabethan period (the late sixteenth century), and some not until the Victorian era (middle to late nineteenth century).

Celtic art preserves for us many depictions of the dress of the early millennia. Illuminated manuscripts as well as carvings show us the costumes of the second to ninth centuries C.E. From these, and from historical and archaeological studies, we can get a good idea of what the average Celt wore from day to day.

Embroidery was a highly prized art, and Celtic clothing, even everyday wear, was often lavishly embellished with symbols of rank, family, country, or spirituality. Though the women usually were given charge of this craft, men were not above taking a needle to fabric when the spirit moved them.

Simple tunics, woolens, and animal furs were worn for everyday use, especially in the northern reaches of the Celtic world where the summertime highs rarely exceed 65°, and the winters are damp and chilly. Sleeves were long, but not flowing, and clothing for warmer weather was usually made from serge or linen (called *srol*). There is mention in several extant sources of a fabric called "Irish Silk" which was wildly expensive and believed to have been prized by the fourteenth-century Queen Clemence of Hungary. It is doubtful, given the climatic conditions, that this silk was the thin, cool fabric we know today.

Women wore long dresses, or ankle-length tunics, unless they were warrioresses, in which case they dressed similarly to the men in breeches or shorter tunics which would leave them free to move agilely in battle.

The Celts were superb metalcrafters, and the more affluent or higher ranking among them wore elaborately carved jewelry usually made from gold or bronze. Archaeologists have uncovered many such pieces which are now on display in the national museums of the Celtic lands.

Males of modestly high rank often wore a neckpiece known as a *torque* (tork), a round, heavy brace of twisted metal extravagantly decorated with Celtic inter-locking designs and usually made of gold or bronze. The highest nobility (read successful warriors and clan chiefs) wore collars called *maniacis,* similar to a *torque,* but which denoted one's clan.

Women of privilege would wear a headpiece called a *niam-lann* (NEEM-lawn), a headband which is often used in modern Wicca as a headdress for the priestess. It was usually crafted of silver, copper, or *findruine* (white bronze), and at its front it usually sported a jewel or design of some kind which rested over the power spot (*chakra*) known in the Eastern traditions as the Third Eye, a center of psychic energy. In its modern incarnation this design is often the three moons of the Triple Goddess.

The "adder's tongue" (*ouion anguinum* in Gaulish) was another pan-Celtic ornament which doubled as a protective charm. It was usually an amulet made from a snake or adder's egg, or sometimes a sea shell or black stone, and was worn on a leather thong around the neck as a charm of protection and as an amulet to help the wearer contact the spirit world.

Wearing a Niam-Linn *on the forehead.*

Drawing of the gold and garnet pendant in the shape of the triskele on display in the British Museum, Haversham, Kent.

Broaches (called *delg* in Irish and Scots Gaelic, and *tlws* in Welsh) were also used and often denoted one's rank in society, and were worn by both men and women. The most famous broach, the Tara Broach, found accidentally by a child, is crafted of gold and precious jewels and is on display in the National Museum of Dublin. It is often copied by Celtic jewelers today. These broaches were usually used to secure cloaks (called "mantles" in Ireland and "kerseys" in Scotland) to the shoulder.

Mantles and kerseys were highly personal items and they were often the one item of clothing to which the most thought was given and the most cost invested. The Irish *Book of Rights,* when outlining the tribute to be paid to kings, discusses in detail the appropriate number and style of mantles permissible to offer for each rank of society. The mantles were decorated to match one's rank, with the highest strata of society favoring cloth embroidered with genuine gold filigree or trimmed with costly furs.

Women had a wide variety of other fine jewelry, ear clasps, bracelets, and even gold-framed mirrors called *scadarcs.* Many of these things can be brought today as fine reproductions from import stores.

Leather goods were also crafted by the Celts and used for belts, boots, and weapon holsters much as they are today. These were embellished with Celtic designs and worn as much as a sign of rank as for any practical purpose.

Most students of Celtic culture are surprised to discover that hair was given a great deal of attention and was often meticulously curled or plaited by both males and females. Males were even known to plait or decoratively twist their long beards. Persons of both sexes often carried around elaborately decorated combs in embroidered *cior-bolgs* (comb bags) for quick touch-ups. Small gold balls were used to decorate or cap the braids of both genders.

The use of the Scottish tartan (*breccan*), a plaid with a specific pattern designating one's clan ties, began early in Scotland but it was not until the Victorian period when the Queen's love of all things Scottish made fashionable the dress tartan as we know it today. Specific plaids began to be adopted by Celtic clans both in and out of Scotland as early as the fifth century C.E., but were not standardized for many hundreds of years, and the one used by one clan in the eastern Highlands might have been used by a rival clan in the west.

Scottish men (and also the men of Ireland and Brittany) began wearing kilts, the plaid pleated "skirts," around the fifteenth century, though plaid breeches were more often seen. Extant drawings and paintings of Scots in battle usually show them sporting breeches.

Scottish women wore plaid skirts of home-woven wool, and both sexes usually wore a *feileadh mor,* a long length of wool plaid thrown over the shoulder like a sash and fastened to the shirt, called a *leine,* with a broach. The shirts and tunics worn today with the kilts and shirts are usually white, but were once a bright saffron yellow, a custom taken from the Picts, who used the herb to color their bodies for ritual occasions.

Today, full dress kilts with all the accoutrements can be very expensive—as much as 1,200 American dollars. The complete outfit includes the plaid wooden knee socks, the *sporan,* lace jabots, *ghille* shoes, argyle jacket, cuffs, and the Balmoral hat (*boneid*). The cost is slightly less for the modern woman's versions of the kilt because all the male dress accents are not included.

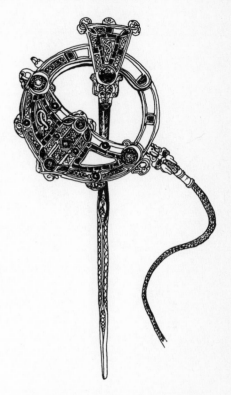

A drawing of the famous Tara Broach.

If you like the look of tartan, you should not hesitate to find the one for your own clan, or just to adopt one for yourself that you happen to like. If the cost of purchasing a ready-made kilt is out of your reach, check out your local yard goods stores for plaid fabric and patterns. A skillful seamstress should be able to put together a kilt in a couple days at a fraction of the cost of buying one.

Celtic charioteers and other warriors often wore metal helmets reaching well down the back to the vulnerable area between the shoulder blades. These helmets were adopted as part of the warrior's dress when they came into contact with the Romans at Gaul. The Celtic versions often had horns (representing the Horned God) or animal totems carved or set onto the tops.

The Druid priests wore long robes of white or blue, the Druidesses ones of white or red. These were believed to have been made of silk or linen and had hoods which could be drawn up over the head for various ritual needs. They also wore or carried a scepter called a *slat* (slawt) made of ritually selected and cut wood, a symbol of their power and rank, and was used like a wand in magick.

In Ireland the wooden staff known as a *shillelagh* was traditionally made of blackthorn wood, a cursed wood among the English Celts. These were usually carried by men and doubled as walking sticks as well as magickal wands. In Brittany the men carried a similar staff known as the *pen-bas,* or cudgel.

The Bretons, like the Scots, also developed their own national dress which utilized the kilt. The Bretons are the people of Brittany, that peninsular part of northwestern France which was

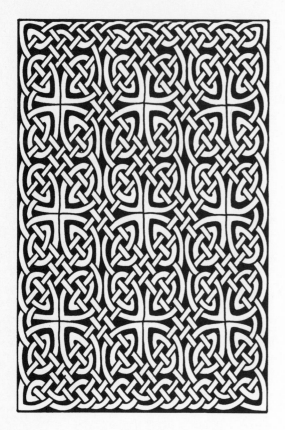 

Two examples of the interlacing knotwork which characterizes Celtic art.

settled by the Celts. The region consists of the departments (provinces) of Finistere, Cotes-du-Nord, Morbihan, Ille-et-Vilaine, and Loire-Inferieure. The Bretons used lots of black woolens in their clothing, and linens were also widely used with embroidered black waistcoats under dark jackets. Women wore dark or white aprons of satin or velvet, plain for unmarried girls, and embroidered for married women. They also lavishly embroidered embellishments on the bodices of their dark blouses.

Their skirts were multi-tiered skirts also woven of a dark fabric. Under these, Breton women wore several petticoats called *pieces*, and these were always in the same color as their skirts (Irish and Scottish women usually opted for many multi-colored slips).

The Breton men still wear the voluminous homespun breeches known as *bragoubras* (usually in blue or brown fabric), which are held at the waist by a wide leather belt and metal buckle. Their waistcoats often depict symbols showing the region of Brittany from which their clan hails, or the mark of the itinerant tailor who made the costume. Broad-brimmed hats finish the costume. A peaked hat indicates it is being worn by a bachelor, and one not turned up on the side is worn by a married man.

If you follow the Breton Celtic path you may wish to develop some embroidered designs which will be meaningful to you to add to your ritual wardrobe.

Elaborate hairstyles were also used by the Bretons, and if one attends a *pardon* (a Breton festival) today, representations of this old style can still be seen as a matter of ethnic pride. These were called by the French word *coiffe,* and were tall columns of hair said to be symbolic of the menhirs, or sacred standing stones, of the region. For daily wear, Breton women often covered their hair with small rectangles of linen lace somewhat like the Spanish *mantilla.* To make one of these for yourself, take a simple white linen handkerchief and add a bit of lace trim to the edge.

Another feminine Breton headdress still seen today is the *bigouden,* the Flemish-styled cap which covers all the hair but the bangs and ties under the chin.

In Wales, a feminine variation of this type of national dress required a tall black hat which resembles a traditional "witch's hat," but which was flat on top and was worn over a mob-cap with a ruffled edge. Over the clothing of both males and females the Welsh wore a full "Red Riding Hood-style" cloak made popular during the reign of Cromwell and his Puritans.

Contrary to popular belief, the Celts were rather fastidious for their time, and references to this are made by the Romans and Greeks as well as in the Celtic myths themselves. Cleanliness was especially important prior to religious rituals, and the idea of a ritual bath is still a popular one in Paganism because of the Celtic influence.

All of these ideas of Celtic ethnic dress are starting points, ideas you can adopt, adapt, discard, or alter to create your own idea of Celtic ambience.

CELTIC ART

From scenes like these,
Old Scotia's grandeur springs.
—Robert Burns

CELTIC ART FASCINATES Celtic and non-Celtic people, artists and those of us who can barely make stick figures. The art is characterized by inter-woven ropes of intricate knotwork which can be seen painted, carved, or placed on fine jewelry or other metalcrafts. Many examples of Celtic art survive, and there is a renewed interest in it. After you have spent some time studying the way the Celts viewed their world, their artwork will seem to suggest to you some of their cosmic beliefs. The waxing and waning energy patterns which are part of all life can be seen in the knots, twists, turns, and swirls of their drawings and carvings. Celtic art probably was unknown on the continent of Europe and no examples of it have been found there, though there is a vaguely similar art form in India. Many art historians believe that the Picts, the pre-Celtic people of northern Scotland, originated the knotwork we think of today as being Celtic.

Today you can inexpensively obtain patterns for Celtic needlework, stenciling, drawing, etc., and learn to create your own designs. Dover Publications prints several books of Celtic-styled patterns designed for use with either cross-stitch, needlepoint, pen, or paint, as well as a number of other practical and aesthetic books on Celtic art. Write to Dover and request a copy of their latest catalog, specifying your subject interest.

Dover Publications
31 East 2nd Street
Mineloa, NY 11501

CELTIC SACRED ANIMALS

Man is never closer to God
than when he bends down
to touch an animal in need—
—Roary Kennedy Smith

ANIMALS, BOTH WILD and domestic, have always had their special place within Paganism. In the Celtic myths are many, many references to sacred and totem animals, including animals created by shapeshifters (see the story of Cerridwen); birds, to represent transformation into the world of spirit (see the story of Blodeuwedd); familiars, animal co-workers in magick and ritual; human-animal hybrids; and totem animals, those used in sympathetic magick and in alignment rituals.

Animals often act as a bridge between the world of the divine and the mundane world, and, among the many Celtic traditions, they are often associated with specific deities. On an earthly level the animal represented the primal power of the deity, and on the spiritual level they exemplified the particular animal's highest attributes. The Celts used alignment rituals to connect themselves with an animal's essential energy to move attributes of the animals into themselves. For example, if one were seeking the qualities of bravery and strength, one might align themselves with a bear. Or if one wished knowledge, a salmon might be chosen.

When wishing to involve a specific deity in their rites, animals could still be used, often with more ease than when attempting to seek out the deity without the aid of an animal familiar. A deity was first chosen who was deeply associated with a particular animal, such as the Goddess Cerridwen and the sow. By connecting with that animal—something the Celts could see and know as opposed to the unseen deity, which was harder to comprehend—they were able to connect with the deity and its energies.

The Celts held numerous animals sacred, and Celtic shamans attempted to work with and transform into these animals. In one of his books on Celtic shamanism, *Taliesin,* Celtic scholar and author John Matthews gives us names of some special animals used by the shamans, and their related astrological attributes:

ANIMAL	PLANET
Horse	Mercury
Stag	Venus
Boar	Moon
Ousel	Mars
Eagle	Jupiter
Salmon	Saturn

You can use the planetary correspondences given by Matthews to begin to understand the animals' character. For example, the salmon was associated with knowledge by the Celts, and Saturn, its corresponding planet, is known as the planet of self-undoing and hidden knowledge. Astrology alone does not tell the entire story of sacred animals. For that we must look to the myths and artwork of the people we are studying. The following are prominent among the Celtic sacred animals.

Bear
An animal associated with royalty, particularly in Scotland. Also associated with King Arthur and with Shamanic Celtic traditions. The name "Art," seen frequently in Celtic mythology, means "bear." This is also seen in the name of the Goddess Artio who is usually depicted with a bear nearby her.

Birds
Associated with death transitions in Celtic mythology.

Boar
The boar is a symbol of masculine power. The meat of the boar was served at Otherworld feasts for the deities.

Bull
Figures heavily in what little Celtic creation mythology survives from Ireland, though this may not be Irish at all, but rather a myth derived from a Middle Eastern source. In the Celtic world the bull was a symbol of virility, sovereignty, and wealth. The famous Irish legend, *The Cattle Raid of Cooley*, surrounds the taking of a famous bull. In ancient Ireland, a *tabhfheis,* or a highly ritualized "feast of the bull," always proceeded the crowning of a new High King.

Butterfly
Associated with Celtic reincarnation myths and reincarnation deities such as Edain.

Cat
Unlike many other Indo-European cultures, the Celts did not revere cats, though there are many references to them in Celtic mythology. Archetypally they serve the same guardian function as demons/angels in the Judeo-Christian myths. Three mythic references to cats which are prominent are; one, a cat which helps to guard the gates of the Otherworld; two, one who is able to shapeshift into a ball of fire, and; three, one called Irusan of Knowth who stole humans like a faery. Cat-like monsters were also believed to dwell in dark caves.

Cow
The principal herd animal of the Celts. So important was this beast to the sustenance and economy of the Celts that cattle deities, such as Aine, were once very highly regarded.

Crane
Numerous Celtic myths tell us of a heroic figure or deity who was changed into a crane such as Aife, the Lady of the Lake, or Munanna. Archetypally this bird means an apparent, rather than substantive, change. A sign of, or punishment for, deception.

Crow
Deeply linked to Crone Goddesses such as Badb, and to Goddesses of war or death like the Morrigan.

Deer/Stag
The deer was the principal animal hunted by the Celts for food. The doe was associated with most woodland Goddesses, such as Saba and Flidais, and is their totem animal. The stag was often seen as the incarnate form of woodland Gods such as Cernunnos. White stags were considered to be from the Otherworld and, in myth, their appearance always heralded some profound change in the lives of those in the story. Considered in Celtic mythology to be among the oldest creatures in existence.

The Celtic art form known as the "bestiary." It uses animal likenesses and weaves them into intricate knotted patterns.

DOG

Sacred to the faeries of Ireland and Scotland probably because they were held in high regard by the Tuatha De Danann. Many Celtic myths involve dogs or dog familiars which belonged to heroic figures or deities, and wars were often fought for and over them such as the one between Fionn MacCumhal and King Arthur. Examples of the importance of Celtic dogs are found in the myths of Gwyn Ap Nuad, Cuchulain, Amaethaon, and Taliesin. Dogs are also the archetypal symbols of shapeshifters.

EAGLE

Eagles were the feared scavengers of Europe and were usually linked to death Gods, such as Beli, in the same way as the crow was linked to death Goddesses. In Welsh mythology, Llew was turned into an eagle at the moment of his murder.

HORSE

Horses were sacred to many Indo-European Goddesses, and often filled the archetypal place given to cats in other cultures. They were linked to the night, the moon, mystery, and magick. Nightmares, a name which is derived from that of the female horse, were thought by the Celts to be brought by a visiting horse Goddess such as Epona or Mare. In most Celtic myths the horses are black or white.

Ousel

(Usually spelled Ouzel in the United States.) This water bird is known for its tenacious and deceptive personality. While it looks harmless enough, it is revered for its ability to staunchly defend itself and its flock. In myth, the Ousel of Cilgwri once picked a smith's hammer down to the size of a small nut.

Owl

Westerners have always regarded the owl as a bird of wisdom and mystery. This nocturnal predator has been associated with both old Gods and crone Goddesses, age being indicative of wisdom gained. Archetypally the owl often heralds the end of a story where a lesson has been learned, such as in the familiar story of Blodeuwedd. Also of note is the Welsh Owl of Cwn Cawlwyd who helped in the search for Olwen.

Ram

Deeply associated with Celtic fertility Gods such as Cernunnos, and with the Bealtaine Sabbat.

Raven

Similar to the crow in that it is deeply associated with death deities. But, while the crow is usually reserved as a spirit form for feminine deities, the raven has been the Otherworldly body for both Gods and Goddesses. Like the crow, it flew over Celtic battlefields as the deity incarnate. The raven is most closely associated with the Irish/Welsh God Bran.

Salmon

While airborne creatures archetypally linked the Celts to the Otherworld, sea creatures linked them to great knowledge, sacred mysteries, and deep emotion (typically, only deities of great wisdom and temperament ruled the Celtic seas). Most prominent among these wise sea creatures was the Salmon of Knowledge. The myths of Nudons and Fionn MacCumhal are among the many dealing with this fish.

Serpent

Represents the cyclic nature of life due to the annual shedding of its skin. It is a phallic symbol, a symbol of the Triple Goddess, and of the earth mysteries. It is important to the Druids, and is found on much old Celtic jewelry. Contrary to popular myth, there *are* snakes in Ireland, though they are pretty much confined to the rugged western region of the island.

Sow

Associated with some Crone/Mother Goddesses, such as Cerridwen, and with Otherworldly feasts. The pig is the archetypal symbol of plenty, healing, and shapeshifting.

Myths also tell us that, for a long time, several animal types lived in the Otherworld and belonged only to the deities. Among these were the deer, the pig, and the dog. They were brought into the human realm only after a lengthy Otherworld battle (see the "Battle of the Trees" in Chapter 6).

Other references to sacred and totem animals can be found in Robert Graves book, *The White Goddess,* when he discusses a calendar of birds used in ancient Ireland, and a Druidic calendar divided into thirty-six periods each represented by a different animal.

Other traditions use the image of either the wren, owl, or fox to represent the energies of the waning year, and the hare, robin, or bear to symbolize the waxing time from Yule to Midsummer. Others use what they believe is an old Celtic system of dividing the seasons into four rather than two parts with a bear for summer, a stag for autumn, a horse for winter, and a cow to symbolize spring.

If you are interested in further exploring the relationship of sacred animals to Celtic Pagan practice, you should begin reading about the many animals which appear repeatedly in Celtic myths. Read with a pen in hand and make note of the animals which appear and how they relate to the story. Before long you will find that you deeply understand the archetypal significance and magickal use of each sacred beast or bird. Then, armed with your findings, you can meditate on their qualities, adopt them as familiars, use their symbols or likenesses as tools for alignment with your deities, or make a mask of them to call their spiritual essence into yourself.

CELTIC MUSIC

Thou'rt the music of my heart, Harp of joy oh harp of my heart,
Moon of guidance by night, Strength and light thou'rt to me.

—Hebridean Love Song

MUSIC IS ANOTHER way to add Celtic ambience of your rituals, and is great for dancing to raise power. The Celtic people have always loved their music. Music was very important at old Celtic gatherings, and fine singers and musicians were prized courtiers of the High Kings and clan chiefs. An entire classification of Druidic study, the Bardic, devoted itself to the art of music and lyric poetry. Today there is never a festival occasion in which the Celts do not have their traditional music predominantly featured.

If you are musically talented you may wish to learn a Celtic instrument such as the bagpipes, harp, or tin whistle. Look up ethnic organizations or music schools in your phone book for more information on lessons available in your area. Also check out the bulletin boards in the music departments of universities and colleges where you can often find notices of students or professors anxious to supplement their income by teaching their art to others.

If you play other instruments, or enjoy singing, printed Celtic music can easily be found in folksong books and in sheet music at better-stocked music stores. (Also see Appendix F in the back of this book for some sample transcriptions of traditional Celtic music.)

By far the easiest way to provide yourself with Celtic music is to buy it prerecorded, and the Resources Guide in Appendix D of this book will give you the names and addresses of companies which sell Celtic music, both recorded and printed. You should also check out your local merchants for recordings by the Chieftains, the Battlefield Band, St. James' Gate, The Tannahill Weavers, Robin Williamson, Christy Moore, Planxty, and other Celtic musical groups and singers.

If you are fortunate enough to live in, or to be able to travel to the Celtic countries, you are bound to find some sort of music festival to attend. Over the past several decades there has been a great revival of traditional music with the full support of the various governments. In Ireland, *Radio na Gaeltachta* has been instrumental in promoting cultural literacy in traditional music, and many young Irishers can sing the old songs which their grandparents' generation nearly lost.

Each May, County Kerry hosts the hugely attended Pan Celtic Week, a gathering of Celtic people and Celtophiles from all over the world who wish to engage in and learn more about traditional Celtic pastimes. Certainly music plays a large part in the festival, but so do dance and

Celtic games such as Hurling. If you are interested in attending, contact the Town Hall in Killarney for more information, or call them at (064) 31622.

Another large Celtic music festival, which attracts up to 5000 musicians at once, is the *Fleadh Cheoil Nah Eireann Buncrana* which is held in County Donegal each August. For more information you may contact the organizers, the *Comhaltas Ceoltoiri Eireann*. Address queries to them at Belgrave Square, Monkstown, County Donegal, or talk to your travel agent.

All these massive Celtic gatherings derive from ancient clan games, and they have become the focus of modern national pride. Celtic Pagans usually associate them with Midsummer or Lughnasadh festivals even though the earliest recorded of these nationally organized festivals took place in Cardigan, Wales, at Yule in 1176. They include traditional Celtic games, music, native crafts, dance, and food. The national festivals are called *Yn Chruinnaght* on the Isle of Man, *Eisteddfod* in Wales, *Mod* of the *An Commun Gaidhealach* in Scotland, and *Oireachtas* of the *Conradh na Gaeilge* in Ireland. Most travel guides can give you information on the time and places of these gatherings.

Don't discount North America when seeking Celtic festivals. The majority of the people now living in the United States and Canada can trace their roots to the Celtic lands, and the Celts are well represented in ethnic and folk music festivals throughout both countries. If you can get to only one of these festivals, you can easily discover where the others are, as Celtophiles tend to run in packs. An excellent place to start is in Nova Scotia. As its name implies, it was heavily settled by the Scots, and each year a huge Highland games and gathering of the clans festival is held there which also features Scottish music, dance, and food.

You have several avenues open for locating other music festivals. You can talk to a travel agent, call tourist offices, subscribe to periodicals likely to carry the information, or check in some of the many newspapers often carried in local libraries.

CELTIC POETRY AND VERSE

For everything is sacred, poetry
of heavenly nature is on these hills....

—Islwyn

VERSE, IN THE form of poetry or song lyrics, can also help add to the Celtic ambience of your circle and set the proper tone for your rituals. It can be placed within rituals to underscore a feeling, concept, or emotion. After all, poetry is words directly from the heart which speak to the very soul of the collective human experience.

Throughout this text there are many snatches of Celtic verse heading each chapter and section. Also check your local library and bookstores for titles of volumes containing Celtic poetry. (The Bibliography of this book contains the names of several older titles which are relatively easy to locate in libraries.)

TRADITIONAL CELTIC DANCE

Come out of Charity,
Come dance with me in Ireland.
—William Butler Yeats

THE FOLK DANCES of the Celtic people are some of the best known in all the western world, for they formed the basis of the folk dances of the lands the Celts migrated to, particularly Australia, Canada, and the United States.

The national dances of Ireland are those most recognizable to Americans, and they are also the ones most untouched by other cultures. (England, Scotland, and Brittany adopted many French movements into their national dances from the sixteenth to the eighteenth centuries.) These movements, seen frequently in the media around St. Patrick's Day, can be learned as they are, or adapted for use in circle dances and coven or solitary celebrations. The Welsh dances are less familiar to North Americans, but they are still practiced all over the world, wherever the Welsh have gathered.

To learn these dances you can check out ethnic catalogs, magazines, and import shops (also see the Resources Guide in Appendix D) for videos or books which teach the steps, or, better still, check the local library and events column in your local newspaper for meetings of ethnic societies which usually teach the dances to their membership either free of charge or for a modest fee. In major metropolitan areas you are likely to find instructors to teach you for a higher price.

Most Celtic music festivals routinely include dances, either impromptu or organized. American and Canadian cities with large Irish populations (such as Chicago, Boston, and Toronto) have many Celtic music festivals or dances, some on a weekly or monthly basis. Again, newspapers and libraries are your best sources for locating these events.

If you are able to travel to, or if you live in, Ireland or Scotland, be sure to read the local newspapers for notices about a *feis* or a *ceilidh* (dance) which is open to the public. There are many of these held each week. You'll find that you will be most welcome and that the locals will be glad to show you a few basic steps.

CELTIC FOOD AND DRINK

I feasted in the hall of Fionn, At each banquet there I saw
One thousand cups upon the board, trimmed in richest gold.
—Irish Folk Song

WHETHER YOU ARE a solitary exploring the mythic figures for yourself, or are part of a larger group, food and drink should always be a part of your festivities, rituals, and magickal ceremonies.

The old Celtic rules of hospitality would not permit anyone—even prisoners and slaves—to go without extravagant sustenance, especially on festival occasions. The sharing of one's bounty, however meager, was a must among these people who believed that to conceal food and drink from a wanting guest was the same as denying it to the deities. In modern rural Ireland this custom still holds, with Jesus replacing the old Gods as the one in want. The Celts also left food and drink libations for deities, elementals, and other discarnates after each ritual or festival meal was finished.

The Celts relied heavily on their herds, and on game animals, especially venison, mutton, and hare, for their food. They scavenged the woodlands for berries and herbs and, being lands of islands and peninsulas, fish and seafood also made up a large portion of their daily diet in the later Celtic period. In the early Celtic period it is believed that water was held in such reverence that its creatures were not consumed for food except, perhaps, on festival occasions. Today, the Celtic people, who live so close to the bounty of sea, stream, and lake, rely heavily on fish and seafood, both for their own diets, and as a means of making a living.

They also made potent wines and, later in their history, cultivated the land for grains and tubers. See Appendix G in the back of this book for a sampling of some traditional Celtic recipes.

WHEN TO DO YOUR CELTIC RITUALS

*The most beautiful thing we can
experience is the mysterious.*
—Albert Einstein

RITUALS SHOULD BE done anytime the Pagan feels the need or desire to perform one. You need not be part of a group or coven to do a ritual. The Celts worked alone, as solitaries, or with their immediate families unless it was a major festival day. Rituals should be done when one is not going to be disturbed, or "discovered," and when one is fully alert and able to focus and concentrate on the process.

Use the times "inbetween," as the Celts did, to your advantage whenever possible, as they are already a part of the Celtic collective unconscious, and utilizing them will make it easier for you to connect with these energies.

WHEN TO DO CELTIC MAGICK

*Three sounds of increase:
the lowing of a cow in milk, the din of
a smitty, the hiss of the plough.*
—From *The 33 Triads*, ninth century

VARIOUS TRADITIONS HAVE different ideas about when magick should be worked. For example, most Pagans are already familiar with the idea of working magick for gain or increase on a waxing moon, and magick for loss or decrease on a waning moon. There are also numerous astrological and meteorological do's and don'ts depending on whom you consult, and many of these concepts were likely part of the Celtic world-view. Use any or all of these if you like, but the best time to make magick is *when you really need it.* Only then will your desire, focus, and intent be great enough to make the spell truly work for you. As long as you are comfortable in your surroundings, you feel safe, and are sure you will not be disturbed, weave positive magick as you see fit.

If you are creating a spell to be worked in a ritual setting, try to use one of the Celtic "between times" discussed above for the most potent outcome.

THE ESSENCE OF CELTIC PAGANISM

Seek first the gifts of the spirit
And those of mankind will surely follow.
—Matthew D. O'Reilly

THE ESSENCE OF any spiritual tradition is in the sincere heart of the seeker who chooses that pathway to help discover the great mystical mysteries which have intrigued human beings since the first of us crawled out of a cave on a starry night and asked ourselves, "Who else is out there?" Only by finding a way to unite ourselves with divine universal forces can we ever hope to answer those ancient primal questions or to evolve into more spiritual beings.

Perhaps Celtic Paganism is that pathway for you. The rest of this text is devoted to helping you find union with those divine forces as perceived by our Celtic ancestors.

CHAPTER TWO

ATTUNING TO THE CELTIC PANTHEON

*Let us contemplate both our forefathers and
posterity, and resolve to maintain the rights
bequeathed us from the former for
the sake of the latter.*

Samuel Adams

HE CELTIC PANTHEON is made up of many individual deities and heroic figures which, all together, make up the totality of power which humans the world over invest in their Gods and Goddesses. In keeping with the beliefs of nearly all other Pagan cultures, the Celts saw each individual in their pantheon as being merely a part of the "whole" deity, each one contributing a piece of the complete being who birthed all things into being and from whom we draw all magickal and ritual energy.

Modern anthropologists now believe there was never any such thing as polytheism, the concept of many unrelated deities making up a single pantheon, but rather that old Pagan cultures practiced pantheism, the belief just described. Therefore many of the surface impressions found in myths about our deities have to be reexamined with this concept in mind. For example, the Goddess takes the God as her lover, but he is also her son (and will be again) and, therefore, is merely reunited with her and, by doing so, perpetuating them/it/her/himself. This duel role concept is also seen in myths from numerous other parts of the world where divine brothers marry their Goddess sisters, etc. Though the mainstream religions have used these stories to point out how evil and vile Paganism is/was, the meaning is not one of incest, but rather of the union of two halves of the whole, the male and female principles of deity combining to make one potent whole.

Of course, this hypothesizing brings us to the eternal question: "Are the deities 'real'?" This is a question debated not only among Pagans, but by everyone who has ever lived. We all sooner or later question the spiritual and seek to work out in our own minds exactly what type of force a God or Goddess is, and just where that being's energy resides.

Certainly the deities are alive and well inside the human psyche, but as to whether they exist outside of this realm, only you will be able to decide for yourself. Indeed, these forces can be harnessed and manipulated by us, but whether that is an inner- or outer-plane function, or a combination of both, has never been answered. Certainly their power can manifest on the outer-planes (the concrete waking world in which we live every day), but how that comes about is definitely because of an inner-plane event such as spellwork or spiritual ritual. Certainly a fair number of the mythological figures we seek to worship or work with were, or were based upon, the lives of real people. But whether the figures lived or not, or whether the stories of their lives have been altered to fit the archetypes we collectively need, is irrelevant to the strength of the power they have waiting for us to tap.

The basic spiritual beliefs of the Celtic people provide a firm working foundation which makes it very easy for us to find ritualized methods to align ourselves with these potent, archetypal powers regardless of where they reside or if they lived "real" lives or not, or whether or not they exist outside of our own minds. The Celts were taught for thousands of years that human beings can indeed all work magick, do effective ritual, and have a deep inner spiritual life by getting to know the deities on a personal level not before taught to humankind.

Each of us contains a bit of divine essence simply because we exist. As Pagans we believe divinity created us as would human parents, and just as we contain a bit of our earthly parents within us, so we each contain a piece of the divine. The rest of the book is devoted to teaching you how to discover and use that God/dess-given power.

LEARNING TO FEEL THE POWER WITHIN

Ni bhionn an rath ach mar a mbionn an smacht
(There is no luck except where there is discipline)
—Irish Proverb

BEFORE WE CAN begin to harness the powers of the individual archetypes which make up the totality of the divine world, we must first learn to feel that power within ourselves. We must learn to recognize the essence of our shared life force, and learn to connect it with our own sense of being. This is done easily through basic meditation or altered state of consciousness.

In many ancient cultures it was prerequisite to prepare for rituals involving the divine with purification baths and/or pre-ritual fasts. While we have no hard evidence that the Celts regularly practiced either, we do have several references from faery tales and nursery rhymes about purification baths being taken on the Sabbats (the solar festivals) or Esbats (full moons). Hunger strikes, as a means for achieving social justice, are recorded in the monastic writings of the Celtic people, though there is no mention of them being used as a part of ritual preparation as was done with great efficacy in Native American cultures. If you enjoy these preparatory rites and feel they enhance your efforts, then use them anyway. Certainly they have a long history of Pagan use in other cultures, and can help put you in a receptive frame of mind.

ALTERED STATES OF CONSCIOUSNESS

Last night, in some lost mood of meditation,
The while my dreamy vision ranged the far
Unfathomable arches of creation,
I saw a falling star....

—James Whitcomb Riley

MEDITATING, OR ACQUIRING an altered state of consciousness, has taken on an unnecessary aura of mystery in our modern world, yet we all do it every day. You have changed your focus of consciousness every night since the day you were born when you went to sleep. During the night you go up and down from the light trance of alpha sleep to the deeper levels of delta and theta sleep. If you were attached to an EEG machine (brain wave scanner) as you read this page, the cycles per second read out would show that you are in an alpha state, a light hypnotic trance (called the alpha level) just below the level of normal wakefulness (the beta level). Likewise, watching the imperceptible light pulsations on the screen during a television show or movie induces a mild altered state of consciousness.

Altering your consciousness for divine alignment exercises, pathworking, or any other type of meditation, spell, or ritual work, is merely a process of learning to consciously control which of these four brain wave levels you function at (usually always alpha and theta for inner-plane work), and deciding for yourself how long you remain in each.

BRAIN WAVE LEVELS

Name	Cycles per Second	Human Condition
Beta	15–18	Normal wakefulness, alertness, study, conversational level (person is aware of all physical sensations and bodily needs)
Alpha	8–12	Light to medium meditation, daydreaming, focused concentration, drowsiness, cat-napping, some astral projection, easy guided meditation, very light sleep, reading, watching television, basic alignment exercises (person finds waking from this level not difficult)
Theta	4–6	Deep meditation, medium to deep sleep, complex astral projection, complex guided meditation, light unconsciousness, deity contact, pathworking (person finds waking moderate to very difficult)
Delta	0.5–2.5	Very deep sleep, coma or deep unconsciousness, near death experiences, anesthesia before surgery (person has little or no consciousness of physical sensations or bodily needs, waking is difficult, maybe even impossible in the deepest level)

To place yourself deliberately into one of these altered states is not a mysterious or frightening trip into dangerously unknown realms which can only be attained and mastered by some great adept. Those who would try to tell you that do not know what they are talking about. *Anyone* can achieve *some* success on his or her first attempt, though, as with any endeavor, you will improve with practice. It is all a matter of focusing your mind on one thing/event/idea to the exclusion of all else. When your mind wanders from the intended focus, don't get upset, just gently bring it back.

With practice in meditation and sustained concentration, your altered states can become longer and deeper, and at the deepest controlled states (the deep theta level) you can do more advanced work such as unguided inner-world explorations, unguided past-life regression work, and serious astral projections. These are very natural states. The only difference here is that you are seeking to gain conscious control of them. The key to all these things is in learning to concentrate for increasing periods of time upon one thing only.

You should now begin this daily practice of sustained concentration, especially if you are not already used to using meditation in your spiritual practice. The better able you are to keep focused, the better success you will have in working with mythic figures. To begin practicing this, go to a place where you will be unlikely to be disturbed for twenty to thirty minutes, gently close your eyes, and hold one image in your mind. Keep it simple. Choose a geometric shape or occult symbol with which you are familiar. Use only one object, symbol, word, phrase, or idea per session, and focus upon it alone. When you master this you will automatically be able to slow the cycle per second waves of the brain, inducing a sort of awakened sleep during which all facets of ourselves are in a heightened state of awareness and receptivity.

When you are able to keep this image in your mind for at least five minutes, then you can create a more complex scene. Add more symbols, motion, color, or even make a mental stage play. Practice this exercise every day, increasing the complexity of your images, and soon your mind will be disciplined enough to take you anywhere at any time.

USING MEDITATION FOR OCCULT PRACTICES

I am a wiseman of the primal knowledge...
I continue to behold God.

—Taliesin

OCCULT MEDITATION IS defined not only as "focused thought," but also the "absence of thought." It is a practice in which you attempt to empty your mind of all thought—a very difficult proposition for an organ which is active twenty-four hours a day all the days of your life. Either way, you are attempting to control your brain patterns so that you connect with a deeper spiritual place within yourself, one which can connect you with other, even outside, forces.

Begin as you did with the previous exercise, only this time choose a symbol of relevance to Celtic Paganism, or a symbol associated with deity (look at the dictionary section for ideas if you come up blank), and focus on that. Suggestions for symbols are the pentagram, the triskele, Arianrhod's wheel, Badb's hooded crow, or Dagda's harp.

When you can sustain the image for five to ten minutes without your consciousness wavering, begin to allow your inner-self to feel a kinship to the symbol. Allow yourself to feel "pulled" toward it. Mentally feel and see every inch of its surface. You can even project your own image into the scene and caress the object. Mentally move your hands over it and begin to get a sense of its subtle energies, and try to imagine the essence of the deity for which it stands. Feel his or her power under your hands, feel it crackle with the divine energy.

Next, step back from the object and view it from a distance. Try to get a sense for the energy it possesses without touching it. Now turn your thoughts deeply inward and try to find that part of yourself which crackles with the same energy as you just felt in the object. When you find it you will know that you have discovered the spark of divinity within yourself.

In keeping with Celtic practice, allow yourself to experience this energy association three separate times before moving on to another symbol.

CENTERING AT WILL

Blest, blest and happy be
Whose eyes behold her face....
—Anonymous Scottish Verse

PAGANS OFTEN USE the term "centering" to describe a deliberately induced altered state designed to bring them into themselves and shut out the outside world. This is usually done just prior to performing any ritual or magickal work. With practice you will find you can do this at will. The very act of preparing yourself for ritual in this way will have you halfway to your goal.

Every Pagan has his or her own method of centering, the most common being to take a deep breath, hold it, and release it while feeling yourself become the channel for a universal (divine?) life energy. Others mentally circulate a vibrant light energy through or around themselves, and still others picture themselves as the trunk of a great tree with their feet being the roots which reach down to infinity, and their head and arms the branches which do the same thing.

When you are ready you will choose a method for yourself. Chances are the choice will be practically an unconscious one, for it will be the natural outgrowth of practice and knowledge.

LEARNING TO FEEL THE POWER WITHOUT

May the blessings of the Light be on you,
Light without and Light within....
—Old Irish Blessing

BY USING THE power we have within, and combining that with a catalyst such as words, sounds, or color, we can begin to get a feel for the subtle divine energies of the universe around us. After all, these things contain an energy and a "life," one that, as Pagans, we believe came from the deities.

What good, you might ask, is there in discovering the power in objects outside yourself when your goal is presumably to feel deity within? The Celts believed that there was tremendous power in the name of a person or thing, that the vibration of something's name not only connected you with it, but also gave you a measure of power over it. There is a great similarity in the words for soul, breath, and name in both the Irish and Welsh languages, showing a decided linking of these functions in the popular mind.

Begin these meditative exercises by selecting an inanimate object and holding it in your receptive hand (the one you *do not* write with, or your left if you are ambidextrous). First study it with your eyes open. Turn it over and examine it. Say its name over and over (preferably in multiples of three) trying to feel the connection between the name of the object and the energy you feel coming from it. Next do this with your eyes closed.

Practice this three times with each object until you are familiar with the energies it emanates.

Next you should practice this with colored objects. These too emit a specific energy separate from whatever object they tint. The names of colors also relate to the energy they emit. For example, think of the word "blue." Let the sound roll off your tongue. You'll probably find that it is a lazy sounding word, slow, languid and not overly energetic. Pagan, occult, and New Age people all associate blue with peace, tranquility, sleep, and passiveness.

Practice this through the entire color spectrum, three times with each color, until you obtain a sense of the subtle energy of each. You can test your progress by holding pieces of colored cloth sight unseen and seeing if you can guess the color by the energy you sense.

BASIC ALIGNMENT EXERCISES

Snow falls on the top of the ice,
the wind sweeps the crest of the near trees;
Fine is the shield on the brave one's shoulder.
—From *The Black Book of Caermarthen*

THE EXERCISES IN which you learn to align with deity are basically the same as those you have just practiced. To do so will, perhaps, make you feel on some deep inner level that you have merged your energies with those of divinity. This exercise is designed to get you used to and comfortable with the energy patterns and sensations of divine forces so that you can begin to learn to work with them on a regular basis.

Basic alignment is also a prelude to evocation and invocation, more advanced work which will be discussed and explained in later chapters. But before we can begin that work we have to develop an understanding of, and familiarity with, the vibrations of divine energy.

For the time being, it is wise to stick with the divinity which corresponds to your own gender for these exercises. Later on you will have the time, and even be encouraged, to explore the energies of deities and heroic figures of the opposite sex. After all, they are all part of us and we need to learn how to be comfortable with them.

Never let anyone tell you that aligning with any particular divine force is inherently dangerous, a practice to be avoided at all costs. While in any occult practice there is some *slight* risk in dealing with powerful universal forces, on the whole you are in much more danger just sitting right where you are reading at this exact moment. Once you are comfortable with basic God or Goddess energy you can begin to expand that knowledge and try aligning yourself with other aspects of those polarized forces. For example, you might try to align yourself with the force of a youthful God, or an aged God, or even the crone Goddess.

Even the so called "dark forces," like the crone, have their place within us. You may hear it suggested by the fearful and uninformed that these dark images are best avoided. Hogwash! This only seeks to perpetuate the self-destructive myth that old women are somehow repulsive and dangerous, and that darkness is evil and hides goodness and truth. The crone is just one aspect of the Goddess, and the dark is merely a part of the light, and to get to know, love, and be comfortable with these dark energies is every bit as important as are knowing and loving the Maiden, the Mother, and the light. They are all a part of the whole, and we must explore each one if we are to become whole ourselves.

For our basic alignment exercises we will not be using any specific deities, but rather the female and male principles which we generically label the "Goddess" and the "God." The Celts believed themselves to be descended from a Mother Goddess and an Otherworld/Underworld God. It is these two potent primal forces with whom we will begin to merge ourselves.

If, like most witches, you keep a Book of Shadows (in Irish it is called the *Oiche Leabher* which means "Book of the Night"), or some other type of magickal/ritual journal, you may wish to record in it the details of your alignment experiences to reexamine later on.

ALIGNMENT EXERCISE 1

THE PURPOSE OF this alignment exercise is to understand that the deities who created you bestowed upon you their characteristics, both good and bad, just as did your biological parents.

Go to your private place and center yourself. Begin breathing deeply and steadily, visualizing each breath you take as being filled with divine energy. See it sparkle with silver and gold light as it enters you. Draw the breath in through your nose and exhale through your mouth. This process has long been believed to set up a powerful energy circuit within the body (i.e., breath becomes energy) which benefits not only your ritual and magickal work, but your overall physical health and well-being as well.

Close your eyes and think of the three principal qualities that you associate with either the Mother Goddess or the Father God *without* visualizing a corporeal vehicle for them. You may want to think of such qualities as strength, fairness, protectiveness, contrariness, sternness, kindness, nurturance, guidance, or love. There will likely be as many different sets of answers as there are people doing this exercise.

Now look within yourself and find as many similar qualities as you can. Meditate on how the way you display these characteristics is like or unlike your perception of deity. When you have done this, sit quietly and still your mind. Begin to deliberately shift your inner-energies so that yours and that of the deity become more similar. You can think of this as being either a temporary alteration, or the first step toward permanent self-change, whichever you wish. Continue doing this until you can clearly sense the divine spark ignite within yourself.

If you like, you may pick another three characteristics and continue the exercise, or experiment with the qualities opposite the ones with which you began the exercise.

ALIGNMENT EXERCISE 2

THE PURPOSE OF this exercise is to feel the power of deity in nature. If you have access to natural land, or even a tree in your own backyard, this is the best place for this exercise. If you don't, you can try this exercise with a large house plant, or with visualization only.

Find a large tree, plant, or shrub to work with, one that is at least as tall as you are. Stand in front of it and study it with your eyes open. Note its size, shape, scent, texture, everything about it that makes it unique.

Now it is time to look into the tree. With eyes either open or closed, peer into the soul of the tree and feel the indwelling spirit. Begin to see the divinity within the tree take anthropomorphic shape. See the head, the arms, the eyes. See the God/dess dwelling there as in all living things.

Now, physically try to put a part of yourself into the tree. Feel how easily you merge with the energies there. Know that this is because you and the tree share the distinction of having been created by the same creative life source.

Do this experiment three times and compare notes on each experience to see if they differ or if they remain the same.

ALIGNMENT EXERCISE 3

THE PURPOSE OF this alignment exercise is to recognize yourself in a true and complete image of the divine, and to understand that you can indeed work magick through this image.

Go to your private place and center yourself. Begin breathing deeply and steadily, visualizing each breath you take as being filled with divine energy. See it sparkle with silver and gold light as it enters you. Draw the breath in through your nose and exhale through your mouth. Do this several times until you are completely relaxed and your brain waves have slowed considerably.

Close your eyes and, in your mind, form a picture of total blackness, the infinite primal void which preceded all life as we know it. Allow it to engulf you, and see yourself at the center of this dark nothingness.

In the far distance imagine now that you see the faintest glimmer of light. As you keep your mind focused upon it, see it coming towards you, moving swiftly across the void. The light is a blinding white, and it pulsates with the energy of all life that ever was or will be. As it gets closer, see it as an oval-shaped being which begins to take a human-like form the closer it gets to you.

Though the being is your own size, its light and life force illuminates everything for many miles around, and soon you see yourself engulfed in this white brightness.

As the being comes to stand front of you, imagine it taking shape in the form of either the Goddess or the God. You can mold this image in any way you see fit. We all have our own mental picture of deity, and now is your chance to utilize that image. Form every detail of him/her in your mind, making the likeness as real as you can.

As you raise your right hand in greeting, so does s/he. As you smile at it, so it does at you. Note that it matches your movements so precisely that you neither feel like its leader nor its follower, and begin to feel the current of sympathetic energy which passes between you. This is often felt as a gentle pull from the solar plexus area. Realize that this is the divine energy in your-self which you share with this image of God/dess-hood. You are neither ruled by it, nor do you rule it. You are partners, kinsmen, a shared presence.

Now, as you continue to watch the being in front of you, begin to see its face change so that it looks exactly like you. It is you and you are it. When you feel this to be so, thank the being for coming to share with you. It may or may not choose to leave or dissipate then. In any case you are now free to end the exercise.

Breathe deeply again and begin to bring yourself out of the meditative state. To do this, some persons like to count up from one to nine, others merely begin to slowly stretch unused muscles, while others recall mundane thoughts. All ways are correct as long as it is not done too quickly. You took the time to properly take yourself down, don't skimp on properly coming up.

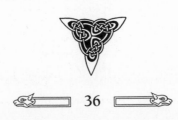

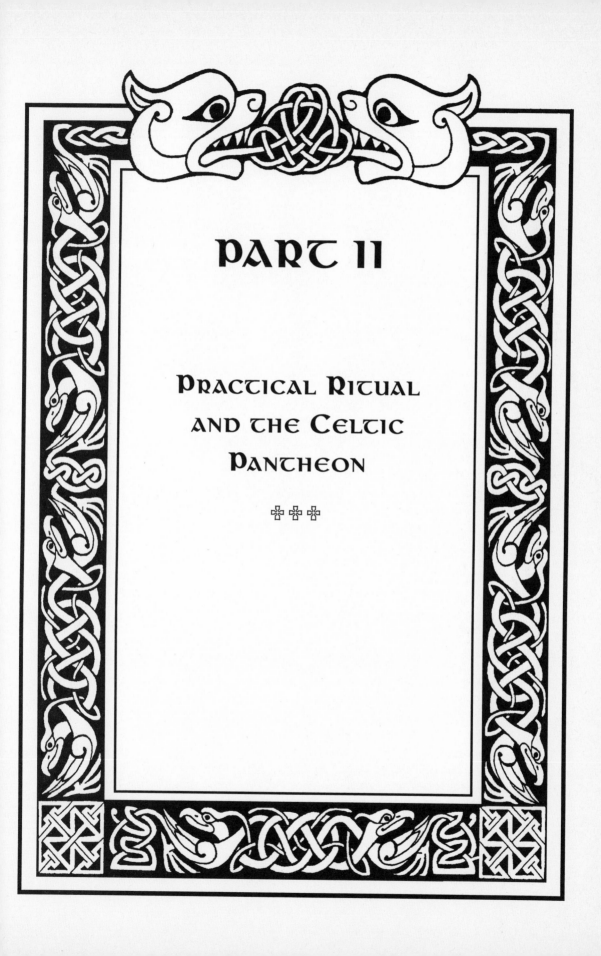

PART II

PRACTICAL RITUAL AND THE CELTIC PANTHEON

✠ ✠ ✠

—

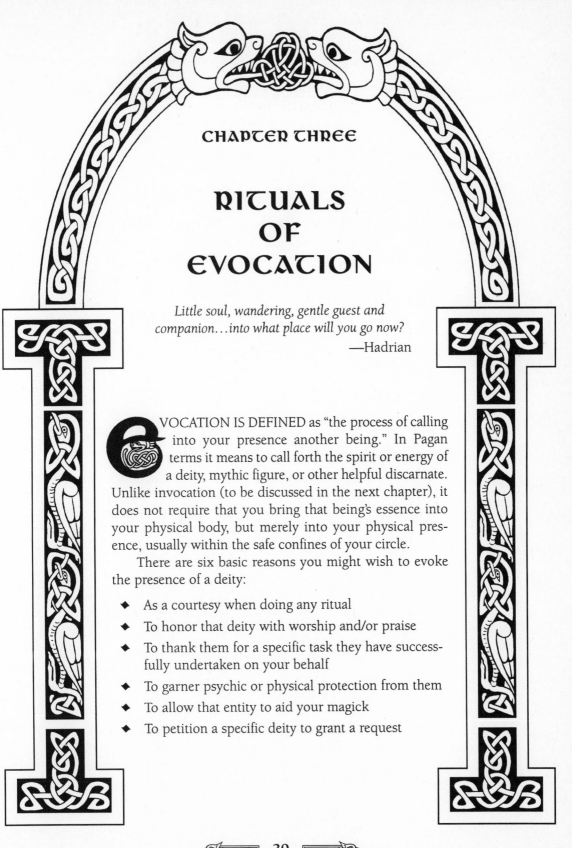

CHAPTER THREE

RITUALS
OF
EVOCATION

*Little soul, wandering, gentle guest and
companion...into what place will you go now?*
—Hadrian

EVOCATION IS DEFINED as "the process of calling
into your presence another being." In Pagan
terms it means to call forth the spirit or energy of
a deity, mythic figure, or other helpful discarnate.
Unlike invocation (to be discussed in the next chapter), it
does not require that you bring that being's essence into
your physical body, but merely into your physical presence, usually within the safe confines of your circle.

There are six basic reasons you might wish to evoke
the presence of a deity:

- As a courtesy when doing any ritual
- To honor that deity with worship and/or praise
- To thank them for a specific task they have successfully undertaken on your behalf
- To garner psychic or physical protection from them
- To allow that entity to aid your magick
- To petition a specific deity to grant a request

COURTESY EVOCATION

The first word from the cauldron, when was it spoken?
By the breath of nine maidens it was gently warmed.

—Taliesin

PAGANS HAVE BEEN evoking elemental spirits to their circles for a long time. Some modern Pagans who jump into ritual without first analyzing the process are often surprised when they later discover that this is what happens naturally during the invitation to the four directions, a process which is part of the preliminary ceremony for virtually all Pagan circle rites.

Some Pagan rituals also request the presence of the God/dess. During the rites deities may or may not be called upon to add their blessings to the ceremony. At the end they are nonetheless thanked and dismissed along with the elemental forces which were also called upon.

This is what is known as "courtesy evocation." It requires no special words or gestures, and the energies of deity are no doubt present, though any specific God/dess archetypes which may be of value to your workings will probably *not* be present.

CELTIC WORSHIP

Celestial as thou art, O pardon, love, this wrong,
That sings heaven's praise with such an earthly tongue.

—William Shakespeare

BASIC WORSHIP OF the generic God or Goddess presence can be viewed as a phase between a courtesy evocation and the process of evoking a specific deity for a specific reason.

As mentioned in the Introduction, some scholars argue that the Celts did not worship their deities as we might think of the term today. We know, however, that no matter how flawed the Celtic God/desses were, we have three solid reasons to believe they were honored and revered:

◆ All cultures have had their special deities and have sought to honor them in some way, no matter how meager that offering might be. We have no reason to believe the Celts were any different.

◆ We know that Celts honored their deities seasonally like other Pagans because we have the traditions of the Sabbats and Esbats which have been handed down to us, both by hereditary Pagans and through Pagan customs found cloaked in mainstream religions.

◆ Drawings, carvings, and other Celtic artwork displays divine figures. Particularly noticeable is the Horned God, the principal male deity of much of western Europe, and images of a pregnant Mother Goddess.

Feel free to honor your God/desses, or your favorite aspect of them, whenever you are moved to do so. The best way to do this is to let words and/or music come from your heart. This is no time to be a slave to written rituals, especially since the arts of evocation and invocation are best accomplished by the solitary practitioner. You should never feel self-conscious in the presence of the divine. Their energy is a part of you (which is one of the reasons why it was so easy to call to you in the first place), and you should rejoice.

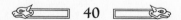

You cannot say the wrong thing, cannot offend, cannot hurt their ears with off-key music and made-up tunes. Even if you haven't figured out the whole relationship, *they* know you are connected, and, like proud parents, are pleased by whatever efforts you offer as long as they are the best you can produce—not the best effort of someone you know who may be gifted with words or music—but your *own* best effort.

THANKSGIVING

Let us be thankful—thankful for the prayers
Whose gracious answers…might fall upon us unawares.
—James Whitcomb Riley

IT IS APPROPRIATE, and even expected, that you will hold a special evocation ritual to formally thank a deity who has successfully aided you in some way. You may thank that being with words, music, dance, libations, incense, or by offering gifts either to them, to something in nature (such as giving plant food to a tree), or by giving to animals or to other people in need.

Again, as long as the thanks come from the heart, you cannot go wrong or offend. In fact, you will get a lot farther by making some gesture, even a token one, than by doing nothing, taking for granted their help when you are in need. Recall how you felt the last time you went out of your way for someone and they walked away without a single word of appreciation?

THE RITE OF EVOCATION

… At the moment two souls merge,
All the universe holds its breath in wonder.
—Rebecca Worrell

TO CALL A specific deity or mythic figure to your circle is not a complex procedure. Once the preliminaries for ritual have been set in motion, whatever forces you might wish to call upon have already been alerted to your intent. Some argue that this is merely because you have alerted your own psyche as to what it is you want it to project, and the psychic forces, often mistaken for the deities, are subsequently called forth. There are some Pagans who accept this theory, and their rites of evocation work just as well. (Remember as you do this, or any Pagan ritual, not to confuse that which is imagined with that which is not real. They are *not* one and the same!)

In any case, your evocation will be accomplished through a ritual specially designed in the Celtic style to manifest the power of the divine into your circle in the form of a specifically named archetype. You will be able to know when you have succeeded in your efforts because you will distinctly *feel* the presence of the mighty energy. Your sense of it may be a bit subtle at first, but with a minimal amount of practice, you will definitely know when you have succeeded.

 **Sample Evocation Rite**

BEFORE YOU BEGIN your ritual you will need to decide which deity you wish to evoke. If you are familiar with the Celtic pantheon, you may already know which being(s) you wish to invite. If not, please scan the Dictionary section of this book, or read some Celtic myths and folktales to get an idea of with whom you wish to connect. Do not worry at this point about whether or not the deity you have chosen to work with is of your own gender or not. You will not be drawing this force into yourself and therefore should not feel at odds with its energy. Think of evocation like a telephone line to divinity—you can call up anyone at anytime just for a heart-to-heart chat.

Next, you will need to cast your circle in your usual manner, calling upon any directions, elementals, etc., which you usually do before beginning any working.

If you are not familiar with the circle casting process, simply take one of your tools or your pointed finger, and walk the perimeter of your work area, moving clockwise, all the while visualizing a bright blue-white protective circle rising around you. Make it real in your mind and it will be real around you, offering you both protection and space in which to contain all the energy you will raise during your rites. It is also recommended that you read several books on Pagan practice so that you will be knowledgeable about the things you will be doing. While it is doubtful that any significant harm will befall you if you make an error, it is better to know in advance what sort of forces you are dealing with and how to handle them.

You also need to have your altar, no matter how simple or elaborate, inside the circle. Again, this is a matter of personal taste or of the dictates of your tradition.

When all your preliminary work is complete, you are ready to evoke the presence of your chosen mythic figure(s)/deities into your circle area.

Select a tool which to you symbolizes the ability to direct energy. This can be a wand, athame, pentacle, or your pointed finger. You will be using this to help focus your intent and to direct the divine energy into your circle.

Stand facing the direction that either you personally, or your tradition, feels is the home of the deities. For some this is the west, where most references to the Celtic Otherworld are made. Others view this as the north, the cold place where the sun never travels, or the east, where the new day's sun rises each morning. Others still will choose a direction based on correspondences of the deity they wish to evoke. For example, when calling to a sun God, they would face south, the traditional direction of the element fire in the northern hemisphere.

Hold your chosen tool in what is commonly called your "power hand." This is the hand you write with. Spread your arms out to your sides and part your legs so that you are in a position roughly resembling the upright pentagram. As you do this, visualize the pentagram around you as if you have stepped into it. See it pulsate with the same blue-white light of which your circle is made.

Center yourself and call out, using appropriate words, to the deity you wish to have come to you. Always phrase your summons as a request or invitation and never make demands. It is traditional in Celtic practice to begin and end the evocation by intoning the deity's name three times. As you call the name visualize your voice being carried off to the far reaches of the universe, then echoing back to you. For example, if you wanted to call Flidais, an Irish woodlands Goddess and protectress of animals, you might say:

Flidais. Flidais. Flidais.

Pause after each intonation of the name to allow for the visualization.

> *Blessed Lady of the woodlands wild, Mistress of the Hunt, guardian of its animal*
> *spirits, protectress of its verdant lushness, and keeper of its many eternal secrets.*
> *I ask that you please come to me here and now in this sacred space. I ask that you*
> *join with me in (state the purpose of your ritual here).*

Raise your tool or finger as high above you as you can reach and imagine that you are catching a part of the universal life force at its tip. Now bring the tool down in a quick arc in front of you and touch it to the ground just inside your circle's perimeter. Tap the ground three times and repeat the deity's name:

Flidais. Flidais. Flidais.

Stand and welcome the deity. Also thank him or her for coming. You should then restate the purpose of your evocation.

Another way to call in the deity is to draw an invoking pentagram three times in front of you while calling the name three times. Though this gesture is most often used to call energies other than the divine, this pentagram configuration is very much a Celtic practice and will not disturb the working.

Next, spend a few moments feeling the powerful presence and attuning yourself to its energies.

The idea of repeating the name and tapping the ground three times has been an accepted part of Celtic evocation rituals for as long as anyone can remember. Though we are all familiar by now with the sacredness attached to the number, most of us have from time to time questioned its dogged use in modern ritual. Interestingly enough, when anthropologist Margaret Murray began researching her book, *God of the Witches,* she turned up a number of transcriptions of witch trials both in Europe and in North America in which the accused (probably actual practitioners of the Old Ways in these cases rather than the hapless victims the powers-that-were usually rounded up) confessed to using a strikingly similar method for evoking whatever spirits they were accused of calling forth.

Many followers of Celtic magickal ways insist that it is an absolute must to feed any being you call out of the Otherworld, be it a human discarnate, an elemental, or a deity. Food and drink can be offered simply in the form of offering it to the evoked being on a plate, through visualization, or through specific offerings. Offerings can be made by pouring a libation onto the ground, ingesting it yourself in honor of the God/dess, paying homage to the food and drink as a physical representation of the deity, or declaring a portion to be taken later to a woods for animals or to be donated to a shelter which needs the assistance. The choice is yours. Do what your tradition, or your own inner-sense, tells you is right.

After your successful evocation, and/or ritual feeding, you may proceed with any other ritual or spellwork you like. The presence of the deity can watch, assist, or lend energy to your project. All you have to do is ask.

✠ ✠ ✠

PROTECTION RITES

Soft, the lonely hours are creeping,
Hill and dale in slumber sleeping,
I, my lonely vigil keeping,
All through the night.
—Welsh Folk Song

HAVING DIVINE FORCES present in your circle is already highly protective, but you can call upon them to offer you an even greater blanket of protection by using a shielding ritual, one which will continue to look out for you even after the ritual has ended.

Shielding rituals are commonplace in Celtic Paganism, and many of our most omnipresent deities are associated with them. When thinking of shields, Cuchulain and Brid immediately come to mind, as do Dagda, Arthur, Fionn, and Maeve.

For this ritual it is more efficacious to choose a deity to work with who is associated with a shield, or at least with having strong protective powers (refer to "Appendix E: Mythic figures Cross-Reference"). In this ritual you will draw the energy of the deity you have present in your circle into an astral shield, one created by your own will and powers of visualization.

 **Shielding Ritual**

AFTER YOU COMPLETE the basic Rite of Evocation, pause and create in front of yourself (visualize) a magnificent full-body shield. Give it form and life with the force of your will. Give it details by adding any decorative touches to it which speak to you of protective powers. You can use Celtic knots, figures of power animals, symbols associated with the deity with whom you are working, penta-grams, crosses, etc. Spend as much time as you need creating this shield. You will wear it always until you decide to dissolve it.

Next, take your tool in your power hand and point it toward the deity, and intone words such as:

Blessed Lady Brid, loving mother, protectress and warrioress, whose energies blaze with the heat of the sacred fire, I ask that a part of your divine essence now enter and remain in my shield, that I may carry with me always the sacred protection of your loving care. Help this shield to deflect the ill-will of my enemies and others who wish to harm me both physically and psychically. Be my shield and my strength, my comfort in time of need. Wrap your loving arms around me through the power of this shield. Enter it now, I ask you.

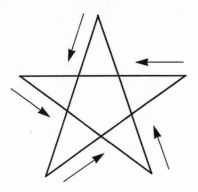

* Start here

The Invoking Pentagram

* Start here

The Banishing Pentagram

Imagine a part of the vast energy of the deity entering your tool. Then take that tool and hold it against the shield which is in front of you. It is best to point the tip of the tool toward your breast bone, as this seems to be the place most of us instinctively choose to point to when doing this ritual. Both see and feel the God/dess energy enter the shield. Visualize it glowing with a vibrant intensity that haloes it with a blinding white-gold light. Continue to visualize exactly how that shield will work for you. Picture the divine energy deflecting harmful energies which come your way, sending them harmlessly away from you.

Be sure to thank the deity whose you help you have asked. After all, they have literally given a part of themselves to you.

To keep the shield functioning at optimum levels, renew the ritual monthly.

✠ ✠ ✠

PECICIONING

Carry my blessing with thee to the west....
—Colm Cille

WHILE YOU HAVE a deity present in your circle with all your ritual accouterments at hand is the ideal time to petition, or request, special favors. These favors are usually referred to as "boons" in most Celtic circles.

Asking a deity for a specific item to manifest or for a special situation to come about is a very, very old concept, one which is still used today in both Paganism and in mainstream religions. In mainstream religion the process is usually called "prayer." The great difference between the two styles of petitioning is that Pagans, especially Celtic Pagans who view their deities as imperfect beings, do not expect the petitioned God/dess to do all the work for them, but rather they know that they will have to back up their requests with mundane efforts of their own. This is not to suggest that one system is inherently a better way of doing things, just that each takes a different approach.

Though the difference sounds simple enough, it has been cause for a great deal of bitter misunderstanding between us and our detractors. I once was acquainted with a woman who called herself a "born-again Christian." She made a habit of spending late nights in a bar which had a notoriously dangerous reputation. Though I have always considered myself to be pretty fearless, I would go out of my way to avoid the part of town where that bar was located, especially after dark. I asked her why she wasn't afraid, and she replied that she prayed each night for the protection of her God. To her, this made perfect sense—as a Pagan, I would not only have prayed for protection, but I would have avoided the obvious danger by going elsewhere.

For Pagans, making a petition to a deity is rather like working a spell in which the petitioner knows that a certain amount of effort and self-involvement will be necessary for the request to manifest. For example, one cannot ask a Goddess of abundance to shower them with riches if all they wish to do with their time is sit at home and stare at a television. At some point the petitioner is going to have to show his or her good faith and intent by going out and getting a job, buying a lottery ticket, or beginning some other enterprise which has the potential of being profitable.

Before you ask for anything keep in mind the old adage, "Be careful what you wish for…you just may get it." Pagans and other witches who have been involved with magick for a long time can all relate stories—mostly humorous ones—of how their magick backfired when their intent was not crystal clear in their own minds and not worded clearly when the petition was made.

If you are not sure just how these things can take a bizarre turn, remember the popular horror fable called "The Monkey's Paw," penned in 1902 by W. W. Jacobs. In this tale, a distraught mother comes into possession of a magickal talisman, the Paw, and is granted a wish. She wishes that her son, maimed and killed in an industrial accident, would be returned to life. Well, he was, but he returned with the hideous maiming still intact. Though this is an extremely exaggerated case, it illustrates very well why we must be careful with our wishes.

Before asking for anything, meditate briefly on the following ideas:

◆ Is this what I really want?

◆ Do I have a clear picture of the outcome?

◆ Is the outcome likely to harm or take away from someone else?

◆ Have I visualized my request well?

◆ Have I worded my request in a way which matches my visualization?

◆ If something goes awry, can I live with the consequences?

◆ If I cannot, then what steps will I be able to take to reverse things?

◆ Have I consulted a divinatory device to double-check my results?

◆ Is the request likely to offend the deity I wish to petition?

◆ Have I chosen the right deity to help me?

Divine magick is one of the most potent and expedient forces we Pagans have at hand to make lasting changes in our lives. Approach the ritual with all the caution you would take before creating any other spell, and then think about it again just to be sure.

Though you should make some preparation in order to have your request properly worded, making sure it reflects as accurately as possible your mental image of the desired outcome, you want the words to sound as if they come from your heart. Your desire and emotional involvement are important to your ultimate success.

Taking the example of Flidais again, here is how you might word a request to her to aid an injured animal. She is already present, so you do not have to repeat the name three times:

> *Flidais, my beloved dog has broken his leg and the vet fears he may never heal properly. I ask that you please send your loving energy over him, infuse him with your divine self, heal his wound, and restore him to me whole, complete, and healthy, his limb functioning perfectly and without any trace of the injury. I ask this with love, for the good of all, and wishing harm to none.*

Notice that instead of just merely asking that the pet recover and be returned, the petitioner asks that the animal show no trace of the injury. In other words, the petitioner has thought out the scenario so that the pet would not have a limp or other disfigurement which might cause him pain and the loving owner more distress.

Always, always, always, think out these things whether you are evoking the divine or merely making a simple bedroom candle spell. It can save a lot of headaches in the end.

When you have finished making your request, it is also traditional in modern Celtic ways to chant three triads in rhyme form over and over again until you can feel a reserve of built-up energy within the confines of the circle. This is similar to the raising of the Cone of Power. But instead of sending the energy you built up mentally into oblivion, send it into the deity. This accomplishes two things. First of all, it further links the deity's energy with you own and with your need, and, secondly, it gives the deity added energy to work with. Rest assured that it will be returned to you threefold.

The three rhyming triads for the request to Flidais might go something like this:

> *Flidais, Flidais,*
> *Hear my plea,*
> *Restore my loving pet to me.*
>
> *Heed my need,*
> *Make him well,*
> *Bind his wound with this my spell.*
>
> *Flidais, Goddess of us all,*
> *For your aid I humbly beg,*
> *Heal complete my sweet dog's leg.*

SAMPLE SPELLS USING EVOCATION

They do all because they think can.
—Virgil, from *The Aeneid*

PAGAN MAGICK HAS long been understood by its practitioners as the manipulation of forces and energies not yet understood by science. For example, an internal combustion engine, the sort that powers the all-too many cars we drive, would have been a fear-inspiring manifestation

of magick several hundred years ago. But to we twentieth-century people who understand the factual scientific principles on which it runs, it is not "magickal" at all. It is simply an occurrence which works on natural scientific principles.

Pagan religions have few rules, but there are two laws which are generally acknowledged by all. When the first law was first uttered is unknown, but it has many first and second cousins among other world religions. It is commonly called the Pagan Rede:

As ye harm none, do what ye will.

This law prohibits a Pagan from doing anything, in magick or in daily life, which might harm any other living being, and most significantly prohibits us from violating any living being's free will. Don't even think to risk manipulating another person through magick, the consequences are just too great.

If you do choose to do something which might cause harm to another, you should remember the second law:

The threefold law.

Pagans believe that any energy sent out from themselves, either for good or for bad, will be revisited on them three times over. This is a type of karmic law, and a good one to keep in mind if you doubt that your spells are entirely harmless. The best way to ensure that your spells will not have some harmful side effect is by doing a divination beforehand to discover the probable outcome. If you are not familiar with all the forms of divination, or do not have one which works well for you, please consult your local bookstore or occult shop for ideas.

Some Pagans will add a line to their spell incantations such as "as it harms none," or "as all will it freely," or something similar to further ensure that they are not violating the Rede.

In many Celtic circles this law is taken a step further and, in keeping with the sacredness of three times three, many believe that any combined energy which three or more persons send out, the essence of that energy will come back to them each nine times over.

The Pagan Rede also means that you have an obligation to keep yourself from intentional harm, and violating any law which you know will bring harm back to you should be considered morally wrong. This is especially important to remember when working directly with the divine, for any magick you do with these forces is more potent, and therefore the consequences of misuse of this power are greater.

Magick requires several things of the spell caster:

◆ Involvement—physically, mentally, and emotionally

◆ Knowledge about how the spell works and how to do it

◆ A strong need or desire for the hoped-for outcome

◆ The ability to sustain a visualization for at least several minutes without your thoughts wavering

All four of these things will be evident in the following sample spells, and in those in Chapter 4. For those of you with no prior experience or knowledge of spellwork, it is best to get some guidance in the form of many good books written on the subject before going very far with the practice. Look for works by Raymond Buckland, Scott Cunningham, or Janet and Stewart Farrar for

solid introductions to the Pagan forms of this art. Also, look to Appendix B in the back of this book for a detailed outline for helping you in constructing spells of any kind.

House Protection Spell

A SOLID HOUSE protection using divine energy can be done similarly to the shielding ritual presented previously. However, this time the ritual is more complex because you will need to evoke four specific deities, each one associated with a different element. In this spell you will draw the divine energy into an imaginary oversized tool or weapon, one which corresponds to the direction, element, and deity, and then you will set these astral tools up at each corresponding compass point of your home.

There are numerous combinations you can use. For balance it is best to use two female and two male deities. For example, try these:

Deity	Element	Direction	Tool to Visualize
Lugh	Fire	South	Candle or spear
Cerridwen	Water	West	Cauldron
Dana	Earth	North	Pentacle or wand
Dagda	Air	East	Sword

Call all the deities into your circle following the Rite of Evocation, each to their corresponding quarter of the circle. Then, beginning with any direction you like, visualize a giant ritual tool standing by your house. For instance, if you begin in the west, see a huge, powerful cauldron there. Using the same technique given above for drawing divine energy into an astral shield, do the same with each astral tool.

Proceeding clockwise around the circle, ask each deity to lend part of themselves to the object you have set in place.

Be sure to phrase your words in the present tense as if the work is already completed. This is a basic must-do in magick, otherwise the energy will forever remain in the future, just out of your reach.

When the spell is done, thank the deities individually for their aid. Renew the spell once a month to reinforce its power.

It is traditional to seal the end of any and all spells with words proclaiming your assurance that the work is done. Words such as "So Mote It Be," "The Rite Is Done," or "As I Will, So It Is Done," are usually chosen.

✠ ✠ ✠

Area Protection Spell

BELLS AS A source of protection are ancient (many decorative items we use today were once protective talismans). Door harps and wind chimes are among the most prominent of the bell talismans which can be found in most gift shops.

Bells were also used similarly by the Celts and there are several extant nursery rhymes and stories from Celtic countries which point up the pervasiveness of the practice.

The use of sacring bells (from the word "sacred") is an old Celtic Pagan custom still in use in the churches of Brittany. These are very small bells which are tied at intervals to the outer rim of a large wooden wheel, ironically often called a Wheel of Fortune. As people walk past, they turn the wheel, releasing the protective energy of the bells. You can buy bells almost anywhere, and you can construct or buy a wheel by utilizing the services of a carpentry, craft, or garden shop. Evoke the power of protective deities as you put it together. The wheel can be turned whenever you feel the need and can melodically ward off unwanted influences and entities.

When the wheel comes to a stop be sure to end the spell with a:

So Mote It Be.

✠ ✠ ✠

 ## Money Spell

BEFORE YOU BEGIN this spell of sympathetic magick, choose a deity to call upon who is associated with abundance or prosperity. Anu, Artio, Cernunnos, Dagda, Habondia, or Liban are good ones with whom to begin.

For this spell you will need a green candle, some matches, and some money—a single coin or a bill is fine.

Evoke the deity who you wish to work with, and petition him or her with your need. Ask for help in working the spell to achieve your goal.

Strike the match to light the candle, feeling the deity with you, lending its energy to the divine spark. Bring it slowly down to light the candle. Again, feel the deity infusing the candle with the power of your need. Place the money underneath the candle holder and say something to the effect of:

This money, as all money I need, is now buried, out of my reach. Help me, (state deity's name), to burn away the obstacles in my way and reach the money I need for (state the purpose of your need). As the candle burns away so does my poverty. As the candle is consumed so is my need, and just as this dollar is free of the weight holding it back, so is the other money I need.

At this point do not use "So Mote It Be," or any other words indicating the end of a rite.

Spend as long a time as possible visualizing the burning away of your financial difficulties as you watch the candle burn. If you cannot sit while the candle burns clear down (and most of us cannot), repeat this spell on consecutive nights until the candle is burned away.

As the candle burns itself out, you should end the rite with the words:

The money I need is released. It flows freely to me now. My need is satisfied.
Thank you, blessed (state deity's name). So Mote It Be.

✤ ✤ ✤

OTHER SPELLS AND SPECIAL NEEDS

REMEMBER THAT YOU are not limited to using only one deity in any single divine magickal operation. You can be as specific as you like with your spells and with whom you choose to aid you in them. For instance, let's say you are trying to get a job with a telephone company. You may wish to work with a prosperity deity such as Habondia, but you might also want to add the influence of a need-specific deity such as, in this case, Oghma, a God of communication.

You might even wish to find three deities whose energies are compatible with your desired outcome in keeping with the Celtic sacred number. These need not be standard triplicities, they need only have energies of which you have need. The following is a list of several possible triple combinations for deities who might be able to help you in a number of hypothetical situations. Study the list, and the energies of the deities chosen for it, to get an idea of how to begin making your own magickal combinations:

- For creating romance with a person interested in horses:
  Epona, Aengus MacOg, Aine
- For getting a job in the defense industry:
  King Arthur, Anu, Scathach
- For creating wealth using communication:
  Habondia, Oghma, Ossian
- For help in the study of history in a university:
  Abelard, Taliesin, Cerridwen
- For aiding a sick child:
  Diarmuid, Deae Matres, Airmid
- For aiding a sick animal:
  Diarmuid, Flidais, Saba
- For help in growing a medicinal herb garden:
  Diarmuid, Cebhfhionn, Flidais

CORD MAGICK AND EVOKING THE DEITIES

Nine powers of nine flowers,
Nine powers in me combined....
—from *Mabinogion*

WORKING WITH CORDS is another practice which is quintessentially Celtic. Cords represent the unifying force of the fifth element of spirit and, properly used, have the ability to draw together all the elements into one great power spot.

In the case of using a cord in evocation rites, you would draw the essence of the deity into it just as you did above in the shielding ritual. The cord can then be used to immediately bring the presence of divinity into any spell you wish to do. Think of it as a source of emergency reserve power for those times when your need is immediate but your time is not.

To make your own cord(s), simply go to any craft store and ask for craft cord. Most of these are unfortunately not made of all natural materials, though you can find these if you look. However, be prepared to pay dearly for them. In this case I believe the synthetic works just as well, and my cord is made largely of polyester. The power in the cord will come from deity and not from nature, so the medium is less important than it might otherwise be.

Celtic cords can be made individually of white, red, or black fabric, or of all three woven together like a braid for wearing or for more potent magick. It is traditional to call into them the three aspects of the Triple Goddess, each evoked at the proper moon time:

CORD COLOR	DEITY	MOON PHASE
White	Maiden Goddess	Waxing
Red	Mother Goddess	Full
Black	Crone Goddess	Waning

The cord is traditionally nine feet long though, but since the measurement of "feet" and "inches" dates back only a few hundred years, it is impossible for us to know exactly what type of measurement the ancient Celts might have used. When casting a circle for solitary work or for small groups, the cord also serves as a measuring device for the circumference of the working area.

When you evoke the presence of the deities and draw them into the cord, make nine knots in the cord, each at one-foot intervals while visualizing the divine energy being tied up in them. Of course, it is best to do this outdoors under the moonlight, but at a window will do just as well.

If you wish to use deities other than the Triple Goddess, Celtic Pagans often choose the colors blue, green, and gray for their cords. Again, these can be made individually and then be woven into one cord. When deciding which deities to evoke and call into each cord, think about what the colors represent to you and which deities best correspond to them.

Blue is usually the color of youth, and is an alternative color for virgin or maiden Goddesses, or for young male Gods. It is a color for issues of beginnings and fresh starts, for dream work, and for the spring festivals. Green is the color of fertility and plenty and would best correspond to Mother deities or Father Gods and virile prime-of-life Gods. Green is best used for acts of general worship and praise, for summer festivals, or for spells dealing with prosperity and fertility. Gray is for sacrificial Gods and older deities, and is best used for dark times, spells of banishment, spirit contact, and winter festivals.

There are numerous other associations for each of these colors and for the deities who might represent them. To begin, you might want to try any of the combinations on the following page.

CORD COLOR	DEITY	ASSOCIATION OF DEITY
Blue	Aengus	God of Young Love
Green	Dagda	Father God
Gray	Arthur	Sacrificial God
Blue	Dwyvan	God of New Beginnings
Green	Mabon	Harvest God
Gray	Balor	Sacrificial God
Blue	Cessair	Goddess of New Beginnings
Green	Arianrhod	Fertility Goddess
Gray	Bo Find	Sacrificial Goddess
Blue	Branwyn	Virgin Goddess
Green	Bran	Fertility and Harvest God
Gray	Badb	Crone Goddess
Blue	Ossian	Adventurous God
Green	Boann	Fertility and Water Goddess
Gray	Fionn	Warrior and Sacrificial God

As you can see from the list, it does not matter if you evoke all male, all female, or a combination into the three cords.

If you should ever decide that your energies and that of a particularly deity you have used in cord magick are not compatible, you should not attempt to reprogram the cord. Certainly, no harm of any kind would befall you if you tried, but making a brand new cord is much more efficacious. By constructing another from scratch, you are investing in it a new intent, removing old energies which might interfere with your magick while purposely and purposefully creating a home for another deity. The results will be much more satisfactory if you take the time to begin again because the energy you want will feel welcome and needed. Imagine that someone offered you a cast-off that someone else they had offered it to did not want. Even if you were glad to have the item, you would no doubt feel better and more comfortable with something made especially for you.

Experiment until you find the right divine combination for your cords. Every few months renew the evocation to keep the cord properly charged to its maximum potential. When not in use store it in a dark place, untouched by sunlight.

You may choose to braid the cords into one rope. This of course combines, or triples, the power in it. The finished cords are usually worn around the waist during rituals as vestments of power. You can also use each cord separately for specific spells, or wear them all together around your waist during rituals when they are not needed for magick. This goes both for those who choose to wear robes and those who practice skyclad.

ENDING THE RITE OF EVOCATION

The lions of the hill are gone,
And I am left alone—alone.
—from *Lament for Deirdre*

ENDING THE RITE of Evocation does not involve any complex visualization or ritual. Simply prepare to end and close your circle in your accustomed manner. Thank the quarters, or any other beings you have called in, and be sure to thank the deities whom you called upon. The deities will depart when they are ready, though when you physically close your circle their energy will noticeably fade.

You can also make the banishing pentagram in the air before you as you release the energy of the deity. Though this pentagram configuration is usually reserved for banishing unwanted energies, no deity would take offense if you used it here for it is a very Celtic practice. Just remember, you cannot force a deity to go or come—only invite.

For those unfamiliar with this closing process, you simply reverse the actions you took to create it. Walk counter-clockwise around your circle, seeing it dissolve, and its blue-white energy fade into the ground. Again, it is best to read some books on basic magickal practice or to find a teacher who can help you learn to do this properly.

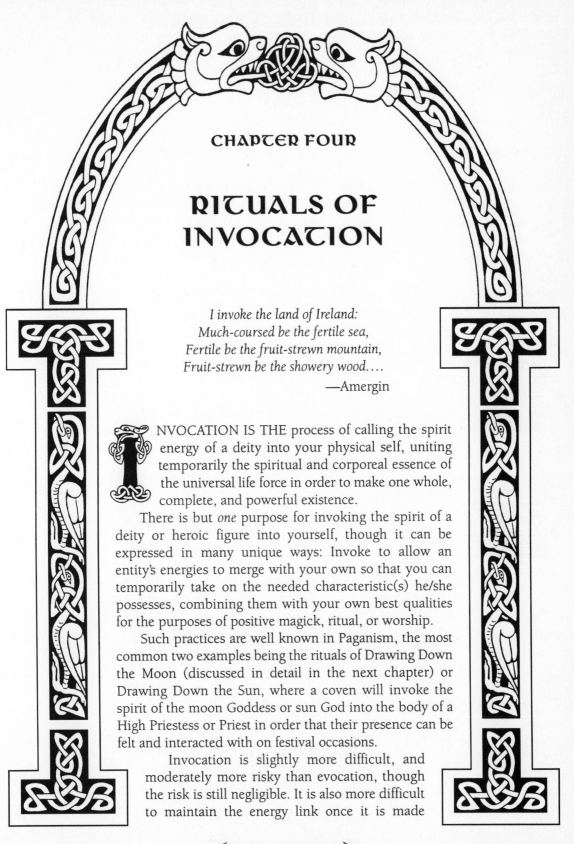

CHAPTER FOUR

RITUALS OF INVOCATION

I invoke the land of Ireland:
Much-coursed be the fertile sea,
Fertile be the fruit-strewn mountain,
Fruit-strewn be the showery wood....

—Amergin

NVOCATION IS THE process of calling the spirit energy of a deity into your physical self, uniting temporarily the spiritual and corporeal essence of the universal life force in order to make one whole, complete, and powerful existence.

There is but *one* purpose for invoking the spirit of a deity or heroic figure into yourself, though it can be expressed in many unique ways: Invoke to allow an entity's energies to merge with your own so that you can temporarily take on the needed characteristic(s) he/she possesses, combining them with your own best qualities for the purposes of positive magick, ritual, or worship.

Such practices are well known in Paganism, the most common two examples being the rituals of Drawing Down the Moon (discussed in detail in the next chapter) or Drawing Down the Sun, where a coven will invoke the spirit of the moon Goddess or sun God into the body of a High Priestess or Priest in order that their presence can be felt and interacted with on festival occasions.

Invocation is slightly more difficult, and moderately more risky than evocation, though the risk is still negligible. It is also more difficult to maintain the energy link once it is made which is why many covens reserve this task for their leaders, the people who are presumably the most experienced in occult practices.

The technical term for invocation is *theurgy* (a Greek word often used in Ceremonial Magick) which means the magickal experience of human union with a divine force.

Until very recently I believed, as do many Pagans, that men are best left to invoking male deities and women to female. It wasn't until I read Ivo Dominguez Jr.'s thought-provoking article, "Sabbats and Sexuality: Sense and Sensibility," in the Spring, 1993, issue of the Pagan periodical, *Green Egg,* that I began to rethink that position. Dominguez tells of his own coven's experiments with non-traditional ritual role assignments. He wisely reminds us that within us all there exist polarities which enable us, on some level, to expand our spiritual potentials.

Soon after reading the article I began to do my own experiments in cross-gender invocation, and, though I will admit to being a bit self-conscious about them even though they were done in private—they became increasingly successful with time. And while I never felt myself to be completely a part of some of the male mythic figures I called into myself, I did discover that they were nonetheless a part of me.

The idea of a large rugged man being a Virgin Goddess, or a delicate young woman being a Father God may take some getting used to, especially for the persons undertaking these roles, but what we can learn from these experiences far outweighs the self-consciousness society has taught us to feel when adopting roles not assigned to us by some part of the larger culture. But keep in mind that, in the Celtic view, all the deities are part of one single power, the power that created all of us. Inside us all are varying aspects of the masculine and the feminine, and it could be that it is necessary to regularly feed this repressed part of our psyches in order to become and to remain whole and balanced. To validate the rightness of this assumption we need only to look at our nightly news broadcasts to see the result of unbalanced, one-sided power (usually masculine power due to the blanketing influence of mainstream religion) running amuck.

THE RITE OF INVOCATION

*Let each of us become
all that he was created
capable of being.*
—Thomas Carlyle

YOU WILL NEED to select a specific deity to invoke before you begin your invocation rites. Whom you choose will depend a lot upon what you wish to do while joined with a God/dess. If this is your first experience with invocation it is best if you choose a major deity such as Dana, Dagda, Arthur, Brid, etc., because their archetypes are better known and understood. They are potent forces which are most easily reached by beginners. Those with more experience in Pagan rites, or who are on familiar terms with the Celtic pantheon, may wish to experiment with some of the minor deities or heroic figures.

Begin your Rite of Invocation in the same way you began your evocation ritual, within the safe confines of your circle with all your needed tools at hand. If you plan to invoke a male force, you will need a wand, athame, or pointed finger, just as you did before. But if you wish to unite with a female force, it is best to have with you some feminine symbol such as a cup or chalice.

Even a drinking glass from your own kitchen is fine to use. Just eliminate from it any mundane energies first by running it under cold tap water and visualizing all the past psychic programming it may have picked up during regular use being sucked down the drain. Spend some time afterward rubbing it and holding it to infuse into it your own energy patterns.

When you have done any preliminary work you wish to do as dictated by your personal habits or your tradition, you may begin the invocation.

Take your chosen tool in your power hand and face the direction you feel is best.

Close your eyes and begin to slow your mind, placing yourself in a medium-level altered state of consciousness. For doing this choose a mantra which reflects your will to unite with divinity. "Mantra" is a Hindustani word meaning a repeated phrase or chant which, when repeated over and over in the mind, alters the brain waves to induce an altered state which is in sync with the desire or idea expressed in the mantra. Though modern Celtic traditions frequently use these mind chants, there is no Celtic word which expresses the process as well as the better-known Hindustani term.

For example, if you wish to invoke the sun God Lugh you might choose a mantra such as "I am one with the sun," or, "Lugh is the light, summer bright." If you want to invoke a fertility Goddess such as Arianrhod you might select something like "I am the same as the grain," or, "Womb of Arianrhod, womb of mine." You might find the mantra easier to say and focus upon if it rhymes slightly as the above examples do. Experiment with various phrases until you find one you like which works for you.

When you feel you are in the proper state of mind you may stop the mantra and continue, eyes open or closed at your discretion. Knowing when it is time to continue is not something anyone can teach you, you must learn to sense it for yourself. Through experimentation, trial and error, you will succeed in doing so.

There are two ways to do an invocation which are fairly easy to learn. The first involves the visualization of the deity coming to stand before you as it did in Alignment Exercise #3 from Chapter 2. The other involves using your tool to direct the energy of the deity into yourself, and this seems to be the preferred method for most.

 ## Invocation Method One

WITH YOUR EYES closed, form in your mind a picture of total blackness, the infinite primal void from which preceded all life as we know it. Allow it to engulf you, and see yourself at the center of this dark nothingness.

Now imagine that in the far distance you see the faintest glimmer of light. As you keep your mind focused upon it, see it coming toward you, moving swiftly across the void. The light is a blinding white, and it pulsates with all the energy of all life that ever was or will be. As it gets closer, see it as an oval-shaped being which begins to take on human-like form the closer it gets to you.

Though the being is your own size, its light and life force is so great that it illuminates everything for many miles around, and soon you see yourself engulfed in this white brightness.

As the being comes to stand front of you, imagine it taking shape in the form of either the Goddess or the God. As before, you can mold this image in any way you see fit. As your raise your right hand in greeting, so does s/he. As you smile at it, so it does at you. Note that it matches your movements so precisely that you neither feel like its leader nor its follower, and begin to feel the current of sympathetic energy passing between you.

Mentally communicate to the deity exactly what you want of it. Tell it not only that you wish to merge with its energy, but exactly what you hope to accomplish by doing so. Also keep in mind that the deity has the right to refuse you this request. Its body, such as it is, is its own possession and it does not have to give it up or merge with you if it chooses not to. You will feel yourself denied very rarely, though it does occasionally happen, usually when there is some reason you should not be doing an intense ritual. Such reasons as illness or lack of preparedness for the undertaking are most often the cause of being denied.

When the deity has given its permission for the invocation, turn around, facing the opposite direction. The deity should now be behind you with the two of you facing the same direction. Begin to feel your energy and the divine presence become one and slowly step back and into the astral body of the deity.

Once you are there, remain very still. Allow a few moments for your life forces to join and align themselves. Again, this is not something anyone can teach you to sense. You will just have to know when the union is completed.

You may now open your eyes and do whatever spell or ritual work for which you called the deity to aid you.

Invocation Method Two

STAND IN YOUR circle facing the chosen direction. Have your chosen tool, one which corresponds to the gender of the deity you wish to invoke, in your receptive hand (the one you do *not* write with). Just as the power hand projects energy, the receptive hand draws it in and it will be used to direct into you the energy of the divine.

As in the evocation rite, you should call out the name of the deity three times, intoning each with meaning while visualizing it echoing out over the vast reaches of the universe and coming back to you.

Now call the life force of that deity to your circle. You will not be calling it in corporeal form as you did with the evocation, but rather you will be inviting the spirit or power part of the deity. This energy will come to your circle in spirit, and will permeate every inch of your ritual space, being contained within the circle's confinement until you choose to do something else with it.

Call upon the deity with words such as:

Blessed Arianrhod, whose womb brings forth life to all things, to whose womb I will someday return to await rebirth, I call upon your mighty spirit to please come into my circle now. Infuse it with your many blessings, cloak me in your mantle of fertile power. Come unite with me in the Rite of Invocation.

Or for Lugh:

> *Powerful Lugh, blessed of the sun, wide shield of protection, bestower of riches and well-being. My Father and my Lord, I call upon your mighty spirit to please come into my circle now. Infuse it with your many blessings, cloak me in your mantle of fiery power. Come unite with me in the Rite of Invocation.*

As with the intonation of the name, be sure to visualize the call going out to the farthest reaches of all space and time. Then, with arms flung wide, wait for the presence to be felt. Don't worry if you don't sense it strongly on your first try. It may be that you are not ready to handle any more energy than has been presented to you, or it could be that you just need more practice with invocation work.

(Note that you stated your purpose—that of invocation—within the call. The fact that you feel a willing presence with you after the call will indicate that the deity has given its permission for the rite.)

Raise the tool in your receptive hand high in the air as directly above your head as you can reach. Imagine that you are trying to shove that tool straight up into the highest reaches of the heavens. Say something like:

> *Lady Arianrhod (or Lord Lugh), please join with me now. Merge your life force with mine, May two halves now be whole.*

Visualize the power of the deity entering the top of the tool you hold. Feel it filling to overflowing with power. Persons doing this often report feeling a tingling in their hands or arms, or a feeling of dizziness as they come into contact with the divine energy. This is normal. It will not hurt you, and it will soon right itself. If it doesn't, it is best to close down the ritual and try again another day. Don't worry that you have invoked a power overload. This is probably just a sign that you are not ready either physically, mentally, or emotionally for this particular invocation. In fact, there was a belief among the Druids that in no magickal operation would any practitioner ever be given more of a challenge than they were capable of handling at any stage of their spiritual development. So do not worry about being overloaded with a power you cannot handle. This simply will not happen.

When you feel that the tool you hold has absorbed all the energy it can hold, bring it down in front of you at chest level, still held upright.

You now need to take that accumulated energy and direct it into your body. The exact place on your body that you use as an entry point is really up to you, though there are traditional and/or recommended places. Use the following guidelines to help you decide where to begin experimenting:

◆ **Female Invoking Female Deity**
   Womb Region
   Genital Area
   Heart Area

- ✦ **Female Invoking Male Deity**
  Forehead
- ✦ **Male Invoking Male Deity**
  Genital Area
  Solar Plexus
  Heart Area
- ✦ **Male Invoking Female Deity**
  Throat Area

Bring the tool to the area you have chosen as the best spot to bring to energy into yourself. Exhale as you touch it gently to the spot, and then inhale. As you draw in the breath, will the divine life energy into yourself. Take several deep breaths until you feel it has been completely drawn in. Do this gently without heaving, huffing, or puffing. Doing so will set up tensions in your body which will pull you out of your altered consciousness.

Many people report feeling a great rush of personal strength and power at this point, and, like them, you may find you have to spend a few moments adjusting to the coursing blood and elevated physiological responses which accompany it. You may even feel sexually excited. This is normal too, and is an excellent indication that you have succeeded in your goal.

If you follow the old Celtic belief that all beings called forth from the Otherworld must be fed, do so now, before beginning any other ritual or magickal workings.

Now that you have the essence of the deity inside you, you are free to continue with your ritual or magickal workings.

DIVINATION WITH THE DIVINE

Part wide the veil
That I might seek the unknowable.
—Riley Wilde O'Manion

WHILE YOU HAVE the power of a deity inside you is an excellent time to experiment with some of your favorite divination tools.

Tarot, Runes, scrying, etc., are all done much more efficaciously during an invocation. The reason is quite simple. First of all, you have inside you added energy for making these devices work, and secondly, you have the advantage of the deity's broader scope and more omniscient view-point to help you in your interpretations.

Experiment with these for yourself, especially when invoking deities who are known to have an affinity for divination work such as Badb, Bran, Cerridwen, or Feithline.

CORD MAGICK AND INVOKING THE DEITIES

No cord nor cable can so forcibly draw, or hold so fast,
as love can do with a twined thread.

—Robert Burton

YOUR CORD CAN also be used as an effective tool for invocation and invocative magick. (The concept and instructions for making a cord are outlined in Chapter 3.)

When your cord is constructed and placed in its traditional place about your waist, you have right next to you the primal power of whatever deity you have invoked into it. As was said before, think of your cord as an emergency reserve of divine power to be used when you need something immediately but do not feel you have any time to waste with a formal invocation.

Invocation through a cord works best when the cord is tied about your bare waist next to your skin. You need to call upon the deity whose energy resides inside it to come into you. To do this simply visualize first and then sense the transfer taking place. This will not be as potent a force as you would have if you taken the time to do a full-blown formal invocation ritual, but it works quite well in a pinch.

To release the energy from you, simply untie the cord from your waist and it will be gone.

When you do this type of invocation you will deplete the cord of its power and it will have to be recharged in another ritual.

SAMPLE SPELLS USING INVOCATION

Three qualities that foster dignity:
a handsome figure, fine memories, morality.

—From *The 33 Triads,* ninth century

IF YOU ARE unfamiliar with the theory and practice of Pagan magick, read the section in the previous chapter on "Sample Spells Using Evocation." This will give you a sound basis with which to begin working and will also direct you to some authors who have written solid, easy to understand books which focus solely on spellcraft.

LOVE SPELL

WHEN DOING LOVE magick we are all at our most vulnerable. There is probably little that we will experience in life quite as painful as unrequited romantic love, and therefore the temptation to use manipulative magick is at its greatest. If you are currently in this situation you are no doubt at this very moment weighing the pros and cons of violating the Pagan Rede. We have all had similar contemplations. It's natural.

But such manipulative acts are best avoided. Ask anyone who has crossed that line to tell you about their own experiences. Most of them do not end happily. Often the object of desire becomes madly obsessive about the one who worked the spell, other times the relationship decays because there was never any common basis for it in the first place. Another prevalent scenario is that the one you wanted so badly is taken away from you by another by either fair means or foul. All these miserable examples illustrate the Threefold Law in action, and none of them are worth the effort or the ensuing misery.

However, you can use love magick to give yourself a fighting chance either with someone you know and like, or to draw into your life that mysterious stranger whom you have been waiting for all your life.

To use a love spell with invocation you need to select one of those gorgeous, irresistible deities whom no man or woman could ever turn away. You might try Diarmuid, Fand, Cliodna, or Fergus for starters. Invoke that deity into a cord that you can carry with you against your bare skin (instructions for charging the cord are in Chapter 3). You can choose to make a smaller cord for this purpose, one which could be worn around your neck or wrist like a piece of jewelry.

The color you choose for a love spell cord is also important as it will indicate the type of romance you are trying to draw to you:

CORD COLOR	ROMANTIC ASPECT ATTRACTED
Red	Passionate, physical, lusty love, good for finding non-monogamous partners
Orange	A basic color for attraction, somewhat lusty
Yellow	An intellectual love based on shared interests, communication
Green	Marriage and family love, attraction to family life and children, good for finding monogamous partners
Blue	Dreamy, sensual, reckless love
Violet	A relationship based more on imagined qualities than on reality
Gold	A protective love, somewhat possessive
Silver	A neurotic love, very possessive, tendency to get a weak, clinging partner
Pink	Sweet, flowery, romantic love
Black	A turbulent relationship with many hidden aspects
Brown	Unsuitable for love magick
White	Chaste, unpassionate, but very faithful love

You can also weave together several colored cords into one to get and balance all the qualities you want to attract.

When you are in the presence of the one whose attention you wish to attract, or are in a situation where you think you might be able to meet the man or woman you want to find, allow yourself to absorb the energy from the cord. Take into yourself the irresistible power of the deity you invoked. Feel yourself to be very beautiful, or handsome, and desirable. Project those feelings outward so that the one you want will notice you. What happens then is first up to that person, and then up to you.

If you want to attract a specific person, this spell will give you a fair shot at them without resorting to manipulation, and it will not draw in anyone else who does not want to respond to you other than to notice the unusual power you are emanating.

HEALING SPELL

TO DO INVOCATIVE healing magick you need to invoke a deity of health and healing, or a mythic figure who was known as a fine physician. You might wish to invoke Airmid, Diancecht, Laeg, Meg the Healer, or Miach for starters.

The concept behind this invocation is simple—you are going to draw right into your own sick body all the knowledge and power of a deity with a reputation for unqualified healings. Some of the stories of the Celtic physician deities are quite miraculous.

Once you have invoked the deity and told it your purpose, simply stand quietly and allow them to do their job. They may heal you all on their own or they may move you to seek out a particular human doctor, drug, or healing herb.

Healing spells work best when they are done in tandem with modern medicine. Use your head. Don't ignore dangerous symptoms while hoping for a miracle cure. Find a doctor you trust, and then allow the deities to aid him or her in the total healing process.

ECO-MAGICK

BY NOW THERE is probably not a person left on the face of this earth who is not aware that our planet is in sad trouble. Pollution is destroying Mother Nature and eroding the resources she needs to sustain life. Pagans were aware of this long before it came to the attention of the general public, and we have long been arbiters for sane environmental policies.

We have also been practicing eco-magick, magick to aid the environment, for many decades. Sometimes we feel we are fighting a losing battle, but we keep trying.

If you can do an invocation ritual in a natural setting it is an ideal time to use the power of that deity to help you project energy to heal the nearby plants and trees. If you cannot be outdoors, send the energy out from wherever you are and it will be received and appreciated.

For best results, choose deities to invoke who are known to have an interest in the environment such as Aine, Druantia, Fand, Flidais, Llyr, or Manann.

CHOOSING PERSONAL DEITIES

Are you a god? Would you create me now?
Transform me then, and to your power I yield!
—William Shakespeare

WHILE YOU ARE certainly free to work with any and all mythic figures, most settle after a while on a small number, usually about a half-dozen or so, with whose energy they most keenly resonate. These are deities which are not only potent archetypes in the broad sense (the macrocosmic level), but who, on the individual level (the microcosmic level) have a special meaning or significance to the one who frequently invokes them.

In Joseph Campbell's classic work, *Hero With A Thousand Faces,* he eloquently makes his argument for the universality of these divine archetypes. He points out that our need for these archetypal heroes and heroines is so compelling that we recreate them over and over in modern versions to whom we become very attached. Most often cited are the widely popular characters from the popular sci-fi adventures *Star Wars* and *Star Trek.* Building on this assumption, several psychologists have used these mythic characters as models for human development, claiming that we learn to identify with a few particular archetypes as children, and that we either learn to internalize and emulate them, or else we seek out others to fulfill those roles for us. Regularly evoking or invoking the deities of your own spiritual tradition can adequately and safely fill this yearning need.

You will probably experiment with several personal deities who appeal to you before settling on your favorites. I most often use Brid, the principal Goddess of my own Wittan tradition; Flidais, a woodland Goddess because of my love for animals (my dogs always know when I am working with her and stay nearby); and Queen Maeve, a figure who represents to me the epitome of feminine power. I am also currently experimenting with invoking various God forms to find one with whom I am best suited to work. So far Taliesin, who shares my passion for music, and Oghma, who shares my love of words, seem to be the best contenders.

Begin by reading through the Dictionary section of this book and familiarizing yourself with the stories and energies of the various deities. Then, if you feel moved to do so, seek out more about them in books on Celtic mythology. Work with several of them, both with evocation and invocation, and begin to build a personal relationship with them.

It may sound like a lot of work, but the result, the indescribable feeling of actually uniting your own being with that of a powerful divinity, is well worth the effort. It has certainly been worth it for me. For several years I worked to build up the sympathetic links with my chosen personal deities, and now I have only to call up the image of Brid's shield to know she is protecting me, and if I call out to Flidais to look after my animals, I can instantly feel her loving energy wrap around them.

Once you begin working with deities on a regular basis, keep alert for signs that one special deity might be trying to let you know that he or she wishes to forge a closer bond with you. I once thought looking for these "signs" was sort of kooky until it happened to me. It happened several years ago when my partner and I decided to take a chance on making a major change in our lives. He quit his very well-paying job, made application to return to university, and we sold our home and moved cross-country. Once settled, it was imperative that we both find other employment—anything!—as soon as possible until our other plans began to take shape. I was having no luck at all in finding work until I spotted a classified ad from the phone company. I wasn't sold on the idea, but I had worked part-time for a phone company many years earlier to help put myself through undergraduate school, and figured if experience counted for anything, it was worth a shot. Besides, I was getting desperate.

When I got out of my car at the phone company offices I spotted a very long silver gray feather lying on the damp grass in front of my car. It was one of the prettiest wild feathers I had ever seen, beautifully formed with a satiny texture, gleaming in the morning sun. It would look nice on my altar, I decided, and resolved to pick it up if it was still there when I came back out. Thirty minutes later I came back to my car and saw that the feather, which I had forgotten about in the angst of the interview, was still waiting for me.

I stooped down to pick it up. As soon as I touched it, I felt a surge of energy course up my arm. In a flash I remembered that air was the element associated with communication—exactly what the phone company was all about. Then I remembered Oghma, the Celtic God of communication. This was also a corresponding symbol of his.

I wanted very much to believe the feather was telling me something, but I wasn't completely convinced. However, three days later I was offered the job.

Since that day Oghma has made his interest in my life known in numerous ways. No matter how you view them, don't sell your Gods and Goddesses short, they are out there, and they are *in there*, too. Human-divine relationships take as much time to grow and build trust as do human-human bonds. Invest time and effort in these relationships and a rich partnership will grow.

CHOOSING A CRAFT NAME

There stands the shadow of a glorious name.
—Lucan, first century C.E.

IT IS CUSTOMARY in many spiritual traditions, not just in Paganism, to select a new name which reflects the new life you have chosen. Some witches will go through several of these before settling on one they feel reflects the true inner-them. Others plan on changing their name many times throughout their lives as they grow and learn in their faith.

If you have not yet chosen a craft name for yourself, or if you feel it is time for a change, you may wish to adopt the name of a special deity as your own. This is an old and honored practice, and since names were of great importance to the Celts, it is a decision a Celtic Pagan should carefully consider.

If you feel a deep connection to more than one deity, you might want to combine their names either in whole or in part. For example, you might feel strongly a part of both Lugh and Taliesin and want to make your craft name Taliesin Lugh or Talilugh.

If you choose to adopt a deity name as your own, you can make the ceremony of name adoption extra special by invoking that deity and merging with its energy, making it truly a part of yourself. You can also align yourself with some of the deities who are linked to the naming process (see Appendix E for assistance in finding these) to help you select something appropriate.

There are as many ceremonies for bestowing a craft name as there are Pagans. All are deeply personal events even if done in the company of a coven, and all are correct if they are meaningful to the one receiving the name.

When you invoke the deity whose name you wish to adopt, you should spend a good deal of time feeling like that deity, allowing yourself to take on their persona, their attributes, and clearly forming in your mind just why you want their name as all or part of your own. Then take whatever ritual tool(s) you wish to use and place it (or them) against your forehead while making a verbal declaration of your name. Say the words that feel right to you. An example of this might be:

> *I am Brid, beloved of Erin, spirit of fire, healer of ills, warrioress of old, protector*
> *of life, woman of power, sovereign Mother of all creation. I create, I inspire, I*
> *make magick. I am old, I am young, I an eternal. I am the All-Power personified.*
> *I am me...Brid.*

Repeat the new name nine times, intoning each one with great feeling, attempting to fully align yourself with the vibration of the name.

You can also add additional names to your craft name which reflect other aspects of yourself or other occult interests you have. For instance, you might call yourself Brid Moondancer because you love to dance your magick under a full moon. Or you might call yourself Taliesin Songweaver because of your love for music and your talent with song spells, or Lugh Firewalker for your affinity for fire magick. If you know something about one of the Celtic languages, or have access to someone who does, you might want to translate your name. For example, Brid Moondancer in Irish would become Brid Gealacrinceoir (pronounced GOOH-loch-RREEN-ker).

ENDING THE RITE OF INVOCATION

As strong as the sea, your fortress shall be,
Your language stays ever with me.
—Hen Wlad Fy Nhadau (Welsh National Anthem)

TO END THE Rite of Invocation you must release the divine energy from your body before you can thank it and close your circle. It is certainly permissible to retain some of that energy for protection, personal power, etc., but the deity itself must be released. Even if you would wish to carry it around with you, it is doubtful that you could sustain the link for long after your visualization was broken.

Ending Invocation One

TO END THE first method of invocation you need merely to allow yourself to feel your energy and that of the deity separating. When you feel it is time, step out of him or her and turn around again face to face.

Thank the deity for the help given and close your circle in your usual manner.

✥ ✥ ✥

Ending Invocation Two

TO END THE second method of invocation you must return the divine energy to the ritual tool you used to gather it. Place the tool in your receptive hand and place that tool against the place you used as an entry point. Allow the energy to depart back into the tool.

When you feel that all the divine energy has been reabsorbed, transfer the tool to your power hand and raise it high above your head. Say something like:

(State name three times), I return you to the sacred space of the circle.

Feel the energy pour out from the tool and into the space around you. Thank the deity and close your circle in your usual manner.

✥ ✥ ✥

CHAPTER FIVE

THE CELTIC PANTHEON AND THE ESBATS

By the moon we sport and play.
With the night begins our day....
—Thomas Ravenscroft

HE ESBAT, OR full moon, has long been seen by Pagans of many cultures and traditions as being an efficacious time for ritual and magick. The word Esbat comes from the French *esbattre*, meaning "to frolic," and is indicative of the joyful and powerful group workings which have become a popular part of modern Celtic Pagan celebrations, even though it is most likely that the majority of Celts honored the Esbat alone or with family. Those following Celtic ways usually believe the impact of the full moon's energy and influence is felt from approximately three days before until three days after the actual moment of fullness.

Invocation has and still does play a large role in Esbat celebrations, as the popular and ancient ritual known as Drawing Down the Moon is nearly always a central part of the festival. This is a rite in which the spirit of the Mother Goddess, who is represented by the full moon, is invoked into a physical body.

The Celtic year was divided by its full moons into thirteen months, one for each moon occurring during the solar year. (This is also one of many explanations for thirteen being the preferred number for members of a coven, though this seems to have been a medieval idea, and not originally a Celtic one.) By learning about the Celtic associations of the full moons we find more opportunities to invoke other deities than the Mother Goddess whose energies are at their peak on certain Esbats.

THE CELTIC TREE CALENDAR

Oh, the oak and the ash and the bonnie
ivy tree, all flourish at home in my own country.
—Yorkshire Folk Song

THE MOON IS humanity's oldest calendar. Evidence of ancient peoples keeping time by the phases of the moon have been found carved into rocks and cave walls the world over. The famous tree calendar of the Celts was such a time-keeping device, and, like other tribal cultures, the Celts found names and associations for their moon which were developed and codified over many years of ritual and experimentation. Each moon phase was assigned a corresponding tree, each tree being sacred to either feminine energy and to the Goddess, or to masculine energy and to the God.

The lunar tree calendar of the Celts has long been a source of controversy among Celtic scholars. Some even claim it was never a part of the old Celtic world, but was an invention of author/researcher Robert Graves. The Druids are generally given credit by other researchers for creating this system. There seems to be no scholarly evidence to prove otherwise, yet many Celtic Pagans feel that the system pre-dates the time of Druidic influence over Celtic religious matters. It is probably reasonable to believe that the truth lies somewhere in between these three extremes. It is most likely that the tree system was in place, with minor regional variations, before the time of the Druids who experimented with it, discovered the magickal properties of each tree, and codified all the information into the system we have today.

The trees the Druids selected for the thirteen months were already trees which were sources of magick and myth in Celtic folklore. Several of the trees are said to be attractive to faery folk, and others were sources of magick herbs or medicines.

There are two major systems of tree calendars, each being popularly credited with being the "true" one, and both can make solid academic arguments for themselves. The one beginning with the sequence Birch-Rowan-Ash is probably the most widely used and accepted today.

When the Celts picked a piece of nature to personify the spirit of the Esbat, why did they pick trees and not plants, herbs, or animals? There are many possible answers to that question. First of all, many cultures in western Europe and the Middle East held trees to be sacred. Many of these cultures had a model mystical scheme of the universe and spiritual progression which they termed a "Tree of Life" or a "World Tree." Trees were a physical representation of unity with all things because of their visible upper parts which reached far into the heavens, and the unseen bottom parts, or roots, which reached far into the ground, were virtually identical to the visible parts. This reflected to many the ancient mystical adage, "As above, So below," which was not originally a Celtic saying, though it was one of their concepts. This saying meant that what is in the world of the unseen could be made manifest in the physical world, and is the operating principle behind all magick.

A twelfth-century drawing of trees with intertwined boughs. Stories about these "lover's trees" are sometimes found in Celtic mythology.

Trees physically unite the heaven and the earth making Earth Goddess and Sky God one, uniting the two halves of the whole and making them a powerful source of creative magick. It is no accident that the leaves or bark of most of the trees in the Celtic calendar are also used as fertility herbs.

The long-lived trees were seemingly ageless to humans, and some of us still can't help but feel awe at their seeming immortality when we are faced with grandeur such as the Giant Redwood trees of California. Each generation knows that these trees were born long before us, and we can see them still strong and thriving as we prepare to depart the earth plane into death.

Trees, more than any other plant in nature, served humankind. They provided fuel for warmth and cooking, boards to make shelters, and provided homes for animals both above and beneath the earth.

Trees also attracted a host of faery life; particularly noteworthy are the Dryads who had a special affinity for a certain class of female Druids to whom it is said they gave their name. Gnomes, the kindly earth elementals of northern Ireland and Scotland, are said to make their homes within the roots of large oak trees and from there to watch over all woodland creatures.

Today the counting of the Celtic tree calendar begins with the full moon nearest Yule. Perhaps it once began with the full moon nearest Samhain since, until the influence of the Norse, Samhain marked the beginning of the Celtic new year. Why the Druids placed the beginning at Yule is a mystery we may never uncover. When you have pinpointed the full moon closest to Yule, count off the thirteen moons of the lunar year and mark them with their Tree

Calendar names. We can further align ourselves with the energy of each full moon by paying attention to the "nicknames" frequently given to each. This will help us to understand the subtle energy the Celts felt at each Esbat. The moon names, polarity, and nicknames are as follows:

MOON NAME	POLARITY	NICKNAMES
Birch Moon	(feminine)	Moon of Inception Moon of Beginning
Rowan Moon	(masculine)	Moon of Vision Spirit Moon Astral Travel Moon
Ash Moon	(feminine)	Moon of Waters
Alder Moon	(masculine)	Moon of Utility Moon of Efficacy Moon of Self-Guidance
Willow Moon	(feminine)	The Witches' Moon Moon of Balance
Hawthorn Moon	(masculine)	Moon of Restraint Moon of Hindrance Summer Moon
Oak Moon	(masculine)	Moon of Strength Moon of Security Bear Moon
Holly Moon	(feminine)	Moon of Encirclement Moon of Polarity
Hazel Moon	(feminine)	Moon of the Wise Crone Moon
Vine Moon	(androgynous)	Moon of Celebration
Ivy Moon	(masculine)	Moon of Buoyancy Moon of Resilience
Reed Moon	(feminine)	Moon of the Home Hearth Moon Winter Moon Moon Which Manifests Truth
Elder Moon	(masculine)	Moon of Completeness

For example, if it is the Ivy Moon (Moon of Resilience) and you are in a situation which requires that you learn to be more flexible, or to bounce back quickly, you know that this is an excellent time to work magick to that end. You can also look through the myths for deities who can teach this quality to you, since that particular power aspect of that deity will be at the peak of its influence on the Ivy Moon Esbat.

Various parts of the tree were also used for herbal magick spells. These, too, can be studied and coordinated with the energies of the deities to help us discover whose power is most easily manifest under the corresponding moon. For example, if you need to do an invocation for protection and it is the Reed Moon, look through your myths until you find a deity who is associated with stories about reeds, or who possesses strong powers of protection. These particular aspects of the deity will be at the peak of his or her power on that night.

This following is a list of the magickal properties generally associated with each tree:

Tree	Magickal Properties
Birch	Protection of children, purification, creativity
Rowan	Healing, personal empowerment, divination
Ash	Prosperity, protection, healing
Alder	Spirituality, teaching, weather magick, duty, mental prowess
Willow	Romantic love, healing, protection, fertility, magick for women
Hawthorn	Fertility, peace, prosperity, binding
Oak	All positive purposes, magick for men, fidelity
Holly	Protection, prophecy, magick for animals, sex magick
Hazel	Manifestation, spirit contact, protection, fertility
Vine	(Property dependent upon the type of vine) Blackberry—Prosperity, protection, sacred to Brid Blueberry—Spirituality, dream magick Grape—Fertility, inspiration, prosperity, binding Thistle—Courage, protection, strength
Ivy	Healing, protection, cooperation, exorcism
Reed	Fertility, protection, love, family concerns
Elder	Exorcism, prosperity, banishing, healing

To help you begin to put this all together, the following pages contain a lengthy list of some of the most well-known Celtic deities with whom to begin experimenting. You can use either evocation or invocation rituals to harness their power. They are listed with one or two of their major magickal associations or teachings along with the Esbat during which this particular aspect of their power should peak. Most deities have more than one aspect with which you can work. Please consult the Dictionary or Appendix E Cross-Reference section of this book for more information on numerous other ways in which each deity can aid you:

WELL-KNOWN CELTIC DEITIES, THEIR ASPECTS, AND CORRESPONDING MOONS

DEITY	ASPECT	MOON
Abelard	Loyalty	Oak
Aengus	Dreams, romance	Vine
Aibheaog	Fire magick	Hawthorn
Aife	Overcoming enemies	Alder/Elder
Aine	Summer festivals	Hawthorn
Airmid	Healing	Rowan/Elder
Ambisagrus	Weather magick	Alder
Amergin	Creativity	Birch/Vine
Andraste	Overcoming enemies	Alder/Elder
Arawen	Friendship, loyalty	Oak
Arianrhod	Binding spells	Hawthorn
Arthur	Self-sacrifice	Alder
Artio	Fertility	Oak
Baile	Communication	Rowan
Balor	Protection	Elder
Ban Naomha	Wisdom	Hazel
Bebhionn	Spirit contact	Hazel
Beli	Divination	Rowan
Beltene	Spirit contact	Rowan
Biddy Mamionn	Healing	Ash/Ivy
Blodeuwedd	Learning lessons	Birch/Alder
Boann	Fertility	Willow
Borvo	Healing	Rowan/Elder
Bran	Protection, divination	Rowan/Reed
Branwyn	Romantic love	Willow
Brian Boru	Leadership	Ivy
Brid	Protection	Vine
Bres	Compassion	Ivy
Caer	Dream work	Vine
Cailleach	Wisdom	Hazel
Cairbre	Creativity	Birch/Vine
Caradoc	Divination	Rowan
Cebhfhionn	Wisdom	Hazel
Cernunnos	Fertility	Oak/Holly
Cerridwen	Shapeshifting	Willow
Coll	Astral work	Rowan

DEITY	ASPECT	MOON (CONT.)
Connla	Wisdom, loyalty	Oak/Hazel
Cormac	Perseverance	Rowan/Oak
Coventina	Divination	Reed
Credne	Creativity	Birch/Vine
Crom Cruaich	Spirit contact	Rowan
Cuchulain	Strength, courage	Oak/Vine
Deae Matres	Children's concerns	Birch
Dagda	Masculine power	Oak
Dahud	Sex magick	Holly
Dana	Faery contact	Willow
Dhonn	Past-life memory	Rowan
Diancecht	Healing	Rowan/Elder
Diarmuid	Romantic love	Willow/Reed
Don	Family matters	Reed
Druantia	Eco-magick	Alder
Edain	Reincarnation	Birch/Elder
Epona	Dream magick	Vine
Evnissyen	Being responsible	Birch/Alder
Fand	Faery contact	Willow
Feithline	Divination	Rowan/Reed
Fergus	Sex magick	Holly
Flidais	Animal concerns	Holly
Figol	Patience	Alder/Ivy
Finvarra	Competition	Birch
Fionn	Overcoming enemies	Alder/Elder
Goibniu	Creativity	Birch/Vine
Grainne	Astral work	Rowan
Grannos	Purification	Birch
Guildeluec	Making choices	Holly
Gwendydd	Divination	Rowan
Gwyddion	Wisdom, magick	Elder
Gwyn Ap Nuad	Spirit contact	Rowan
Habetrot	Healing	Ash/Rowan
Isolde	Making choices	Holly
Laeg	Loyalty	Oak
Lavercam	Loyalty, duty	Oak/Alder

DEITY	ASPECT	MOON (CONT.)
Leucetios	Weather magick	Alder
Llewellyn	Faery contact	Oak
Llyr	Water magick	Ash
Lugh	Fire magick	Hawthorn
Mabon	Harvest festivals	Vine
Macha	Strength of wisdom	Holly
Maeve	Feminine power	Ash/Willow
Manann	Eco-magick	Alder/Ash
Meg the Healer	Healing	Elder/Ash
Melusine	Compassion	Ivy
Merlin	Teaching, magick	Oak/Reed
Miach	Healing	Rowan/Elder
Nantosuelta	Fertility	Willow
Nessa	Feminine power	Willow
Niamh	Leadership	Ivy
Nomenoe	Serving others	Alder
O'Carolan	Creativity	Birch/Vine
Oghma	Communication	Rowan

DEITY	ASPECT	MOON (CONT.)
Ossian	Courage	Vine
Owen Lawgoch	Self-sacrifice	Alder
Pryderi	Loyalty, duty	Oak/Alder
Pwyll	Fairness, justice	Hazel
Ratis	Courage	Vine
Rhiannon	Fertility	Willow
Rohand	Loyalty, duty	Oak, Alder
Robin Ddu	Mental prowess	Alder
Rosmerta	Communication	Rowan
Saba	Eco-magick	Alder
Scathach	Teaching	Alder
Sheila-na-gig	Feminine power	Willow
Sin	Strength	Oak/Willow
Stine Bheag	Weather magick	Alder
Taillte	Fertility	Willow
Taliesin	Understanding time	Rowan/Alder
Veleda	Leadership	Ivy

THE BATTLE OF THE TREES

I have been in the battle of Goddeu,
with Llew and Gwyddion,
They changed the forms of the
elementary trees....

—Taliesin

IF YOU ARE truly interested in working with the tree symbolism and energies on an in-depth basis throughout the year, it might be worth your time to study the mythic poem known as *The Battle of the Trees* (or *Cad Goddeu* in Welsh). It is also sometimes called the Battle of Achern or Ochren which are alternate names for the Welsh Otherworld. The poem is attributed to the famous bard, Taliesin.

The battle took place during a war which was fought to secure three things for humankind—dogs, deer, and the lapwing—all creatures considered sacred to various highly placed deities and in the sole possession of the Otherworld. The end result of the battle was not only the bringing into the physical world of these animals, but it also set up a hierarchy of sacred trees which was used by the Celts and their Druids for worship and self-attunement to the seasons from ancient times until this very day. Studying and meditating on the poem will help you further sort out and understand the energies of the thirteen sacred trees. (Also look into the myths of Pryderi, Gwyddion, Llew, and Arawen for more fragments of the battle story.)

Discussing the implications of the Battle of the Trees and all the nuances of the tree calendar goes far beyond the cope of this work. Persons interested in a more in-depth look at this calendar, the Ogham Alphabet which corresponds to it, tree divination, and other associated rituals, should consult Pattalee Glass-Koentop's *Year of Moons, Season of Trees,* or Edred Thorsson's *The Book of Ogham.*

CAKES AND ALE

Bring us in good ale, bring us in good ale,
For our Blessed Lady's sake, bring us in good ale.
—English Folk Song

THE CEREMONY OF Cakes and Ale is very ancient in both concept and practice. So deeply ingrained was its symbolism and so widely spread was its usage throughout Europe that the early Christian Church was forced to adopt it as their own Communion ritual in order to keep the converts interested in their new religion. It is unknown just when in time the Ceremony of Cakes and Ale became an established part of Celtic Esbat celebrations, but today nearly all Celtic Pagans use some form of this old ritual to end their full moon rites.

The cake (or bread, or cookies, etc.) is symbolic of Mother Earth, and the ale (or juice, or wine, etc.) is a symbol of water and of the moon. Ritually blessing and uniting these items within ourselves—by eating and drinking them—is a token symbol of our unity with the Mother Goddess whose full moon we are honoring, and reaffirms our desire to allow the Goddess to be manifest within ourselves and our lives.

The practice also ties in with the Pagan concept that what one consumes will be made manifest, or reborn, a belief whose roots are buried in deep in antiquity. Celtic warriors used to consume parts of their dead soldiers so that they could be reborn into the clan. Certain parts of hunted animals were consumed ritually so that the herds would flourish and that their energy would be carried inside the hunter. In the Irish myth cycles we read of Edain being accidentally ingested by Etar and being reborn as a mortal child.

In the Celtic traditions, the Ceremony of Cakes and Ale is observed while still inside the protection of the circle *after* the rest of the Esbat ritual and magickal work has been completed.

There are various ways to bless the cake and ale before it is eaten; many of these depend upon personal taste or your tradition's views on the rite. The following is a sample of a solitary Cakes and Ale ritual which can be copied or adapted as you see fit:

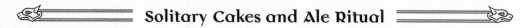
Solitary Cakes and Ale Ritual

BEFORE BEGINNING, HAVE your cake and your ale, in whatever form you prefer, sitting on your altar. Open your circle in your usual manner and do whatever preliminary work you normally do. Stand before your altar and address the Goddess. You may look at the moon to do this if you are outdoors, or you may look at the cake and ale:

Blessed Mother of us all, I come into this sacred space and stand before this altar on this, your special night, to offer you my love, my allegiance, and my blessings, and to reaffirm that I am your child. Tonight I will consecrate and consume the cake of your earth and the ale of your moon that I might carry your essence within me, that your love and will might be carried by me into the mundane world.

Take a piece of the cake and hold it in your receptive hand. If you are outdoors, allow the moonlight to wash over it:

Mother, I thank you for the bounty of your earthly body which sustains me with food. From your womb flows all life and all manner of life's sustenance. Allow me to use this symbol to fill myself with your boundless presence. Be in and of me always.

Eat a bite of the cake, then break off another small piece and hold it up in your power hand. You are going to give this portion as a libation, a traditional offering both to the Goddess and to the nature spirits and animals which may be nearby:

This bit of life-giving grain from your womb I give back to you now in humble thanksgiving. May you and your creatures of the wild partake and enjoy.

If you are outdoors, set the libation of cake on the ground. If you are inside, have a plate ready to collect the offering so that you can place it outside later.

Now hold up the ale in your receptive hand. Again, if you are outdoors, allow the moonlight to reflect over its watery surface:

Mother, I thank you for the mysteries of your watery realm which sustains my spirit and imagination, for this blood of your womb which brought forth all life. By your blood all living things are blessed and made sacred. Allow me to use this symbol to fill myself with your boundless presence. Be in and of me always.

Take a sip of the ale, then transfer the receptacle into your power hand and say:

These precious drops of life-giving water from your womb I give back to you now in humble thanksgiving. May this symbol of your blood give life renewed to all who partake with pleasure.

If you are outdoors, pour a bit of the ale onto the ground near the cake. If you are inside, transfer the liquid into something which you can take outdoors later and pour onto the earth.

Now take the ale receptacle in your receptive hand and the cake in your power hand and say:

Behold, the Triple Goddess is one!
Maiden, Mother, and Crone.
Earth and heaven are one!
The womb and blood.
I am one with them.
I am the child of the Goddess.
In me may she always be manifest.

Dip a piece of the cake into the ale and allow the cake to soak up some of the liquid. Think of the unity of the Goddess as you do this, of her earthly womb and heavenly blood being united inside you, ready for any acts of creation. Then eat a portion of the unified part. By doing so you are signifying your willingness to be a vessel for the manifest creative power of the Goddess.

Complete your ritual with these or similar words:

Behold, I am Goddess.
Behold, I am the Creative Principle.
Behold, I am divinity.
The Triple Goddess is one.
She lives in me.
I live in her.
So Mote It Be!

You should now eat whatever portion of this feast you wish, or you may simply sit quietly and meditate on the ritual you just performed. Afterwards, you are free to close your circle.

✤ ✤ ✤

CHE DIVINE ESBAC RICUAL

When the white moon first peeks her fair face
over the tops of the pine,
what joy fills my heart.

—Rebecca Worrell

Time: At night anytime three days before, until three days after the actual moment of the full moon

Colors: Silver, white, violet

Symbols: Chalice, blood, horns, cauldron, mirrors, bread, cake, all liquids

Meaning: The fullness of the Mother Goddess' power, the full power of the feminine, secrets and mysteries

Deities: Mother Goddess, Triple Goddess, a deity associated with the tree calendar of that particular Esbat

BECAUSE THIS BOOK has been written with the solitary practitioner in mind, you will find a few gaps in the following ritual text. This is to allow you to fill in your own expressions, songs, gestures, needs, or any other material you feel is appropriate and which is best suited to helping you invoke the divine.

Though some covens regularly meet at Esbats to make magick, and even Draw Down the Moon with great success, it is my feeling that the energies of the divine, both the subtle and the potent, are best experienced in a solitary setting. In many (but certainly not all) of the Celtic traditions, the Esbats are a private time during which the individual is invited to connect with the universal forces of nature alone.

 ## Esbat Ritual

TO BEGIN, HAVE your altar set up in your circle, oriented to whichever direction you like. You can have it facing the moon if you prefer, but remember that this is a fairly lengthy ritual and the moon travels swiftly across the night sky. If you orient your altar to the moon at the beginning it may be significantly out of physical alignment by the time you are done. Don't worry if you have no way to be outdoors. The full moon's power is quite potent and will not be lost to you if you are not standing in its direct light.

If you wish to invoke a particular deity in correspondence with the tree calendar, it is nice to have some item on your altar which corresponds to that deity's energy. This could be a leaf, branch, or wand cut from the tree, or a symbol of the particular power of the deity you wish to invoke, such as a romantic picture for making love magick with Branwyn, or a small blaze for calling upon the fiery power of Brid.

The steps we will follow for this ritual are:

◆ Opening of the circle

◆ Calling the quarters or doing other preliminary work as desired

◆ Statement of purpose and blessing of the Moon Goddess

◆ Blessing of the deity associated with the tree calendar if you are going to be working with one

◆ Acknowledgement of the moon's special aspects as determined by the tree calendar

◆ Drawing Down the Moon and/or invocation of another deity (It is best to pick only *one* deity to *invoke* each moon cycle, but you may evoke as many as you can keep track of)

◆ Working any magick needed

◆ Releasing any evoked deities, and then releasing the invoked ones

◆ Doing the Ceremony of Cakes and Ale

◆ Closing of the circle

Everyone's concept of the *exact* purpose of their Esbat ritual will be different. Not only does everyone approach the rites in a slightly different frame of mind and with varying expectations, but the magick you wish to do, and any other deity you wish to call upon, will make your ritual unique.

Here is an example of how you might state your purpose and bless the Goddess:

> *Behold! I stand here tonight in the light of my Goddess' love and light to worship in the ancient way, to make moon magick, and to invoke her primal power that my rites will be successful. Hear me now, my Mother, I bless your bounty and your goodness, bless me in turn with you eternal power and love. Wrap me in your warm silvery light. Hold me forever in your boundless arms.*

If you will not be invoking the Moon Goddess's energy, but have decided to invoke another deity based on tree calendar associations, you should offer a similar blessing to him or her. However, if you merely want to *evoke* this deity's presence and not *invoke* it, you may also do the invocation of Drawing Down the Moon. Which you choose will depend largely on what sort of magickal or other rites you have in mind. For instance, if you are looking for strength from Cuchulain under the Vine Moon, you should say so now.

After that you should honor the moon through its Celtic attribute. There are many ways to do this. The simplest is to hold in your hand an object which you feel corresponds to this particular Esbat's energy and make a blessing such as:

> *Blessed be the Oak Moon. Blessed be the Moon of Strength in its full flowering of glory. As its light shines on me, may its energy and blessings fill me in this sacred space tonight. Bless me in turn, and impart your strength to me this sacred night, the Esbat of the Oak Moon.*

Spend a few moments feeling your connection to the energy of this moon. Allow yourself to feel filled with its attributes. When you are finished, place the item back on your altar.

You are now ready to Draw Down the Moon, unless you have chosen to invoke another deity's power. If you have, you will do that instead, constructing a ritual designed by yourself based on the model in Chapter 4. It is recommended that if you have not had any practice with Drawing Down the Moon that you begin with this most basic of invocations before attempting other Esbat-associated invocations, just so you can get used to the feeling of having this concentrated power inside yourself.

The purpose of Drawing Down the Moon is threefold:

◆ It is a time, astrologically speaking, to merge with the Mother Goddess at the peak of her power

◆ To allow the Mother Goddess to help you with all magick being done under the full moon's influence

◆ It provides a connection to the ancient fertility rites of the Celts, who made such magick under the full moon's light because the full moon represents the mid-point of a woman's monthly cycle, the time when she is most fertile

You may use any tool you choose to direct the moon energy down into you. Some like a pointing tool such as an athame or wand, others prefer the feminine symbolism of the chalice or cup filled with a liquid—usually the ale from the Cakes and Ale ritual which will follow. If you do not already have a tool you use regularly for Drawing Down the Moon, you should pick one now and be consistent with it as the energies absorbed by it will make each subsequent moon invocation easier.

Stand as near to the center of your circle as is possible and turn to face the moon. Allow its light to flood your face. If you are not outdoors, simply look up and visualize the power of it coming in through your ceiling and washing you in its light. If you are using an athame, etc., raise it and point it at the center of the moon. If you are using a chalice, hold it in front of your face so that you can see the moon's light reflected in the surface of the liquid inside:

Blessed Mother Goddess, your silvery light washes over me, it permeates my being with your living, vibrant life energy. Enter this consecrated tool and prepare to merge with me, your child. Come to me, my mother. I now Draw Down the Moon.

Mentally see the tool filling with moon energy. Visualize it happening and know that it is real. Open yourself to the Goddess' presence. When you feel her essence has entered your tool you are ready to bring it into yourself. If you are using an athame or other pointing tool, or if you are a man using a chalice, pull the tool to your breast. If you are a female using a chalice you may use the breast or the womb region as the entry point:

I Draw the Moon into Me. I am divinity incarnate.

You may chant this couplet over and over while the divine energy fills you.

Feel the Goddess spirit entering you and the two of you becoming one. If you have done this right you will immediately begin to feel a little different. Often persons report an odd static electricity within the circle and about the person who has Drawn in the Moon while the Moon Goddess is joined with them.

When you feel you have absorbed all the energy from the tool, you may put it back down on your altar. Repeat the words, "I am divinity," or some other affirmation about what has happened such as:

I am Goddess. Love is my creed. Let all positive and pleasurable acts commence, for these are my sacred rites, my gifts to my children. Let laughter ring from the dark hillsides. Let all hearts be light and all earthly cares foresworn. Let magick be afoot, for this is my will.

If you wish to evoke the presence of other deities, you may do so now. Some persons familiar with the rites of evocation prefer doing them while the Moon Mother Goddess is within them. The extra power you have as Goddess helps facilitate this as does the fact that you now resonate on a level more attuned to the energy of the other deities. Experiment with this if you like and see if it works for you.

Whether or not you use evocation, it is now time to make any magick you need, or to make magick for others. You will find spells for things such as healing, fertility, romance, and peace are especially efficacious under the full moon's influence.

When you have concluded your magick, it is time to release any energy, either evoked or invoked. Release the evoked deities first.

To reverse the Drawing Down the Moon process, simply hold your tool against the place you used as an entry point and visualize the Goddess energy flow out of you and back into the tool. Raise the tool back toward the moon, visualize the energy returning from whence it came, and allow and feel yourself returning to normal consciousness.

Be sure to thank the Goddess, and any other deities you called upon, before dismissing your circle.

Hold the Ceremony of Cakes and Ale, and then close your circle in your usual manner.

⚜ ⚜ ⚜

ONCE YOU ARE comfortable with the invocation of the Mother Goddess at the Esbat ritual, try writing your own rituals for the waxing and waning moons to invoke the essence of the Maiden Goddess (waxing moon) and Crone Goddess (waning moon). These, too, can be potent experiences for both men and women. The energy you feel while being united with them will be noticeably different from that of the Esbat. Keep a record in your Book of Shadows of your feelings and experiences during each moon ritual to help you better understand the energies of each aspect of the Triple Goddess.

CHAPTER SIX

THE CELTIC PANTHEON AND THE WHEEL OF THE YEAR

The earth turns,
So night follows day.
—Gwion

THE OLD CELTIC word for the solar calendar was *bleidonii,* and the passage of its time was symbolized by a wheel. Today "The Wheel of the Year" is a very common Pagan metaphor, the conceptualization of the ever-turning cycle of life, death, and regeneration, the primary infrastructure on which all seasonal ritual is hung. The Celts viewed this wheel as being turned by a great Crone Goddess in the Land of the Dead. In Ireland this Goddess is Badb, "the boiling one," who also presides over the great cauldron to which all life goes at death and from which it waits to be reborn. In Wales it is Arianrhod of the Silver Wheel who turns the ancient wheel, and in Cornwall it is Cerridwen. Even when the Celtic myths underwent changes through patriarchalization, the image of the wheel persisted through the story of Dagda and his circular harp which made time move.

The Wheel has two conceptualizations in Celtic Paganism, the one you choose to use as your mental plan for the sacred year is a personal one. One is circluar, flowing clockwise through the seasons; the other is shaped like a swastika, or sun wheel (the origin of the Brid's Cross), and the seasons follow a zigzag pattern.

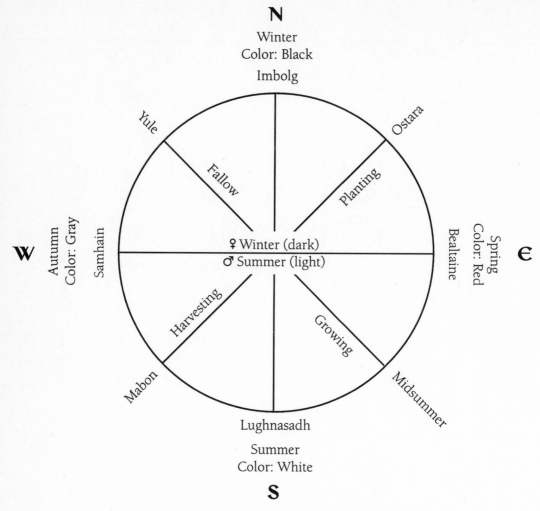

N

Winter
Color: Black

Imbolg

Yule

Ostara

Fallow

Planting

Autumn
Color: Gray

Samhain

Spring
Color: Red

Bealtaine

W

♀ Winter (dark)
♂ Summer (light)

E

Harvesting

Growing

Mabon

Midsummer

Lughnasadh

Summer
Color: White

S

Circular Celtic Wheel of the Year which flows clockwise through the seasons.

CHE CELCIC CONCEPC OF CIME

And if you like to return
You will be, for a time, a Druid, perhaps.
—Anonymous Irish Poem

THE CELTS BELIEVED in reincarnation, but the form and method in which it occurred was considerably different than most of today's Pagan attitudes towards rebirth. For the majority of Celts, it was rebirth into one's own clan which was to them the most sensible way in which reincarnation could occur. For a few others, it was rebirth somewhere else in their native land, never outside it. For the Druids, it was the immediate transmigration of the life essence into another nearby lifeform. Certainly the most common of these ethno-centric Celtic beliefs was the idea that one would return to be reborn into their own clan. In Old Irish the word for this specific type of reincarnation was *aithghen,* a word whose root means "to repeat."

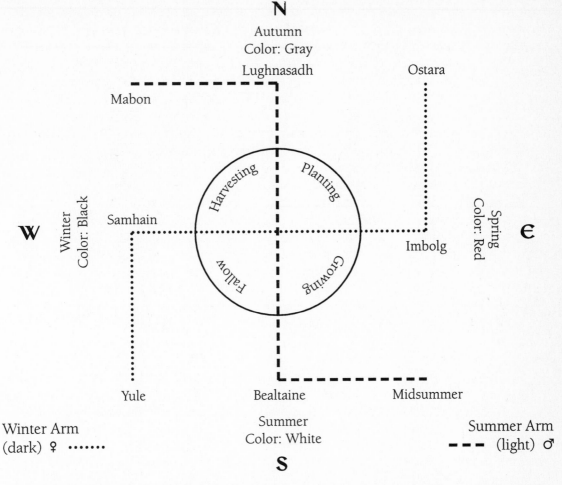

Swastika-shaped Celtic Sun-Wheel (origin of Brid's Cross) in which the seasons follow a zigzag pattern.

All of these rebirth concepts were based upon the underlying belief that time was not linear as it appears to be, but rather one great omnipresent *now* in which we all live many concurrent lives, all of them connected to all other lifeforms—human, animal, and plant.

When attempting to interpret or discuss Celtic concepts of time and reincarnation one runs up against more resistance than in any other area of conflict in Celtic studies. The reason is twofold. First of all, there are many sensitive toes out to be stepped on when attempting to unravel and explain this most basic of human beliefs—that of life and afterlife. We all have our own ideas about them, most of those hard-won after many hours of study and contemplation. Simply put, we do not like to have that little corner of our personal theology tampered with. The other reason is that the Celtic concepts of time are so complex and esoteric that they are hard to describe even to someone who might agree with your own point of view.

We must look again to the myths of the Celts in order to understand how time was seen and to verify Celtic acceptance of reincarnation or transmigration.

In many Celtic myths we see the phenomenon known as shapeshifting, in which a divine or magickally talented human being transforms themselves temporarily into another creature.

While in these transformed states they were able to cast spells, level a geise, or work other magickal feats of which they seemed incapable while in their anthropomorphic forms. When we compare these Celtic myths to other cultures whose beliefs in shapeshifting have survived over the centuries, such as those of many of the Native American people, we find that those cultures all view time as a non-linear phenomenon. They all believe that in order to shift one's shape one must first transcend time by reaching that part of the mind which makes us see time linearly, and turn it off so that we can transcend not only time, but space as well. This would require "bending" time, turning it back on itself like a giant ball of twine where the many strands overlap and cross, but are unseen from the normal, everyday conscious perspective.

We also have the verse of the famous bard Amergin who sang of being numerous other people and animals—not in succession—but all *now*. Amergin was a teacher and leader of his people, one highly qualified to attempt to explain spiritual beliefs in song.

Another common transformation theme in Celtic mythology is that of taking the form of a bird upon one's physical death. To the Celts birds were a symbol of transformation from the state of living to the state of death. Reread some of the myths such as those of Aife, Blodeuwedd, Bran, Cliodna, Edain, Laustic, Liban, or Llew, while keeping in mind that at the moment of their transformation they actually died, and you will see them in an entirely different light—one which speaks of reincarnation, not merely shapeshifting.

Probably the most well-known example of Celtic belief in reincarnation are the "Sleeping Deities," Gods and heroes (and sometimes Goddesses and heroines) who served their people well and who are believed not to be dead, but merely sleeping, waiting until the time they are needed again to rise and lead their people. When thinking of such mythic figures, even people who are not well-versed in mythology can immediately call to mind King Arthur of the legendary Camelot. There are numerous other sleeping deities, most notably Fionn MacCumhal, Owen Lawgoch, and the Irish Goddess, Bo Find.

It is interesting, and even baffling, to note that no shapeshifting myths make any reference to a "soul" as we have been taught to think of one by the mainstream religions. Therefore the implication is that we humans are, in some way, immortal. If we do not really go to a Land of the Dead and wait rebirth, if that is merely a metaphor to help us accept a time process which to our limited minds appears linear, then we must accept that we exist somewhere else. And if we are somewhere, but we do not have "souls" which move about after release from our physical being, and if we live all at once—past, present, and future—can we not be said to be immortal?

These are questions with which many will feel profoundly uncomfortable. (And I confess to being no different. Every time I think about it too long I get a monstrous headache.) If you do wish to ponder this at length, spend some time before each Sabbat ritual meditating on the question, "If all time is now, am I immortal?" You may discover that some surprising insights occur to you.

Within their elaborate concept of time, the Celts saw three worlds in parallel and simultaneous existence:

◆ The Upperworld
◆ The Mundane World
◆ The Otherworld

The Upperworld was a realm of the divine, the Mundane was the earth plane, and the Otherworld (also called the Underworld) was the Land of the Dead. Upon physical death one might enter any or all of these, leaving a "shadow self" in the other two. The idea of shadow self being left behind from any and all of one's earthly incarnations is one reason given for how the Celts so readily accepted spirit contact as a very real possibility.

A fourth realm, *Mide* (the "center"), a powerful place where all worlds converged was symbolized by the institution of the main Celtic government at Tara near Ireland's center in County Meath, "meath" being a variant form of *mide*. It was at Tara where the Sabbat celebrations began with the lighting of the ritual fires.

The original Celtic solar festivals may have began on the fifteenth of the month rather than on the first. There are several theories as to how the observances got moved back:

◆ It was done to conform to other solar festivals in Europe

◆ Dates were shifted when the heavens realigned themselves as they do periodically in relation to the solar calendar

◆ Changes, deletions, and additions to calendars over the years made the changes come naturally

All of these theories are valid, and make no difference to the ways Celtic Pagans worship today.

The one central concept in all of the major Celtic myths is the movement from darkness to light, then back to darkness. The Celts believed that each new "day," the beginning of a new twenty-four-hour period, began at sunset, not at midnight. Night, the darkness, came first. Therefore each festival would commence at sunset the night before and end at sunset on the next evening. The reason given for this is that Celtic cosmology teaches that the night was created before the day, hence it is first and therefore symbolic of beginning. Many other old cultures also share this view, and even today Jews go to their Sabbath and festival worship at sundown.

[**Note:** Cosmology is a word meaning the way the beginning of creation is viewed within any culture. In the case of the Celts, exact cosmological beliefs can only be inferred or surmised, for they appear to be one of the very few cultures on earth without a native creation myth. Of course, this does not necessarily mean that they never had one. It may have been lost along with other myths, or was at such variance to the creation stories taught by the Church fathers that it could not be reconciled to the new ways and was summarily destroyed. Probably no one will ever know for sure just what happened.]

SABBAT RITUALS

The Scots are steadfast—not their clime.
—Thomas Campbell

THE WORD SABBAT comes from the Greek *sabatu*, meaning "to rest." Sabbats are the solar festivals which mark various points along the Wheel of the Year, usually when the sun reaches a point of balance or of extremes, such as at the solstices or equinoxes, though there have been other Sabbats added to various Celtic calendars from time to time. Each Sabbat generally corresponds to some stage in the eternal, ever-renewing, life of the Goddess and the God.

The Sabbats were all fire festivals because of their association with the phases of the sun. Fire, usually in the form of balefires (ritual bonfires) were lit in a specified manner depending on which Sabbat was being observed.

The eight Sabbats featured in modern Celtic Paganism are:

Samhain	October 31
Yule	Winter Solstice
Imbolg	February 1 or 2
Ostara	Vernal Equinox
Bealtaine	May 1
Midsummer	Summer Solstice
Lughnasadh	August 1 or 2
Mabon	Autumnal Equinox

Sabbats are most certainly best celebrated with others, if for no other reason than to experience the joy of being alive for another season. But whether you do or do not have others with whom to celebrate the day, you can always allow yourself private time to honor your deities whose lives the Sabbats commemorate.

The Celts celebrated their Sabbats with food, drink, dance, song, and all other pleasurable acts. It was a time to put aside the concerns of work, a day for the larger community to gather to worship and give thanks, to rest and rejoice, relax and renew old acquaintances. Many Celtic Pagans will not do any work on these days, and even attempt to be excused from their mundane jobs in order to comply with their religious beliefs. Magick is also work, much more so than many realize, and many believe it is also taboo to work magick on these sacred days. Evocations and invocations done on the Sabbats can be powerful experiences, but because this is a time of rest, you should not ask the deities for their aid in magickal "work" unless there is a dire emergency which needs immediate attention.

Also, every Celtic tradition has slight variations on the central theme of each Sabbat, though the overall concepts remain the same, and, as mentioned, others add or eliminate minor Sabbats depending upon their seasonal beliefs and associations. Of necessity the ritual suggestions which follow are created so as not to interfere with the teachings of any specific pathway. For example, the Caledonii tradition celebrates Ostara as the time of power of the warrior God, while Witta views it as a time for the awakening of fertility deities.

Again, because this is basically a guide for the solitary practitioner, I have avoided providing detailed scripted rituals. Solitary practice, while needing a certain amount of structure in order to be workable, has the added bonus of allowing the worker a certain scope of spontaneity unknown in most coven settings. Therefore practices will be suggested rather than fully pieced together. And since this is a guide to harnessing the energy of the deities, the suggestions will concern incorporating them into common and already established Celtic Pagan Sabbat practices.

Hopefully, after reading through these, you will begin to develop your own ideas on how to bring evocation and invocation more directly into your seasonal rites whether they are solitary or not. If you do not know a lot about the Sabbats, or do not already have solitary rituals you like, you can find information and/or fully written rituals in many books on Paganism. Two good guides to begin with are *Wicca: A Guide for the Solitary Practitioner,* by Scott Cunningham, and my own, *The Sabbats: A New Approach to Living the Old Ways.* Also, look to Appendix A in the back of this book for a detailed outline to help you in constructing rituals of any kind.

Basically, Celtic Sabbat rituals will follow this form:

- Opening of the circle
- Calling the quarters or doing other preliminary work as desired
- Statement of purpose
- Evocation or invocation of any deities which will be utilized
- Lighting of a ritual fire
- Celebration, recreation, enactment, etc., of the symbolic meaning of the season
- Releasing any evoked deities, and then releasing the invoked ones
- Ritual feasting and offering of libations
- Offering of thanks to deities or others called
- Closing of the circle

SAMHAIN

I heard the dogs howl in the moonlight;
I went to the window to see the sight;
All the Dead that ever I knew
Going one by one and two by two.
—William Allingham, Bard of Donegal

Date: October 31

Other Names: Hallowmas, Samana, Samhuinn, Samonios

Colors: Black and Orange

Symbols: Cauldron, jack o'lantern, mask, balefire, besom

Deities: Crone Goddesses, Dying/Aging Gods, Sacrificial Gods, Death and Otherworld Deities

SAMHAIN (SOW-in or SAV-ayn) MARKED THE beginning of the old Celtic new year, and many Celtic Pagans still observe Samhain as the renewal of the Wheel of the Year.

This was the night that the old God died, returning to the Land of the Dead to await rebirth at Yule, and a time when the Crone Goddess would go into mourning for her lost son/consort, leaving her people in temporary darkness.

As in days long past, Celtic Pagans believe that the veil between the world of the living and that of the dead is at its thinnest on this night, and that the spirits of our departed loved ones walk the earth, visit family and friends, and join in the ritual celebrations. This makes Samhain a prime night for any type of spirit contact rituals (see Raymond Buckland's *Doors to Other Worlds* for all sorts of ideas on how to go about this at any time of the year).

The feeding of the dead is a widespread practice, even in modern Celtic lands. In Brittany and Ireland food is always left out for these spirit travelers, and candles are placed in windows to guide them along their way, and these were the origins of the modern Halloween customs of the jack o' lantern and trick-or-treat.

If you wish to use invocation to make your Samhain ritual more meaningful, you can try invoking the Crone Goddess in one of her guises as the deity who watches over the Land of the Dead (such as Badb). Invoke her according to the model in Chapter 4 and, with her power in you, do whatever rituals of spirit contact you like. On Samhain, when the spirits are all about, all the Goddess has to do is call out to them and they will come to the edge of your circle.

There are then several ways you can take your ritual with an eye toward using divine energy:

◆ After invoking the Goddess, open your arms to the dead and offer to help escort them to the Land of the Dead when they are ready to go back

◆ Or, you can welcome them back to earth and offer your blessings on their journey

◆ Tell each of them why they are missed by you and why the evoked Goddess is happy to receive them into her Otherworld home

◆ Offer them a libation of food in her name

◆ Light a candle in her name for each of them to carry away—astrally, of course—to help light their journeys

◆ Create a ritual around a number of masks to show that though the crone is now old and lonely, she is still many other Goddesses also, reaffirming her eternalness and the turning of the Wheel of the Year

You can evoke or invoke any God and build a ritual around his demise. With evocation you can:

◆ Watch the old God die and offer him comfort and blessings

◆ Light a candle for him which you will keep burning until his rebirth at Yule

◆ Offer to carry a part of him within you until Yule and create a ritual to do so using invocation methods

With invocation you can be the dying God. Just don't get too carried away with your role! You can then:

◆ Dramatize his death and then release his energy, symbolizing that you, as part of him, still live on

◆ Experience a small part of divine death to help you understand the cycles of life, death, and rebirth

◆ Evoke the crone to mourn over you and then offer her your comfort after you have released the God energy

◆ Offer the spirits of the night food, shelter, and light

YULE

Sing reign of Fair Maid,
with gold upon her toe—
Open you the West Door,
and turn the Old Year go.

—Scottish Yule Song

Date: Winter Solstice

Other Names: Midwinter, Sun Return, Fionn's Day

Colors: Red, green, and white

Symbols: Evergreen, wreath, Yule log, holly, spinning wheels

Deities: Newborn Gods, Triple Goddess, Virgin Goddesses

YULE IS ONE of the oldest and most widely observed of all the Sabbats, yet, oddly enough, it was not a part of Celtic year until the Norse invaders made it so. It celebrates the rebirth of the God as symbolized by the sun which will begin to wax anew after this night of peak darkness. The Celts, for reasons unknown, waited until Imbolg to celebrate the sun's return.

After the Norse brought Yule into prominence it nearly replaced Samhain as the date of the New Year, and many modern Celtic covens still honor Yule in this way. The Nordic-influenced Celts celebrated Yule with many of the trappings we associate with modern Christmas observances; decorated evergreen trees, wreaths, holly, mistletoe, feasting, and dancing.

They also believed that on this night the Holly King, as the God of the waning year, would battle the Oak King, the God of the waxing year, and lose. Often Yule coven rituals have members reenact this fight.

If you wish to enjoy the battle, but are alone by choice or chance, you can:

◆ Evoke both of these deities to your own circle and enjoy the fight

◆ You may even wish to invoke the winner when you are through and do your ritual to celebrate the newly waxing year with its new God being a part of you

This is also a night to honor the Triple Goddess, especially in her virgin guise. You can invoke the Triple Goddess if you like and:

◆ Give yourself the Celtic Threefold blessing. This is when each aspect of the Triple Goddess reaches into a cauldron and anoints you with the consecrated water of life (*eau de vie* in Brittany) which is inside. The Maiden anoints your feet to set you on right and straight pathways, the Mother anoints your womb or genital area for fertility in all your endeavors, and the Crone anoints your head for wisdom and to help you connect with all the cosmic mysteries

◆ Experience the symbolic birthing of the sun God through the virgin's eyes and mind

IMBOLG

Mother and maiden
Was never none but she;
Well may such a lady
God's bride be.
—Anglo-Scottish Folk Song

Date: February 1 or 2

Other Names: Oimelc, Imbolc, Brid's Day, Bride's Day

Colors: White, silver, pale yellow

Symbols: Candles, brides, grain dolly, burrowing animals, ewes

Deities: Virgin or Child Goddesses, Gods as Young Men or Boys

IMBOLG (EM-bowl'g) IS THE Sabbat which honors the Goddess as the waiting bride of the returning sun God. Before the Nordic influence, it was also the Sabbat in which the Celts saw the sun as being born anew. In Ireland it was, and still is, a special day to honor the Goddess Brid in her guise of bride. The modern Irish know this as St. Bridget's Day, St. Bridget being a vaguely disguised and Christianized version of the old Goddess.

Celts would often dress grain dollies, representations made from dried sheaves from the previous harvest, as brides, and set them in a place of honor within their homes. They were usually placed in cradles called Bride's Beds, and nuts, symbols of male fertility, were tossed in with them.

This is also a Sabbat where candles are lit in profusion, often within a wreath, another symbol of the Wheel of the Year. These are symbolic of the heat and light of the returning sun.

At Imbolg the deities are still youthful and not yet joined as one through sacred marriage. They are innocent and fun-loving, and are waiting just as anxiously for spring as are we.

If you wish to invoke the bride you can:

◆ Become her and call out welcomes and blessings to the approaching sun God

◆ Sing a spontaneous love song in his honor

◆ Light a candlewheel, a wreath holding lit candles, in the God's honor as a form of sympathetic magick to lure him back to you

If you wish to evoke the bride you can try:

◆ Allowing her energy to infuse the grain dolly

◆ Playing "games" with her as a child would like

If you wish to work with the God energy you might try:

◆ Evoking the God energy into the candlewheel and feel him returning to the cold earth

- Invoking the God and singing a spontaneous song of love and return to the waiting bride
- Bring his energy into the nuts which have been tossed in the Bride's Bed as your symbolic hope for their sacred marriage at Bealtaine

OSTARA

T'was but a hint of spring—for still
The atmosphere was sharp and chill....
—James Whitcomb Riley

Date: Spring Equinox

Other Names: Eostre, Lady Day

Colors: Pastels

Symbols: Egg, equilateral cross, butterfly

Deities: Youthful Deities, Warrior Gods, Deities awakening to sexuality

OSTARA WAS ANOTHER Sabbat which was not originally a part of the Celtic year, and all its associations were given to Bealtaine until recent times. Because it is named for the Teutonic Goddess of Spring and New Life, Eostre, it is assumed that it was brought to prominence in the Celtic world by the Saxons.

Modern Celtic Pagan practice has adopted Ostara whole-heartedly, and different Celtic traditions have different ways of observing this Sabbat. Primarily it is a night of balance in which night and day are equal, with the forces of light gaining power over the darkness. One tradition honors the God in his guise as a warrior on this date, while another views it as a time of the courtship between the God and Goddess, a relationship to be consummated at Bealtaine.

There are numerous ways you can use evocation and invocation to bring the power of the deities to your Ostara celebration:

- Evoke or pathwork (see Chapter 8 for complete details on pathworking) with the presence of a warrior teacher such as Scathach to come and teach you her battle skills
- Invoke a warrior or warrioress and allow their power to fill you, to make you feel invincible
- Invoke a youthful deity or mythic figure and allow yourself to remember the strong feelings and emotions of sexual awakening
- Bring the power of a fertility Goddess into an egg and keep it on your altar until Bealtaine when its symbolic promise is fulfilled
- Evoke the God or Goddess, whichever is the opposite of your own gender, and do a courtship dance with him/her

Another Ostara custom of uncertain origin which has gained popularlity in Celtic circles is that of awakening mother earth. The youngest person present is asked to take a stick or wand and walk to the far northern point of the circle, the coldest compass point in the northern hemisphere, the place where the sun never travels, and tap on the ground three times. The youngster then entreats mother earth to "wake up." In keeping with the Celtic beliefs about the sacredness of three times three, this gesture is repeated twice more. After this is done you may wish to evoke or invoke the earth mother and make her the center of your Ostara festivities, celebrating her presence as the embodiment of spring.

BEALCAINE

If not a bowl of thy sweet cream,
Then a cup to bring me cheer,
For who knows when we shall meet again
To go Maying another year.
—Cornish Folk Song

Date: May 1

Other Names: May Day, Beltane, Rudemas, Giamonios, Bhealltainn

Colors: Red and white

Symbols: May Pole, egg, baskets, flowers, butterchurn

Deities: Flower Goddesses, Divine Couples, Deities of the Hun

THE FIRST OF May has been celebrated in song and verse for longer than human history has recorded the date. It is a time to celebrate new life in all its forms, and the time when the Goddess and the God are united in sacred marriage, their relationship consummated, an act which symbolically fertilizes the animals and crops for the coming year.

The most common ritual act which celebrates this union is known as The Great Rite. It is the symbolic union of the male and female principles of creation, the union of the two halves of the All-Power which unite to bring all things into being. The Great Rite is usually performed by ritually placing a male ritual tool, usually the athame, into a female ritual tool representing the cosmic womb. A chalice or small cauldron is usually chosen for this purpose. Couples working together will often invoke the deities into themselves and perform The Great Rite *de facto,* which is also acceptable.

The dancing of the May Pole is another May Day Celtic custom practiced both within and outside of Paganism. The weaving of the red and white ribbons around the pole, like the Great Rite, symbolizes the union of Goddess and God.

In recent years there has been some debate within the Pagan community as to just how old the May Pole custom is, and if it is really Celtic or not. Remember that no culture ever has, or ever will, exist in a vacuum, and it is likely that the May Pole came to the Celts from the southern Teutonic Pagans who also revered trees. Written references to this "quaint country custom" date from the Elizabethan period (1558–1603), and from as early as the late seventeenth century we have extant wood carvings depicting the revival of the communal May Pole after the fall of the Puritan Commonwealth. Most likely, the May Pole as we know it today dates to Britain of the late 1300s when, after the devastating march of the Black Plague through Europe, people were ready to celebrate the renewal of life once again. Perhaps there was an underlying belief that somehow the new religion had failed them and that maybe the old ways were worth another look.

Customs change with time and with the people who use them. Whatever the May Pole ritual might have been prior to the 1300s is anybody's guess. Certainly the post-plague generation put their own spin on it, as did the Elizabethans. No doubt modern Pagans will continue to change and modify these traditions again as time passes and human needs change.

Deities of the hunt, of the woodlands, and of animals, are also honored at Bealtaine (Ball-TAWN, BEEL-teen, or BELL-tayn).

For using deity energy at Bealtaine here are several ideas which you can begin exploring:

- Evoke the presence of the God and Goddess into your circle and allow them to perform The Great Rite themselves
- If you are into sex magick you can invoke one of these creative principles into yourself and evoke the other for The Great Rite
- You can also evoke the presence of a deity of the hunt and allow him/her to pursue you
- You can invoke this deity of the hunt and pursue a goal of yours
- You can invoke a woodlands deity and offer fertility and blessings to the nature around you.
- You can evoke or invoke a deity of animals and bless your pets or livestock, particularly if you have animals which you breed for your livelihood

MIDSUMMER

My meadow lies green, and my corn is unshorn,
My barn is to build and my babe is unborn.
—Scottish Folk Song

Date: Summer Solstice

Other Names: Litha, Gathering Day, Feill-Sheathain

Colors: Green

Symbols: Fire, mistletoe, solar disk, feathers, blades

Deities: Gods at their Peak of Power, Pregnant Goddesses

MIDSUMMER IS ANOTHER Pagan Sabbat which was, oddly enough, not originally a part of the Celtic year. The Norse and the Saxons brought it into prominence as they did with Yule.

Midsummer is the time when the sun reaches the peak of its power, the earth is green and holds the promise of a bountiful harvest. The Mother Goddess is viewed as heavily pregnant, and the God is at the apex of his manhood and is honored in his guide as the supreme sun.

But don't overlook the Celtic sun *Goddesses* in your celebration. The Celts are one of several cultures known to also have had female deities to represent the power of the sun. The Celtic languages are some of the *very* few in which the names for the "sun" are feminine nouns, which attests to the one-time prominence of these Goddesses. A number of the myths surrounding these ladies of light have been preserved. Among the most well-known are Sul (Anglo-Celtic), Dia Griene (Scottish), the Princess of the Sun (Breton), and Grian and Brid (Irish).

Just as the Holly and Oak Kings battled for supremacy at Yule, this ever-repeating fight is reenacted at Midsummer, this time with the Holly King, as king of the waning year, victorious.

You can honor the Goddess as mother-to-be by:

◆ Evoking her to aid you in lighting the ritual balefires

◆ Invoking her and feeling the power of all creation growing in her womb

◆ Performing a ritual designed to honor her in this guise, invoking her at the end to bring those blessings into yourself

You can honor the God by:

◆ Invoking him and feeling the power of manhood at its peak

◆ Bring his energy into the balefire through which animals, tools, etc., are traditionally passed for his blessing

◆ Designing a ritual to honor him at his peak. Evoke him so that he might be a part of the proceedings

◆ Evoke the Holly and Oak Kings to do battle in your circle. Mourn the Oak King, and honor the Holly King, knowing that they are but two aspects of the same God

◆ You can also perform a ritual known as Drawing Down the Sun. This is performed the same way as Drawing Down the Moon was in the previous chapter, only this time you invoke the energy of the Father God through the full power of the sun. Follow the instructions for Drawing Down the Moon using masculine tools such as the wand or athame in place of the chalice

Aine, the Irish Goddess most often known as a cattle deity, can also be worked with at this time. Cattle deities were extremely important to cultures which relied on herd animals for a major portion of their food, as did the Celts.

LUGHNASADH

Idle days in summertime, In pleasant sunny weather,
Amid the golden colored corn, Two lovers passed together.
—Bugeilio'r Gwenith Gwyn

Date: August 1 or 2

Other Names: Lammas, August Eve, Elembiuos

Colors: Gray, gold, green, yellow

Symbols: All grains, breads, threshing tools

Deities: Harvest and Grain Deities, New Mother Goddesses

LUGHNASADH (Loo-NAHS-ah) IS NAMED for the Irish sun God, Lugh, and is usually looked upon as the first of the three Pagan harvest festivals.

Lughnasadh is primarily a grain harvest, one in which corn, wheat, barley, and grain products such as bread are prominently featured. Fruits and vegetables which ripen in late summer are also a part of the traditional feast. The Goddess, in her guise as the Queen of Abundance, is honored as the new mother who has given birth to the bounty, and the God is honored as the Father of Prosperity.

The threshing of precious grain was once seen as a sacred act, and threshing houses had small wooden panels under the door so that no loose grain could escape. This is the original meaning of our modern word "threshold."

Ways in which you might utilize divine energy at Lughnasadh are:

◆ Bring the divine energy into your ritual breads, of which a part is traditionally offered as a libation to faery folk and animals

◆ Giving honors to Lugh, or his Welsh/Cornish form Llew, by evocation or invocation

◆ Honoring the Goddess as the Queen of Abundance

◆ Taillte, the mother of Lugh, can also be honored in her fertility guise

MABON

Earth is here so kind, that just tickle her
with a hoe and she laughs with a harvest.
—Douglas Jerrold, from *Land of Plenty*

Date: Fall Equinox

Other Names: Wine Harvest, Feast of Avalon

Colors: Orange, russet, maroon

Symbols: Apple, wine, vine, garland, gourd, cornucopia, burial cairns

Deities: Wine Gods, Harvest Deities, Aging Deities

MABON (MAY-bone or MAH-bawn) IS NAMED for the Welsh God and it is seen as the second of the three harvests, and particularly as a celebration of the vine harvests and of wine. It is also associated with apples as symbols of life renewed.

Celebrating new-made wine, harvesting apples and vine products, and visiting burial cairns to place an apple upon them, were all ways in which the Celts honored this Sabbat. (Avalon, one of the many Celtic names for the Land of the Dead, literally means the "land of apples.") These acts symbolized both thankfulness for the life-giving harvest, and the wish of the living to be reunited with their dead.

There are many ways to utilize the power of the deities at this Sabbat of balance:

◆ Invoke the Goddess at a cemetery where loved ones are buried and place the ritual apple on their headstones as her promise of life renewed

- ◆ Evoke Mabon, or his mother Modron, and honor them as the deities who brought forth the second harvest
- ◆ If you like making wines, make specific ones to be consecrated to the deities of Mabon, and use them in ritual
- ◆ Pathwork (see Chapter 8 for full explanation) with these deities to gain an understanding of the Otherworld and of reincarnation

✠ ✠ ✠ ✠ ✠

The best way to approach all the Sabbats is to read more about them and all the varied ways the Celts have observed them both past and present. Then see if you are inspired to devise other ways in which harnessing the power of the deities can make the symbolism of the seasons more meaningful and real to you.

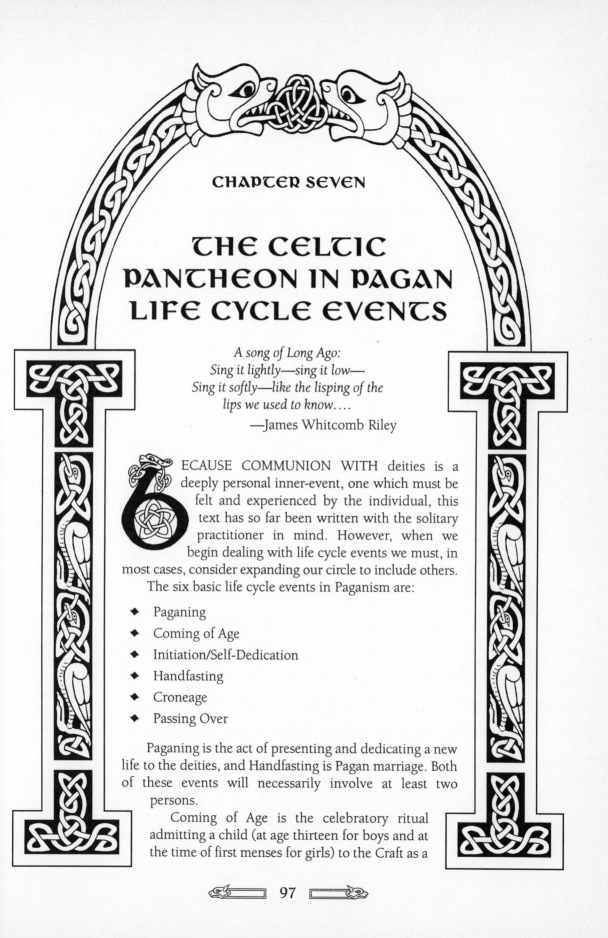

CHAPTER SEVEN

THE CELTIC PANTHEON IN PAGAN LIFE CYCLE EVENTS

A song of Long Ago:
Sing it lightly—sing it low—
Sing it softly—like the lisping of the
lips we used to know....
—James Whitcomb Riley

ECAUSE COMMUNION WITH deities is a deeply personal inner-event, one which must be felt and experienced by the individual, this text has so far been written with the solitary practitioner in mind. However, when we begin dealing with life cycle events we must, in most cases, consider expanding our circle to include others. The six basic life cycle events in Paganism are:

◆ Paganing

◆ Coming of Age

◆ Initiation/Self-Dedication

◆ Handfasting

◆ Croneage

◆ Passing Over

Paganing is the act of presenting and dedicating a new life to the deities, and Handfasting is Pagan marriage. Both of these events will necessarily involve at least two persons.

Coming of Age is the celebratory ritual admitting a child (at age thirteen for boys and at the time of first menses for girls) to the Craft as a willing member, and Initiation/Self-Dedication is the act of admitting an adult to the Craft. While these too can be solitary events, they are often done in the presence of others, though the participation of others makes no difference to the outcome or meaning of these rituals.

Croneage is a celebration of the cessation of a woman's menstrual cycle, a time when she is often scorned and reviled by mainstream society, but which was celebrated and revered in Pagan cultures as it has been for many thousands of years.

Passing Over commemorates a human life which has ended its current incarnation and has passed over into the Land of the Dead. These memorial services can also be done in a coven or other group setting, but are often most meaningful when done alone.

In all of these events our deities are frequently called upon (evoked) to witness or aid in the ritual. They can also be invoked in many instances, and doing so can add a mind-expanding dimension to the old ritual forms.

Again, all of the following ritual outlines are merely suggestions which it is hoped will trigger your own creative spirituality.

PAGANING

I sigh that kiss you,
For I must own
That I shall miss you
When you are grown.
—William Butler Yeats

WHEN A CHILD is born to, or adopted by, a Pagan individual or couple, those parents, like parents of all religions, usually want to make some sort of formal presentation or dedication of their child to their deities. The difference being that in Paganism, the ceremony does not eternally bind the child to the path of the parents, but allows for his or her free choice in the future. Therefore, Paganing (also called Wiccaning) involves the presentation to the deities, petitioning aid and guardianship of them, and making a vow to help steer the child onto the positive path he or she is meant to take in this life.

In the old days, Pagan children were brought to the altars of the old deities in much the same way as mainstream children today are dedicated in a church or synagogue. Confirmation in the faith, what we Pagans call Coming of Age, takes place in the teens when the child is deemed old enough to make their own spiritual decisions.

The following ritual is written for the participation of one parent and the child, but it can be adapted to use by both parents or by larger groups.

 **Paganing Ritual**

A CIRCLE SHOULD be cast with some type of altar in the center oriented to whichever direction you are accustomed. Some like to orient to the east, the direction associated with new beginnings. The choice is yours, no way is "wrong."

On the altar you will need a chalice, or some type of receptacle to hold water, a masculine tool such as a wand or athame, a small circle of lit candles with one unlit candle in its center, matches, and a candle snuffer of some kind for it is considered rude in most traditions to blow out ritual candles.

Evoke the Triple Goddess and a God of your choosing, or use the generic male principle. They will need to be present to bless the child.

Hold the baby in your arms and stand (or kneel if it is easier) before the altar. Verbally present your child to the deities with his or her given, legal name, and then with any magickal or Craft name you might wish to choose to bestow. It is customary for the child to use that name until Coming of Age, at which time he or she will choose a magickal name of his or her own. Pick something which reflects either the personality of the child, or the hopes you have for its future. Remember that names were very important and powerful to the Celts, and that magickal names were often kept secret.

The presentation might sound something like this:

Old Ones, I welcome you to this circle. In this sacred space I present to you my son/daughter, (insert name), who will be known among the magickal folk as (insert child's magickal name). I ask your blessings on him/her now as I dedicate him/her to you as a child of the Old Ways. This is not to bind his/her will, or to manipulate or coerce him/her onto my chosen path. But rather it is an act of love, as I give him/her to you to watch and protect until he/she is wise enough to choose for him/herself by what names he/she shall call you, and in what manner he/she will offer you praise.

Hold the child up before the God and ask his blessing on the child. Take the athame, point it towards the God and feel his energy merge with the tool. Then place the tool lightly on the crown of the child's head.

In the name of (insert the God's name), I give you the blessings of strength, perseverance, and truthfulness. I bestow upon you the qualities of love, kindness, and mercy. I hope for you loving family and friendships. I bequeath you knowledge, loyalty, and a quick tongue. Blessed Be.

Replace the athame on the altar and move the water-filled chalice within reach. Now you are ready to present the child to the Triple Goddess. You will be giving the child the Threefold Blessing in her name in much the same way as it was outlined in the suggestions for the Yule ritual in the previous chapter.

Take your right hand and get a small bit of the water on your fingertips. Place your wet fingers on the child's feet and say:

In the name of the Maiden, I bless your feet that they might always walk along the straight and blessed path. Blessed Be.

Place some water on the child's womb or genital area:

In the name of the Mother of us all, I bless your womb (or "loins" for a male child), your creative center, that you might be fertile and fruitful in all your endeavors. Blessed Be.

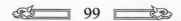

Lastly, place some water on the child's forehead:

> *In the name of the Crone, I bless your head that it might always seek knowledge and truth so that you might grow in wisdom. Blessed Be.*

Next, take a match and prepare to strike it:

> *Little (insert child's magickal name), you are now one of the magickal people. May you be forever surrounded by their love and support, and always know you may turn to your Goddess and God in time of need or thanksgiving.*

Light the candle in the middle of the circle of lit candles to symbolize the child's dedication to the Old Ways. See it as being representative of the child's lifelight surrounded by the strength and support of the Pagan people and their deities.

You can also evoke the presence of a guardian deity to look after the child, or bring some divine protective energy into an amulet or talisman which you can present to the child now as a Paganing gift.

✤ ✤ ✤

COMING OF AGE

> *Away this little boy is gone,*
> *as fast as he could run...*
> *Where is my daughter fair,*
> *that used to walk with me?*
> —from a Breton Ballad

A MODIFIED FORM of the old Coming of Age Ritual is gaining popularity among even the most mainstream people, especially as mothers attempt to remove the culturally imposed fear of menstruation from their daughters. Instead of shielding their entrance into womanhood with secretive whispers and actions which bring to mind shame, they are treating these young women to dinner, new clothes or commemorative jewelry in order to communicate a positive attitude about their developing bodies.

The Celts celebrated Coming of Age for both male and female children. For females it was at the time of first menses, for males it was age thirteen by the solar calendar. At this time the child, who has presumably been raised to know and understand both Paganism and as many other religions as he or she has come into contact with, is ready to dedicate his or her life to the Pagan path. After this ceremony they will be considered full-fledged spiritual adults able to take on any and all roles within spiritual life whether they choose to practice as a solitary, are part of a coven, or are operating strictly within a family tradition.

In some modern Celtic covens the Coming of Age rite has been postponed to coincide with the age of legal adulthood (anywhere from age 16 to 25 depending in which part of the western world one lives). At age thirteen or first menses the youngster is given a Puberty Rite at which he or she announces their chosen craft name and their intent to study and follow a Pagan life-style, but, in this case, the ceremony honors them only as physical adults.

Like the Paganing Ritual, the Coming of Age Ritual can be adapted for two parents or for larger gatherings. If other relatives, such as grandparents, are present, allow them to feel a part of the spiritual life of the young person by giving them active roles to play whether they are Pagan or not.

 **Coming of Age Ritual**

THE COMING OF Age Ritual traditionally need not be done inside a circle. In fact, some traditions send their children out on a quest which requires that they travel fairly far from the ritual site. But if you wish to make the ritual special by invoking the power of the Goddess or God into the new adult, you will need the protection of the circle. Then, if you wish to send the young person forth on a quest, a door can be "cut" in the circle with a ritual tool to allow exit and reentry.

Allow the ritual to begin with the young person doing the talking, perhaps making a statement of purpose, or explaining why he/she has elected to follow a Pagan spiritual path.

Then formally ask the young person something like:

Are you, (insert the child's old Paganing name), ready to dedicate yourself to the ancient ways of the old Goddesses and Gods?

Wait for the young person's response after each question is asked:

Are you willing to accept all of the many responsibilities of adult spirituality?

Are you ready to allow the Pagan Rede of Harm None to govern all your thoughts, words and deeds?

Are you ready to accept full responsibility for your actions and thoughts? For all energy which you send forth consciously or unconsciously?

Are you ready to accept that any harm or help you give will return to you three-fold?

Are you ready to take your place as a spiritual adult, a brother/sister of the divine, beside me and others of the Pagan community both near and far?

Are you ready to stand here, in this sacred space, before me (or "before us," as the case may be) and before the Old Ones, and to declare openly your choice of the Pagan lifepath, discarding your old life and beginning a new one with a new name?

Presumably the young person will answer each question in the affirmative.

At this point it is traditional in some circles to ask the person to perform some task to demonstrate their readiness and worthiness. Sometimes this is a simple scavenger hunt for magickal items, other times it is a full-blown vision quest in the wilderness, and other times it is the performing of some act of ritual or magick.

Whether this is included in your Coming of Age Ritual or not is up to you and the young person involved. It is certainly not mandatory.

Give the young person the Threefold Blessing and then proclaim that he or she is now a spiritual adult. Then ask the person what Craft name he or she has chosen to adopt. Allow the name to be stated, then greet him or her with that name saying something such as:

> Bright Blessings upon you, sister/brother (insert name). May you never hunger and never thirst.

As a spiritual adult, the young person is now mature enough to participate in evocation and invocation rituals. To formally seal your acceptance of that person as an equal, draw into them the essence of the God or Goddess. For the time being keep the choice gender specific as young teens are still discovering their own sexual identity, and being asked at this point in time to deal with the identity of the opposite sex can be very confusing.

Using the Drawing Down the Moon model from Chapter 5, invoke the spirit of deity into the young person. Allow them to role play once the act is complete, let them feel that divine power and reinforce it by telling them that they are indeed God/dess.

When they are finished doing whatever it is they wish to do with the invoked energy, hand him or her the chalice with water and allow them to give you the Threefold Blessing for the first time. This little bit of ritual goes a long way in making the young person feel they are truly a spiritual adult and and equal to you within the sacred circle.

Coming of Age Rituals, like B'nai Mitzvah and Christian Confirmations, usually end with gift giving. The gifts chosen by Pagans are usually things which the young person can use within the framework of their chosen religious practice. Suggestions for such items are Tarot cards, Runes, athames, Pagan jewelry, or a silver chalice. Avoid the giving of wands as it is a Celtic tradition that wands are to be found or made by the person who is to use them.

INITIATION/SELF-DEDICATION

Is buaine focal na toice an t-saeghail
*A word is more lasting than all
the riches of the world.*
—from a Connacht Love Song

WHEN A PERSON is part of a coven or other Pagan group, that group usually already has its own initiatory rituals which they may or may not allow you to adapt to suit your own tastes. Therefore the following ritual is designed for solitary practice, and may be used whether or not you are part of a larger group which had its own initiation procedure. In it you will not only

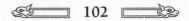

dedicate yourself to whichever tradition of the Celtic Craft you choose to follow, but you will also call to your circle the deities you feel most aligned with, and you will make them a conscious part of your new life.

Initiation is traditionally held a year and a day after study of the Craft has begun because many Celtic myths use the time of a year and a day when describing the time between great events. This time frame is a good basic guideline, but many will wait longer if they feel they are not ready to make the final commitment. There are no hard and fast rules. When it comes to spirituality we are all on our own schedule.

Pagans are often confused about the value of initiations done by either themselves or others and they often question the validity of one over the other. They worry whether or not they are a real witch if they have not been trussed up like Thanksgiving turkey for the rite or if no Grand Master First Degree High Priestess muttered the sacred words over them. Most simply put, if you wish to follow a tradition which requires initiation—or any special formula of initiation—and/or has specific degrees of advancement, you *must* be initiated within that tradition in order to be considered a member of it by others following that path. If, on the other hand, you wish to follow a more solitary path, an eclectic Celtic tradition of your own making, or follow a tradition that does not consider group initiation a necessity, then your sincere self-dedication will be valid, and you should let no one in their ignorance tell you otherwise.

If you truly desire a group initiation ceremony, even if you later plan to follow a solitary path, you should check with some of the networking groups listed in Appendix D or make queries at Pagan gatherings for someone who can do the initiation for you.

 ## Dedication Ritual

SELF-DEDICATION IS best done at the inbetween times which the Celts held to be so powerful. These are times such as midnight, dawn, dusk, seasonal changes, etc., all times when it is hard to tell if it is really day or night, or winter or summer, etc. Doing your dedication at these times symbolizes your willing entrance into a life which consciously walks the fine line between the seen and unseen worlds.

Cast your circle in the usual way and have your altar set up in any quarter you like. Have on hand some salt water, an item which has been very popular in Self-Dedication Rituals over the past several decades. It represents the union of the elements of earth (the salt) and of water, and is also a time-honored purifying force.

Begin as you did with the Coming of Age Ritual, with your personal statement of purpose to the deities.

Before the ritual began you should have spent some time contemplating which deities of the Celtic pantheon you personally feel most aligned with at this stage of your spiritual development. You can discover these affinities through reading myths and folktales, alignment practice, or mediation on the question. Evoke these deities to your circle. You can bring in as many as you are comfortable with, or as many as you can visualize at one time. Be sure you are comfortable aligning yourself with each one, for they will be a part of this Self-Dedication Ritual.

When they are all present, stand before them proudly. Do not kneel in supplication, as this habit would have been alien to the Celts. Announce again your desire to initiate yourself into the Pagan faith, declaring this intent with your chosen new name. You might say something like:

> Blessed Old Ones, I stand before you, sure and steadfast in my desire to dedicate the beginning of my conscious life as your child, to initiate myself into the mysteries of the Celtic way (or you can insert the name of the tradition you follow). Henceforth, I will be known among the magickal folk as (state your new name). Old Ones, I seek knowledge in the light, and revelation in the darkness. As I step from darkness into light, bless, guide, and guard me in my never-ending quest for understanding.

The Threefold Blessing is also appropriate here. You may wish to add words to it which reaffirm your self-dedication such as:

> And as my feet walk in your ways, may they remain steadfast in their honor of Goddess and God and all that my chosen spirituality symbolizes.

Using one of the alignment exercises from Chapter 2, align yourself with each deity present, feeling their essence to truly be a part of your own. Since you have dedicated yourself to each deity's magickal traditions, the experience will be stronger because you have literally aligned all parts of your being with their energies on a deeper inner-level than any you have ever experienced before.

You may also choose personal, or mascot, deities if you like, ones with whom you feel a special affinity, whom you call upon frequently, who teach and share your interests and even some of your personality. Call their energy into a talisman or amulet and wear it as a keepsake of your dedication. You might even want to amend your Craft name to proclaim yourself as that deity's child. For example, you may wish to call yourself Tara Daughter of Brid, or Brian Son of Lugh.

There are many other ways you can choose to dedicate yourself, and these are only suggestions. Whatever else you do in your Self-Dedication Ritual, remember to use the energies of the Celtic pantheon to enhance the ceremony and to bind you more closely with their power.

✠ ✠ ✠

HANDFASTING

My love is like a red, red rose,
that's newly sprung in June.
My love is like a melody
that's sweetly played in tune.
—Robert Burns

HANDFASTING IS SO called because the priest/ess who "married" the old Celtic couples literally bound their hands together for the duration of the ritual. It is also the origin of the phrase giving one's "hand in marriage."

Couples were not bound for life as they are in today's mainstream religions, but rather for a duration of time chosen by them. For the Celts this was usually nine years, in keeping with the idea of incorporating the sacred three times three in any ritual proceedings. The bonds of union were renewable only if both parties agreed. And no matter how many times the bond was made or renewed, it was an excuse for celebration and rejoicing among the Celtic clans.

Though a nine-year Handfasting is traditional, other common durations chosen by Celtic Pagans for this union are:

◆ Three years, always renewable by mutual agreement

◆ Six years, always renewable by mutual agreement

◆ Nine months trial Handfasting, renewable to three years, followed by a life-time commitment with mutual consent

◆ A year and a day trial Handfasting followed by a life-time commitment

◆ Three years trial Handfasting followed by a life-time commitment

Unfortunately modern law has made legal Handfastings almost impossible to obtain unless one commits for life at the onset. Because of this legal quirk, many Pagans have ceased to care about the legality of their unions and have opted to be Handfasted only by the tenets of their faith, united by a priest/ess or by themselves.

The following ritual is written for two and *is not* legally binding according to the laws of any state or province, unless it is used by a licensed member of the clergy. If you are interested in legality, check with the networking entries in Appendix D or ask around at Pagan festivals. Licensed priests and priestesses often will have lots of ideas for music and ritual to deeply personalize your Handfasting ceremony, and can show you ways in which other family and friends can have active roles.

Many Celtic traditions have broken away from the rigid idea of the male-female marriage mold and will also accept group and gay marriages. This openness and eclecticism is, for many of us, one of the great attractions of Paganism. Always adapt your Handfasting rituals to reflect your own needs and situation. But for a special touch, the true microcosm of the joining of parts of the supreme macrocosmic power, always remember to invoke deity.

 **Handfasting Ritual**

BEGIN, AS ALWAYS, with a cast circle. It is a nice touch to hold a Handfasting in a natural setting, but if this is not possible, bring as much of nature indoors as you can without straining your budget or harming the plants.

You will need on hand a chalice with water if you wish to add the Threefold Blessing to the ritual. You will also need some vine, garland, or strip of silk for binding your hands, gifts to exchange (usually in the form of wedding rings, but you can be creative if you like), a basket with a handle, and, if you wish, a written contract of your vows specifying the duration for which you have agreed to be Handfasted.

You will also need to have already made decisions about what type of "marriage" you want. You can select vows to reflect a choice to be monogamous, or both of you can retain the right to pursue relationships with others outside of the union. The choice is for the two of you alone to make. Just make it honestly. Don't say you want monogamy, meaning you want your partner to be monogamous while you are planning to cheat behind his or her back. Decide on a lifestyle and be faithful to it, or at least include a clause in your vows or contract specifying how lifestyle changes will be decided upon.

For example, one of my best friends and her husband are monogamous, but both are very free to pursue their own outside interests and non-sexual friendships. In other words, they don't see marriage as being eternally joined at the hip and they realize that no one single person can be expected to satisfy all one's emotional and psychological needs. But they also recognize that the time may come when one of them may wish to explore other romantic or sexual relationships within the bounds of their union. They have agreed to discuss such changes openly so that no sneaking around is involved. That way the other partner will have the opportunity to decide if they want the change in the rules of the relationship or if they wish to look elsewhere for a partner who shares their own desires in a union. It is only fair, and in keeping with "Harm None," in these days of AIDS be completely open with a partner if you are having sexual relations with someone else. They have the right to decide if they wish to risk further contact with you because, in essence, in they would not only be sleeping with you, but also with your new partner and all the partners that other person has ever had.

With all these preliminaries out of the way, you are ready to begin the ritual.

Pagan marriage has always seen the union of a couple as the union of the Goddess and the God, the joining of the two halves of the All-Power into a new creative whole. To add a new dimension to the Handfasting rite, you can each invoke the Goddess and God and finish your Handfasting Ritual as deity incarnate.

Begin by stating your intention to take the other as a partner for the specified duration. Verbally acknowledge the other as God or Goddess incarnate, offering some token of honor and showing that you realize your Handfasting is much more than the mere joining of two earthly bodies.

Next, take the vine, garland, or strip of silk and bind together your left hands. The left hands are usually the ones considered to be the receptive ones. The exception to this would be if both of you were left-handed, then you would probably do better to bind your right hands together. Make a statement of the symbology of the joining of your hands such as:

Hand to hand we are bound, as heart to heart we have loved for many lifetimes. Hands to hold, hearts to cherish. Here we stand, Goddess and God, female and male. We have been ever apart, seeking always to be united again. In this effort we rely on our children who stand here now asking to be joined as one creative power—the whole—the All-Power. Through the receptivity of our willing hands we feel the energy of the All-Power pass between us. We are deity. We are one. So Mote It Be!

It is customary in many cultures, including the Celtic one, for a bride and groom to exchange a token of some measurable value to seal their vows. Wedding rings are most commonly chosen, though they often come under fire from both Pagans and feminists. A wedding ring is a circle, a sacred space encircling the finger which many ancient people believed contained a vein running directly to the heart. Therefore, it is not a brand of ownership, as some would have you believe, but a magick circle which guards a sacred place and which creates upon the giver a *geise,* or honor vow, to uphold the Handfasting oaths they have just taken.

You may add any other vows you like after you make your initial pledge to one another. These can be as personal or as broad, as mundane, or as detailed as you care to make them. You may also share a cup of wine, a loaf of bread, kiss, dance, or do anything else which are you moved to do when creating this ritual together.

In many cultures, the basket represents the unity of the masculine and feminine creative forces. Those who have read the popular occult novel, *Medicine Woman,* by Lynn Andrews, will recall her pursuit of the elusive "marriage basket" which would represent the fulfillment of her fundamental power. Today, marriage baskets are often a part of Handfasting rites in Celtic ceremonies. The basket can be hooked over the bound hands of those being joined, can be offered to them as a wedding present to be taken home and put in a place of honor, or the couple can add symbols of the elements to it and "mix" them to symbolize their union. Nearly every Handfasting you attend will utilize the basket in a different way, yet the end meaning is the same. Be creative with yours, doing with it what will mean the most to you.

You may also have the couple "jump the broom" at the end of the ritual. This fertility rite is a common addition to nearly all Pagan weddings, though the custom originated in Africa and not with the Celts.

Finish your Handfasting with The Great Rite, symbolically if you are in the presence of others, and *de facto* if you have privacy. Do not release the invoked energy until The Great Rite has been concluded.

✠ ✠ ✠

CRONEAGE

When Age comes on!—
O tide of raptures, long withdrawn,
Flow back in the summer floods....
—James Whitcomb Riley

CRONEAGE IS A ceremony which, in most tribal cultures, is reserved for women, to be aided by women, and in the presence of only women. Such secretive practices once reinforced feminine power, but over the past millennia have done a lot to feed the ridiculous fear many people—male as well as female—feel toward older women.

There is nothing frightening about the elderly, other than a projection of our own morbid fear of aging which has been imposed on us by a youth-oriented world. When people in old Pagan cultures aged they were seen as coming into their full power; they were wise, all-knowing, and had many potent secrets gained over a lifetime to impart to any young person lucky enough to be selected as their apprentice. For women, it was the time of menopause, when women were seen as keeping the power of their sacred blood locked inside themselves rather than letting it flow outward—a very potent symbolic situation.

Because men do not menstruate there are no known precedents (the operative word here is "known") for similar rituals for aging Pagan men, but that does not mean they cannot be created to be just as powerful and meaningful as they are for women. If you are a man who is interested in such a ritual for yourself, use the following ritual, or other Croneage Rituals, as a model. Pick a time in your life which you feel corresponds to female menopause (some medical and psychological studies say men do have a menopause, but its symptoms are more subtle), a time when you feel you have gained great wisdom from living, and allow that to be your Croneage time.

Rites to mark the wisdom and aging of men have been tried in some modern covens, and many report the ceremonies to be very moving. The term "Saging" has been the only label which has so far been placed in the rite, but the expression does not seem to carry the same spiritual weight as "Crone." Men are still seeking the proper expression of this rite of passage and, perhaps, through solitary rituals and experimentation one will emerge which speaks eloquently of all the mystery and power the aging process confers on older male Pagans.

Other covens have adopted uni-sex rituals to honor their Sages and Crones as "Elders," though the lack of recognized sex differentiation seems to take away from the power of both sexes without adding to either.

What little we know about elders in Celtic society point towards them being held in high esteem. The Brehon Laws even specified what portion of the clan's time and goods had to be contributed to elder family members in their care (though by today's affluent standards these allotments seem quite parsimonious). Elder females were the wise women, the healers of the body and mind, the keepers of herbal knowledge, the symbol of the single motherblood which bound together the clan and through which the oral traditions were passed along. The role of male elders is more obscure, though it is reasonable to assume by reading the myths that older men were believed to have equally strong magickal powers, greater ease in contacting Other-world beings, and frequently served as mentors to young warriors.

Croneage Ritual

BEGIN INSIDE YOUR cast circle. Have on your altar symbols of your life's achievements. These can be honors, awards, degrees, pictures of grandchildren, etc., anything which to you signifies your accomplishments. Also have on hand your Book of Shadows or some other compilation of your spiritual wisdom, a small mirror, and, in the center of your altar, place several lighted candles in a circle around an unlit one. Visualize each candle as a center of power, and see the center candle as yourself.

Invoke into yourself a Crone Goddess. (If you are a man you might pick a sleeping deity such as King Arthur or Fionn MacCumhal.) Allow her energy to fill you, feel her wisdom as she welcomes you as herself, a woman of age and power.

Make a bold statement of your personal power such as:

I am Crone. I am Wise. Iam Powerful. I am Beautiful. I am Strong.

Look into the mirror and see the power of the invoked Crone Goddess reflected in your face. See your wrinkles as badges of honor, your crow's feet as symbols of wisdom. Remember that these scars of life were once a woman's ticket to community leadership. Smile at the old woman who is looking back at you, who is a part of you, and realize you have not come to the end of life, but rather you are embarking on a brand new part of it. Remind yourself that you are far from finished on earth, and that you can make of the rest of your life anything you wish it to be, perhaps even fashioning it to be the best time yet.

Pick up one of the candles in the lit circle and name it, giving it the verbal label of a particular kind of power. Name it, for example, "wisdom." Then use that candle to light the unlit center one which represents yourself, and feel its power bringing all your own life's wisdom to the surface of your consciousness.

Snuff out the named candle and replace it in the circle.

Moving clockwise, take the next candle and give it a name, for instance, "strength," and use it to "light" the already-lit center candle. Again, feel the power of your strength coming to the surface. Keep in mind that these are not qualities you are being given anew, but ones you have earned and harbored throughout your life.

When the circle is completed you should have a circle of dark candles with your own shining brightly in the center. Feel all that power being concentrated in yourself and repeat your affirmations. You can chant them over and over if you like, building around yourself a cone of power:

I am Crone. I am Wise. I am Powerful. (etc.)

You may even wish to select a specific Crone Goddess as your personal deity. Invoke her power into a talisman or amulet to wear which will remind you always of your own inner-strength. You will need this psychological boost in a world which still, sadly, denigrates and despises the power inherent in old age.

⚜ ⚜ ⚜

PASSING OVER

Now Voyager depart, (Much, much more for
thee is yet in Store)…Depart upon thy
endless cruise old Sailor.

—Walt Whitman

SCOTTISH AUTHOR AND poet Thomas Campbell wrote, "To live in the hearts we leave behind is not to die." Keeping the memory of loved ones alive and well, and aiding both them and ourselves in this transition, is the purpose of a ritual of Passing Over.

Celtic Paganism has occasionally been accused of being a cult of ancestor worshippers. While this is not exactly true, ancestor lore and remembrance was deeply a part of the Celtic religion, one kept alive by today's witches. Paganism does not view death as an ending, or even as a beginning, but as just another phase on the ever-turning wheel of existence. We come, we go, we come again, we go again. Look into the stories of the High Kings of Ireland and Scotland, to the myths of the various sun Gods, or to the tales of reincarnation deities such as Edain to find these concepts echoed over and over again.

Pagan Passing Over Rituals differ dramatically from the funeral services of today's western people in which the whole purpose is to make one feel as if the loved one is not really dead. Phrases such as, "He looks just like he's asleep," or, "The make-up artist did such as nice job," only serve to further this unhealthy illusion of death denial. Some Pagan traditions refer to the Passing Over Ritual as a *requiem*. Though the word is often used today as a synonym for funeral, the word originally referred to the musical or chanted escorting away from the earth of the soul of the deceased.

Paganism accepts death as a natural phase of life. Though we still grieve deeply at the loss of a loved one, we recognize the transition for what it is and seek to aid the loved one in making it, realizing that they may be having as much trouble adjusting to it as are we.

Passing Over Ritual

CAST YOUR CIRCLE and sit before a single lighted candle which will represent your loved one. It is traditional to orient your altar to face the west since this is where the Land of the Dead, or Otherworld, is located in Celtic mythology.

Mentally evoke the presence of the spirit of the loved one. This should be easy to do if you were close and that person was expecting this ritual from you. Try not to be afraid if you feel a slight breeze or even a spectral touch. This is to be expected. If this was a loved one, he or she will certainly wish you no harm.

Begin with a statement of purpose and offer your blessings to the loved one. Tell them that this ritual is in their honor as you are saying your final farewells before they pass into the Otherworld. There are many ways to do this, each one as personal as the individuals involved. In the tradition of the Irish Wake, you may wish to recall good times you had together, tell a lively story of a special memory you have of that person, or share with them some food and drink. You may wish to sing some songs the spirit loved in life, or you might choose to recite excerpts from some of the spirit's favorite literature.

Mentally ask the spirit if it is ready to pass on to the Otherworld at this time. The answer is almost always a resounding yes.

Evoke the presence of a Goddess associated with the Otherworld. A good choice is Badb, who is the traditional guardian of the great cauldron of life, death, and regeneration into which the Celts believed all souls had to pass to await rebirth. You will later ask this Goddess to escort your loved one to the Otherworld.

At this time offer the beloved spirit your final blessings, loving words, best wishes, hopes for reincarnation and for the spirit's eventual reunion with you, etc. Some Pagan periodicals feature lovely ritual verse which you might wish to use or adapt for this purpose. Or you may write the words yourself, even compose or adapt music to sing them, or you can use any of the death-ritual verse so easily found in any poetry volume. Outside of romance, death is the single most common poetic theme.

You may also utilize an elemental blessing in which the four elements are entrusted with the care of the spirit. An example of such a blessing is:

> *May the gentle breezes over the western sea carry you safely into (insert here your tradition's name for the Land of the Dead here). May her warm waters comfort you, her loving earth receive you, and her eternal sacred fires create for you a joyous life anew. So Mote It Be!*

Lastly, turn to the evoked Goddess and ask her to please escort your loved one safely to the Land of the Dead. This Otherworld has many different names within Celtic traditions. Some of these have subtle distinctions in their exact meaning, therefore several of them might be used with any single tradition. These are some of the more common names and euphemisms from which you might choose:

COMMON NAMES FOR THE OTHERWORLD

Aberffraw (also a royal seat)

Abred (also a magickal term)

Achern

All World

Annafn

Annwn

Aoncos

Avalon (Land of Apples)

Avilion (Land of Apples)

Badb's Isle

Bardsey (an isle associated with Merlin)

Caer Arianrhod

Caer Feddwid

Caer Golud (Castle of Riches)

Caer Sidi (Castle of the Sea)

Caer Vedwyd (Castle of Revelry)

Caer Wydyr (Castle of Glass)

Dark Plain, The

Gateway, The

Gresholm Island

Gwlad Yr Haf

Hy Breasail

I-Breasil

Isle of the Blessed

Isle of the Ever-More

Isle of Nowhere

Isle of the Strong Door

Land of the Blessed

Land of the Dead

Land of the Gods

Land of Illusion

COMMON NAMES FOR THE OTHERWORLD (cont.)

Land of the Great
    Cauldron
Low Road, The
Mag Mell
Ochren
Otherworld, The
Realm of Glamour, The
Tir Tairngire

Tir Tairnigiri (Land of
    Promise)
Tir-na-nBan (The Land
    of Women)
Tir-na-nOg (Land of the
    Ever-Young)
Tir-nam-beo (Land of
    the Alive)
Tirn Aill (The Other
    Land)

Somerset
Spirit World, The
Strong Door, The
Summerland, The
Uffern (The Cold Place)
Underworld, The
Ynys Mon (also a name
    for Anglesey)

When you feel the spirit of your loved one is gone, snuff out the candle. You may wish to save the stub to burn on Samhain when loved ones return to the earthly plane and expect you to provide a light to guide them on their nightly rounds.

☩ ☩ ☩

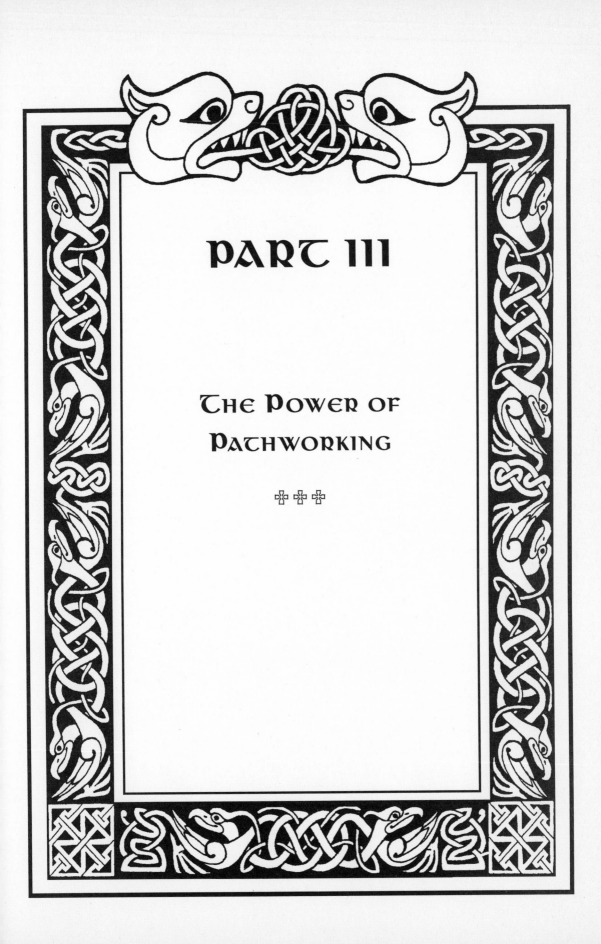

PART III

THE POWER OF PATHWORKING

✣ ✣ ✣

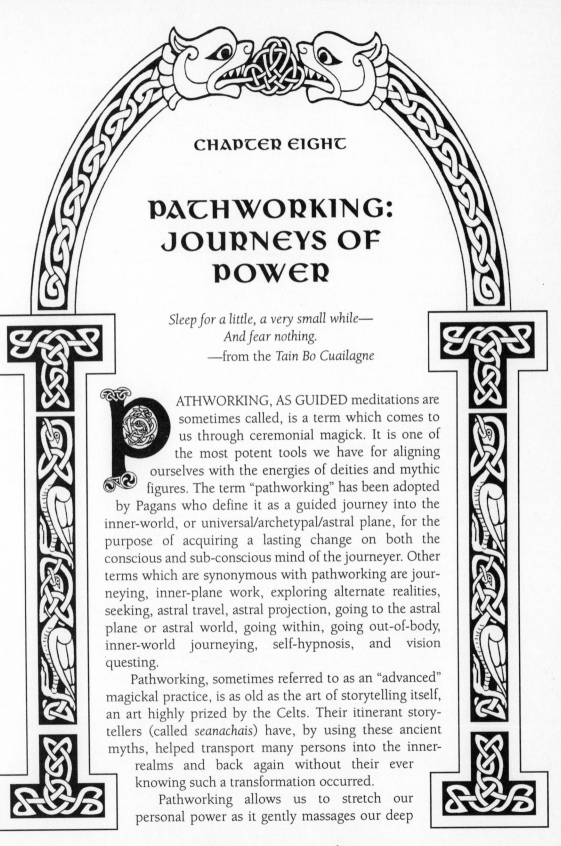

CHAPTER EIGHT

PATHWORKING: JOURNEYS OF POWER

Sleep for a little, a very small while—
And fear nothing.
　　　—from the *Tain Bo Cuailagne*

PATHWORKING, AS GUIDED meditations are sometimes called, is a term which comes to us through ceremonial magick. It is one of the most potent tools we have for aligning ourselves with the energies of deities and mythic figures. The term "pathworking" has been adopted by Pagans who define it as a guided journey into the inner-world, or universal/archetypal/astral plane, for the purpose of acquiring a lasting change on both the conscious and sub-conscious mind of the journeyer. Other terms which are synonymous with pathworking are journeying, inner-plane work, exploring alternate realities, seeking, astral travel, astral projection, going to the astral plane or astral world, going within, going out-of-body, inner-world journeying, self-hypnosis, and vision questing.

Pathworking, sometimes referred to as an "advanced" magickal practice, is as old as the art of storytelling itself, an art highly prized by the Celts. Their itinerant storytellers (called *seanachais*) have, by using these ancient myths, helped transport many persons into the inner-realms and back again without their ever knowing such a transformation occurred.

Pathworking allows us to stretch our personal power as it gently massages our deep minds to stimulate meetings and interactions with mythic figures, but also to provoke creativity, aid in other astral projection, facilitate past-life recall, energize spell work, open channels for divination, and many other endeavors of importance to seekers on any spiritual path.

Jungian psychologist Edward C. Whitmont summed up the essence of pathworking in his book, *The Symbolic Quest*, when he began his chapter, "Archetypes and Myths," with these words:

> In order to affect a constructive and lasting change in our lives we must strive toward a transformation…by reaching [our] archetypal cores. Such transformation can occur only when we have gone beyond the personal dimension to the universal. This process is sustained by guidance from the objective psyche through dreams and fantasies.

Pathworking provides these fantasies and takes us from the personal to the universal because, above all else, it forges a link between the conscious and sub-conscious minds, allowing each access to the memories and capabilities of the other. This has benefits beyond the performance of magick and ritual. It has lasting effects, reaching far beyond the boundaries of the working itself into the everyday life of the journeyer. After all, this is the place where the divine beings of the Celtic pantheon can step out of the withered and yellowed pages of library tomes to live and breathe, speak and hear, show and teach. Once you train your mind to send forth its consciousness to them, once you learn to roam freely and safely in the inner-realms, and once you learn to understand divine archetypes and the meanings they have for you, you can roam these worlds without aid of a guide and explore new ideas, meet new entities, and expand all your potential.

Archetypes are universal. They are defined by Funk and Wagnalls as a "standard pattern" or a "prototype." Archetypes speak to us in an ecumenical language. They are the images which cloud our dreams, they are the inherent power of our deities, and they are the machinery which make Tarot and all forms of divination possible. Archetypal images are used heavily throughout pathworking, for this is the only language our sub-conscious (sometimes called our super-conscious or deep mind) can understand, utilize, and with which it can communicate back to our conscious minds. In the following pathworkings many of these powerful images are taken directly from the archetypal imagery inherent in the stories of the Celtic myths.

To begin your pathworking exercises you need two things:

◆ A pre-written journey rife with potent mythic and archetypal symbolism to be read to a journeyer, or group of journeyers

◆ the ability to allow one's self to be placed in a light to deep meditative state, or altered state of consciousness, for a prolonged period of time

These things can be easily obtained by the serious Pagan student. This book will provide you with three journeys, and will explain how to achieve an altered state of consciousness.

DEITIES AND HEROIC FIGURES IN THE PATHS

We are companions of the heart,
Fellows of the same bed….
—from the *Tain Bo Cuailagne*

THE THREE PATHWORKING texts presented in this volume are loosely based on the mythological stories of Cuchulain, Queen Maeve, and the magician, Merlin. By using their archetypal images, we can meet with them, join forces with them, and, by extension, bring them out of the realm of the archetypal and into our concrete lives. Through pathworking we can not only learn from them by hearing their words, but we can merge with them in a oneness of spirit and actually experience their trials, their pains, their joys, and their triumphs.

The inner/astral world should never be mistaken for being somewhere which is not "real," or where the inhabitants are also somehow less than "real." The archetypes we humans have created on these inner-planes over the centuries are indeed real, and even sentient, creatures. If they were not real, then how would we be able to go to these places, draw energy or information from them, and bring that change or knowledge back into our concrete world?

The deities also reside on the inner-planes, perhaps more solidly than they do in any other world. It is there that they are best contacted and conjoined. Keep in mind that any being you meet on an inner-journey, whether it is divine or elemental, or one you whom intended to meet or not, should be approached with respect, and even a little bit of caution. (As long as you are on pre-written journeys, you should not encounter unexpected beings, though you will when you begin journeying on your own.)

PUTTING FEARS TO REST

We have nothing to fear but fear itself.
—Franklin Delano Roosevelt

THERE ARE A lot of people, some Pagans included, who have an unnatural fear of altered states (see instructions for basic meditation, also known as an altered state of consciousness, in Chapter 1), and especially of inner-world journeys. Possibly this is because it is strange and new, and possibly because they have been taught by someone in the larger mainstream society that it is evil or that they will "lose control" of themselves or even become lost in the inner-worlds, or not be able to awaken to deal with emergencies. All of these fears are basically groundless.

If you want to get the feeling of a guided meditation before attempting an actual pathworking you can try tape recording a simple scene for yourself to practice with. A scenario which you live out every day is the best choice. Try taping yourself coming home from work. Start with seeing yourself getting into your car, bus, or cab. Feel yourself actually doing it. Imagine the ride home—feel it. Hear the sounds, smell the smells, see the people and things around you. Put in as much detail as possible for you to better capture the actual feeling of the ride home. Take yourself right to the front of your own home. Picture the entrance. See it all. Hear the neighbor's dog barking at you, smell dinner cooking down the street, see the neighborhood children playing ball in the driveway. Then feel the cool metal of the keys in your hand, and remember how it feels to place your hand on your own doorknob. Recall what it feels like when you walk in the door at the end of this long day. Do you sigh, collapse, cuddle your pet, kiss your partner, read the paper, greet your kids, turn on the TV, snack? Feel and see yourself doing it all. If your mind wavers, gently, but firmly, bring it back to the images you choose.

Such simple exercises as this will not only help put aside your fears, but will help also you begin to discipline your mind to prolonged concentration, and help you to follow, without lagging behind, the narration of a pathworking.

Some people also excessively fear the creatures they meet in the inner-world. While it cannot be over-emphasized that the inner-planes are in the mind but are still a very *real* place, there is no more to fear there than there is in your own home. You must always be respectful of the deities and other beings you encounter on the inner-planes, but you should never overtly fear them. Most of them are benevolent or, at worst, neutral to your presence. If you do encounter a being in whose presence you feel uncomfortable, simply move yourself slowly away from it. Also keep in mind that you voluntarily entered this altered state, and you can voluntarily leave it. In other words, if you ever do feel excessively threatened all you have to do is "wake up."

There are three phenomena in the inner-world which many first time and new travelers often find disconcerting, but these, too, are nothing to fear. These three things are:

- ◆ Form distortion
- ◆ Omniscient sight
- ◆ Time distortion

The first two things you can learn to control, the last you cannot.

Some persons find that when they look down at their astral bodies from an inner-world perspective, that they are not fully in their human form, or that they are nude. Remember that the inner-plane is a fluid world, one that responds almost instantly to thought-forms. While in this realm you can give your astral body whatever form you choose. Make it your ideal, but it is recommended, however, that you stick to a human form or a become a simple sphere. Trying to be an animal form or the form of another person is risky. In doing so many persons' rational minds have become distorted and they have endured varying periods of dementia upon their return to normal consciousness. (Many written pathworkings will tell you how you should appear and you should conform your thoughts to that ideal insofar as is possible.)

If you are nude and are bothered by this (and most of us are), then simply mentally clothe yourself in a simple gown or robe. A robe with a hood is a good idea if you experience a phenomenon called omniscient sight, or 360 degree vision. If you ever wanted to have eyes in the back of your head, then this is your chance. However, most people find this view of things somewhat distressing. You can either try to will it away, or mentally draw a hood up around your head to block the view.

Time distortion is the other problem, and the one which cannot be overcome, and this is often the experience people have which makes them feel they have been "lost" in the journey. It is a fact of the inner-world that time has no meaning. Anyone who has ever tried meditation and felt they have only been at it for several minutes, only to find they have been down for an hour or more, knows just how disconcerting this phenomenon can be. Even while sleeping—another inner-world function—you can occasionally forget time, and are shocked when you awaken at how short or long a period you have slept.

Modern physics theorizes that time does not exist outside of our known universe, and the inner-world seems to be just a step removed from our idea of the universe. How this is, no one has adequately explained, but it may have something to do with the omniscience of the collective consciousness—that universal store of all knowledge which many of us believe exists.

Some persons have experienced or read about others who have become "stuck" on the inner-plane and unable to return to their bodies. Generally this does not happen because *you* are not out of your body, only your consciousness is elsewhere, and since consciousness is controlled by you, you always have the choice of where to take it. Being stuck "out" is a mental blockage caused by one's own fears and it can almost always be overcome by relaxing and simply thinking yourself back into yourself in rather the same way that you force yourself to awaken from a bad dream.

For those who have a sincere fear of not being able to handle such a situation on their own, I suggest you practice these, and any other inner-plane workings, with a trusted friend nearby. If you express an inability to return all your friend has to do is "come in" *verbally* and take you back out with them. This is done by talking to the one who is "stuck" and telling them that you are coming, following their same path, and that you now see them. Ask them to take your hand and then "return." This is a method used by hypnotists who are faced with subjects who will not snap out of their hypnotic states and it is virtually one hundred percent effective.

In the altered state induction given in this book you will be given a "quick return suggestion" which will enable you to return instantly whenever you feel the need. Getting lost should never be a problem. If you find it is, you might consider seeking psychiatric help to find the cause of the blockage. Look for a professional who has some knowledge of past-life therapy or who is sympathetic to occult practices.

Another method of removing a blockage in your path is to stop and perform any type of banishing ritual you feel best gives you the feeling of vanquishing an astral entity. These include gestures such as raising before you a flaming pentagram, holding up a protective talisman, mentally "frying" the creature or malevolent entity with a beam of energy from yourself or from a ritual tool. You can also call upon the name of a deity to remove your obstacles. Or you may tell the being or entity, in a firm and commanding voice, to step aside and let you pass. This often works amazingly well. After all, astral beings are largely made up of our collective thought forms.

If you still have any concerns about your safe return there is one more related precaution. Before you take off on your own inner-world paths, traveling away from the confines of a pre-written pathworking, be sure you are adept at returning to your normal consciousness without being told to. You can practice this by willing yourself out of the altered state with the quick-releasing suggestion given in the induction. When you find you can do that consistently without fear or difficulty, you are ready to strike out on your own.

Just keep in mind that you are always in control and you should experience few, if any, problems. If an emergency or other event which needs your attention arises while you are pathworking, you will be able and ready to awaken and deal with it. You can and will return to your full normal consciousness at *any time* you choose.

PREPARING FOR PATHWORKING

*I have but one lamp by which my feet are guided,
and that is the lamp of experience.*
—Patrick Henry

NO ELABORATE PREPARATIONS are needed to begin your pathworking journeys, but, as with any magickal ritual, there are a few preliminaries which are helpful.

It is best to start with journeys which are written from your own physical gender point of view. If you are male, start with a neutral or male-centered tale, and if you are female start with a neutral or female-centered tale. Neutral in this instance means a pathworking which is not written to be gender-specific, but uses non-gender oriented words when referring to the journeyer. For women this is especially important as women are generally not taught to see themselves in strong, heroic roles as are young males, and beginning with same-sex heroic figures is easier for them to accept. Eventually, when you are comfortable with the idea, it is important to go ahead and work through the paths oriented to the opposite sex in order to better integrate the male and female aspects of the personality. This is necessary to become a whole being. After all, the yin and yang, the animus and anima, the feminine and the masculine, are already a part of each of us, and we must learn to love that "other" part of ourselves if we are to progress spiritually. But in the beginning, stick to those meditations which are of your own sex until you are used to the jarring effect of seeing yourself in a *very* unfamiliar body.

The one absolute requirement for pathworking is *quiet privacy*. You must *not* be disturbed. The effect of being jolted out of a journey will be like that of suddenly being awakened from a deep sleep and you will feel drowsy, disoriented, and grumpy. You may also find you are timid of going into another altered state for fear of being jolted awake again. This happened to me when I was first learning to meditate and it was a long time before I could fully relax again.

Usually your ritual/magical site is a good choice unless it tends to be very cool there. Having a warm place to go is also necessary. The inert body cools quickly. A few blankets usually do the trick for most of us.

It is also best to do pathworking—or any ritual—on a relatively empty stomach. As with sleeping, a full tummy tends to prevent one from fully slipping into a deep altered state until the food is completely digested. Also, many foods contain salts or sodium, a very grounding (earth-centered) element. Salt has been used in occult circles for thousands of years to end rituals and ground the conscious mind in the present, everyday, waking world. Avoid all salts for at least twelve hours prior to pathworking.

Wearing loose clothing or going nude also helps you achieve the proper state of mind. This is only common sense. Tight, binding clothing is a distraction to any kind of relaxation. It is hard to get comfortable when your clothing is cutting into you.

You should choose a time for pathworking when you are not overly tired. These altered states are very relaxing, and there is sometimes a great temptation to fall asleep. If you become tired while on the journey and wish to quit, simply use the trigger words given in the induction to bring you home. If you fall asleep, no harm will befall you, in fact, your deep mind will probably continue on without you, returning when you awaken, but your conscious mind will not reap any of the benefits you seek. If you tend to get too drowsy in an altered state, try sitting up instead of reclining. Either position, as long as you are comfortable and relaxed, is fine.

Other tips which can help you more easily achieve the proper mood are to use incense or music while you travel. Scent has a powerful effect on the memory centers of the brain and can be a very effective way to aid yourself into an altered state of consciousness, especially if you use the same scent every time you do a particular working. A list of scents which best correspond to each deity or heroic figure are listed with their entry in the dictionary section of this book. But don't limit yourself by these choices. If you feel a scent is appropriate then you should use it. There are no rights or wrongs here, only suggestions gleaned from generations of persons who have been successful with this art, and who know only what worked for them.

If you wish you may also play some "New Age" music softly in the background. Soft, seemingly non-metered music boosts concentration for many, and can certainly help to drown out the sounds of the mundane world. Again, it is a personal choice. If you feel any of these things will distract you, then avoid them.

THE ACTUAL PATHWORKING

We…must live in two worlds:
The World of Form and the Otherworld of Force,
for a true existence involves the constant intercourse of both.
—from *The Yellow Book of Ferns*

THERE ARE A number of ways to take these inner-journeys. You can relax and read the path to yourself, or have a friend read it to you. Having it read to you will allow you to fully concentrate on focusing your thoughts inward and outward, and is the recommended method. You may also tape record the path and play it back to yourself. If you are working with a partner you might consider each taping the pathworkings for each other. Often times we find the sound of our own voices to be unfamiliar and, therefore, distracting. Any of these ideas will work. Which one you choose is a matter of personal preference.

The first part of the pathworking is an induction which I am fond of for slowing brain activity. It has many cousins among occultists and, again, no one is right or wrong. You may use any one you like, but you must *not* skip this crucial part of the journey. Pick a method you like to get to the astral/inner-plane, or use the one printed here, and use it *every* time. Again, the repetitiveness will condition your mind to the changes about to take place, making this state easier to achieve each time. And since the way you go into the inner-world will determine the way to leave it, it is important to know it well.

If at any time during the pathworking you feel uncomfortable, nervous, or frightened, try increasing the protection of your physical body with a strong protective energy such as a white or gold light visualization. If you are still not comfortable, it is probably best that you return to full waking consciousness, or what some might term "returning to your body." Write down all your impressions and try to discover what it was you found bothersome before you attempt the pathworking again. Keep in mind that you will be in control the entire time and fully able to return to your normal waking consciousness at any time. (Trigger words for returning will be given to you in the induction.)

After the induction you will progress to the body of the path. Do this smoothly. Mark the pages so there is no break in the material being read. The journeyer should sense no break in the continuity of the experience, and the reader should try to facilitate this natural, flowing feeling.

Do not read the introduction material to each path in the actual pathworking itself. This material explains symbols, gives pronunciations, and readies you for any unusual phenomena you will encounter. Its purpose is explanatory and it should have been read beforehand by anyone intending to work the path.

In the body of the pathworking are sections marked in brakets [ ]. These enclose instructions to the reader and should not be read aloud. They indicate points at which to pause while the journeyer is involved in some special event, perhaps receiving a message from another being, or it can show where simple sound effects might be added to enhance the working.

You should return from the inner-world gently—always—and for the sake of your rational mind, return by the same route you entered. This is a time-honored occult practice. The only exception to this will be when you will yourself out of an altered state because of some fear or other difficulty. (Instructions for this will be given in the induction and should be similarly written into any pathworking which you write for yourself.)

WRITING YOUR OWN JOURNEYS

I am the son of the mountain, lover of the wind and snow,
heir to the haunts my fathers wandered in long ago....

—Eifion Wyn

THE MOST POWERFUL inner-journeys are the ones you create for yourself out of your own needs and ever-evolving spiritual perspective. Refer to Appendix C in the back of this book for ideas on how to create your own pathworkings.

The elements of myths are a universal phenomena, enough so that anyone—even persons without so much as a drop of Celtic blood—can connect with, use, and understand the symbology of pathworkings using Celtic figures, and derive all the intended benefit from them. It was Carl Jung—again—who first hypothezised that myths were based on human dreams and need-fulfilling fantasies, and since all human minds share a similar structure this may account for the often spooky similarities in mythic themes and events throughout the world. Therefore, it matters not if our personal mythic hero is the Greek Zeus or the quintessentially Celtic Cuchulain, our mind cannot actually separate them, but seeks only to gain profit from their tales and exploits.

When you write your own journeys you can make it easy on yourself by using names which resonate with your consciousness. Since we all like that which is familiar to us, it is possible, and even encouraged, that you substitute deity names, place names, etc., for the ones you may find in any myth according to your own tradition or inner-guide. For example, you may want to call *Tir-na-nOg*, the Irish Land of the Dead, by names such as Summerland or Avalon.

THE BEGINNING...

In the spot where heart travels now,
How I do love my blue island....

—Scottish Folk Song

THE NEXT CHAPTER gives the complete texts for beginning and ending the pathworkings. If you do not have a method which you like for entering these inner-realms, you should try using these. But keep in mind that whatever method you choose to begin your pathworking should also be used for your returning. The conscious and sub-conscious minds seem to agree that this time-honored occult practice of one way in, one way out, is the best way to proceed.

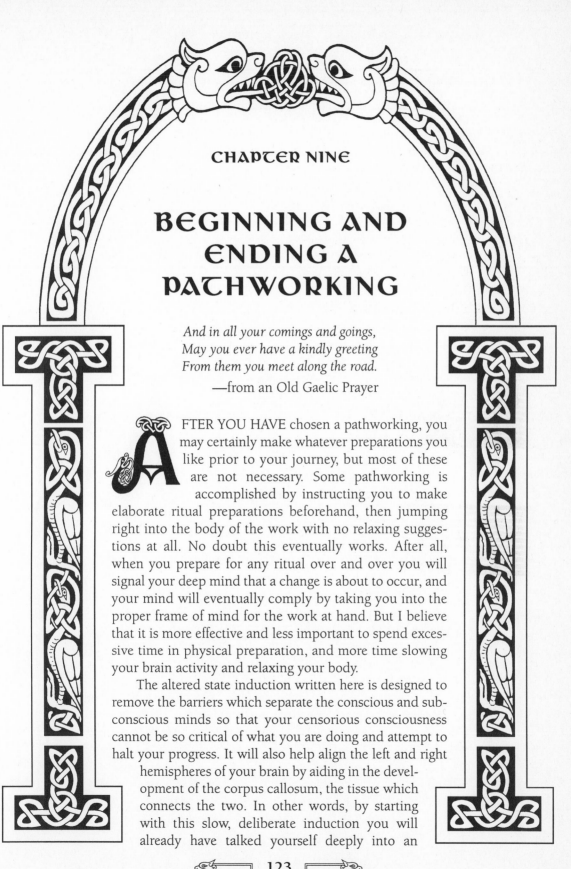

CHAPTER NINE

BEGINNING AND ENDING A PATHWORKING

And in all your comings and goings,
May you ever have a kindly greeting
From them you meet along the road.

—from an Old Gaelic Prayer

AFTER YOU HAVE chosen a pathworking, you may certainly make whatever preparations you like prior to your journey, but most of these are not necessary. Some pathworking is accomplished by instructing you to make elaborate ritual preparations beforehand, then jumping right into the body of the work with no relaxing suggestions at all. No doubt this eventually works. After all, when you prepare for any ritual over and over you will signal your deep mind that a change is about to occur, and your mind will eventually comply by taking you into the proper frame of mind for the work at hand. But I believe that it is more effective and less important to spend excessive time in physical preparation, and more time slowing your brain activity and relaxing your body.

The altered state induction written here is designed to remove the barriers which separate the conscious and subconscious minds so that your censorious consciousness cannot be so critical of what you are doing and attempt to halt your progress. It will also help align the left and right hemispheres of your brain by aiding in the development of the corpus callosum, the tissue which connects the two. In other words, by starting with this slow, deliberate induction you will already have talked yourself deeply into an altered state of consciousness well before the first word of the main body of the pathworking is spoken, and have aligned these brain/mind spheres as completely as possible. Repeated practice with the altered state induction, written out for you in this chapter, will help condition your mind to the attaining and maintaining of a medium to deep-level altered state.

In this induction, the imagery of a rainbow bridge is used as a channel to the inner-world. The rainbow is also an archetype in its own right, symbolic of spiritual and universal knowledge, and of the promises of goodwill of the deities in many different cultures. For many of us it makes the perfect link between the physical and inner-worlds.

In the induction, the inner-world will be referred to as the "astral world." Though the two are synonymous, we are are used to visualizing the astral as being removed from ourselves, and it is this imagery of being directed outward which is necessary for us to succeed.

Sections of italicized type set apart between brackets [*italicized type*] are instructions to the reader and are *not* to be read as a part of the actual pathworking.

And remember: *start each new pathworking at the beginning…with an altered state induction.*

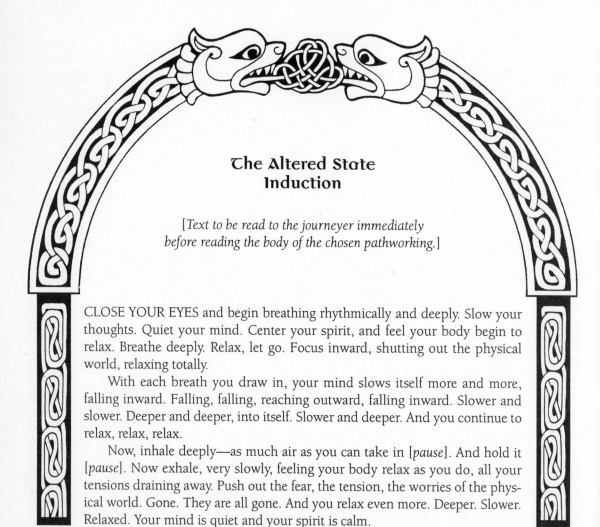

The Altered State Induction

[*Text to be read to the journeyer immediately before reading the body of the chosen pathworking.*]

CLOSE YOUR EYES and begin breathing rhythmically and deeply. Slow your thoughts. Quiet your mind. Center your spirit, and feel your body begin to relax. Breathe deeply. Relax, let go. Focus inward, shutting out the physical world, relaxing totally.

With each breath you draw in, your mind slows itself more and more, falling inward. Falling, falling, reaching outward, falling inward. Slower and slower. Deeper and deeper, into itself. Slower and deeper. And you continue to relax, relax, relax.

Now, inhale deeply—as much air as you can take in [*pause*]. And hold it [*pause*]. Now exhale, very slowly, feeling your body relax as you do, all your tensions draining away. Push out the fear, the tension, the worries of the physical world. Gone. They are all gone. And you relax even more. Deeper. Slower. Relaxed. Your mind is quiet and your spirit is calm.

Inhale again, very deeply this time. Hold it for a few seconds [*pause*]. Now exhale, very slowly. All the tensions of your physical body have fallen away. You are relaxed and growing less and less aware of your physical shell.

Once more—inhale as deeply as you can and hold it [*pause*]. Now exhale slowly, allowing the last hold to your physical consciousness to slip away with the breath. Your mind is quiet, receptive, open, and your body still and relaxed. Release it all. Relax, go deeper. Deeper into the inner-worlds. Relax.

As the last gasp of breath leaves your body you notice a tingling of energy deep within you. This is not a remnant of tension from your physical life which is beginning to stir within you, but an energy which is new and exciting, rather like a fire ignited by a divine source. Suddenly you feel yourself surrounded and empowered by this energy. It is the protective energy of your Goddesses and Gods which now encircle your body in an egg of golden light which throbs and sparkles about you as if kissed by the sun and blessed by the full moon. This egg of protective energy is born of the divinity that has always been within you and it will never desert you. In times of stress or fear it will only glow brighter, its defenses stronger. It is all-knowing and far-reaching. It will protect your inert body as you travel to other realms, and it will also go with that part of you which is now ready to journey forth.

You have no fear because you know that you are always in control. You know that if for any reason you wish to return to your body, and to your normal waking consciousness, you can do so by saying to yourself the words, "I am home." The words, "I am home," will trigger both your sub-conscious and conscious minds that you wish to return immediately to your normal consciousness—and it will immediately happen. Know this. Trust it. The words, "I am home," will absolutely, always, bring you home, and you can then open your eyes and go about your daily life unharmed.

But right now you are so relaxed that you have no fears, no worries, no concerns outside of your pathworking goal. So feel yourself relax even more and go deeper…deeper…deeper into an altered state. You have never felt so relaxed and peaceful before.

Feel yourself sinking—sinking so deep into yourself that you feel you can fly. So deep that you know you will not be attached to the physical world much longer. You have never felt so relaxed or so peaceful.

Now become "unaware" of your physical shell. For one last moment know it is a part of you, and then let it go. Release it. It is not needed now. Become "unaware" of your legs [*pause*]. Become "unaware" of your arms [*pause*]. Become "unaware" of your back and stomach [*pause*]. Relax your neck and shoulders and then become "unaware" of them. Feel them fall away from you like old clothes, and you relax even more [*pause*]. Relax your eyes, your throat, and then forget them.

As you feel yourself sinking deeper and deeper you are ready to call upon your deities for the protection you need as you traverse the astral realms.

With your mind, call out to the Goddess Brigid, valiant and faithful protectress, inspirer of all creative endeavors, and ask her blessing upon your venture as you seek entrance to the astral world [*pause*]. Feel her approval. Accept her blessing. Feel her protective energy come to you, as sure and as safe as if you have just been placed into the arms of a loving mother. As if in answer to your plea you notice above you a large pentagram. It blazes strongly with a blue-white flame. It is impenetrable by any but yourself, and with that knowledge you are able to relax even more…deeper, more relaxed.

Already the veil which separates your everyday world from the astral plane is blurred, and you can feel the astral coming closer and closer. You sense its subtle energies. You know you will be there soon and you relax even more…deeper, more relaxed.

With your mind call out to the God Lugh, the shining warrior God, blessed of the sun, and ask his blessing upon your venture as you seek entrance to the astral world [*pause*]. Feel his strength and his assurance that you are safe and well, and that your journey is blessed. Like a kindly father, he places his hand on your head with love and approval. As if in answer to your plea you notice that a bright golden shield has been raised over you, glowing golden like the August sun. On the shield are carved intricate knots and penta-grams, and animals of strength and courage, the same which protected the Celtic heroes and heroines of old. It is impenetrable by any but yourself, and with that knowledge you are able to relax even more…deeper, more relaxed.

With the glowing shield of Lugh, the pentagram of Brigid, and your own innate protective energy pulsating around you, you feel warm and and very sleepy, and yet incredibly energized. You know you are safe and protected, and you know that soon you will step from inside yourself into the mysterious and ethereal astral realm—a plane of existence wherein everything is possible.

Suddenly you realize that your physical body is completely numb. You are now so deep in an altered state that you can no longer feel any sensations of your physical body, it has no connection whatsoever with you. That mortal shell is now forgotten, and your separation from it is nearly complete. You are so deep into yourself that your mind is reaching outward, stretching towards new worlds and new experiences. And you feel yourself begin to sway. That part of you which is able to go forth and travel unhindered by your physical being is anxious to begin the journey. It wants to leave. As you sway you feel a sense of lightness and buoyancy which draws you closer to the astral world.

As you continue to sway you feel a weightless sensation in the pit of your stomach, and suddenly you find you are no longer part of that heavy shell. You feel light and free, and you move slowly upward. Upward, out of, and away from, your physical self.

You travel out a few yards enjoying the sense of lightness and freedom, and you find that you are above your body looking down at it. You see that it is safe and protected, and you know it will remain that way until you decide to return. You are ready to go now.

You turn and fly through your ceiling feeling happy and carefree. You rise up and up and up, flying free, and the air becomes thinner and thinner. Up and up you fly, reveling in your freedom. You are now in a whitish mist which you know borders the entrance to the higher astral world. As you think to yourself "the astral world is my destination, the astral world is my destination," a swirl of rainbow-like colors begin dancing around your flying form as if wanting to play.

You slow your upward flight and float gently along in this misty world. You watch in fascination as the rainbow colors begin to come together to form the bottom of a beautiful astral rainbow. The rainbow rises from you so high into the mist that you cannot even see up to where it begins to arch. The colors are vibrant and clear, and the rainbow sparkles beautifully as if it has been kissed by moonbeams. It is so light, so incredibly buoyant and beautiful. All your hopes and dreams and aspirations are a part of this beautiful swirl of colors which can lead you anywhere in time or space where you wish to be. This rainbow bridge is your passport and pathway to all that ever was, is, or will be.

A great joyfulness overtakes you, and you began to fly upwards again, following the beckoning rainbow which rises high up into the white mist. Up and up and up you fly, going higher and higher, up and up, until you reach the rainbow's apex. Like a playful child, you sit on the rainbow and start to slide down the other side. It is a long, long way down, but the ride is fun. You are so light that you feel like you are riding on air. The soft wind blowing in your face is exhilarating, you feel energized by it.

As you slide down further you notice a world forming below you and you are coming closer and closer to it. You know this is a part of the astral world, the higher astral world, where the deities, beings, and experiences you wish to contact reside, and you are about to step off the rainbow bridge and into this mysterious and magickal place.

[*Now proceed smoothly to the actual body of a chosen pathworking.*]

Returning Home

[*Read this immediately after the body of any pathworking, making as smooth a transition as possible.*]

SUDDENLY, FEELING VERY light again, you step off the ground and find that you can fly. You fly back up the rainbow, watching the astral world disappear, receding into the white mist below you. This world no longer pulls at you to remain, and you discover that you are anxious to return home. Up and up you fly, only you and the sparkling rainbow can be seen in the white mist around you. You feel the pulsating glow of protective energy around you and know that you are about to return safely to your body and to your normal waking consciousness. You are looking forward to being soon able to contemplate and record your feelings and experiences from this powerful pathworking.

Mentally you make a note to yourself that you will not forget anything of value which you learned on your journey. All that you experienced will forever be a part of you.

Soon, you again reach the apex of the rainbow bridge. When you do, you sit down to slide down the other side, back into your waiting body.

Down you go. Riding as if on air, through the mist, down, down. And as you travel downwards the air becomes thicker, denser, and a sense of solidity begins to make itself known. Below you, the barest traces of the physical world are starting to become clear to you. And down, down, down you slide.

You can now look below you and see your home. You know where you are and are ready to finish the journey.

When you are right over your home, you hop off the end of the rainbow bridge, and fly gently down towards it. Something deep within the pit of your stomach compels you to keep moving downward. You enter the ceiling of the room in which you lay as if asleep, and you begin to remember the sensation of being a living, corporeal human being. You again see your resting body surrounded by the golden light, the pentagram, and the shield, all of them doing their job for you just as they were when you left.

You move slowly over your waiting body, as glad to see it as if you were suddenly rediscovering an old friend. Hovering gently, you begin to lower yourself, and you melt into it saying to yourself the words, *"I am home."*

Feel the awareness of your physical self return—your legs, arms, back, stomach, and neck. Flex them all and relish in the joy of being a living human being.

You are once again part of the waking physical world, and you open your eyes and feel exhilarated, energized, and glad to be home.

[*Make a loud noise like hand clapping or bell ringing to alert your sub-conscious that you have returned to your normal consciousness. This helps prevent any bleed-over between the two worlds, and it also helps frighten away any astral entities which may have followed you home. It is a wise and preferred practice to make whatever statement you, or your tradition, normally uses to end rituals, such as* "It is Done," *or* "The Rite is Closed," *or* "So Mote It Be" *to further get the message across that you are back in the physical world.*]

CHAPTER TEN

PATHWORKING ONE:

CUCHULAIN THE WARRIOR

Let Erin remember the days of old...
When her kings with standards of green unfurl'd,
Led the Red Branch Knights to danger.
　　　　　　　　　　　　—Thomas Moore

[*Do not read this introductory material to the path when doing the actual working itself. This material is only intended to explain symbols, give any needed pronunciations, and in general to ready you for any unusual phenomena you will encounter. Its purpose is purely explanatory and it should be read well beforehand so that the pathworker will completely understand the quest he or she is undertaking.*]

CUCHULAIN IS PROBABLY the most celebrated hero in Celtic folklore next to the mysterious King Arthur. Many tales exist of his heroics and fantastic exploits, a few of which will be explored in this pathworking.

Cuchulain will be a figure with whom you will merge your own personality. By doing this you will be able to understand his choices, learn as he learns, and, in the end, you will hopefully find your "true" name just as he did.

Some myths tell us he was the son of Lugh—when in need, he will call upon this God to aid him and lend him the powers he needs to survive and deal with his challenges.

We will pick up Cuchulain's story as a young man, just about thirteen, just before he slays the aggressive and beloved hound of Cullan and earns his own magickal or power name. Then we will follow him to the Hebrides Islands of Scotland to the mysterious warrior school of the Goddess Scathach. We will stay with him as he learns the skills of a Celtic warrior and hears the prophecy spoken that will declare him the leader of the Red Branch warriors.

Before the pathworking is over, you will be instructed to move out of the body of Cuchulain and merge with your own spirit self in order to try to obtain a glimpse of your own power name.

Also remember *not* to read aloud the material bracketed off [ ]. These are instructions to the reader and are not a part of the pathworking.

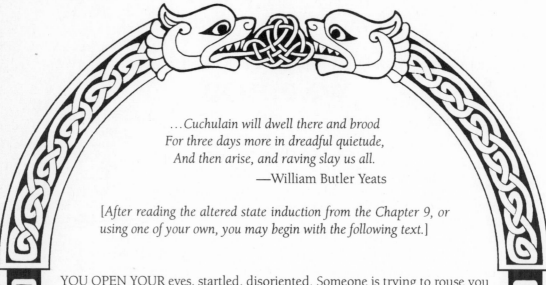

…Cuchulain will dwell there and brood
For three days more in dreadful quietude,
And then arise, and raving slay us all.
—William Butler Yeats

[*After reading the altered state induction from the Chapter 9, or using one of your own, you may begin with the following text.*]

YOU OPEN YOUR eyes, startled, disoriented. Someone is trying to rouse you with a name most unfamiliar to your ears.

"Setanta [Se-TAWN-tah]. Setanta. Wake up, lazy."

You sit up and find yourself on a bed of cool green grass on a bright sunny morning. From the angle of the sun you know it is early yet. Habitually, you stretch a leg which also startles you by its appearance. It is the sturdy limb of a young, well-developed man, perhaps thirteen years old. Yet the limbs before you are maturely muscular and virile, as if they belong to a slightly older lad.

The other man speaks again, giving you a not-so-gentle shove. "Why is it you insist on sleeping outdoors when King Conor provides well for us within the comfort of the castle?"

Unsure of how to answer, you choose to ignore the question.

As you stand and stretch again, you can feel the youthful potential of great strength pulsing through your nimble limbs. Slowly, you begin to feel that you really are this Setanta. You try the name on for size [*pause*]. It doesn't seem to fully fit, but you decide it is good enough for now.

The other man, who seems to be several years older than you, appears impatient. You notice that, though you are younger, you are much taller.

"Would you hurry yourself, Setanta, or we'll be late. Did you forget we are to ride to Quelgny [QUEL-nee] this day to the home of Cullan for a feast to honor our blessed mentor, King Conor?"

As he speaks, your memory as Setanta returns in full, and you rush to the stable to ready your horse for the ride. You remember that you are a student at the court of King Conor, and it is your duty to ride with the other young people of the court to the feast.

When you emerge from the stable you find yourself in the company of others: young and old, warriors and warrioresses, nobles and peasants, parents and children, and also there are other court students like yourself, all ready for the day's ride to Quelgny. Quickly, you mount your large, roan horse and join the group. As you move away from the court others join your ride, all in high spirits. Some come in groups carrying proudly a banner of their clan.

You ponder this as you examine the various banners. Why do your people set such store by names? Why is it that yours doesn't seem to quite fit, yet it is what you are called? And why can you think of no other you would prefer? Though you are the nephew of a great chieftain, why have you never felt a part of the clan? Even the gold and green banner of your mentor, King Conor, which blazes proudly ahead of you, often fails to stir in you a sense of chauvinism.

You continue thinking about these questions as you ride.

When you are not more than a league from the court, you feel a sense that something beneath you has given way. It is your saddle girth. It snaps in the middle and you are tossed to the ground. After some good natured teasing, you announce that you must return to the castle for repairs and that you will catch up later with the group.

You walk the horse back to the stable and make the necessary repairs. You like working with your hands, and rethreading the leather strap gives you pleasure. You like the feel and the smell of it. You are also rather glad of this inconvenience for you enjoy riding alone even though it has its dangers.

When you finish your repairs you saddle up the roan and take off for Quelgny. The Irish northern countryside of Ulster is in the full bloom of a warm spring, and you deeply inhale the scent and feel of the place. Flowers cover many of the knolls. They bob and dip as you go by as if in greeting.

But as you cross these gently rolling hills and go past terraced villages, you realize it is now later than you thought, and that you will arrive at the fortress of Cullan much later than you had hoped. The sun is low in the west and will surely set before you arrive at your destination.

You use your muscular legs to urge the horse faster. It is not safe to ride alone after dark, and you do not want to miss the magnificent feast Cullan will no doubt have waiting for the visiting court.

Night falls and on you ride, slowing your mount appropriately. You are sure you are not very far now. As you crest a steep hill, glowing torch lights in the distance tell you that you have arrived and that the feast is indeed in progress. As you get closer you can hear the sounds of the pipes and *bodhran [pronounced "BAOW-rawn," it is the traditional Celtic goat skin drum]* echoing off the old stone walls, making the still night air come alive. The sound of singing and the pounding cadence of dancing feet accompany the joyful rhythm.

You trot your mount happily into the open gates of the fortress and tether your horse near the others. You are most anxious to get into the banquet hall and are thinking only of your stomach when you are startled by the sound of an ominous low growl coming from behind you.

Slowly you turn, and your knees grow a mite weak at the sight of the most massive hound dog you have ever seen, standing in front of you effectively blocking your way into the hall. His teeth are bared, his eyes glow red, and the hackles on his back are raised. His powerful back legs are tensed, ready to spring for your neck at the slightest provocation.

You are aware that this is the famous hound of Cullan, a massive Irish Wolfhound you only have heard about before, the faithful friend and protector of Fortress Cullan. Why the animal is loose on this night, with nearly all the warriors in Ulster present, is a question you do not have time to ponder.

You have been told that you have a way with animals, and you bend down to try and reassure the beast of your good intentions.

Just then it springs. You are taken by surprise, but you have no doubt that the dog means to kill you, and you have no choice but to defend yourself or die. You feel its huge teeth begin to dig into the soft skin of your neck. There is no time to draw your sword. You must act quickly.

Mustering all the strength you possess, you place your large hands around its bulky neck and, with all your might, hurl it away from you.

As the dog goes sailing through the air, you are surprised at how easy this task was for your strong arms. You watch—partly in relief, and partly in sorrow—as the beautiful animal twists in mid-air, letting out a snarling howl of rage, and then it lands, head first, against the stone post of the fortress gate.

The animal lays still. All is quiet for a brief moment, and then the others inside the banquet hall, roused from their festivities by the commotion, pour through the doors of the dwelling to see what has transpired. Leading them is Cullan. The kindly, well-to-do smithy slowly approaches his slain dog with unashamed tears in his eyes.

A hush falls over the crowd as their host kneels to tenderly stroke the broken neck of the beast. He lowers his head to mourn his faithful hound.

You do not know what to say to this man, whom you know by reputation sets great store by this dog. He is a good man, and your host, and you fear you have grievously betrayed the sacred trust of Celtic hospitality.

Your breathing slows, your mind clears and, at length, you find your voice. "Forgive me, sir," you say without any other explanation.

Cullan stands and looks directly at you, but his eyes hold no malice, no hatred. "The hound did what he had to do, son, and so did you." Cullan looks again at the huge beast and then at you, and you can see that he is evaluating your youth. "But how…? You are but a boy? How did you slay my hound without bloodshed?"

You have no answer for the grieving man, but behind you, you can hear for the first time the whispers of awe and respect in the voices of your comrades. But you do not have to answer. Cullan truly wants no answer, and his sorrowful eyes travel again to his beloved dog. "Oh, my friend," he whispers to the hound, "what shall I ever do without you?"

You not only see this man's grief, but you are beginning to feel it. Now you are sure of what you must say: "It is I who shall have to do something, Cullan. Give me a whelp of this hound so that I might train it up to be a dog who is at least the equal of this one which I have taken from you. And I lay a *geise* [*pronounced "gaysh" or "gesh," it is an honor vow, a magickal and sacred bond*] upon myself that until the time when that whelp is ready to take over the duties of its father, I shall stand in its stead. I will be your hound and guard your fortress as if it were my own. With the shield of Brid and the spear of Lugh I will stand fast at your gate. I will serve you well."

The silent crowd around breaks into cheers and applause at your unselfish actions; your *geise* has found favor.

King Conor himself smiles upon you and comes to stand near Cullan who now says, "I accept your *geise,* Setanta. So mote it be."

Another cheer arises from those around you. For the first time you feel a sense of belonging. You are a warrior now, accepted, brave, taking on a man's job with an adult's honor.

King Conor, who has hereto remained silent, steps forward. In his right hand he holds a small snakeskin pouch. He reaches inside and produces a shiny stone with alternating bands of red, white and black which seem to pulsate from deep within. You have heard of such stones, but have never seen one. It seems to radiate a power all its own.

"Do you know what this is?" he asks you.

"An adder's egg?" you answer tentatively.

He nods. "That is what it is called. But it is really a stone of blessed earth of our Ulster. Its bands represent our Goddess and possessing it binds us to her honor. It is kept in the snakeskin to show its link to change over time. Like the snake, it often sheds its skin, takes on new hues, finds new associates, and moves ever onward. It is also a long-cherished amulet of protection which is given only to those who earn it. You, Setanta, have earned it this night. I could be no more proud of you than if you were my own child."

King Conor raises his voice so that all may hear. "Tonight Setanta has slain an enemy, made a *geise,* and thus has earned the right to enter into adulthood with us. Henceforth he shall be called a warrior of his people. His name shall no longer be Setanta, but, by his own admission, he is now the Hound of Cullan. Let his name forevermore be Cuchulain [Coo-HOO-lyn or Coo-COOL-lyn]— the Hound of Cullan. Let all who hear it honor him for it."

A servant of Cullan comes forth with a jewel-encrusted silver chalice of meade [*pronounced "meed," it is a potent honey ale*], and the three of you, Cullan, yourself, and the King, drink to bind the agreements just made.

Another cheer rises from the crowd, and you are ushered into the banquet hall where you are now the guest of honor.

But you do not stay at the celebration long. For that night you begin your *geise* by standing guard at the gates of Fortress Cullan while the rest of the court sleeps the sound sleep of revelers.

Time passes quickly for you, and soon it is a year and a day from the time of your *geise,* from the night when you slew the hound and earned your power name. The son of the great hound has been well trained by you, and Cullan is very happy with him and loves him as much as he did the predecessor. He has also come to love you who have served him well and with honor.

You know that the time has come for you to leave Cullan's service, but admit only to yourself a fear of such a bold step. Where will you go when you leave? What direction should your life take? Should you return to court? Return to your clan? Or should you marry the young woman, Emer, whom you have courted?

On the last night of your *geise,* Cullan comes to you as you and the hound are standing guard at your place by the fortress gates.

"My young friend," he says, "I regret that this is your last night at Fortress Cullan. But I feel great things are resting on your horizon, Cuchulain."

You are proud of your new name, and even after a year, you never tire of hearing it used. You also wish you shared his confidence in your future. Some inner-sense of pride will not let you show him your insecurity.

"A messenger arrived today from King Conor's court," he tells you. "The King has heard of the demands of the woman Emer that you perform acts of heroism in order to win her. Whether she is worth that effort or not is up to you, but certainly you have proven that your skills as a warrior are second to none. King Conor wishes you to seek out Scathach (SCAH-yah'k) in the Isles of Shadow and let her polish the skills you will need—not just for Emer, but for Ireland. Will you go, son?"

The words which have been spoken soak in slowly. Scathach. The legendary warrioress. Some say she is a Goddess, that she has been teaching warriors for many lifetimes. A burning excitement rises within you. All the greatest warriors of the Celts have all been taught by her. You know it is only proper that you learn at her hand rather than from the men at the court. It is a long-standing tradition that women teach men and men teach women the skills of battle, prowess, and heroism. How could you refuse such an offer?

"Yes, Cullan, please inform the King that I will leave tomorrow to seek out the Isles of Shadow."

Cullan smiles proudly, but with obvious reservation. Just the act of seeking the Isles is one fraught with danger, but you are sure you can find it, and will be accepted and learn much from Scathach.

At daybreak you offer petitions for your success to Lugh, you bid farewell to Cullan, and set out to the east with only your bronze sword and your silver shield to find the secret Isles.

You travel over the Irish Sea, and across an Otherworldly desert where unseen monsters chase you. But still you press on. Cold and heat sap your resources making you tired and sore, but you dare not let your guard down. You know that the isle could be under your feet at this very moment, hidden; cloaked in the mists of mystery. You look with your eyes, ears, and your warrior's intuition, traveling forward, always looking for the Isles of Scathach.

On the infamous grounds of the Perilous Glen you are forced to slay a

monster who blocks your path. At first you greatly fear it, it is huge and seems to embody within its face all the fears of your childhood nightmares. But as you fear it more and more, you see that it grows, and you realize that you must destroy this manifestation of your own anxiety if you are to continue on. You grab it by the neck and, with a fierce toss, you dispatch it as you did Cullan's hound. When it crumples, it disappears, fading harmlessly into Mother Earth.

Finally, nearly a year and a day later, you come to the bog-covered land known in legends as the Plain of Ill-Fortune. You know that the school of Scathach lies beyond. But you look at the endless mudhole knowing that to put foot onto it would mean you would sink slowly into its depths. Clutching your spear tightly you go within yourself to seek an answer.

Suddenly, you are jolted from your contemplation by the sound of spectral hoofbeats beating the air. In the distance, riding rapidly towards you, is a huge man dressed all in yellow. His golden horse snorts fire as it rides on air, its orange hoofs never quite touching the ground. Rays of light shine from the man's face and his kindly eyes glow with a combination of power and compassion. You do not fear him, but you are awed by his presence.

The man dismounts and raises his right hand in a greeting which you return. Then, without further explanation, he reaches onto the back of his horse and brings down to you a large wheel of gold.

"I am here," he announces, "to aid you in crossing the Plain. Take this wheel and all will be well."

You look skeptically at the odd, shiny wheel. "And just how will this help me?" you ask.

The man smiles cheerfully. "But roll it before you and the heat of its core will dry the earth, making it solid for you to cross."

You are not completely convinced, but the magnificent figure seems to know of what he speaks. You thank him and he rides away without waiting to see the outcome of your venture. Cautiously, you set off across the Plain.

The wheel works perfectly and soon you have crossed to the other side. You are now in the Isles of Shadow.

When you arrive you see old friends from the court of Conor playing a game of hurling on a golden field. They rush towards you and greet you happily, asking news of Ireland.

When the small talk is over you tell them you have come seeking teachings from Scathach. All your friends announce that she is indeed the best teacher, though very strict and mysterious. Many of her lessons can be quite deadly, they inform you. They also tell you she comes to them only when she is ready, from her castle over the infamous Bridge of the Leaps.

You look at the bridge as your friends explain that it will hurl you back to shore if you set foot upon it without knowing its secrets. Or worse, it will throw you down into the rocky gorge where hungry monsters lurk.

You announce to all with a bravado you keenly feel that you intend to cross the bridge. After coming all this way you cannot and will not wait another day to see Scathach.

Your friends laugh. "Cuchulain, the Bridge is the last skill Scathach will teach us—that will be after three years of study. Then, if you can cross it and live, you have a chance to win from her the Gae Bolg [*pronounced as it looks, it is a famous magickal sword*]. No one has won it yet, we're sorry to tell you."

You refuse the offers of games, drink, and food as you contemplate just how you are going to cross the Bridge of Leaps. After a while you step cautiously onto the boards, but you are hurled viciously back to the far shore. Again, with more determination you try, but are again repulsed by the stubborn bridge. Before trying again you stop to think about the bridge itself—its name—the Bridge of Leaps. What is its secret? Like most magickal secrets you have learned, you know that often secrets are most obviously placed out for all to see. This is the best way to hide them, of course. So what could this one's secret be?

You think about it deeply, mulling the name over and over in your mind. Leap? Leap! That must be the key, you decide. The name.

Mustering all your energy, you take a long ferocious jump, and hurl yourself into the center of the narrow overpass. Before the bridge can snap and send you to the bottom of the gorge, you take another stupendous leap, and miraculously, you arrive on the shore of Scathach's Isle.

But you have little time to revel in your accomplishment for, immediately, you feel a potent presence near you. You turn and see the one whom you seek. Scathach stands before you, the gleaming ruby- and emerald-studded Gae Bolg clutched in her right hand. Her dark eyes peer out at you from an ageless face, her red cape shrouding her in formless mystery.

"How did you cross my bridge, young Cuchulain?" she asks in a voice which belies age and time.

You wonder for a moment how she knows your name. "I did as it asked me to—I leaped."

A mirthless chuckle erupts from her. "So you did, young man, so you did. You are a clever one, I will grant that. Perhaps you are the one I have sought for so many years, the one whose coming was foretold long ago."

You aren't about to argue with the powerful woman, though you have no idea about what she is speaking.

"I have come to learn," you announce, drawing yourself up to your full impressive height.

"And so you shall, Cuchulain, so you shall. You shall learn well or die trying. Like all endeavors worth seeking, this one will not come easily. You will work hard and study hard. You will eat well and sleep soundly the sleep of the exhausted. Are you prepared for this task?"

"I am, my lady."

"Then get a good night's sleep, Cuchulain, for tomorrow will be the longest day of your life."

You stay in the Isles of Shadow and study with Scathach for the promised three years. During that time your muscles bulge, your mind quickens, and you now look like a Celtic warrior. None of your peers can best you in the war games, and you enjoy an unprecedented respect. Your name is honored and you have the best place at the table.

Scathach says little, but her shiny black eyes tell you that she is pleased with you. The night before you are to leave the Isle she comes to your chamber.

"Cuchulain," she says, "as I thought three years ago, you are the one whose coming I have been expecting for more years than you would believe possible. I have never held back with you. You have been given the best I have to offer. A lesser warrior would have been killed. I have a gift for you if you can answer but one question correctly."

From inside the ever-present red cloak she draws out the Gae Bolg and presents the hilt to you. "Gae Bolg is yours if you have become as wise as you are strong."

You swallow nervously. Games of wit have never been your strong suit, and you would dearly love to be the first ever to gain the magickal sword. Possessing the Gae Bolg has been the dream of every Celtic warrior for centuries.

"When you leave here you will return to Ulster," she prophesies. "While you have been away she has gone to war against Connacht and badly needs your aid. You are going to form an elite band of warriors whom you shall call the Red Branch. Can you tell me why you will call them this and why this completes all your life's study up to this point? Can you tell me, Cuchulain [*emphasize the name Cuchulain as you speak or read the previous sentence*]?"

You stop to think. You hear the accent on your name. Your name? Red Branch? You close your eyes and think, trying to remember all the knowledge ever gained by you in your many studies, both the physical and the esoteric. Suddenly you realize that this Red Branch is a special name, the third special name which has, or will have, a profound effect on your life. You open you eyes and smile wisely at your patient teacher.

You speak slowly and clearly to her. "When I became Cuchulain I earned my name through valor. That was the first of three lessons in naming. When I arrived at the Isles of Shadow I allowed the name of the bridge to teach me its secrets. That was the second of three lessons in naming. Now I shall lead the Red Branch warriors. Red for the blood which must be spilled in the defense of Ulster, and, like the many branches of a mighty oak tree, we shall grow and spread and grow, each limb giving birth to new ones, and we shall be victorious. This is the third of three lessons in naming. A cycle is complete. My lessons of naming are through."

Scathach raises the Gae Bolg and you grip its golden hilt. As you do, an electrifying power rolls up your arm and you feel, for just a moment, at one with Scathach, and the combining of your lifeforces creates a power surge within the confines of the room. Small ghostly wisps of lightning fire off the old stone wall. Scathach releases the sword and you raise it high, pointing it towards the heavens, and give an offering of thanks to Lugh and Brid who have guided you to this day.

"Go now, Cuchulain of the Red Branch. Your lessons here are done. I can teach you no more. But remember, there are other lessons to be learned, other realms to conquer. Never think you have ever finished learning merely because one cycle is through. There is much which will befall you in the life ahead. Much to learn, both to your joy and to your sorrow. Go in peace, strength, and honor, my Cuchulain."

As you leave the Isle the Bridge of Leaps seems to bow down before you as you begin to cross. It makes no attempt to toss you. In fact, it seems to be chanting farewell to you.

As you walk on, you suddenly seem to separate from yourself, and you notice that you are looking down on yourself as you continue to walk west toward Ireland. From this distance you are able to remember who you are, your current incarnate identity. You could only share this brief time with Cuchulain, and learn his lessons with him. You have to be yourself.

You keep drifting further away, thinking about the lessons of naming. You drift peacefully into a white mist which seems to have no beginning and no ending. As you do you seek to discover your own personal power name. Perhaps you have already had the life experience in which your name is to be found. Perhaps you are just learning it now. Or maybe you are not ready for it, but need to be pointed in the right direction. You know it exists, and you will it to come to you now. [*Pause and allow the pathworker time to discover his or her name. It may come as a psycho-drama, a symbol, a memory from this or another life, or it may be bestowed by a spirit who will come to the journeyer now.*]

You thank whatever presence aided you in discovering the knowledge which you have just gained, and are now ready to return to yourself. Beside you a shimmering rainbow of iridescent color appears.

[*Follow the "Returning Home" reading from Chapter Nine, or some other reading for returning to your own consciousness. Always come home by the same route you left. When you are awake, make some loud noise, eat, go to the bathroom, or do anything else "earthly" to reinforce the idea to your subconscious that you are back.*]

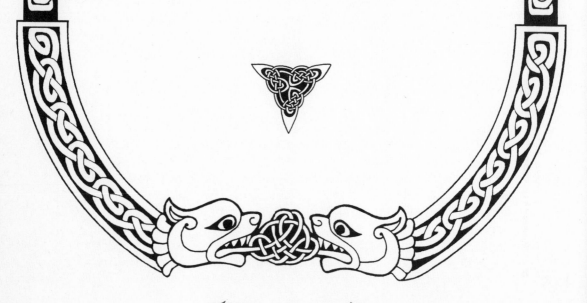

CHAPTER ELEVEN

PATHWORKING TWO:

QUEEN MAEVE THE WARRIOR

Maeve walked through that great hall, and with a sigh
Lifted the curtain of her sleeping-room,
Remembering that she too had seemed divine
To many thousand eye, and to her own....
— William Butler Yeats

[Do not read this introductory material to the path when doing the actual working itself. This material is only intended to explain symbols, give any needed pronunciations, and in general to ready you for any unusual phenomena you will encounter. Its purpose is purely explanatory and it should be read well beforehand so that the pathworker will completely understand the quest he or she is undertaking.]

HE CHARACTER WE know as Queen Maeve of Connacht had her roots in an earlier, long-lost Goddess of sovereignty. No King of Connacht could rule without her as Queen. Her sexual union with these favored men created heroes and rulers alike. For many, she is the single best archetype of the full power of Celtic womanhood. Maeve was a fine warrioress, she had an almost unlimited sexual capacity, she could out-drink and out-fight all of her warriors, she was complete and whole unto herself, and she alone decided who would govern her lands and who would be King.

The major myth involving her, The Cattle Raid of Cooley, is probably the most popular legend in Irish literature, and it has been explored, analyzed, written, and rewritten about *ad nauseum*.

For this pathworking we are going to step outside of the known myths and work with Maeve as a female heroic figure in her own right. This will result in our placing more emphasis on the heroic aspects of her life and less on archetypal imagery. As with Cuchulain in the previous chapter, you will merge your personality with hers for the duration of the working.

For women of the baby boomer generation (the majority of Pagan women fall into this age group), raised on a steady diet of Donna Reeds and June Cleavers, it is important to our emotional and psychic development to allow ourselves to feel internally the power of a warrioress. Unlike boys of our generation, we were discouraged from viewing our bodies as instruments of power and viewing ourselves in heroic fantasies. This narrow scope of internal experience is not only a detriment to our social development, but also to our spiritual one. How can we ever hope to be proficient at magick and ritual if we cannot conceive of ourselves as strong channels for power?

For men of this generation, also raised with the same restrictive feminine stereotypes, it is equally as important to view women as powerful beings. After all, the feminine is fully half of deity, and men cannot hope to draw full power from the Goddess if somewhere deep inside they feel that she is lesser.

In comparison with the larger society, Pagans are generally much more advanced in their thinking where women are concerned, but there are still many cultural boundaries to be crossed. This pathworking, it is to be hoped, will be one of the bridges across them.

We will follow Maeve as she leads her court on a dangerous hunt for the Wild Sow of the Wilderness. Sows were sacred to a number of Celtic Goddesses, and slaying and consuming a sow were acts of sympathetic magick designed to bring the power of that deity into one's self. Therefore, the hunt she leads is as much a spiritual one as a quest of power. We will remain with her as she fights off the Ulster raiders like the fine warrioress she is, and takes on numerous sexual partners while she remains a potent symbol of feminine sovereignty.

In general, pigs in Celtic mythology archetypally represent abundance, wealth, rank, and linkage to the Otherworld.

Also remember not to read aloud the material bracketed off [ ]. These are instructions to the reader and are not a part of the pathworking.

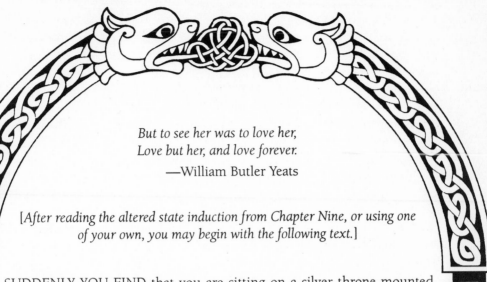

But to see her was to love her,
Love but her, and love forever.
—William Butler Yeats

[After reading the altered state induction from Chapter Nine, or using one of your own, you may begin with the following text.]

SUDDENLY YOU FIND that you are sitting on a silver throne mounted high on a flat stone. The cool metal is hard beneath your thick silk skirts. For a moment you are taken aback. What are you doing here in such a foreign-looking place? You look around at the heavy stone walls which surround you and wonder if you are in some sort of cave. There are elaborately woven tapestries covering them, all made of rich velvet.

As you try to puzzle it all out, a young woman dressed in the fine clothing of a courtier enters the room and kneels before you.

"My Queen," she says, "is there anything I can get you?"

Queen? You wonder if she is really talking to you.

"Queen Maeve, a hunting party is being formed in the courtyard at your request. They wonder if you wish them to remain."

As she speaks the name Maeve, you suddenly find you have all the memories of this legendary Queen. You are sitting in your throne room in Rathcroghan [Rahth-CRAW-han], your royal home. A mischievous smile breaks over your beautiful face. A hunt! "Tell them to wait. I will be joining them shortly."

With your silks flying, you bound off to your chambers to change into clothing more to your liking. As you race down the narrow, tall corridors of your Connacht castle, those you pass bow in deference to you. You take their homage for granted as you have only one thing on your mind—the hunt.

In your chambers two maidservants await your orders. They help you change into a warrior's tunic. The short doeskin sheath is comfortable and allows you full range of movement. It feels sensual over your tall and muscular body, its softness complimenting your hard contours.

You carelessly toss your jewel-encrusted crown on your well-padded bed, and tie your loose yellow hair back with a velvet ribbon so it will be out of your way. On your feet you place stout leather boots, your athame tucked in the one side resting securely against the rippling hard muscle of your calf. At your side you tie on your sword. Its scabbard carries your crest, a crowned wheat sprig on a triple field of green, red, and purple. Lastly, you place over your shoulder your quiver of arrows. Grabbing your sturdy crossbow in your large and capable hands, you are ready to go, anxiously anticipating besting your finest warriors.

You are a champion in all your undertakings, and it gives you great pleasure to win. You are not necessarily conceited about your accomplishments, you just know your own talents and your worth.

When you are dressed, you go out to the courtyard where your groom is holding your horse for you. You call the animal by the name *Geansai* [*pronounced GAWN-see, it means "jumper"*] and he is the largest and strongest horse in all of Connacht, perhaps in all of Ireland. His coat is as white as milk, and today he wears the red and purple plumage of your rank.

"Are you ready, my Queen?" asks the groom.

You only smile smugly at him, mount your horse unaided, and command, "Huntsman, sound the charge."

From the gleaming post horn of your chief huntsman sounds the royal charge to the hunt, piercing the air with a loud whine, making the hairs on the back of your arm rise with a delightful shiver. Moving as one, the horses bound forward with you, the earth rumbling with the rolling thunder of your mounted host.

You are leading the pack, the wind and warm sun in your face, the speed exhilarating. Looking over your broad shoulders, you cast a pleased eye back at those you are quickly leaving behind. Many times you have challenged your court to race you for the lead, but try though they might, they all have failed against the power of the majestic white horse under your command.

Beneath you Geansai's hooves slam the ground with a vigorousness that is almost sensual in its appeal. You move as one with him, feeling your own animal power rise as you leave your court further and further behind.

At the crossroads some three leagues from the castle, you pull to a halt and dismount to pay quick homage to Flidais, Goddess of the Hunt, and to leave an offering for Epona, the Horse Mother, before the rest of the court catches up. You like to keep your faith private and never like to be seen in overt acts of worship. [*Pause to allow the pathworker some time to mentally make these offerings in his or her own way.*]

No sooner do you finish your tasks, than you hear the approaching hoofbeats of the court. They ride to a halt around you.

"Where to today, my Queen?" the huntsman asks.

"To the Forest of the Bottomless Cauldron," you respond almost too casually. "I feel like tracking the Wild Sow of the Wilderness."

The huntsman's face momentarily shows a hint of fear, which you pretend not to notice. The Sow you seek is a large and vicious beast whom many have sought to kill, but none have managed. A few have died in the effort. Today, you have decided that killing her is just what you will do, and you usually get what you want.

"Yes, my Queen," the huntsman acknowledges your command and turns to inform the rest of the court, many of whom ask to be excused from the games.

With regal benevolence you let them return to the castle. If they are afraid of a mere pig then you have no need of them anyway. Twelve warriors, anxious to prove their prowess against the Wild Sow, remain with you, all men whom you deem highly worthy of the challenge. You resolve that each who proves his bravery today will be rewarded later, a reward which will be as pleasant for you as for any of them.

"Well, my friend," you announce to Geansai when the others are out of earshot. "Shall we ride on?"

The huntsman again blows the call to the hunt, and wild war whoops arise from the warriors and you turn Geansai to the northwest to lead the way towards the dark and dense Forest of the Bottomless Cauldron.

The terrain becomes more difficult as you ride on. The ground is rockier and steeper, and many times you have to leap hedgerows. The huge horse carries you effortlessly over them. The sensation is exhilarating. In each single airborne moment, you feel as if you actually have the power of flight. For several leagues more you drive on at a reckless speed, and you can sense the admiration from your twelve followers as you fly along, heedless of any danger.

Soon you reach the crest of a steep hill. You pause so that the others might catch up and briefly rest their mounts as you plan your descent. Beyond this hill the land smooths out; it is a lush dark green as if the essence of night has been captured inside each verdant leaf and grass blade. A telltale hint of moisture is felt in the subtle breeze which touches your cheeks. Beyond this place, called by your people the Valley of the Vanished, lies the Forest of the Bottomless Cauldron from which few return unscarred.

You have been to the Forest before, usually at the challenge of someone foolish enough to think you would pale in fear. Before the dares were over, it was inevitably your challenger who would turn tail and run, leaving you to bask in your bravery.

"How do you wish to proceed, Queen Maeve?"

Your sharp eyes roam expertly over the area. Little escapes you. "I think we shall go down to the north near the stream and then tether the horses there. The Forest is too thick and dangerous for them."

You know that large horses would be all day hacking their way through the dense forest. You can move more quickly and quietly on foot.

You lead your band down the green hill by the stream and dismount. Your huntsman sees to Geansai's needs while you peruse the area and check your crossbow one more time.

Then you stop to peer into the thick Forest. You can understand so well why it got its name—The Forest of the Bottomless Cauldron. It is an exceptionally dense forest, large in scope and very overgrown, where often the bright sunlight of midday is obscured by the heavy veil of trees. Just looking at it from the edge of the Valley of the Vanished, one could see no more than a few yards into it. It is not unlike the bottom of a mystical black cauldron. It is a place which has held much life and death, and whose mysteries are reserved for only the few brave enough to seek them out.

You inhale deeply. Forests always smell of the earth, wet and green, pulsating with living secrets. And inside lives the Wild Sow of the Wilderness, your elusive prize, one who has never yet bowed to human arrows.

You call to your party to ready themselves for the hunt, and then you lead them cautiously and silently into the edge of the Forest.

As you step in among the looming trees, it is as if you have just closed a door to the outside world behind you. Immediately a worshipful silence, broken only by the distant calls of forest creatures, engulfs you. Like the dimness itself, it is a sensation which is as alive as yourself. Instinctively, all your senses sharpen like finely honed steel. Like a wild jungle predator, you are alert to every nuance of sight and sound around you. Your hearing is keen, your mind alert, your eyes ever-scanning for movement and signs of your prey or any other wildlife which might threaten you here.

Behind you the twelve large men tread as uneasily, all of them tensed and ready to draw their bows. You know they are all wondering who will return from this adventure, and that each of them wants the elusive Sow as much as you do.

You wander deeper and deeper into the Forest, sure now that you are picking up the trail of the Sow. If you were asked how you knew, you could not answer. But some inner-sense you long ago learned to trust tells you it is so.

That same inner-sense now begins to ring an alarm in your ears. You halt. Your warriors halt behind you, all of them knowing your uncanny knack for foresight, and they too are now alert, waiting.

Without warning you hear a scream, a cry to battle, and thirty-three Ulster warriors, obviously on a raid into your kingdom, leap from behind the trees, their swords and clubs drawn for battle.

Without a second's hesitation, you unsheath your own sword and join in the fray. To you a good fight is better than a good hunt any day. The adrenaline courses wildly through your veins, your rounded arm muscles strain under the weight of the shiny sword, and your well-trained body responds to your mind's every split-second command.

The largest of the Ulstermen, recognizing you as Queen Maeve, pairs up with you and begins to battle in earnest, intent on killing you for the honor of Ulster. You sense that he is anxious to pit his skills against those of the famous Queen Maeve. He strikes several blows which you agilely deflect.

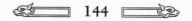

After a few moments you have had time to assess his battle skills and, you note with mirth, he is foreshadowing each movement he makes so that you can easily prepare ahead your defense. Is this the best that Ulster can send against you, you wonder smugly.

Slowly you turn so that you maneuver his back to a thick oak tree, then you thrust your sword, taking the offensive stance. The warrior pulls back to escape your thrust, but is blocked by the bulk of the tree. Your sword meets its mark and the man slumps to the ground at the base of the old tree.

But you have no time to rest on your laurels. From behind comes a shout. You spring around and start to find a thorny club poised over your head. With a quick handspring and ground roll, you land far away from the club and find yourself near Conor MacDiarmuid, your most favored warrior. The two of you dispatch the remaining Ulstermen who are trying in vain to slay you, but the invaders are taking a beating and soon route themselves for a hasty retreat.

You are not about to let them get away so easily.

Grabbing their leader by the throat, you are able to halt the battle.

Conor takes him and holds him to the sword, awaiting your next command.

Drawing yourself up to your full regal height, though you are still panting from your exertion, you address the invader. "What, pray tell, are you doing in these woods, Ulsterman? Certainly you know you are on Connacht land. Speak up."

The captured warrior is trying in vain not to appear fearful. "Yes, My Lady."

"Who sent you here? Ulster's cowardly King, no doubt?"

"No, My Lady."

You know he is protecting his leader, but you let the question pass.

"I hope this little raid was worth the effort. Two thirds of your men lie dead. I am sure their bodies will make fine scavenge for the wild pigs. Count yourself lucky that I will allow the rest of you to escape with your wormish lives."

Clearly this is more generosity than he had hoped for. "Thank you, My Lady."

"Don't thank me yet," you order regally, your proud breast swelling with the essence of your royalty; your eyes glittering golden like the sun burning into your enemies. "In order for me to honor your safety out of Connacht, you must make a *geise* [pronounced "gaysh" or "gesh," *it is an honor vow, a magickal and sacred bond*] upon yourself that if you return to Connacht uninvited you will submit to servitude in my castle for nine years, and your three firstborn after you. Do you accept this *geise* or do you and your remaining warriors wish to be pig food also?"

You know the open-mouthed man has little choice, and he accepts on behalf of the ruined raiders. You also are aware that many of your warriors are eager that he refuse. On the way back to Rathcroghan from the hunt they will want to come and collect the heads for display on the gateposts of your stronghold. [*Celtic mysticism placed great value in the human head, and it was their war custom to take the heads of their enemies and display them on spears, gateposts, or fenceposts.*]

"Gawlail!" you call to another warrior. "Pick three men and disarm these bandits, then please escort them to the borders of Connacht."

"It will be a pleasure, my Queen."

You look around at your remaining eight warriors. All thirteen of you survived the attack with no more than a few scratches. You are fiercely proud of each of them and they will be rewarded well.

After the four Ulster escorts leave, you and the remaining eight continue your quest for the Wild Sow of the Wilderness. Conor and your huntsman are near you so poised that you can almost hear the flow of the blood through their veins. The thought excites you deeply.

Soon you come upon a small clearing in front of the mouth of a dark round cave. You gasp and halt and you spy the quarry you seek sitting peacefully in the cave's mouth.

Your inadvertent gasp alerts her and she stands, head lowered, teeth bared, poised for a fight. You have no doubt she knows what she is about. This ageless animal has eluded human capture for longer than you have lived. This is no ordinary sow. She stands two heads above any other wild pig you've ever seen, her prickly coat is harsh and an unusual hue of blackish-red. Around her neck is a band of yellow and white. Her eight withered teats hang low beneath her tight belly, and her emerald green eyes are narrow and alight with an alarming intelligence. Through her nose is a ring of woven silver. No one knows for sure how the ring came to be there, but its value is said to be enormous, and you would dearly love to add its value to the coffers of your already prosperous kingdom.

The Sow lowers her head and prepares to charge.

Without further warning she races towards your band, scattering your warriors, though you remain steadfast. Several of the men take wild shots at it, but it either dodges them, or her tough wiry hide deflects the arrows like a divine shield of bronze.

Holding fast to your battle position, you draw your crossbow. Your hands are steady as you peer down the sights of your instrument at the angrily snorting beast.

The great Sow turns directly toward you as if she knows your intent. Then with a great bellow she charges you. Her cloven hooves beat the mossy ground with quick staccato beats. Still you hold your ground. Holding and aiming carefully, you point your finest honed arrow at a point between the eyes and, at the last possible moment, you fire.

The arrow makes a whipping sound as it flies and hits its mark.

For a moment, all breaths are held as the pig stumbles, rights herself, and then falls over dead.

You smile, deeply satisfied with your kill, and your warriors breathe a collective sigh of relief and then kneel and cheer you.

Conor reminds you, "The honors are yours, my Queen."

You reach into your boot and draw your athame and go to stand over the Sow's belly. With one bold stroke you cut into the chest and pull out the still warm heart and make an offering of it to Flidais, Goddess of the Hunt.

Your huntsman leads the hunting party back to the castle with the Sow for the night's feasting and with the heads of the fallen Ulstermen.

Once you are home, you change again into your silken gown and go to the banquet hall where the first taste of the roasted Sow is yours. You offer the second portions to your warriors.

Immediately afterwards you leave the festival and retire to your chamber where you will honor the eight warriors who returned from the hunt with you. Your lady's maid disrobes you before a huge roaring fire, brings you a tall silver chalice, and then you recline naked on a luxuriously thick sheepskin blanket.

You smile thoughtfully as you anticipate your warriors coming to you one at a time seeking favors which, as Queen, are yours to dispense. How many times have you bragged that you can take on thirty men in one night? And how many times have you made good on that boast? You recall the excitement of the hunt and look forward to the night to come.

The first knock comes on the door.

"Enter," you call.

Your favorite, Conor, enters and kneels before you, his eyes cast down.

"What is it you wish, my friend?" you ask.

"Whatever it is of which you deem me worthy, my Queen."

"Conor, you have served me well. It is time for you to have your own sept. I will give you the Roscommon sept to rule over for you and your descendants forevermore. I offer you the gift of sovereignty."

Conor rises and you motion him over on the blanket where you bless together the wine in the silver chalice with his athame, then you share a drink. You take the chalice, set it aside, and then you begin to disrobe him. Only by uniting with you in the Great Rite can he hope to claim the rulership of his new land.

You enter all your sexual encounters with enthusiasm and boundless energy, the power is yours to give, and you revel in the pulsating spirit of the event.

One by one, all of the heroes of the day come to you seeking boons, and it seems so short a time before you have so honored all eight.

When you are alone before the fire, sated and drowsy, you suddenly notice that you are floating over yourself watching Maeve on the blanket below. As you move further and further away, the castle receding against the background of night, you remember that you are not she, but yourself. All the memories of your current incarnation identity return to you. You are glad to be you.

You float upward until you are surrounded by an endless mist of white reflecting on your adventures as the Queen of Connacht, remembering what it was like to be a woman of power when, beside you, a shimmering rainbow of iridescent color appears.

[Follow the "Returning Home" reading from Chapter Nine, or some other reading for returning to your own consciousness. Always come home by the same route you left. When you are awake, make some loud noise, eat, go to the bathroom, or do anything else "earthly" to reinforce the idea to your subconscious that you are back.]

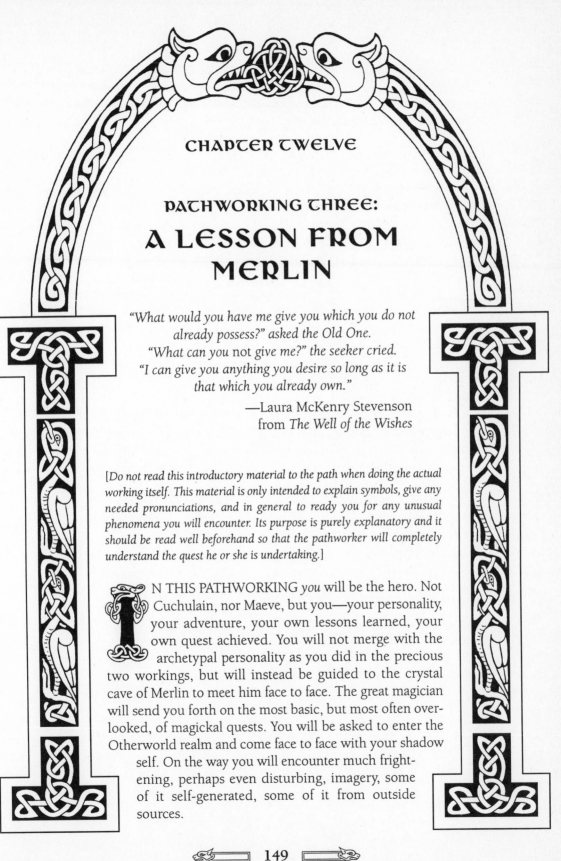

CHAPTER TWELVE

PATHWORKING THREE:
A LESSON FROM MERLIN

*"What would you have me give you which you do not
already possess?" asked the Old One.
"What can you not give me?" the seeker cried.
"I can give you anything you desire so long as it is
that which you already own."*

—Laura McKenry Stevenson
from *The Well of the Wishes*

*[Do not read this introductory material to the path when doing the actual
working itself. This material is only intended to explain symbols, give any
needed pronunciations, and in general to ready you for any unusual
phenomena you will encounter. Its purpose is purely explanatory and it
should be read well beforehand so that the pathworker will completely
understand the quest he or she is undertaking.]*

N THIS PATHWORKING *you* will be the hero. Not
Cuchulain, nor Maeve, but you—your personality,
your adventure, your own lessons learned, your
own quest achieved. You will not merge with the
archetypal personality as you did in the precious
two workings, but will instead be guided to the crystal
cave of Merlin to meet him face to face. The great magician
will send you forth on the most basic, but most often overlooked, of magickal quests. You will be asked to enter the
Otherworld realm and come face to face with your shadow
self. On the way you will encounter much frightening, perhaps even disturbing, imagery, some
of it self-generated, some of it from outside
sources.

This type of journey in Irish and Scottish myth is called *Immram,* the story of an adventure in the Otherworld, and they became very popular in the oral traditions during the Elizabethan period. However, their broad appeal waned through the efforts of Oliver Cromwell and the Puritan Commonwealth who abhored such tales of mere mortals adventuring in what they percieved to be their Hell.

While there are many reasons one might wish to visit this mystical realm, the most basic purpose of an Otherworld quest is to learn to overcome fear. Fear is one of the most destructive and hindering emotions, and all lifeforms are subject to its disease. Fear builds hatred, fuels wars, creates barriers, turns the pernicious gossip mills, and separates human beings from each other and from their inner-selves. For magickal folk, it can hinder spiritual progress, inhibit power flow, and interrupt altered state work. We *must* overcome fear, no matter what its source, if we are to be effectual and successful in our ritual endeavors.

Some fear is healthy. Fearing to walk down the proverbial dark alley after dark is a smart and healthy fear. But fearing various spiritual practices because of cultural conditioning or because of an imagined boogeyman hiding in the closet is destructive fear. Hopefully, this pathworking can be the first step in eliminating your ruinous fear, and will allow you to emerge stronger and more self-assured.

The quest to overcome fear is not a new concept. It is echoed repeatedly throughout world mythology. Renowned mythologist Joseph Campbell repeatedly pointed out the universality of the story of a hero who falls into paranormal situations, triumphs, and returns to the mundane world with God-like powers, able to grant boons to humanity, both the real and metaphorical.

In this case you will be returning from your quest with a special amulet, born of yourself, designed to protect you in times of need or fear and to aid you in your magickal endeavors. You will physically have this in the pathworking, and you will be instructed on how to retrieve its astral essence when you need it in your everyday life.

In many pathworkings and folktales, Merlin is often cast in the role of teaching this valuable lesson. Perhaps he is an archetype which we have learned to trust over the centuries. We usually view him as a kindly old man even though most of the myths about him do not show him in this light. This pathworking will attempt to bridge the gap between the two conceptions of this potent figure.

The pathworker should also be thinking about the one thing he or she fears the most. It is this which will have to be faced and conquered on this journey. Don't skimp on this part or try to substitute something else which you "sort of" fear. This defeats the purpose of the working. You need to think about that which you fear above all else and prepare how you will visualize it when the time comes. For example, if you are herpaphobic, envision a huge venomous snake; or, if you fear failure, find a way to best visualize it at its worst.

Also remember not to read aloud the material bracketed off [ ]. These are instructions to the reader and are not a part of the pathworking.

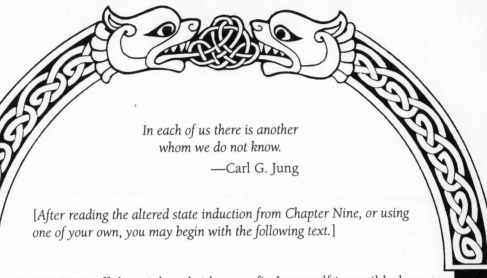

*In each of us there is another
whom we do not know.*

—Carl G. Jung

*[After reading the altered state induction from Chapter Nine, or using
one of your own, you may begin with the following text.]*

AS YOU STEP off the rainbow bridge you find yourself in a wild place at
evening. The bright orange sun is sinking low in the western sky, riding the
crest of the horizon like a floating ball of fire. Its orange glow is familiar
and pleasing to look upon.

Stopping to get your bearings, you see that the land you are in is a
mixed one. There are softly rolling hills to the east, mountains to the north,
red rocks to the south, and a churning sea to the west.

The landscape looks vaguely familiar. You view it with as sense of
surreal *deja-vu,* as if you have been here before in a vivid dream. Somewhere deep inside yourself, you associate this land with a purpose and you
begin to feel you were drawn here for a specific reason.

On the dusky breeze you seem to hear your name being called. The
voices grow louder and more persistent. They seem to want you to come
with them. At first you wisely hesitate to follow. What if they are
pranksters from the land of faery whose purpose is to lead you astray? You
are aware that you are in a place where such a thing could easily happen.

As you think these words, the tenor of the voice changes, becoming
lower in pitch, less strident, more reassuring, but still persistently calling
to you.

Keeping in mind that you know how to return home at any time if you
feel uneasy, you decide to chance following the mysterious voice. You
follow it up an overgrown path between the mountains and the sea which
winds back on itself until you are completely unsure of which direction
you are heading.

With a sparkling laugh the voice leaves you there, and you find yourself all alone in an unfamiliar land where night has fallen. You decide to
continue along the path which you can barely see now in the rising moonlight. It leads up the side of a gently sloping mountain to the mouth of an

old cave whose outer formations make it look like a yawning mouth with two huge canine teeth growing down from its upper lip. From somewhere deep inside its murky depths you think you see a faint blue light glowing, beckoning your presence.

You decide you have little to lose at this point, and the light seems harmless enough, so you step into the coolness of the cave's interior and move towards the light.

Feeling your way along the walls of a short narrow chamber you emerge into an egg-shaped room with smooth stone walls that shine like fine crystal. In the center of this room is an older man in a blue robe stirring something in a large iron cauldron. Over the boiling pot hangs a lovely blue light which appears to be suspended in mid-air. There are no other lights visible in the chamber, and yet there is light everywhere. You realize it is emanating from the crystalline walls.

Without looking up from his potion, the man addresses you by name: "[*Insert pathworker's name here*], it is about time you got here. I've been expecting you for some time—that is, if time interests you."

You are dumbstruck and do not know how to respond. Despite the strange situation in which you find yourself, you have no fear of the man and his cauldron, only an intense fascination.

Finally you find your tongue. "Who are you?" you ask.

He looks up at you for the first time. "Who do you think I am?" Several answers come to mind, none of which you feel like trying to explain.

He shakes his head at your apparent ignorance. "I am called by many names, but you know me best as Merlin."

You are flabbergasted. "Merlin? The Merlin? King Arthur, the Lady of the Lake, the Sword in the Stone and all that?"

He seems unimpressed with your knowledge, and suppresses a bored yawn. "That is one of my guises, yes. But, like you, I am much more."

"Why am I here?" you ask.

"That was to be my question to you," he responds.

"But you said you were expecting me."

"I was. Is this your first trip here?"

You answer as best you can since you are not sure exactly where you are. [*You should also answer this question based upon how much experience you have had with these types of pathworkings. Though the imagery is slightly different in each, you are always in roughly the same place.*]

Merlin removes the long wooden spoon from the boiling cauldron and places it on a nearby table. He then walks towards one edge of the room and sits down on a large crystal rock which looks like a great throne carved into the side of the cave wall. He motions for you to sit at his feet and you eagerly do so. After a few moments of gathering his thoughts, he speaks:

"You are a spiritual seeker who wishes to expand your power and your knowledge. These desires are good in most. But so many fail them. Either they get discouraged and fall short of their goals, or they lose their hard-won gifts through ignorance and arrogance. They never return to them. Instead they often fall prey to the teachers of hatred who tell them their goals were evil in the first place. They teach them to revile that which is a part of themselves rather than showing them how to understand it and change it."

Sitting at his feet, you are not at all sure you follow this speech, but you continue to listen without interruption.

"Do you truly wish to understand yourself? To do so requires finding yourself in ways and places which you have never imagined." he asks.

You answer that you do wish this.

"Are you willing to learn to overcome the most basic impediments to your progress?"

You again answer that you do.

"Are you willing to do this even at some personal risk? Can you face that which you fear the most? Can you face yourself?"

You hesitate briefly before saying yes.

He stands and returns to the side of his cauldron. Leaning over its thick lip, he stares into its steamy depths. "Come, take a look."

You cautiously follow him over and peer inside. There you see yourself traveling through a land of shadow and mist in which eerie and nebulous forms swirl and twist.

"This then is your quest." He stands and looks hard at you. "You must travel to the Otherworld and retrieve for yourself an amulet of your personal power. In doing this you will face many choices, and you will be asked to overcome many of your deepest anxieties and fears. This amulet will tell me that you went there, and it will forevermore be yours and will aid you in time of need. It is a powerful amulet, and a powerful experience, one which few can complete."

You ask, "Then I may return at any time?"

"You may, but when you do you only make subsequent quests more difficult for yourself, until finally, like the others, you will give up."

You tell him you wish to go anyway.

Merlin studies you carefully for a moment. "Very well. To begin your journey you must start where all those who leave this life start. Travel down the path in front of the cave going northwest until you come to the fenced clearing. The way from there will be up to you. Return here before dawn with the amulet."

He turns back to you, ignoring you as if you had never entered the room.

Determined to prove yourself worthy of the amulet, you jog out to the mouth of the cave and, in the dim light, find the path of which Merlin spoke. It slopes gently downward past a pleasant but dark woods and you are starting to feel that this night's work might be easier than you had anticipated.

Suddenly you find yourself at the edge of the clearing. Just in front of you is a small, well-tended cemetery. The headstones look to be very old, and ancient trees stand among the lonely graves. You realize that this is the place of which Merlin spoke for your journey's beginning—the place where we all begin when we leave this life—the grave.

You are here, but now what? You have no idea what to do next.

Attempting to center yourself, you call upon your personal deities for protection and aid, asking for some sign of which direction you should proceed. [*Pause for the pathworker to do this. Allow two or three minutes.*]

When you are finished, you look around you, more sure than ever that a clue to your next step must be in evidence. Yet there is nothing but the night woods, the lonely graves, and the sound of an owl hooting nearby. Your ears strain in the quiet, listening for a hint of answer.

Your ears hear another noise, one which is as yet undiscernible. In the far distance you think you hear something coming rapidly towards you from the west. As it approaches, the wildlife in the night woods falls hushed, and you sense in the silence a respect rather than a fear.

Turning your eyes to a small parting in the far side of the woods, you wait to see what will come. In the meantime you take precautionary cover behind a large oak tree. You are acutely aware that you have no weapons, not even magickal ones, with which to defend yourself, and a rising apprehension grips you.

The sound you hear is definitely hoofbeats. As they approach the cemetery they slow. Within a minute a shadowy equine figure enters the clearing. It is a large horse as black as the night itself. There is no rider, nor is there any tack [*saddle, bridle, halter, etc.*] on the animal.

You emerge from behind the tree and the horse paws the ground as if in greeting. You walk closer and reach out a hand to stroke her, but she pulls away and dances anxiously in front of you moving in little counter-clockwise circles. She is obviously trying to communicate something, and you realize she may be the next step in your quest.

Snorting as if you are the stupidest creature she has ever met, she kneels, clearly offering you her back.

Now you are sure this is the step you were meant to take. You realize too that you have reached the point of no return. This is the time to decide if you really wish to endure this night-long quest, or return home to your warm bed. For a brief moment you waver, weighing all your options, then you move to the mare, and climb onto her broad back.

She rises and runs back to the trail from which she came, carrying you swiftly westward through a dense woods. In order to keep from being hit by low hanging foliage and branches, you lean over her shoulder, your hands clutching her silky mane. She travels with a sense of purpose and seems to know exactly where she is going. You try to relax and trust in her, but you find it difficult.

Soon the pathway emerges onto to a flat sandy plain. A few cairns [*Celtic stone burial mounds*] are scattered here and there among sparse trees bare of their foliage. In the distance you hear the sound of the restless sea battering the shore.

The black mare does not slow as she approaches the rocky coastline, and your eyes scan the surroundings looking for what will come next, but you see nothing. The mare continues running and, at the water's edge, charges out over the sea as if a sturdy path remains under her rhythmic hooves.

You grip her tightly, waiting to sink, but, unbelievably, you stay on top of the obsidian surface holding your breath at the phenomenon. Soon she comes to a halt on a sandbar far enough from shore so that you can just see the cairns outlined there in the moonlight.

She whinnies impatiently for you to dismount. You do, and she races off to the north, disappearing in the dark as if blending into it: sky, water, and horse, all a murky, mutable black.

You are now alone on this lonely stretch of sand, too far out to swim back, and far enough out that you are not tempted at this point to give up. For a moment you are alarmed, wondering if you would be able to summon your rainbow bridge home at this point. You are tempted to test this, but decide that it would be an act of cowardice, and you are here to learn about facing fear.

Well, you decide, so far you are getting a taste of something—if not fear, at least a severe uneasiness.

What is next? you wonder, looking about for some clue.

Suddenly you are startled by the feel of a tug on your clothing. You look down and are surprised to see a mermaid [*or a merman for female travelers*] floating nearby. She [*He*] is the most beautiful creature you have ever seen. For a moment you think that to be with her [*him*] for only one night you would gladly give up any quest, any effort, any prize.

"Don't be afraid of me," she [*he*] offers with a seductive smile. "I can show you the way you are seeking. Come." She [*He*] offers you her [*his*] hand, reaching up imploringly.

Maybe this is the next step—lucky you. Your hand moves closer to hers [*his*], and you notice a faintly triumphant look behind her [*his*] sea-blue eyes. But she [*he*] is so beautiful you refuse to consider all the implications of this.

Just before your hands meet, a deep voice from behind you cries out, "*No!*" You spin around to see a small ball of red fire floating just above the surface of the water. "Do not go with this one," it cries. "This is the way to disaster and woe. Wait for the Bird of Paradise."

You look again toward the beautiful figure floating in the water, a petulant look about her [*his*] sensual lips. Then you look again at the ball of fire. How are you supposed to know who tells the truth?

The red fire speaks again. "That way will take you to the Otherworld, but not the way you wish to get there. Wait for the Bird of Paradise."

You still hesitate. The mermaid [merman] pleads again for you to come with her [him].

Again the voice of fire counters, "Wait for the Bird of Paradise." The red fire then fades away, only a warm spot in the air remains where it hovered.

You force yourself to look away from the sea creature in order to clear your head. What to do? The fire—the element of protection—offered you warning. Three warnings, no less. Three. You think about the metaphysical implications of the number. The mermaid [merman] merely beckons with seduction. Merlin said you would face choices. Obviously this is one of the big ones, but no one ever said it would be easy to decide.

You think some more and you remember that fire, by its nature, is protective, and that water is the realm of change…and of death.

You turn again to the beautiful sea creature and, summoning all your will power, you banish it: "Be gone, sea faery, tonight is not for us. Be gone, sea faery, your way lies disaster. Be gone, sea faery, for yours is not the path I seek." You make a banishing pentagram with your hands and finish with, "So Mote It Be."

Slowly the faery sinks from your sight beneath the waves, and you breathe a sigh of relief. You have made the right decision.

But now you are back where you started—alone in the middle of the silent sea. Only the water lapping at the edge of the bar can be heard. Even the waves which are crashing on the distant shore can barely be heard this far out. Overhead the stars have come out, dotting the heavens like someone were out there holding up a million tiny candles against a large black cloth. Somehow, that thought makes you feel less alone.

Now your ears hear another distant sound which rapidly approaches. The noise hits your ears like the rhythmic whipping of heated air. Your peer into the dark night trying to see what is coming, knowing there is nowhere for you to hide this time.

Looking to the west, you can just make out the outline of a giant black bird coming towards you, its monstrous wings beating a windy cadence in the air over the sea. The bird resembles an inky crow, only much, much larger. It circles above you three times, then lands in the water beside you.

It regards you with eyes so wise you think it could speak. Clearly it wishes you to crawl upon its back. Riding a wild horse through the woods was one thing, but you are not all that anxious to mount the back of some strange bird in the middle of the sea and have it carry you away. Suddenly the path of the mermaid [merman] seems much more sane.

You also realize that this bird may be your only way off the sandbar, so you take a deep breath and crawl upon its back.

As soon as you are settled the bird lets out one mighty caw and takes to the air.

You fly high and fast above the dark ocean and you feel that you are losing all sense of perspective. Above you the sky is black, below you the ocean is black, the bird you ride is black. Only the glow of stars above keeps you balanced and oriented upright.

On and on you travel until the air about you becomes misty with low hanging clouds. After a long time you begin to feel that you are making a descent. Certainly you must still be well out over the ocean, and you feel a bit of panic set in. You would dearly love to see where it is you are going, but the surrounding fog blocks your view.

With a slight jolt, the bird lands on what you know is solid ground. It makes clear that you are to dismount.

Reluctantly, you step off and let go of this lifeline to your own world. As you expected, the bird flies away and you are left alone again.

The place you are in has a boggy ground, and the fog is still so thick that your visibility is not as good as you would like. But, as your eyes adjust to the gloom, you can make out a few features in the landscape. There are gnarled old trees here and there, vines on the ground without fruit, and barren gardens. Looking down at your feet you notice that you are standing in the center of a crossroads with a path leading off in four different directions.

To move on you know you must choose one road to travel. You would like to know which direction they each go, and you search about for clues. Then you notice a signpost low to the ground. One arrow points west and says: To The Cauldron. One points north and says: To The Cairn. Another directs you east and says: To The Answer. And the fourth points the way south and says: To The Hearth.

You have no idea which way to proceed. Since you have come seeking answers, you decide to go east.

You travel along a path which winds eastward, deeply into a dark valley. The winds whips around you more strongly the deeper you travel. Sometimes they are bonechilling, at other times dry and hot. You see no light to guide you, no sign of life, and you come upon no other signposts. If there are answers of any kind this way, you do not know how to find them.

You turn around to go back to the crossroads.

Now you hear tiny voices on the winds, all of them whispering advice to you. They attack you like a well-trained fighting machine until you are so confused you just want to sit down and give up. "Stay, go, come, here, there, no, yes…" they all cry.

You know that the only way you will arrive at the crossroads with your sanity intact is to shut them out. You stop dead in your tracks and go deeply into yourself to seek your answers in your own inner-resources. Suddenly, one loud and clear voice from within speaks: "Go south."

You return unmolested to the crossroads and turn with the arrow which points you "To The Hearth."

You find that this path is lit for you by torches, and they lead to a small inviting cottage. There is a welcoming light in the window and you go inside.

You find you are in a typical Celtic cottage with whitewashed rooms and a thatched roof. In the center of the room is a huge stone fireplace with a warmly blazing peat fire. There is an old handhewn rocking chair in front of it, and you decide a brief rest is in order until you can figure out what to do next.

You stare lazily into the fire focusing on your next step. Suddenly, you are startled by a face which appears in the flames. It is Merlin. He looks at you as if he knows you are resting there and are not following your quest.

He speaks: "Remember your quest. You must find your shadow self and retrieve your personal power amulet from I-Breasil [*You may substitute any other name you like for the Otherworld. See Chapter 7 for other Celtic name for this realm if you are not familiar with them.*] and return to me before dawn. Time grows short. Seek your shadow in the north."

The image fades away as quickly as it came, and, though reluctant to leave the comfort of the hearth, you set off for the crossroads to head north.

As you go north the fog deepens and an uneasiness of spirit pervades. Merlin said you must find your shadow self in I-Breasil. That, you know, is one of the many names for the Land of the Dead. Certainly you cannot really be in the Otherworld, you are a human being…aren't you? So much has happened to you this night that you are not really sure about anything. Still, you know the Otherworld is the only place where a shadow self can be.

Again you question your choice of coming on this trip. But you also know that if Merlin sent you for a personal power amulet, then it must be worth having. You also know spirits speak in metaphor, and you sharpen your eyes and other senses to be alert for anything which might become an amulet for you. You have come too far to fail now.

As you travel along the overgrown path, you know you are not alone. Spirits surround you. Their subtle forms are silent, but taunting. They dance before you and alter their forms. Your throat is dry. They jeer, and cry, and keen. Some know your name, both the revealed one and that which you have kept hidden, and they call to you. You freely admit to yourself that these mutable forms which change on a whim scare you. They seem to know what form to take which will frighten you the most, and you try to clear your mind so that they cannot read your thoughts which are naturally straying to all which you fear.

Even through the dense fog, you can see that just ahead the path curves, and you hope that once you round it you will leave the spirits behind.

Forcing yourself to maintain an even pace, you round that bend. Then you stop dead in your tracks as you face the most terrible monster yet— that which you fear most. Rising up, blocking your way, it stands. You swallow hard and try to maintain a facade of calm, but you are more terrified than you have ever been before. Here is your worst nightmare standing before you, ready to consume you. See it, know it is real, and that you *must* now find a way to deal with it. [*Pause for a moment so that the pathworker can visualize that which they most fear. This is an exercise which is difficult for everyone, and we all tend to go with an image which is not the worst for us. However, not facing your greatest fear here defeats much of the purpose of the pathworking.*]

You know that you should stand and fight, but you find yourself fighting the urge to turn tail and run. Even traveling through that spirit realm again would be better than this. Anything would be better than this.

You have no weapon but your wits so, instead, you make a mental list of all the reasons that this fear really is not so bad. As you do so, you begin to notice that it loses a bit of its bravado. Gaining confidence from this, you continuing using visualization to diminish the vision. Know that this is real. The monster is fading. [*Pause again for pathworker to use creative visualization to slay their personal dragon. This can be done in any way the journeyer sees fit. Allow three to five minutes.*]

At last the image is gone, and your path is clear once more. You know it is not gone for good, but you also now know that you will be able to find ways to deal with it when it comes again. You can defeat it.

You continue along until you come to a land of neglected cairns all side by side covering the plain in front of you for as far as you can see. You really don't want to walk among them, but you know you must.

Armed with your new-found confidence, you stride among them, wary but brave. Dark human-like forms dart in and out among the stones, some of them watching you while others flee from your unexpected presence. They appear to be the mere shadows of mortals. You are in the realm of the shadow selves. Certainly yours must also be here. Slowly you walk on, looking right and left for some hint that you have found yourself. What a strange feeling, you think, to be searching for yourself.

Suddenly you are stopped short by a dark figure standing directly in front of you. You stand with morbid fascination as you find yourself looking at a dark image of yourself. You sense that it has your same fears, loves, hopes, and joys. It shares your strengths and it projects all your faults. It is you—your own shadow self which always lives in the Otherworld. You now realize that facing yourself is the hardest thing you have ever done. There is so much about yourself you do not wish to see which is now all laid bare. This would have been an easier task if your shadow had been your direct opposite, or very good, or very evil. But it is not. It is just you. You stand and watch all your faults, lies, dogmas, and problems being reflected in your shadow eyes. [*Pause*]

You decide you will remember what you are seeing so that you can do something about those things you do not like.

You find that you do not know what to say to this image, and it does not speak to you. You stand there for a long time looking at each other until you realize that you must speak or stand here eternally.

"I have come seeking my personal power amulet," you tell your other self. "Do you know where that can be found?"

The shadow does not speak, but walks toward you, closer and closer. You do not want it to touch you, and yet you seem frozen, you cannot move. It keeps coming closer until the two of you merge.

For a brief moment you feel a surge of great power as your mind is connected to all levels of awareness. You feel that you can do or be or have anything. You feel like a God [*or Goddess for females*]. Answers to all the questions you have ever asked pass rapidly through your expanded mind, but you cannot latch onto even one of them. The power reaches a peak which you can barely contain, and then the shadow self emerges from you.

Between you on the ground is a small glistening gem which seems to have been born of your union. You kneel and pick it up. It is a chameleon of a gem which seems to change colors with your feelings. This must be your power amulet—a stone born of two worlds—a potent magickal device indeed.

You stand and thank your other self, then you turn to leave this boggy world of shadow.

Gripping the prize stone tightly in your hand, you walk back to the crossroads. No fear images assault you, though the shapeshifting ghosts are still there. They seem to sense the presence of your stone and back away.

Back at the crossroad you stand wondering what to do next. You have your amulet and you would like to return to Merlin as quickly as possible. Certainly dawn cannot be long away.

Nothing seems to be happening, and you realize that you are going to have to figure out your own way home from this place. Your mind races through all the Celtic myths you have ever heard concerning I-Breasil. The only way you know by which anyone emerges from this place is through rebirth from the Great Cosmic Cauldron of the Crone Goddess who rules this land.

Knowing what you must do, you go west, following the arrow which reads, "To The Cauldron."

The trail winds through an ever-changing terrain which shapeshifts constantly as you walk through it. You watch in fascination, unsure if you find it more interesting or more disconcerting.

Finally the trail emerges into a wooded clearing. At the center of this clearing is a large old woman standing over a huge black and silver cauldron. At her side are eight other old women who stand regarding you passively, their robed arms folded over their chests. They radiate sovereignty and prerogative and, again, you have the urge to turn tail and run.

With trembling voice, you address yourself to the tall center figure. She looks up at you with clear and wise old eyes. Her entire being radiates power and self-assurance. She knows she is Queen here. And you know that she is your only way back home.

"My Goddess, I am a traveler in your world in need of aid."

She steps forward and asks that she might see what is in your hand. You show her your amulet and you can see that she approves. She places her withered hand over the stone in your palm. You are surprised by the strength of it, and a surge of force rushes from her hand into yours. When she removes her hand you see that the gem glows with a gold-green brightness.

"You have done very well," she tells you. "I will send you home."

"Who are you?" you ask, feeling that you just have to know.

She stares deeply into your questioning eyes. "I am ageless and known by many names, but you know me best as Rhiannon. [*You may substitute the name Badb, or Macha, or any other Goddess whom you associate with this task of presiding over the cauldron of life, death, and regeneration.*] It is I who decides who goes back to the Mundane World and when they should go. But you do not belong here and you must go back. There are things here you may not see."

You are not in a mood to argue with her.

"Close your eyes," she commands, "and visualize where you wish to be."

You do as she asks and focus your thoughts on Merlin's cave.

"Open your eyes and walk toward the cauldron," she tells you.

You again do as she asks and head towards the large steaming pot. When you get close enough, the eight old women grab you and hoist you in. A terrified scream erupts from your mouth as you are tossed like some storybook character into the pot. Down, down, down, you fall as if the cauldron has no bottom. Images come and go past you so rapidly that you cannot make them out. And still you fall. You are still screaming, sure that you are lost, part of the cosmic mix.

Just when you decide you will never stop falling and are resigned to your fate, you stop with a thud.

You crawl onto your knees and look around. You are sitting on rocky grass. When you look over your shoulders you find that you are sitting just outside of the cave of Merlin. In your hand you still grip the hard-won amulet.

Rising to your feet you race into the cave like an excited child, anxious to show the great magician your prize.

You scurry down the short narrow way and burst in on him where you left him, huddled over his cauldron.

"Back so soon?" he asks blandly without looking up. You are disappointed that he seems so little interested in your achievement.

"Yes, I'm back," you tell him, proudly striding towards him. "And I've got my amulet."

He still does not look up. "So you do."

You have to fight a rising anger. After all you have achieved, after all you have been through, he seems not the least interested in any of it.

As if reading your mind, he looks up at you for the first time since your return. "[*Address pathworker by name*], don't ever think you need me or anyone else to validate your experiences or your achievements. I know you went though a great trial tonight, and you emerged victorious. You have a right to feel proud. Few can do what you have done. But you don't need me to cheer you. I share your joy. I am happy for you, but you only need this sharing—*not* my admiration."

The old man smiles warmly for the first time and, despite his words, you know he is proud of you.

He beckons to you to his crystal throne where you sit at his side this time, rather than at his feet, and he asks to see the stone.

You hold it out in your palm and it now glows a vibrant blue-violet.

You ask: "What do I do now? You said the stone would be mine forever. How do I keep it? How do I use it?"

He answers: "You know, I presume, that you cannot take an object from one world into another? But you still may call that astral, or etheric, part of it to you in time of need. For example, say you are doing a ritual designed to bring you courage. Simply call upon the stone to come to you."

"But how?" you ask, feeling very much like all your efforts were going to be for nothing.

Out of the folds of his blue robe he pulls a black thong and instructs you to tie it in quarters around the stone. When you are finished, he asks you to place it around your neck.

"That stone will always hang there," he tells you. "No matter what you wear, or where you go, it will be there, its power center resting on your breast bone. It can never be removed except by you. Remember that it is an aid to personal power. When you need it you need only visualize it being there, and tap it three times to awaken it. You may then draw from its resources. It will know what you need of it because it is a part of all you are on every level. In time, it may even reveal its name to you. Speaking this name three times in succession will also awaken its energy. It is also your link to other worlds for it was born of your completeness—your mundane self and your shadow self. It has great power. Never abuse it or use it for harm or it will fade away."

You ask: "Could I get it back then?"

He pauses before answering. "Maybe. But if you thought the way was difficult this time, it would be three times as hard next time. Such temporal power can be taken by any one, but lasting power comes to those with the wisdom to use it for the good of all. Remember this always."

For a moment the old man seems distracted. "It is nearly dawn. You should return home now."

You stand and offer your thanks. After saying good-bye, you walk happily out of the cave's entrance.

You step outside the cave and are surprised to see that it is indeed early morning. The warm golden sun sparkles on the dewy ground, kissing each blade of grass with a dot of silver. Before you start back, you turn to bid Merlin one last farewell, but you see that the cave behind you is empty. No lights, no cauldron, and no Merlin.

Knowing the extent of Merlin's abilities, you are not really surprised by this turn of events.

You turn and walk a few more feet away from the mouth of the cave. Then, beside you, the familiar hues of the shimmering rainbow bridge appear.

[*Follow the "Returning Home" reading from Chapter Nine, or some other reading for returning to your own consciousness. Always come home by the same route you left. When you are awake, make some loud noise, eat, go to the bathroom, or do anything else "earthly" to reinforce the idea to your subconscious that you are back.*]

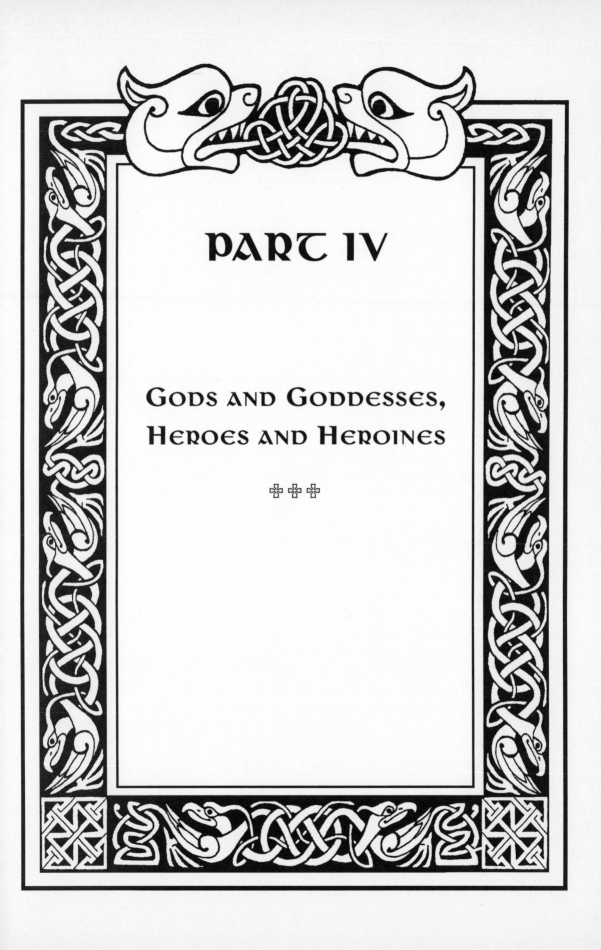

PART IV

GODS AND GODDESSES, HEROES AND HEROINES

✠ ✠ ✠

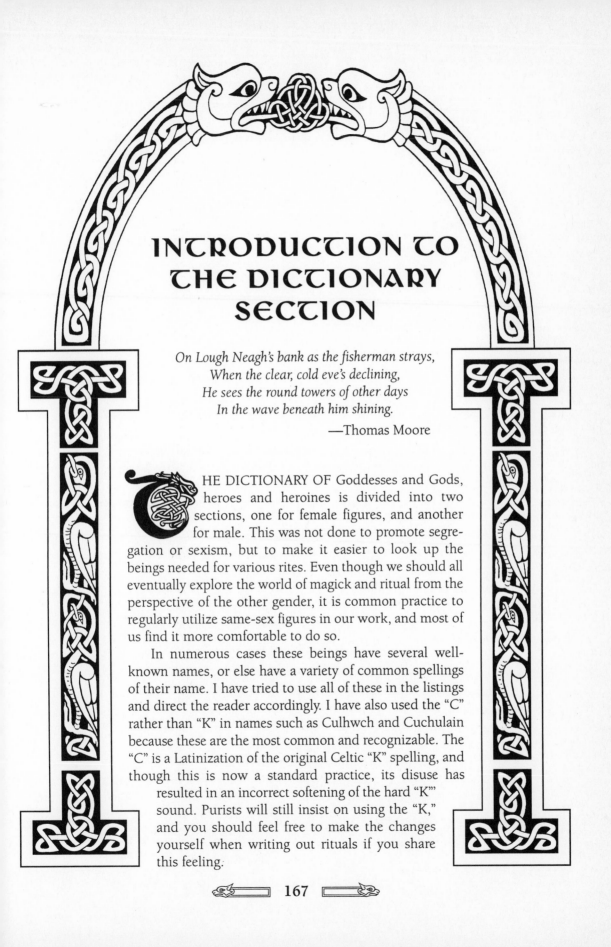

INTRODUCTION TO THE DICTIONARY SECTION

On Lough Neagh's bank as the fisherman strays,
When the clear, cold eve's declining,
He sees the round towers of other days
In the wave beneath him shining.

—Thomas Moore

HE DICTIONARY OF Goddesses and Gods, heroes and heroines is divided into two sections, one for female figures, and another for male. This was not done to promote segregation or sexism, but to make it easier to look up the beings needed for various rites. Even though we should all eventually explore the world of magick and ritual from the perspective of the other gender, it is common practice to regularly utilize same-sex figures in our work, and most of us find it more comfortable to do so.

In numerous cases these beings have several well-known names, or else have a variety of common spellings of their name. I have tried to use all of these in the listings and direct the reader accordingly. I have also used the "C" rather than "K" in names such as Culhwch and Cuchulain because these are the most common and recognizable. The "C" is a Latinization of the original Celtic "K" spelling, and though this is now a standard practice, its disuse has resulted in an incorrect softening of the hard "K'" sound. Purists will still insist on using the "K," and you should feel free to make the changes yourself when writing out rituals if you share this feeling.

As many Celtic deities, heroes and heroines are included here as could be found which have practical magickal/ritual applications. Heroic figures are also embraced as long as their feats of derring-do move beyond the historical and into the archetypal realm of myth. For example, Brian Boru and MacBeth are such figures, but Robert the Bruce and King Malachi are not.

Each mythic figure is listed with a reference to the area/sub-culture of the Celtic world from whence they came. These divisions are:

- ◆ Anglo-Celtic
- ◆ Breton
- ◆ Continental
- ◆ Cornish
- ◆ Irish
- ◆ Manx
- ◆ Pan-Celtic
- ◆ Scottish
- ◆ Welsh

Some deities are part of several cultures or will be associated with only a small portion of one of these areas such as the Hebrides or the Channel Islands. These distinctions are also made. Others undoubtedly had their origins in far off places such as the Middle East or India. This is simply because no culture ever has or ever will exist in a vacuum, and our archetypal memories travel with us wherever we go, merging and blending with other similar tales until new ones, bearing faint resemblances to their parents, are created. Celtic figures with these possible origins are duly noted.

Other Celtic deities had their origins on the European continent, particulary in Gaul where the Celts came into contact with Roman Paganism. The Saxon and Norman invasions of England also helped to merge some local deities with other figures. With each of these events, two cultures blended for a time, inevitably contributing their ideas of deity and mythic heroics to the other. Separating some of the Roman and Saxon deities from the Celtic ones can be a difficult task, and it is noted wherever the origin is questionable. (Invasions after about the eleventh century had little or no effect on Pagan mythology, as by this time most of Europe was Christian, at least in name.)

A rough phonetic pronunciation of many of the names is provided. However, the Celtic languages all contain sounds which are not found in other languages, including English. And because the Celtic languages are not the only ones spoken in their homelands, the variations in regional dialect greatly affect the already complex rules of pronunciation.

The pronunciations given here are a basic guide only and, if you wish to work with a particular deity on a regular basis, you should consider investigating the rules of the language of her/his native land. The Celts put a great deal of emphasis on the importance of a name. Certainly there is power in uttering a divine name, but there is also power in the intent behind the words. Focusing on the energy and associations of the one you are calling upon is every bit as important, and will work nicely until you can better understand the language from which the name comes.

A number of the deity names have more than one accepted pronunciation. This can probably be accounted for from years of popular usage in circles which began using "wrong" pronunciations, and spread them until they became the standard. For example, the name of the Irish Goddess Dana is called THAY-nah, DAY-nah, DAWN-ah, DON-nah, and JAWN-ah. All of these are perfectly correct depending upon whose circle you are in.

Many of the deities listed here will have other Celtic counterparts who are no more than vaguely diguised versions of the other. This is particularly true of the Irish and Welsh deities. Mythologist Charles Squires writes:

> The Celts, both of the Gaelic and Brythonic branches, were split up into numerous petty tribes, each with its own local deities embodying the same essential concepts under different names.

References are made to these counterparts so that these names can be looked up later for comparison.

In a few cases you will come across an entry which says "equated with _____." This means that Celtic mythologists see that particular deity as having the same attributes and associations as another more well-known one, usually from "classical" (Greco-Roman) mythology. These references are included so that you may get a quick overall picture in your mind of what affinities the deity you are reading about governs. For example, most westerners can relate a solid mental image to the names Poseidon and Eros, but are less certain about the names Manannan MacLir and Aengus MacOg, deities who respectively share their attributes. This does not mean that the named deity was taken whole and untarnished from those other cultures (though this did happen in a few instances), but rather that these figures share similar archetypal imagery or analogous mythic stories and functions.

Do not assume that because a deity is considered a minor one that this means they were of little importance. Many Celtic communities and geographical regions had local Gods and Goddesses who were every bit as important and revered as the major deities. The difference is that they were local, rather than being a deity which was widely worshipped over a larger area.

Also listed are several lesser Celtic deities/heroic figures whose tales are important in helping to understand the scope, tone, family groupings, and mind-set of Celtic myth and folklore, but who really are not potent enough archetypes to stand on their own as powers in magick or ritual. They are included here in order to make this as comprehensive a listing of Celtic mythological figures as is possible; however, trivial and very minor figures have been excluded due to space considerations.

Keep in mind that there is not a Celtic God of all Gods, a chief Goddess, or any set hierarchy of Celtic deities. Looking for these will only result in frustration. Some folktales or myths might suggest an ordered organization, but these can easily be contradicted by other myths and oral traditions. To quote contemporary Celtic researcher and author R.J. Stewart, "much of the significant evidence [for a hierarchy] is in the form of allusions, asides, single images or references."

The listings also contain basic information about the major myths and folktales which surround each figure. Because of space considerations, not all of the available information could be included, nor could all of the many versions of the myths. In most cases the one which was chosen was the most accepted and well-known version. And since some mythic figures have epic and involved stories, the information presented about them here has been edited to include only the part of the story most relevant to the magickal or ritual uses of the being. Following that is a list of suggestions for incorporating that particular being into your practical work, including any known correspondences which are generally associated with her/him. These are gleaned from many popular sources, some modern, and others quite old. They can also be used to facilitate contact. For example, Brid (Brigid) is associated with her sacred plant, the blackberry, and these can be brought into your spell/ritual/rite as a food, incense, wine, or altar piece to help you align yourself with her.

In Appendix E you will find cross-references which can further help you find exactly the right mythic figure to work with for any need or goal.

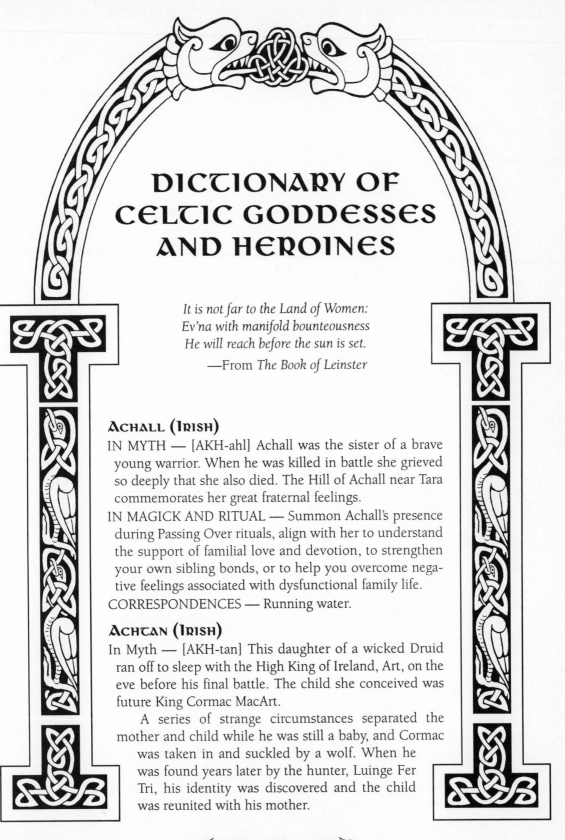

DICTIONARY OF CELTIC GODDESSES AND HEROINES

It is not far to the Land of Women:
Ev'na with manifold bounteousness
He will reach before the sun is set.

—From *The Book of Leinster*

ACHALL (IRISH)

IN MYTH — [AKH-ahl] Achall was the sister of a brave young warrior. When he was killed in battle she grieved so deeply that she also died. The Hill of Achall near Tara commemorates her great fraternal feelings.

IN MAGICK AND RITUAL — Summon Achall's presence during Passing Over rituals, align with her to understand the support of familial love and devotion, to strengthen your own sibling bonds, or to help you overcome negative feelings associated with dysfunctional family life.

CORRESPONDENCES — Running water.

ACHTAN (IRISH)

In Myth — [AKH-tan] This daughter of a wicked Druid ran off to sleep with the High King of Ireland, Art, on the eve before his final battle. The child she conceived was future King Cormac MacArt.

A series of strange circumstances separated the mother and child while he was still a baby, and Cormac was taken in and suckled by a wolf. When he was found years later by the hunter, Luinge Fer Tri, his identity was discovered and the child was reunited with his mother.

ACHTAN (CONT.)

Achtan then knew that she had to make the dangerous journey with him over the Mountains of Mourne to Tara, where her son could claim his rightful kingship. Along the way they were protected by the wild animals who had known Art as a babe. Later Achtan married her son's rescuer.

IN MAGICK AND RITUAL — Achtan can teach us about the strength of mother love and help us to have the perseverance to seek the best for our children.

ACHTLAND (PAN-CELTIC)

IN MYTH — [AHKT-lawnd] Achtland was a Goddess queen whom no mortal man could sexually satisfy, so she took a giant from the faery realm as her mate. Legend says she took great pleasure in combing his long, fair hair.

IN MAGICK AND RITUAL — Invoke her for sex magick or for taking the female role in the Great Rite.

ADSULLATA (BRETON)

IN MYTH — [AWD-soo-LAWT-ah] A Goddess of hot springs who came to Brittany from Celtic Gaul. She is the origin of the Anglo-Celtic sun Goddess, Sul, and was most likely a minor sun Goddess in her own right before the time when the Celts relegated the majority of their sun images to male deities, and moon images to female ones.

IN MAGICK AND RITUAL — Call on this lady for purification rites, and for all manner of magick relating to solar energies.

AEBH (IRISH, WELSH)

[Aev] Also spelled Aobh. The mother of Fionnuala and her three brothers by Llyr (Lir in Irish). She died birthing her daughter. The four children became the subject of one of the "Four Sorrows" of Irish mythology when they were changed by Aife, Llyr's jealous second wife, into singing swans.

AERTEN (CORNISH, ANGLO-CELTIC, WELSH)

IN MYTH — [AER-teen] Also spelled Aerfen. A Goddess of fate who presided over the outcome of war between several Celtic clans. She had a shrine at Glyndyfrdwy on the banks of the River Dee, where legend says that three human sacrifices had to be made every three years to ensure success in future battles.

She is often equated with the Three Fates of Greco-Roman mythology.

IN MAGICK AND RITUAL — Work with Aerten to overcome your enemies and to make peace.

CORRESPONDENCES — The double-bladed axe.

AERON (WELSH)

A Goddess of war who may be only another name for Aerten.

AEVAL (IRISH)

IN MYTH — Also Aebhel. This Goddess came into popular legend as a faery, a Munster queen who held a midnight court to hear the debate on whether the men of her province were keeping their women sexually satisfied or not. The problem, she deemed, was that the men were both prudish and lazy, and commanded that they bow to the women's sexual wishes.

IN MAGICK AND RITUAL — Call on Aeval to aid you in spells of lust, sex magick, and wisdom in making judgments.

Agrona (Anglo-Celtic, Welsh)

Goddess of slaughter and war often equated with the Morrigan. Though her name bears the root of the modern English word "agronomy," the name for the scientific study of land cultivation, no evidence of her as a harvest/fertility Goddess can be found today.

Aibell (Irish)

IN MYTH — [AW-bel or EE-bel] Aibell, whose name means "most beautiful," was a Goddess of Munster whose legends were almost completely lost until she was "demoted" to regional faery queen.

      She possessed a magickal harp which did her bidding, but which human ears could not hear or else the eavesdropper would soon die. A large gray rock in Killaloe, known as *Dal gCais* is her reputed home, telling us that she was probably once a mother earth Goddess whose image was stamped out by the monasteries.

      Modern legend says she is now the guardian spirit of Clan O'Brien.

IN MAGICK AND RITUAL — Cultivate Aibell for protection and for aid in making music magick. Her energies are also compatible with earth magick and eco-magick.

CORRESPONDENCES — Stones, leaves.

Aibheaog (Irish)

IN MYTH — [AWV-ay'ok] This fire Goddess from County Donegal is also known by the name *Tobar Brid,* a term which combines the Irish word for "well" with that of the widely worshipped Goddess Brid. The waters of Aibheaog's sacred well contained mighty healing powers, especially effective against toothache so long as the petitioner leaves a small white stone at the well to represent the decayed tooth.

IN MAGICK AND RITUAL — Use the energy of this Goddess for spells of healing or for Midsummer well rituals popular within some Celtic traditions.

CORRESPONDENCES — Wells, the number five.

Aidin (Irish)

IN MYTH — [AW-deen or AE-deen] Aidin was the wife of Oscar, a grandson of Fionn MacCumhal who died in the Battle of Gabhra. When she heard of his passing, she also died of grief, and they were buried together by Ossian. An Ogham stone marks their joint grave as an eternal testament to the power of romantic love.

IN MAGICK AND RITUAL — Love spells.

Aife (Irish, Scottish)

IN MYTH — [AW-fah or EE-fah] Also spelled Aoife. Aife was a Goddess and queen of the Isle of Shadow, an honor she shared with her rival and sister Scathach. Scathach operated a school on the isle where she trained fighters, including the nearly invincible Red Branch warriors. Aife also ran a school for warriors, but was much less successful than her sister.

      Aife was not vulnerable to magick, and commanded a legion of fierce horsewomen. She had a son by Cuchulain whom she kept from Cuchulain until the boy was of age to join the Red Branch.

AIFE (CONT.)

Other sources place her as a consort of the sea God Manann or of one of his sons, and say she stole an Alphabet of Knowledge from the deities to give to humankind. For this transgression, and her general meanness, she was transformed into a crane by the elder deities. Some legends say she haunts the countryside in this form to this day, others that she was accidentally killed by hunters.

IN MAGICK AND RITUAL — Call on Aife for protection, for general knowledge, or for aid in teaching. Through pathworking, she can also help teach us lessons of the Threefold Law.

CORRESPONDENCES — The crane, the lance.

AIFE (IRISH)

She succeeded her older sister, Aobh, as the wife of the sea God Llyr. She was jealous of her step-children (who were also her nieces and nephews), and turned them into swans for nine hundred years. Numerous sources feel she is the same as the Aife mentioned above.

AIGE (IRISH)

IN MYTH — A woman from oral tradition who was turned into a fawn by an angry faery, though some sources say it was a Druidess who did this. Afterwards she ran wild across the island and plunged into the bay which today still bears her name. By doing so she grounded forever the evil power of the faery who changed her. The only detail the accounts of her leave out is whether or not her drowning was a deliberate act or an accident. Other accounts say she was slain by a hunting party of a High King.

IN MAGICK AND RITUAL — Call on her to help ground negativity or to work banishing or staying spells.

AILBE (IRISH)

IN MYTH — [AWL-buh or EEL-buh] This daughter of Cormac MacArt was known for her brilliance and clever wit. She was able to answer a set of trick questions posed to her by Fionn MacCumhal who became so enamored of her sagacity that he fell in love with her and asked her to come share his home.

IN MAGICK AND RITUAL — Ailbe can help strengthen your mental prowess. Call on her before tests or other events which need brain work. She can also aid you in overcoming obstacles and bestow the gift of blarney, the cherished Irish art of glib gab.

CORRESPONDENCES — The throat chakra.

AILLE (IRISH)

IN MYTH — [Awl or AWL-uh] When Aille's husband, Meargach of the Green Spear, was killed in the battle of Knock-an-Air by Oscar (Fionn MacCumhal's grandson), this clan chieftain had her chief Druid, Fer Gruadh, administer a sleeping potion to Fionn so that he could be taken captive. The Fianna warriors pursued the Druid, but his magick was greater, and soon the warriors were all under his control. Eventually the spell ran out, Oscar slew the Druid, and Aille committed suicide.

IN MAGICK AND RITUAL — Merge with Aille when you need to think up a clever way to thwart an enemy, or to teach you to temper your need for revenge.

Ailinn (Irish)

IN MYTH — [AW-leen or EE-leen] This romantic heroine was a Princess of Leinster, the grand-daughter of a local king, and the lover of Baile of the Honeyed Speech. An evil faery falsely told each partner of the death of the other so that they would each die of broken hearts. The trick worked, and they were buried in adjoining graves where two trees, an apple and a yew, grew and entwined.

Later generations of Pagans used limbs from these trees to make wands for love, death, and binding spells.

IN MAGICK AND RITUAL — Call upon Ailinn to make love magick or to bless your own magickal wands. If you feel your romance is being threatened, she is also used efficaciously as a protectress of lovers.

CORRESPONDENCES — Sliced apples.

Aimend (Irish, Scottish)

[AW-mend or EE-mend] A minor Celtic sun Goddess who was said to be the daughter of the king of the region known as Corco Loidhe.

Ain and Iaine (Irish)

IN MYTH — [Awn and Ee-AWN-ay] These pre-Celtic princesses married their own brothers so that no other family would be able to rule the island. They are credited with inventing war in order to claim the rest of the land for themselves. As a result of this, the Brehon Laws were instituted which gave women high status including the right to own property. Among these laws was one which said no child could be called illegitimate. This was enacted so that any lands owned by offspring of Ain, Iaine and their brothers would be entailed to them and their dynasty.

IN MAGICK AND RITUAL — Unite with these energies to protect your family, land, and/or property.

Aine (Irish)

IN MYTH — [AW-nay or EE-nay] Aine is an Irish cattle, sun, and fire Goddess who is still very popular in her native Munster. She is sometimes called by the name Aine of Knockaine. She is strongly identified with Midsummer on which night torchlight processions are still held in her honor. The torches were also waved over Midsummer fields to ensure their growth. Because of these associations, she is also thought to have once been worshipped as a deity of the waning solar year, a twin to Grian.

She was raped by Ailill Olum, a Munster king, but her vast magickal arts destroyed him for his violation of her.

Aine made a *geise* (a sacred honor vow) never to sleep with a man with gray hair. She became infatuated with the handsome young warrior Fionn, but her jealous sister tricked him into an enchanted lake that grayed his head. Saddened by this, Aine still kept her promise and did not sleep with him.

Some also claim that she is or was a minor moon Goddess, or that she might have later merged into the Goddess Anu. She is credited for giving meadowsweet its delicate scent.

IN MAGICK AND RITUAL — Aine is a protector of women and a ruler of the faeries known as the Dinnshenchas (either named for or the namesake of the famous Irish mythology book).

AINE (CONT.)

She can also be called upon for Midsummer rites, as a protectress of animals and environment, and for aid in keeping promises. Aine can also aid in banishing spells or any magick ruled by the sun.

CORRESPONDENCES — Cattle horns, faery burghs, illuminated writings, the color brown, milk, the waxing moon, balefires.

AINE (IRISH)

A Goddess of love who may or may not be the same as the more famous cattle Goddess. This Aine is said to be a daughter of Ouel, a sage and seer of the Tuatha De Danann.

AIRMID (IRISH)

IN MYTH — [AWR-meet or EER-meet] A daughter of the God of medicine, Diancecht, this Goddess of the Tuatha De Danann was adept at medicine and all healing arts. She was looked upon as a magician and herbalist of great repute. After the death of her brother Miach, she tended the grave on which all the herbs of the world grew and as she harvested them, they spoke to her and assisted her in their uses. She laid them out on a cloak by their properties, but her jealous father came along, shook out the cloak, and scattered away nearly all of the knowledge.

She was also a craftswoman who, with her brother, helped forge the famed silver hand of Nuad.

IN MAGICK AND RITUAL — Call on Airmid for general aid in magic, for healing, learning herbalism, or understanding family loyalty. She can also inspire craftspeople.

CORRESPONDENCES — The caduceus wand, silver, hazel, chamomile, rosemary, number seven.

ALMHA (IRISH)

[AHL-vah] Almha and her attendant myths are lost to us. We only know she was a Goddess of the Tuatha De Danann and that a hill in southern Ireland was named for her.

AMERACH (IRISH)

IN MYTH — An Ulster Druidess who cast a spell of agelessness over Fiongalla.

IN MAGICK AND RITUAL — Agelessness in Celtic myth is often a metaphor for time manipulation, a shamanic art. Call on Amerach's energies to teach you to put aside your perceptions of linear time and peer through the veil to other worlds.

CORRESPONDENCES — The number two.

ANCASTA (ANGLO-CELTIC)

A Goddess who survives in name only through an inscription on a stone in Hampshire. She is possibly related to Andraste.

ANDRASTE (BRETON, ANGLO-CELTIC, CONTINENTAL)

IN MYTH — This war Goddess' name means "the invincible one." Her presence was evoked on the eve of battle to curry favor, and possibly ritual sacrifices were given her.

Queen Boadicea of the Iceni offered sacrifices to Andraste in a sacred grove before fighting the Romans on her many campaigns against them.

IN MAGICK AND RITUAL — Overcoming enemies.

Anu (Irish)

IN MYTH — [AW-noo] (Also spelled as Ana and Catana.) Anu is the virgin aspect of one of the Triple Goddesses of Ireland. Her mother aspect is Dana, or Danu, and her crone aspect is Badb.

She was known as a Goddess of prosperity and abundance, which suggests that her name was also associated with the mother aspect of this triplicity.

IN MAGICK AND RITUAL — Call on Anu for fertility magick.

CORRESPONDENCES — The waxing moon, emeralds, blood, moonstones.

Ardwinna (Breton, Continental)

IN MYTH — This woodland Goddess haunted the forests of Ardennes riding a wild boar. She demanded a fine for any animal killed on her land, yet asked for animal sacrifices on her feast day.

Though we no longer know her exact function in the Celtic pantheon, we can surmise that she was a continental version of Ireland's Flidais, a woodland and animal Goddess.

Her popular Gaulish name is Dea Arduinna.

IN MAGICK AND RITUAL — Use Ardwinna's energy when making magick for animals or to aid you in finding a familiar.

CORRESPONDENCES — The Strength Tarot card.

Argante (Welsh, Cornish, Breton)

IN MYTH — [Ar-GAN-tay] Little is known about Argante other than that she was a healer of Avalon, and probably a powerful Druidess.

IN MAGICK AND RITUAL — Healing magick and ritual.

Ariadne (Continental)

IN MYTH — [Awr-ee-AWD-nah] This Goddess of ancient Crete is the only Greek deity known to have been worshipped in Celtic Gaul. Her name is derived from the genus name for the spider, *arachnid*. In one of the few threads of extant Celtic creation myths, Ariadne spins the universe from the primordial darkness like a spider spins her web, a theme with echoes in the creation myths of many other cultures. Therefore this particular myth strikes many scholars and Pagans as being very un-Celtic, and it may have been a remnant of Indian mythology brought with the Celts on their long journey across the European continent.

In Greek myth Ariadne was a daughter of Cretan King Minos who aided Theseus on his quest through the dark labyrinth to kill the Minotaur. She was the consort of Dionysus, God of wine and the vine.

In *Adriadne's Thread*, author Shekhinah Mountainwater links her to the great loving earth mother, a bastion of safety and protection, the archetypal thread which guides spiritual seekers into the dark maze to learn lessons and complete quests, then shows them the way out again.

IN MAGICK AND RITUAL — Assistance in protection rites, manifestation magick, and learning the art of time manipulation.

CORRESPONDENCES—The spider web, sulphur, thread, yarn.

ARIANRHOD (WELSH)

IN MYTH — [AHR-ee-an-r'hod] Arianrhod's name means "silver circle." This major Welsh Goddess is the Goddess of reincarnation, the Wheel of the Year, the full moon, fertility, and a primal figure of female power. Some Celtic scholars believe her story represents the shift from woman-centered clans to patriarchal power.

Her heavenly star/island, Caer Arianrhod in the Corona Borealis, is believed in some Welsh traditions to be the place where dead souls go to await reincarnation. There she lives with her female attendants presiding over the fates of the departed.

She is sometimes depicted as a weaver, which links her to lost creation myths and to magickal practice, sometimes called "weaving a spell."

Arianrhod mated freely with whomever she chose and was not questioned until the magician Math claimed she had conceived two children she had not borne. By jumping a staff she gave birth to Llew and Dylan. Dylan left immediately to go to the sea. Arianrhod denied the remaining son, Llew, the right to a name or arms, as was a Welsh mother's right to bestow. She was later tricked into bestowing both.

She married her brother Gwyddion, and she is the daughter of the great Welsh mother Goddess, Don.

IN MAGICK AND RITUAL — Arianrhod can be invoked to help females find their own feminine power. She can also assist you with spirit contact, sex and fertility magick, and past-life knowledge. Because her myths are linked with jumping the broom, an event which is part of Pagan marriage, she can be called upon to bless Handfasting rites.

CORRESPONDENCES — Wheels, silver, wheat, full moon, blood, geode stones, moonstones.

ARNAMENTIA (ANGLO-CELTIC)

A Goddess of spring waters who was probably once a minor solar deity, or a Goddess of healing and purification.

ARTIO (CONTINENTAL)

IN MYTH — This bear Goddess was the consort of Essus. A shrine to her once stood in what is now Berne, Switzerland. Like Eostre, she probably was originally a Teutonic deity.

She is depicted as being surrounded by full baskets and animals, therefore it can be surmised that she was a fertility and harvest Goddess, and a Goddess of wildlife.

IN MAGICK AND RITUAL — Call upon Artio for fertility spells, animal magick, and personal strength and courage. Align with her if the bear is one of your personal totem animals or familiars. The word "art" in her name means bear, a sacred totem animal of the Celts associated with strength and courage.

CORRESPONDENCES — The bear, particularly the claws and teeth, geode stones, the Strength Tarot card.

> *Peace mounts to the heavens,*
> *The heavens descend to earth,*
> *Earth lies under the heavens,*
> *Everyone is strong....*

—Badb's victory song from *The Book of Fermoy*

BADB (IRISH)

IN MYTH — [Bayv, Bibe, Bive, or Beev] Badb, also spelled Badhbh and Badb Catha, is a crone aspect of the Triple Goddess who is often called "The Fury." Her Gaulish names are Cauth Bodva and Catubodua.

Her archetype as a war Goddess is particularly strong, and she is a part of the dreaded Morrigan, a triplicity of crone Goddesses associated with death, destruction, and battle. She is often linked with the death portent faery, the Beansidhe (usually written in English as "Banshee"), who was seen washing the armor of soldiers who would perish in the upcoming battle. Badb usually appeared over the fury of the battle as a hooded crow, but sometimes ran wild among the fighting in the guise of a wolf. In her own battle, she is one of the deities who drove the Formorians (sometimes called the Formors or the Formorii) out of Ireland forever.

A daughter of Ernmas, she is called the "one who boils," as in boiling the Otherworld cauldron of death and rebirth which she is thought by many to preside over, deciding the fate of those who have passed over into its great cosmic mix. In Celtic eschatology (end of world beliefs), it is Badb who will cause the end of earthly time by causing the great cauldron to boil over, engulfing the planet in a great wasteland.

Badb prophesied the downfall of the deities (the Tuatha) to the humans (the Milesians), and many believe she also prophesied the Great Famine of 1845–1849.

IN MAGICK AND RITUAL — Call on Badb at Samhain to aid you with spirit contact and to learn about past-lives. Through divination she can tell you your time of death if you really wish to know.

CORRESPONDENCES — The carrion crow, the staff, the scythe, garnets, bloodstone, Samhain, the Tower Tarot card, apples.

BAN-CHUIDEACHAIDH MOIRE (IRISH)

IN MYTH — [Ban C'HOO-dayk-haw MOY-ruh] This old Goddess appears in modern Irish legends as the midwife who assisted the Christian Virgin Mary with her birth, and was also a title applied to St. Bridget (a thinly veiled disguise of the Goddess Brid). This deity is accepted now as a once forgotten Goddess of childbirth.

IN MAGICK AND RITUAL — Call upon her to aid in childbirth.

BANBHA (IRISH)

IN MYTH — [BAHN-na or BAHN-vah] A warrior Goddess who protected Ireland from invaders, and one in a triplicity with Eire and Fodhla. Of the three she is the earth aspect whose name means "a land unplowed for a year."

Banbha was a gifted magician and, as such, went out to meet the Milesian invaders when they first came to Ireland. Her mission was to keep them from taking over, but she

BANBHA (CONT.)

was unable to show any feat of power with which to impress them, and they ignored her pleas to name the conquered island for her.

Their extant story is a later addition to the myth cycle when the God Dagda was seen as having birthed the Triple Goddess rather than the other way around. According to one oral legend she is the first woman to have discovered Ireland after the primordial flood.

IN MAGICK AND RITUAL — Banbha can enhance qualities of leadership, teach us to keep memories alive, and bless earth magick. As a magician she can aid in all spellwork.

CORRESPONDENCES — Olivine.

BASILEA (CONTINENTAL)

An ancient Celtic queen who is credited with "civilizing" her subjects.

BEAN NAOMHA (IRISH)

IN MYTH — [Ban NO-vah] In County Cork there lies the Well of the Sun, called *Tobar Ki-na-Greina*. In it swims Bean Naomha in the form of a trout, a symbol of great knowledge. As such, she is the Goddess of supreme wisdom, but answers from her do not come easy. One must follow an elaborate ritual of crawling deosil (sunwise or clockwise) around the well three times, taking a drink with each pass, and each time laying a stone the size of a dove's eye on the rim of the well. Then one must form a question in the mind and glance into the well for the answer.

The Salmon of Knowledge, always perceived as male, once may have been her consort.

IN MAGICK AND RITUAL — Bean Naomha could possibly be helpful in divination, but if the ritual given above is any indication, she is a difficult Goddess from whom to obtain aid.

CORRESPONDENCES — Fresh water fish.

BEBHIONN (IRISH, WELSH)

See Vivionn.

BEBO (IRISH)

IN MYTH — A faery woman whose affair with a king of Ulster made the region prosper.

IN MAGICK AND RITUAL — Though Bebo is not a well-known mythic figure, her archetype as the bringer of abundance is a very strong one. Ask her aid in prosperity or fertility rites, invoke her for sex magick rituals, use her to bless animal, crop, or human reproduction. Honor her at the harvest Sabbats.

CORRESPONDENCES — Blood, geode stones.

BECHOIL (IRISH)

This Goddess, whose legends have all been lost, may have been a very early version of Dana.

BECUMA (IRISH)

IN MYTH — This Tuatha De Danann deity was the Goddess of magickal boats who had a weakness for sleeping with High Kings at Tara. At that time in history most kings ruled by permission of their consorts and thus the act of her sleeping with them gave these human men permission to rule over the divine Tuatha. Among her own people, Becuma was an outcast for her behavior, and eventually, the Milesians took over Ireland, supplanting the Tuatha altogether.

She also had a torrid romance with Gaiar, a son of Manann. For this Manann banished her to the human world where she married Conn of the Hundred Battles. She was fiercely jealous of his pride in his son, Art, and sought to banish him from Conn's kingdom, but when she saw her plans fail, she left. She now lives in the Land of Promise, one of the names for the Otherworld.

IN MAGICK AND RITUAL — Let Becuma teach you lessons about unnecessary jealousy, and use her energies as you would any Goddess of sovereignty.

Becuna Cneisgel (Irish)

IN MYTH — [NAYSH-gel] A faery mistress of King Art whose need to avenge herself on her husband's people inspired her to bring mass infertility to Ireland. She plays the archetypal role of the crone who must be replaced with the maiden in order that prosperity might again come to the land. (Compare her to the sacrificial Gods.)

IN MAGICK AND RITUAL — Evoke Becuna's presence at Samhain when her power as crone is strongest.

Belisama (Anglo-Celtic)

Also Belisma, the Goddess of the Mersey River.

Bellah Postil (Breton)

IN MYTH — This young magician gave her fiance, Houran, two of her three magickal objects, which would warn him if he was in danger as he went off to seek riches before their wedding. She only kept for herself a magickal staff which could instantly take her anywhere she wished to go.

While traveling, Houran ran afoul of an evil old woman known as the Groac'h (a corruption of an old Brezonek name for the crone Goddess) who took joy in imprisoning men in various creative ways. She decided to change Houran into a frog.

Knowing the danger, Bellah traveled to him on her staff and killed the old woman, claiming her treasure for herself. She then restored all the imprisoned men to their original forms and returned them to their homes.

Bellah and the old woman can archetypally be seen as being one and the same, the young Goddess replacing the aging crone in her guise as the devourer.

IN MAGICK AND RITUAL — Bellah can aid you in love magick and astral projection, the latter being a synonym for her traveling by staff. Invoking her is the best way to enlist her help for astral travel.

Bellona (Scottish)

This battlefield Goddess is mentioned in the second scene of Shakespeare's *MacBeth*. Her name is probably a Latinized or corrupted form of Ireland's Badb, a Goddess with similar properties.

Berecyntia (Continental)

IN MYTH — Primarily an earth Goddess, and possibly a Gaulish version of Brid.

IN MAGICK AND RITUAL — Elemental earth magick, fertility.

BIDDY EARLY (IRISH)

IN MYTH — Biddy is sometimes called the "White Witch of Clare." She was an old wise woman who lived near the mountains of Echtaghe in the nineteenth century. She has several early forms which link her to the crone Goddess. This latter is the best known Biddy who, though a contemporary figure, has ancient archetypal roots.

Biddy was in possession of a blue bottle which contained powerful magick. Before she died she tossed it into a lake near the hills where it still rests, waiting to be reclaimed.

IN MAGICK AND RITUAL — Biddy's bottle archetypally represents the loss of feminine power and the suppression of the magickal life in general. She can be a great aid in all forms of magick. Invoke her when you study Pagan subjects, or when attempting to reclaim lost Pagan arts and legends.

CORRESPONDENCES — Blue glass, the chalice, the cauldron.

BIDDY MAMIONN (IRISH)

IN MYTH — A midwife of Innishsark who had a gift for healing. The faeries once took her to heal a sick child for them, and she was on friendly terms with them ever after, and they shared lots of healing lore.

IN MAGICK AND RITUAL — Healing, aid in childbirth.

CORRESPONDENCES — Knives, bloodstones.

BIROG (IRISH)

[BEE-roge] This powerful Druidess aided Cian in a campaign of vengeance against Balor.

BIRREN (IRISH)

Mother of Cessair, wife of Bith.

BLAI (IRISH)

IN MYTH — [Blaw or Blee] Ossian's Tuatha mother. She probably represents a personal or mascot deity for him, as his earthly mother was Saba. (Compare this to the relationship of Cuchulain and Lugh.)

Today she is known as a faery queen with a burgh of her own in Drumberg.

IN MAGICK AND RITUAL — Aid in faery contact.

BLANCHEFLOUR (CORNISH, BRETON)

The mother of Tristan and sister of King Mark the Good.

BLATHNAT (IRISH)

IN MYTH — Also Blanid. A daughter of Midhir who helped Cuchulain steal her father's magick cauldron. Her name means "little flower" and she is probably a form of the better-known Welsh Goddess, Blodeuwedd.

She traveled the island with three cows tied to her cauldron, and demanded that warriors perform feats of superhuman proportions for her amusement. She was captured in battle by the Red Branch warriors where she, like so many before her, fell in love with Cuchulain.

When the spoils of the latest raid were divided Cuchulain forgot to include Cu Roi MacDaire in the cut, so he stole Blathnat away and forced her to marry him. She feigned love for him and was able to bind him until the Red Branch returned to their fortress to avenge themselves. But one of Cu Roi's servants grabbed her and jumped off a cliff with her to their deaths.

IN MAGICK AND RITUAL — The triplicity of the three cows, images of abundance, linked to the cauldron, clearly tie Blathnat to the energies of fertility.

CORRESPONDENCES — Roses.

> *The moping owl does to the moon complain....*
>
> —Thomas Gray

BLODEUWEDD (WELSH)

IN MYTH — [BLODE-uh-oo'th] Blodeuwedd, whose name means "flower face," was created from the flowers of oak, broom, and meadowsweet by Gwyddion and Math as a wife for Gwyddion's nephew Llew. This arose because Llew had been cursed by his mother, Arianrhod, that he would never win a bride of his own people.

While Llew was away one day Blodeuwedd saw Gronw hunting in the woods and the two fell madly in love at first sight. She and Gronw made plans to kill Llew, but because he was no mere mortal, Gronw asked his lover to discover for him the secret of his death. Blodeuwedd coaxed the information out of Llew, and not only passed the information along to Gronw, but tricked Llew into being at the right place at the right time. At the moment of his death, Llew turned into an eagle and flew away.

Gwyddion sought out Blodeuwedd to seek revenge, and for her punishment decided he would turn her into a bird, one which only lived by night, a carnivore whom other birds shunned and feared. Thus she became an owl.

She can be viewed as a May Queen, bound in sacred marriage to the sacrificial king who must eventually be sacrificed to her and through her, to his people.

IN MAGICK AND RITUAL — Blodeuwedd can teach us that we must always be responsible for our actions and that that which we seek will cost us. Perhaps she learned this lesson as we now view the owl as a wise old bird.

CORRESPONDENCES — Owl, hawthorn, Death Tarot card, emeralds, blood.

BO DHU (IRISH)

See also Bo Find.

The black cow Goddess who helped bring fertility to barren Ireland.

BO FIND (IRISH)

IN MYTH — The name of this very old Goddess literally means "white cow," and this is how she appeared long ago on the barren and fruitless mass that would become green and verdant Ireland. She came from the western sea with her sisters, the red cow Goddess, Bo Ruadh, and the black cow Goddess, Bo Dhu. These colors are those of the Celtic Triple Goddess, whom they represent.

The black cow went to the south of Ireland, the red to the north, and Bo Find to the center. When Bo Find arrived at the site that some say is actually near present-day Tara, she gave birth to twin calves, a male and female who would feed her people forever. Then she retreated with her sisters back to the sea.

A Celtic-style drawing of a winged cow, after the original in The Book of Kells.

BO FIND (CONT.)
The sacred well *Tabor-Bo-Find* is named for her.

IN MAGICK AND RITUAL — Call on her to ward off hunger, or to bring prosperity and fertility, especially if you breed or raise animals. Honor her at Mabon.

BO RUADH (IRISH)
(See also Bo Find.) The red cow Goddess who helped bring fertility to barren Ireland.

BOADICEA OF THE INCENI (ANGLO-CELTIC)
IN MYTH — Also Boudicca. She was a famous, red-haired, warrioress queen of the first century Celts who led a rebellion against what she felt were injustices in the Roman government in Southern England. Her name means "victorious."

Her patron Goddess was Andraste, a war Goddess she evoked on the eve of battle whose name means "the invincible one." Boudicca offered her sacrifices, usually captured enemies, in a sacred grove before fighting the Romans on her many campaigns against them.

Her totem animal was the hare which she would release from her cloak to alert her followers to rebellion. Later, in her own rebellion against the English crown, the ill-fated Mary Queen of Scots similarly chose the hare to symbolize herself.

IN MAGICK AND RITUAL — Ask her aid in overcoming enemies, for help in choosing your own totem animals, or align with her to aid you in your own rebellions.

CORRESPONDENCES — Shields and armor, hares.

BOANN (IRISH, CONTINENTAL)

IN MYTH — Also spelled Boanne. Bouvinda was her Gaulish name. She is the water Goddess for whom the River Boyne is named. In later myths she was relegated to the sea where she was queen of the ancient Formorian invaders, a race later driven into the sea by the Tuatha De Danann where they became sea monsters.

She was a virgin Goddess in the old sense of the word, meaning a woman whole and complete unto herself. She was the mother of Aengus MacOg. The mating with the Dagda which resulted in his birth took place on November 1, the day after Samhain.

The source of the Boyne River is a pool where the Salmon of Knowledge resides, fed on nuts from the grove of the nine hazel trees which guard its source. Boann got her "position" by approaching the grove into which even deities were forbidden to go. There at the Well of Segais she was drowned when she ate the nuts.

Boann's is another universal theme in mythology, the idea of the "tree of knowledge" or "tree of life" of which no one is allowed to partake. The concept of knowledge being a special attainment, a guarded gift from the deities, is a very potent archetype.

It is said she sleeps until her people need her again and call upon her aid.

She is also a fertility deity.

IN MAGICK AND RITUAL — Ask Boann's aid in fertility rituals, water magick, and she also can teach us when it is worth it to take chances.

CORRESPONDENCES — Hazel nuts, blood.

BODUA (CONTINENTAL)

A war Goddess similar to the Irish Badb.

BRANWYN (WELSH, MANX)

IN MYTH — Also Branwen. A daughter of Manann and Iweridd whose name means "fair bosom." She is often equated with the Greek Aphrodite and is a Goddess of love, sexuality, and of the sea.

She was married to Mathowch, a king of Ireland who fought a battle with Bran after a wedding feast insult. Her son Gwern was put in his place but immediately killed.

She died of a broken heart during the war between Wales and England, which began with an insult at her wedding feast, was her fault. It had, in fact, been the deliberate act of Evnissyen, a jealous courtier who thrived on malicious mischief.

IN MAGICK AND RITUAL — Ask Branwyn's help with water magick, love spells, and sex magick.

BRENGWAIN (IRISH, CORNISH)

The Lady in Waiting who accompanied Isolde to the Court of King Mark and accidentally gave the love potion intended for the king to Tristan, causing the two young people to fall madly in love.

BRI (IRISH)

IN MYTH — A queen of the Tuatha De Danann, today considered a burgh-dwelling faery queen.

IN MAGICK AND RITUAL — Aid in making faery contact.

A straw-woven Brid's Cross.

BRIANT (ANGLO-CELTIC)
Goddess of the river which bears her name.

BRID (IRISH, SCOTTISH)
IN MYTH — [Breed] Also Bridget, Brigit, Bride, and Brighid. Her name comes from the old Irish *brigh*, meaning "power." Her Gaulish name is Brigindo, and she is probably the source of the Anglo Goddesses Brigantia and Brittania.

She was the great mother Goddess of Ireland. At one time in history most of Ireland was united in praise and worship of her. She probably was one and the same with Dana, the first great mother Goddess of the Irish.

Brid represents the supernal mother, fertility, and creative inspiration. She has also been worshiped as a warrioress and protectress, a healer, a guardian of children, a slayer of serpents, a sovereign, and a Goddess of fire and the sun. Still other sources say she was the Goddess of agriculture, animal husbandry, medicine, crafting and music.

She was credited with inventing the Irish mourning wail called *caoine* (keening) when she mourned for her son Ruadan, her child by her husband Bres, who was killed in battle. Part of her essence is still said to reside in the Beansidhe, the faery spirit whose keening can be heard at night before a death.

In the fifth century her shrine at Kildare was desecrated and adopted as a holy site by Christian missionaries who turned her into their Saint Bridget. They latched onto her sky Goddess aspect and nicknamed her the Queen of Heaven. They took her Sabbat, Imbolg, and created their own feast days for her, *La Fheile Brid* in Ireland, and *Laa'l Breeshey* in Man. She was adopted by the Romans as their Minerva, and also was worshipped in the western Scottish Highlands as a Goddess of childbirth.

IN MAGICK AND RITUAL — Brid can aid you in virtually any endeavor you wish to undertake. Call on her for assistance in fire magick, crafting, inspiration, animal magick, fertility, healing, and childbirth. Honor her at Imbolg.

CORRESPONDENCES — Fire, blackberries, Empress Tarot card, wells, milk, shields, lambs, and the heart (an ancient symbol of feminine power).

BRIGANTIA (ANGLO-CELTIC)

IN MYTH — The Goddess whose face and sovereignty are the source of the appellation Brittania for Great Britain. As a Goddess of sovereignty, she is usually thought of as the Brid of England.

In 1667 Charles I had her face placed on the coinage where it remains today, reviving an old custom, first instituted by the invading Romans who adopted her as their own.

IN MAGICK AND RITUAL — Call on her to learn to be strong as sovereign, to take control of your own being, and to serve and inspire those who look up to you. Also to protect your land, and for prosperity.

CORRESPONDENCES — The lioness, from whom the British symbol is taken, and also Strength Tarot card.

BRIGINDO (CONTINENTAL)

See Brid.

BRITANNIA (ANGLO-CELTIC)

See Brigantia.

BRONACH (IRISH)

IN MYTH — A crone Goddess linked to forgotten Samhain rituals.

IN MAGICK AND RITUAL — Reclaim this Samhain Goddess at your own seasonal rites.

CAER IBORMEITH (IRISH)

IN MYTH — [Kyair] Caer's name means "yew berry castle," and she is usually called a Goddess of sleep and dreams, perhaps a less violent version of Mare. She was the daughter of Ethal Anubail, a faery king from Connacht.

She often took the form of a swan who lived on a lake called Dragon's Mouth, and wore a copious golden chain with one hundred and thirty golden balls on a silver chain about her slender neck. She was loved by Aengus MacOg, the God of young love. When he awakened from a dream of her he sought her out. After he found her, he too became a swan, and the two of them sang the sweetest, most restful music ever heard upon this earth. Together they flew away to *Bruigh na Boinne,* his megalithic site north of Tara, where they sang so wonderfully that the whole of Ireland fell into a peaceful sleep for three days and three nights.

IN MAGICK AND RITUAL — Call on Caer to aid you in dream work, prophetic dreaming, aid in falling asleep, and music magick.

CORRESPONDENCES — The horse, the moon.

CAILLEACH, THE (SCOTTISH, IRISH, MANX)

IN MYTH — [COY-luck or CALL-y'ach] The word means "old woman" or "hag" and is used as a generic Gaelic name for the crone Goddess. She is called Carlin in Lowlands, Hag of the Beare in the Highlands, Cally Berry in northern Ireland, Black Annis in England, and Cailleach ny Groamch on Man. Other appellations are Cailleach Bolus, Cailleach Bheur, Digi No Duineach, Digne, Cailleach Bui, and Cailleach Corca Duibhne. Her name also appears in Scottish and Welsh Triads (wisdom written in triunes which appear in this volume). Even in the faery stories about her we see her as the Triple Goddess, as the hag who dies of old age and is reborn over and over again into the body of a young woman. *The Book of Lecan* emphasizes the cyclic nature of her being by telling us that she had seven youthful periods with seven different mates. She was also thought to have control of the seasons and the weather.

In patriarchal times the Cailleach's image has been distorted to one which resembles the traditional Halloween witch. She is now depicted as having a black and blue face, one large eye in the middle of her head, green teeth, tangled white hair, and a pronounced dowager's hump. This once potent Goddess has also been stripped of her mighty powers, and in folklore often appears as an evil faery who brings death and winter.

IN MAGICK AND RITUAL — Call on this Samhain Goddess for seasonal rites, wisdom, and weather magick. Do not fear working with her. Some say it is best to leave alone this dark aspect of divinity, but be assured there is nothing to fear. We must learn to love her and work with her as much as with the virgin or mother aspects in order to be whole. Treat her with the respect her age and wisdom have earned.

CORRESPONDENCES — The raven, the staff, the crow, the waning moon, winter, turnips, dried foliage, apples.

CAIREEN (IRISH)

IN MYTH — A champion and defender of youth, probably once a protective mother Goddess, a patron of children.

IN MAGICK AND RITUAL — Evoke her presence to assist in protective spells for children.

CORRESPONDENCES — Holly leaves.

CALLY BERRY (IRISH)

Also see Cailleach.

IN MYTH — Cally Berry is often equated with the Cailleach Bheur of Scotland, and yet, in northern Irish legends she also appears as a maiden Goddess, a divinity of spring, the hunt, and as a guardian of animals. Contemporary mythologist Katherine Briggs hypothesizes that she might possibly be a derivative of Artemis/Diana, and that the crone images were grafted onto her at a later date when the churchmen were attempting to purge her image.

In her faery form she could take the form of a crane to fly high and predict storms.

She is credited with being the builder of the Irish mountains, traditionally seen as the crone's earthly home.

IN MAGICK AND RITUAL — Call on Cally Berry for magick for animals or for eco-magick.

CAMPESTRES (CONTINENTAL)

This was the Roman name of a lost Goddess of fields and was probably a fertility or harvest deity in Celtic Gaul.

CANOLA (IRISH)

IN MYTH — Thought to be one of the oldest of the Irish deities, Canola was the inventor of Ireland's long cherished symbol, the harp. Legend says that she fell asleep outdoors one day while listening to beautiful ephemeral music. Upon waking she realized the music was being made by the wind beating upon the sinews of a gutted whale, and she was inspired to craft the instrument to recreate the splendorous sound.

IN MAGICK AND RITUAL — Canola can aid us with music magick and dream work, and in gaining and giving creative inspiration.

CAOLAINN (IRISH)

IN MYTH — [KAY-lawn] A local deity who was the guardian/queen of a magickal well in County Roscommon in western Ireland. She was known for helping to grant wishes, usually ones which taught the wishers that they didn't really want what they thought they did. For example, one folktale tells us that a young man passing by admired her eyes and wished for them for his own beloved. Immediately she plucked them out and, with warm blood dripping, threw them at him.

Her myth is the origin of the popular wishing well, an image taken from the birth canal of the great mother earth from which all existence is born.

IN MAGICK AND RITUAL — Caolainn serves as a magickal reminder—be careful what you wish for or you just might get it. The story also goes on to tell us that she was able to regenerate new eyes, therefore she might also have some connection to healing powers. She is also a mother and fertility Goddess.

CORRESPONDENCES — The wishing well, falling stars.

CARLIN (SCOTTISH)

See Cailleach.

CARMAN (IRISH)

Also see the Morrigan.

IN MYTH — A County Wexford Goddess and source of name for Loch Garman, who was once honored at Lughnasadh. Some scholars believe she has roots in the Greek grain Goddess Demeter.

Modern Irish legend portrays her as a Goddess of evil magick, one who can destroy anything by thrice chanting a spell. This is also the manner in which the Morrigan, particularly Badb, can destroy. But this is not a manifestation of evil intent, but an end of the world prophecy common to many cultures.

IN MAGICK AND RITUAL — Invite Carman to share in your harvest rites and to aid you in magick for decrease.

CORRESPONDENCES — Grains.

CARRAVOGUE (IRISH, BRETON)

IN MYTH — Also Garbhog and Gheareagain. A local crone Goddess from County Meath who was turned into a huge snake for eating forbidden berries. Her original purpose as a Goddess is lost to us because her stories became absorbed by Christian legends which attempt to make her a Celtic Eve. They tell us that St. Patrick killed her with holy water

CARRAVOGUE (CONT.)

which melted her, but (you can't keep a good Goddess down) from which she will rise again. As persistent as the Eve/Carravogue image is to the modern mind, hers is a story about the acceptance of self-responsibility, not one of punishment.

Feminist researcher Patricia Monaghan believes St. Patrick may have been the one who tampered with this legend, one of many about a virgin Goddess of spring who banished each year the crone she would eventually become, in order to further his own aims.

Carravogue was also worshipped in Brittany.

IN MAGICK AND RITUAL — Call on Carravogue for seasonal rites and to help teach you self-responsibility. Keep in mind the snake image of her which links her to reincarnation and earth Goddesses.

CORRESPONDENCES — The number nine.

CARTIMANDUA (ANGLO-CELTIC)

IN MYTH — A British warrior queen of the Brigantes who fought against the Roman invaders, and she is possibly a heroine whose stories were confused with those of Brigantia or Boadicea.

Her name means "silken pony," and the horse Goddess Epona may have been her patron deity or another legend which merged with her own.

IN MAGICK AND RITUAL — Feminine power, overcoming enemies, serving country. The horse image links her to the realm of night and dream magick.

CATHUBODIA (BRETON)

IN MYTH — Sometimes seen as a Breton version of the Irish earth Goddess Banbha, most likely with origins in Gaul. Also thought to be a war Goddess who shares Badb's energies.

IN MAGICK AND RITUAL — Experiment with the two diverse forces attributed to Cathbodia to try to reclaim her original power.

CAUTH BODVA (CONTINENTAL)

This name means "war's fury," and she is believed to be another name for Badb, an aspect of the Morrigan.

CEBHA OF THE WHITE SKIN (IRISH)

IN MYTH — Also spelled as it is pronounced, Keva. The delicate daughter of Fionn MacCumhal who was given in marriage to Goll MacMorna for his daring rescue of several of the Fianna warriors. Since Goll became a Fianna leader after this, Cebha functions archetypally in this story as a Goddess of sovereignty.

IN MAGICK AND RITUAL — Seasonal rites.

CEBHFHIONN (IRISH)

IN MYTH — [CAVE-f'ohn] Her name means "of the white" or "of light." She was a Goddess of inspiration who was often found next to the legendary Well of Knowledge, from which she filled an endless vessel. She kept this magickal water from humans, feeling they could not handle its power. Merely to taste of the waters meant to instantly possess great knowledge, wisdom, and divine inspiration.

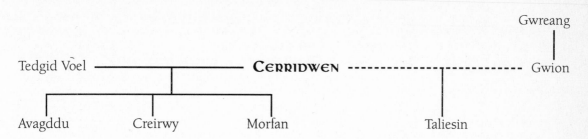

The generally accepted family tree of Cerridwen.

The well here functions archetypally like some of the famous cauldrons of Celtic myth, as a source of knowledge and regeneration.

IN MAGICK AND RITUAL — Astrally petition her for admission to the healing Well's side. She is also useful in rituals for the inspiration of self or for enhancing your mental powers.

CEITHLEEN (IRISH)
The wife of Balor, possibly another name for Dana.

CERRIDWEN (SCOTTISH, WELSH)
IN MYTH — [KARE-id-oo'in or KARE-id-win] Cerridwen is a sow Goddess, famous for her great cauldron of knowledge. She is also a moon and grain deity with many crone and mother attributes.

Her cauldron's name was *Amen,* in which her potion of wisdom called *greal* was made, the origin of the Halloween image of the cauldron-stirring witch and witch's brew. To make her potion of knowledge, the brew had to simmer for a year and a day. This is a common passage of time in Celtic lore, and the source of the traditional study period before formal initiation. Her servant, Gwion, was sent to take care of it, but splashed some on his fingers. Without thinking, he licked his fingers and ingested three drops of the potion. Instantly he gained all knowledge, including that of being able to see into the future and past, and knew he had to flee.

Cerridwen discovered this and pursued him through many forms until, when Gwion became a speck of grain, she became a chicken and consumed him. The grain took root and she gave birth to him as the great bard Taliesin.

Some Pagans believe this mystic chase relates to various levels of Druidic initiation rites, and it parallels the teaching of Merlin to the young King Arthur as he is allowed to inhabit various animal bodies in order to gain knowledge.

Cerridwen lived on an island in Lake Tegid (named for her husband) with her children.

She is often equated with the famous Greek crone, Hecate, and to the Irish Badb. She is also sometimes related to the Greek Muses, only in a more violent and dark form.

IN MAGICK AND RITUAL — Cerridwen is at home during harvest rites, in all spells for wisdom and knowledge, and at waning moon festivals. She can also help teach us about past lives and aid in divination.

CORRESPONDENCES — Pigs, cauldrons, vervain, the dark moon, hens.

CESSAIR (IRISH)

IN MYTH — [KAY-Sawr] Also Cesara, Sesara, and Kesair. A member of the race known as the Partholans who were among the first to occupy Ireland, she is considered to be the first ruler of Ireland. She was probably once a well-known pre-Celtic mother Goddess figure like Dana. Most sources cite her as the wife of Fintaan, and the daughter of Bith and Birren.

She led an expedition of Partholans to the "western edge of the world" forty days before the great flood, among them her husband and one hundred and fifty mothers of the world. This myth shows how Pagans saw the mother Goddess as source of regeneration and life renewal.

Her "I was here first" image was so pervasive among Irish Pagans that when the Christians could not eliminate her, they made her the granddaughter of their flood savior, Noah. By their version, instead of Cessair repopulating the world when her armada of ships arrived back in Ireland, she was drowned as were her daughters. They say she cursed the Christian God as she went down.

Since the native myths say Ireland was spared the ravages of this world-wide flood, Cessair was possibly once seen as a water deity who had the power to save Ireland from flooding.

IN MAGICK AND RITUAL — Cultivate Cessair for her powers of strength, perseverance, leadership, and foresight. Honor her as a deity of new beginnings.

CORRESPONDENCES — The rising sun, the cauldron.

CETHLION (IRISH)

IN MYTH — [KET-leen] Also Cetnenn. A Goddess of the Formorians who is called "crooked teeth." She prophesied the downfall of her people to the Tuatha De Danann.

IN MAGICK AND RITUAL — Ask Cethlion to aid you in divination.

CHLAUS HAISTIC (IRISH)

An old Goddess of unknown function who came down to us as a powerful witch. Probably a crone Goddess, a Goddess of magick, or a Druidess.

CIGFA (WELSH)

See Kicva.

CLIODNA (IRISH, SCOTTISH)

IN MYTH — [KLEE-nah] Also spelled Cleena and Cliodhna, and Cliodna of the Fair Hair. A Tuatha sea and Otherworld Goddess who often took the form of a sea bird and, as such, symbolized the Celtic afterlife. As the ruler of the waves, she was believed to be embodied in every ninth one which broke on the shore. This wave was believed to break higher and stronger than the others.

Many folktales exist concerning her, nearly all of them contradictory in nature. In her native Munster she was a Goddess of beauty and was viewed as a very lusty woman who often took her mortal lovers to the Otherworld. She escaped the Otherworld with her favorite mortal lover, Ciabhan of the Curling Locks, just before the Cailleach was ready to send her back. The Cailleach sent her faeries to lull the girl to sleep on an Irish beach while a giant wave washed her back to the land of the dead (some versions of the myth say

Manann had a hand in this). She has since existed in Irish mythology as a minor sea Goddess, doomed by the Cailleach never to return to Ireland in mortal form.

Today she is thought of as a faery queen in County Cork with her own resident burgh. The rocky coastal Irish landmark *Tonn Cliodhna* ("The Wave of Cleena") is named for her.

She is attributed to be the daughter of the handsome Druid Gebann, and is also a Goddess of beauty in her own right.

IN MAGICK AND RITUAL — Ask Cliodna's aid in spirit contact, especially as she is said to still long for contact with the spirits though she is now bound to her beloved earth. She can teach us an appreciation for life, a direct contrast to what modern societies teach us that to live is only a bitter pill to take before we go forever to Heaven. Invoke her to enhance personal appearance or to aid you in water magick.

CLOTA (SCOTTISH)

IN MYTH — [CLOOD-uh] Popular Goddess and namesake of the River Clyde. In England she was called Clud and Cludoita, and in Wales, Clwyd. The waters in which she ruled were believed to be especially useful in controlling seizures.

IN MAGICK AND RITUAL — Water magick.

CORRESPONDENCES — Lobelia. This herb, although poisonous, was frequently distilled by old-time herbalists to control seizures. It is best to refrain from ingestion of this herb as the negative consequences far outweigh any benefits.

CLOTHRU (IRISH)

Also Clothra. Clothru is one of the three women attributed with being the mother of Lugh by the God Iuchar. She also carried on an affair with her three brothers and gave them a son who became the High King Lugaid Riab nDerg. Though she cherished her brothers, she loathed her pregnant sister, Ethne, a minor fertility Goddess, whom she drowned.

COINCHEND (PAN-CELTIC)

IN MYTH — [KOEN-chend or KON-hend] A giant semi-divine warrioress whose home was in the Otherworld. She was married to Morgan, an Otherworld king, and was the mother of Delbchaem.

IN MAGICK AND RITUAL — Spirit contact.

CONDWIRAMUR (WELSH, CORNISH)

IN MYTH — [KOND-oor-uh-moor] An archetypal guardian of the feminine mysteries and a Goddess of sovereignty who appears briefly in the Grail legends as the wife of Sir Percival. He weds her and beds her, then immediately sets off for the Grail castle to which he is finally admitted. After wedding her, Percival becomes the ruler of the Grail kingdom, acknowledging Condwiramur's sovereign role.

The idealistic son of this union, Loherangrain, is dubbed Knight of the Swan, and sets off on a quest to right all wrongs.

IN MAGICK AND RITUAL — Women can align with Condwiramur to discover their own feminine power, and males can utilize her energy to help them discover the ancient Grail mysteries.

CORRESPONDENCES — The chalice.

CORCHEN (IRISH, MANX)

IN MYTH — A very old snake Goddess about whom little is known. Because of her linkage to the serpent image, she was probably once a regional mother earth Goddess, or a Goddess of rebirth. Others speculate that her lost legends were once part of forgotten creation myths.

IN MAGICK AND RITUAL — Reclaim her image by asking her to assist you in uncovering your past-lives, or for making earth magick.

CORRA (SCOTTISH)

IN MYTH — A Goddess of prophecy who usually appeared in the form of a crane. Similar Irish Goddesses such as Aife and Cally Berry also took this form, and did so to symbolize transcendent knowledge and transitions to the Otherworld.

IN MAGICK AND RITUAL — Aid in divination.

COVENTINA (ANGLO-CELTIC, SCOTTISH)

IN MYTH — Coventina is probably Roman in origin, though she is one of the most potent of the Celtic river Goddess archetypes. Shrines to her sprang up along Hadrian's Wall into which coins, trinkets, and other offerings were made.

Whatever the original myth might have been has been long lost. It is known that she was looked upon as the queen of river Goddesses, particularly of the watershed where the Celts believed the power of the river deity could be seen and its energy most keenly felt. She was most closely associated with England's Caldew River.

Like other river deities, she represented abundance, inspiration, and prophecy. The coins offered to her appear to be sacrifices made in the hopes of sympathetic magick in which like attracts like.

In Scotland she was also the Goddess of featherless flying creatures which may have represented some type of blockage to passing into the Otherworld.

There is evidence of her having been worshipped in Celtic Gaul where reliefs have been found depicting her reclining on a floating leaf.

IN MAGICK AND RITUAL — As a Goddess of the watershed she has the energy associated with the ebb and flow of time, with new beginnings, life cycles, and making wishes. She can also be asked to aid in magick for the protection of birds, divination, and for inspiration of self.

CORRESPONDENCES — Coins, broaches, lily pad, mud.

CRED (IRISH, SCOTTISH)

IN MYTH — Also Creide. This faery queen Goddess is associated with Dana's mountains, the Paps of Anu. She promised never to sleep until she found a man who could create for her the most magnificent poem ever penned. It not only had to be perfectly crafted, but describe in vivid detail her home and all its contents. The catch was that no man was allowed within her dwelling's guarded walls (possibly a reference to one of the Otherworld realms known as The Land of Women).

Coll, one of the Fianna warriors, finally overcame these obstacles and wrote her the desired poem. She was so greatly impressed that she married him and they now make their home together in the Otherworld.

In another myth, she was given a ring by an exiled visitor named Cano. The two fell in love, and before Cano left for his home in Scotland, he told her that the ring contained his very life and that she was to guard it carefully. Cano did not return, and in her anguish, Cred accidentally dropped the ring and broke it. Cano died three days later.

IN MAGICK AND RITUAL — Cred can help us with love magick, teach us about searching for the perfect mate, keeping secrets, and she can aid us in making spirit contact from her Otherworld home.

CORRESPONDENCES — Yew, rose oil, the color pink.

CREIDDYLAD (WELSH)

IN MYTH — [KRAYTH-ee-lahd] The daughter of sea God Llyr. She is another May Queen Goddess over whom two men must fight, and one die, in order for the fertility of the land to survive. In her myths there was a famous rivalry of the Gods Gwyn and Gwyrthur over her each Samhain and Bealtaine. This is one of the origins of the Holly King and Oak King duel which is commemorated each Yule and Midsummer in most Celtic covens. (See Holly King for details.)

She defied her father's wishes to marry the man of her choice, and became the inspiration for Cordelia in Shakespeare's *King Lear.* In Geoffrey of Monmouth's stories about her, she came to live on earth after Llyr's death.

It is believed most of her original oral legends have been lost.

IN MAGICK AND RITUAL — This strong-willed woman can imbue us with the courage to stand up for ourselves and our rights and wants. Invoke her for strength of will.

CORRESPONDENCES — Hawthorn.

CREIRWY (WELSH)

IN MYTH — [KRAY'R-oo'ee] Creirwy was the daughter of Cerridwen and Tegid; the most beautiful child in the world while her brother, Avagdu, was most ugly. Her name means "dear one."

IN MAGICK AND RITUAL — Invoke her to boost your self-esteem and to aid in personal appearance.

CORRESPONDENCES — Amber.

CROBH DEARG (IRISH)

[Crove Dairg] This war Goddess' name means "the red claw." She is a sister of Latiaran, possibly a form of the crone Goddess of battle Badb. A Leinster fortress was named for her.

CYHIRAETH (WELSH)

IN MYTH — [KEER-uh-eeth] Once a Goddess of streams, she later became thought of as a faery spirit who was a portent of death, very much like Ireland's Beansidhe or Cornwall's Washer at the Ford. Both of these specters are seen or heard just prior to a nearby death.

IN MAGICK AND RITUAL — Evoke her presence for Passing Over rituals, aid in faery contact, or for water magick, especially when the goal is some type of inner-transformation.

CORRESPONDENCES — Primrose, cowslip.

CYMIDEI CYMEINFOLL (WELSH)

IN MYTH — [KEEM-uh-day KEEM-een-vol] Her name means "big belly of battle." She is a war Goddess who is always paired in stories with her husband, Llasar Llaesyfnewid. Together they own a magickal cauldron into which they would cast warriors killed in battle. From the cauldron these dead soldiers would come forth to life again, but minus their power of

CYMIDEI CYMEINFOLL (CONT.)

speech. In later myths, the cauldron became a peace offering to end a war with Ireland. This image marks her as one half of the creative principle.

As Wales' supreme war Goddess, she gave birth to its warriors, one every six weeks.

IN MAGICK AND RITUAL — Cymidei's energy can give you the strength to continue in whatever battles in which you are embroiled. She can also teach you about past-lives and help with creative magick.

CORRESPONDENCES — The cauldron.

DAHUD-AHES (BRETON)

IN MYTH — Also Dahut. Her adoring father, King Gradion (or Gradlon) of Cornwall, built for her the city of Ker-Ys ("city of depth") off the coast of Brittany in order that she might escape the persecutions of the monks who had declared her a witch for her violent opposition to their Christianization of her kingdom.

Modern legends tell that her city was swept away by a wave caused by an intervening Christian saint. Pagan stories tell how she asked a city of Korrigans, the Breton sea faeries, to disguise her sea world until it was safe again for them to emerge again in a world without religious persecution. In this way she is similar to the sleeping deities, such as King Arthur, who lie in a state of suspended animation waiting until their people call upon them again.

Dahud was dubbed a Goddess of "debauchery" by her detractors, while some more recent legends go so far as to make her the destroyer of her own realm through her excesses and her worship of "idols." Patriarchal legends say her father, recognizing her as evil, either escaped her world or drowned her.

She is hailed as a Goddess of earthly pleasure by her followers. Archetypally she can be viewed as a mother Goddess cradling the reborn infant of the Old Religion, and as a rebel against patriarchy and its new rules.

Breton fishermen claim to occasionally see her city beneath the French seas, and believe that she will indeed return someday.

IN MAGICK AND RITUAL — Dahud can teach us to have responsible pleasure without guilt. When persecution strikes, call on her for courage to maintain your Pagan lifestyle and fight for the right to practice it openly as you please. Summon her presence to aid with water magick, sex magick, or sea faery contact.

CORRESPONDENCES — Shells, primrose.

DAIREANN (IRISH)

[DAWR-ee-ahn] Also Darine. This daughter of Bov the Red fell in love with Fionn MacCumhal. He rejected her suit because he wished to wed her sister. Daireann brewed him a cup of poisoned tea which drove him insane. When the effects of the tea wore off, he had her kidnapped and reported dead so that he could wed her sister Saba.

DAMARA (ANGLO-CELTIC)

An English fertility Goddess associated with Bealtaine.

DAMONA (CONTINENTAL)

A cow Goddess about whom little is known. Cow Goddesses were linked to fertility and abundance.

Dana (Irish)

IN MYTH — [DAWN-uh, DAY-na, THAY-na, or JAWN-uh] Also written as Danu [DAWN-oo], the dative form of the name. She was the first great mother Goddess of Ireland, who was later renamed/absorbed by Brigid. Some scholars believe she is the most ancient of the Celtic deities of whom we have extant knowledge. The root "dan" in Old Irish means "knowledge," an important insight into her archetypal traits.

Today Dana's tri-form usually assigns her the name Danu, the virgin aspect of the Triple Goddess with Brigid as mother and Badb as crone. Later folktales also tell us that she is the daughter of Beltene, rather than his mother or consort.

Many Celtic Pagans still view her as the sovereign, singular, great mother who birthed all things into being.

She is equated with Don, the first mother Goddess of Wales.

IN MAGICK AND RITUAL — Dana's very powerful presence can aid you in achieving anything you desire. She is especially strong in her association to motherhood, fire, crafting, fertility, manifestation magick, the healing of children, inspiration of self, sovereignty, and other creative endeavors.

CORRESPONDENCES — Empress Tarot card, amber, blood, holey stones.

Deae Matres (Breton, Continental)

IN MYTH — [DEE-uh MOT-rays] Her name means "mother Goddesses," a triplicity of earth Goddesses given this singular Latin name on the continent. None of the legends about her survive, though there are many inscriptions and sculptures which attest to the pervasiveness of her worship. It is believed her cult was successfully decimated by the Romans when they took Gaul.

The trio are shown as robed figures bearing baskets of flowers, fruit, and grain, items which represent the bounty of three non-winter seasons.

She is sometimes equated with Habondia.

IN MAGICK AND RITUAL — Call on her to be a part of your harvest ritual and your fertility magick, or to gain prosperity.

CORRESPONDENCES — Wheat sheaves, geode stones.

Dealgnaid (Irish)

IN MYTH — Also spelled as it is roughly pronounced, Dalny. She was the wife of Partholan, the earliest invader of Ireland, and the queen of his subjects.

IN MAGICK AND RITUAL — Invoke her power for taking on effective leadership roles.

Dechtere (Irish)

IN MYTH — Also Dechtire. This Goddess exists as a triplicity unto herself. Throughout her myth she alternately takes on the images of maiden, mother, and crone.

She is one of three women in myth who is credited with being the mother of Cuchulain, an honor usually given solely to Taillte by Celtic Pagans. A stray mayfly, containing the "soul" of Lugh, fell into her wine glass. When she drank it she became impregnated with Cuchulain. However, she birthed Cuchulain by vomiting him up and, therefore, remained always a "maiden."

She is described as a woman of "large proportions," a detail which tells us that she

DECHTERE (CONT.)

shared the attributes of a mother and fertility Goddess, or possibly a deity of abundance with roots in antiquity.

She had the ability to transform herself and her entourage into birds for swift travel and, predictably, they could fly to the Otherworld and back in this form. However, wherever they stopped to feed they nearly decimated the land, and this links her to the dark side of the Goddess of abundance—that of the devourer.

IN MAGICK AND RITUAL — See the entry for Triple Goddess for suggested uses for Dechtere's energies.

CORRESPONDENCES — The shamrock, the Triple Goddess' colors: white, red, and black.

DEIRDRE OF THE SORROWS (IRISH)

IN MYTH — [DEER-druh] The tragic heroine of this folktale is one of the stories in the legends known as "Four Sorrows of Erin," and it is by far the most famous of the quartet. Several versions of the myth exist today.

Deirdre was the most beautiful woman in the world, but was cursed so that only sorrow could come from her beauty. Because others feared her, she was banished by King Conchobar to the far edge of the island. While there she began having prophetic dreams, particularly of a young man with black hair, red lips, and white skin. The man was Naoise, one of three brothers.

He and Deirdre fell in love and escaped to Scotland, but there a jealous king wanted her for himself. Before the Scottish king could take action, word reached the pair that King Conchobar would permit their return to Ireland and, having nowhere else to go, they went, though Deirdre's dreams told her only misery would result. Upon their return Conchobar had Naoise and his brothers killed. While Deirdre was being taken away, she stood in the wagon and killed herself by allowing her head to be bashed against a tree.

The story makes very clear that, at her death, her blood was spilled on the land in the manner of a sacrificial God while Naoise embodies the Triple Goddess aspects.

IN MAGICK AND RITUAL — Invoke Deirdre at bedtime to have prophetic dreams. Align with or invoke her to enhance personal appearance. Pathwork with her to overcome the ludicrous idea that that which is beautiful is always dangerous.

DELBCHAEM (IRISH)

IN MYTH — This daughter of the warrioress Coinchend and Morgan, an Otherworld king, was stolen away from her Otherworld home by Art MacConn. Her return caused the old faery woman, Becuna, who had blighted the land with infertility, to flee, and therefore return prosperity to Ireland.

Archetypally, she is a May Queen image, the young bride of the God sent to vanquish and replace her older crone aspect.

IN MAGICK AND RITUAL — Fertility magick.

CORRESPONDENCES — Blood, emeralds, hawthorn.

DEOCA, QUEEN (IRISH)

IN MYTH — Also spelled as it is pronounced, Decca. Her story is part of one of several endings to the tale of "The Sorrow of the Children of Llyr," one of the famous "Four Sorrows of Erin."

This consort of Munster's King Lairgnen was asked to have possession of the Four Children of Llyr after they had been changed into beautiful singing swans by Aife's jealous rage. When they were seized and taken to the castle, a Druid changed them back into human form, but they were transformed into humans with all their nine hundred years showing. The shocked queen and king fled Munster in terror never to return again.

IN MAGICK AND RITUAL — Without anything magickal being involved, Deoca's story reminds us of the ancient adage known to all practitioners of magick: be careful what you ask for or you might get it.

DERBFORGAILLE (IRISH)

The lover of Diarmuid. When they eloped they opened the door to the Norman invaders.

DERBFORGAILLE (IRISH)

IN MYTH — Also spelled Devorgilla and (similar to the pronunciation) Dearvorgawla. The daughter of King Lochlann who fell deeply in love with Cuchulain only by hearing of his daring exploits. With a servant, she has them transformed into two swans joined by a golden chain. When they arrived at the lake where Cuchulain and his Red Branch warriors were camped, one of them threw a stone at them which hit and turned them back into humans. When Cuchulain sucked the stone from her, he also inadvertently consumed her blood and therefore could not marry her for they were united by female blood like kinsmen. The Celts had a taboo against marrying within one's own clan which was defined for many centuries as being linked by a woman's blood.

IN MAGICK AND RITUAL — Invoke her to teach you the mysteries of spiritual kinship.

DEVONA (ANGLO-CELTIC, CORNISH)

Goddess of the rivers of Devon.

DIA GRIENE (SCOTTISH)

IN MYTH — This daughter of the sun—or possibly of a sun God—was called by the name "the sun's tear." This is probably the remnant of a myth which has been lost to us. We do know that she was held against her will in The Land of Women, a synonym for the Otherworld. She was released by the Cailleach who rules there, allowed to leave in the body of a fox because a young man, named only as Brian, wanted her in the mundane world again.

Archetypally her story serves as a metaphor for reincarnation.

IN MAGICK AND RITUAL — Dia Griene's energy can help us in uncovering past-lives.

CORRESPONDENCES — The vixen, an animal associated by many cultures with shrewd intellect; and sunstones, an orange quartz.

DIL (IRISH)

A very old cattle Goddess about whom nothing is known today. She possibly was a derivative of the nearly forgotten Damona of Gaul.

DOMNU (IRISH)

IN MYTH — A Goddess of the Formorians, who are sometimes referred to as the *Fir Domnann* ("Men of Domnu") in her honor. This race was one of the occupiers in the five-fold Invasion cycle of Irish myth. Her son was killed by Oghma in battle.

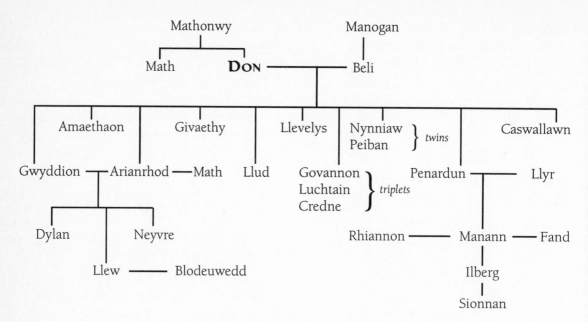

The generally accepted family tree of Don.

DOMNU (CONT.)

Her name means "the deep," making perfect sense since the Formorians were banished by the Tuatha De Danann to became grotesque sea monsters off the Irish coast.

IN MAGICK AND RITUAL — Domnu can teach leadership skills, and aid you contacting the numerous Celtic sea faeries.

CORRESPONDENCES — St. John's Wort.

DON (WELSH)

IN MYTH — Don [pronounced with a long "o"] is the Welsh form of Ireland's Dana, though it is believed by some scholars that Don has roots in the Goddess Danae of the Greeks, while Dana's origins are believed to be Peloponnesian.

With her consort, Beli, Don is the mother Goddess from whom the Britons believed themselves to be descended. Her children taught the arts to the Brythons. The *Mabinogion* lists among her famous divine offspring Arianrhod, Gwyddion, Amaethon, and Govannon.

The Donwy River is named for her.

IN MAGICK AND RITUAL — See Dana for full discussion.

CORRESPONDENCES — Empress Tarot card.

DREM (WELSH)

IN MYTH — Drem was a prophetess employed at the Welsh court who had the power to mentally view aggression against her country.

IN MAGICK AND RITUAL — Invoke Drem to aid you in divination, in conjuring prophetic dreams, or help in serving your country, clan, or other group about which you care.

CORRESPONDENCES — Mistletoe berries.

DRUANTIA (BRETON)

IN MYTH — A fir tree Goddess who probably had her origins in Gaul. The root of her name, *drus,* means "oak," and links her also with oak trees and with the Druids. Today she is associated with the Dryads, the tree faeries, and reigns as their queen. The Dryads protect their native trees by punishing those who show disrespect.

Archetypally she is an aspect of the eternal mother as seen in the evergreen boughs.

IN MAGICK AND RITUAL — Call on Druantia and her legions to aid you in eco-magick and with help in understanding the complex tree calendar of the Celts, and the magickal properties of each.

DUBH (IRISH)

[Doov] A Druidess who magickally drowned her husband Enna's lover when she discovered his infidelity. In retaliation, Enna killed her by a blow from a slingshot. She fell into a lake which was named Dubh's Pool, *Dubhlinn* in Irish, often cited as the derivative of the name of the modern capitol city of Ireland.

DUBH LACHA (IRISH)

[Doov LAH-kah] An early Irish Goddess of the sea about whom little is known. Possibly another version of the Druidess Dubh.

DWYVACH (WELSH)

IN MYTH — [DOO'ee-vahk] Also Dwyfach. With her husband Dwyvan, they built the ark called *Nefyed Nav Nevion* in which they and their animals escaped the great flood caused by the dragon king Addanc. In Welsh their names simply mean God and Goddess.

Welsh legend says that she and her husband were each part of one river which flowed into Bala Lake which was at one time called Lake Dyfrdwy, from the term *dyfr-dwyf* meaning "water of the divinity." This confluence image links them to lost creation myths. Dwyvach embodies the feminine principle of creation.

IN MAGICK AND RITUAL — Think of Dwyvach as one half of creative magick, needing her consort to complete the work. Call upon them when working as a couple in ritual or spell-work or to enhance sex magick.

EADON (IRISH)

IN MYTH — [AE-don, with a long "o"] A Goddess of poetry who may have also been a bard. Female bards were known, but most of their legends have not survived.

IN MAGICK AND RITUAL — Invoke Eadon to open your own creative channels.

EBHA RUADH NI MURCHU (IRISH)

IN MYTH — [EE-va ROO-ah Nee MUR-hoo] A fierce warrior queen who has been shoved into the back pages of history.

IN MAGICK AND RITUAL — Women who wish to merge with a genuine heroic figure and are as yet uncomfortable working with male forces might wish to align with Ebha instead.

CORRESPONDENCES — Shields.

EBHLINNE (IRISH)

IN MYTH — [EV-leen] This Goddess of Munster was, until recent times, honored at the Midsummer Sabbat in her mountain home in County Tipperary. Though all her myths have been lost but for a few minor references, she was probably once a sun or fire Goddess.

According to the *Dinnshenchas,* the Twelve Mountains of Ebhlinne were her domain. She was given in marriage to a king of Cashel, but ran away with his son.

IN MAGICK AND RITUAL — Invite Ebhlinne to actively participate in your Midsummer rituals or to assist you with fire magick.

CORRESPONDENCES — Sunstones.

ECHTGHE (IRISH)

Also Aughty. She is believed by some sources to be another form of Dana, the first great mother Goddess of Ireland. Her lover gave her the hills which bear her name to this day, the *Slaibh na Echtghe.* She was the daughter of Nuada of the Silver Hand.

> *Pale-faced, alone upon a bench, Edain*
> *Sat upright with a sword before her feet....*
> —William Butler Yeats

EDAIN (IRISH)

IN MYTH — [EE-dawn or AY-deen] Also Etain. She was the beautiful blonde queen of the Tuatha De Danann in Ulster, and a superb horsewoman for which she earned the name Edain Echraidhe (Edain the Horse-Riding). She was wooed out of the human world (or stolen, or won in a chess game, depending upon which version of her story catches your fancy) by faery King Midhir.

Midhir took her to his crystal mansion in a faeryland burgh called *Bri Leith.* The Ulster king, Eochaid, followed them, but Midhir disguised his many faeries to look like Edain so that she could not be found among them.

Aengus MacOg was finally able to rescue her by disguising her as a butterfly. In this form she fell into a tankard of ale consumed by Etar and, through her, was reborn in the human world.

A third story concerning her took place when High King Eochaid heard of her famous beauty and went to see her. When he set eyes on her he fell deeply in love and bestowed upon her a huge dowry. In this version of the tale he dug up Midhir's burgh and rescued her himself, but she did not wish to leave.

The three major stories about her have caused some students of myth to think she is three separate figures. Instead she is a triplicity who is the archetypal personification of reincarnation.

Her story was immortalized in Fiona MacLeod's drama, *The Immortal Hour.*

IN MAGICK AND RITUAL — Ask Edain to help you with past or future life explorations, invoke her to enhance personal appearance.

CORRESPONDENCES — Lilac oil, the butterfly; and the serpent, especially one with tail in mouth to symbolize the eternal cycle of reincarnation.

Stylized shamrocks from a medieval English prayer book.

EDAIN OIG (IRISH)

Edain's daughter. Some stories claim she was hidden away for her barrenness, yet she gave birth to one daughter who would be the mother of King Conaire Mor.

EIBHIR (IRISH, MANX)

[EE-ver] The first wife of Ossian who is described as a being a yellow-haired "stranger from another land." She is quite likely a forgotten sun Goddess.

EILE (IRISH)

[EL-lee] The sister of Queen Maeve of Connacht.

> *I seek her from afar.*
> *I come from temples where her altars are;*
> *From groves that bear her name—*
> —Edna St. Vincent Millay

EIRE (IRISH)

In Myth — [Air-uh] or Eriu [AIR-ee-oo]. The dative form of her name, Erinn or Erin, has been the poetic name for Ireland for centuries.

Eire has been worshipped by Irish Pagans as the Goddess/protectress of their island.

She was a daughter of the Dagda and Delbaeth, the maiden/spiritual part of a triplicity with Banbha and Foldha, and was the third of the three to be approached by the Milesian invaders. Eire's magick was so potent that she was able to toss mud balls down on her enemies whereupon they turned into hundreds of fierce warriors when they shattered. Eire won the battle, but lost the island. However, out of respect for her display of power, the Milesians agreed to name the island Eire in her honor.

She was the wife of MacGreine whose name means "son of the sun," indicating that she may once have been part of a creation myth.

IN MAGICK AND RITUAL — Call on Eire for her qualities of leadership, to aid you in keeping memories as in keeping one's name alive, and for finding creative ways to overcome enemies.

CORRESPONDENCES — The harp and shamrock, the age-old symbols of Ireland. Also the color green.

EITHNE (IRISH)

IN MYTH — Also Ethleen, Ethlinn, and Ethniu. Her name means "nutmeat." She is an old Goddess whose original form likely traveled with the Celts across the continent over many

EITHNE (CONT.)

generations from the Middle East. These legends say she lived off nothing but the milk of a sacred Indian cow and was protected by a spirit who chased away all would-be suitors.

When she fell in love with Cian, she was locked in a tower by her father who believed her sons would kill him. Here the father represents a sacrificial God not wanting to do his duty and allow the new God/king, who is only another aspect of himself, to come to power. In this version of her myth all her children were killed as infants by their grandfather.

She is sometimes thought to be one and the same as the Goddess Ethne, who is one of the several women credited with being the mother of Lugh.

Her last pregnancy ended along with her life when she was drowned by her jealous sister, Clothru.

She was also a minor fertility and moon Goddess—equated with the Welsh Arianrhod.

IN MAGICK AND RITUAL — See Arianrhod for full discussion of Eithne's attributes.

CORRESPONDENCES — Silver.

ELEN (CORNISH)

IN MYTH — She is the daughter of King Eudaf from whom all the Cornish kings claimed descent. Her children melded into the Arthurian legends, with Elen herself sometimes linked romantically to Merlin. Her charitable work on behalf of her people caused her to be merged with Christian legends in the region.

IN MAGICK AND RITUAL — Invoke her to gain her qualities of leadership and compassion.

ELPHAME, QUEEN OF (SCOTTISH)

IN MYTH — Also Elphlane and Elphane, which some claim is a corruption of the world "elfland." She is a Goddess of death and disease who is often equated with the famous Greek crone Goddess Hecate. As the crone image began to deteriorate in Europe with the coming of the Church, she became a Goddess of "the witches" and of evil. In Robert Graves' classic, *The White Goddess,* he tells of several sixteenth century Scottish witchcraft trials in which accusations of having "dealings" with the Queen of Elphame brought the death sentence.

In the past few hundred years the Queen of Elphame has been seen as a Scottish faery queen and associated with Bealtaine. Thomas the Rhymer always maintained that she appeared to him on a May Eve all dressed in diaphanous green silks and riding a white horse with fifty-nine silver bells tied in its mane (an odd association since Celtic faeries have always been thought to shun the ringing of bells).

IN MAGICK AND RITUAL — As a potent crone Goddess her energies are associated with death, destruction, plague, battle, and the Otherworld. By extension, her Bealtaine associations link her to concepts of rebirth. Respectfully harness her powerful energy as you would any crone's. Also call upon her as a May Queen and for aid in faery contact.

CORRESPONDENCES — The moon, silver, the number five, vetivert, rue, the pentagon, primrose, cowslip.

EMER (IRISH)

IN MYTH — [EE-mer] A heroic woman of great pride in all she accomplished, which was considerable. She was beautiful, intelligent, witty, and multi-talented, all traits of which she well aware. Cuchulain became fascinated with her, but before he could court her she demanded of him a string of heroic and dangerous exploits in order to prove himself worthy of her.

In a dream Cuchulain saw her burning body being tossed from his fortress of Emain Macha. He rushed there to reassure himself. He found Emer to be well, though she told him he must not go out again, for what he saw was really a prophecy of his own end. She begged him to remain at the fortress, but he left, and Emer's prediction of his demise came true.

IN MAGICK AND RITUAL — Ask Emer's help when you need a boost of self-esteem and self-pride. It really is all right to blow your own horn occasionally. She can also help you to release your own creative spirit and aid your mental prowess.

Enid (Welsh)

IN MYTH — Enid is one half of a famous romantic couple in Welsh legends, her name eternally paired with her lover Garient. They met when Garient was poised to fight Edern Ap Nudd for deliberately insulting Queen Guinevere. Guinevere, not really caring for the fight over her honor, took pity on Enid and kept her under royal protection during the battle.

Garient won his fight and married Enid, but soon came to distrust her feelings for and loyalty to him.

Also a part of the Enid/Garient tale is the legendary White Hart, an all-white deer archetypally associated with messages from the Otherworld. King Arthur kills the beast, as is his right as a member of the royal Pendragon clan, in the middle of their story which always heralds a major change of Otherworldly proportions within the lives of the people whose tale is being told.

Their tale appears both in the *Mabinogion* and in Chretien de Troyes' *Erec and Enid*.

IN MAGICK AND RITUAL — Cultivate her aid in couples work, sex magick, romantic love spells, and when issues of fidelity are involved.

CORRESPONDENCES — Rosemary, striped agates.

Eostre (Pan-Celtic)

IN MYTH — [ESS-trah or Y'OSE-tree] Eostre is an Anglo-Saxon Goddess, the one for whom the Ostara Sabbat is named. When the Saxons invaded Britain, they brought this vigorous Goddess with them and she was eventually adopted into the Celtic pantheon.

She is seen as spring personified, a Goddess of rebirth, new beginnings, and fertility. The word for animal menstruation, "estrus," meaning "fertile period," is derived from her name, and as such, she is also a Goddess of animal reproduction. The Christian holiday of Easter is also her namesake, and the concept of the Easter Bunny came from another of her legends.

IN MAGICK AND RITUAL — Call on Eostre for assistance in your Ostara rites, in the Great Rite, in fertility matters for you or for your pets and livestock. Her association with spring makes her energy compatible with blessing new ventures or for celebrating reincarnation and new life.

CORRESPONDENCES — The equilateral cross, the egg, the rabbit, baskets.

Ride a cockhorse to Banbury Cross
to see a fine lady upon a white horse,
With rings on her fingers and bells on her toes
she shall have music wherever she goes.

—Anglo-Celtic Nursery Rhyme

Epona (Pan-Celtic)

IN MYTH — [Ey-PONE-ah, AY-paw-nah or Ay-PAWN-uh] With roots in Celtic Gaul, this horse Goddess was vigorously adopted by conquering Pagan Rome whose cavalry called upon her to aid them. She is the only Celtic deity known to have actually been enshrined and worshipped in Rome where they made her a triple deity known as the Eponae.

Her Irish name is Mare [MAH-ray], and there she is the bringer of dreams both good and bad. The English word "nightmare" is derived from her Irish name. So ingrained was her horse image with night terrors that English artist Henry Fuselli incorporated her more disturbing images into the famous painting, *The Nightmare*.

She is rarely depicted as being the white horse itself, but as reclining or sitting upon it, often carrying a serpent, with a dog riding at her side, and with corn in lap. These images tell much of how she was seen. She was also a Goddess of fertility and abundance, and, because white horses are symbols of spiritual mastery, that her mounting of the beast indicated her high rank among the deities. The horse, particularly male horses, have always been seen as potent sexual symbols. Epona's sitting astride the animal links her to unlimited sexual performance.

Epona was also a Goddess able to bestow sovereignty on Celtic kings, and old rites existed marrying the kings to her. Ulster kings once had to declare their own sovereignty by mating with a horse which was killed afterwards—says thirteenth century Welsh writer Giralus Cambrensis. In other incidents the horse, as her totem animal, was used as a mate by a God in order to gain rulership from the sovereign Goddess.

Jean Markale, author of the superb work on Celtic Goddesses, *The Women of the Celts*, believes she may have been the first mother Goddess of Celts, even predating Dana.

The ancient hill-cut drawing of a horse at Uffington, England, is thought to be an ancient shrine to her, as is a chalk cutting at Cambridge depicting a woman with four breasts.

An interesting folk custom survived in western Ireland until the early twentieth century. Legend said that if you sat in a perfectly oriented crossroads just before dawn, lit fires at the four quarters leaving room for a rider to pass between, rode three times around the intersection on a besom, then sat to wait, one would see a dark woman in black upon a white horse fleeing west at the approaching rays of the morning light. This is probably a survival of the Epona legends in her guise as the bringer of nightmares in the realm of night.

In Scotland she is referred to as Bubona, and in England Lady Godiva is thought to be another version. Carvings of Epona also appear in Germany, and the Anglo-Saxons may also have adopted her in the form of their horse Goddess, Horsa. Other horse-associated Goddesses such as Macha, Edain, Rhiannon, and Maeve may have grown out of her myths.

The pervasiveness of Epona worship has been cited as a possible reason for the British reluctance to eat horse meat, a revulsion which was passed on to the cultures of her colonies.

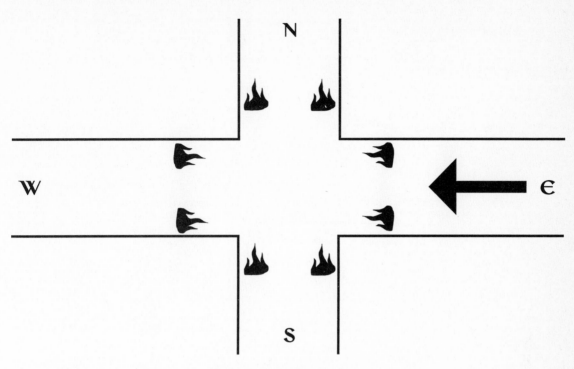

Epona's pre-dawn ride.

IN MAGICK AND RITUAL — Call on Epona for dream work, fertility, war, use her to help banish nightmares in children. As a self-triplicity she can teach women the needed lesson of being whole and complete within themselves, and to be sovereign. Men can "mate" with her to help attain similar strengths. She is also compatible with sex magick and divination.

CORRESPONDENCES — Horses, azurite, purslane, vervain, oats, valerian, and the colors white and black.

Erce (Anglo-Celtic)

IN MYTH — [AIR-chay] An earth mother and harvest Goddess symbolized by a womb or by an over-flowing Horn of Plenty who is believed to be Basque in origin.

IN MAGICK AND RITUAL — Ask Erce to your harvest festivals, and allow her to lend her aid to earth magick.

CORRESPONDENCES — The cornucopia.

Eri of the Golden Hair (Irish)

IN MYTH — Eri was a virgin Goddess of the Tuatha De Danann. One day she was at the bank of a river when a man in a silver boat floated down to her on a beaming ray of the sun. Eri was so overcome with emotion at the sight that the two of them fell into the boat and made love. The man, probably an unnamed sun God, left Eri pregnant with Bres. He also left her a golden ring (a sun symbol) to remember him by.

IN MAGICK AND RITUAL — Utilize Eri's energy as the feminine principle of creation. As the mate of the sun she can be linked to moon mother images.

ERIU (IRISH)
See Eire.

ERNMAS (IRISH)
IN MYTH — [AIRN-maas] The granddaughter of Nuada of the Silver Hand who was the mother of several Triple Goddesses depending upon which story one reads. Her name means either "murderer" or "she-farmer," again depending on which version of Old Irish etymology one embraces. Her reputed children were Anu, Badb, and Macha, The Morrigan or Banbha, Eriu, and Fodhla, all fathered by Delbaeth. She was also the mother of Fiacha, her only son.

IN MAGICK AND RITUAL — "She-farmer" relates her to fertility rites, and the "murderer" to the dark mother. Use her energy for fertility and earth magick spells.

CORRESPONDENCES — Virgin earth, blood.

ESS EUCHEN (IRISH)
IN MYTH — This powerful woman had three sons who were all killed by Cuchulain. She listened to the worst gossip about their death experience and allowed herself to believe she was justified in seeking vengeance. Turning herself into a crone, a symbol of power and retribution, she waited for Cuchulain on a lonely, narrow mountain path. When he approached, she stepped in front of him and demanded that he step aside and let her pass.

Cuchulain stepped to the very edge of the dangerous path where Ess Euchen intended to push him to his death. But using one of his teacher's, Scathach's, magickal leaps, he jumped up and killed her instead.

IN MAGICK AND RITUAL — Align with her to understand the need for and pitfalls of vengeance. Flying off the handle and seeking to do someone else bodily harm may have been an idea prized by Celtic warriors, but it is hardly sound practice for modern Pagans who—hopefully—have evolved into beings able to reason out differences. Pathwork with Ess Euchen to change the outcome of her story and to learn to overcome the temptation to engage in or listen to gossip.

ETAIN (IRISH)
See Edain.

ETAN (IRISH)
A daughter of Diancecht who married Oghma.

ETAR (IRISH)
The woman who drank Edain when, as a butterfly, she fell into Etar's ale. She later gave Edain rebirth in human form.

ETHNE (IRISH)
IN MYTH — A daughter of a servant of love God Aengus MacOg. When Aengus tried to rape her, she escaped him by becoming a being of pure spirit or light. When she vanished from humanity she took with her the Tuatha's Veil of Invisibility which had protected them from the invading Milesians.

IN MAGICK AND RITUAL — Her powers of invisibility are usually a metaphor for astral projection (though there is a tradition of utilizing other types of invisibility spells in Celtic magickal practice). Call on her to aid you in this endeavor, or invoke her when you wish to go about unnoticed.

FACHEA (IRISH)

IN MYTH — A Goddess of poetry and patron deity of bards.

IN MAGICK AND RITUAL — Invoke Fachea to inspire creativity in yourself or others.

FAND (IRISH, MANX)

IN MYTH — Fand, a faery queen, was once married to the sea God Manann. After he left her, she was preyed upon by three Formorian warriors in a battle for control of the Irish Sea. Her only hope in winning this battle was to send for the hero Cuchulain who would only agree to come if she would marry him. She reluctantly acquiesced to his wishes, though when she met him, she fell as deeply in love with him as he was with her.

Manann knew that the relationship between the human world and the world of faery could not continue without it eventually destroying the faeries. He erased the memory of one from the other by drawing his magickal mantle between them.

Fand was also a minor sea Goddess who made her home both in the Otherworld and on the Isle of Man. With her sister, Liban, she was one of the twin Goddesses of health and earthly pleasures.

Some scholars believe she was a native Manx deity who was absorbed in Irish mythology.

Her nickname was "Pearl of Beauty."

IN MAGICK AND RITUAL — Call on Fand for healing, and for the assurance that you can have pleasure without guilt if you act responsibly. She can also aid you in making faery contact and water magick.

CORRESPONDENCES — Sea salt, pearls, mother-of-pearl, aquamarine, coltsfoot, maidenhair.

FEA (IRISH)

[Fee] See also the Morrigan. This war Goddess, whose root name means "the hateful one," is a subordinate deity of the Morrigan. She is the daughter of Elcmar and Brugh.

FEDELMA (IRISH)

IN MYTH — Fedelma was a faery queen from Croghan in Connacht who prophesied to Queen Maeve of her victory over Ulster and the death of Cuchulain.

She is described as having yellow hair falling below her knees, wearing a golden dress and a green mantle, and carrying a chariot pole.

IN MAGICK AND RITUAL — Invoke her to increase your own psychic abilities.

CORRESPONDENCES — Glass.

FEICHLINE (IRISH)

IN MYTH — [FAY't-leen] An emissary from the Otherworld who appeared to Queen Maeve to foretell her of her death. She may be a faery figure, as many of them are recorded in Celtic legends as portents of one's demise. She appeared in a white gown with a gold crown and seven golden braids, and is likely another form of Fedelma who foretold to Maeve the downfall of Ulster.

IN MAGICK AND RITUAL — Call on her for divination and aid in spirit contact. She can also

FEITHLINE (CONT.)

tell you the time of your own death, if you really care to know.

CORRESPONDENCES — Nightshade, yew.

FIAL (IRISH)

[FEE-ahl] The older sister of Emer whom Emer wished to have marry before her. She offered Fial to Cuchulain, but he refused the offer.

FINCHOEM (IRISH)

IN MYTH — Finchoem swallowed a worm she found crawling over a magickal well in hopes of conceiving. She was successful, and the child born to her was Conall of the Victories.

Archetypally she is a well guardian, wells being associated with the birth canal of the mother earth Goddess.

Compare her story to that of Nessa.

IN MAGICK AND RITUAL — Fertility magick.

FINDABAR (IRISH)

IN MYTH — Also Findbhair. Findabar's name comes from the same roots in the Giodelic language as Guinevere does in the Brythonic. Both approximately mean "white shadow" or "fair eyebrows."

Findabar was a Princess of Connacht, the daughter of Queen Maeve and her ineffectual consort, King Ailill. Ailill opposed his daughter's choice of a husband and sought to halt the marriage, wishing her to wed Ferdia instead. Findabar, showing the same spirit and determination as her famous mother, married Froach anyway.

She helped her lover slay a water demon, a synonym for battle with the Formorians.

IN MAGICK AND RITUAL — Females can align with her to have the courage of their convictions and to help them be strong enough to have and live with their choices. Men can pair themselves with her to have a strong partner for overcoming adversity.

FINNCAEV (IRISH)

Her name means "fair love." She was a minor Princess among the Tuatha De Danann, perhaps a Goddess of love or beauty.

FIONGALLA (IRISH)

IN MYTH — The name of this Goddess of southwestern Ireland means "one with fair cheeks." She was placed under a spell by an Ulster Druidess named Amerach so that she would never grow a day older. Amerach extracted a vow from her that she would sleep with no man until he presented her with yew berries, holly boughs, and bouquets of marigolds from a magickal spot. A man named Feargal managed this feat and the geise was released.

The three items requested represent the Samhain, Yule, and Midsummer Sabbats respectively; this, and her agelessness, indicate that she was a regional Triple Goddess and that Feargal was her region's sacrificial God/king.

IN MAGICK AND RITUAL — Call upon Fiongalla for seasonal rites. Bring her her required items to evoke her presence (but not if pets or children will be in attendance, as those items contain toxic properties).

FIONNUALA (IRISH)

IN MYTH — [FEE-onn-OO-lah] Her names means "the fair-shouldered one." She plays a leading role in one of the "Four Sorrows of Erin" in Irish mythology.

Fionnuala and her three brothers were the children of Llyr and Aebh. After Aebh's death, Llyr married Aife, who was so jealous of Llyr's love for his children that she turned them into swans for a period of nine hundred years.

Fionnuala took care of her brothers throughout their exile and taught them to sing. They learned to sing so sweetly that all Ireland was enchanted by them. At one point she feared she'd lost her brothers in a storm. Before she found them again she was credited with one of the most beautiful laments ever known. An English language version of this, *Silent O'Moyle*, was written by Thomas Moore.

They were freed by Druidic magick, but once released from their enchantment, fell dead from old age.

IN MAGICK AND RITUAL — Fionnuala can be invoked to give us the strength to aid our family and keep them together.

CORRESPONDENCES — Water birds, the throat, the nonagon.

FITHIR (IRISH)

The youngest daughter of a High King whom the King of Leinster wished to marry. Because she had an unwed older sister, Darine, the High King said no to the match. In retaliation for the rejection, the Leinster king kidnapped Darine, claimed she was dead, and subsequently married Fithir. When Fithir came upon Darine years later she died of shock and Darine died of heartbreak.

FLAND (IRISH)

The daughter of woodland Goddess Flidais, Fland was most likely a lake Goddess, and is viewed in modern folklore as an evil water faery who lures swimmers to their death.

FLAITHIUS (IRISH)

IN MYTH — Her name means "royal," and she is part of one of the most dramatic romantic stories in Irish myth.

One day, when Niall of the Nine Hostages and eight of his warriors went out riding, they came across an old hag. She demanded they all get down from their mounts and kiss her. To humor the woman they did as she asked, and she immediately transformed into beautiful Flaithius, an archetypal Goddess of sovereignty who gave Niall the legitimacy to rule his sept. (She is also symbolic of the life cycle of the Triple Goddess who becomes the young woman and mates again with her God.) She correctly prophesied that he would become one of the greatest High Kings known to Ireland.

IN MAGICK AND RITUAL — Divination.

CORRESPONDENCES — Catnip.

FLIDAIS (IRISH)

IN MYTH — [FLEE-daws] The shape-shifting Goddess of the woodlands. The wife of Adammair, she is occasionally depicted as the consort of the Horned God, she is the equivalent of Greco-Roman Diana/Artemis.

FLIDAIS (CONT.)

Flidais traveled in a chariot/sleigh pulled by deer. She gave her gifts of love to those who cherished her beasts. She had a cow which could supply milk for thirty people each day. The animals obeyed her and served her needs.

IN MAGICK AND RITUAL — Flidais can aid you in magick for animals, the environment, and in learning to give. She is also a Goddess of the hunt and a feminine version of the Holly King/Santa Claus.

CORRESPONDENCES — Bow, antlers, wormwood, myrtle, the Strength Tarot card.

FODHLA (IRISH)

[FOAL-tah] Also Fotia and Folta. One of a triplicity with Eire and Banbha. She was the second of the three sisters to approach the invading Milesians, but, because she could display no power with which to impress them, they passed her by, ignoring her plea to name the conquered island for her. She was the wife of MacCecht.

FRANCONIAN-DIE-DRUD (IRISH)

A Druidess associated with the horse Goddess Mare, the bringer of dreams.

FUAMNACH (IRISH)

IN MYTH — The jealous faery wife of Midhir who turned his captured bride, Edain, into a pool of water, a brown worm, and a mayfly. In some versions of Edain's myth she was not rescued from Midhir's burgh by Aengus MacOg, but blown away in a furious storm raised by Fuamnach.

IN MAGICK AND RITUAL — Fuamnach was a master at weather magick. Call on her aid to practice this art.

GARBH OGH (IRISH)

IN MYTH — [Garv Ahg or GAR-oo Oeg] A giantess and Goddess of the hunt whose chariot was drawn by elks. Her diet consisted solely of deer milk and eagle breast, and she hunted deer with a pack of hounds which had all been given birds' names.

Garbh Ogh built herself a triple cairn of stone and heather, and went inside to die. Robert Graves says she is a woodland Goddess to whom the Horned God is sacrificed, perhaps his consort.

Her name translates as "rough youth."

IN MAGICK AND RITUAL — Eco-magick, seasonal rites involving the sacrificial God.

CORRESPONDENCES — Animal horns, the Strength Tarot card.

GARMANGABIS (ANGLO-CELTIC)

This Goddess was brought to Britain with the Romans and survives only through cryptic inscriptions. She was worshipped in the Lancashire region of northwestern England, though her function and archetype are now unknown.

GENOVEFA (WELSH, CORNISH, BRETON)

IN MYTH — An Arthurian figure who rode an Otherworldly white deer with her brother Edern, to mark out their respective kingdoms before dawn. When Genovefa saw Edern was riding faster than her, she encouraged a cock to crow, heralding dawn and ending the competition.

Archetypally she is a dark earth Goddess loath to relinquish or share her domain with her consort. She is also linked to the White Hart, a mystical white deer who is linked to Otherworld messages.

IN MAGICK AND RITUAL — Earth magick.

GILLAGRIENE (IRISH, SCOTTISH)

IN MYTH — Also Giolla Griene. A "daughter of the sun." She was the offspring of a sunbeam and a human man. When she learned of her unorthodox parentage, she threw herself into Lough Griene (The Lake of the Sun) and floated to an oak grove where she died.

IN MAGICK AND RITUAL — Fire magick.

GODIVA, LADY (ANGLO-CELTIC)

IN MYTH — Also Godifu. The legends of Lady Godiva riding naked through the streets of Coventry until her husband, a political leader, agreed to reduce the people's taxes, is a corruption of the May Day processional rituals which precede the sacred marriage and sexual union (The Great Rite) of the Goddess and God.

IN MAGICK AND RITUAL — Lady Godiva is a May Queen for seasonal rites. See Epona for further discussion of her attributes.

CORRESPONDENCES — Emerald, blood, horses, the May Pole, hawthorn, and the color white.

GOEWIN (WELSH)

IN MYTH — The Goddess of sovereignty who held the feet of Math while he reigned. She was only exempt from doing so when he went to war.

In old northern and western European cultures kings were often semi-divine beings having need to rest their feet in the lap of a queen by whose grace they ruled. When Goewin was kidnapped by Gilfaethwy, he also captured the means of stealing the throne.

She is equated with Queen Guinevere.

IN MAGICK AND RITUAL — Approach Goewin as a Goddess of sovereignty and May Queen.

CORRESPONDENCES — The chalice, hawthorn.

GOLEUDDYDD (WELSH)

IN MYTH — [GO-loo-theeth] A sow Goddess, the mother of Culwch who ran in an insane rush to the deep woodlands to give him birth.

When she was about to die, she made her husband, Kilydd, promise that he would not remarry until a briar bush with at least two heads sprang from her grave. Such briars do not grow heads until their seventeenth year of maturity. In Celtic mysticism the number seventeen related to the splitting of clans. Every seventeenth year the oldest women and strongest warriors were allowed to branch off from the old clan if they wished.

She was also an aunt of King Arthur.

IN MAGICK AND RITUAL — Cultivate her to strengthen family ties, or to help you know when it is time to leave your family to begin your own.

GRAINNE (IRISH)

IN MYTH — [GRAW-nuh] Also Graine, whose name means "sunny." Grainne was promised in marriage to Fionn, but at their wedding feast she saw Diarmuid and the magickal spot hidden under the hair on his forehead which would make any woman fall in love with him.

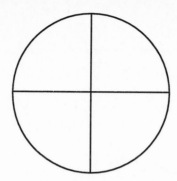

A solar disk. This simple figure represents the four major turning points of the year: the two solstices and the two equinoxes.

GRAINNE (CONT.)

In the most widely accepted version of the myth, Grainne then slipped a sleeping potion into the drinks of all those present and convinced Diarmuid to escape with her. At first he hesitated, but she reminded him of his geise never to refuse a woman in need.

They traveled the length and breath of Ireland, pursued by Fionn and his Fianna warriors, for seven years until Aengus MacOg pleaded their case and won their reprieve.

The two Gods in this tale represents the young king replacing the elder as the consort of the eternal Goddess.

Though their legends differ, she and Grian may have been the same entity.

IN MAGICK AND RITUAL — Feminine power, love, and invisibility spells.

CORRESPONDENCES — Sunstones, mugwort, solar disk.

GRAINNE NI MALLEY (IRISH)

IN MYTH — [GRAW-nuh Nee MAAL-ee] This pirate queen who preyed on English ships has become so legendary that it is nearly impossible to distinguish fact from fiction in her folk-lore. Her story is further clouded in the long and bloody history of rebellion movements by the conquered Irish.

Legends say that Queen Elizabeth I invited Grainne to her court and plied her with gifts in exchange for her promise not to rob English vessels. Grainne scorned the efforts and returned to Ireland, where she captured an English noblewoman until the British admiralty acknowledged her sovereignty over the Irish seas.

She took lovers at will, a new one each year, and in this and other ways has absorbed some of the qualities of Queen Maeve.

IN MAGICK AND RITUAL — Grainne shares the attributes of the many Goddesses of sovereignty, and can aid you in serving your country, or discovering the divine feminine power inside yourself.

CORRESPONDENCES — The Jolly Roger, the chalice.

GRIAN (IRISH)

IN MYTH — [GREE-awn] This faery Goddess from County Tipperary is still believed to live in a burgh beneath Pallas Green Hill. Her name means "sunny," and she was undoubtedly at one time long past a potent regional sun deity. Her nine daughters lived in homes called *griannon,* or sun houses. Though her legends have been lost, some scholars believe she is a twin of Aine who represented the waning year, while Grian was queen of the waxing year.

IN MAGICK AND RITUAL — Call on Grian and Aine to be a part of seasonal rites. If you prefer a feminist slant on your spirituality, they can easily replace the Holly and Oak Kings' function.

CORRESPONDENCES — The sun, gold, sunstones, copper, marigolds.

GROAC'H (BRETON)

This "evil old woman" appears in several Breton folk legends. Her name is a corruption of the Brezonek word for the crone Goddess.

GUILDELUEC (BRETON)

IN MYTH — [G'HEED-uhl-uhk] Her story is part of one of the *Lays* (epic romantic ballads) of Brittany penned by that region's famous poet, Marie de France. She was the wife of the knight Eliduc, who, while he was banished from Brittany, fell in love with a young princess named Guillardun.

When discovering this, Guildeluec agreed to enter an order (probably a nearby school for Druidesses, not a convent) in order that her husband might be able to leave her and be happy with his new love. She restored her young rival, who was thought dead, by placing a blood colored flower in her mouth.

IN MAGICK AND RITUAL — Evoke her to learn lessons of unselfish love, compassion, and as an aid to general magick.

GUINEVERE, QUEEN (WELSH, CORNISH)

IN MYTH — Also Gwenhwyfar and Gueneva. Her name means "white shadow," the sovereign power behind the throne of King Arthur.

While the Camelot stories surrounding her, King Arthur, and his rival, are romantic in nature, these modern incarnations demean the status of the sovereign Goddess in their telling. She was the sovereign who gave Arthur his right to rule simply by being with him. When she left him he pursued her not for love, but because without her his kingdom would crumble for lack of leadership. The role of Goddess of sovereignty is more clearly seen in her legends than in many others. Her duty is to blend the king's energy with the energy of the land. It is in many myths that when the king forgets where his power comes from, that the queen will seek other champions and lovers to remind him as she gladly did.

She is also a May Queen who is occasionally thought of as a female Gwyn Ap Nuad, an Otherworld king and God of the hunt.

Original Welsh legends list three different queens for Arthur all named Guinevere, making her a triplicity unto herself.

IN MAGICK AND RITUAL — Seasonal rites.

CORRESPONDENCES — White hawthorn, emeralds, cat's eyes, blood, the crown, pillows, the May Pole.

GWEN (ANGLO-CELTIC, WELSH)

A young woman who was so beautiful that almost no one could live if they gazed upon her for long. She was possibly a minor sun or moon Goddess or a Goddess of light.

GWENDYDD (WELSH, CORNISH)

IN MYTH — [GWEN-eth] A sister of Merlin who married King Rydderch. She was the only one who could approach her brother once he had gone to the woods to live, and, eventually, she joined him there. He taught her the art of prophecy.

Some sources believe the character is a vague disguise of Vivienne, Merlin's lover.

Her English name is Gandieda.

IN MAGICK AND RITUAL — Divination.

CORRESPONDENCES — Yarrow.

GWENDOLYN (WELSH, CORNISH)

See Vennolandua.

GWENNOLAIK (BRETON)

IN MYTH — Gwennolaik deeply loved her foster brother, Nola, who was away at sea serving his country. She waited patiently for his return, not knowing that he had been drowned. All the while she lived with her cruel foster mother who made her work hard and did all she could to destroy the innocent faith and beauty of the girl.

Magickally, Gwennolaik received a ring she recognized as being Nola's, which contained a message that he would come for her in three weeks and three days. In the meantime, her foster mother decreed that she should be married, and told her to forget about Nola.

That night Nola came to her in spirit and, turning them both into silver birds, took her away to the Otherworld where they lived happily ever after with her family.

IN MAGICK AND RITUAL — Evoke her for romance spells, couples work, and spirit contact. Loyalty and family love and ties can also be strengthened in ritual with her that can teach that family is more than blood ties, but is love and caring.

CORRESPONDENCES — Rose oil, the color pink.

GWYAR (WELSH)

IN MYTH — King Arthur's sister and the wife of Llud. Her root name means "shedding blood" or "gore." Both images link her to Arianrhod in her aspects of mother and death Goddess.

She is called Morgawse by Sir Thomas Malory, and Anna by Geoffrey of Monmouth, who tells us that she had two sons: one good and one wicked. Other than that, the fragments of her myths have been lost.

IN MAGICK AND RITUAL — Spirit contact, Passing Over rites, and childbirth.

HABETROT (ANGLO-CELTIC)

IN MYTH — Habetrot was a "spinning" Goddess. Spinning is both Pagan lingo for spell casting, and for the turning of the Wheel of the Year. She may have been a Goddess of magick or a seasonal mother/creatrix figure since spinning women are usually linked to Pagan creation myths.

Habetrot is best known for her powers of healing which were linked to her skills with weaving fiber. All who wore the clothing she made would never fall ill.

IN MAGICK AND RITUAL — Call on Habetrot for aid in healing spells, to be a part of seasonal rites, or to commemorate creation.

CORRESPONDENCES — The spinning wheel, the spider web, the octagon, wool.

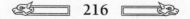

HABONDIA (ANGLO-CELTIC)

IN MYTH — [Hahb-OEN-dee'uh] Also Abondia, Abunciada, and Habonde. She was a Goddess of abundance and prosperity, demoted to a "mere witch" in medieval English lore in order to strip her of her great power in the minds of the rural folk who depended upon her benevolence for their crops and herds.

   She is descended from a Germanic Goddess of the earth.

IN MAGICK AND RITUAL — Use the spirit of Habondia in seasonal harvest rituals, fertility rites, for prosperity spells, or to make earth magick.

CORRESPONDENCES — The cornucopia, wheat.

HARIMELLA (SCOTTISH)

A Goddess of Tungrain origin who was worshipped in Dunfriesshire. Most likely a Goddess of protection. Also called by the name Viradechthis.

Heloise, wicked heart, beware!
Think on the dreadful day of wrath,
Think on thy soul; forbear, forbear!
The way thou tak'st that of death!

—Ancient Breton Ballad

HELOISE (CONTINENTAL)

IN MYTH — [H'ell-o-EEZ] This daughter of the canon of Paris fell in love with the gentle Breton scholar Abelard. She used her fine powers as a magician to keep them together against those who said that a Breton scholar could not marry a Parisian. They were killed together by his uncle and buried in one tomb.

   Their courtship and death is said to have taken place in Nantes, a well-known center for a school of Druidesses. Heloise was probably a student Druidess and, in the original tale, was unable to control or extend her magick to protect herself and her lover. Her story is often compared to the folktale of "The Sorcerer's Apprentice," a work immortalized in the program piece of the same name by Paul Dukas (see Walt Disney's 1940 animated classic, *Fantasia,* for a wonderful visual interpretation).

IN MAGICK AND RITUAL — Call on Heloise for couples magick, Druidic magick, love spells, aid and wisdom for students, and for Handfasting rites.

HENWEN (ANGLO-CELTIC)

IN MYTH — [HEN-oon] A sow Goddess much like her Welsh counterpart Cerridwen. She is the deity who brought abundance to the land by giving birth to an assortment of "litters" throughout England. For example, she left a litter of bees in one spot, wheat in another, barley in another, eagles in another, etc. But she did not produce dogs, pigs, or another animals thought to be the sole possession of the Otherworld inhabitants (refer to "The Battle of the Trees" in Chapter 5 for more on these Otherworld animals).

IN MAGICK AND RITUAL — Fertility rites, childbirth assistance, and prosperity magick.

IAINE (IRISH)

See Ain.

IGRAINE (WELSH, CORNISH)

IN MYTH — [EE-grawn or EE-grawn-uh] Also Igerna. She was King Arthur's mother by King Uther Pendragon of Cornwall. Merlin cast upon Uther an enchantment which made him appear to Igraine as her husband Gorlois. The two spent one night together and Arthur was the result.

IN MAGICK AND RITUAL — Igraine is the eternal mother Goddess who is both mother and lover to her child. Call upon her for seasonal rites involving the birth and death of the father God.

INGHEAN BHUIDHE (IRISH)

Also see Latiaran.

IN MYTH — [EEN-awn BOO-ee] Her name means "yellow-haired girl." Though much of her story has been lost to us, we know that she was the middle girl of three sisters who made up a Triple Goddess.

She represented the coming of summer, or Bealtaine by the Celtic calendar, and for many years she was honored with rituals involving a sacred well on May 6, the original date of the Sabbat.

IN MAGICK AND RITUAL — Use her energy in Bealtaine rituals, for flower festivals, or to bless spring planting.

> Spin for me a thread so fine, Pour for me the red mulled wine
> That you and I should find at last, The promise made in a long-dead past.
>
> —Rebecca Worrell

IRNAN (IRISH, MANX)

IN MYTH — She was one of three aged daughters of a Tuatha De Danann magician named Conaran. As the girls were all powerful magicians, they were asked to go out and capture some of the Fianna warriors. They accomplished this feat easily by spinning a large web which entrapped an advance scouting party as they rode through the countryside, though the gossamer threads allowed the horses to pass through unmolested.

Goll MacMorna rode up shortly afterwards and saw what had been done to his comrades. In a fit of rage he slew Irnan's two sisters. Irnan bargained for her life by promising to release the captured warriors, and Goll reluctantly agreed.

When Fionn and the rest of the Fianna came along, Irnan changed herself into a huge scaled monster and laid a geise on them that they must fight with her individually rather than as a group. Most of the warriors backed off in fear. Only Goll accepted the challenge, and won. He was rewarded with the hand in marriage of Fionn's daughter Cebha.

Goddesses like Irnan who are associated with webs and spinning can usually be linked to very old creation myths.

IN MAGICK AND RITUAL — Irnan is a powerful source of magickal energy, and also shares most of the attributes of the Triple Goddess and the Morrigan.

CORRESPONDENCES — The web, thread.

ISOLDE (IRISH, CORNISH, BRETON)

IN MYTH — Spelled Yseult by the Bretons, Iseult by the Irish, Esyllt Vyngwen ("of the fine hair") on Man, Ysolt in Cornwall, and Ysonde in France. Isolde is her Germanic name, the one by which she is largely known due to the efforts of German composer Richard Wagner.

Isolde is the tragic romantic heroine in the famous romantic tale, *Tristan and Isolde*. The legends surrounding the lovers appear to date from a twelfth century Breton writer named Beroul. Since his time, literally hundreds of different versions of their story have been recorded.

Isolde was the daughter of Irish king who was promised in marriage to King Mark of Cornwall. Mark's nephew, Tristan, was asked to go to Ireland and escort the young lady to her new home. Fearing Isolde would be unhappy in her marriage, her mother, a powerful magician, gave her Lady in Waiting a philter, or love potion, to be given to the couple on their wedding night. During the voyage to Cornwall, the servant accidentally gave Isolde and Tristan the potion, and they fell deeply in love.

Isolde married King Mark, but continued to meet her lover in secret, able to fool King Mark for a while.

Stories of how the lovers met their mutual demise are as varied as the tales about them.

Fans of this legend have been known to make pilgrimages to Castle Dore in Cornwall, the reputed site of the tragic events.

IN MAGICK AND RITUAL — Invoke these two in Handfasting rituals, and ask their aid in couples work, sex magick, and love spells.

Iweridd (Welsh, Anglo-Celtic)

[Y'OO-er-eth] A Goddess about whom little is known. She was one of the wives of Manann in the Welsh versions of his lore but her name, oddly enough, means "of Ireland."

Kele-De (Irish)

IN MYTH — [KAY-lay-day or KAY-lee-day] Also spelled Ceile De. She is an ancient Goddess steeped in mystery. The early church allowed her all-female cult, known as the *Kelles,* to flourish for a time in remote areas of Ireland. Among their practices were that her high priestesses reserved the right to take any and all lovers they chose. Yet, oddly enough, she was probably a crone image in Ireland, and was linked in popular mind as a counterpart to the male creation principle. Some scholars believe she is a corruption of the Indian Goddess Kali.

In an effort to adopt and eradicate her memory, an early sect of Irish and Scottish monks adopted her name.

IN MAGICK AND RITUAL — Call on Kele-De to raise feminine power or for sex magick.
CORRESPONDENCES — Rocky crevices, holey stones.

Kicva (Welsh)

Also Cigfa. The wife of Pryderi and the daughter-in-law of Rhiannon.

Lady of the Lake, the (Welsh, Cornish, Breton)

IN MYTH — The Lady of the Lake is by some accounts a faery woman, by others a potent deity of life, death, and regeneration. She was the possessor of the sword Excalibur (called Caliburn in Brittany), the magickal blade of King Arthur. As the most true archetype of a sovereign Goddess we have in Celtic myth, it is this act of taking the offered sword which grants Arthur the right to rule, and it is she who claims the blade again when his role as sacrificial king must be fulfilled.

The Bretons claim she was a Breton addition to the Arthurian myths and that she never appeared in the original Welsh versions of the legend. Contrary to the widely popular

LADY OF THE LAKE, THE (CONT.)

"sword in the churchyard stone" legends, the Breton version tells us that Merlin and Arthur rowed out to the center of the Dosmary Lake in Cornwall, and that it was there that Excalibur was presented to him, the sword embedded in floating stone. When he pulled it out, he reversed the act of the Great Rite, separating the female and male principles of creation which were not to be united again until Arthur's death.

The Lady of the Lake is also attributed with being the foster mother of Sir Lancelot, one of Arthur's knights, also a Breton addition to the myth.

She is described as sitting on a throne of reeds in the center of the lake's depths.

Among her many magickal credits is that of healer.

IN MAGICK AND RITUAL — The Lady of the Lake is a powerful archetype of sovereignty. Harness her energy for purification, healing, the Great Rite, and many other magickal acts associated with the feminine elements.

CORRESPONDENCES — The crane, water lilies, marble.

LASSAIR (IRISH)

IN MYTH — A Goddess of Midsummer, part of a triplicity with her sisters Latiaran and Inghean Bhuidhe. Her name means "flame."

IN MAGICK AND RITUAL — Seasonal rites.

LATIARAN (IRISH)

IN MYTH — She was the youngest of three sisters who made up a Triple Goddess. Latiaran represented the first harvest of Lughnasadh; her sister Inghean Bhuidhe (also known as Crobh Dearg), the middle daughter, represented the beginning of summer at Bealtaine; and Lassair, the eldest, was the symbol/Goddess of Midsummer.

The only surviving story about Latiaran tells us that each day she carried a seed of fire to a nearby forge. One day, while she was at the forge, her apron caught fire and she melted into the ground, her place marked by a heart-shaped stone.

Archetypally this legend represents a form of female Goddess/queen sacrifice comparable to that of the sacrificial God/kings. She may also have been a Goddess of the forge, a feminine counterpart to Gods such as Luchtain, Wayland, and Vulcan.

IN MAGICK AND RITUAL — Seasonal rites and fire magick.

LATIS (ANGLO-CELTIC)

IN MYTH — She was originally a lake Goddess who became a Goddess of ale and meade. Evidence of her worship remains at Birdsowald, England.

Latis fell desperately in love with a salmon, a totem animal representing knowledge, and, out of pity for her, the other deities turned him into a warrior. However, each winter he must submit to becoming a salmon again until spring.

His returning to fish-form archetypally represents the demise of the old God who is always condemned to die at winter's beginning (Samhain). He is resurrected in spring (Bealtaine) when the Goddess ceases to mourn and is his mate once more.

IN MAGICK AND RITUAL — Ask Latis' assist in your understanding the Wheel of the Year. Call on her for Samhain rites or to add her voice to the mourning of the old God.

LAUDINE (WELSH, CORNISH)

A friend of Owain in the Arthurian myths who was instrumental in facilitating Ossian's marriage with the Lady of the Fountain, a well Goddess.

LAVERCAM (IRISH)

IN MYTH — This poetess and bard was employed by the court of King Conchobar. She was born a slave and was said to have been very ugly, but her wit and talent raised her status. She was also very sturdy and swift, so much so that she could run the length of Ireland in one day and report back to the king all she had seen and heard.

When Deirdre of the Sorrows was banished from Ireland, Lavercam was assigned to go along and look after her. It was she who introduced Deirdre to her lover Naoise.

During the exile her loyalties shifted from the King to Deirdre. She even lied to the King on her behalf, telling him that Deirdre had grown ugly in her hardship. When they set out to return to Ireland, Lavercam accurately predicted doom.

IN MAGICK AND RITUAL — Lavercam can aid you in divination, creative endeavors, and spells and rituals to invoke loyalty. Evoke her energy to bless binding and secrecy rituals within your coven. She can also subtly help us to remember that looks are less important than other qualities.

CORRESPONDENCES — Hemp, garlands, silk, the Moon Tarot card.

LeFAY (WELSH, CORNISH)

IN MYTH — LeFay was a Goddess of the sea and of the Isle of Avalon. She was a efficacious healer, and drinking water blessed by her provided an instant cure for all ills. Scholars debate whether the word "fay" in her name refers to faery, fate, or some blending of both.

IN MAGICK AND RITUAL — Healing.

CORRESPONDENCES — Aquamarines.

LIADIN (IRISH)

A poetess who was mated with the poet Cuirithir. Their story parallels that of Abelard and Heloise.

LIBAN (IRISH, MANX)

IN MYTH — Liban and her twin sister Fand were the Goddesses of health and earthly pleasures.

IN MAGICK AND RITUAL — Healing.

CORRESPONDENCES — Chamomile.

LIBAN (IRISH, MANX)

IN MYTH — [LEE-bahn] Also Li Ban. Her name means "beautiful woman," and she was a faery queen who guarded Ireland's sacred wells. One day she forgot to guard the well, and the ensuing flood formed Lough Neath in Northern Ireland, formerly a plain which had been scooped out by the giant hands of Fionn MacCumhal (which he tossed into the Irish Sea where it became the Isle of Man).

Liban was able to take the form of a salmon at will, an animal which represents knowledge. The shapeshifting and the well imagery may mean she was once a reincarnation deity. When she became a fish, her loyal dog transformed himself into an otter, and they lived happily until she wished to go to earth again.

LIBAN (CONT.)

Modern versions of the tale say that they were captured by fishermen and displayed as curiosities until her dog/otter was killed. Heartbroken, Liban returned then to her human form and also died. She is believed now to haunt the sea as a bird whose mournful cries can be heard when sea animals are in danger.

IN MAGICK AND RITUAL — Liban makes an excellent subject for pathworking to learn about knowledge, transformation, and loyalty. She can also aid you in finding a familiar.

LOCHA (IRISH)

Maidservant to Queen Maeve who died defending her mistress in Connacht's war with Ulster.

LOGIA (IRISH)

The Goddess of the Lagan River.

LOT (IRISH)

A Formorian war Goddess with the characteristic hideousness—by human standards, at least—of the race. She is described as having lips on her breasts and four eyes on her back. She often led the Formorians into battle.

LUATHS LURGANN

IN MYTH — [LOO-ahs LOOR-gahn] This warrior Goddess' name means "the speedy-footed one," and she was known as Ireland's fastest runner. She was also the aunt of Fionn MacCumhal and midwifed his birth.

Because many were fearful of the great prophecies which surrounded him, she took him to live deep within the woods where she taught him the warrior's art and her secrets of speed until she grew too old and fragile to continue.

One day, when they were being pursued, he picked her up and ran with her so fast that she disintegrated. All that was left was a thigh bone which he used as the center point around which grew the lake called Lough Lurgann.

IN MAGICK AND RITUAL — Call on her to overcome enemies, strengthen family or loyalties, for aid in teaching, for gaining physical fitness, or for learning astral projection.

CORRESPONDENCES — Thistle.

LUNED (WELSH)

IN MYTH — An enchantress who frees Sir Owain from imprisonment at the hands of the Black Knight by giving him a golden ring which makes him invisible. In return, he later rescues her from being burned at the stake for sorcery.

IN MAGICK AND RITUAL — Ask Luned to teach you the art of astral projection for this is truly the art of invisibility.

CORRESPONDENCES — Mugwort.

MABB (WELSH)

This warrioress is believed to be a Welsh version of Ireland's Queen Maeve. However, she has come into present-day Welsh folklore as a faery who brings nightmares and as a midwife to the Welsh faery folk, the Twlwwyth Tegs.

She left a long-abiding curse
On the chiefs of the Red Branch....

—From *The Dinnshenchas,* "The Story of Macha"

MACHA (IRISH)

IN MYTH — [MAAX-ah)] Macha is the personification of her name which means "battle." She is also one of the Morrigan, the crone Triple Goddess of death, disease, strife, and destruction.

The famous Ulster fortress of the Red Branch warriors, *Emain Macha* (AE-meen MAAX-ah, meaning "twins of Macha"), was named for her. As a Goddess of death and destruction, she was the guardian of the *mesred machae,* the pillared fortress gate on which the heads of conquered warriors were displayed. She is also associated with a County Armagh stronghold known as *Ard Macha* (for which the county was named) which became a Christian center during the reign of England's James I. At this site she had an eternal flame dedicated to her which was attended by the temple maidens. This task was later taken over by nuns who created a shrine to a local saint at her holy site.

When she was heavily pregnant, she was forced to race against the fastest horse in Ireland. She completed the course, but died at the end post while giving birth to twins. As her life ended, she cursed all the men of Ulster to have great labor pains whenever danger threatened so that they would be unable to fight. Only the famous warrior Cuchulain was immune to the curse, but the rest of his warriors fell under the spell and were subsequently defeated by Connacht.

Macha has three husbands credited to her, Nemed, Nuada, and Crunnchu. Each time she remarried was after a profound self-transformation, which which archetypally links her to reincarnation.

IN MAGICK AND RITUAL — Cultivate Macha to aid you in childbirth, to gain wisdom, to help you overcome your enemies, or to uncover past-lives.

CORRESPONDENCES — Belladonna, the Tower Tarot card, the waning moon, serpents, apples.

MAER (IRISH)

A Druidess who fell in love with Fionn MacCumhal. In an attempt to trap him into a relationship with her, she sent him a charm made of nine nuts. Fionn was suspicious of the offering and gave it to his dogs instead.

She could have called over the rim of the world
Whatever woman's lover had hit her fancy....

—William Butler Yeats, from "The Old Age of Queen Maeve"

MAEVE, QUEEN (IRISH)

IN MYTH — [Mayv] Also spelled Medb and Medhbh and Madb. She is the Queen of Connacht who personifies the heights of feminine power. She was no doubt once a powerful Goddess who merged with a later historical figure. Her name means "intoxicated woman," and she was known for her long golden hair, fiery temperament, and iron will.

Of the many legends surrounding, her the most famous is *The Cattle Raid of Cooley.* In this myth, her coveting of a famous Ulster bull began a war with Ulster.

MAEVE, QUEEN (CONT.)

As an archetypal sovereign, her aging husband, the ineffectual King Ailill, seems as if he would be replaced by Cuchulain who resists the sacrificial role, and battles her instead. She wins the battle, and Cuchulain's blood is spilled on earth in the manner of all sacrificial Gods.

Her sexual images are also strong, and she often boasted that she could sexually exhaust thirty men each night. As evidence of her feminine power, battles would pause while she menstruated. Ancient peoples believed this time to be the peak of a woman's power.

Maeve was not only a powerful leader, but also an expert warrioress, huntress, and horsewoman. Animals, particularly horses, are often depicted with her.

IN MAGICK AND RITUAL — Involve Maeve in sex magick and spells for leadership skills. Call on her power to gain perseverance and strength, or to ward off enemies. Pathwork with her to understand your own, or your partner's, feminine power.

CORRESPONDENCES — The colors yellow, red, and purple; the crossbow, the Star tarot card.

MAEVE LETHDERG (IRISH)

This Leinster queen, who surname means "half-red," was the wife of nine different High Kings in succession. She would allow no king to sit at Tara without her as his wife. Though she is usually thought of as being separate from Queen Maeve of Connacht, they probably both have their roots in the same ancient Celtic Goddess of sovereignty.

MAGA (IRISH)

A daughter of Aegnus MacOg, wife of Ross the Red, and mother of Fachtna.

MAGH MOR (IRISH)

A FirBolg princess/Goddess, the grandmother of Lugh.

MAGOG (ANGLO-CELTIC)

IN MYTH — The consort of Gog. They were two mountain deities of which she was the more important. Britain's Megg's Hills are named for her, and several hillside chalk effigies portray her. She is usually depicted as a four-breasted woman astride a horse. Some speculate that her name may mean "mother deity," and that she was once a fertility and mother Goddess.

In patriarchal times she became England's St. Margaret.

IN MAGICK AND RITUAL — Call on them for fertility or couples magick, and for casting spells with the earth element.

MAIRE NI CIARAGAIN (IRISH)

A warrior queen of the Irish whose legends have been largely forgotten.

MAL (IRISH)

There are many high and jagged cliffs along Ireland's western coast, and Hag's Headland is the most famous of them all. Mal was the Goddess who ruled over them, deciding the fate of all those who ventured there. The most famous story about her tells of her pursuing a much younger man whom she never catches (the chase kills her) up and down the rugged coast.

MALA LIATH (SCOTTISH)

IN MYTH — [MAH-lah LEE-ah] Another name for the Cailleach in southwestern Scotland. She tended a herd of pigs all sired by the famous wild boar of Glen Glass. She is often equated with Cerridwen.

IN MAGICK AND RITUAL — See Cerridwen and the Cailleach for full discussion.

Marcassa, Princess (Breton)

IN MYTH — This Princess was assaulted by Luduenn, a servant of a Breton king, who was on a quest for a bird which had the power to heal the ailing monarch. Later, after she had given birth to his son and had gone looking for him, it was discovered that only by sleeping with this Princess would the King be cured of his disease.

> The Princess refused and went into her own hibernation until the old King died. She then woke up and married Luduenn.

> This story represents the Goddess as crone, sleeping through winter, and being reborn as the maiden in spring when she re-mates with her young consort.

IN MAGICK AND RITUAL — Healing, sleep/dream magick, or seasonal rites.

Marcia Proba (Anglo-Celtic)

IN MYTH — This English Goddess' Roman name means "deep march" or "long march," a Celtic warrior queen who lived around the third century B.C.E. Her laws, known as the Marcian Statutes, were similar to Ireland's Brehon Laws in that they were very fair and gave equal status to women. Though some scholars claim these statutes laid the ground work for the Magna Charta (eleventh century), an English bill of rights, the newer version ignored women's status.

IN MAGICK AND RITUAL — Invoke Marcia Proba when you are called upon to make judgment and mete out justice. Allow her to teach you about fairness and equality.

CORRESPONDENCES — The balanced scales.

Mare (Irish)

See Epona.

Matrona (Continental)

Also see Modron. The Goddess of the Marne River. Her name means "divine mother," and this was probably the very early continental name of Modron.

Meg the Healer (Scottish)

IN MYTH — Meg was a famous healer, so famous that even the local faery folk called upon her when faced with illnesses they could not cure. She was one of the very few humans ever allowed to walk freely into the realm of faery and back again. Occasionally, when working in faeryland, she would spot a human held captive there. On these occasions she would ask the famous Wizard of Reay to release them, for he knew ways of enchanting them out that no other person could ever duplicate.

> Meg lived to be a hundred years old, at which time she was taken into faeryland where it is believed she still resides.

IN MAGICK AND RITUAL — Call on her for healing, herbal knowledge, or to aid you in faery contact.

CORRESPONDENCES — Chamomile.

MELUSINE (BRETON, SCOTTISH)

IN MYTH — [Mel-oo-SEEN] Also Melsuline. A serpent Goddess brought to common awareness through the writings of randy French author Rabelais. She was the daughter of Elinas, a King of Scotland, and a Breton faery woman named Pressine or Pressina.

When Elinas discovered Pressine was a faery, he banished her and their three daughters, of whom Melusine was the eldest. The banished daughter led her sisters to revenge when they locked their father inside the Brandebois Mountains (a mock sacrifice ritual).

The mother, in her outrage, placed a spell on her for this act against the father. The spell would make Melusine appear as a serpent from the waist down on Saturdays. When she married she made a condition that her husband never ask where she was on this day, as her mother had asked before, so that her husband would not know what she was. When he discovered, she sprouted wings and flew away in sorrow, leaving her three cherished sons behind.

She and her sisters, Melior and Palatina, are a triplicity.

IN MAGICK AND RITUAL — Compassion, also knowledge of when vengeance is not right or just, or none of your business.

CORRESPONDENCES — Mermaids, white roses; also snakeskin, snail shells and other natural, shed animal housing.

MESSBUACHALLO (IRISH)

IN MYTH — [MESS-boo-HAHL-la] The granddaughter of Eochaid and Edain, daughter of their only child Edain Oig. She was fostered by a cow-herder who taught her the art of embroidery and, as such, she is linked to cow Goddess images and to needle arts which tie her to lost creation myths.

She remained hidden with the herder for fear of her true identity being discovered. Later a king received a Druid's prophecy that she would bear him a son, though he did not know of her own royal lineage at the time.

A bird from the Otherworld came to tell her this news, and she went to the King and bore him Conaire Mor.

IN MAGICK AND RITUAL — Fertility, general aid to magick.

MILUCHRACH (IRISH)

The sister of the Goddess Aine who tricked Fionn MacCumhal into an enchanted lake, which grayed his hair and made him taboo for Aine, who was under a geise never to marry a man with gray hair.

MODRON (WELSH)

IN MYTH — Her name means "great Mother," and she is one of the most potent of the Celtic archetypal mother Goddesses. She is also a fertility and harvest deity often equated with Greece's Demeter or Ireland's Dana.

She was the mother of Mabon who was stolen away from her when he was three days old and rescued later by King Arthur.

IN MAGICK AND RITUAL — Call on Modron for all mother Goddess magick and ritual needs. She is also at home at harvest rites, childbirth beds, and in sex magick.

CORRESPONDENCES — Sunflowers, civet, poppy, patchouly, and the number three.

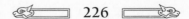

Momu (Scottish)
A Highland Goddess of wells and hillsides.

Moingfhion (Irish)
IN MYTH — [MOYN-f'onn] Also MongFinn. Her name means "white-haired one." She is associated with the crones of Samhain and a with a Pagan feast called *Feile Moingfhinne*.

In later legends she tried several times to kill her step-son, Niall, who functioned as a
sacrificial God. Archetypally she was playing the role of the crone who must mourn the
dying God. In the end, it was she who died by accidentally drinking the poisoned tea she
had made for him.

In modern Ireland, it is a Halloween custom to say prayers to protect one's self from her
wrath, especially if one has children in the house.

IN MAGICK AND RITUAL — Evoke her presence for Samhain rites, and ask her to aid you in
gaining her vast wisdom.

CORRESPONDENCES — Color orange, masks, apples.

Morgan LeFay (Welsh, Cornish, Breton)
IN MYTH — She was the daughter of LeFay, a glamourous Welsh sea Goddess. As the half-sister
of King Arthur, she possibly was once a Goddess of Glastonbury Tor, a sacred Pagan site intimately associated with the Arthurian myths. Archetypally, Glastonbury functions as a
gateway to the Otherworld.

The root of her name, *mor*, means "sea," and she was a sea Goddess, the place one must
cross to reach the isle of the Otherworld. In Brittany, sea sprites which lure sailors to their
deaths are called *Morgans* after her.

Today she is generally thought of as a Goddess of death, equated with the Morrigan, and
this was how she was brought into the written Arthurian cycles as a plotter of his death.

As a Goddess of sovereignty, she backed the Green Knight to take over the kingdom of
Camelot.

Her Breton name is Morgause.

IN MAGICK AND RITUAL — Morgan's energy is compatible with music magick, sovereignty
rites, Passing Over rituals, spirit contact, and water spells. She can also help teach us the
destructive nature of gossip and bigotry. Call on her to put a stop to this if it is ruining your
coven or Pagan organization.

CORRESPONDENCES — Mother of pearl, the High Priestess Tarot card.

Morgay (Scottish, Anglo-Celtic)
IN MYTH — A harvest Goddess from the Scottish/English border region.

IN MAGICK AND RITUAL — Seasonal rites.

Moriath (Irish, Manx)
IN MYTH — This princess' name means "sea land," a term which combines the names of the
two feminine elements: water and earth.

When she fell in love with Labriad, she won him with a magickal song spell.

In another legends she is daughter of a Gaulish king and the lover of Moen the Dumb.

IN MAGICK AND RITUAL — Cultivate her assistance for making your own music magick.

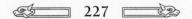

Over his head is shrieking
A lean hag, quickly hopping
Over the points of the weapons and the shields;
She is the gray-haired Morrigu.

—from the *Tain Bo Guilagne*

MORRIGAN, THE (PAN-CELTIC)

IN MYTH — Also the Morrigu. She is a Triple Goddess made up of three crone Goddesses of war, battle, death, and destruction. They were Badb, Macha, and Nemain. Their collective name means "the phantom queen."

    The Celts believed as they engaged in battle, the Morrigan flew shrieking overhead, often in the form of a carrion crow or a raven, calling up a host of slain soldiers to a macabre spectral dance. When the battle ended, the soldiers would leave the field until dawn so that the Morrigan could claim their trophies of heads, euphemistically known as "the Morrigan's acorn crop."

    Many Celtic folksongs and nursery rhymes refer to three black birds or ravens, which is how their legends were safely disguised and preserved during the times of persecution.

IN MAGICK AND RITUAL — The Morrigan are a powerful force which most prefer to separate and work with one-on-one. Call on them for Passing Over rituals, or to help you overcome enemies. Servicemen and women can call upon their energy when in battle. They are also a potent force for waning moon and banishing magick. However, be cautioned that their collective energy can turn violent.

CORRESPONDENCES — The raven, the carrion crow, obsidian, rubies, the waning and dark moons, yew, onyx, nightshade, henbane, black dogs.

MUIREARTACH (IRISH, SCOTTISH)

IN MYTH — A Goddess of battle often associated with the Morrigan. Her name means "eastern sea," and she personified the storm-tossed seas between Ireland and Scotland. (Interestingly, a similar word in modern Irish, *muirneach*, means "beloved.") Today an entire race of unpleasant Scottish sea faeries bears her name. She is depicted as a one-eyed crone with a black and blue face and a scaled body.

    The Fianna claimed she would occasionally fly in from over the sea and fight on their side in battle.

IN MAGICK AND RITUAL — See the Morrigan for full discussion.

MUNANNA (IRISH)

IN MYTH — This powerful witch left her boring husband for a dashing Viking pirate, but the Norseman, fearing the woman's power, pushed her overboard and she drowned. Today she is said to be heard crying out for revenge as she flies in the shape of a crane over the cliffs of Inishkea.

IN MAGICK AND RITUAL — Though not a potent archetype, Munanna can be helpful to us in understanding and overcoming our culturally bred fear of powerful women.

MURIGEN (IRISH, SCOTTISH, MANX)

A lake Goddess associated with the deluge myths.

MURNA OF THE WHITE NECK (IRISH)

IN MYTH — A daughter of Goll MacMorna who eloped with Cumhal against her father's wishes. She feared for the life of her unborn child and, when it came time to give him birth, fled deep into the forest. The boy, Demna, was born in the heart of the woodlands. Later his name would become Fionn MacCumhal.

IN MAGICAK AND RITUAL — The birth in the woods links her image to fertility, woodland, and fertile earth Goddesses. Call upon her for fertility, or eco- and earth magick.

NAAS (IRISH)

This Goddess was a wife of sun God Lugh. She died in County Kildare at a site which still bears her name.

NAIR (IRISH)

IN MYTH — [Nawr] This Goddess is less a Goddess than a personification of the concept of regicide, the king-killing which many ancient peoples, including the Celts, believed had to be done every so many years so that the sovereign's blood could fertilize the land. Legends said that all kings who slept with her would die.

She is best-known for escorting High King Crebhan to the Otherworld where she bestowed on him great treasures. Archetypally she represents the devourer image of the Goddess, the dark side of the crone.

Her name means "modesty."

IN MAGICK AND RITUAL — Ask Nair's aid in making spirit contact, assisting your Samhain rites, and in prosperity rites.

CORRESPONDENCES — The exact moment of the dark moon.

NANTOSUELTA (CONTINENTAL)

IN MYTH — Also Nantsovelta. Her Breton name is Nataseuelta. She is a river Goddess from Celtic Gaul whose name means "of the meandering stream." The root of her name, *nant,* is the modern Welsh word for "stream."

Some sources claim that her consort was Sucellos, a river God about whom nothing survives except his name. She is depicted carrying a cornucopia, and was probably also a fertility/prosperity Goddess, and a personification of the waters of the cauldron of rebirth.

IN MAGICK AND RITUAL — Fertility spells, harvest rites, and water magick.

NEHALENNIA (BRETON, ANGLO-CELTIC)

IN MYTH — A dog Goddess who was the patron deity of sea traders, possibly an image derived from Sirius (the Dog Star), once an important navigational star. The word "dog" is used frequently in terms related to British sailors and their effects (examples: salty dog, a drink; sea dog, a sailor).

IN MAGICK AND RITUAL — Call on Nehalennia for protection on the water.

NEMAIN (IRISH)

Also see the Morrigan. [NIM-awn or NIM-vahn] Also Neman and Nemhain, which means "venomous one." She is one of the three crone Goddesses of battle and strife which made up the Morrigan.

Sing louder around
To the bells' cheerful sound,
While our sport shall be seen
On the echoing green

—William Blake

NEMETONA (ANGLO-CELTIC, CONTINENTAL)

IN MYTH — Her name derives from the Gaulish word *nemeton,* meaning "sacred space." She is the guardian deity of all sacred places such as circles or magickal groves.

A shrine to her was erected at Bath, England, where she was depicted as seated and surrounded by three hooded figures and a ram. The three figures represent the Triple Goddess and the ram is a male fertility symbol often linked to Cernunnos, the Horned God.

IN MAGICK AND RITUAL — Call upon Nemetona for blessing your circle and for bestowing protection on all your sacred spaces.

CORRESPONDENCES — The circle, the pentagram, rings.

NEMONTONA (ANGLO-CELTIC, BRETON)

See also Nemain. Also spelled Nemona. A war Goddess who was called "the venomous." Associated with the Morrigan as a subordinate deity, most likely a lesser-known name for Nemain.

NESSA (IRISH)

IN MYTH — This promising scholar's original name was Assa, meaning "the gentle," but when Cathbad, a wicked Druid, murdered her tutors, she changed her name to Nessa, meaning "the ungentle."

After her name alteration, she became a great warrioress, defeating many kings who sought her hand by force. She did this by combining her physical skills with the mental ones taught by her tutors.

Cathbad eventually captured her and made her his concubine, but she refused to bear his children. Instead, she impregnated herself with two worms she found crawling on the rim of a sacred well. When her son, the future King Conchobar, was born he held in his hands two worms.

Nessa married Fachtna, then left him to wed his half-brother Fergus when he agreed to allow her son to become the next High King.

IN MAGICK AND RITUAL — Invoke her as a Goddess of sovereignty, feminine power, strength, and courage. Ask her aid in overcoming enemies, increasing mental prowess, and in helping you to look out for the interests of your children.

NIAMH (IRISH)

The wife of Conall of the Victories who became Cuchulain's last mistress. Badb put a staying spell on her—one which caused her to be lost and disoriented—so that she could beseech Cuchulain to save Ulster from the Connacht warriors.

NIAMH (IRISH)

The daughter of Celtchair the Druid. She married a warrior who possessed the secret of not being killed in battle. After she discovered his secret, she told it to her father who was then able to kill him. She married Cormac, the son of King Conchobar.

The winds awaken, the leaves whirl round,
Our cheeks are pale, our hair is unbound....

—William Butler Yeats,
Niamh's call from "The Hosting of the Sidhe"

NIAMH OF THE GOLDEN HAIR (IRISH)

IN MYTH — [NEE-ahv] The name of this daughter of Manann means "beauteous" or "lustrous." A Goddess who befriends warriors at the time of their death and leads them to Tir-na-nOg, a name for the Otherworld. As one of the names for the Land of the Dead, Tir-na-nOg is the realm of the ever-young where souls go to be rejuvenated.

Niamh took Ossian to the Otherworld to visit and, while they were there, she had two sons and a daughter by him. They lived happily there together while his Fianna friends in Ireland grew old and died. When Ossian wanted to visit earth once more she gave him a horse to ride which she said he could not for any reason dismount. When he disregarded her warning and left his mount, he immediately aged and died.

IN MAGICK AND RITUAL — Niamh can aid you in naming rites, spirit contact, working love magick or assisting in Passing Over rituals.

NICEVENN (SCOTTISH)

IN MYTH — A crone Goddess associated with Samhain. In later times she has been called a "witch" or "evil faery."

IN MAGICK AND RITUAL — Samhain rituals.

NIMUE (WELSH, CORNISH)

See Vivienne.

NOCTILUCA (CONTINENTAL)

A Goddess of magick from Celtic Gaul about whom nothing else is known. She may have originally been Roman.

OANUAVA (BRETON, CONTINENTAL)

An ancient earth Goddess from Celtic Gaul. She was probably a mother Goddess who was regionally worshipped as the source from which all life flowed.

ODRAS (IRISH)

IN MYTH — This Connacht girl refused to allow her cow to be mated to Slemauin the Smooth, the famous bull belonging to the Morrigan. The Morrigan took the cow away, and Odras followed them in anger to the gates of the Otherworld where the Morrigan turned her into a pool of water which remained to purify newcomers to that realm.

IN MAGICK AND RITUAL — Since the Morrigan are the supreme death and battle deities of the Celts, Odras' tale teaches us that death cannot be cheated or halted, no matter how we protest. When Odras' livelihood was taken (symbolized by the cow), she died (symbolized by her return to the elements), even though she tried in vain to fight the death Goddesses. Use her to learn about accepting the inevitable cycles of time rather than fearing them. This does not mean one should not fight for life, but we must be wise enough to realize when the struggle must end.

OLWEN (WELSH)

IN MYTH — [O-loon] Also Olwyn. A daughter of the king of the Giants, Ysbadadden. Her name means "the golden wheel," which makes some see her as an opposing force to Arianrhod of "the silver wheel." Her other nickname was "Lady of the White Tracks" because wherever she walked the trefoil plants commonly called shamrocks would pop up. This indicated that she may have been a Triple Goddess unto herself with several other associations long lost to us.

Olwen can aid you in making faery contact, or enhance Bealtaine
    The hero Culhwch was a suitor of Olwen's who went on a mythic journey to find her after her father, who knew he would die if their marriage took place, hid her. In this part of the myth she is a May Queen, a partner of the new sacrificial God who takes the place of the old one.

    Olwen also had adventures in faeryland after she was captured by horse-riding faeries. She was rescued by her father after a year and a day of captivity. (May Queens are often linked to the faery kingdom.)

IN MAGICK AND RITUAL — Olwen can aid you in making faery contact, or enhance Bealtaine rituals, and she can help women learn to tap into their own feminine power.

CORRESPONDENCES — The hawthorn tree, the trefoil.

ONAUGH (IRISH)

IN MYTH — Also Oona. She was the faery wife of Tuatha leader Finvarra. She tolerated his cheating with mortal women and seemed totally asexual herself, which may be a later addition to the myth since the Tuatha faeries are generally portrayed as very sexual creatures. She is always described as having golden hair so long it touches the ground. Onaugh is now popularly known as a Munster faery queen.

    She and Finvarra were probably once mighty creation mother/father images, and Onaugh may have origins in the Gaulish earth/mother Goddess Onuava.

IN MAGICK AND RITUAL — Assistance in faery contact.

OSTARA (PAN-CELTIC)

See Eostre.

PENDARDUN (WELSH)

A daughter of the Welsh mother Goddess Don. Little is known about her except that she was one of the several wives of Manann and is sometimes considered to be the mother of Bran and Branwyn. After she left Manann she married Eurosswyd and gave birth to the twins Nisien and Evnissyen, one of whom loved peace as the other cherished discord.

PLUR NA MBAN (IRISH)

IN MYTH — [Ploor nah Vawn] The daughter of Ossian and Niamh of the Golden Hair, born in Tir-na-nOg, the Otherworld realm which means "land of the ever-young." Her name means "woman of flowers," and she may have once been honored as a Goddess of Bealtaine, equated with Rome's flower Goddess Flora.

IN MAGICK AND RITUAL — Experiment with her youthful energy at the spring Sabbats or at Pagan flower festivals.

PRESSINE (BRETON)
[Pray-SEEN] The Breton sea faery woman who was the mother of Melusine by the King of Scotland.

PRINCESS OF THE SUN, THE (BRETON)
IN MYTH — Also called Princess Starbright. She was placed under an enchantment by some Nains (hideously misshapen and wicked Breton faeries) so that she could not appear as anything but a swan except for a short time at sundown.

She pleaded with the Miller of Lac de Leguer to free her by spending three nights in the Nains' haunted castle. She offered him the protection of the last of her magick and he agreed to the task. When it ended she gave him treasure and told him that she would return in a year and a day to marry him, which she did by flying in in a fiery chariot from the heavens.

She is also viewed as a minor sun and fire Goddess.

IN MAGICK AND RITUAL — Call on her for aid in overcoming enemies, for couples work, lessons in cooperation (often needed in coven settings), and for protection.

RASHINCOATIE (SCOTTISH)
IN MYTH — Rashincoatie is a Celtic Cinderella who lived with her nasty step-mother and two jealous step-sisters. Like her better-known counterpart, she was miserably treated and abused by them until, assisted by a friendly faery woman, she stole off to a grand ball where she met and married a prince.

IN MAGICK AND RITUAL — Pathwork with Rashincoatie to help you overcome your own childhood traumas. There's a lot to be said for visualizing yourself in a happy ending—whatever you choose it to be.

RATIS (ANGLO-CELTIC)
IN MYTH — A Goddess of protective fortifications whose name means "of the fortress." She is remembered today because the Britons set up shrines to her at various places along the Roman fortification known as Hadrian's Wall which ran the east-west length of northern England for the purpose of keeping raiding Scottish warriors on their own side of the border. Ratis' most notable worship sites were near the towns of Birdoswald and Chesters.

IN MAGICK AND RITUAL — Use the energy of Ratis when you need to build up and/or enhance your defenses. Call upon her to protect the boundaries of your sacred circle.

CORRESPONDENCES — Red jasper.

RHIANNON (WELSH, CORNISH)
IN MYTH — [R'HEE-awn-on] Rhiannon's names translates as "divine" or "great queen." She is a potent symbol of fertility, yet she is also an Otherworld and death Goddess, a bringer of dreams, and a moon deity who is symbolized by a white horse. Her father was Heveydd the Old, and she was married to both Pwyll and Manann.

Rhiannon, riding her pure white horse, appeared to her future husband Pwyll three different times before he was allowed to catch her. Though promised in marriage to Gwawl Ap Clud, a minor sun deity, she was determined to have Pwyll. He went to ask for her hand, but instead was tricked into giving her to Gwawl as a matter of honor. A year and a day later Rhiannon used her magick, a bit of conspiracy, and the guise of honor, to get away from

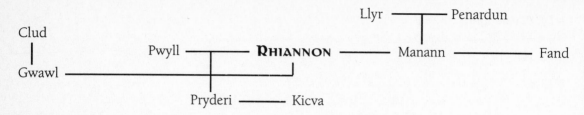

```
                                          Llyr ────┬──── Penardun
                                                   │
Clud                                               │
 │              Pwyll ────┬──── RHIANNON ────── Manann ────── Fand
 │                        │
Gwawl ───────────────────┤
                          │
                     Pryderi ────── Kicva
```

The generally accepted family tree of Rhiannon.

RHIANNON (CONT.)

Gwawl. Gwawl followed them, but Pwyll caught him up in a bag and then tried to have him slain by telling everyone he was a badger.

Rhiannon was falsely accused of killing her infant son, Pryderi, who was actually kidnapped. All six of her handmaids fell asleep when the child disappeared and, fearing they would be punished for their negligence, killed a dog and smeared her with the blood, sat bones near her bed, and accused her of eating the child. She was deemed guilty, but Pwyll, instead of having her killed, stood her at the gate of his city to carry people in on her back like a horse.

Her lost child was returned years later when a servant discovered him on Bealtaine. His relieved parents named him Pryderi, which means "trouble."

In her guise as a death Goddess, Rhiannon could sing sweetly enough to lure all those in hearing to their deaths, and therefore she may be related to Germanic stories of lake and river faeries who sing seductively to lure sailors and fishermen to their deaths. Her white horse images also link her to Epona, and many scholars feel they are one and the same, or at least are derived from the same archetypal roots.

Rhiannon's original name is thought to be Rigatona (Gaulish), also meaning "great queen," indicating a much higher status in the Celtic pantheon than she enjoys today. Some sources say she was once a sun Goddess.

The stories about her appear in the *Mabinogion*.

IN MAGICK AND RITUAL — Rhiannon can aid you in overcoming enemies, exercising patience, working magick, moon rituals, and enhancing dream work.

CORRESPONDENCES — Mares, silver, blood, the waning moon, jasmine, moonstones, the color white.

RHIANNON RHIN BRANAWD (WELSH)

IN MYTH — The possessor of a sealed vial of magickal potion needed to aid Culhwch in the search for his beloved Olwen. Archetypally she is a guardian of the feminine mysteries.

IN MAGICK AND RITUAL — Invoke or pathwork with her to learn more about the feminine mysteries.

ROSMERTA (ANGLO-CELTIC, CONTINENTAL)

IN MYTH — Rosmerta was a Goddess of both Celtic and Roman Gaul. After Rome conquered the region, Rosmerta was adopted into the local Roman pantheon where she became a consort of their God Mercury. In Roman depictions of her she carries a caduceus wand, an indication that she was adept in the healing arts.

In Celtic England her images are confused, and she is considered to be a Goddess of either water or the sun indicating that she may have been associated with hot springs.

IN MAGICK AND RITUAL — Cultivate Rosmerta to aid in healing and communication.

CORRESPONDENCES — The caduceus wand.

Saba (Irish)

IN MYTH — Also spelled Sadhbh, Sadv, and Sadb. A daughter of Bov the Red and wife of Fionn MacCumhal who was lured away from their house by forest faeries while she was pregnant. After she was hopelessly lost in the wild, the faeries turned her into a deer. She remained in the woodlands and gave birth to Ossian, the poet, who was born in human form and with his creative gifts already in evidence. He was later returned to his father.

Saba was also able to return to Fionn when he prevented her death at the hands of hunters. She went back home with him and became his mistress even though he had remarried and she retained her deer form.

IN MAGICK AND RITUAL — Magick for animals, aid in finding a familiar.

Sabrina (Anglo-Celtic)

See Savern.

Saitada (Anglo-Celtic)

(See also Scathach.) Her name may mean "grief", and she is known only from one inscription in the Tyne Valley. It has been suggested that she may have been a Goddess of mourning, or part of the Scathach legend.

Savern (Cornish, Anglo-Celtic)

Also Sabrina. She became the Goddess of the River Severn when she was drowned there by Vennolandua. She may be one and the same as Sequana.

Scathach (Irish, Scottish)

In Myth — [SCAH-yah'k] Also Scathach nUanaind, Scathach Buanand ("victorious"), and Skatha. Her name means "shadowed one" or "one who strikes fear." She lived on the Isle of Shadow in the Hebrides where she had a school to which the greatest of Ireland's warriors came to be trained. She was famous for invincible battle methods such as the magickal leap and the battle yell, a technique also employed effectively by the Native Americans (the war whoop), and by the Confederate soldiers (the rebel yell) during the American Civil War.

Cuchulain, possibly Ireland's greatest warrior hero, was one of her students, as were many of the other Red Branch warriors. Like the Lady of the Lake in the Arthurian sagas, she bestowed on her most deserving pupil a magickal sword (see Chapter 10 for more on this part of the legend). Scathach did not train women because of a Celtic belief which stated that only women could teach men effective battle skills, and only men could teach them to women.

Scathach was Amazonian in size and seemingly ageless. She was also a powerful magician, a rival of her sister Aife.

IN MAGICK AND RITUAL — Call on Scathach for weaving potent magick, to learn fighting skills, to offer protection, or invite her to aid you when you are the teacher.

CORRESPONDENCES — Shields, swords, garnets.

SCEANB (IRISH)

The wife of Craftiny. Craftiny killed Sceanb's lover, Cormac, in a jealous rage.

SCENA (IRISH)

IN MYTH — The wife of the bard Amergin who once had a shrine at the mouth of the River Kenmare. She was probably once worshipped as a Goddess of confluence.

IN MAGICK AND RITUAL — Experiment with her energies as a Goddess of mergers and subtle changes.

SCENMED (IRISH)

After Cuchulain eloped with her step-daughter, Emer, Scenmed raised an army to follow him to Ulster and steal the girl back. She was slain by him for her unsuccessful efforts.

SCOTA (IRISH)

IN MYTH — She was probably once a mother Goddess in her native Egypt, but her myth and origins today are shadowy. The general agreement is that she was the daughter of the Pharaoh Cingris, after which the stories about her diverge, some even merging her with Christian Biblical figures. In most tales she is the mother of Amergin the bard, though she is said to be the wife of both Milesius and Niul. She died in the Milesian invasion and is thought to be buried near a dolmen (a primitive stone altar) in County Kerry.

The Ankh.

The name Scoti, derived from her own, was once a designation for the Irish, and later became the name of the Scottish people.

IN MAGICK AND RITUAL — Call on her to aid you in finding the right names for yourself and other things. Experiment with her energies as a mother Goddess.

CORRESPONDENCES — The ankh, the Egyptian symbol of life.

SEQUANA (ANGLO-CELTIC, CONTINENTAL)

IN MYTH — Also Sequena. An earth Goddess who lived beneath the rivers of Britain and could be seen only if the rivers were drained or low from drought. Originally she was a continental deity who ruled the Seine Valley. Each year at a festival held in her honor, her image, appearing very like a duck, was paraded down the river, and trinkets and coins tossed to her in mock sacrifice.

Later she came to Britain where she remained the Goddess to the many other river Goddesses.

IN MAGICK AND RITUAL — Call on Sequana for prosperity rites, or for making earth and water magick. Use her presence to purify your circles. Invoke her for prosperity rites.

CORRESPONDENCES — Rue and salt water, the latter a time-honored purifier.

SGEIMH SOLAIS (IRISH)

This High King's daughter's name means "light of beauty." When she married a Desi, a rival "race," she began a war between her father's followers and the Fianna.

SHEILA-NA-GIG (IRISH)

IN MYTH — Little is known about this curious deity except that she was a pervasive image found carved on Irish doorways and stones, presumably for protection or blessing, or as an invitation to the feminine mysteries. Her figure is a crude rendering of a woman holding wide her vulva in a triangular pattern.

Many of these carvings were used by nuns to adorn the doors of early Irish convents. When these were discovered by horrified churchmen, they were broken off and destroyed. A hundred years ago an archaeologist found a pile of them buried near the ruins of an old church.

Today she is seen by Celtic Pagans as a Goddess of regeneration, akin to the Goddesses of the great cauldron of the Other-world.

Archetypally her yawning vulva represents the gateway to the feminine half of the All-Power.

IN MAGICK AND RITUAL — Use her image for harnessing feminine power, or to help reveal past and future lives.

Sheila-na-gig.

CORRESPONDENCES — Doors, portals, passageways, caves—the archetypal symbol of the womb of the great mother.

SIN (IRISH)

IN MYTH — [Shin] This one-time patron Goddess of warriors has been reduced to being a minor faery who feeds on war, similar to the Morrigan. The oldest legends about her portray her as a powerful deity who could make wine from water and swine from leaves in order to feed and fortify her fighting forces.

Traces of folklore exist that link her to the feminine half of the All-Power which, if the antiquity of these can be proven, would tie her to some of the oldest Goddess images of the Middle East. In Kaballistic mysticism the Hebrew letter *shin* (a similar word with the same pronunciation) symbolizes the fire of creativity made by the God and Goddess merging as one divine force. In modern Irish the word *sin* is the demonstrative form of the word "that."

The Hebrew letter "shin."

IN MAGICK AND RITUAL — Call on her for stamina and strength to fight problems, to help handle legal matters, or overcome enemies. Also ask her for protection and prosperity. Evoke her as a patron Goddess if you give your time and energy to aiding the hungry or the homeless.

SIONNAN (IRISH)

IN MYTH — [SHON-nahn] Also Sineand and Sinnan. A granddaughter of Manann who was the Goddess and namesake of the River Shannon. She went to a magickal well to perform an unspecified ritual, but she came unprepared and irreverent. Worse yet, this well was the great well of knowledge, sacred to the Cailleach. Sionnan's actions so outraged the well's waters that they rose up and sucked her into themselves. She was washed up on the banks of the River Shannon. For her effrontery she was denied entrance to the Otherworld, and now resides in her river as the queen of the well spirits of Ireland.

SIONNAN (CONT.)

Her story parallels that of Boann.

IN MAGICK AND RITUAL — Ask her to aid you in faery contact or in well rituals.

CORRESPONDENCES — Wells, river stones, river sand.

SIRONA (BRETON, CONTINENTAL)

IN MYTH — Also spelled Dirona. Her name means "star." She was a Goddess of the many bene-ficial hot springs in southern France from which her few extant legends came. She was also a sky Goddess, probably a deity of the sun.

She was the mother of Borvo, who usurped her position in patriarchal times.

IN MAGICK AND RITUAL — Healing and purification.

CORRESPONDENCES — Fire, boiling water.

SMIRGAT (IRISH)

In Myth — One of the many wives of Fionn MacCumhal. She told him that if he ever drank from a horn he would die. The horn to the Celts was a vessel of completeness, a symbol of the womb of the mother Goddess inside and the phallus of the father God outside. After this warning Fionn always drank from a bowl or cup.

Archetypally she represents the guardian of feminine mysteries.

IN MAGICK AND RITUAL — Tap into her power to gain feminine power and learn the mysteries.

CORRESPONDENCES — The cauldron.

STINE BHEAG O' TARBAT (SCOTTISH)

IN MYTH — This old woman, who lived near Tarbat Ness, was said to be very powerful, with special mastery over the weather. As her story came into modern times she was reduced to a vindictive old hag or baneful faery who used her powers for spite rather than assistance. In the modern stories about her, those who come to her for help address her as "mother." It is reasonable to assume that she was once a Scottish Pagan leader, perhaps a highly placed Druidess, or even a local mother Goddess.

IN MAGICK AND RITUAL — General aid in magick, and for making weather magick.

SUL (CONTINENTAL)

IN MYTH — Also Sulla, Sulis, or Sulevia. The root word of her name, *siul,* means "eye," a word archetypally linked to the sun in Celtic lore. She was a Goddess of hot springs whose sacred waters always ran hot. Prince Bladud built a shrine to her near Aquae Sulis where the popular modern-day spa is located. The waters were once believed to hold powerful healing magick, and a perpetual fire burned near them in her honor.

Sul is depicted in bas-reliefs with a foot on an owl (a symbol of death and disease to the Romans), and wearing a hat made of the head of a bear (a symbol of strength and power to the Celts).

The Romans adopted her and called her Sul Minerva, a deity later associated with Imbolg and with Ireland's Brid. She may be one and the same as Adsullata.

IN MAGICK AND RITUAL — Invite Sul to Imbolg rites and ask her aid in healing rituals.

CORRESPONDENCES — Sacred fires.

Taillte (Irish)

IN MYTH — [TAWL-tay, TAHL-y'uh-too, or TELL-tay] Also spelled Taultiu, Tailtu, and Telta. A Goddess of the Lughnasadh Sabbat associated with the harvest of first grains, particularly of wheat, a feminine fertility symbol. She is cryptically said to be the foster mother of light. This has been interpreted by some to mean the physical being of Lugh, an Irish sun God, but it may also be a remnant of an even older creation myth in which the Goddess gives birth to the sun itself.

Taillte lived at Tara, and was there revered as an earth deity and patron Goddess of competition. She had the Plain of Oenach Taillten cleared of its woods in order to create a playing field. Annual games festivals were held at this site (now called Teltown) until 1169; formal, organized games considered to be an Irish Olympics. (Some Celtic scholars say these were originally associated with Passing Over rites for reasons which are not completely clear.) The games were revived in the late nineteenth century when a renewed interest in Irish culture flourished.

Medieval trial marriages—for a duration of a year and a day—were held on her sacred site to promote fertility. Lack of fertility was the primary reason these marriages were dissolved at the end of the trial period.

Taillte was the daughter of the FirBolg, Magh Mor, and wife of Duach the Dark of the Tuatha De Danann.

IN MAGICK AND RITUAL — Taillte's energy is compatible with seasonal and harvest rites, fertility magick, and enhancing strength for competitive games.

CORRESPONDENCES — Wheat, blood, geode stones, holey stones, bistort, and game pieces.

Tamara (Cornish)

IN MYTH — The Goddess of the River Tamar which divides the Duchy of Cornwall from the rest of England. She was probably as much of a protective force as she was a water deity.

IN MAGICK AND RITUAL — Call on the energy of Tamara when you need to create or fortify your own boundaries.

Tamesis (Anglo-Celtic)

The Goddess and namesake of the River Thames, later replaced in patriarchal times by Llud, for whom Ludgate Hill in London is named.

Taranis (Continental)

IN MYTH — A death Goddess to whom human sacrifices were offered. Some etymologists say that when her name is broken down to its roots it means "tsar of the west," which would link her to the realm of the Otherworld. She should not to be confused with Gaulish God Taranus.

IN MAGICK AND RITUAL — Involve Taranis in Passing Over rituals.

CORRESPONDENCES — Cairn stones, nightshade, yew.

At Tara today in this fateful hour
I place all heaven with its power.

—St. Patrick

Tea and Tephi (Irish)

IN MYTH—Tea [Tee or TEE-uh] and Tephi [T'hee] were co-founders and protectors of the sacred site at Tara. Current Irish legends say they named the site after themselves, though some claim it was named for Tara, a star Goddess of India whose myths traveled west with the Celts. Originally Ireland's Tara was called *Temair* or *Tea Mur* meaning "the wall of Tea."

However, as a fortification, Tara dates to around 2000 B.C.E. (and it remained the Irish royal stronghold until the ninth century). This pre-dates these two Milesian deities who are often referred to as "princesses" in modern tales.

IN MAGICK AND RITUAL — Call on these two to protect sacred spaces or to aid you in seeking to find your sacred space. They also share a connection with the ancient Celtic powers sleeping in wait at Tara which can be connected with through deep meditation and path-working.

CORRESPONDENCES — Cut stones, cornerstones.

Tlachtga (Irish)

IN MYTH — [T'LACH-t'gkah] The Daughter of Mog Ruith, an Arch-Druid, and a gifted magician in her own rite. She died giving birth to triplets by three different fathers.

She is a sacrificial Goddess associated with Samhain, and Samhain rites were once held on her sacred hill in County Meade, a site which once bore her name. Today it is known as the Hill of Ward.

IN MAGICK AND RITUAL — Call Tlachtga to your Samhain rituals and invoke her during Croneage rites of passage.

Triduana (Scottish)

IN MYTH — This Goddess of Edinburgh plucked out her eyes to destroy her own beauty rather than submit to the advances of Nechtan, King of the Picts.

She is thought by many to be an eastern Scottish version of the Irish Goddess Brid.

IN MAGICK AND RITUAL — See Brid for full discussion.

Be mindful of the name of the Trinity
And none shall ever overcome you.

—Taliesin

Triple Goddess, The (Pan-Celtic)

IN MYTH — The Triple Goddess is known and worshiped in Pagan cultures the world over (though a few cultures worship a female foursome). She is eternal, yet always in a state of flux, only her names and faces change. Like the moon which represents her, she shows a different face throughout her eternal cycle, yet she is always the same moon. At once she is the Maiden, Mother, and Crone, the creatrix who births all things into being, who devours all at its ending, and who provides life anew when the cycle begins again.

Many different colors are attributed to her, but in Celtic Paganism they are white for the Maiden, red for the Mother, and black for the Crone.

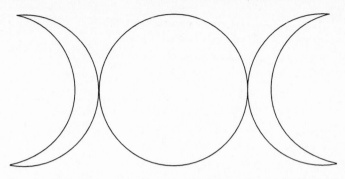

The symbol of the Triple Goddess: The waxing, full, and waning moons.

Throughout the Celtic lands many ancient remnants of her preeminence remain. One of the best examples survives at Corleck, County Cavan, Ireland, where an ancient and weathered stone is carved with three faces. Each face looks out to a different direction.

IN MAGICK AND RITUAL — When working magick in sync with the moon phases, draw into yourself the appropriate aspect to aid you. By doing this any magickal goal can be aided.

CORRESPONDENCES — The moon, the entwining of her three colors (red, white, and black), menstrual blood, silver (the metal), moonstones, all things which come in threes.

Tryphyna, Princess (Breton)

IN MYTH — [Truh-PHEE-nuh] This princess was claimed as bride by King Conomor, also known as Comorre the Cursed, a giant king who was believed to have slain his four previous mates. In order to keep peace in her kingdom, Tryphyna reluctantly agreed to the marriage. As a wedding gift from her family, she was given a golden ring which would turn black if she were ever in danger.

All was fine until she told Conomor that she was to have a baby. Conomor was afraid of the child because he had been told by a Druid that any son of his would slay him. This was the reason he killed his previous mates.

When Conomor heard of Tryphyna's pregnancy, the ring she wore turned deep black, and she ran off to pray near the graves of her husband's four late wives. When she finished her pleas, their spirits rose from the graves, and they each gave her means of escape and lesson in how to use them: poison (water element), fire (fire element), rope (air element), and a stick (earth element).

By taking the advice of her predecessors she managed to escape Conomor and, later, gave birth to the child who, predictably, slew his father.

This legend is yet another story of the old king who would not step down when it was his time, but instead feared the young God who was to replace him. Archetypally Tryphyna is another May Queen, the representative of the earth to whom the blood sacrifice must be made. As in all Pagan legends, the mother becomes the consort of her grown son until he, too, must die.

IN MAGICK AND RITUAL — Tryphyna can teach us to wield the power of elements, to overcome enemies, and to work with all forms of elemental magick. Evoke her spirit into a ring for protection.

CORRESPONDENCES — The alchemical symbols and all circular protective devices.

TURREAN (IRISH)

IN MYTH — Also Tureann. This lovely Goddess was transformed into the first large, shaggy Irish Wolfhound by a jealous faery queen named Uchtdealbh. But the spell had its flaw: Turrean not only turned into a dog but, quite literally, became the most beautiful bitch ever seen on earth. Turrean was kept a prisoner at the faery's home in Galway Bay until her brother, the warrior chief Fionn MacCumhal, rescued her and her two sons, Bran and Sgeolan, who retained the shape of dogs for the rest of their lives. (The sons are often portrayed as guard dogs seated near Fionn.)

Turrean and her tormentor archetypally represent the maiden and crone Goddess, the former which must replace the latter when the year begins anew.

Do not confuse this Goddess with the God Tuirrean.

IN MAGICK AND RITUAL — Pathwork with Turrean to learn to make the best of a bad situation, to help you in the care of dogs, or for working with dog familiars. Call upon her maiden form for New Year's rites.

CORRESPONDENCES — The Irish Wolfhound.

UAIREBHUIDHE (IRISH)

A bird Goddess about whom little is known. Because of the Celtic association of birds and death, she was probably a death or Otherworld Goddess, or perhaps a consort of the better-known bird God Nemglan.

UATHACH (IRISH, SCOTTISH)

IN MYTH — A Goddess who taught warriors to fight. She was the daughter of Scathach, and her right hand at the warrior school on the Isle of Shadow. Her name means "specter."

One day in training, Cuchulain accidentally broke Uathach's finger. Her screams of pain summoned her lover, the Scottish warrior Cochar Crufe, to fight on her behalf against the perceived insult. Cuchulain killed him and Uathach and Scathach made Cuchulain replace him as the guardian of their island for a year and a day. During that time Uathach became his mistress, one of many Cuchulain would have over his lifetime.

IN MAGICK AND RITUAL — Protection and strength.

VAGA (ANGLO-CELTIC)

The Goddess of the River Wye.

VARIA (IRISH)

IN MYTH — Varia was a woman of extremely bad temperament. One day her husband, Donagha, made her so mad that the blast from her fit of temper propelled him from their home in Kerry to the far northern end of Ulster. When she realized what she had done she was sorry, but Donagha refused to return to her.

IN MAGICK AND RITUAL — Learn from Varia the right use of temper in magickal intent.

VELEDA (CONTINENTAL)

IN MYTH — Veleda was a warrior queen of a continental Celtic people known as the Bructeri. At the time she ruled, the Celts were at war with Rome. Her military prowess and skillful leadership inspired her legions to steal a Roman ship and tow it home up the River Lippe to her.

IN MAGICK AND RITUAL — Call upon Veleda when you need to enhance your leadership skills, inspire others, or lead troops.

VENNOLANDUA (CORNISH)

IN MYTH — The wife of Cornwall's King Locrin who dumped her to marry his mistress, Estrildis. Vennolandua killed Locrin in combat and drowned the mistress and her daughter, Savern (Savern then became the Goddess of that river, the Severn). Vennolandua then ruled as High Queen of Cornwall until Maddan, her son, came of age.

Her Welsh name is Gwendolyn.

IN MAGICK AND RITUAL — Call on her for reclaiming feminine power, or for exercising leadership roles.

VERBEIA (ANGLO-CELTIC)

The Goddess of the Wharfe and Avon Rivers.

VIRADECHTHIS (SCOTTISH)

See Harimella.

VIVIENNE (WELSH, CORNISH, BRETON)

IN MYTH — Also spelled Nimue (Malory's name for her), Niniane, or Chwimbian. She was the lover of Merlin who is sometimes associated with attributes of the Lady of the Lake, and some legends claim she is the Lake Lady's daughter.

She was a more powerful magician than her famous lover, but she was unscrupulous, and craved more power. To hold onto him she convinced him she had him captive in a tower when they were actually in an open wood. In Cornish legends, she used her wiles to gain Merlin's secrets of magick and shape-shifting, and used them to trap him in his cave. In Brittany, she enticed him to meet her in the Forest of Brocelaide, where she entombed him in stone. Needless to say, all these attempts at magickal manipulation were either thwarted or backfired on her.

Some believe Merlin's romance with her was not originally a part of the Arthurian legends, but a spurious one added to round out the romantic themes.

In Breton legend, Vivienne is the woman who escorts Arthur to Avalon at his death. In this guise as a death Goddess she is often equated with Rhiannon.

IN MAGICK AND RITUAL — Vivienne can be a boon to sex or couples magick despite her negative press. She can also teach us about the dangers of manipulative magick of any kind, but especially in love where we are all tempted.

CORRESPONDENCES — The throne.

VIVIONN (WELSH)

IN MYTH — Called Bebhionn in Ireland. This young giantess was the daughter of Treon who resided in the Land of Women, one of the many synonyms for the Otherworld. On her fingers she wore thick gold rings, large enough for a person to live within. Against her wishes she was engaged to marry Aeda, a dwarf king, after which she ran off and sought the protection of the Fianna.

VIVIONN (CONT.)

She was killed by Aeda by a blow in the eye when she refused his hand in marriage, and was buried with full divine honors at a place known as the Ridge of the Dead.

IN MAGICK AND RITUAL — Evoke her for assistance in Passing Over rituals.

CORRESPONDENCES — Yew.

WACHILT (ANGLO-CELTIC)

A minor sea Goddess, later called a "witch" in English mythology. She is the mother of Wayland the Smith, a German God honored in England.

YSEULT (BRETON)

See Isolde.

⚜ ⚜ ⚜ ⚜ ⚜

This dictionary of Goddesses and heroines is in no way intended to be the final word on Celtic mythology. Your own tradition may have a unique view of the feminine mythic figures and tailor its rituals accordingly. This is as it should be. Likewise, your own individual viewpoints and mythic experiences are important to your spiritual practices. The following blank pages are provided for you to jot down these feelings and insights so that you can conveniently keep in one place as much information about the Celtic Goddesses as possible.

Notes

NOTES

Notes

NOTES

Notes

NOTES

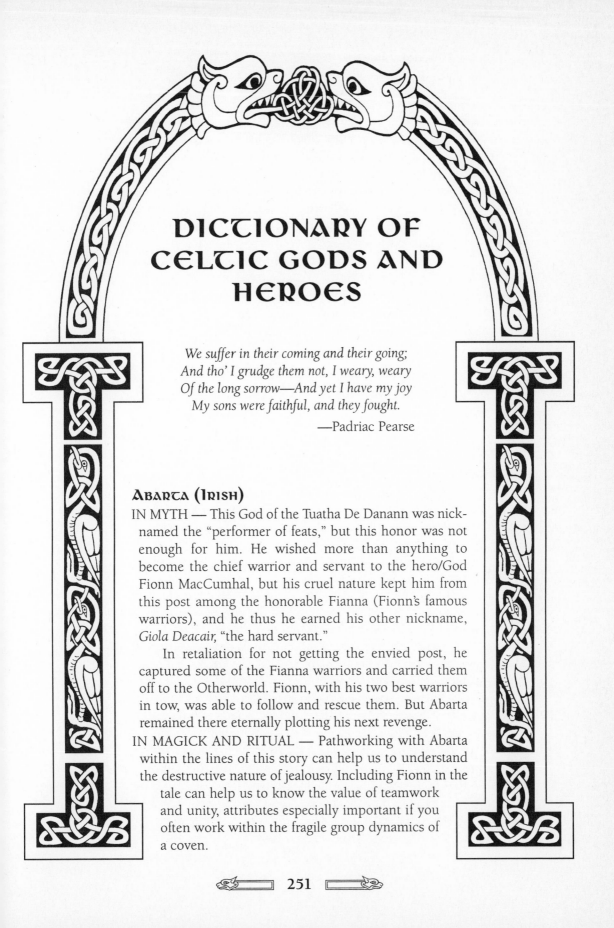

DICTIONARY OF CELTIC GODS AND HEROES

We suffer in their coming and their going;
And tho' I grudge them not, I weary, weary
Of the long sorrow—And yet I have my joy
My sons were faithful, and they fought.

—Padriac Pearse

ABARTA (IRISH)

IN MYTH — This God of the Tuatha De Danann was nick-named the "performer of feats," but this honor was not enough for him. He wished more than anything to become the chief warrior and servant to the hero/God Fionn MacCumhal, but his cruel nature kept him from this post among the honorable Fianna (Fionn's famous warriors), and he thus he earned his other nickname, *Giola Deacair,* "the hard servant."

In retaliation for not getting the envied post, he captured some of the Fianna warriors and carried them off to the Otherworld. Fionn, with his two best warriors in tow, was able to follow and rescue them. But Abarta remained there eternally plotting his next revenge.

IN MAGICK AND RITUAL — Pathworking with Abarta within the lines of this story can help us to understand the destructive nature of jealousy. Including Fionn in the tale can help us to know the value of teamwork and unity, attributes especially important if you often work within the fragile group dynamics of a coven.

ABELARD (BRETON)

IN MYTH — [AB-uh-lard] Abelard was sent by the Duke of Brittany to study with the great scholars of Europe in France. In a short time he found he hated France, and was appalled at the offhanded way in which the natives killed their deer, an animal his people held sacred. Despite his hatred of the country, he flourished as a brilliant scholar.

While in France, he fell in love with Heloise, a daughter of a canon of Paris, a scholarly disgrace which caused him to be mutilated by his angry uncle. Since he was an apprenticed student he was not legally allowed to marry, and the uncle was angry because he felt he was betraying Brittany, which sent him there.

He and Heloise died together and are buried in one tomb. They were faithful in their love until the end, determined that they could have both worlds. Two trees, one dark-barked and the other light, are said to grow entwined above their joint grave.

IN MAGICK AND RITUAL — Call on Abelard for aid in magick for love, loyalty, or mental prowess. Couples, or other covens of two, will also find these two archetypes useful.

ACCASBEL (IRISH)

IN MYTH — A Partholan who is credited with creating the first tavern, or public house (pub), in Ireland. He was likely an early God of wine or meade.

IN MAGICK AND RITUAL — Cultivate Accasbel at Mabon to celebrate the vine harvest or at Bealtaine for the blessing of the meade.

CORRESPONDENCES — Ale, meade, wine.

ADAMMAIR (IRISH)

IN MYTH — [AD-ah-mawr] The husband of the mistress of the beasts, Flidais. He was such a virile lover that in her absence he needed seven mortal women to satisfy him.

IN MAGICK AND RITUAL — Ask for his aid in sex magick and stamina.

CORRESPONDENCES — Dill.

ADDANC (WELSH)

IN MYTH — [ATH-ank or AV-anhk] Also spelled Affanc. Flood/deluge myths are almost a universal phenomenon in world mythology, with the best known in the west being the one concerning Noah in the Judeo-Christian tradition. Addanc is part of the Celtic flood myth, a primordial giant/God/faery (some accounts call him a dragon or demon) who created and rode the crest of the flood near his home on the Lake of Waves.

The God/Hero Dwyvan, and his wife, the Goddess/Heroine Dwyfach, escaped the flood in an ark. Depending on your version of the myth, Addanc was slain either by oxen belonging to Hu the Mighty, or by Peredur, and the waters receded.

Though he has been reduced to faery or evil demi-God by recent mythological scholarship, he was probably once a deity worshipped by the people of the lake region. Today Addanc is a word used to describe any evil fresh water-dwelling faery of Wales.

IN MAGICK AND RITUAL — Addanc can help you when you wish to erase an event, person, or other memory from your mind. Allow his flood waters to wipe away unwanted thoughts providing a fresh start.

CORRESPONDENCES — The number five, driftwood.

Adna (Irish)

IN MYTH — This bard was one of Ireland's great poets, and the father of another poet, Neide. He was in the employ of King Conchobar.

IN MAGICK AND RITUAL — Invoke him to get your own creative juices flowing.

Aeda (Welsh)

[AE-vah] The dwarfish faery king who sought the hand of the giantess, Vivionn, whom he later killed.

Aedan (Irish)

IN MYTH — [AY-dan] Also spelled Aidan. Aedan is the warrior who killed Mael Fhothartaig of the Red Branch. Mael was the son of Ronan, who was jealous of his own offspring. This is one of the many stories in Celtic myth which depicts a son or grandson whom the father or grandfather fears because of the elder's archetypal sacrificial role. The jealous elder deities or heroes often seek to kill the usurper and postpone or cancel their own deaths, even though the enlightened reader recognizes the two as merely opposite aspects of the same being.

Aedan was killed by Mael's sons in revenge, and Mael's line took the throne.

IN MAGICK AND RITUAL — This myth can teach us much about the passing of time, though its most potent archetypes are those of the main characters. Use Aedan and Ronan if you belong to a coven which role plays the sacrificial battles of Midsummer and Yule.

Aedh (Irish)

IN MYTH — [A'ee] A fourth century B.C.E. king of Ireland who ruled jointly with his two brothers, Cimbaeth and Dithorba, making up one of the little-known male triplicities in Celtic lore.

IN MAGICK AND RITUAL — Men who are uncomfortable working solely with a Triple Goddess might wish to try connecting with Aedh and his brothers. Women who feel ready to explore other aspects of their inner-selves might also benefit from this contact.

Aedh Dubh (Irish)

See Arca Dubh.

Aengus MacAedh (Irish)

IN MYTH — A brother of the faery Goddess Fand who was able to use his own magickal songs to cure her lover Cuchulain's illness.

IN MAGICK AND RITUAL — Aengus' energy lends itself well to healing and music magick.

CORRESPONDENCES — Mistletoe.

Aengus MacLamh Gabuid (Irish)

IN MYTH — [Mac LAHV GA-boo-ee] A warrior who challenged Cet to a bragging contest in retaliation for his cutting off the hands of Aengus' father. Bragging contests were popular among the Nordic deities, and this myth may have been influenced by the Norse invaders.

IN MAGICK AND RITUAL — If you are low on self-esteem, invoke this God of arrogant verbosity to bolster yourself.

> *I went out to the hazel wood*
> *Because a fire was in my head,*
> *And cut and peeled a hazel wand....*

—William Butler Yeats,
from "The Song of Wandering Aengus"

Aengus MacOg (Irish)

IN MYTH — [AWN-ghus or AING-uhs] Also spelled Oenghus and Aonghus. MacOg means literally "son of the young," though it has also been translated as "son of the virgin." That is virgin in old sense of the word, a woman intact, whole, complete unto herself, and fully independent.

Aengus was the handsome and witty harpist of the Tuatha De Danann, the son of Dagda and Boann, usually called the God of young love. He was a patron God of poets and musicians, though he does not seem to have been a bard in his own right.

Aengus tricked his father into giving him Newgrange Cairn (*Bruigh na Boinne*), and the stone bowl in its inner-chamber is often associated with his magick. The Dagda grew jealous of him and coveted the cairn for his own. This Cairn is a type of ritual burial site properly referred to as a *tumulus* or "barrow." It exists today and is a cherished and protected ancient site in Ireland.

In one of the most well-known myths involving him, Aengus helped the fugitive lovers, Diarmuid and Grainne, escape Fionn MacCumhal's vengeful wrath. He pleaded their case to Fionn and secured their freedom from his pursuit. He also abducted the unhappy Edain, the wife of Midhir, from her imprisonment in faeryland.

Sometimes he has been called a God of death or, more accurately, of fatal love, and he is often discussed in terms which credit him with powers similar to those of both Mabon and Apollo. He is most strongly equated with the Greek love God Eros.

IN MAGICK AND RITUAL — Call on Aengus for music magick, aid in romantic love, protection of lovers, dream work, creative inspiration, or music magick.

CORRESPONDENCES — Bowls, sapphires, cinnamon, clay, red roses, copper, rose quartz.

Aesun (Irish)

[AEE-son] An early Irish God whose name means "to be." He was probably part of a lost creation myth. Aesun was also known by the early Persians and in Umbria and Scandinavia.

Ai (Irish)

IN MYTH — [Aw or Ee] Also spelled Aoi. He was a bard and poet of the Tuatha De Danann who fulfilled a Druidic prophecy with his great talents and magickal powers of music. The prophecy said that if a great wind rocked the home where his pregnant mother dwelled, that he would be this gifted person. A local king, fearing the boy's talents, ordered him slain, but he was saved by his father Olloman.

IN MAGICK AND RITUAL — Ai is an excellent source of energy for the making of music magick.

Aichleach (Irish)

[AWHK-leehk] Also spelled Ailach. The killer of Fionn MacCumhal during a Fianna rebellion.

AILILL AGACH (IRISH)

[AW-leel or EL-yell AG-ohk] The father of mythic voyager Mael Duin. He is also referred to as Ailill Edge-of-Battle, and he was killed by a rival clan from Leinster before his son set out on his famous adventure.

AILILL DUBH-DEDACH (IRISH)

IN MYTH — [Doov DAY-dock] A warrior who reputedly could be harmed by no known weapon, yet, like his Greek counterpart Achilles, had one single weakness to which the myths only allude. He was killed during his quest to win the hand of Princess Delbchaem.

IN MAGICK AND RITUAL — Though he has no strong magickal archetypes, his story can provide us with the reaffirmation that no one is invincible or perfect.

AILILL, KING (IRISH)

A king of Leinster who was poisoned by Cobthach, a king of Bregia. His own son, Moen, was forced to eat his carcass.

AILILL MACMATA, KING (IRISH)

The husband of Queen Maeve of Connacht. His taunting cajoled his jealous wife to go to war with Ulster over a prize bull. This story is told in the famed Irish legend, *The Cattle Raid of Cooley*. He was killed by Conall of the Victories.

AILILL OLOM (IRISH)

This Munster king raped the Munster Goddess Aine and she killed him for it.

AINLE (IRISH)

One of Naoise's two brothers who was slain with him at the Red Branch encampment.

AITHERNE (IRISH, MANX)

IN MYTH — [AWTH-hern] A bard who stole King Midhir's infamous Three Cranes of Denial, Deceit, and Churlishness. Birds were the principal vehicle by which travel to the Land of the Dead was possible. Archetypally, this theft cuts off Midhir's access to the Otherworld and leaves him vulnerable.

IN MAGICK AND RITUAL — Call on Aitherne to help symbolically disarm your enemies.

ALBION (ANGLO-CELTIC)

A giant fathered by a forgotten Celtic sea God who may have been part of a lost creation myth. He once was said to rule the Celtic world, and his name became the poetic name for Britain.

> *But if my lips no longer frame*
> *The glories of our Alain's name,*
> *My heart shall ever sing his praise,*
> *Who won the fight and wears the bays.*
>
> —Villemarque

ALIAN BARBE-TORTE (BRETON)

IN MYTH — [Ah-Lee'AWN Barb-TORT] A celebrated red-headed tenth-century war chief who drove the Norse from Brittany in a decisive victory. He is sometimes called Alian the Fox, or

ALIAN BARBE-TORTE (CONT.)

Alian of the Twisted Beard, named for a common style of Celtic facial hair dress. The French poet Villemarque wrote a ballad about the event supposedly taken from a story told him by a soldier who fought with Alian. For his service Alian was crowned Arch-chief, or a minor king, of Brittany in 937.

IN MAGICK AND RITUAL — Alain can teach us lessons about serving our country.

ALISANOS (CONTINENTAL)

IN MYTH — A Gaulish God of stones about whom little is known. He was most likely a deity of the standing stones of Brittany or the consort of a Celtic continental earth Goddess. His phallic stone impregnated the mother earth.

IN MAGICK AND RITUAL — Fertility.

CORRESPONDENCES — Barley.

AMAETHAON (WELSH)

IN MYTH — The Welsh word for ploughman is *amaeth,* and Amaethaon has always been the patron deity of the farmers of Wales. He was a master magician, the son of the Goddess Don, and brother of Govannon and Gwyddion, the latter to whom he taught the art of magick.

Amaethaon was one of the few beings, deity or mortal, permitted to venture into Annwn, the Land of the Dead, and return to the earth plane again without being harmed or greatly changed. However, while he was there, he stole away a sacred dog and a stag. This act was the direct cause of one of the most famous events in Welsh mythology, the Battle of the Trees (*Cad Goddeu*).

His other famous fight was against Bran, another agricultural God, and this may have been another case of the elder God trying to slay his successor.

Amaethaon was encouraged to try to earn the hand of Olwen, for many of his fellow Gods believed only he was capable of performing the forty monumental tasks required to win her. He refused the offer.

IN MAGICK AND RITUAL — If you are seeking to improve your magickal skills, try aligning yourself with Amaethaon. However, keep in mind that his story teaches, above all else, that one must handle magick responsibly.

CORRESPONDENCES — Ploughs, oxen, oleander (poisonous).

AMBISAGRUS (BRETON)

IN MYTH — This deity was originally from Gaul, where his Celtic identity was lost during the Roman takeover. Instead, Ambisagrus took on all the characteristics of the Roman God Jupiter. Jupiter's name (Jove in Latin) means "supreme God." He was a deity who was seen presiding over the city/state matters of Rome and of the realm of the deities.

Other than his Jovian associations, Ambisagrus was primarily a weather deity who controlled the functions of rain, wind, hail, and fog.

IN MAGICK AND RITUAL — Call on Ambisagrus for making weather magick. Also invoke him if you are seeking to imbue yourself with leadership qualities.

CORRESPONDENCES — For Jupiter: The Wheel of Fortune or Magician Tarot cards, cedar, the swastika, scepter, fan, olive, nettles, unicorns, the square.

> *Oh, listen to the tale of a poor Irish harper,*
> *And scorn not the strings in his old withered hand;*
> *But remember those fingers could once move more sharper,*
> *To waken the echoes of his dear native land.*
>
> —Thomas Campbell

AMERGIN (IRISH)

IN MYTH — [Am-AWR-geen] Also spelled Amairgin. Amergin was the chief bard of the Milesian invaders credited with the composition of the poem "I Am the Stag of Seven Tines." He was also known as a harper, magician, and seer. Many other poems still exist which are attributed to him, many of which carry reincarnation themes.

In the invasion myths of Ireland, it was he who places the Gaels' demands to the leaders of the Tuatha De Danann. He granted the departing wish of the Tuatha triplicity of Eire, Fodhla, and Banbha that Ireland (named Eire and pronounced AIR-uh) be named for them so that the glory of the Tuatha would not be forgotten.

Some mythologists feel he may be another version of Taliesin.

IN MAGICK AND RITUAL — Make wish-magick with Amergin, or invoke him when you face a writer's block or other creative impediments. Also ask his guidance in helping you choose a magickal or craft name. This latter can be especially effective if you are male.

CORRESPONDENCES — The quill, the circle.

AMORGIN (IRISH)

Another poet, not to be confused with Amergin. This father of Conall of the Victories boasted in song of his wisdom, wealth, and quick tongue. He praised his son for staying in the midst of battle even though he was wounded to stay with his dying leader.

ANIND (IRISH)

IN MYTH — [AWN-eenth or AWN-eenj] This son of Nemed could not be bound to his grave. He sprang to life as soon as it was being dug. Later, he was enshrined at *Dun na Sciath* (The Fortress of Shields), a circular stone fort (*rath*) in the west of Ireland.

IN MAGICK AND RITUAL — Anind represents the reborn sun God, and was probably honored at Yule or Imbolg, who would die only to be reborn again. Use him in your own seasonal rites or to uncover the secrets of your own past incarnations.

ANLUAN (IRISH)

IN MYTH — [AWN-lwan] Anluan was a Connacht warrior who fought against Ulster's famed Red Branch warriors. He led Queen Maeve's three thousand troops into battle against Ulster where he was beheaded, but victorious.

IN MAGICK AND RITUAL — Align with Anluan for his bravery and leadership qualities.

ARANNAN (IRISH, CONTINENTAL)

[Ahr-RAWN-on] A son of Milesius, who climbed to the top of the ship's mast during the invasions of Ireland. He fell and was killed. Some legends attribute his death to a Tuatha De Danann protection spell.

Softly we glide along,
Softly we chant our song,
For a king who to resting is come.

—Scottish Folk Song

ARAWEN (WELSH)

IN MYTH — [AIR-uh-oo'en] Also spelled Arawyn, Arrawn, and Arawn. He was the King of Annwn, the Otherworld. His name means "silver-tongued."

He fought in the Battle of the Trees (*Cad Goddeu*) with Bran against Amathaon and Gwyddion. Arawn, like most Otherworld Gods, was a master hunter who rode a pale horse and rode with a pack of white hounds with red ears. The archetypal purpose of the hunt was to gather souls for the Otherworld if the quarry was not smart enough to evade the chase.

Arawen possessed a magick cauldron of regeneration, later captured by King Arthur.

He bestowed on Pwyll the title Pen Annwn for his assistance and loyalty in time of need.

IN MAGICK AND RITUAL — Arawn can help you in picking magickal names, in making magick for strengthening friendships, or in facilitating spirit contact. He also has attributes of reincarnation deities.

ARCA DUBH (IRISH)

IN MYTH — [AR-ka Doo, Thoo, or Doov] Also Aedh Dubh. His name meant "on our black." He was a king of a minor Irish kingdom known as Airgialla and was in possession of a great magickal shield called Dubhghiolla ("the black servant"). On the top of the shield sat Badb, the Irish Goddess of war and death, in her crow form. No known force could penetrate this mighty shield.

He is also thought to be one and the same as Goll ("one-eyed") MacMorna, a fierce Fianna warrior, who killed Fionn MacCumhal's father and became the new leader of the Fianna. This can be seen as a sacrificial king succession tale.

Though he was partially blind, he was the greatest seer in Celtic history.

IN MAGICK AND RITUAL — Divination. Call upon Aedh to shield you with Dubhghiolla for protection.

ARD GREIMME (IRISH, SCOTTISH)

His name means "high power" or "high sun." He is the father of the famed warrioress sisters Aife and Scathach, and was probably once a sun God in his own right.

ARGETLAMH (IRISH)

See Nuada of the Silver Hand.

ART MACCONN (IRISH)

IN MYTH — Art was the son of King Conn and a marvelous chess player, a game beloved by the Tuatha De Danann. He lost a gambling game to his father's faery lover, Becuma, who entreated him to go to a "distant island" (the Otherworld) and return with Delbchaem, the daughter of Morgan, whom she knew would unleash great terrors on the land in retaliation.

Under this geise, Art went to the distant land and found that he would be allowed to take the girl if he could choose the right one of three cups of wine. Each cup was held by a

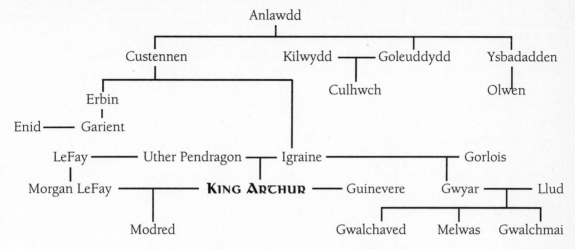

The generally accepted family tree of King Arthur.

woman, one vinegar, one poison, and the other a fine wine. Warned by another faery, he chose correctly, beheaded the girls' mother, and took Delbchaem back to Ireland.

Becuma was so angered at his success that she left Ireland and prosperity returned.

Art eventually became High King in his own right.

IN MAGICK AND RITUAL — Art means bear, a sacred totem animal of the Celts associated with strength and courage.

Artaius (Continental)

A God of sheep and cattle herders from Celtic Gaul. For reasons which are not completely clear, the Romans identified him with Mercury.

> *And in the moon athwart the place of tombs,*
> *Where lay the mighty bones of ancient men....*
> —Lord Tennyson, from *Morte d'Arthur*

Arthur, King (Welsh, Cornish)

IN MYTH — The search for the truth behind the persistent legends of King Arthur and his Camelot have consumed humankind since the Middle Ages. The stories we know today as Arthurian are largely Christianizations of older Celtic myths, and we are familiar with them through the medieval writings of Tennyson, Malory, and Geoffrey of Monmouth. Arthur is probably based on a seventh-century king named Artorius who led the fight to drive the Saxons from Britain, and later his myth and imagery was merged with that of a now-forgotten father/sacrificial God. Because of the pervasiveness of these legends, more strong archetypal associations have been placed on him, and the characters who people the myths surrounding him, than any other single mythic figure. He is at once a God, a father figure, a warrior, a leader, a sacrificial king, a protector, and the gallant defender of justice and mercy.

Arthur was the son of King Uther Pendragon and Igraine, the Duchess of Cornwall. He was taught and protected by the magician/Druid Merlin, married Guinevere, a Triple

ARTHUR, KING (CONT.)

Goddess/May Queen figure, and was mortally wounded in battle by his son Modred (by Morgan LaFay). Arthur's body was carried to Avalon to sleep and await the time when he is needed. Therefore he is a sacrificial God/king in the purest sense.

Other stories say he was changed into a raven upon his death, and Celtic folklore often sees dead figures turned into birds, an archetypal symbol of the transition to the spirit world.

Writing at the end of the nineteenth century, Celtic mythologist Sir John Rhys believed the Arthurian stories parallel that of Fionn MacCumhal of Irish lore (i.e., the Round Table compares with the Fenian warriors), and also parallels most of the old tales of Gwyddion. Of all the major Welsh folk heroes, only Gwyddion is conspicuously absent from the Arthurian legends. Rhys also asserted that the "Knights of the Round Table" are barely disguised Welsh deities made acceptable to a medieval audience.

In recent times author Mary Stewart has offered another interpretation of Arthur, and Geoffrey Ashe has searched for him historically as well as mythologically.

The oldest legends surrounding him are found in *The Black Book of Caermarthen*.

IN MAGICK AND RITUAL — Virtually any magickal need can be aided by Arthur.

CORRESPONDENCES — The scepter, the Emperor Tarot card.

ARTUR (IRISH)

A son of Nemed who led his people into battle with the Formorians for possession of Ireland.

ATHAIRNE (IRISH)

Also known as Atharine the Importunate, he was an arrogant bard and Druid who ordered King Mesgegra to give him his wife, Queen Buan, so that he could have her blessing of sovereignty. Her name means "eternal," and she was probably a Goddess whose powers Athairne needed to compliment his own. The King's refusal to comply began a war of vengeance. He was foster father to Amergin and he may once have been the same as Aitherne.

AVAGDU (WELSH)

IN MYTH — [AV-ahg-d'hoo] Also spelled Afagddu. He was the son of Cerridwen and Tegid, dubbed the ugliest child in the world while his sister, Creirwy, was most beautiful. He made up for his shortcomings when his mother brewed him a great cauldron of inspiration and knowledge so that he would be the most learned man in the world. Unfortunately, there are many twists and turns in this tale, and Avagdu never did get his gift of wisdom, though the story makes clear that much of the gift he wanted was within him all the time.

IN MAGICK AND RITUAL — The moral to this myth is straightforward enough—there is more to everyone than can be told by mere physical appearance. Always look deeply into yourself and into others. Work with him to discover the hidden wisdom inside yourself.

> *No waiting maid should ever spread*
> *Baile and Aillinn's marriage bed....*
>
> —William Butler Yeats

BAILE OF THE HONEYED SPEECH (IRISH)

IN MYTH — [BAWL-uh] This Ulster warrior was quite literally the God of Blarney, the glib speech so valued in Irish culture. He was also the lover and fiance of Aillinn. Aengus

MacOg, the God of love who lived in the Otherworld, wanted the couple to come and live happily with him. He told each of them the lie that the other had died so that they would each die of broken hearts.

The trees that grow over their reputed joint graves entwined, and their branches have been used for magick wands, especially for love magick.

IN MAGICK AND RITUAL — Work with Baile when you need to think quickly and clearly, when you have to make a speech, promote an idea, verbally impress someone, or engage in any other mental activity, especially when it involves speaking. His energy is also compatible with love magick, protection for lovers, and for the blessing of magickal wands.

CORRESPONDENCES — The Blarney Stone, yew trees.

Balin (Welsh, Cornish)

IN MYTH — Often called the "wild knight" of King Arthur's Round Table, he sought shelter from his Grail quest in the castle of King Pelles where he killed the King's brother, Garlon, a Druid who knew the secrets of invisibility, by using the magickal weapons of spear and chalice. The blow causes the coming of the Great Wasteland of Arthurian legends.

IN MAGICK AND RITUAL — Through pathworking, Balin can teach you the proper use of the elemental weapons.

Balor (Irish)

IN MYTH — Also called Balor Beimann, meaning "Balor of the Mighty Blows." Balor's life and kingship were dependent on him keeping his giant evil eye shut. This poisonous eye could kill merely by looking at a living thing, and his lid was so heavy that it took four warriors to lift it when needed. The dreadful eye was the result of a curse laid on him when, as a child, he peered into his father's magician's chambers when he was warned not to.

Balor engaged in a mighty battle with his grandson, Lugh. After a whole night of fighting, Lugh won by striking Balor with a stone so hard that his eye flew into the sky and, in a remnant of an old creation myth, became the sun. Balor and Lugh are both considered to be sun Gods. By some accounts, this event occurred at the second Battle of Magh Tuireadh (Moytura). Both of these battles were fought between the Formorians and the Tuatha De Danann for the kingship of Ireland. Archetypally, this is a common story in Celtic mythology, that of the old sacrificial God not wishing to relinquish his reign to his successor.

He is believed to dwell on Balor's Castle, an island off Donegal where legends say the Formorians now make their capital. His Welsh equivalent is Beli who, in some stories, first colonized Wales.

IN MAGICK AND RITUAL — Call on Balor to protect you from your enemies—an "evil eye" protection. Also to know when it is time to step aside to allow others to lead.

CORRESPONDENCES — The sun, the omniscient eye, heliotrope.

Barinthus (Anglo-Celtic, Welsh)

A charioteer to the residents of the Otherworld who was once probably a sea or sun God. He is mentioned by Geoffrey of Monmouth in his *Vita Merlini*.

Baruch (Irish)

A Red Branch warrior who met the tragic Deirdre and her lover Naoise when they returned from their exile in Scotland. He delayed Fergus, who was escorting them to Emain Macha, by

BARUCH (CONT.)

inviting them to a feast so that his own forces could attack the encampment. The ruins of his *dun* (pronounced doon) lie on the banks of the River Moyle.

BEALCU (IRISH)

IN MYTH — [BAY'L-koo] A Connacht warrior who, when returning from an raid into Ulster, was attacked by Conall of the Victories. The two engaged in hand-to-hand combat which ended with Conall seriously wounded. Conall begged to be killed, but Bealcu refused, saying he would not kill a man who could not defend himself.

Bealcu took him home and nursed him back to health telling him that when he was well they would fight again. However, Bealcu's three sons, fearing their father would lose the fight, contrived to kill Conall, but Conall tricked them into killing their father instead.

IN MAGICK AND RITUAL — Lessons of compassion and honor.

BEDWYR (WELSH, CORNISH)

IN MYTH — [BED-oor] A knight in King Arthur's court who accompanied Culhwch in his search for Olwen. He severely wounded the great giant Ysbadadden, Olwen's father, who did not wish his child to marry and produce the heir who would someday dethrone him.

IN MAGICK AND RITUAL — Archetypally, Bedwyr is the catalyst by which the Wheel of the Year turns and the young God supplants the old.

BEL OR BILE (SCOTTISH)

See Beli.

BELANOS OR BELINAS (ANGLO-CELTIC)

See Beli.

BELENUS (CONTINENTAL)

See Beli.

BELI (WELSH)

IN MYTH — [BIL-ay or BEEL-ay] The primary Welsh father God, husband of Don, and father of Arianrhod. Also a minor sun God who some feel is the Welsh equivalent of Balor. Other scholars cite his name as being the origin of the name for the Bealtaine Sabbat, though most of his associations are now deeply linked with Samhain.

Now Beli's principal role is that of the God of death and king of the Underworld. He is also linked to several of the legends concerning the sacred Pagan site of Glastonbury Tor where balefires were lit on Bealtaine and Samhain up until the Commonwealth period (1640–1660). Some legends say this site is the home of the death God Gwyn Ap Nuad, and that Beli purifies this site with his fires each Sabbat.

IN MAGICK AND RITUAL — Beli can help you seek knowledge of the Land of the Dead, help you to contact the spirits of those passed over, or purify your ritual sites. Call on him to help protect you from your enemies. Because of the association of Beli with the all-seeing eye, he can also aid you in astral projection or with past-life memory. Use his presence to enhance the Bealtaine or Samhain Sabbat festivities.

CORRESPONDENCES — Black, the scythe, balefire, the omniscient eye, Samhain/Bealtaine, mandrake (poisonous), ash.

BELTENE (IRISH)
See Beli.

BEN BULBEN (IRISH)
The owner of the wild boar which killed Diarmuid who was under a geise never to slay a pig of any kind.

BENDIGEID VRAN (WELSH)
See Bran.

BITH (IRISH)
Son of Noah, father of Cessair (the first Queen of Ireland) and the husband of Birren. His symbol is the banner.

BLACK KNIGHT, THE (WELSH, CORNISH)
IN MYTH — A mysterious figure in Arthurian legend who battles Cymon and knocks him from his mount. The following day, Owain seeks him out, but the wounded knight flees, imprisoning Olwen in his castle walls.

Archetypally, the Black Knight represents the dark side of our own personalities, the shadow self, with whom we must meet, and perhaps battle, in order to be initiated into the greater mysteries.

IN MAGICK AND RITUAL — Evoke the Black Knight to help you seek your own shadows.

BLADUD (WELSH, ANGLO-CELTIC)
IN MYTH — This "flying king" was probably a regional sun God. He is associated with the sacred English hot spring known as Aquae Sulis, an area occupied heavily by Roman forces which appropriated many of the local deities. He is depicted in a famous stone carving near the spring as a very virile male figure with flaming hair, the radiant features making him unmistakably a sun God.

Several Goddesses were also sacred to this hot spring, including Brid, whom the Romans called Minerva.

IN MAGICK AND RITUAL — Bladud can be invoked for protection, gaining employment, or other endeavors governed by the sun.

CORRESPONDENCES — Sunstones.

BOBH, KING (IRISH)
The father of Aebh and grandfather of Fionnuala and the children of Llyr who turned Aife into a crane (sometimes called an "air demon") for turning the four children of his daughter into swans. This tale is part of one of the stories comprising the "Four Sorrows of Erin."

BORMANUS (CONTINENTAL)
This was probably one of the earliest of Celtic Gods, about whom nothing is known today. He may have later surfaced as Borvo, a Breton God of hot springs. His name appears in cameo in old manuscripts and carvings.

BORVO (BRETON)
IN MYTH — Borvo's name means "to boil" (similar to Goddess Badb), and he was a God of the

BORVO (CONT.)

hot springs. He replaced his mother, Sirona, in this function when her story was patriarchalized.

The spring he ruled had tremendous healing powers.

IN MAGICK AND RITUAL — Healing.

CORRESPONDENCES — Fire, the sun.

BOV THE RED (IRISH)

IN MYTH — [Bove] Also written as Bodb Dearg or Bodb the Red. A warrior of the Tuatha De Danann who is mostly connected with the Munster region, also a brother of the Dagda who succeeded him as king of the Tuatha.

With his great skill in magick he helped Dagda seek out a maiden he saw in his dreams. Today he lives in a faery burgh in the Galtee Mountains.

IN MAGICK AND RITUAL — Evoke him for faery contact, or as an aid in general magick.

Men of Harlech, lie ye dreaming?
See ye not their falchions gleaming?
While their pennons gaily streaming,
Flutter in the breeze.

—Welsh Folk Song

BRAN (PAN-CELTIC)

IN MYTH — Also Bran MacFebal and Bran the Blessed. His name means "crow." He was the son of Llyr, and in the Welsh sagas he is also the child of the Goddess Iweridd.

This giant of a man set out with an army to avenge the ill-treatment of his sister Branwyn by her husband, King Matholwch of Ireland who blamed her for an insult they endured at their wedding. Nothing would stop his army's progress, and he once laid down across the Shannon river so his forces could use him as a bridge to walk cross.

In the Battle of the Trees, he could not be defeated unless someone could guess his name (a common mythological ploy in western Europe) and Gwyddion was able to do this. His forces won the battle, but he was fatally wounded by taking a poisoned arrow in the foot.

His grieving troops took his head to their stronghold at Harlech for a period of seven years where it talked and offered warnings and divinations. It then sat eighty-seven years at Gwales (place unknown today), then it was taken to London where it was set facing France so that it could warn of invasion.

The Celts revered the human head as not only a seat of learning, but also as the seat of the immortal spirit and therefore a repository for all knowledge which retained the personality of the person for as long as it remained intact. In death as in life, it was believed that the attributes of a person of strength and agility (such as a warrior) was able to be utilized as a continuing protective force. The early Celts were headhunters, and these prized battle spoils were preserved in cedar oil and hung on gateposts as talismans of protection and divination. Many such sacred skulls have been found when sacred wells and Celtic fortresses have been excavated.

In the Breton story he was imprisoned by the Norse and killed there. He would return as a crow and tell the birds of the land to be happy, for at least when they ended their days they would die in Brittany unlike him.

Bran's Gaulish name was Brennus.

IN MAGICK AND RITUAL — Protection, divination, service to country, perhaps a God of the waning year.

CORRESPONDENCES — Grains, sword, the raven.

Breasal (Welsh, Cornish)

IN MYTH — A High King of the entire planet who made his home in the Otherworld which is sometimes called Hy- or I-Breasal in his honor. Some scholars have wondered if Breasal and his mystical western island might not have been the legendary and controversial continent of Atlantis. His world was visible to humans on only one night every seven years.

An apocryphal legend says that so pervasive were these myths of the Celtic deities who lived on the western isle which was the Otherworld, that when Portuguese explorers reached South America they mistakenly thought they had landed in Breasal's world and named the land they discovered "Brazil" in his honor.

IN MAGICK AND RITUAL — Help with namings, spirit contact, guidance and protection for travelers and explorers.

CORRESPONDENCES — Mugwort, yew.

Bregon (Irish)

A minor Celtic figure who plays a role as either the human son of Milesius or the divine father of Bile and Ith.

Brenos (Continental)

A war God to whom the victories at Allia and Delphi were attributed. He may also be one and the same as Brennus, the Gaulish version of Bran.

Bres (Irish)

IN MYTH — Bres was the handsome son of an Otherworld father and Tuatha mother (Eri), and the husband of the mother Goddess Brid. He became king of Tuatha, but lost the throne due to his lack of generosity, compassion, and his generally despotic ways.

When he was satirized by the magickal music of Cairbre the bard, huge boils appeared on his face and he had to abdicate the throne since only the physically perfect were permitted kingship in Ireland.

IN MAGICK AND RITUAL — Without using magick, you can allow him to teach you lessons of compassion, and the ugly result of power hunger.

Brian (Irish)

This oldest son of Tuirrean and the Goddess Brid killed Cian, Lugh's father, with the help of his two brothers Iuchar and Iucharba. In payment for their deed they were required to go on a nearly impossible eight-fold quest. Even though they fulfilled their quest, they returned to Ireland only to die. This story is one of the "Four Sorrows of Erin" in Irish literature.

That royal Cashel is bare of house and guest,
That Brian's turreted home is the otter's nest....

—O'Rahilly

BRIAN BORU, KING (IRISH)

IN MYTH — Brian was a historical figure whose potent images as warrior, ruler, protector, and sacrificial king have made him almost divine.

He drove the Norse from Ireland in 1014 at the Battle of Clontarf. However, he was killed in the battle as were his son and grandson, making him a triple sacrificial God figure.

IN MAGICK AND RITUAL — Call on Brian for developing your warrior skills, for protection, overcoming an enemy, for acquiring leadership skills, or for showing you the best way to serve your country.

BRIAREUS (WELSH, CORNISH)

This guardian warrior from the Arthurian myths stands faithful watch over Merlin's sleeping body.

BRICCRIU (IRISH)

[BRIK-roo] Also Briccriu of the Poisoned Tongue. He coveted the leadership of the Red Branch warriors and spread lies about Cuchulain to create hostility toward him from the warriors. He was an adept high magician who summoned demons to aid him in his efforts which were mostly unsuccessful.

BRITAN (IRISH, ANGLO-CELTIC)

IN MYTH — A Nemed warrior who left Ireland after his people's victory over the Formorians. He settled in Britain and gave it his name.

IN MAGICK AND RITUAL — Evoke him for the ritual of name giving.

BUIC (IRISH)

IN MYTH — One of the two Connacht warriors in the service of Queen Maeve who is credited with finding the Brown Bull of Cooley and turning it over to Connacht. Archetypally this is symbolic of bringing prosperity and abundance to the land.

IN MAGICK AND RITUAL — Prosperity spells.

BUSSUMARUS (ANGLO-CELTIC, BRETON)

A God originally from Celtic Gaul who is identified with Jupiter. See Ambisagrus for full discussion.

BWLCH (WELSH, CORNISH)

IN MYTH — [Boolk] A warrior of King Arthur's court who possessed one of the three sharpest and most potent weapons in the kingdom. The other holders of these items were Cyfwlch and Syfwlch.

IN MAGICK AND RITUAL — Aid in the selection and blessing of magickal tools.

CADOG THE WISE (WELSH)

IN MYTH — Cadog was a master magician whose specialty was dealing with animals and settling disputes. He had an extraordinary herd of horses which could travel hundreds of miles in a very short time. They were made of wood and required only an occasional painting to keep them happy and faithful.

Cadog successfully helped settle a dispute between King Arthur and a fugitive who had slain three of Arthur's knights by magickally changing brown cows into red ones. These were to make a required punitive payment, and were changed at Arthur's request.

In the way of numerous Celtic mythic figures, Cadog was adopted by the Christians as a saint.

IN MAGICK AND RITUAL — Call on Cadog to help settle disputes or when you wish to work with animals.

CORRESPONDENCES — Dragon's Blood.

Cadw (Welsh, Scottish)

[Kah-DOO] A Pict who was the only man allowed to shave the death-fearing giant/God Ysbaddaden.

Cadwaladr, King (Welsh)

Another version of the sleeping king, like Arthur, waiting only for the call to serve his country once more. But unlike Arthur, Cadwaladr was not a great success. He waged an unsuccessful war on the Angles of Northumbria in the seventh century. No mention of him is found in any of the Welsh cave legends where the other sleeping kings are mentioned. His father was the much-revered King Cadwallon.

Cadwallon, King (Welsh)

IN MYTH — Another sleeping deity who was a seventh century king. He was able to unite the kingdoms of Wales. The legends about him say that when Wales again needs him, he will awaken from his sleep and lead them.

IN MAGICK AND RITUAL — Call upon Cadwallon's power to unite scattered forces.

Caier of Connacht, King (Irish)

He was deposed of his throne through trickery by his brother Neide, and later died of shame to be seen with the blemished face which caused the loss of his throne.

Cailte (Irish, Manx)

[CAWL-tay] Also Caoilte, a warrior and chief poet of the Fianna warriors. He killed the sea God Llyr.

Cairbre (Irish)

A Tuatha warrior who led an unsuccessful revolt against the Milesians.

Cairbre, Son of Etan (Irish)

IN MYTH — [CAWRB-ruh] Also spelled Cairpre. The bard who deposed the oppressive King Bres with his magick music spell. The spell caused blemishes to appear on Bres' face and he was forced to abdicate since only the physically perfect could hold the High Kingship of Ireland.

He fought against Osgar, Fionn MacCumhal's son, and they slew each other.

IN MAGICK AND RITUAL — Music spells.

CALATIN (IRISH)

IN MYTH — Calatin was the Connacht Druid highly skilled in magick who was sent by Queen Maeve to cast an incapacitating enchantment over Cuchulain during the Cattle Raid of Cooley. However, older myths credit this to a curse of Macha's, and hers is the most widely accepted version of the myth.

Calatin was happy to oblige his Queen, for Cuchulain's Red Branch warriors had slain his entire clan.

IN MAGICK AND RITUAL — General magickal assistance.

CAMULOS (ANGLO-CELTIC)

A war God from the region of Colchester, which was once called by the Latin name Camulo-dunum ("place of Camulos") in his honor.

CAMULOS (IRISH)

IN MYTH — A king of the Tuatha De Danann who is often identified with Cumhal, the father of Fionn. Some speculate that Camulos is the original "Old King Cole" of nursery rhyme fame. He came to Ireland from Gaul where his name was spelled Camulus, a word which meant "heaven." The Gaulish Romans equated him with Mars. Camulos had an invincible sword, linking him to the Anglo-Celtic war God of the same name.

IN MAGICK AND RITUAL — Call on Camulos to help you when searching for Pagan lore amongst folk songs and nursery rhymes, or for overcoming enemies and protection.

CORRESPONDENCES — The smoking pipe.

CANO (IRISH, SCOTTISH)

IN MYTH — Cano was the son of a Scottish king who was forced into to exile in Ireland. While staying with an Ulster chieftain, he fell in love with his host's daughter Cred, and she with him. She came to his bed, but he refused to sleep with her and violate the hospitality of the household.

Before he returned to Scotland, he gave her a ring as a token of his pledge to return to her. The ring's stone, he said, contained his very life, and that she must guard it well.

Cred waited and waited for him, but he never returned. In her grief, she dropped the ring, shattering the stone. Cano died three days later.

IN MAGICK AND RITUAL — Cultivate Cano for love magick, and the strength to keep a geise.

CARADOC (WELSH)

IN MYTH — Also spelled Caradawg and Caradawc. A son of Llyr who was nicknamed "Strong Arm." He appears in the *Mabinogion* as a first cousin and advisor to what some believe are the first written references to King Arthur.

IN MAGICK AND RITUAL — Divination, wisdom.

CARNE (BRETON, CORNISH)

Carne is most likely another version of Herne, a horned God of the hunt. See Cernunnos for a complete discussion.

CASWALLAWN (WELSH, ANGLO-CELTIC)

IN MYTH — Also Caswallon. A son of Beli and Don who deposed the sons of Llyr from the throne of Britain. He was also reputed to have led the Catuvelauni against Julius Caesar in 54 B.C.E. This revolt took place while Matholwch and Bran were fighting in Ireland. Bran, the rightful ruler, dies in the battle, and Caswallawn inherit his throne.

IN MAGICK AND RITUAL — Leadership, and aid in serving one's country.

CATHBAD (IRISH)

IN MYTH — An unscrupulous Druid in the employ of King Conchobar who usually worked his great magick for harmful purposes. He was the father of Dechtere, one of the women credited with being the mother of Cuchulain.

He had great powers of divination.

IN MAGICK AND RITUAL — Use his aid for great divinations, but avoid using them to gain power over others as he did.

CELTCHER (IRISH)

[KELT-yar] Also Celtchair and Keltchari. The son of Uthechar and husband of Brig Brethach. While under the laws of hospitality at Tara, this Red Branch warrior killed Blai Briuga, his wife's secret lover. King Conchobar knew he could not let this violation of law go unpunished and he placed him under a geise to rid Ireland of three plagues: an enemy of Ireland known as Conganches MacDedad, a vicious dog, and a rabid dog. He succeed in eradicating all but the last, and the sick canine's blood killed him.

CERNUNNOS (PAN-CELTIC)

IN MYTH — Cernunnos is a Greek name, one of the many names of the European Great Horned God. Whatever his original Celtic name might have been has been lost in history.

He is portrayed on many Celtic artworks and artifacts from as far back as they can be recovered, the most well-known being the famous Gundestrup Cauldron. As the Horned God he is depicted with the antler of a stag or horns of a ram, and was probably the most widely worshiped God-form in European Paganism. Sometimes he is drawn with a sack of coins which he is pouring onto the bare earth, or with a club.

He was the randy goat representing the fertility rites of Bealtaine, and the master of the hunt who came into his full power in late summer and early fall. He was the primal fertility God, consort to the first Great Mother, and the male creative principle. He is also honored as a death deity, and the hunt is sometimes viewed as metaphor for rounding up the souls of the living to take to the Otherworld. He has also been cast as the role of guardian of the Otherworld's gates, and as a God of the woodlands, animals, revelry, and male fertility.

His stories are sketchy and come largely from oral sources. Herne is his British name. His Anglo-Celtic name was Herne, and his Gaulish name was Dispater.

He is equated with the Greek God Pan whose name means "all." Both Cernunnos and Pan became the prototype for the Christian anti-God, Satan. This was not a judgment on the attributes of these deities, but rather a device for frightening the European populace away from the Old Religion.

IN MAGICK AND RITUAL — Hunt, woodland, fertility, magick, sacrifice, and animals.

CORRESPONDENCES — The stag, pan pipes, oak leaves, ram's horns, antlers.

CET MACMAGA (IRISH)

A warrior who was always looking for a evil deed to do. He aided King Mesgegra's prophecy that his head would revenge his own death.

CIAN (IRISH)

In Myth — [KEE-awn] This son of Diancecht, the God of medicine, went to retrieve a cow which had been stolen by Balor. While at Balor's castle, Cian discovered that Balor had imprisoned his daughter Ethne in a tower because he feared a prophecy that he would be slain by his own grandson. Cian rescued Ethne and they married, producing the God Lugh who did eventually slay Balor.

IN MAGICK AND RITUAL — Love magick.

CIMBAETH (IRISH)

[KIM-bayth] Also Kimbay and Cimboath. This Ulster king was the founder of the Red Branch fortress of Emain Macha, and was married to its namesake, the Goddess Macha, who was also his sister. The fortress was laid out like a broach, which is what the word "emain" approximates.

He was to share rulership of Emain Macha with his brother Dithorba, but when it was Dithorba's turn, Cimbaeth went to war with him instead. They make a triplicity with their brother Aedh, and their fighting is no more than the same being fighting the inevitable changes in time.

CLUST (WELSH)

IN MYTH — A warrior with acute hearing who accompanies Culhwch in his search for Olwen.

IN MAGICK AND RITUAL — Invoke Clust if your clairaudience (psychic hearing) needs a boost.

COCIDIUS (CONTINENTAL)

See Segomo.

> From some dead warrior's broken lance:
> I turned it in my hand; the stains
> Of war were on it, and I wept....
>
> —William Butler Yeats

COLL (IRISH)

IN MYTH — Coll was the Fenian warrior who was able to bring to the Goddess Cred the poem she required of her lover, describing her Otherworld dwelling in minute detail. He most likely accomplished this magickal feat through astral projection or scrying, as no mortal was allowed near her heavily guarded home.

They married and made their home in the Otherworld.

IN MAGICK AND RITUAL — Call on Coll to make love magick, to inspire yourself and others, as a general aid to magick, and invoke him to help you learn the art of astral projection.

CONAIRE THE GREAT (IRISH)

IN MYTH — Also Conary and Conaire Mor meaning "big." A High King who was the great-grandson of Eochaid and Edain, and the son of Messbuachalla and the bird God Nemglan.

Before taking the throne, Nemglan appeared before him and laid a long series of geise upon him including that he would not allow a man or woman alone to enter any place he was dwelling after sunset.

Conaire achieved a measure of peace among the warring Celts, and legends tell us that during his reign no murder was committed, no blizzards blew, no floods ravaged, and no crops or herds were blighted. (Compare this utopian scene to the popular image of Camelot.) His own three brothers were the ones who often broke the new laws of peace, and the Tuatha, who also benefitted from his reign, asked for their deaths which Conaire could not bring himself to do. When he refused, the Tuatha tricked or cajoled him into breaking all of his geise one by one.

Conaire also possessed a sword which sang prophecies and helped him cast spells. The story of his murder is related in the romantic tale *Bruidhen Da Derga* ("The Destruction of Derga's Fort") when he broke the last of his geise.

IN MAGICK AND RITUAL — Learn from him the importance of the keeping of a geise, an honor vow of great importance in Celtic mythology.

CONALL OF THE VICTORIES (IRISH)

IN MYTH — Also Conall Cearnach. The warrior Conall cut off the head of Leinster's King Mesgegra and wore it, but then found he could not remove it from his shoulders (some versions of the myth say this was the head of Mac Da Tho), so he had the brains taken out and used them as a magickal talisman. He used another part of the brain as a slingshot ball to kill King Conchobar.

He had a protective magical shield which didn't protect the arm not holding it in battle.

Conall avenged the death of Cuchulain and, as a warrior, the legends about him are almost equal to those of Cuchulain.

IN MAGICK AND RITUAL — Call on Conall to offer you protection, to overcome enemies, or to discover the masculine power within yourself.

CONAN MACMORNA (IRISH)

A swaggering warrior characterized as an inept buffoon who, like most braggarts, is really a coward.

CONCHOBAR MACNESSA (IRISH)

IN MYTH — A king of Ulster and leader of the Red Branch who was friendly with the faeries. His mother, Nessa, agreed to marry Fergus when he acquiesced to her terms of allowing her son Conchobar to be High King for a year and a day. Fergus, who desperately wanted Nessa for his wife, agreed.

When the year was up Conchobar refused to return the throne to Fergus, and mustered his warriors to drive his rival into exile.

He banished the beautiful Deirdre of the Sorrows from Ireland when she would not have him. Later he arranged to have killed Naoise, her lover, and his brothers.

Conchobar owned a famous shield named Ochain (literally "the moaner") which let out a pitious wail whenever its master was in peril.

The Book of Leinster tells of his death at the hand of Conall of the Victories who hit him with a talisman from a slingshot so hard that the ball became deeply embedded in the King's

CONCHOBAR MACNESSA (CONT.)

brain. Seven years later, during one of his famous temper fits, he died.

He may be the same figure as Conaire Mor.

IN MAGICK AND RITUAL — Call on Conchobar to shield you with Ochain for protection. While not relating directly to magickal practice, we can easily glean the didactic meaning of this myth: that the keeping of one's word is important, and that one cannot force their will upon others without having it eventually backfire.

CONDATIS (CONTINENTAL)

IN MYTH — A God of confluence whose sacred sites were wherever two rivers or bodies of water met. These places were one of the "inbetween" places which the Celts knew held great power.

IN MAGICK AND RITUAL — Water magick, a deity to be honored at the inbetween times.

CONN (MANX, WELSH)

A son of Llyr who should not be confused with Conn of the Hundred Battles.

CONN OF THE HUNDRED BATTLES (IRISH)

A High King who archetypally played the role of sacrificial God.

CONNLA CAINBHRETHACH (IRISH)

IN MYTH — Also Conlai. The son of Cuchulain and the Goddess Aifa who, by some accounts, became a Brehon judge. Connla grew up in Aifa's custody, and it was not until he was a man that he went searching for his father in the mortal world to fulfill his mother's promise to his father that, when he was of age, he would be given to the Red Branch to study the ways of a warrior. Cuchulain had asked Aife to put the boy under a geise that he would not reveal himself when he came to Ulster. When Connla was grown, Aife kept her promise and sent him to Emain Macha. Cuchulain, not recognizing the boy, kills him as a spy.

Because he was raised on the Isle of Shadow, he was said to possess a visionary knowledge of the past.

IN MAGICK AND RITUAL — Ask Connla to share with you his wisdom, invoke him to help you see past-lives.

CONOMOR, KING (BRETON, WELSH)

IN MYTH — Also Kynvawr. This king from the sixth century, who was several times a widower, has a tale very similar to that of other Celtic kings. He married the young and beautiful Tryphyna, daughter of the King of Vannes. She was aware of the rumor that he murdered all his former wives when they became pregnant, so when she became with child she fled. Conomor caught her and cut off her head which was restored by the magick of a Druid.

Her son, Tremeur, was born, grew up, and slew his father in revenge. Hence, Conomor was yet another aging king who did not want to sacrifice himself for his country, fearing his successor.

Christian additions to this myth tell that it was St. Gildas who destroyed Conomor's castle and all its occupants.

IN MAGICK AND RITUAL — Knowing when to step down, knowing place in ritual, knowing the responsibility of accepting leadership. Call his spirit to function as a sacrificial God at Samhain rites.

Dead Cormac on his bier they laid: —
"He reign'd a king for forty years,
And shame it were," his captains said,
"He lay not with his royal peers."

—Samuel Ferguson

CORMAC MACART (IRISH)

IN MYTH — Cormac was the illegitimate son of a High King who slept with his mother, Achtan, only once: on the eve of his final battle. After being separated from his mother, he was suckled and raised by a wolf pack. When a hunter found him many years later and returned him to his mother, he followed her over the mountains to Tara, where he could claim his rightful place as High King. On the journey they were protected by the wild animals with whom he had lived.

Cormac was a great supporter of the Fianna during the time in which Fionn MacCumhal was their leader.

He was also a third century king whose legends have merged with with the mythological archetype.

IN MAGICK AND RITUAL — Leadership, magick for dogs, and perseverance.
CORRESPONDENCES — Canines.

CRAFTINY (IRISH, SCOTTISH)

IN MYTH — Also Craftine. A mute Ulster harper who was given a love poem written by Moriath, the daughter of the king of the region known as Feremorc, in which she spelled out her passionate feeling for Moen. When he set it to music, he was so overcome with its beauty, that he broke into song and was cured of his muteness.

IN MAGICK AND RITUAL — Call on the energy of Craftiny to help you make musical spells and to heal throat ailments whether they are physical or psychological in nature.

CREDNE (IRISH)

IN MYTH — A God of metallurgy and smithing who worked in bronze. He made all the Tuatha's weapons with the goldsmith Goibniu and the woodworker Luchtain.

IN MAGICK AND RITUAL — Call on Credne for knowledge of self-defense, inspiration for your artistic endeavors, or for blessing your magickal tools.

Around Cromm Cruaich
There the hosts would prostrate themselves;
Though he put them under deadly disgrace,
Their name clings to the noble plain.

—from *The Voyages of Bran*

CROMM CRUAICH (IRISH)

IN MYTH — [Crom CROO-ach] Also called Lord of the Mound and Crom Dubh. An ancient deity about which little of fact is known, and he is therefore a great source of controversy in Celtic studies. His name may be associated with the popular Irish festival loaf called *bram brac*. His feast day has been Christianized in Ireland and takes place on the last

CROMM CRUAICH (CONT.)

Sunday in July. Pilgrimages are still made up St. Patrick's Hill (Croagh Padriac in County Mayo) on this day.

His name means "bowed one of the mound," and his image is often linked to a mythological golden idol to which sacrifices may have been made. He is still seen by Pagans as a harvest, death, and sacrificial God to whom it is believed human sacrifices were once made at Samhain.

Some sources relate him to Zeus, a Greek heaven/sky God of Gods, though there is little evidence to support this link. The *Dinnshenchas* tell us that once at Meg Slecht, a standing stone of solid gold was erected to him with twelve stone idols surrounding him (thirteen is still the traditional number for members in a Celtic coven). King Tigernmas led the worship at this site.

IN MAGICK AND RITUAL — Call on Cromm for successful harvest, evoke his presence during the dark festivals. His image as a death God makes his energy compatible with Passing Over rituals and Otherworld contact.

CORRESPONDENCES — Standing stones, rye, animal blood.

CRONOS (ANGLO-CELTIC)

A minor harvest and sun God with Greek roots who was imprisoned with his subordinate deities on a western island which may have been a Land of the Dead. He appears to have no connection to the Greek God of time who has the same name.

CRUNNCHU (IRISH)

[CRUN-hoo] One of the consorts/husbands of Macha.

> *Cuchulain cried, "I am the only man*
> *Of all this host so bound from childhood on."*
>
> —William Butler Yeats

CUCHULAIN (IRISH)

IN MYTH — [Coo-HOO-lyn or Coo-COOL-lyn] The heroic tales of Cuchulain are so old that they were almost forgotten when they were revived by a seventh century bard named Sechan Torpeist.

Cuchulain was born Setanta, but his name was changed when he placed a geise upon himself to take the place of a dog he had killed which belonged to Cullan. His new name means "hound of Cullan." (See Chapter 10 for a more detailed version of this tale.)

Several women in Celtic myth are said to be his mother, some human and others divine. The God Lugh is said to be his father, but this relationship appears to be more of a spiritual link than a biological one, and Cuchulain also has a human father, Sualtam.

He studied under the warrior/Goddess Scathach on the Isle of Shadow and returned to Ulster to be a great warrior and leader of the Red Branch, a semi-chivalrous order of the warriors of Ulster whose exploits make up an entire cycle in Irish mythology. He became semi-divine himself through his adventures, and is now honored as a Pagan God.

Many of his stories are recorded at length in *The Book of the Dun Cow*. A statue in Dublin portrays his dramatic demise in battle when, while his men were asleep, he held off Maeve's armies single-handedly by being tied to a tree to remain standing. Cuchulain's image may have once been that of a minor sun or sacrificial God. His great enemy, the sovereign Queen Maeve of Connacht, seemed ready to replace her husband with Cuchulain who resisted the sacrificial role and battled her instead. Predictably, she won the war, and his blood was spilled on earth in the manner of sacrificial Gods. During his death battle he failed to recognize the Morrigan flying over him, and many believe that was really what killed him—failure to realize the role he was born to play as symbolized by the death-bird images of the triple crone.

He had many loves including Aife, Emer, and the faery woman, Fand.

IN MAGICK AND RITUAL — Cuchulain can be invoked to teach you where your own masculine power lies. He can also help you find stamina, perseverance, strength, and guide you in overcoming enemies. He was the only one of the Red Branch warriors imper-

A man wrestling with a beast. Drawing from The Book of Kells.

vious to Macha's curse, and his energy can be evoked to aid in spells designed to ward off negative energy from others.

CORRESPONDENCES — The spear and sword.

CULHWCH (WELSH)

IN MYTH — [KILL-hugh] Also Kulhwch and Kilhwch. He was the son of the sow Goddess Goleuddydd, a daughter of Prince Anllawd, and Kilydd, grandson of Prince Kelyddon. The moment Goleuddydd was pregnant with him, she ran mad seeking lonely places. She ran to a pigsty where she gave birth. The pig keeper carried the child back to the court. (The pig in Celtic myth is a symbol of health and plenty and was highly prized, as well as being sacred to many Goddesses.)

When his mother died, his stepmother hated him so much for refusing her daughter that she laid a geise on him to marry no one but Olwen, whom she knew had been hidden away by her fearful father, Ysbadadden. Ysbadadden lived in fear of a prophecy which said Olwen's son would kill him, so he tried to prevent her from ever marrying, though this impediment never stopped dedicated Celtic lovers any more than it stops anyone today.

When the two met they fell deeply in love and Ysbadadden hid her again.

Culhwch gathered King Arthur and several other warriors and went out on an epic quest in search of her. In his path lay thirteen obstacles engineered by her father which comprise one of the longest extant legends in Welsh lore.

Olwen eventually married Culhwch against her father's wishes and, predictably, their son displaced his grandfather.

IN MAGICK AND RITUAL — Perseverance, love magick, couple's work.

CORRESPONDENCES — Mullein.

CUMHAL (IRISH)

IN MYTH — [Cool] The husband of Murna of the White Neck, father of Fionn, and leader of the Fianna. He was also the respected and feared chief of Clan Morna. He was killed in the Battle of Knock, now the site of the town of Castleknock near Dublin.

IN MAGICK AND RITUAL — Leadership skills.

CUNEDDA (WELSH)

IN MYTH — [KOON-uh-tha] Also Kwnedda. Cunedda is a figure from early Welsh mythology which tells us that he came to the region with his eight sons, and the nine of them carved out the nine Welsh kingdoms. His stories parallel that of Milesius and his eight sons who conquered Ireland. Archetypally he represents the potent force of a triple triplicity.

IN MAGICK AND RITUAL — Men who wish to work with a triplicity, and are not as yet comfortable invoking the feminine Triple Goddess, might wish to experiment with the energies of Cunedda and his sons.

CU ROI MACDAIRE, KING (IRISH)

Also Curoi MacDaere. A king of Munster under High King Eochaid, who was friendly with the faeries. His name means "dog king." He stole Blathnat away from the Red Branch when they forgot to cut him in on the spoils of a raid, and was killed by Cuchulain for his efforts.

He is the Irish version of Wales' Sir Gawain, who is challenged by the Green Knight. See Gawain and the Green Knight for a full discussion of the archetype.

CYMON (WELSH, CORNISH)

IN MYTH — Also Kymon. A knight in the court of King Arthur whose myth has been greatly influenced by the medieval codes of chivalry and combat.

When riding out seeking a fight, he came across a one-eyed, one-armed, one-legged man (an accurate description of an unpleasant Scottish faery known as the Fachan) who told him to go to a nearly fountain and gather some water in a silver bowl. Then he was to toss it onto a nearby marble slab, after which a violent storm would boil up and a dark knight would appear to him thundering from the west on a black horse.

The Black Knight appeared, but instead of the heroic victory he expected, Cymon was wounded and limped back to court.

IN MAGICK AND RITUAL — Cymon set out to find an unnecessary battle and was told by the faery that if it was trouble he sought, he should find it with the Black Knight or it did not exist. Though he can provide little in the way of ritual energy, we can allow ourselves to learn from Cymon's foolish mistake.

CYTHRAWL (WELSH)

IN MYTH — [KEETH-rawl] In Welsh cosmology, Cythrawl archetypally symbolizes the opposing male creative force which represents destruction rather than creation. While this sounds very negative to non-Pagans, Pagans accept the energy as leading towards nothingness, and being as necessary to existence as that which leads towards creation.

Cythrawl's energy has been personified as deity, and his home is in the Otherworld where his energy is first manifested before appearing in the concrete world.

IN MAGICK AND RITUAL — Call upon this very powerful divine force when you wish to banish something from your life. This "destructive" magick can have just as much of a positive, unharmful effect as so-called "positive magick." You can also merge with his energy when you wish to be reincarnated with a loved one.

Cyvarnion (Welsh, Breton)

A Welsh bard who fled to Breton and married a Druidess. They were the parents of Herve the Blind, the tamer of wild wolves.

Da Derga (Irish)

The lord who owned a wealthy stronghold near Tara where Conaire was murdered when he broke the last of his geise. The story is related in the tragic romantic tale *Bruidhen Da Derga* ("The Destruction of Derga's Fort"). Da Derga's home had seven doors and three persons named "Red" in residence, a configuration which made up the last of Conaire's forbidden geise.

Dafyd Meirig (Welsh)

A young drover who accidentally stumbled onto the sleeping place of Owen Lawgoch. He took some gold from the spot against the instructions of a Druid, and then he was never able to find the cave again.

> *Out of Murias was brought the Dagda's cauldron:*
> *No company ever went away from it unthankful.*
>
> —Taliesin

Dagda, The (Irish)

IN MYTH — Also Daghdha, whose name means "the good God," and Eochaidh Ollathair, meaning "the all-father." He is one of the principal deities of the Tuatha De Danann whose archetype is that of a potent father God figure.

He owned a magickal harp which made the seasons come and go, possibly a patriarchalization of the Goddess' spinning wheel, both symbolizing the Wheel of the Year. This symbolism is further seen by the club he carried which was a wheel mounted on an eight-pronged staff, one prong for each solstice, equinox, and cross-quarter festival.

He acquired his famous harp when he traveled to the Otherworld and brought back to Tara the Cauldron of Abundance, named *The Undry* (associated with the Grail of the Arthurian legends), in which all found food according to their merits, and not one left hungry. Also taken from the Otherworld was The Stone of Destiny (the *Lia Fail*), and the Sword of Nuada. These four items represent the four elements.

In early myths he was likely the personification of the male creative principle, the consort/son of the mother Goddess. In later additions to the myth cycles he is the father of Brid and her sisters (a Triple Goddess). He was also mated with the Morrigan, another triplicity. Both images make it clear that the Dagda was also once a triplicity in his own right, for in most all mythologies the God who mated with a triplicity either carried a trident or was a triune himself.

When the Tuatha were finally defeated by the Milesians, he led the Tuatha underground to the burghs (faery mounds) where they remain as a rich part of present-day Irish folk beliefs. He was deposed as their leader by his brother Bov the Red.

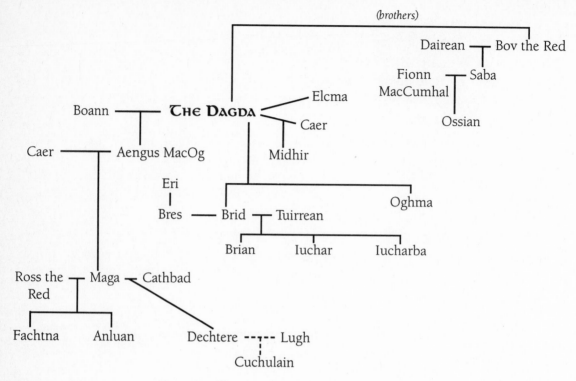

(brothers)

Dairean — Bov the Red

Fionn — Saba
MacCumhal

Boann — THE DAGDA — Elcma

Caer

Ossian

Caer — Aengus MacOg — Midhir

Eri
|
Bres — Brid — Tuirrean

Oghma

Brian   Iuchar   Iucharba

Ross the — Maga — Cathbad
Red

Fachtna   Anluan   Dechtere ---ᵣ--- Lugh
                              |
                          Cuchulain

The generally accepted family tree of the Dagda.

Dagda, The (cont.)

The Dagda is usually described as wearing a short tunic which reveals his buttocks. Despite his great power he was often the butt of jokes (no pun intended) or ridicule in keeping with Celtic God concepts of divine beings possessing human flaws.

There are many written and oral myths concerning him, as well as a large body of folklore which contains hundreds of dissimilar tales about him. Pagans today revere him as a God of knowledge and wisdom, as well as a potent creative power.

IN MAGICK AND RITUAL — You can use Dagda's energies for almost any purpose you might need. Call on him for wisdom, for magick for animals, for warrior skills, to aid children, for fertility or protection, to make music spells, to assist faery contact, for elemental magick, or to increase mental prowess.

Steve Blamires, author of *The Irish Celtic Magical Tradition*, also links Dagda to the physical actions of labor, eating, and sex.

CORRESPONDENCES — The harp, the elder tree, the sun wheel, the alchemical symbols, the High Priest Tarot card, and the triangle with the apex up.

Dara (Irish)

The owner of the famous Brown Bull of Quelney, over whom the Cattle Raid of Cooley epic battle was fought.

DARONWY (WELSH) SEE TALIESIN

The "Song of Daronwy," in *The Book of Taliesin,* relates exploits of this God who does not appear elsewhere in Celtic mythology. Many scholars believe Daronwy is actually Ossian.

DEGAD (IRISH)

IN MYTH — Also Dedad. This Munster chieftain was the greatest warrior of the region who founded a military dynasty of conjoined clans known as the Deged warriors. Upon his death his son Li took over, but was unable to hold the group together.

IN MAGICK AND RITUAL — Call on him for his skills in leadership, overcoming enemies, or for strengthening family ties.

DELBAETH (IRISH)

In patriarchal myths, he was the father of Dana, though in old Ireland it is almost a certainty that he was her son/consort. He is also sometimes said to be father of Boann and of the Morrigan.

DERMOT OF THE LOVE SPOT (IRISH)

See Diarmuid.

DESA (IRISH)

The foster father of Conaire, the leader of a fierce tribe known as the Desi who were often at war with the Tuatha and the Gaels.

DHONN (IRISH)

IN MYTH — [Doe'n] Also spelled Donn and Don. Dhonn is a lord of the Underworld, a death God, and a consort of the crone Goddess Macha. He is the son of faery King Midhir. His own son, Diarmuid, was given to Aengus MacOg to raise.

IN MAGICK AND RITUAL — Spirit contact, past-life memory.

CORRESPONDENCES — Onyx.

DIANCECHT (IRISH)

IN MYTH — (DE'on-keht) The master physician of the Tuatha De Danann. The evil serpent children of the Morrigan, who were extremely venomous to touch, were threatening to kill all the cattle. Diancecht slew the serpent children by drowning them in the River Barrow and dispersing their power.

He and his children, Miach and Airmid, were always on duty at the Spring of Health concocting healing spells and charms. He loved his children and was proud of them until his son Miach fashioned King Nuada a new eye and Airmid replaced his severed hand with one made of silver. Diancecht eventually killed Miach. Airmid fled from him, eventually becoming a greater healer than her father. Meanwhile, Diancecht was blamed for denying the world the cure to all illness by killing Miach and breaking up the successful male/female partnership Miach had with his sister. He scattered to the winds the great body of herbal knowledge Airmid had gathered.

IN MAGICK AND RITUAL — Call on Diancecht for healing minor illnesses and treating sick animals. He can also remind us of the evils of jealousy rather than cooperation. However, his energy is a good one to draw upon for banishing negative influences.

CORRESPONDENCES — The color purple.

DIARMUID O'DUIBNE (IRISH)

IN MYTH — [DEER-meed Oh DOO-nee] Alternately spelled Dairmuid, Diarmaid, Dermot, and Diarmait. Also known as Dermot of the Love Spot for a mark on his forehead, hidden by his hair, which would make any woman instantly fall in love with him if she saw it.

Diarmuid was raised by a faery king, and the king's son was his foster brother whom he accidentally killed. The son was transformed into an unbristled boar who was under a geise to lead Diarmuid to his death, at which time the boar would also die.

The High King's daughter, Grainne, was betrothed to the giant warrior, Fionn MacCumhal (Diarmuid's uncle), but at a banquet given for the couple, Grainne fell in love with Diarmuid. Diarmuid was unsure if he should flee with her, but she reminded him that he was under a geise never to refuse to help a woman. The couple knew that in order to remain together they would have to flee and hide. Their legendary flight took them all over the length and breadth of Ireland for seven years, and numerous dolmens in Ireland are named for the couple.

When Fionn found them, he set a wild boar upon Diarmuid and killed him. Diarmuid's body was taken to *Bruigh na Boinne* (the famous cairn at Newgrange) where Aengus MacOg breathed life back into his body.

IN MAGICK AND RITUAL — Go on an inner-journey as Diarmuid to determine how strong the bonds of your romantic attachments really are. Could you make a promise to leave your love alone forever even at the cost of your life? He can also give us strength for keeping a geise.

DISPATER (CONTINENTAL)

IN MYTH — Also Dis Pater. This Gaulish God, whose name means "the father," was a primal God of creation who later merged with both Don and Cernunnos, the Horned God. The Gauls all believed themselves to be descended from him.

IN MAGICK AND RITUAL — As a father God he can aid in fertility magick, and in magick in general. If you follow a Gaulish Celtic tradition, include him in your ancestor rites.

DISSULL (WELSH, CORNISH)

A giant whose beard hair was woven into the only leash which could restrain the hunting hounds belonging to Mabon. The beard was destroyed by Mabon's enemies.

DITHORBA (IRISH)

One of the brothers of Red Hugh, the father of Macha, who together ruled Ulster in turns when Emain Macha was founded. Macha decided she was not going to give up their throne after her father stepped down, and she battled Dithorba for it and killed him.

DIWRNACH THE GAEL (IRISH, SCOTTISH)

IN MYTH — [DOOER-nochk] This Gael briefly captured Dagda's magickal cauldron of abundance from which all the persons of the world could be fed. He was probably once a harvest God or a deity of abundance who was grafted onto an historical figure.

IN MAGICK AND RITUAL — Prosperity.

DRUTWAS (WELSH)

IN MYTH — [DROOT-oois] Drutwas was a knight in King Arthur's court who was jealous of the

King's position. He married a faery woman who, as a wedding gift, gave him three magickal birds who understood human speech and would do any task he asked of them. Discovering their power, he challenged Arthur to a duel, then he instructed his birds to tear to pieces the first person they saw at the duel site. Arthur had no intention of showing up, so when Drutwas appeared to watch his birds do their job, they turned on him and killed him instead.

IN MAGICK AND RITUAL — Such stories as these are not uncommon in Celtic folklore. They point up the high price which is always paid for the wrong use of magick and clearly illustrate the Threefold Law in action. Pathwork with Dwutwas to discover healthier and better ways of handling negative emotions.

DUACH THE DARK (IRISH)

A member of the Tuatha De Danann who built the Fort of the Hostages at Tara. He was married to Taillte, the foster mother of Lugh.

DUBHTHACT DOELTENGA (IRISH)

A Red Branch warrior who was always gossiping and causing dissension among the warriors. He enjoyed infighting and thrived on discord. His surname means "one who backbites."

DUNATIS (CONTINENTAL)

IN MYTH — A Gaulish Celtic God of fortifications. He was probably also a protector of sacred spaces.

IN MAGICK AND RITUAL — Evoke Dunatis to protect your own sacred spaces and hiding places during rituals.

DWYVAN (WELSH)

IN MYTH — Also Dwyfan. Dwyvan and his wife, Dwyfach, are the heroes of the Welsh flood myth. Together they built an ark, filled it with animals, and survived the great flood caused by Addanc, a lake God/dragon/faery. Though later versions of this myth are distorted in order to make it conform to the Biblical version, the old story shines through and we see that Dwyvan was the personification of the male creative principle which has taken over for the older sacrificed God.

The Welsh deluge legend says that he and his wife were each part of one river which flowed into Bala Lake which was at one time called Lake Dyfrdwy, from the term *dyfr-dwyf* meaning "water of the divinity."

IN MAGICK AND RITUAL — Call on Dwyvach not only for perseverance and stamina, but think of him as one half of creation, needing his consort to complete the magick. Call upon them when working as a couple in ritual or spellwork or for sex magick.

DYLAN (IRISH, BRETON)

IN MYTH — The guardian deity of the mouth of the River Conway whose name is sometimes linked to the sea God Llyr. The *Mabinogion* story tells us he took off for sea as a newborn (he was son of Gwyddion and Arianrhod) where he could swim like a fish immediately and was beloved of these creatures. No wave ever broke beneath him and so he was called *Dylan Eil Ton,* "the son of the wave." In other stories he married the Lady of the Lake who bore him Vivienne, Merlin's great love.

DYLAN (CONT.)

Romanticized stories grew up around his death, thanks in part to the efforts of the bard Taliesin. The Welsh believe that the restless crash of the sea is an expression of longing to avenge his death. Around River Conway this roar is still called "Dylan's death groan."

In some stories he is one and the same as Math Ap Mathonwy.

Dyonas is his Breton name.

IN MAGICK AND RITUAL — Call on Dylan for water magick or to help contact sea faeries.

DYONAS (BRETON)

See Dylan.

EASAL (IRISH, MANX)

IN MYTH — A God of abundance and prosperity who came into myth as the King of the Golden Pillars. He gave the sons of Tuirrean seven magickal pigs, which would miraculously reappear the day after they were eaten. This story figures in one of the "Four Sorrows of Erin."

IN MAGICK AND RITUAL — Prosperity.

ECCA, KING (IRISH)

Also Erc. A king who kept a flood gate near Lough Neagh, over which he placed a young woman to stand guard. She was only to open them when someone needed water, but due to her carelessness, the lake flooded, killing all on the plain where Ecca's castle sat, with the exception of his daughter, Liban. This parallels the Greek myth of Pandora.

ECNE (IRISH)

A grandson of Dana. His name is sometimes translated as "knowledge," and sometimes as "poetry." Ecne's triple-father was Dana's son.

EDERN (WELSH, CORNISH, BRETON)

An Arthurian figure who became Brittany's St. Edern. He rode an Otherworldly white deer with his sister Genovefa, to mark out their respective kingdoms before dawn. When Genovefa saw Edern was riding faster than her, she encouraged a cock to crow heralding dawn. The deer in this myth is probably the legendary White Hart, an archetypal Otherworld messenger and harbinger of profound change.

EFFLAM (BRETON)

IN MYTH — A servant of the king who was sent out on a quest to solve the mystery of why the morning sun was red. He ventured to the golden palace of Mother of the Sun, who protected him on his quest. She told him the sun was red because of the brilliant radiance of her daughter, the Princess of the Sun. When the sponsoring king wished to marry the Princess, Efflam went on an adventure to seek her out, enduring three great trials.

The Princess thought the king too old, and suggested she kill him and restore him to life as a twenty-year-old. He agreed, but she chose to leave him dead and marry Efflam instead.

Efflam archetypally represents the young God who takes over for the dying God.

IN MAGICK AND RITUAL — Evoke him to enact this battle at Yule or Midsummer.

ELATHAN (IRISH)

IN MYTH — A chief of the Formorians who was described as attractive, a very unusual trait in a race which became known as grotesque sea monsters after they were banished from Ireland. He was tall, muscular, and golden-haired, and always wore a mantle made of spun gold. Around his neck were gold necklaces and he had silver, bronze, and gold spears.

He married a Danann and tried to keep peace between these two tense factions. He was a fair and honest ruler who loathed gossip and hearsay other than by his appointed spies.

IN MAGICK AND RITUAL — Evoke his presence to bring peace, and connect with his energy for overcoming prejudice and gossip, a difficult feat since prejudice against other tribes was actually valued by the Celts as with most early societies.

ELATHA (IRISH)

Elatha was the son of a Formorian king who had an affair with Eri. Bres, a Tuatha leader, was the son born of their union.

ELCMAR (IRISH)

The Dagda sent Elcmar to sleep with Boann because of a prophecy he had been given that their child would be of value to him. The two fell in love and married, but the Dagda cast a spell upon them so that nine months would pass in what would seem like a day and they would not know of the birth of the child. The boy was Aengus MacOg, of whom the Dagda ended up being jealous and covetous.

ELFFIN (WELSH, CORNISH)

In Myth — Also Elphin. Elffin was a poor young man out on a routine fishing trip with his father when his hook caught a leather bag. He reeled it in and found inside the infant Taliesin, who he decided to raise as his own. With Taliesin under his roof, he grew in power and wealth, but his love for the boy he took in never wavered. Taliesin's first poem sang of his love and adoration of Elffin.

Elffin began bragging about his new-found status: his wealth, his bards, his beautiful and faithful wife; and soon he raised the jealousy of King Arthur, who had him imprisoned. Taliesin tricked the knight, Rhun, sent to seduce his foster mother, and wove a spell of music magick which rendered Arthur's knights dumb and caused the chains to fall from Elffin's hands.

IN MAGICK AND RITUAL — This story is complex; on the surface it seems to be reminding one to stay humble, yet Elffin was not permanently punished for his bragging, a talent valued by some cultures. The deeper meaning seems to be the old adage that good deeds will be rewarded. Evoke Elffin to teach you to love and care for your own children, to see them as your wealth.

ELIDUC (BRETON)

IN MYTH — One of the Lay (epic romantic ballads) of Brittany as penned by that region's famous poet, Marie de France. Though this Lay has been Christianized to a great extent, we can still see through to its Pagan origins.

Eliduc was a knight who was maligned out of jealousy by his peers. Without giving him a chance to respond to the charges, the Breton King banished him. He left his wife, Guildeluec, behind while pledging his undying fidelity to her.

ELIDUC (CONT.)

He ended up in Lourdes, where he met the King's only heir, a daughter named Guillardun, who was pledged to marry a rival King in an attempt to bring peace to the region. To protect her, the King of Lourdes had her shut in a tower. Eliduc offered to protect her, and in doing so, fell in love with her as did she with him. He decided not to tell her he was married, but also refused to consummate the relationship.

Guillardun asked her father to release her from her engagement and he agreed, but when permission was granted, Eliduc refused her. She pursued him, unable to understand why he no longer desired her.

When it was time for Eliduc to return to his own country, she wanted to come, but he refused to take her. Guillardun stowed away on the ship to be with him. Well out to sea, a great storm ensued. Some of the sailors, believing this stemmed from Eliduc's unchivalrous behavior, tossed the couple overboard. They became separated in the sea, and Eliduc made his way home alone to his wife who immediately realized something was wrong.

Eliduc thought Guillardun dead, but she had been taken in by his wife, who found her washed up on the shore. She was restored to consciousness by his wife's placing a red flower (blood-colored) in her mouth. When the two women met and talked, Guildeluec offered to enter an order (probably a nearby school for Druidesses, not a convent) in order to step aside so that her husband could be happy with Guillardun. Eventually Guillardun came to join her, as did Eliduc.

IN MAGICK AND RITUAL — Pathwork with Eliduc to study the risks of indecision and of lying to others for our own selfish purposes. Also work with Guildeluec for her qualities of compassion and unconditional love.

ELINAS, KING (BRETON, SCOTTISH)

The King of Scotland who fathered the Breton Goddess Melusine.

EMRYS (WELSH)

See Merlin.

EOCHAID (IRISH)

To the eternal confusion of students of Celtic folklore, more than a dozen Eochaids appear in Irish myth and history, most of them as rulers. One was a FirBolg's High King who fathered Taillte. He was overthrown by the Tuatha at the First Battle of Magh Tuireadh. Another was a Desi who fought against Cormac MacArt, lost, and his clan was exiled. Yet another was a second century king of Leinster.

EOCHAID, KING (IRISH)

IN MYTH — [Y'OH-key or Y'OH-hee] Also Eochy and Eochaid Airen. A High King who was one of the husbands of Edain. His name means "horse," and is believed to be the etymology of the English word "jockey."

When he lost Edain in a chess game to Midhir, a faery king, he tried to prevent Midhir from taking her away, but he could not stop the faery, and watched helplessly as the two changed into swans and flew away.

Eochaid ventured into the Otherworld to try to rescue her; his actions resulted in a faeryland war. When the battle was over, he discovered that Edain was not there. She had been hidden by Midhir in a faery mound which he spent nine years digging out with his bare hands.

IN MAGICK AND RITUAL — Archetypally the story of Edain is about death and rebirth, and Eochaid represents the living force of love which compels her return to the living. Work with him to forge eternal bonds with your own loved ones.

Eoghan (Irish)

IN MYTH — [EE-gan] Eoghan was a Connacht king killed in one of the numerous battles with Ulster. His warriors buried him on the border facing Ulster as a talisman of protection and of warning against other attacks.

IN MAGICK AND RITUAL — Protection. See Bran for a full discussion of Celtic beliefs about the head.

Epos Olloatir (Pan-Celtic)

IN MYTH — A horse God often seen as either a male form of the widely worshipped Goddess Epona, or as her consort.

IN MAGICK AND RITUAL — Horse deities are linked to the night and to dream magick. Call upon Epos when you wish to work with dreams as a magick tool.

Eremon, King (Irish)

Sometimes spelled Herimon. First king of the Milesians, son of Milesius, the conqueror of the Tuatha. He was the first human, male ruler of the island. Queen Cessair was its first human ruler.

Essus (Breton, Continental)

IN MYTH — Also Esus. A harvest God worshipped in Brittany, and in Gaul by the people known as the Essuvi. He was the consort of Artio.

He is connected with a vague and lost myth about the penalties for the cutting down of trees, and was associated with the totem animals of crane and bull, symbolizing his fertility principle and his links to the Otherworld.

Extant altars to him date to the third century B.C.E. The Romans recorded that sacrifices were made to him on these. When we consider his image as a fertility and Otherworld one, it is reasonable to assume that the sacrifices were made as an exchange to persuade him to released loved ones from the Otherworld.

He died by being hung on one of his sacred trees like the Norse God Odin with whom he is often equated. His legends eventually merged with those of Jesus in the early centuries C.E., and eventually his own myths were lost.

IN MAGICK AND RITUAL — Call on Essus for fertility and harvest rites. Evoke him with rituals designed to facilitate spirit contact or to bind yourself to passed over loved ones with whom you wish to reincarnate.

CORRESPONDENCES — The crane and the bull.

Evnissyen (Welsh)

IN MYTH — Also Efnisien. A Welsh schemer who gravely insulted the bride at the wedding feast of Math and Branwyn. He also cut the ears, lips, and tail off Matholwch's horse. When

EVNISSYEN (CONT.)

the Irish discovered this, they began a war to avenge the couple's honor, a war which Evnissyen felt guilty for sometime later. He atoned for the error by sacrificing himself in order to destroy the cauldron of regeneration through which the Irish were replenishing their warrior ranks. His tactic worked. The Welsh won and killed all their Irish enemies, however, only seven Welshmen were left alive at the battle's end.

IN MAGICK AND RITUAL — Learn from Evnissyen the value of self-sacrifice and for learning lessons about the acceptance of responsibility.

FACHTNA (IRISH)

IN MYTH — This Ulster king was the son of the evil Druid Cathbad, though he was raised by his foster father, King Conchobar. He had a passionate affair with Nessa, whom he later married. His reputation was one of a great lover and fine magician.

IN MAGICK AND RITUAL — Cultivate him for sex magick and as a general aid to spellwork.

FEARGAL (IRISH)

IN MYTH — Feargal is the Munster man who brought the specified magickal items to Fiongalla, and broke the spell of agelessness which was cast upon her. Feargal in this story probably represents a sacrificial God/king who has returned to his Goddess bride when she returns to her virgin form.

IN MAGICK AND RITUAL — Evoke him and Fiongalla for Yule or Imbolg rituals.

FEINIUS FARSAIDH (IRISH)

IN MYTH — [FINE-ee-oos FAHR-see, or FAHR-saw] This very wise man was such a superb teacher that he was invited to travel to Egypt and teach Pharaoh Cingris and his court. His son Niul married the Pharaoh's daughter Scota (other sources make her the wife of Milesius).

IN MAGICK AND RITUAL — Invoke Feinius to learn his wisdom, and call on his magickal powers to boost all your spells.

FELIM MACDALL (IRISH)

This high-ranking chieftain was the father of Deirdre of the Sorrows. He forever regretted asking Cathbad to perform a divination at the birth of his daughter, wishing he had never known in advance of her unhappy fate.

FER CARTNA (IRISH)

A bard employed by Cu Roi who ran off with Blathnat. Cu Roi forced the two of them to leap together off a cliff to their deaths.

FER GRUADH (IRISH)

IN MYTH — [Fear GREW-ah] When clan chieftain Aille's husband, Meargach of the Green Spear, was killed in battle by Fionn's grandson Oscar, she had her chief Druid, Fer Gruadh, administer a sleeping potion to Fionn so that he could be taken captive. The Fianna warriors discovered the plot and pursued the Druid, but his magick was greater, and soon the warriors were all under his control.

IN MAGICK AND RITUAL — Invoke or evoke Fer Gruadh to aid in any spell, especially binding or staying spells.

CORRESPONDENCES — Garlands.

FERDIA (IRISH)

IN MYTH — A friend and sidekick of Cuchulain's who studied with him at the Isle of Shadow under the tutelage of Scathach. During the war between Connacht and Ulster he sided with his native Connacht, though he tried to avoid battle with his Ultonian friend. However, Queen Maeve forced a one-to-one struggle between them in which Ferdia was killed.

Ferdia's death was a symbolic sacrifice for Connacht. When Cuchulain fell down exhausted and heart-sick from the battle with Ferdia, the Connacht legions stormed the borders, overtaking Ulster.

IN MAGICK AND RITUAL — Use Ferdia's energy for overcoming enemies and for learning lessons of loyalty.

FERGUS (IRISH)

IN MYTH — Also Feargus. The virile and insatiable husband of Flidais, Goddess of the woodlands and its beasts. It took many mortal women to sexually satisfy him when Flidais was not around.

IN MAGICK AND RITUAL—Invoke Fergus to contribute to your sexual stamina, or to be a part of any sex magick practices.

FERGUS THE GREAT (SCOTTISH)

IN MYTH — The first monarch outside of Tara to be crowned while standing on the Lia Fail, the Stone of Destiny, reputed to give out a leonine roar when the rightful ruler stood upon it. The current British royal family claim him as an ancestor, and are thought to be coronated on the same stone which now sits in Westminster Abbey. (The other reputed residence of the stone is in Perth, Scotland.)

IN MAGICK AND RITUAL — Invoke Fergus into the body of your own High Priest or Priestess to aid him or her during her tenure as your leader.

FERGUS MACLEDA (IRISH)

IN MYTH — An Ulster king who got into a battle with Iubdan, a faery king, and imprisoned him. Fergus and the countryside were plagued by the faeries until he agreed to Iubdan's release. The faeries, claiming no hard feelings, offered peace in the form of a pair of shoes which could bear the wearer safely over water. Fergus used them frequently, but he was maimed by a sea monster while walking on the ocean and had to relinquish the throne.

IN MAGICK AND RITUAL — Though Fergus is not a potent archetype, his folktale has much to teach about dealing with the faery kingdom.

FERGUS MACROI (IRISH)

IN MYTH — A king of Ulster who was supposed to reign in turns with Fiachna and Conchobar. He was to succeed Conchobar as king, but Conchobar did not want to relinquish the crown to him. As a result, Fergus sided with Connacht during their great war, but a long-held geise forced him to refrain from battle. He endured exile for the sake of his love, Nessa, after she was banished by Conchobar.

He was the teacher of Cuchulain, and is often thought to be one and the same as Ferdia, Cuchulain's loyal friend.

IN MAGICK AND RITUAL — Teacher, love magick, wisdom, keeping of geise.

FIACHA (IRISH)

IN MYTH — [FEE-ahk-uh] An Ulster warrior who fled to Connacht in protest over the oppressive rule of King Conchobar. However, when he saw Cuchulain being held down by twenty-eight warriors, Fiacha became enraged and cut off the right hands from the restraining warriors in one great blow.

Fiacha gave his great sword to Fionn MacCumhal and taught him its secrets. The magickal blade was for Fionn what Excalibur was to King Arthur.

Fiacha's myths blur with those of Ferdia and Fergus MacRoi. They may have been one and the same, or a long lost triplicity.

IN MAGICK AND RITUAL — Call upon for Fiacha for overcoming enemies, to find or consecrate magickal tools, or for invoking loyalty.

CORRESPONDENCES — Sweetpea.

FIGOL MACMAMOS (IRISH)

IN MYTH — A chief Druid of early Tara during the time of the wars with the Formorians. He magickally took two-thirds of the strength from the enemy, and increased, with each breath they drew in, the strength and valor of the Tuatha De Danann's forces so that they could win. He did this by sending "three streams of fire" into the enemy's faces. It took seven years for the Tuatha to prepare for this war.

IN MAGICK AND RITUAL — Summon Figol for learning patience and for assistance with all magick, especially staying spells.

CORRESPONDENCES — Woad, saffron, Dragon's Blood, the color blue.

FINEGAS (IRISH, SCOTTISH)

IN MYTH — He is called Fingus in Scotland. He was a bard and teacher who taught the arts of poetry and music, as well as the hard sciences, to his most famous pupil, Fionn MacCumhal. Finegas fished the great Salmon of Knowledge from the waters of the Irish Sea and gave it to Fionn to cook for him without knowing what it was. Fionn burned his thumb on the fish. When he sucked at the pain, he instantly acquired great knowledge. Seeing this, Finegas realized the Salmon was not meant to be eaten by himself, so he gave it to its rightful recipient—Fionn.

IN MAGICK AND RITUAL — Invoke the essence of Finegas when you must be the teacher, to use your native wisdom to fullest capacity, to gain compassion, or to increase mental prowess. Call on him to help you find the Salmon in your inner-journeys.

FINGAL (SCOTTISH)

See Fionn MacCumhal.

FINTAAN (IRISH)

IN MYTH — The husband of Cessair, the first human occupant and Queen of Ireland. They left with their entourage for the "western edge of the world" forty days before the great flood which engulfed all the world except Ireland. He survived by changing himself into a salmon, and some scholars argue that he was the Salmon of Knowledge, which is occasionally called by his name.

IN MAGICK AND RITUAL — Use Fintaan's energy to gain knowledge, wisdom, and endurance skills. Invoke his wit when your survival is at stake.

FINVARRA (IRISH)

IN MYTH — [FIN-var or Fin-VAR-uh] Also Fionnbharr. A mighty God who became known as a faery king of the Tuatha De Danann. He used games of chess (the old Irish version known as *fidchell*) to gain power over his enemies. He loved the sport of hurling, but needed a mortal on the team in order to win and he usually asked his good friend Ossian to join.

He was also a warrior who intervened in the war between Midhir and Bov the Red. He was probably once a father God who, today, rules the burgh at Knockma with his wife Onaugh.

IN MAGICK AND RITUAL — Call on the spirit of Finvarra to assist you in all competitions, for increasing mental prowess, and for aid in faery contact.

CORRESPONDENCES — Primroses, and all game equipment and pieces.

> *All Eire does tremble to the beat of the steeds,*
> *The wild, fearless ghosts charging forth as they heed*
> *The spectral call of the ancients, and then,*
> *"Ride to victory!" cry out Fionn's warrior men.*
>
> —Moirna Carol O'Reilly

FIONN MacCUMHAL (IRISH, MANX, SCOTTISH)

IN MYTH — Also Finn MacCool or McCual; Fin on the Isle of Man, and Fingal in Scottish. His original name was Demna, the son of Murna of the White neck and Cumhal, the Fianna leader. Fionn plays a leading role in Irish mythology, appearing in many stories, even when only in cameo.

Fionn is the legendary giant God/warrior of Ireland who foresaw the coming of the Milesians, and banished an invading giant from Scotland. He married Grainne, a master herbalist and sun Goddess who was the daughter of King Cormac, but he went on to take many other wives and lovers including Fand, a faery queen.

He took over the leadership of the Fianna from his father. (The Fianna are also called the Fenians, from which the twentieth-century Irish rebels took their name.)

When he was a child he burned his finger on the Salmon of Knowledge which his teacher, Finegas, had unknowingly given him. He sucked on the burn, and instantly acquired vast knowledge and wisdom.

One of Fionn's earliest achievements was the creation of Lough Neagh in northern Ireland, which he scooped out with his two bare hands, and tossed into the Irish Sea where it became the Isle of Man. He later destroyed all of Ireland's serpents, a story later appropriated by St. Patrick, which represents the destruction of Druidic power. (It may also be a patriarchal legend which symbolizes the dismantling of feminine power with which the serpent has long been associated.) Fionn killed the snakes only when they rose up and threatened to eat the island's food supply.

Archetypally he is another sleeping God/king who is supposed to rise with his Fenian warriors when his people need him.

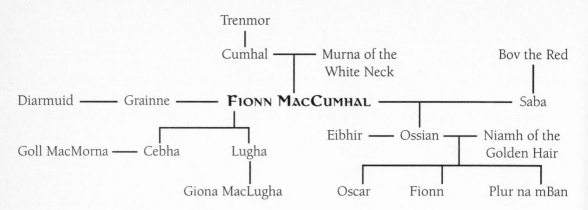

The generally accepted family tree of Fionn MacCumhal.

FIONN MACCUMHAL (CONT.)

Legends say he lived for two hundred years. It is a long-standing Irish tradition to honor his memory at the Yule Sabbat.

IN MAGICK AND RITUAL — Wisdom, overcoming enemies, creation, protection, knowledge, and divination.

FISHER KING, THE (WELSH, CORNISH)

IN MYTH — The Fisher King plays a central role in the Arthurian Grail legends. It is his palace which holds the sacred object where it is guarded by three maidens.

The Grail legend further tells us that the Fisher King's kingdom fell under a curse where all living things became barren—the land, the animals, and the people. He himself lay in pain and agony with a wound in the thigh, a metaphor for his impotency.

In order to find the Grail, a questing knight had to first find the way into the palace, had to eat and drink with the King, and then ask all the right questions of his host. The questions not only concerned the Grail, but a lance which lay nearby it that always dripped with blood, a metaphor for a wounded phallus.

Archetypally the Fisher King is not only the guardian of the Grail mysteries, but is a father God whose potency is restored when the feminine principle, which is also a part of him (as manifested in the Grail), is freed, and when it is reunited with the masculine principle as symbolized by the lance. It is only when his wound heals that fertility and abundance are restored.

IN MAGICK AND RITUAL — Fertility, knowledge, and prosperity.

CORRESPONDENCES — Coins, ripe grains.

FOILL (IRISH, SCOTTISH)

The young man who was killed by Cuchulain in the Ulster hero's first battle. Cuchulain tied Foill's head to his chariot as a talisman of protection.

FORBAY (IRISH)

When both Queen Maeve's husband and favorite lover had been slain in her eighty-eighth year of rule, she left her Connacht castle and retreated to seclusion on an island called Inis

Clothrann (now called Quaker's Isle). Forbay is the Ulster warrior who killed her with a blow from his slingshot while she was bathing in a pool on her island retreat.

FROACH (IRISH)

IN MYTH — This figure is the hero in the epic tale, The Cattle Raid of Cooley. He was the husband of Princess Findabar, the daughter of Queen Maeve. Their union was opposed by her mother and King Ailill who went so far in their resistance as to plan his demise in a lake with a carnivorous dragon.

Froach was led to the lake and took a swim. Predictably, the dragon attacked, but he was rescued by Findabar who rushed in to save him. When she pulled him from the water, a host of Otherworld deities came and took him back with them in order to nurse him back to health. Meanwhile the divinities intervened and convinced the reluctant parents not to oppose the marriage.

IN MAGICK AND RITUAL — Perseverance and courage. Also couples and sex magick with Findabar's energies.

GABAIGLINE (IRISH)

IN MYTH — [GAHV-aw-len-ee] A blind man who was the chief prophet and seer for Clan Degad who confirmed that Macha's curse of pain on the warriors of Ulster would hold in battle.

IN MAGICK AND RITUAL — Divination.

GADEL (IRISH)

IN MYTH — An ancient Milesian king credited with dividing the Gaelic language into five separate dialects; one each for poets, historians, warriors, healers, and the common folk. Some credit him with originally being a Middle Eastern deity from Achaea near the Black Sea.

IN MAGICK AND RITUAL — Call on his energy for effective communication and for overcoming communicative barriers.

GAIAR (IRISH, MANX)

A son of Manann whose affair with Becuna caused their banishment from the Otherworld.

GALAHAD, SIR (WELSH, CORNISH, BRETON)

IN MYTH — As the son of Lancelot and Elaine LeBlanc, Galahad is a medieval addition to the Arthurian myths and did not appear in the original tales. He may have been based on several of the original minor characters.

In the medieval interpretation, it is he who is the sole finder of the Grail, even though earlier tales give both Percival and Gawain the same honor. Other legends say he finds the Grail before Percival but dies when he touches it.

Galahad fought with the Green Knight at Yule, and the seasonal colors of green and red are deeply linked to his myth. He is protected by a green garter which became his emblem, wore red armor, and pulled his mighty sword from a block of red marble floating in the river. The color association may link him to the battle between the waxing and waning energies who fight at Yule and Midsummer.

IN MAGICK AND RITUAL — Seasonal rites.

CORRESPONDENCES — The green garter.

GARIENT (WELSH)

IN MYTH—Also Gerient. Garient, a warrior, is one half of a famous Welsh romantic pair. Their tale appears in the *Mabinogion* and in Chretien de Troyes' *Erec and Enid*.

They met when Garient was poised to fight a hand-to-hand combat with Edern Ap Nudd over an insult to Queen Guinevere. As the issue of insult was settled, the love between Garient and Enid grew.

The legendary White Hart, an all-white deer associated with the Otherworld and with messages brought to earth from that realm, appears to them.

His story is believed to be based upon the life of a fourth-century Dumnonian king who was involved in battles with the Anglo-Saxons.

IN MAGICK AND RITUAL — Call on Garient for couples and sex magick, and for love spells.

GARLON (WELSH, CORNISH)

IN MYTH — A Druid who mastered the art of invisibility. He was the brother of King Pelles, and it was in his castle that he was slain by Balin, a Round Table Knight. His death brought about the great Wasteland of Arthurian myth, an archetypal linkage to the God's death at the beginning of winter, the "dead season."

IN MAGICK AND RITUAL — Learning astral projection.

GAVIDA (IRISH)

A minor God of the forge, sometimes thought to be one and the same as Goibniu.

> *From the rocks rebounding,*
> *Let the war cry sounding,*
> *Summon all at Cambria's call....*
>
> —Welsh Folk Song

GAWAIN, SIR (WELSH, CORNISH)

IN MYTH — Also Gwalchmai or Gauvain. Since his strength peaked at midday after which it waned, this knight from King Arthur's Round Table was probably once a regional sun deity.

He was the first to swear an oath to seek out the Holy Grail, the supposed drinking cup used by Jesus at the Passover meal known as the Last Supper. The archetypal Grail is a cauldron, a vessel of feminine power which was needed by mythic kings in order for them to rule legitimately.

Gawain was a nephew of Arthur's, once portrayed as courageous and self-sacrificing, though later legends made him an ineffectual boor. Sometimes he is linked romantically with Lady Loathly, a thinly disguised moon Goddess. He functioned as Arthur's *tanaiste* (an Irish word), or heir, whose duty it was to look out for his inheritance against treachery to the king. This was a prevalent Celtic custom. In this role, Gawain challenged the Green Knight to save Arthur's throne.

He discovered the Castle of Wonders, where the Grail in all its archetypal glory as "the keeper of the greater mysteries" was hidden. In the very oldest of the Arthurian tales, he alone managed to battle through the many illusions, diversions, and obstacles deliberately placed there to lure the seeker way from the true spiritual goals. When he found the Grail and the bloody lance near it, he symbolically reunited the male and female principles of creation, returning fertility to the land.

IN MAGICK AND RITUAL — Use Gawain's energy for protection, sex magick, and for guidance towards spirituality as and he can help clear away the murky clouds for the sincere seeker. Evoke his aid for the male role in the Great Rite, for that was what the reunion of Grail and lance symbolized. Pathwork with him to learn to overcome spiritual obstacles. He can also help you think clearly.

CORRESPONDENCES — The white rose.

Gebann (Irish)

IN MYTH — [GOHV-ahn] Also Gabann and Gebhann. This Druid, known for his great beauty and his house of many mirrors, was the father of Cliodna, an Irish Goddess of beauty. One of his great feats of magick was the ability to manipulate time.

IN MAGICK AND RITUAL — Invoke him to enhance personal appearance, for making mirror magick, and for learning lessons in time manipulation.

CORRESPONDENCES — The mirror.

Gilla Stagshank (Welsh)

A famous leaper who was sent for by Culhwch to aid him in his quest to find Olwen.

Gilvaethwy the False (Welsh)

Also Gilfawthwy. He coveted Math's foot maiden, Goewin, and plotted to steal her so that he could steal the throne through her blessing of sovereignty. (Celtic royal bloodlines were often traced through women, even though the men were the highest rulers of the land.)

His brother Gwyddion knew how he felt, both about the throne and the lovely Goewin, and he agreed to help Gilvaethwy win her. They sought out Math, and through a series of lies and deceit, convinced him to use trickery to obtain the magick swine herd of King Pryderi. Math agreed to the plot, but his actions began an unforeseen war. While the others were away fighting, Gilvaethwy stole Goewin. Finally Math, aware of the deceit and tired of the lies and quarrels, turned Gilvaethwy into a deer for a year, then a pig, then a wolf. Each year he had to return and give Math one of his young.

The story of this son of Don is recorded in the *Mabinogion*.

Giona MacLugha (Irish)

IN MYTH — A grandson and pupil of Fionn MacCumhal who learned magick from him, and the warrior's art from his warrior mother, Lugha. When he was given command of the Fianna, the power went to his head and he became lazy, selfish, and tyrannical. His men lay down their arms and refused to fight until he was replaced. Fionn placated them, then taught lessons of wise leadership to his grandson who eventually became a good and well-loved leader.

IN MAGICK AND RITUAL — Pathwork this story to learn to rule wisely.

Glewlwyd of the Mighty Grasp (Welsh, Cornish)

IN MYTH — A warrior with a devastating grip that could crush iron. He guarded the gates of both the fortress where Ysbadadden hid his daughter Olwen, and also Arthur's abode.

IN MAGICK AND RITUAL — Evoke his guardianship during circle rites.

GLUEU (WELSH)

One of the seven survivors of the Irish-Welsh war fought over the insult at the wedding feast of Matholwch and Branwyn. His father was said to be Taran, a corruption of the Gaulish God Taranis. Other sources link him to Etirun, an Irish name for a long-forgotten Welsh father God.

GOG (ANGLO-CELTIC)

The consort of Magog and her male fertility principle.

> The Danann children laugh,
> in cradles of wrought gold....
> —William Butler Yeats

GOIBNIU (IRISH, WELSH)

IN MYTH — His Welsh name is Govannon. A master goldsmith at Tara who, along with his brothers Luchtain and Credne (a triplicity), made nearly all of the weapons used by the Tuatha De Danann. The smith's craft was associated with potent magick by the Celts, and he is the deity credited with being the founder of the arts and is the patron God of Irish crafts-people.

He was also known as an ale or meade maker whose drink bestowed both invincibility in battle, and release from illness and death for the one who imbibed. This brew was served at Manann's Feast of Age at which no one who sat at his table ever grew old.

IN MAGICK AND RITUAL — Creativity, magick, crafting, protection, blessing and making of meade or magickal tools.

CORRESPONDENCES — The anvil.

GOIDEL (IRISH)

IN MYTH — Also Gael and Gaeldhal. A Son of Niul and his Egyptian bride, Scota. Legend says Goidel is the common ancestor of the Goidelic Celts—speakers of Irish, Manx, and Scottish—whose language he was said to have invented.

As a God of the basic means of communication—speech—his image was appropriated by the local Christian leaders, and legends abound which link him to both Moses and St. Patrick.

IN MAGICK AND RITUAL — Communication skills, creativity, or courage when public speaking. Invoke him to get all to speak truth in gatherings.

CORRESPONDENCES — The staff.

GOLL MACMORNA (IRISH)

IN MYTH — Goll is a complex character with several roles in the Fennian Myth cycles. In one he is the leader of the Fianna between Cumhal and Fionn. He killed Fionn to obtain his position then married Fionn's daughter Cebha. Though he was an unpopular leader, he was tolerated until he killed one of Fionn's sons. In other myths he was the great friend and loyal subordinate to Fionn, even rescuing him from an enchanted cave and being given Kicva as his wife for his heroic efforts.

He fought off several magickally manifested attacks when his battalion took refuge from a storm in what we would today call a haunted house.

IN MAGICK AND RITUAL — Call on Goll to help you see through illusion, for protection, courage, and to help you out of dangerous or uncertain situations.

GONEMANS (WELSH)

A warrior teacher who trained many of the Welsh fighting men including Percival.

GORLOIS OF CORNWALL (CORNISH)

Husband of Igraine, the mother of King Arthur. It is his likeness which was assumed by Uther Pendragon in order to father Arthur. Gorlois was killed in battle before Uther became king.

GOUVERNAYL (CORNISH)

The loyal servant of Tristan who can be compared to Laeg in the tales of Cuchulain.

GOVANNON (WELSH)

See Goibniu.

GRANNOS (SCOTTISH, ANGLO-CELTIC, CONTINENTAL)

IN MYTH — An early continental God of mineral springs whose shrines have been found in the English town of Musselburgh, in Auvergne, France, and near Edinburgh, Scotland.

On the continent he was a minor sun God and God of the healing arts. Like many people today, the early Celts sought out mineral springs for their healing benefits, particularly for degenerative muscle ailments or arthritis.

Grannos is also given a role as a harvest deity in a children's rhyme sung at harvest bonfire which calls Grannos friend, father, mother, and child.

He is sometimes the consort of Sirona.

IN MAGICK AND RITUAL — Purification, harvest, or healing.

CORRESPONDENCES — Dried corn sheaves.

GREEN KNIGHT, THE (WELSH, CORNISH)

IN MYTH — This mysterious figure in the Arthurian legends posed one of the few serious threats to Arthur's rulership. He fought a beheading game with Galahad who challenged him to protect the throne. Galahad won that round, but the Green Knight does not remain dead. He rises with his head in hands each year and demands a rematch.

The Green Knight contains many qualities of the Holly King: he appears at Arthur's court at Yule, is depicted as dressed in evergreens, and his totem animal is the wren.

IN MAGICK AND RITUAL — The Green Knight teaches us that many challenges will come our way and that we must not fear them nor flee. They must be undertaken in order to move onward. The fact that the Green Knight lives through these encounters underscores that these are but natural events in the cycles of time.

CORRESPONDENCES — Holly berries, the wren.

GREEN MAN, THE (PAN-CELTIC)

IN MYTH — His is an image which transcended all the other Celtic God forms and became a version of the Christian Devil every bit as potent as the Horned God. His appearance is rather like that of the advertisement of the Jolly Green Giant®, a leafy figure in verdant green with green skin and hair. His face is ringed with verdant leaves, and superstitious folk still say they see him in the summer foliage, from which they flee. His randy woodland image was firmly linked in the minds of the churchmen with "evil" witches who cavorted with him under the light of the full moon.

He is possibly an Oak King image, a symbol of fertility and of the waxing year. He is also linked to Cernunnos, the Horned God of the wild. Archetypally he is the male fertility principle of the earth mother.

IN MAGICK AND RITUAL — Eco-magick, fertility, male mysteries, and masculine power.

GRONW PEBYR (WELSH)

IN MYTH — [GRAWN-oo PAY-bur] The Lord of Penllyn and lover of Blodeuwedd. He and Llew fought a battle in which both were killed, but Llew was resurrected in what many believe is yet another version of the semiannual Holly King/Oak King battle.

IN MAGICK AND RITUAL — Seasonal rites, love magick.

GRUFFYDDAP LLYWELYN (WELSH)

IN MYTH — He was the last High King of Wales who reigned from 1029–1063. Though engaged in constant warfare, he eventually managed to unite Wales for a time under one royal house. When dissension divided the country again, he was defeated by the English and killed by his own men.

IN MAGICK AND RITUAL — Evoke his spirit—which has taken divine proportions—to unite your working groups.

GUAIRE (IRISH)

IN MYTH — [GW'AWR-ee] Also Guary. A guardian God/spirit of *Bruigh na Boinne* (Aengus MacOg's Newgrange Cairn), and father of Ebhlinne.

IN MAGICK AND RITUAL — Protection.

GUGEMAR (BRETON)

IN MYTH — Gugemar is the hero of one of the Lay (epic romantic ballads) of Brittany as penned by the famous poet, Marie de France. He was made a knight by King Arthur and fought for him in Flanders.

When hunting one day in his native country, he shot at a white, unblemished doe who was protecting her fawn (a Goddess image of uncertain origins). The arrow bounced out of her own wound and imbedded itself deep in Gugemar's thigh. She came and spoke to him saying that because he killed her, he would never be healed but by the woman who loved him, and that they would both suffer much sorrow before they would have joy.

Gugemar, having no interest in romantic entanglements, hobbled away. He ended up on an enchanted boat which took him to another land where he met a young queen with whom he was smitten. She healed his wound.

For a year and a day he stayed with her. Before they parted they tied each other in special garments with a knot which only the other knew the secret of undoing. On that same day, the angry king discovered them and Gugemar was banished back home. Back in Brittany, his family wished him to marry, but he insisted he could only wed her who could untie his knot.

The queen escaped the angry king in an enchanted ship and came to Brittany with faulty memory. When questioned about her knotted garment, she said only that she must wed the one man who could untie her. Eventually the two stories were put together and the lovers reunited. They untied the knots, regained full memory of each other, and finally lived happily ever after.

IN MAGICK AND RITUAL — Use Gugemar in loyalty, love, couples magick.

GUINGAMOR (BRETON)

IN MYTH — This Breton knight was the boon companion of the king's nephew. The two of them were the favored of the queen who had fallen in love with Guingamor. When he refused her advances, she sent him on a dangerous hunt to kill a wild white boar from which no one who ever set out after it had returned.

While on the quest, he found a lovely woman bathing in a pool and stayed with her. She was a faery woman and kept him with her for three hundred years, though he thought only a few hours had passed.

When Guingamor finally left her, she warned him not to eat or drink anything while he was away. When he did, he fell down dead.

IN MAGICK AND RITUAL — Guingamor can teach us several things. One, that one must use caution when dealing with faeries, obey the rules of the Otherworld, and that, when approached properly, there are good things to always come from bad. Since he knows all the pitfalls of human-faery relationship, he can help protect you from them.

GWALCHMEI (WELSH)

IN MYTH — Also Gwalchmai. His name means "the hawk of May," and he was King Arthur's nephew, a peacemaker and arbiter for his court. He is believed to have become Sir Gawain in the medieval legends.

IN MAGICK AND RITUAL — Peace magick. Invoke him when you are called upon to settle disputes.

GWAWL AP CLUD (WELSH)

IN MYTH — Also Gwawn. The son of the Goddess Clud whose name means "of light." He fell in love with Rhiannon and was promised to her in marriage, but when it came to blows, he lost her to Pwyll.

Because of his name, it is reasonable to assume that he was once a minor sun God.

IN MAGICK AND RITUAL — Experiment with how the energies of Gwawl relate to solar-influenced magick.

GWERN (WELSH)

The son of Matholwch and Branwyn who was given the throne of Ireland in an attempt to make peace between between Ireland and Wales. He was cast into a fire at age three, and the battle was renewed.

GWION BACH (WELSH)

IN MYTH — [GOO'ee-ahn] This son of Gweang of Llanfair was charged with keeping the contents stirred inside Cerridwen's great cauldron where a potion of knowledge was being brewed. When he accidentally splashed out three drops on his fingers and sucked them, he acquired all knowledge.

Realizing what had happened, he fled in fear, but Cerridwen pursued him. First he turned into a hare to escape, but she became a greyhound. Then he took the form of a fish, and she an otter. Then he became a bird, and she a hawk. Lastly, he turned himself into a grain of corn, and she became the hen who consumed him. He took root inside her and was reborn from her as Taliesin.

Druidic lore relates this chase to their initiatory rites and others as a metaphor for reincarnation.

IN MAGICK AND RITUAL — General magick, wisdom, and past-life explorations.

CORRESPONDENCES — Honeysuckle and dogs.

GWRHYR (WELSH)

IN MYTH — A magician who spoke all the languages of the world.

IN MAGICK AND RITUAL — Call upon him for mental prowess or for communication needs which further understanding or seek to avoid misunderstandings.

> *I was spellbound by Gwyddion,*
> *Prime Enchanter of the Britons.*
> —from the *Mabinogion*

GWYDDION (WELSH)

IN MYTH — [GWID-ee-ohn or GWITH-ee-ohn] Also Gwydion Ap Don and Gweir. A son of Don, and the uncle of Llew who changed his wife Blodeuwedd into an owl. Perhaps all the Arthurian legends were once attributed to him, but they were eventually grafted solely onto King Arthur.

Gwyddion was very wise, especially in music magick, and he once rescued Llew by singing an enchantment. He was referred to as master of illusion, a helper of humankind, and a fighter against the greedy and small-minded. He supported the cultural arts and learning, and tried to stamp out ignorance. Because of all this praise, he is sometimes called the Druid of the Gods.

He got his own education from his uncle Math. Like many other Pagan cultures, it was customary for the mother's brother to teach the sons.

Gwyddion and his brothers fought in the Battle of the Trees to ensure that the dog, deer, and lapwing he took from Annwn could remain on earth. His last foray into the Otherworld resulted in pigs (sacred to many Goddesses, most notably Cerridwen) being brought to humankind.

IN MAGICK AND RITUAL — Cultivate Gwyddion for making music spells and general magick, and to gain mental acuity.

CORRESPONDENCES — Clover.

GWYDDNO (WELSH)

IN MYTH — This one-time sea God came down in myth as a monster or faery of the ocean. He had many treasures on his sea floor home, one of which had to be obtained by Culhwch if he wished to have Olwen for his wife.

His world is known as "the drowned kingdom," and the story may also be one which refers to the intriguing and controversial lost continent of Atlantis.

IN MAGICK AND RITUAL — Water magick.

> *I have been where the soldiers of Britain are slain,*
> *From the east to the south — I am alive,*
> *They in their graves!*
>
> —from *The Black Book of Caermarthen*

GWYN AP NUAD (WELSH)

IN MYTH — His name means "white son of darkness," and he was the child of the sun/death God Llud, also called Nuad or Nudd, the leader of the hunt.

Gwyn is a God of war, death, and the hunt, and a patron God of fallen warriors. He is equated with Ireland's Fionn MacCumhal as both Gwyn and Fionn mean "white." As the master hunter, he rode a wild horse and had three massive hounds; one red, one black, and one white. In an early Welsh poem he is a God of battle and of the Otherworld, the escort of dead souls to Annwn. Rural people claim they can sometimes hear his wild chase at night. (The hunt is a metaphor for gathering souls for the Otherworld.)

Gwyn appears in the *The Black Book of Caermarthen*, *The Red Book of Hergest*, and is featured in the Arthurian legends as the abductor of Creiddylad. He is forced to engage in hand-to-hand combat over her with Gwyrthur Ap Gwreidawl, their sentence being that they must fight until the end of time. Whoever is the victor at that time may have her. This is another waxing/waning year battle in which Gwyn is the waning or dark force.

Today is he often thought of as king of the Tylwyth Teg, the faeries of Wales who can be equated with the Tuatha of Ireland. Modern legend has him living on the summit of high Welsh hills looking down at his people.

IN MAGICK AND RITUAL — Spirit contact, strength, Passing Over rituals, and seasonal rites. Pathwork with Gwyn's archetype to venture into the Otherworld.

CORRESPONDENCES — Dogs, mandrake roots.

GWYNGELLI (WELSH, CORNISH)

IN MYTH — A courtier of King Arthur who was a master of animals. He was able to subdue the wild boar, Twrch Trwyth, and to befriend and gain the trust of other beasts.

IN MAGICK AND RITUAL — Call on him for working with totem animals, finding a familiar, or making magick for animals.

GWYRTHUR AP GWREIDAWL (WELSH)

IN MYTH — A rival deity of Gwyn Ap Nuad. A solar deity who was sentenced to battle eternally for the hand of the Creiddylad, daughter of Llud. The two combatants represent the polarities of dark and light and as such are the personification of the Holly King/Oak King who

GWYRThUR AP GWREIDAWL (CONT.)

fight for rulership of the winter and summer halves of the Celtic year.

This tale is told in *The Red Book of Hergest*

IN MAGICK AND RITUAL — Seasonal rites.

HAVGAN (WELSH)

He was the rival of Arawen for the kingship of the Otherworld. He was defeated at the hands of Pwyll.

HEILYN AP GWYNN (WELSH)

IN MYTH — Heilyn opened the forbidden door at Harlech where the eighty-years feast of "Entertaining the Noble Head" of Bran was going on. Like Pandora in Greek mythology, he brought the enchantment to an end and made all present realize the pain of their loss as if it had happened only yesterday.

He was one of the seven sole survivors of the battle between Wales and Ireland fought because of Evissyn's insult at the wedding feast of Matholwch and Branwyn.

IN MAGICK AND RITUAL — While he has little archetypal function, he can teach us about curiosity, when it is right and when it is wrong.

HEININ (WELSH, CORNISH)

The chief bard at King Arthur's court before the arrival of Taliesin.

HERNE (ANGLO-CELTIC)

See Cernunnos.

HERVE THE BLIND (BRETON)

IN MYTH — The son of the Welsh bard, Cyvarnion, and a Breton Druidess. Blind from birth, he was led around by a wolf, whom later patriarchalized tales tell us he converted to Christianity. It is more likely that they both served a mother Goddess, probably one who was a woodland deity or patroness of animals.

When a wolf scare hit Brittany, Herve did not flee, but convinced a farmer to use an attacking wolf to pull his plough. The wolf was instantly tamed and lived peacefully with the farmer forever after.

IN MAGICK AND RITUAL — Evoke Herve for making magick for animals, for aiding you in communicating with them, and for assistance in securing a familiar.

CORRESPONDENCES — The wolf.

HEVYDD HEN (WELSH)

The father of Rhiannon. The word *hen* means "ancient," indicating that he was once a part of a very old oral tradition which has been lost to us.

HOLLY KING AND OAK KING (PAN-CELTIC)

IN MYTH — The Holly King and the Oak King are two sacrificial Gods who, in the manner of such deities, are two aspects of the same being. The Holly King represents the waning year, and battles the Oak King at Midsummer (probably once at Bealtaine) for rulership. Likewise, the Oak King is the God of the waxing year, and battles with the Holly King at Yule (probably once at Samhain) for the same honor.

Numerous other stories, for example the rivalry of Gwyn and Gwyrthur or the fight between Sir Galahad and the Green Knight, tell us this same story with different names and settings as it is a very common Celtic mythic theme.

Today most Celtic witches see these two as faeries or spiritual energies rather than as divine beings since only snatches of folklore and custom, rather than mythology, define them.

IN MAGICK AND RITUAL — Bring them to your circle to enact their semiannual battle.

CORRESPONDENCES — Respectively: wren and robin, holly berry and acorn, red and gold. Green is the color shared by both aspects.

Horned God, the (Pan-Western European)

See Cernunnos.

Hu the Mighty (Welsh, Cornish)

IN MYTH — Also known as Hu Gadarn and Hugh Guairy. In many myths he is portrayed as the common ancestor and father God of the Cymry (the Welsh). He came to Wales from the "east," possibly meaning India or Constantinople, and became part of the Welsh deluge myths.

Hu taught his people to plough, farm, and work the land, and to sing old sacred songs, especially as an aid to memory for transmitting oral traditions.

A team of Hu's oxen dragged Addanc, the faery/monster/God, from his lair in Llyn Llion Lake after the great flood.

IN MAGICK AND RITUAL — Call on Hu to gain personal strength, for helping to honor ancestors, for fertility of the land, and for casting music spells. Hu may also be viewed as a "father" earth God, and you might wish to experiment with this aspect of this energy.

CORRESPONDENCES — The yoke.

Ialonus (Continental)

IN MYTH — Ialonus was a fertility God who ruled over all cultivated fields, personified by the summer stalk of heavy uncut fruit.

IN MAGICK AND RITUAL — Fertility. Evoke his spirit to give life to your own gardens.

Ian the Fisherman's Son (Scottish)

IN MYTH — The lengthy folktale of Ian begins when a old down-on-his-luck fisherman named Duncan is promised by a sea faery that he will receive fish if he will agree to turn over his first-born son to her. Being very old, as was his wife, he told the faery he had no son, nor anything else of value to offer. She ignored his protest and gave him a potion to make his wife, horse, and dog fertile. A year and a day after the encounter Ian was born.

When Ian was eighteen, he fled for fear of being claimed by the faery. On his travels he aided three hungry animals who promised to give assistance whenever he was in trouble. Over time he not only needed their help, but the help of their friends as well, and they were able to outwit the faery. Eventually he married a princess and became a minor King.

IN MAGICK AND RITUAL—Though this tale is long and strong, Ian is not a potent archetype on his own. However, pathworking through his story may teach us the importance of compassion and team work.

IAN OG MacCRIMMONS (SCOTTISH)

IN MYTH—The faery music dubbed the sweetest in Scotland comes from a burial cairn near Glen Elg on the Isle of Skye where the noted family of pipers, the MacCrimmons, lie buried. Ian's family were all famous pipers who were once given a silver chanter by the faeries. The family founded a famous piping school at Borreraig which operated until the early twentieth century.

IN MAGICK AND RITUAL—Music magick and faery contact.

CORRESPONDENCES—Bagpipes, tinwhistles, and air tools.

IBATH (IRISH)

A Nemed who is thought to be a Tuatha De Danann ancestor/father God.

ID (IRISH)

IN MYTH—Id is the faery brother of Cuchulain's charioteer Laeg. He worked for Conall of the Victories and displayed the same fierce loyalty to his master as did his more famous brother.

IN MAGICK AND RITUAL—Loyalty and friendship.

IDATH (IRISH)

IN MYTH—This son of Froach was a Connacht warrior and fertility God who married the cow Goddess Bo Find, the Goddess who gave birth to the first living things in Ireland.

IN MAGICK AND RITUAL—Fertility magick.

CORRESPONDENCES—The bull.

IDRIS THE GIANT (WELSH)

IN MYTH—A master astrologer who could foretell everything to the last days of time simply by observing the stars. He is said to live on the mountain of Cader Udris (Chair of Idris) near the village of Dolgellau. Welsh legends say that those who sleep overnight on the mountain on a starry night will be driven insane by morning light.

IN MAGICK AND RITUAL—Call on Idris to help you time magick, for interpreting astrological charts, or invoke him before performing stellar divinations.

IFAN GRUFFYDD (WELSH)

See Ysbadadden.

ILBERG (IRISH)

IN MYTH—This son of Manann became the king of the Donegal faeries. He fought four other contenders to take Dagda's place as the chief Tuatha king, but lost the race.

IN MAGICK AND RITUAL—Faery contact.

IOUENN (BRETON)

IN MYTH—Iouenn was the son of a greedy merchant who sent him out to gain riches for the family. The son did as he was asked, and was on his way back home when he encountered a dead man who lay unburied because of lack of money. Iouenn, feeling compassion for the deceased, paid the man's debts and saw to it that the body was decently buried.

On the boat home, he discovered a princess who was about to be sacrificed by the sailors as tribute to a greedy sea serpent. Taking pity on her plight, he ransomed her free.

By the time he returned home, he had lost all the money his father wanted by doing good deeds. His angry father cast him out.

He found and married the rescued princess, but later, when returning from other adventures, was shipwrecked on a rock in the middle of the sea. The dead man came to him promising to take him home if he would give him a part of all he had in a year and day. Iouenn agreed.

In a year and a day the dead man came to claim his part of the treasure and also his "part" of the couple's child. He asked Iouenn to cut a section of the child off for him. Remaining true to his word, he began the ugly task, but was stopped before flesh could be cut. The dead man declared Iouenn a man honor for keeping his word, and left Iouenn with all his possessions and his child intact.

IN MAGICK AND RITUAL—Iouenn's tale compares with the Judeo-Christian myth about Abraham, whose patron also demanded a display of allegiance by sacrifice. Some argue that the real meaning of the story is to question divine demands, others say it is one of unquestioning obedience. In any case, the rewards of keeping one's promises is the principal lesson of this story, as are the qualities of patience and compassion.

Irgalach (Irish)

IN MYTH—An old warrior and teacher who led a guard of one hundred and fifty elder warriors to Emain Macha to teach the Red Branch warriors some finer points of combat. He was valued for his wisdom, compassion, and sound advice.

IN MAGICK AND RITUAL—Compassion, wisdom, and the needs of teachers.

Iubdan of the Faylinn (Irish)

IN MYTH—[YOUB-dahn] An Ulster God usually known in popular legend as the king of the Ulster faeries. His wife, Bebo, had an affair with an Ulster king which resulted in great prosperity for the region. He is the antagonist in the Ultonian Myth Cycle story of King Fergus MacLeda and the faeries.

IN MAGICK AND RITUAL—Faery contact, and lessons in safely and smartly dealing with the faery world.

Iuchar, Iucharba, and Brian (Irish)

IN MYTH — Several versions of myth surrounds these three brothers. One, that they were jointly fathered by Lugh (by either Clothru, Ethinu, or Anu); others, that they murdered Lugh's father Cian for which crime they had to endure the *eric* (honor quest) to secure the treasures of the Tuatha.

IN MAGICK AND RITUAL — Because they took responsibility for their actions in the death of Cian, and fulfilled their eric, they can teach us lessons of responsibility which we must accept in order to live by the Pagan Rede.

Jud-hael, King (Breton)

IN MYTH — An aging king who had a prophetic dream in which he asked, then heeded, the advice of the bard Taliesin to step down from his fine rulership to allow his son, Judik-Hael, to rule. This is a rare example of a younger king replacing an older one without a battle ensuing.

IN MAGICK AND RITUAL — Jud-Hael can teach us wisdom, and help us to know where to turn in time of need.

Kai (Welsh, Cornish)

IN MYTH — [Kae] Also Sir Kay and Cei. He was the surly knight of Arthur's Round Table believed to be a disguised version of the God Kai who, in the Arthurian legends, murdered Arthur's son Llacheu. In his divine form, he is a personification of fire. In the Arthurian stories his fire aspect was confined to his possessing a great inner-heat, and whatever he carried in the rain stayed dry with him. When his fellow knights were cold, they would warm themselves near his body.

With his sword he killed Gwrnach the Giant.

IN MAGICK AND RITUAL — Fire magick and Midsummer rituals.

Keevan of the Curling Hair (Irish)

Also Cebhain. The lover of Cliodna who may have once been a God of fertility and of the hunt. With the exception of his connection to Cliodna, all myths about him have been lost.

Kilydd (Welsh)

Father of Culhwch and consort of sow Goddess Goleuddydd.

Cuchulain told his charioteer
to awaken the men of Ulster.
—from *The Yellow Book of Lecan*

Laeg (Irish)

IN MYTH — [Lay'k or Lae'g] Laeg grew up in the Otherworld realm of Tir-na-nOg (Land of the Ever-young) as the child of a divine mother and a faery father.

As a grown man, he became Cuchulain's charioteer and also his devoted servant and friend. When Cuchulain knew he was about about to die in battle, he asked Laeg to lash him to a tree so that he could face death on his feet still fighting. Laeg protested, instead wanting to help Cuchulain escape his fate. Cuchulain refused the offer and Laeg did as he asked.

After Cuchulain's death, the broken-hearted Laeg traveled many worlds spreading the stories of Cuchulain's heroics and kept his memory alive.

Laeg was a healer, and the mere touch of his hands could halt bleeding where all mortal physicians had failed.

IN MAGICK AND RITUAL — When you work with Laeg, think of the words fidelity, loyalty, friendship, healing, and far memory. All of these were well within his energy grasp. Ask him to teach you to heal, to strengthen a friendship, and to maintain loyalty. Call upon his presence at Passing Over rituals so that he might help keep and spread the memory of your loved one.

CORRESPONDENCES — Yellow roses, elder, the Chariot Tarot card.

Laery (Irish)

[LAY-ree] Laery was a reluctant warrior, the son of King Ugainy, who earned the jealousy of his brother Corvac when he inherited the kingdom. Corvac killed him, claiming that one so timid was not fit to rule. Years before, Laery had refused to complete the Test of Champions, a rigorous and often dangerous test for warriors.

LAIRGNEN (IRISH)

IN MYTH — [LAWR'G-nen] After Deoca became the wife of this Connacht king, she asked him to make her a wedding gift of the four singing swans who were really the enchanted children of Llyr in one of the "Four Sorrows of Erin." He did as she asked, but in the end fled with her in terror when their Druid restored the quartet to their human form and all their nine hundred years of age were visible.

IN MAGICK AND RITUAL — Though there is no magickal archetype to latch onto, this myth can teach us a lesson about the consequences of selfish, manipulative magick.

LANCELOT, SIR (BRETON, WELSH, CORNISH)

IN MYTH — Lancelot is a character from France, perhaps from Normandy; he is not part of original Celtic Arthurian mythology. In fact he probably did not appear in the myths until the high medieval period when he came into the the story as the lover of Queen Guinevere.

Cornish and Breton stories tell us that he was fostered by the Lady of the Lake, who taught him to live a chaste and pure life. Since eunuchs were not a part of the Celtic mindset, these same characteristics made him the perfect choice for the task of protecting Queen Guinevere. Medieval legends show him wavering between his love for her and his duty. This indecision causes his downfall.

Older stories tell of him as a usurper to the throne who deviously courts a Goddess of sovereignty whom he needs in order to rule. Lancelot almost succeeds in the great quest for the elusive Grail, but is denied it because he loves a human woman more. In Celtic mythology, a man may have only have one sovereign, and he chose the Queen over the greater power symbolized by the chalice.

In battle he was said to shine like the sun and be an unbeatable warrior.

IN MAGICK AND RITUAL — Overcoming enemies, love magick.

LAOGHAIRE MACCRIMTHANN (IRISH)

[L'air] A Connacht warrior who aided Fiachna in the rescue of his wife and daughter who had been captured by Goll. He not only killed Goll, but married Fiachna's daughter Der Greine.

He may be the same as Fianna warrior Laery.

LAUSTIC LE ROSSIGNOL (BRETON)

IN MYTH — Laustic's story is one of the Lay (epic romantic ballads) of Brittany as penned by that region's famous poet, Marie de France.

This hero's name means "the nightingale." He was a knight whose best friend, another knight, lived across a stone wall from him. Laustic fell in love with his friend's wife, though he tried very hard to fight the feeling. When spring came, he could no longer resist her, and would appear under her window whenever the nightingale sang. The wife would go nightly to the window and hear him sing of his love for her.

Her husband, angry that she was not in bed, questioned her, and she said she only wished to hear the nightingale's song. The jealous husband had the bird killed, and she grieved because she associated its singing with her poetic, but chaste, love.

Because he knew the cruelty of his friend, Laustic stopped seeing his love, and remained silent of song and poetry forever more in order to protect her. He died shortly afterward, at which time another nightingale reappeared nightly at the lady's window.

LAUSTIC LE ROSSIGNOL (CONT.)

IN MAGICK AND RITUAL — Awaken the powers of this hero for the magick of loyalty, and for finding a true love which cares more for other's welfare than for self. He is also a bard whose energy is compatible with music magick and creative endeavors.

CORRESPONDENCES — All night birds.

LEN OF THE MANY HAMMERS (IRISH)

IN MYTH — Len was the goldsmith for his step-brother Bov the Red, whose name lives on in the Locha Lein, the picturesque lakes around Kilarney. Whenever he worked, rainbows would form around him, just as they often do in the misty region around the lakes which bear his name.

IN MAGICK AND RITUAL — Smithing deities have always had a special status connected to creative magick. Goldsmiths in particular are linked to the sun and the element of fire. The rainbows symbolize a far-reaching spirituality.

A sixteenth-century woodcut showing a witch working weather magick to create a destructive storm.

LEUCETIOS (CONTINENTAL)

IN MYTH — A thunder and storm deity equated with the Norse God Thor.

IN MAGICK AND RITUAL — Weather magick.

CORRESPONDENCES — For Thor: rubies, nettles, sulphur, tobacco, chains.

LIA (IRISH)

The treasurer of the cherished booty of Clan Morner. He lost the clan's wealth when he was killed by Fionn MacCumhal in revenge for the death of Fionn's son. Fionn made off with the treasure.

LIAGIN (IRISH)

IN MYTH — A runner and spy for the Fianna.

IN MAGICK AND RITUAL — Liagin's attributes may not only have been those of an athlete, but of an expert at astral projection. Cultivate him for both needs.

LIR (IRISH, MANX)
See Llyr.

LITAVIS (BRETON)
A God of the forge similar to Rome's Vulcan. See Goibniu for a full discussion of his attributes.

LLASAR LLAESGYFNEWID (WELSH)
IN MYTH — [LASS-ar LEES-guhf-n'oo-ud] This Welsh battle God is always paired with his wife Cymidei Cymeinfoll whose name means "big belly of battle." Together they owned a magickal cauldron into which they could cast warriors killed in battle. From the cauldron these dead soldiers would arise to life again, but, curiously, minus their powers of speech.

   The image of the cauldron links them to the primal creative powers which birthed the universe, and to which all life must return before it can move on to other incarnations. In later myths, the cauldron became a peace offering during a war with Ireland.

IN MAGICK AND RITUAL — Llasar's energy can give you the strength to continue in whatever battles in which you are embroiled. He can also teach you about past-lives and help with creative magick.

LLEVELYS (WELSH, CORNISH, BRETON)
IN MYTH — Also Llefellys. A son of Beli, Llevelys was the ruler of Brittany, a land which was under the curse of three plagues: the screams of two battling dragons on May Eve, provisions missing nightly from the royal household, and an evil race of sub-humans called the Corandians.

   With his brother Lludd, a British God/ruler, they devised a way to end the troubles. They got the dragon drunk on Meade, a Bealtaine potable; spread poison insects for the Corandians to eat; and discovered the name of the wizard who was stealing from the royal household.

IN MAGICK AND RITUAL — Invoke Llevelys for creative problem-solving.

> *There grows an oak on a highland plain*
> *Not warmed by sun, nor drenched by rain—*
> *May his trial soon be o'er,*
> *And Llew restored to us once more.*
>
> —Attributed to Gwyddion

LLEW (WELSH)
IN MYTH — Also known as Llew Llaw Gyffes which means "Llew of the steady hand." Also spelled Lleu Gwalchmei, and nicknamed the "Falcon of May." He was the son of Arianrhod and her brother Gwyddion (or her uncle Math in some versions) whose story is told in the *Mabinogion*. Llew's major myths have to do with the fact that his mother would not name him, cursed him never to marry; and that he could only be killed a certain, secret way.

   Llew was a great archer, a prized skill among the Celts. Arianrhod, his mother who refused to name him as was the mother's right, was tricked into naming him by seeing his archery skills. To be nameless was frightening to the Celts, who equated a name with a spirit essence and true being, one of the reasons many Pagans even today keep their craft names a closely guarded secret.

LLEW (CONT.)

Llew's father, Gwyddion, and Uncle Math decided to make a wife for him who would be beyond the control of the curse of not marrying. But the wife, Blodeuwedd, fell in love with Gronw. They plotted to discover the one way in which Llew could be killed. Blodeuwedd tricked him into telling her the details. He could only be slain by a spear which took a year to make, and the murder must occur while Llew was under a thatched roof, just after bathing, with one foot resting on the back of a goat.

After Blodeuwedd and Gronw killed Llew by the prescribed method, he turned into an eagle and flew away. He was later rescued from his bondage by Gwyddion. Celtic legends often show human souls becoming birds upon death. Therefore his restoration is a metaphor for reincarnation, and may be one of the many versions of the seasonal Holly King/Oak King battle.

Llew was also worshipped in Celtic Gaul. He is generally thought to be the same as the more well-known Irish God, Lugh.

IN MAGICK AND RITUAL — Seasonal rituals.

LLEWELLYN (WELSH)

IN MYTH — Llewellyn and his friend Rhys often went out hunting together. One night Rhys took off on his own, claiming he heard some unusual music he wished to investigate. Llewellyn, assuming his friend only wished to carouse, let him go alone. Rhys didn't return and, within the year, Llewellyn was accused of his murder.

With the help of a wise old farmer, Llewellyn searched out his friend and found him dancing in a faery ring where he had been imprisoned for a year and a day. The villagers were able to rescue him, and the charges against Llewellyn were dropped.

He should not be confused with Prince Llewellyn.

IN MAGICK AND RITUAL — Llewellyn can be called upon to help us think clearly in tough situations, and also to help us learn how best to deal with the capricious world of faery.

LLEWELLYN, PRINCE (WELSH)

IN MYTH — Prince Llewellyn liked to think he was a fair man. He was happy, with a beautiful and intelligent wife, a newborn son, and a hunting hound he adored with all his heart. One day when he wanted to go hunting he couldn't find the dog, Gelert. Gelert deliberately did not respond to the sound of the hunting horn because the baby's mother and nurse were out and he felt he ought to guard the child instead.

A wolf, bent on eating the child, entered the nursery and Gelert fought him off, killing him, but barely escaping with his own life.

Just then the Prince came into the nursery and, seeing the panting dog and all the blood, jumped to the conclusion that his dog had killed the child. Gelert, hurt and unable to explain himself, stood by while the angry Prince ran him through with his sword. Just then the baby cried, and the Prince, going to him, saw the dead wolf nearby. He fell to his knees in anguish over the injustice he had done his faithful dog.

IN MAGICK AND RITUAL — There is an old Welsh proverb which says, "Before the revenge, first know the cause." Call upon Prince Llewellyn to help you learn lessons of justice and fairness, for it is said he will lament his actions for all time.

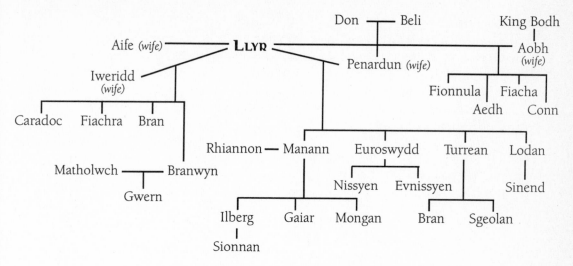

The generally accepted family tree of Llyr.

Llud (Anglo-Celtic)

IN MYTH—Also spelled Lludd, Ludd, Nuda, and Nudd. A river God and minor king for whom Ludgate in London is named. He replaced the Goddess Tamesis as God of the River Thames, and may be the same as the death God Lludd.

He aided his brother, Llevelys of Brittany, in ridding that land of three plagues.

Sometimes nicknamed "Llawereint the Silver-handed." He is often equated with Nuada of the Silver Hand in Ireland.

IN MAGICK AND RITUAL — Call on him as a temporary Guardian of your space or person, for overcoming enemies, or when in need of creative wisdom.

CORRESPONDENCES — Gates, sapphires.

Lludd (Welsh)

IN MYTH — A son of the death God Beli who is also a death God in his own right. Lludd was the ruler of Celtic Britain while his brother, Llevelys, ruled Gaul. Together they outwitted three plagues sent to Gaul.

A temple to Lludd once sat on the site of St. Paul's Cathedral in London (near Ludgate). This Lludd and the Llud listed above are almost certainly the same entity.

IN MAGICK AND RITUAL — Summon Lludd for the qualities of leadership or wisdom, to assist with spirit contact, or for Passing Over rituals.

Llwyd Ap Kilcoed (Welsh)

A Druid who attempted to avenge the death of Gwawl Ap Clud (at Pwyll's hand) by turning his followers into mice to consume the fertile fields of Pryderi's kingdom, Dyfed. His plot failed when one of the mice, who was in reality Llwyd's wife, was captured and about to be killed.

Llyr (Pan-Celtic)

IN MYTH — Spelled Lir in Ireland and Man, but he is better known by his Welsh name. Llyr was the powerful God of the sea, and the father of sea God Manann who was probably more

LLYR (CONT.)

widely known and worshipped than his father. Llyr had several wives in succession including Iweriadd, Penardun, Aebh, and Aife. Four of his children (by Aebh) are part of the folk tales known as the "Four Sorrows of Erin."

He is thought to be the prototype for Shakespeare's King Lear.

IN MAGICK AND RITUAL — Water magick, contacting sea faeries.

CORRESPONDENCES — Beryl, the trident, the conch shell.

LODEN (IRISH)

One of the sons of the sea God Llyr, and the father of the river Goddess Sinend.

LUCHTAIN (IRISH)

IN MYTH — Also Luchtar. A minor war and death God, and a master carpenter and wheelwright of Tara under the Tuatha De Danann.

With his two brothers, Credne and Goibniu, who were also smiths of various types, the trio fashioned the weapons of the Tuatha.

IN MAGICK AND RITUAL — Call on Luchtain for the gift of creativity, for making spirit contact, or for an added boost of energy for the making of your own magickal tools.

CORRESPONDENCES — Anvil, hammer, numbers five and thirteen, onyx, woodworking tools.

LUDUENN (BRETON)

IN MYTH — Luduenn, whose name means "drudge," was part of a story which was the prototype for the fairy tale of Sleeping Beauty. He was a servant in the employ of an ailing king who was sent on a dangerous quest to find a mythic bird named Dredaine, who could cure the monarch. Luduenn's travels took him to a castle which had three courtyards, each with three obstacles and three rooms, all filled with food and tables which never were emptied. In one room he found the beautiful Princess Marcassa, who was in a death sleep. Giddy with a never-ending cup of wine, he made love to her.

Ludenn took the bird back to the king, but then the king discovered that he also needed to sleep with the Princess to be healed. Ludenn, having fallen in love with the Princess since leaving her, refused to go back for her.

In the meantime, the Princess awakened, had a son, and set out in search of her boy's father. She cured the king and then married Luduenn.

IN MAGICK AND RITUAL — While there are many powerful archetypes to explore in this story, including that of the sleeping Princess, we can build on this foundation to discover other hidden Pagan tales disguised as modern fairy tales with patriarchal morals attached.

LUGAID RIAB nDERG (IRISH, SCOTTISH)

IN MYTH — [LOO-gawj or LOO-geed] Lugaid was the foster brother of Cuchulain who married Derbforgaille in his brother's place because Cuchulain had accidentally consumed some of her blood, making it taboo for them to wed.

Lugaid was the son of Clothru by her three brothers. When he grew to manhood he had three distinct parts of himself, each one resembling one of the fathers. His names means "of the red stripes," and he represents a masculine version of the Triple Goddess.

IN MAGICK AND RITUAL — Lugaid can be worked with as a masculine representation of triplicity. Males who are as yet uncomfortably aligning themselves solely with a Triple Goddess may wish to work with Lugaid instead.

> *Bring me my bow of burning gold,*
> *Bring me my arrow of desire,*
> *Bring me my spear, O clouds unfold!*
> *Bring me my chariot of fire.*
>
> —William Blake, from *Jerusalem*

Lugh (Pan-Celtic)

IN MYTH — [Loo] Lugh's name literally means "the shining one." He is also called Ioldanach or Samhioldananach, meaning "master of all arts," or Lamhfada (La-VAH-dah), "the long-armed."

A God of the sun, light, and the grain harvest, who is honored at the Sabbat which bears his name: Lughnasadh. Like Brid, he is a deity of many skills and was even said to be able to come into human form to worship among the Druids for whom he was a primary deity. He is also worshiped as the God of fire, metallurgy, crafting, weaving, and as a protector of the weak.

Because of his many talents, he was able to be admitted to Tara at a time when only the most skilled in the land could gain entrance. He went to the door and asked the gate keeper if they had a scribe. Yes, the gate keeper answered, they did. Well, Lugh asked, did they have a seer? Again, the answer was yes. Lugh went through an exhaustive list and found that each of his skills was possessed by another. Then he asked if Tara had one person with all those talents. They, of course, did not, and he was admitted. Archetypally, these skills were transmuted into the powers of the land which humans could garner with the proper reverence and knowledge.

Some scholars believe he was originally a king of the Formorians who was adopted by the Tuatha De Danann and then by the Celts. He sided with the Tuatha in the Second Battle of Tuireadh (Moytura) and led their forces against the Formorians. It was here that he killed his grandfather Balor, a sacrificial God whom Lugh was destined to replace.

Though he was a divine being, he was said to have an earthly father. Because of this association, he is seen as a bridge between human and the divine worlds.

More statues and holy sites were erected to him than to any other Celtic deity, and many of these sites remain for us today. His continental name was Lugus. He is often equated with the Greek God Apollo.

IN MAGICK AND RITUAL — Invoke and evoke at Lughnasadh to honor him at the harvest. Call on him when you need any powers associated with the sun such as money, strength, or energy. Evoke his aid for new beginnings, especially business ventures, and for protection. Most any magickal need can be well assisted by Lugh.

CORRESPONDENCES — Sapphires, gold, topaz, grains, bread, threshing houses, obsidian, looms.

Lugus (Breton, Continental)

See Lugh.

Vine design carved on stone, Northumberland, England. Vines are symbolic of the Mabon Sabbat.

LUINGE FER TRI (IRISH)

IN MYTH — The hunter who discovered young King Cormac MacArt being raised by wolves. He returned him to his mother, Achtan, whom he later married.

IN MAGICK AND RITUAL — Pathwork with him to learn the lessons of compassion rewarded.

> *Out of tears' and tempests' reach*
> *Alun Mabon sleeps secure;—*
> *Still lives on the ancient speech,*
> *Still the ancient songs endure.*
>
> —Ceiriog

MABON (WELSH)

IN MYTH — [MAH-bahn or MAY-bone] Also Maponos and Maponus. Mabon means "great son," the child of Modred whose name means "great mother." He was stolen from Modron at three years old and later rescued by King Arthur.

Mabon's myths overlap those of Gwyn Ap Nuad, and they may have once been the same deity. Mabon rode wild horses, had prized guardian hunting hounds, and he may have been an actual ruler of Wales who later came into myth.

He is also a minor sun God, yet he represents the power in darkness. His images transcend all the life stages of other Gods. He is a king of death and the Otherworld, a deity of the harvest and fertility, and was once called "The Divine Youth" by his followers. He represents innocent youth when young, strength and virility as a young man, and the sacrificial God when elderly. His image is linked to hierarchies of sacred animals, and he may have once figured heavily in long lost Celtic creation myths since he is equated with the expelling of and control of the darkness and of storms.

Some Celtic traditions see him as the original being, the first God, the first life carved out of the primal void of the divine womb.

He was adopted by the Anglo-Romans as Maponus and was honored at Hadrian's Wall.

Mabon is sometimes equated with Gwyn Ap Nuad for his death images, or with Cernunnos, for his associations as a God of liberation, unity, and music. He is also occasionally equated to love God Aengus MacOg. Sometimes he has been called a masculine Persephone, or the Celtic Dionysus because of his linkage with the grape harvest.

IN MAGICK AND RITUAL — Mabon can be called on to aid in you most any endeavor. He can be part of seasonal celebrations and can assist in fertility rites. As a God of the hunt, he is in his death God role, a metaphor for taking souls to the Otherworld, and he can aid in spirit contact. Honor him at the grape harvest and at his Sabbat of Mabon.

CORRESPONDENCES — Vines, grapes, wine, the equilateral cross.

> *Worthy to be a rebel, for to that*
> *The multiplying villanies of nature*
> *Do swarm upon him....*
>
> —from Shakespeare's *MacBeth*

MacBeth (Scottish)

IN MYTH — MacBeth was an eleventh-century warrior, a member of the nobility asked by King Duncan of Scotland to lead troops against the Danes. He was victorious, but became ego-inflated by the prediction of three old witches (the Morrigan?) that he would become King of Scotland as a reward for his heroics. Instead of waiting for this to come to pass, he pushed the prophecy by killing the King and by engaging in other underhanded stratagems. He was eventually found out and killed by the new king.

IN MAGICK AND RITUAL — Pathwork with MacBeth for learning right use of will, force, and magick. The consequences of our actions is a strong lesson in the threefold law.

MacCecht (Irish)

IN MYTH — A son of Oghma who was the God of the plough for the Tuatha. He was married to Fodhla, the mother aspect of the Triple Goddess symbolizing Ireland.

He killed Mechi, son of the Morrigan, in order to stop the dreadful prophecy that when he grew to manhood that the three snakes which surrounded his heart would break free and devastate Ireland.

He also avenged Conaire Mor's death.

IN MAGICK AND RITUAL — Fertility magick for crops, protection magick.

CORRESPONDENCES — The plough, stalactites and stalagmites.

MacCuill (Irish)

IN MYTH — [Mawk-KWIL] A minor sea God of the Tuatha De Danann symbolized by the hazel branch. He was the husband of Banbha, the crone aspect of the Triple Goddess representing Ireland.

IN MAGICK AND RITUAL — Water magick.

CORRESPONDENCES — Beryl, hazel wood.

Mac Da Tho (Irish)

IN MYTH — Also MacDatho and Mesodra. A Leinster king who owned two much-coveted hounds and a large boar. He agreed to sell the hounds, one each to Connacht and Ulster, in order to keep peace among the kingdoms. He invited the rival leaders to a feast to prove his good faith. When the Connacht and Ultonian legions arrived they found that Mac Da Tho had killed and was roasting his magnificent boar they had each hoped to steal. Rather than seeing this as an act of friendship and peace, they felt cheated because their own wicked intentions had been thwarted, and they began a battle over the animal.

MAC DA THO (CONT.)

Mac Da Tho lost all three animals, but kept peace in Leinster by setting his enemies to war with each other.

IN MAGICK AND RITUAL — Invoke Mac Da Tho for his qualities of sound wisdom, judgment, and peace magick.

MacGREINE (IRISH)

In Myth — This son of Oghma was a minor sun God of the Tuatha and the husband of Eire, the maiden aspect of the Triple Goddess symbolizing Ireland.

His name means "son of the sun," and he may have once been a part of the Lugh myth. He was killed by Amergin.

IN MAGICK AND RITUAL — Call on MacGreine for all the attributes of sun deities, particularly prosperity.

CORRESPONDENCES — The balefire.

MacKAY (SCOTTISH)

IN MYTH — MacKay's myth is possibly a reworking of an old story about a fire God. MacKay was the leader of Clan MacKay credited with bringing fire to Scotland, and also for making the little faery lights known as the will o' the wisp impossible for humans to catch.

MacKay was desperately trying to start a fire to feed his family when he spotted the faery lights dancing on the horizon. He decided if he could just capture those lights he would never again have to spend time trying to strike a spark.

In time he caught the lights and brought fire to Scotland, but the faeries were so outraged that humans had found their sacred fire, that they vowed forever to tease humans with their elusive light and never to allow themselves to be caught again.

The motto of Clan MacKay to this day is "Sons of Fire."

IN MAGICK AND RITUAL — Invoke him to make faery contact and to gain the powers attributed to the sun.

CORRESPONDENCES — Leeks.

MacKINELY (IRISH, SCOTTISH)

An equivalent of Cian, son of Balor by Danu or Ceithlenn.

MacMOINCANTA (IRISH)

This Tuatha warrior challenged the Dagda for the rulership of Tara. Depending upon which myth one reads, he either won or lost his bid. Today he is seen as a minor faery king whose great rival is Finvarra.

MAEL DUIN (IRISH)

IN MYTH — [Male DWEEN or MALE doon] Also Maeldun. His tale is so old that Celtic scholars believe it to be one of the very oldest stories from the oral traditions. His name means "enclosure of riches." His tale was first recorded in the ninth century in a manuscript known as *Immram Curaig Maile Duin,* and it appears in *The Book of the Dun Cow.* The adventure was popularized by Alfred Lord Tennyson's poem, *The Voyage of Maeldune.*

Mael's myth concerns a mythic voyage taken by him to avenge the death of his father, Ailill MacOwens of the Aran Isles, who died before his birth. He set out in the company of his friends in a *curragh,* an animal skin-covered boat which, in Irish legends, has several archetypal associations, including that of being a means of travel to and from the Otherworld.

The company at first thought a storm would drive them back, but they persisted. They ventured to thirty-four different islands, among them the Islands of the Slayer, the Ants, the Giant Birds, the Vicious Beasts, the Monstrous Horses, the Stone Door, the Glass Bridge, the Flaming Tower, and of Women. Each of these islands were metaphors for various aspects of the Otherworld and/or faeryland.

At one island he and his entourage were welcomed by a queen and her seventeen daughters, seventeen being a dynastic number in old Ireland. She told them to remain there and they would never age, an image which links the place to the Otherworld name of Tir-na-nOg which means "land of the ever young." They stayed for three months of winter which seemed like three years.

Mael's adventurers were gone for nine years before returning home, never having avenged Ailill, but bringing home miraculous tales which fed Irish mythology for a long time to come. He has been Christianized as St. Brendan.

IN MAGICK AND RITUAL — Mael Duin is first of all a symbolic bridge to the Otherworld and to the faery and elemental kingdoms, as well as being a master storyteller and protector of travelers. His story can teach us how to blend and use the energies of the elements. Path-working with his many adventures can be very illuminating and exciting. Women, too, should not hesitate to take these inner-world journeys in his guise.

Mael Fhochartaig (Irish)

Mael was killed because of a lie perpetuated by his stepmother whose counsel he rejected. Because of this his father had him killed, but his death was avenged by his three sons.

> *Rivers pour forth a stream of honey*
> *In the land of Manannan son of Llyr.*
>
> —from *The Voyage of Bran*

Manann (Irish, Manx, Welsh)

IN MYTH — [MAN-ahn, Mawn-AWN-ahn, or MAWN-ahn] Also Mannanan MacLir and Oirbsen, the latter being his Galway name which is still reflected in that region's Lake Oirbsen. He was a chameleon-like sea God for whom the Isle of Man was named, and the son of sea God Llyr.

It is Manann who decreed that the world of faeries and the world of humans should forever remain separated when his wife (one of many in succession), Fand, fell in love with the hero Cuchulain.

Manann had a self-propelled ship known as the Wind Sweeper, and a seahorse named Splendorous Mane. His favorite haunts were the Isle of Man (given to him by Fionn MacCumhal), the Isle of Arran, and the Firth of Clyde where it was said he has a sacred apple grove called Emain Ablach where he kept his conch shell throne.

MANANN (CONT.)

He owned a yellow and a red spear, and a sword called the Retaliator which never missed its mark. No weapon could penetrate his mail and breast plate, and two magick jewels of yellow gold flashed from his helmet. He also owned a mantle which made any who wore it invisible at will (a metaphor for astral projection?). Once every thirty-three years he held the Feast of Age, a banquet to ensure that those who ate would never grow old.

Some sources say said he once ruled Elysium, a mythical kingdom beneath the sea, now thought of as a home for faeries and for the banished Formorians who became sea monsters. He was not a popular God until the Celts, largely a herding people, went to sea in equal numbers. The sea power of the Celts was destroyed by the Romans, and therefore Manann became associated with Irish and Welsh waters rather than all the oceans like the Roman's Neptune. Once the Celts latched onto his archetype, he became a frequently mentioned deity in mythology with many stories attributed to him, several of them contradictory.

Unlike other deities, he did not leave the sea to fight the Tuatha De Danann's land battles with the other Gods.

Called God of the Headland, he remained a patron deity of sailors well into the Christian period.

His Welsh name is Manawyddan.

IN MAGICK AND RITUAL — Call on Manann to help erase someone from your memory, to learn astral projection, for environmental or elemental magick, for protection, especially when at sea or from faeries. Merge with him for water spells or weather magick.

CORRESPONDENCES — Irish Moss, seahorses, cloaks, the trident, conch shells, the Chariot Tarot card.

MANAWYDDAN (WELSH)

Also see Manann. Second husband of Rhiannon, Goddess of Fertility and the Otherworld. The Welsh name for the Irish God, Manann.

MANDRED (CORNISH)

IN MYTH — In Cornish legends, Mandred is the true name of God which, when pronounced, draws the All-Power to the one speaking it. Such legends have parallels in Jewish and Arabic mythology, two cultures who will not even attempt to pronounce the name of their God for fear of the power it will unleash.

IN MAGICK AND RITUAL- Call on this primal divine energy—which is really neither male nor female—to aid in all magickal and ritual endeavors.

CORRESPONDENCES — The Triangle of Manifestation.

MAOL (IRISH)

IN MYTH — This bald Druid and master magician was employed by Laoghaire to teach the magickal arts to his daughters Ethne and Fedelma.

IN MAGICK AND RITUAL — Call Maol to your circle to teach you the secrets of Druidic magick, and as a boost to all your spells.

MAON THE DUMB (IRISH)

IN MYTH — [MAY-un] When Corvac killed his brother Laery in order to steal the High King's throne he, like most usurpers, began to fear others who might have a legitimate claim to the kingship. Most feared was the child Maon, a son of Ailill, whom he ordered captured and brought to him. Corvac tortured the boy by making him eat the hearts of his slain father and brothers, along with several small rodents. So traumatized was Maon that he was struck dumb. Seeing this, Corvac ceased to worry, since no one with a physical affliction could claim the High King's throne.

Maon escaped to Gaul with his father's supporters and was raised there as a crown prince. When he grew to manhood, Gaul mustered an army to send to Ireland, a country deeply divided since Maon's father's death.

When Maon's forces won, Corvac asked who their leader was. When he was told, he asked if Maon could speak. Maon answered him.

He married Moriath and reigned as High King for ten blessed years.

IN MAGICK AND RITUAL — Cultivate Maon for the powers of leadership and for overcoming enemies. On other levels he can teach us the power of silence.

Mark the Good, King (Cornish)

IN MYTH — Mark was the wealthy royal uncle of Tristan. He took the boy in after he returned home to Cornwall, not knowing that this was his nephew. He was also the husband of Irish princess Isolde, who fell in love with Tristan due to a mix up in a magickal love potion.

Mark has been portrayed as an unsympathetic, dull-witted character, and as a decidedly evil figure in Malory's *Morte d'Arthur,* written in 1469. Cornish legends tell us that he was a beloved leader who brought much prosperity to the land.

There was an historical King Mark of the sixth century who may or may not be the same man in the legend.

He is equated with the Greek's King Midas.

IN MAGICK AND RITUAL — Prosperity.

> *There are few who know*
> *Where the Magic Wand of Mathonwy*
> *Grows in the Grove.*
>
> —from the *Mabinogion*

Math Ap Mathonwy (Welsh)

IN MYTH — A master magician from the *Mabinogion,* and a king of Gwynedd, a Cymric kingdom. As a brother of the mother Goddess Don, he is also sometimes seen as a minor ruler of the Otherworld. His name means "coin" or "money," and in myth he is the deity who brought wealth and prosperity to Wales, and who is credited also with bringing pigs to that country for the first time. This stemmed from a common Celtic belief that all wealth (and pigs) originated in the Otherworld, to whose leaders they belonged. He had super hearing, and if any sound was cast into the wind, his ears could catch it.

Math could not live (read "rule") unless his feet were placed in the lap of a maiden, though there was a provision made for times when he had to be away at war. This stems from a very ancient Celtic concept which views rulers as the deities incarnate. Kings had to have the approval of their queen, in her guise as Goddess of sovereignty, in order to be legitimate rulers. Many old drawings of Celtic rulers depict the king resting his feet on the lap of

MATH AP MATHONWY (CONT.)

the queen. In one myth concerning him, his footholder was stolen away and he lost the throne until he could retrieve her.

He is most famous for having helped his student, Gwyddion, fashion Blodeuwedd as a bride for his nephew Llew.

In some stories he is one and the same with Dylan, the "Son of the Wave."

IN MAGICK AND RITUAL — Call on Math to aid you in magick, to guide you as a teacher, and for understanding of the origins of power. Math's energy is one of the best with which to work towards personal prosperity.

CORRESPONDENCES — The crown.

MATHOLWCH, KING (IRISH)

IN MYTH — [MATH-oh-law] A King of Ireland, married to Branwyn, the sister of Bran. When the couple was insulted by a Welsh guest, Evnissyen, at their wedding, a great war ensued. In one version of the story Matholwch blamed Branwyn for this and put her to work in the kitchens until the war's end.

He lost the battle against Bran and his forces, though only seven Welsh survived the conflict, and he was killed also. The Irish allowed his infant son Gwern to succeed him in order to appease Bran and end the war with Wales, but Gwern was soon killed by Bran.

After Matholwch's death, Bran gave Ireland a magickal cauldron as a peace offering. Its image as an instrument of regeneration links Matholwch to reincarnation themes.

IN MAGICK AND RITUAL — Exploring past- and future-lives.

MATHONWY (WELSH)

IN MYTH — [MAYTH-on-oo'ee] A father God who, in later myths, became the single being from whom the family of the great Welsh mother Goddess Don was descended. In the original myths it was likely that the two were paired, and he was her eternal consort/son who was sacrificed for his people each autumn and reborn to Don at Midwinter.

The root of his name means "coin," and he was probably also a prosperity God.

IN MAGICK AND RITUAL — General aid in prosperity spells and magick, and assistance in the honoring of ancestors. Also evoke his image at his death at Samhain and his rebirth at Yule or Imbolg, whichever of these two your tradition acknowledges as the rebirth of the sun God.

MATHU (IRISH)

Thought to be a less developed Irish version of Wale's Math Ap Mathonwy.

MAELDUINE (IRISH)

See Mael Duin.

MECHI (PAN-CELTIC)

This son of the Morrigan was the object of a death quest because of a prophecy that he would bring disaster to Ireland when the three serpents which encircled his heart grew up and broke through. He was captured and killed by MacCecht, a son of Oghma.

Melwas (Cornish)

IN MYTH — Also Meleagant in a Breton epic poem, but he seems to be a figure in Arthurian myth unique to Cornwall. He was a "dark God" who lay in wait for an entire year to carry off Guinevere to his palace in Avalon. Some stories have him executing the kidnapping at Modred's (Arthur's nephew) request.

Others call him a God of the Summerland, a popular euphemism for the Otherworld.

IN MAGICK AND RITUAL — Call on him to aid you in making spirit contact and in assisting in Passing Over rituals.

All that we see or seem,
Is but a dream within a dream.
—Edgar Allen Poe

Merlin (Welsh, Cornish, Anglo-Celtic, Breton)

IN MYTH — Also Myrddin, Merlyn, and Emrys. The Merlin of myth and folklore has many faces, often as blurred and contradictory as his historical origins. He is bard, magician, wizard, seer, and Druid. He became the spiritual teacher and advisor of young King Arthur only in later versions of the myth.

His human origins are mysterious, and it is possible he once was a long-forgotten Druid whose legends eventually merged with the mythic archetype. It is likely that he was once worshipped as a God, yet no hard evidence exists that he was ever revered by Celts any more than as a very powerful and wise Druid. Some scholars point to his possible origins as a pre-Hellenic God of fertility and the harvest. Ancient Welsh poetry refers to Britain as *Clas Myrddin,* "Merlin's Enclosure," creating links to earth or sovereign deity images.

Merlin took the role of a sacrificial God when Vivienne, his contrary lover, embedded him in rock. The lament she sung over him was overheard by Sir Gawain, who took word of Merlin's fate to Arthur who set out on a quest to rescue him.

When he retreated (or was imprisoned as some stories tell) into his secret cave to die (possibly intended originally to make him another sleeping God) he took with him the Thirteen Treasures of Britain lost to humans. They included a sword, a basket, a drinking horn, a chariot, a whetstone, a garment, a pot, a serving platter, a mantle, and a chess board.

Born of an earthly mother and Otherworld father, he is an archetypal bridge and mediator between the realms of spirit and matter, and has sometimes been viewed as a minor God of light.

Historian and mythologist Sir John Rhys, who lived in the late nineteenth century, likens him to a Celtic Zeus. Rhys attests that Merlin was once worshipped at Stonehenge, but Rhys stands alone in this theory of early Merlin worship.

IN MAGICK AND RITUAL — There is almost no task in which Merlin cannot aid you. In one myth or another his powers cover the vast range of human need and desire. He is also an excellent temporal guardian of your sacred spaces.

CORRESPONDENCES — The wand, the triscale.

Mervyn (Welsh)

IN MYTH — Mervyn was a highly placed servant (some accounts call him a knight) in the service of the king (some accounts say a patron God) of Breconshire, who was asked to go to a distant city to ascertain whether the reports of the decadence and lack of responsibility heard about the place were true. Mervyn went and, upon his arrival, found rumor to be at best an understatement.

Then he happened upon a small baby and his heart went out to the innocent life that would have to perish when the king destroyed the wicked place. He stayed up all night with the child cuddling it and playing with it, hoping to make its last night a happy one.

At dawn Mervyn set off to report back to his king all he had found, but about halfway home he realized he had forgotten his gloves, and that they must still be with the child. Because they were a gift from the king, he valued them highly, and he set back toward the city to retrieve them. When he arrived, he discovered that the king had already magickally leveled it, all except one small cradle floating on the lake that now covered the city (Llangorse Lake). In the cradle were the baby and the gloves.

IN MAGICK AND RITUAL — Mervyn teaches us that loyalty and compassion have their rewards and that irresponsibility eventually destroys. Call on him to help you discover your own compassion and to strengthen your loyalties to those you serve.

Mesgegra, King (Irish)

IN MYTH — Also Mesgedra. A king of Leinster under High King Eochaid who was friendly with the faeries. He predicted that his death would be avenged by his own head. His killer, Conall Cerach, died by the magick of his severed head when part of it was used as a talismanic stone in a well-aimed slingshot.

IN MAGICK AND RITUAL — Divination and overcoming enemies.

Miach (Irish)

IN MYTH — [MEE-ack] The gifted son of Diancecht the medicine man, and also a great healer in his own right. He and his sister, Airmid, made Nuada's silver hand to replace the severed one because no one with physical flaws could ever take the High King's throne.

When his magical skills outstripped those of the father, Diancecht grew jealous and killed the youth. If one can find his grave, it is said that grass growing over it contains tremendous healing powers. It was there that his sister, grieving over the loss of her beloved brother, began cataloging the herbal knowledge which was soon after lost due to another act of her father's jealous rage.

IN MAGICK AND RITUAL — Call on Miach for powerful healing, for inspiration, and for honing your craftsman's skills. If you work as a couple, invoke Miach and Airmid for an unbeatable union of the healing powers.

CORRESPONDENCES — Mistletoe.

O fair lady! will you come with me
To a wonderful country which is mine,
Where the people's hair is of gold hue,
And their bodies the color of virgin snow?

—Midhir's song to Edain,
from *The Yellow Book of Lecan*

MIDHIR, KING (IRISH, MANX)

IN MYTH — [MEED-er, MY-tir, or MY-deer] Also Mider and Midir, and Midhir of Bri Leith. An Otherworld/faeryland God/king, the son of the Dagda and Boann. His wife was Edain, the queen stolen from the human world though a game of chess. Aengus, the love God, rescued her. When she escaped, Midhir cursed her lineage, an act which forced her great-grand-daughter, Messbuachallo, into hiding.

Midhir owned three birds, the Cranes of Denial, Despair, and Churlishness, who refused hospitality to travelers, a definite breach of the Celtic rules of social intercourse. He possessed a magick cauldron (a symbol of triumph over death) which his daughter Blathnat helped Cuchulain steal from him.

He is seen today as both an Otherworld God and a faery God, equated with Pluto.

IN MAGICK AND RITUAL — Faery contact and prosperity spells.

CORRESPONDENCES — Jewels and the traditional pirate's treasure chest.

MILESIUS (IRISH)

IN MYTH — [Mile-EES-ee-us] Also called Mil and Mile and Golamh. He was the leader of the Milesians who conquered the Tuatha De Danann. His son Eremon was their first king.

He came to Ireland from Spain when he learned of the death of one of his sons, Ith, at the hands of the Tuatha. The Gaels believed themselves to be descended from him.

IN MAGICK AND RITUAL — Leadership.

CORRESPONDENCES — Flint and iron, a taboo metal for the Tuatha.

MILLER OF LAC DE LEGUER, THE (BRETON)

IN MYTH — The miller was asked to aid an enchanted princess/magician who had been placed under a spell by a Nain, a hideously misshapen Breton faery, which made her appear as a swan. She asked him to spend three nights in an evil haunted castle in order to break the spell. He went even though he was afraid, and she vowed to protect him from the Nains with what was left of her magick.

He underwent three terrifying nights in the castle. When he emerged, the princess, in her lovely human form once more, told him to give her a year and a day, and then she would return to marry him. She gave him a vast treasure for his help and then departed.

He waited in good faith and she returned. Then he had to endure another three day ordeal of eating bad fruit before they could marry.

IN MAGICK AND RITUAL — Summon the miller for loyalty, patience, perseverance, compassion, and overcoming fear.

MIODCHAOIN (IRISH)

A warrior who lived alone on a steep hill with his three sons. They were murdered by the three sons of Tuireann, beginning one of the epics known as the "Four Sorrows of Erin." Archetypally, the murder of the three by the three may represent a corrupted version of the old/dying triplicity being dispatched to make way for the new/reborn one.

MOCCUS (BRETON, CONTINENTAL)

IN MYTH — A pig god of the continental standing stones who had his cloudy origins in Celtic Gaul. He was, perhaps, a masculine version of, or consort to, the popular goddess known as Cerridwen. He had his own feast day in Celtic Gaul.

IN MAGICK AND RITUAL — A guardian of sacred spaces.

MODRED (WELSH, CORNISH)

IN MYTH — Also Medrawt and Mordred. He was King Arthur's nephew, the son of his half-sister Morgan, and the lad who fought with and gave him his fatal wound.

In other myths he attempts to take the crown by marrying Guinevere, Arthur's Goddess of sovereignty by whose say-so he rules.

Archetypally Modred is the young God seeking to replace the older, sacrificial one.

IN MAGICK AND RITUAL — Seasonal rites.

MOG RUITH (IRISH)

IN MYTH — [Mok ROO-ee] An Arch-Druid of Ireland, right arm of the High Kings. He brought back fragments of the magickal stone wheel, known as *Roth Fail,* being used for magickal demonstrations in Rome. They may still be seen in the town of Rathcoole near Dublin.

IN MAGICK AND RITUAL — Summon Mog Ruith as a general aid to magick, and as a guardian of magickal tools.

MONGAN (IRISH)

IN MYTH — A son of Manann and a king of a tribe called the Dal nAraidi (also the Delradi). The circumstances of his birth are similar to those of King Arthur in that his mother was tricked into mating with his father. Like his father he had great magickal powers and was able to control sea faeries.

Other stories say he is the reincarnation of Fionn MacCumhal.

IN MAGICK AND RITUAL — Convene with Mongan to aid you in magick of all types, especially when working with the water element, also for assisting in sea faery contact.

MORANN (IRISH)

IN MYTH — [Mor-AN] This Druid became the chief Brehon judge in Ulster during the time of the Red Branch. When he was born with a caul over his head, a layer of thin tissue which people all over the world have associated with the birth of a prophet or magician, his father was afraid of him and tried to drown him.

Morann was rescued by a local silversmith and raised as his son. He was known for his wise and fair judgments and, today, the Moran family of Ireland claims him as their common ancestor.

IN MAGICK AND RITUAL — Invoke Morann when you have to mediate a dispute, sit in judgment, or when you need an extra dose of wisdom.

MORCA (IRISH)

IN MYTH — The Formorian king who routed the Nemed out of Ireland. When the battle was finished, only thirty Nemed remained alive.

IN MAGICK AND RITUAL — Overcoming enemies, banishing magick.

CORRESPONDENCES — Vetivert, rue.

MORDA (WELSH, SCOTTISH)

The blind servant of the sow Goddess Cerridwen whose duty it was to keep the fire lit under her cauldron of knowledge. He may have once been a fire God in his own right. His myths merged with Gwion's.

MORFAN (WELSH)

IN MYTH — A son of Cerridwen and Tegid who was so hideous that he joined King Arthur's warriors, sure that no one would raise a sword to him for fear of the power in his ugly face.

IN MAGICK AND RITUAL — Just like wild animals puff themselves up to appear as more than they are in the face of danger, you can invoke Morfan to accomplish the same thing.

MORGAN (IRISH)

An Otherworld king who was married to the hideous, giant warrior woman Coinchend. He was the father of Delbchaem, a beautiful Otherworld princess.

MORVAN LEZ-BREIZE (BRETON)

IN MYTH — The knight's tale of "the prop" or "hatchet of Brittany" who fought the Francs, is an epic one recounted in detail in the *Barzaz-Breise* by Villemarque. After Morvan left home to follow the knighthood, his mother died of a broken heart. When he returned home ten years later he found his sister there alone, and tried, out of guilt, to stay there to help her. However, he found he was very unhappy not fighting, and he left again.

In a one-on-one battle with the King of the Francs he was beheaded, but still living. He went to the home of a hermit whom he was told could replace his head. The hermit did so while incanting a blessing from the deities.

The hermit then told him he had to do penance for killing his mother by working for him for seven years. He gladly did this, and at the end of the seven years a woman on a white horse (probably Epona) rode by with eyes full of tears. She took him away to await the time his country would need him again.

IN MAGICK AND RITUAL — He is an archetypal sleeping God who can teach us about patience, perseverance, keeping of a geise, and the serving of country.

MUINREMUIR (IRISH)

IN MYTH — One of the Red Branch's most popular and successful warriors. He was the first warrior to accept the challenge of a dark knight who sought to battle to the death by the severing of the loser's head. (Other stories credit this act to Cuchulain.)

Muinremuir's root names mean "neck of the sea" relating him to the watery realm of Manann and Llyr, and to the confluence points in which the Celts believed was great power.

IN MAGICK AND RITUAL — Call on him for overcoming enemies, wisdom.

Three interlaced male figures from the Irish Book of Kells.

MUIRCHERTACH, KING (IRISH)

A king in a Christianized story about a young witch who turned out his wife and children and did battle with a local bishop who has magickal powers similar to those of the Druids. The story tells of how she bewitched King Muirchertach into doing things against his will. He was probably once a sea faery or minor sea God.

MULLO (BRETON, CONTINENTAL)

IN MYTH — The patron deity of teamsters. He is associated with jackasses, and with the Roman God Mars.

IN MAGICK AND RITUAL — Call on him to protect you as you drive to and from work, or if you drive for a living you might wish to adopt him as your personal deity. His energy is also compatible for the protection of travelers and for work animals.

CORRESPONDENCEs — The whip.

MYRDDIN (WELSH)

Also see Merlin. A possible sixth-century bard, sometimes a minor goat-footed God like Cernunnos, also another version of Merlin.

MYRDDIN WYLLT (WELSH)

A woodland God who deliberately grew feathers so he could leap from tree to tree. He is often equated with Ireland's Suibhne.

NAOISE (IRISH)

IN MYTH — [NAY-see] Also Naisi, Naisii, and Noisiu. The ill-fated husband of Deirdre of the Sorrows who, with his brothers, was murdered by King Conchobar.

He and his two brothers, Ardan and Ainle, represent a unique male version of the Triple Goddess. When Deirdre was walking outdoors on a snowy Yule morning long before she met him, she saw a raven picking over a bloody carcass in the snow. This rather gruesome scene inspired her to wish for a mate with hair as black as the raven, lips as red as blood, and skin as white as snow—the Triple Goddess colors—which Naoise fulfilled. Such subtle hints at triplicity are well-known in folk tales and are most strongly seen today in the old story of Snow White and her seven dwarves.

Deirdre knew that part of her fate was that she could have any man she wanted except Naoise, if she wished to live in peace. Despite her intuitive sense of doom at returning from their exile in Scotland, she agreed to go back with him.

IN MAGICK AND RITUAL — Evoke Naoise for making love magick, or for rites of loyalty. Work with him and Deirdre for couples or sex magick.

Nar Chuathcaech and Ochall Ochne (Irish)

IN MYTH — Nar the swineherd's name means "the shameful." He was in the employ of Bov the Red of Munster, and was the great rival of Ochall Ochne, the chief swineherd of Connacht. The two carried on their battle through many incarnations, linking them both to other reincarnation archetypes, and to the reborn son images of the sow Goddess. It is likely that both men were once the guardians or consorts of regional sow Goddesses similar to Cerridwen.

IN MAGICK AND RITUAL — Protection of sacred space and exploration of past-lives, particularly where they involve unresolved quarrels.

Natchrantal (Irish)

One of the two Connacht warriors in the service of Queen Maeve who is credited with finding the Brown Bull of Cooley and turning it over to her.

Nechtan (Scottish)

IN MYTH — A Pictish king who sought the hand of the Goddess Triduana, both because she was beautiful, and because he wished to control his Celtic neighbors through her. He was a water deity, and in some legends is the husband of the Irish river Goddess Boann.

IN MAGICK AND RITUAL — Water magick, purification rites.

CORRESPONDENCES — Basil.

Nede MacAdnai (Irish)

Also Neide. A bard who schemed to get the throne of Connacht away from his brother King Caier. To do so, he asked of the King an impossible request at a magickal time when wishes could not be refused. When the King could not grant the request, Nede was free to compose a satire (such as Cairbre did to depose Bres) in order to cause the King to become blemished so that he could no longer rule. No Irish king or queen could sit on the throne who was not physically perfect.

He was also jealous of his low position at court and fought Fer Credne for the honor of being chief poet.

Neit (Irish)

IN MYTH — [Nayt] Also Net. A Tuatha war God who is seen as both the husband of Nemain and of the entire Morrigan triune. He was killed in a battle with the Formorians.

IN MAGICK AND RITUAL — Fertility rites.

CORRESPONDENCES — The trident which, in Celtic mythology, makes one not a God of the sea, but a fertilizing principle of the Triple Goddess.

NEMED (IRISH)

The leader of one of the Irish invading races in the five-fold Irish invasion myth cycle which bears his name. He died in a plague started by the immune Formorians who won the island from Nemed's people. He was the husband of war Goddess Macha.

NEMGLAN (IRISH)

IN MYTH — A bird God who was the father of Conaire Mor. He placed a geise on his son that when he made his way to Tara to offer himself in the service of his country, that he must walk there naked carrying only a slingshot and one single stone for a weapon. Nemglan promised that if he did this he would one day be High King.

Archetypally, birds represent a transition from the human realm to the Otherworld.

IN MAGICK AND RITUAL — Call on this Otherworld God to aid you in divination, fertility, or for initiating spirit contact. Make offerings to him through the hungry birds in your own backyard.

CORRESPONDENCES — Feathers, mercury.

NERA (IRISH)

IN MYTH — A servant of Queen Maeve who was asked by her to go tickle the feet of those hanging upside down in her torture house. Nera did as he was asked, but took pity on one man who begged for water. He carried the man to a nearby house and let him drink. Fearing that his disloyalty to Maeve would be discovered, Nera blew—with one mighty breath—the remaining water over the house like a deluge, killing all the occupants.

As Nera was taking the prisoner back to the torture house, the man told Nera to go to a certain faery burgh where he would find a woman who would free him from his servitude. There Nera found and married a faery queen. The faery queen told him the drowned house and its people were only shadows, but would become real if he did not destroy her rival faeries on the next Samhain. Nera sent Fergus MacRoi to destroy the burgh, all but his wife and child, to whom he returned to stay with forever.

IN MAGICK AND RITUAL — Faery contact.

NIALL OF THE NINE HOSTAGES (IRISH)

IN MYTH — Also Niall Noighiahhach and Neil. This youngest son took over as High King in the fourth century from his father Eochaid and became the founder of the powerful O'Neill dynasty, known in Ireland as Clan Ui Neill. He is known to have sent armies into both Britain and Gaul, but it is there that the lines separating the historical and mythic figures of Niall blur.

As a youth he escaped the evil intents of his stepmother Mongfhionn, and was raised by an itinerant bard named Torna Eices. He was taught the art of divination by a Druid.

The most dramatic of the stories concerns he and eight of his warriors who were out riding one day when they came across an old hag. She demanded they all get down from their mounts and kiss her. To humor the woman they did as she asked, and she immediately transformed into Flaithius, a beautiful Goddess whose name means "royal." She symbolizes the sovereign who gave Niall the legitimacy to rule. She also prophesied that he would become one of the greatest High Kings known to Ireland.

IN MAGICK AND RITUAL — Leadership and secrets of divination.

NISSYEN (WELSH)

IN MYTH — Also Nisien. He always sought peace and harmony. His brother, Evnissyen, was of an opposing disposition, and loved discord. Evnissyen was responsible for a war between Wales and Ireland.

IN MAGICK AND RITUAL — Call on Nissyen for peace rituals.

NOLA (BRETON)

In Myth — Nola loved deeply his foster-sister Gwennolaik, but he died at sea in the service of his country before he could return to rescue her from his hateful mother.

He returned later in spirit and whisked her away to the Land of the Dead where she was reunited with her family and lived happily with him forever.

IN MAGICK AND RITUAL — Cultivate Nola for loyalty, spirit contact, love magick, and for couple's work.

NOMENOE (IRISH, BRETON)

IN MYTH — A ninth-century Breton chief originally from Ireland who led a revolt against the King of the Francs, Charles the Bald. After he beheaded the king in a surprise attack, he washed his blood-stained hands in a nearby stream while stating that by this act he freed the Bretons. This last was a ritual of release, purification, and a fitting end to a spell for the defeat of his enemies. An epic poem by French poet, Villemarque, commemorates these events.

IN MAGICK AND RITUAL — Cultivate him to help release old prejudices, fears, etc. Also for purification rites, overcoming enemies, and for strength in serving your country or another organization about which you care deeply.

N'OUN DOARE (BRETON)

IN MYTH — N'Oun Doare means "I do not know," which was all he could say to the Marquis of Coat-Squiriou when he was found and adopted by him. When the boy came of age, the Marquis set out to buy him a fine sword, but N'Oun found an old rusted one which he begged to have. At the hilt the words, "I am Invincible" were engraved. Next the Marquis wished him to have a fine horse, but he chose an old broken-down horse instead.

N'Oun stole the crown of a king, which his horse told him not to do. When he was found out he had to go on a long quest to right the wrong he undertook willingly. Along the way the horse guided him, and the good deeds he performed (mostly kindness to animals) earned him their help in aiding his quest. In the end he was rewarded with a princess, riches, and then a kingship.

IN MAGICK AND RITUAL — He can help you find tools which will serve you well, and maybe teach you how to avoid traps of greed, a lesson he learned the hard way. Also lessons of responsibility and reaping the proverbial rewards of good deeds.

NUADA (IRISH)

IN MYTH — This Arch-Druid of Cahir Mor was a king in his own right and the great grandfather of Fionn MacCumhal. Nuada was respected and honored for his great magickal powers.

IN MAGICK AND RITUAL — Call on him to assist you in all your magickal efforts.

It is that hand touched with silver
Which most easily caresses the moon....
—Moirna Carol O'Reilly

NUADA OF THE SILVER HAND (IRISH)

IN MYTH — Also spelled Nuad Argetlam, meaning "the silver-handed." He was the last king of the Tuatha De Danann, a God of war who owned a sword from which no enemy could escape alive once it was trained on them. He was also a minor sun or moon deity.

He was forced to abdicate his throne to the Milesian invaders after a lengthy battle in which he lost his hand (the First Battle of Mag Tuireadh). Unfortunately for him, Irish kings had to be physically perfect to rule. The great healers Airmid and Miach fashioned him one of silver so that he could rule.

He is one of the three men who were married to Macha.

IN MAGICK AND RITUAL — Overcoming obstacles, perseverance, and leadership.

CORRESPONDENCES — Chameleons, lizards.

NUDONS (WELSH, ANGLO-CELTIC)

IN MYTH — Also Nodens, Nodonti, and Nodente. A sea God equated with Poseiden, rather than Manann or Neptune, also thought to be the same as the death and river God Llud.

Libations were given to him at his sacred sites where he was worshipped by both the invading Romans and the native populace. The Romans built him a shrine on the banks of the Severn where he was pictured as youthful with a shine around his head like a halo, and flying near him were his faery hosts. The Britons gave him a shrine overlooking the Thames where he was depicted as being beardless (the Roman influence) and driving a chariot while holding reigns and scepter. Near him were a fisherman hooking a salmon, and other marine animals.

Shell trumpets were blown to honor him.

IN MAGICK AND RITUAL — Eco-magick, water magick.

NWYVRE (WELSH)

A husband of Arianrhod about whom nothing is known but his name. The name itself translates as "sky" or "firmament," indicating that he was likely once a father sky God.

NYNNIAW AND PEIBAW (CORNISH)

IN MYTH — Sons of Beli who were rulers of two adjoining areas of the Duchy. They got into a quarrel over the meaning of the stars and planets and their significance to the fate of their country, and on which lands their herds had grazing rights. The argument led to a war in which both Kings' lands were totally destroyed.

An unnamed God turned them both into oxen as punishment for their actions. As such they worked the land yoked together to restore some of what they had taken.

IN MAGICK AND RITUAL — Pathwork with this pair to learn lessons of self-responsibility and the need for overcoming prejudices. Think of their story as an example of the Threefold Law in action.

OAK KING (PAN-CELTIC)
See Holly King and Oak King.

> *Harper Composer Poet Singer*
> *Our Great Solace In Our Great Need*
>
> —epitaph, O'Carolan's tombstone

O'CAROLAN (IRISH)
IN MYTH — His first name was Turlough, though he was always known as O'Carolan or just Carolan. He was one of the last great Irish bards, often referred to as "the last harper," and though he lived from 1670–1738, he is as much a fundamental bardic archetype as any Druid in mythology.

O'Carolan passionately believed in the faery folk of his country and frequently sought out their inspiration. He deliberately slept on a Manx faery burgh one night, and forever after had faery tunes running through his head, many of which he committed to paper. His music and poetry honored the character of Irish and Manx myth, and he was particularly fascinated by the exploits of the Fianna.

He was known for his wit, and his lyrics reflect a brilliant combination of pathos, passion, and urbanity.

His four-day wake was a time of rare peace in Ireland, when Protestant, Catholic, Celt, and Anglo all came together to celebrate and mourn this monumental talent. O'Carolan is buried in the churchyard at Kilronan Abbey near Lough Meelagh.

IN MAGIC AND RITUAL — Call upon the spirit of this great bard to help you in magick, music magick, faery contact, or gaining mental prowess.

OCHALL OCHNE (IRISH)
See Nar Thuathcaech.

OCTRIALLACH (IRISH)
A Formorian who sealed off Diancecht's medicinal spring which was restoring the Tuatha De Danann's dead warriors to life. Nonetheless, he died fighting the Tuatha.

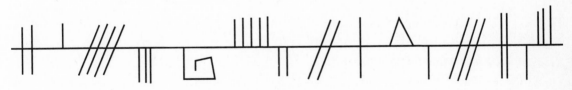

A sample of Ogham writing.

OGHMA (SCOTTISH, IRISH)
IN MYTH — [OHG-mah or OW-ma] The God of communication and writing who invented the Ogham Alphabet and gave it to the Druids. He is sometimes thought of as the patron deity of poets. Writing was considered a very sacred and holy act by many early people including the Celts. It is for this reason that the Celts had a strong oral tradition, even among their magickal folk, as very little was believed safe to commit to paper.

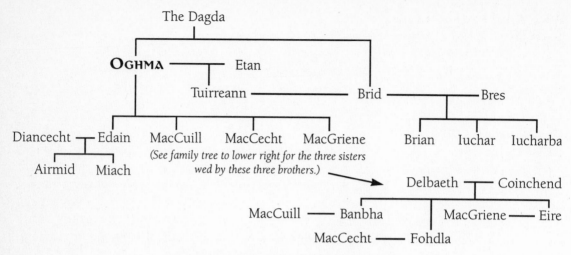

The generally accepted family tree of Oghma.

OGHMA (CONT.)

Aside from Oghma's literary association, he was a warrior of Tara who fought with Lugh against the Formorians. He was also given a role in myth of helping to escort the recently dead to to the Otherworld.

He had two nicknames which tell much about his character. One was Cermait, which means "the honey-mouthed," relating him to the Irish gift of glib gab known as blarney; and the other is Grianainech, "the sunny-faced," believed to come from his great wisdom.

Ogmios was the Continental name for Oghma where his principal role was that of combatant. An inscription saying "Ogmia" was also found in the north of England.

IN MAGICK AND RITUAL — Call on Oghma to gain wisdom, creative inspiration, overcoming writer's block, aiding communication, or if you wish to be touched with the blessing of blarney without having to travel to Ireland to kiss the Blarney Stone. His energy is also compatible with Passing Over rituals and spirit contact.

CORRESPONDENCES — Mercury, feathers, quills.

OGMIOS (CONTINENTAL)

See Oghma.

OGYRVRAN (WELSH, CORNISH)

IN MYTH — One of the two men credited with being the father of Queen Guinevere. This one divine, the other human.

Ogyrvran shares many aspects with rulers of the Otherworld. He was of gigantic size, he possessed a magick cauldron from which three Muses were born, he was a patron of the arts and of bards who worshipped him as the founder of their craft. His name contains the roots of the words "evil raven," the raven being the bird which is most often seen as the harbinger of death in Celtic mythology.

IN MAGICK AND RITUAL — Call on Ogyrvran for a role in Passing Over rituals or for making spirit contact. His powers are greatest near Samhain.

OL (WELSH, CORNISH)

IN MYTH — A teacher and huntsman attached to King Arthur's court. Arthur highly praised and valued Ol's talents, claiming no dog could sniff out prey or escaped prisoners as well as he.

IN MAGICK AND RITUAL — Invoke Ol to help you find lost objects, persons, or pets.

OSCAR AND FIONN (IRISH)

IN MYTH — Also Osgar and Finn. The sons of Ossian and Niamh of the Golden Hair who were born in the Otherworld.

Oscar was one of the Fianna's greatest warriors. Under his command was a company known as the Terrible Boom, so named for their refusal to retreat until the battlefield was swept clean of living enemies. High King Cairbre grew nervous of the power of the Fianna and engaged them in battle. The Fianna were crushed, but not before Oscar decapitated Cairbre. Fionn also died in the battle.

Fionn MacCumhal, the Fianna's most well-loved leader, came from the Otherworld to mourn the fallen hero and personally escort him to the Otherworld.

IN MAGICK AND RITUAL — Protection, leadership, and courage.

> *For neither death nor change comes near us,*
> *And all listless hours fear us...*
> *For these were ancient Osian's fate*
> *Loosed long ago from Heaven's gate....*
>
> —William Butler Yeats

OSSIAN (IRISH, SCOTTISH, MANX)

IN MYTH — [USH-een] Also Osian and Oisin, and Oshin on Man. His name means "fawn." Ossian is the son of Fionn MacCool and Saba.

Saba, Ossian's mother, was lured away from Fionn by forest faeries and turned into a deer before Ossian's birth. Ossian was born from her in human form, and eventually returned to his father as a gifted poet.

He returned again to the Otherworld with his second wife, Niamh, where she gave birth to two sons, Fionn ("the white") and Osgar ("lover of the deer"), and a daughter, Plur na mBan ("woman of flowers"). His first wife was Eibhir, who is described as a yellow-haired "stranger from another land," possibly meaning she was once a sun Goddess.

Ossian became a Fianna leader, and the Fennian Cycle of Irish mythology is often referred to as the Ossianic Cycle in his honor.

Faeries would often seek him out for company, especially to play the Irish game known as hurling. Finvarra, the faery king, was an intimate of his, and enjoyed engaging him in a game of chess. Ossian died when he ignored his wife's pleas to always remain mounted in the human world.

Aside from the body of mythology surrounding him, Ossian's tales have been immortalized in numerous works of poetry and fiction. One of the most famous of these is James MacPherson's 1760 collection, *Fragments of Ancient Poetry Collected in the Highlands*.

OSSIAN (CONT.)

IN MAGICK AND RITUAL — Call on Ossian to enhance creativity, overcoming fear, and assisting in spirit contact. Ossian maintained a demonstrative love for animals all his life, and he can be called on to work magick for animals, especially healing rituals.

CORRESPONDENCES — The stag.

OWAIN (WELSH, CORNISH)

IN MYTH — Also Sir Owain. He was a knight in King Arthur's court who ran off to slay the Black Knight. After that episode, he began a series of adventures which made him a symbolic consort of the Triple Goddess. He was first the lover of Luned, a maiden who helped him escape prison by teaching him the secrets of invisibility. He then wedded the Lady of the Fountain, a well/mother Goddess. He lived with her happily for three years until his fellow knights came to take him back to court.

When the Lady of the Fountain came shrieking after him for his lack of fidelity, he fled to the woods in shame. While there, he found an aged Luned who was imprisoned with twenty-four other women who were sentenced to be burned at the stake. Owain redeemed himself by rescuing them all.

In *The Dream of Rhonabwy*, the most famous myth in which he is involved, he was portrayed as a fine warrior who was given three hundred ravens which formed the core of his battalion.

IN MAGICK AND RITUAL — Protection. You might also wish to experiment with his father God energies.

OWEN LAWGOCH (WELSH)

IN MYTH — A sleeping king/God, like King Arthur, whose myth is even more pervasive in some parts of Wales because it was based on a real hero nearer to our own time, one whose historical personage blended with an older archetypal king who may have been Arthur. Others claim he is based on Owen Glyndwr, a knight who fought in the French army, but the dates have never been able to prove that one definitely antedated the other.

The mythological Owen was a warrior and minor king who fought against the invading Saxons. He was killed by his nephew in the heat of combat and was carried off to a cave to sleep and await his country's call. Other legends say he sleeps with his entire retinue waiting to rise together to fight again. Owen will be roused by a "trumpet blast and a clash of arms" at which time he will arise and lead the Brythons to victory. (Trumpet blasts have long associated with Otherworld messages, and similar horns are still used by modern-day Spiritualists in their spirit communications.)

Owen's own sword, said to have been passed down from the ancient kings of Prydain, never lost a battle, a sidearm comparable to Arthur's Excalibur.

IN MAGICK AND RITUAL — See King Arthur for a full discussion of Owen's attributes.

PARTHOLAN (IRISH)

IN MYTH — The leader of the third of the invader races in the five-fold Invasion Cycle of Irish mythology. He came to the island with a force of only twenty-five men and twenty-four women warriors.

Though he was ruthless in his quest for power, even to the point of killing his own parents, his people (the Partholans) are credited with bringing agriculture and craftsmanship to Ireland.

Partholan went off to war and left his wife, Dealgnaid, with his male servant, Togda. They had a passionate romance in his absence, yet when he returned, he accepted the responsibility for the incident because it was he who chose to leave.

IN MAGICK AND RITUAL — Pathwork with Partholan to teach you the valuable lesson of learning to accept responsibility for own actions.

Peibaw (Cornish)

See Nynniaw and Peibaw.

Pelles, King (Welsh, Cornish)

(Also see Pryderi, also Pellean.) The King whose castle is the scene of a battle which starts the coming great Wasteland of Arthurian legend. Before the myths of Sir Percival, he was the Keeper of the Grail and its mysteries, equated with Pryderi.

Percival, Sir (Welsh, Cornish)

IN MYTH — Also Parzifal and Peredur. Percival, sometimes nicknamed the "perfect fool," is one of King Arthur's knights who managed to capture the elusive Holy Grail. With it he healed the mythical great Wasteland, and then became the guardian of the Grail itself.

Percival was unknown in Celtic myth until Breton writer Chretien de Troyes penned this addendum to the Arthurian legends in 1175. The model for him was Peredur, the warrior/God who was the seventh son of a seventh son. The Welsh root of his name, *per,* means "bowl," and archetypally he represents the guardian force surrounding the Goddess and the cauldron (Grail) of regeneration.

Peredur is also noted for his legends concerning acts of vengeance.

IN MAGICK AND RITUAL — Align with Percival to become a keeper of the Grail and to seek its mysteries.

Peredur (Welsh, Cornish)

See Percival, Sir.

> *In Aber Gwenoli is the grave of Pryderi,*
> *Where the waves beat against the land.*
>
> —from *The Black Book of Caermarthen*

Pryderi (Welsh)

IN MYTH — [PREE-dair-ee] The son of Pwyll and Rhiannon, the latter of whom was punished because it was believed she had killed him by devouring him while the castle slept. He was later found to have been kidnapped. Called Gwri of the Golden Hair by his foster parents, when he was finally returned safely to his family they gave him his adult name which means "care" or "trouble."

Pryderi took Bran's side in conflict with Matholwch, and was one of the seven survivors of that battle. He married Kicva, and was friends with Manann after he married Rhiannon.

PRYDERI (CONT.)

He even offered Manann part of his kingdom of Dyfed (now Pembrokeshire) when Manann was dispossessed of his undersea realm.

While the four of them were at a banquet, a great desolation overtook the land, and they set out on a series of quests to reverse it. The curse was laid by Llew. When the foursome were successful in their quest, Llew lifted the enchantment, promising never again to blight the land of Dyfed. (This story can be equated with most of the world's flood/deluge myths.)

Archetypally, Pryderi represents the dark forces in opposition to, and as a part of, the light. He lost in the Battle of the Trees (Gwyddion was victorious), and is equated with King Pelles who lost the Grail to the archetypal forces of light.

Pryderi is the only mythic figure to be mentioned in all the various branches of the *Mabinogion.*

IN MAGICK AND RITUAL — Call on Pryderi for lessons in loyalty, or draw him into you as you set out on your own quests.

CORRESPONDENCES — The number seven.

PWYLL (WELSH)

IN MYTH — [POO-ul] The father of Pryderi and first husband of Rhiannon. He was the King of Dyfed (now Pembrokeshire) who became the King of Annwn, a synonym for the Other-world.

Pwyll claimed ownership of a stag not felled by his own hounds. When caught in the act by Arawn, king of the Otherworld, he was very contrite and asked how he could repay the transgression. Arawn said that he wished for Pwyll to go to the Otherworld and take his place in fighting Havagan, his rival. To make the task easier, Arawn even agreed to work a spell to make Pwyll appear as Arawn to all who looked upon him.

Pwyll not only accepted the task and kept his word, but did not violate Arawen's wife for the year and a day he was there, and he ruled well and justly. Arawen so marvelled at this friendship that they became as close as brothers, and Arawen bestowed on him the title of *Pen Annwn,* the "head of Annwn."

IN MAGICK AND RITUAL — Call on Pwyll to draw into yourself the positive qualities of justice, fraternal love, the keeping of a geise, and loyalty. He can also aid you in making spirit contact with the Otherworld.

CORRESPONDENCES — Masks, bronze.

RAGALLACH (IRISH)

This Connacht king attempted to kill his daughter in fear of a prophecy which said he would die at the hand of his own grandson. Archetypally he is yet another in a long line of sacrificial God/kings who is unwilling to step down for his successor.

RAYMOND OF POITOU (BRETON)

The husband of the Goddess Melusine who breaks his promise not to look upon her on Saturday.

RHONABWY (WELSH, ANGLO-CELTIC)

IN MYTH — [R'HONE-ah-bwee] A prophetic dreamer in the *Mabinogion* who foresaw the invasion of King Arthur's knights and correctly predicted the victor. The majority of the dreams concern an intense game of chess played between King Arthur and Owain, the game symbolic of war strategy.

IN MAGICK AND RITUAL — Invoke Rhonabwy before you go to sleep to induce your own prophetic dreams.

Rob Roy MacGregor (Scottish)

IN MYTH — The great swordsman and wielder of the claymore who was challenged by Black Roderic, a man jealous of any swordsman claiming they possessed greater skill than he. Rob Roy hated fighting without reason, but accepted the challenge since he knew Roderic would certainly kill him if he refused. Rob's arms were so long that Roderic couldn't get close enough to inflict even the most minor scratch, and Rob managed to cut off Roderic's sword arm at the shoulder. After that no one else challenged him without cause.

IN MAGICK AND RITUAL — Pathwork with Rob for knowing when to fight and when not to, and for strength and assistance when you must.

Robin Ddu (Welsh)

IN MYTH — [Thoo] Robin was a great wizard/Druid whose name means "bright flame of black." His fame was great, and people far and wide sought him out for his wisdom and magick. One day a stranger came to the Welsh village where Robin lived, declared that he did not think the man a wizard at all, and set out to prove his point.

By pure luck Robin managed to avoid being caught up in any of the stranger's traps and, as a result, his fame spread even further. Finally, the word of his fame reached the ears of a queen who had lost a very precious ring, and she sent for Robin to find it for her. By using his logic and his physical senses, Robin was able to discover that the ring had been stolen by a servant girl. Taking it from her, he planted it in the belly of a bird which he commanded the queen to kill and eat and she would find her ring.

IN MAGICK AND RITUAL — "Reality" is a word not well defined, as Robin's story shows us. His tale teaches us the lesson that magick comes in many forms, principally through what is believed to be real by us and others around us. Cultivate him to help you use your logic and to remind you that all acts of magick require our physical efforts as well in order to manifest.

Robin Goodfellow (Anglo-Celtic)

Also see Cernunnos. Though often thought of today as the goat-footed faery king of the woodlands, Robin was probably once another name for the Horned God, and he is believed to be the source for the folktales about the forest-dwelling hero Robin Hood.

Roc (Irish)

IN MYTH — Roc was the servant of Aengus MacOg who fathered a son by Dhonn's wife. In a fit of rage, Dhonn killed the child by crushing it against a tree. Roc wove a spell, using a magick wand, which restored life to the boy in the form of an earless, tailless boar, who exacts his renege by killing Dhonn's son Diarmuid.

IN MAGICK AND RITUAL — Use Roc's energy to help overcome enemies and as a general aid to magick, especially when using wands.

ROHAND (CORNISH)

IN MYTH — Rohand was the vassal of Roland Rise, who took Tristan out of Cornwall in fear for his life. In their exile, he became the faithful servant of Tristan, and returned him home only after he was grown. In the meantime, he instructed the boy in knightly pursuits and music, and claimed him as his own son.

IN MAGICK AND RITUAL — Loyalty.

ROLAND RISE (WELSH, CORNISH)

The Lord of Ermonie, father of Tristan, and chieftain of a small Welsh duchy. He won the hand of Princess Blancheflour, a sister of King Mark, in a tournament.

RON CER (IRISH)

A Leinster warrior who was the slayer of High King Aedh.

ROSS THE RED (IRISH)

IN MYTH — The human king of Ulster who wed Aengus MacOg's daughter, Maga, a woman of the Tuatha. He is credited with organizing the first Red Branch warriors of Ulster from the men of his own clan.

IN MAGICK AND RITUAL — Call upon the potent force of Ross to aid in you in forming organizations, protecting yourself, overcoming your enemies, and discovering the hidden strengths within your own family.

RUADAN (IRISH)

The son of Bres and Brid. He wounded the Tuatha goldsmith, Govannon, at the Second Battle of Magh Tuireadh, though he was later slain in the same combat. Brid came to the battlefield and began to weep over him, the legendary beginning of the practice of *caoine* (keening), or lamenting the dead.

RUADH (IRISH)

IN MYTH — Ruadh [ROO-ah] sailed from Ireland in three ships which ran into a storm that depleted the ship's food and fresh water provisions. After he reassured his frightened crew, he set off swimming for land. He soon ran into an island which was populated by nine women. He stayed there for nine nights, in which time one of the women bore him a son and asked him to return when his mission was done. Ruadh did not return to the island, and the woman sought him out and beheaded him.

IN MAGICK AND RITUAL — Pathwork through Ruadh's myth for personal adventure.

RUDRAIDHE (IRISH)

IN MYTH — The eldest son of Partholan who is considered to be the founder of the royal line of old Ulster. The Ultonian rulers were often known collectively as Clan Rudraidhe after him.

IN MAGICK AND RITUAL — Use the power of Rudraidhe for making new starts or for invoking leadership skills.

SAINNTH (IRISH)

In later myths, he was the father of Macha, the powerful Goddess who cursed the warriors of Ulster.

SALOMON (BRETON)

IN MYTH — A celebrated ninth-century war chief who drove the Saxons and the Danes from Brittany. Like many other historical mythic heroes, his tales merged with those of the archetypal heroes of mythology. He is equated with Ireland's King Brian Boru and, on a lesser scale, with the hero Cuchulain.

IN MAGICK AND RITUAL — Overcoming enemies and protection.

SAMALITIATH (IRISH)

IN MYTH — The Partholan warrior and magician who was the first to brew meade in Ireland. Meade (pronounced "meed") is a rich, honey ale associated with Bealtaine, Esbats, and Handfasting rites. Meade has had sacred uses in all of the Celtic countries.

IN MAGICK AND RITUAL — Call on the spirit of Samalithiath to celebrate the wonders of meade, ale, wine, Irish whiskey, or any other Irish potables. Evoke him during the Great Rite, or whenever drink is used as part of the ritual. Honor him at the Mabon grape harvest.

SANDDA (WELSH)

IN MYTH — [SAHN-tha] A guardian of King Arthur's stronghold, a later addition to the Arthurian myths. He was reputed to be an angel and, therefore, the enemies of Arthur feared to attack while he was on duty at the gate.

IN MAGICK AND RITUAL — Invoke Sandda when you feel the need to increase your own protective aura.

SECHNASACH (IRISH)

The son of Mor ("the big"), Queen of Munster, who fled in terror of prophecy of doom surrounding his birth. He was born in a dark, isolated cave, and rescued from his distraught mother by friendly faeries. Caves are symbolic of the womb of the earth mother.

SEGDDA SAERLABRAID (IRISH)

A son of an Otherworld king and queen who were said never to have had sexual relations except at his conception.

SEGOMO (CONTINENTAL)

A war God also called by the name Cocidius. His image is always seen with birds of prey such as the hawk or falcon.

SEITHYNIN VEDDW (WELSH)

IN MYTH — This drunkard inadvertently unleashed the sea into the Otherworld because he raped a young woman who stood guard over its magickal fountain.

IN MAGICK AND RITUAL — Allow Seithynin's myth to remind you that the consequences of our actions often have greater significance than we might at first realize.

SEMION (IRISH)

IN MYTH — Semion was the patriarch of the FirBolgs, one of the old races of Ireland, from whom all of that people believe themselves to be descended. At one time long past he was likely their chief father God and the embodiment of the male creative principle.

IN MAGICK AND RITUAL — Honor Semion as a father deity, and call upon him for all types of creative magick or to aid in male fertility rites and spells.

SGILTI (WELSH)

IN MYTH — Called "Lightfoot," he was a runner in King Arthur's court. No one could beat him for he could run through solid objects and over tree tops at a speed which visually reduced him to a blur.

IN MAGICK AND RITUAL — Ask Sgilti's aid in learning astral projection, which for which his fast running skills are a metaphor.

SHONEY (SCOTTISH, IRISH, MANX)

IN MYTH — Though the Shoney are now thought to be sea faeries living off the coast of Scotland and northern Ireland, they were once personified as a single God of the North Sea. Documentation exists showing that local fishermen continued to offer libations of ale to him as late as the nineteenth century.

IN MAGICK AND RITUAL — Experiment with Shoney's energies as a sea God, and call upon him to aid you in water faery contact.

SION, LLEWELLYN (WELSH)

IN MYTH — [SEE-ohn] This famous bard is the reputed author of the *Barddas,* a famous compilation of bardic and Druidic knowledge. His works are the basis of the teachings of the bardic schools which functioned until well into the seventeenth century.

IN MAGICK AND RITUAL — Sion can help you get your own creative energy flowing and help open the doors to sacred knowledge.

SITHEHENN (IRISH, SCOTTISH)

IN MYTH — [SHEE-thah-in] A Druidic prophet who encouraged Niall of the Nine Hostages to set fire to his forge. When, as predicted, Niall emerged from the conflagration unscathed and carrying the hot anvil, Sithehenn declared that he would one day become High King of Ireland.

IN MAGICK AND RITUAL — Divination, fire magick, blessing and creation of magickal tools.

SLAINE (IRISH)

IN MYTH — [SLAWN-ay] In Irish *slainte* means "health," therefore it is reasonable to assume that this son of Partholan was once a deity of healing and the medical arts.

IN MAGICK AND RITUAL — Experiment with his energies in healing rituals.

SOMHLTH (IRISH, SCOTTISH, MANX)

IN MYTH — In folklore, Somhlth is a deity who had no corporeal incarnation, a representation of pure masculine, divine energy.

IN MAGICK AND RITUAL — Invoke his energy to enhance your own masculine powers.

SRENG (IRISH)

The Formorian minister who was sent to negotiate with the Tuatha De Danann when they landed in Ireland. Though he was fearful of the Tuatha's superior weaponry, he could not come to terms with them. He fought a battle with Nuada of the Silver Hand which resulted in the severing of Nuada's hand (the silver one was made to replace it).

SUCELLOS (CONTINENTAL)

A river and death God about whom nothing but his name survives. Some sources do claim he was the consort of Nantosuelta, whose name means "of the meandering stream." Others see him as a personification of death.

SUIBHNE (IRISH)

IN MYTH — [SWEE-nee or SUV-nee] A Dal Riada warrior driven mad by the horrible wounds he took during the Battle of Moira. He ran the entire length of Ireland looking for a peaceful place where he would no longer feel the urge to flee from himself. He is finally able to find what he seeks in the solitude of a virgin forest.

IN MAGICK AND RITUAL — Peace and eco-magick.

TADHG (IRISH)

[TAW'eeg] Tadhg inherited the role of chief warrior of Munster as the son of Cian. Cormac MacArt tried to woo Munster into an alliance against Connacht by offering Tadhg any amount of land in his kingdom which he could encircle in his battle worn chariot. Cormac knew Tadhg coveted Tara, and the High Kingship which owning it represented, and he bribed the charioteer with three bags of gold to make a circle which would exclude Tara.

This story was in the oral tradition for hundreds of years before it was written down. It is believed to date to the third century. In the original the Goddess Cliodna appears to him and asks that he temper his greed.

TADHG (IRISH)

The son of Nuada of the Silver Hand who became a famous Druid and was the maternal grandfather of Fionn MacCumhal.

TALHAIARN (PAN-CELTIC)

IN MYTH — A magician greatly admired by the bard Taliesin, the only being he regarded as his superior.

IN MAGICK AND RITUAL — Use Talhaiarn's energies as an aid to your own magickal spells.

As for those who made the attack,
with their chieftain,
for a year I'll prepare the song
of their victory….

—Taliesin

TALIESIN (PAN-CELTIC)

IN MYTH — [Tal-ee-ESS-en] Taliesin is considered by many to be the greatest of all the Celtic bards with the possible exception of Merlin. His name means "radiant" or "shining brow." He was the son of Cerridwen, who gave birth to him after swallowing her errant servant Gwion. Because his divine archetype merged with a historical figure, many men are credited as being his father. Among these are Caradawc the Strong-Armed, and Henwg, another bard of the sixth century. The historical Taliesin was known to have been educated at Llanvithin in Glamorgan.

TALIESIN (CONT.)

Taliesin sang often, and with full knowledge, of being various animals and inanimate objects. In other words, he was saying the deities gave him conscious knowledge of all his incarnations which seemed to co-exist. He tells many of his stories as an eye witness, and boasted that since the creation of time, he had been present for any event of importance, past or future.

He was also a fine magician, and regarded Cerridwen, his mother, as his patron deity of inspiration. He was also an admirer of Talhaiarn, a great magician, and the only being he regarded as his superior.

IN MAGICK AND RITUAL — Call on Taliesin for knowledge and mental prowess because he was born as a result of it. He can also teach you to know your own value without resorting to arrogance. Also compatible with his energy are past-life knowledge, creative inspiration, making music magick, and help in understanding non-linear time. Taliesin is also a archetypal guardian of tradition. If your Celtic path is a secretive one, have him present as you initiate your members to secrecy. Call on him to help them keep their vows.

CORRESPONDENCES — The ousel, the harp.

TALIESIN (WELSH)

A minor barley God worshipped through the sixth century. He should not be confused with the famous bard, though some of the great bard's attributes were grafted onto him.

TANNUS (BRETON, ANGLO-CELTIC, CONTINENTAL)

IN MYTH — Also Tinnus and Taranus. A thunder God who has origins in Celtic Gaul under the more well-known name Taranis. He is not to be confused with the Goddess of the same name.

In early Gaul human sacrifices were offered to him to influence the weather. He was also a God of the wheel who was associated with the strong oak tree, and was also a God of fertility and a sky God.

He is equated with the Nordic God of thunder, Thor, and sometimes with Rome's Jupiter. His feast time was Yule.

IN MAGICK AND RITUAL — Call upon Tannus for seasonal rites because of his association with the wheel of the year. Invoke him when working weather magick or fertility spells.

CORRESPONDENCES — The wheel, oak leaf, the lightning bolt.

TEGID VOEL (WELSH, CORNISH)

The husband of Cerridwen, and father of the ugliest child in world, Avagdu, and the most beautiful, Creirwy. Another son was Morfyn, a warrior so hideous that challengers were afraid to fight him.

TETHRA (IRISH)

IN MYTH — A king of the FirBolgs after they were banished into the sea where they became known as grotesque sea monsters or ocean-dwelling faeries. He owned a sword named Orna which was death itself, a blade crafted for him by Oghma. It was captured from him by Lugh.

He is now seen as a minor death God like the smith Luchtain, and is said to be the King of Lochlann, the mythical undersea home of the banished Formorians.

Like Manann, his Tuatha counterpart, he did not leave the sea to fight in the FirBolgs' battle for kingship as did the other Celtic deities.

IN MAGICK AND RITUAL — Call on Tethra at the seaside (which can, of course, be visited astrally) and call him to you to aid in water magick or to aid you in contacting faeries of the sea. His energy is also compatible with weather magick at sea or near water.

CORRESPONDENCES — Fish, starfish.

Teutates (Continental)

IN MYTH — A Celtic God of Teutonic origin whose name root means "the people." Julius Caesar equated him with Mercury, and his original image was probably that of a tribal God during the Celts' sojourn into Switzerland on their migration across the European continent.

Caesar wrote about him as a God of the arts, protector of travelers, and a "helper in trade or the gaining of money."

IN MAGICK AND RITUAL — Invoke Teutates before a delicate business deal, or when contemplating making a major purchase. Use his energy for your own crafting projects, and draw his energy into travel talismans and amulets. Since he is so strongly connected to Mercury, a God of communication, ask Teutates to lend his energy to communicative needs.

CORRESPONDENCES — Chalcedony.

Teyrnon (Welsh, Cornish)

IN MYTH — Also Ternan. Teyrnon is associated with Bealtaine fertility rites. In ancient myth, he was the one who released the sacred stallion on May Eve which would mate with the divine mare, possibly a reference to Epona. On Bealtaine day a foal would be born to the pair.

In Welsh folklore, he was the one who found the child Pryderi, the stolen son whom his mother, Rhiannon, was accused of eating. The child was found in a stall and was raised by Teyrnon and his wife until they discovered his true identity.

The stories surrounding Cornwall's St. Erney came from the myths of Teyrnon. The saint's sacred site on Bodmin Moor was once a shrine to this Pagan God.

IN MAGICK AND RITUAL — Call on Teyrnon for fertility rites, and pair him with Epona for couples or sex magick. He can also be evoked as a guardian of your sacred sites. Work with his energy at Bealtaine or for enacting the Great Rite.

> *There came Tigernmas, King of Tara yonder,*
> *On Samhain with his many hosts,*
> *And cause of grief to them was the deed.*
>
> —from *The Book of Leinster*

Tigernmas, King (Irish)

IN MYTH — Also Tiernmas. A fourth-century ruler sometimes called the "culture king." He is credited with bringing music, goldsmithing, fabric dyeing, silversmithing, and art to the Celts.

He died mysteriously along with three quarters of the adult males of Ireland while worshipping Cromm Cruiach at Meg Slecht, a deity whom he is said to have brought into

TIGERNMAS, KING (CONT.)

Ireland. The monastic interpretation was that Tigernmas was slain in a Pagan religious "frenzy," a chilling tale intended to eliminate "idol" worship.

References to his life and death can be found in *The Dinnshenchas*.

IN MAGICK AND RITUAL — Call on him for making music magick or for inspiration in the crafting arts.

TORC TRIATH (IRISH)

See Twrch Trwyth.

TORPEIST, SENCHAN (IRISH)

The seventh century bard who saved the ancient legends of Cuchulain from extinction.

TREON (WELSH)

[TRAY-on] The father of the giantess Vivionn who lived in the Land of Women, one of the Other-world realms.

TRISTAN (IRISH, CORNISH, BRETON)

IN MYTH — Also Tristram and Trystan. His name means "child of sorrow," so named because his father was killed shortly before his birth. He was the lover of Isolde in the epic romantic tale made famous by the opera of German composer, Richard Wagner, and by the many writings of Sir Walter Scott.

Tristan was a knight of Lyonesse, a duchy off the coast of Cornwall. When Rohand, his foster father, came back with him to Cornwall after teaching him to be a knight and harper in exile, Tristan had also became a keeper of the old ways, and was openly appalled at the way stags were indifferently killed. Like the Native Americans, the Celts respected the spirit of their animals. Tristan retaught the Cornish the old ways, and insisted on killing stags with reverence and ceremony, and with honor to the spirit.

All his skills bought him to attention of King Mark, who took him in not knowing this young man was his nephew. (Rohand eventually told the King the lad's identity.)

Mark was glad to have him back and tried to dissuade him from avenging his parents' deaths. He did end up fighting a succession of battles for King Mark against the Britons, and was appointed heir.

When he wished to leave Cornwall again, he was provided with a ship which landed him near Dublin and there he met Isolde, a daughter of the Irish King. When Tristan returned to Cornwall he made so much over the beauty and talents and mind of Isolde, that King Mark wanted her for his wife, and he sent Tristan to fetch her. On the way home he accidentally was given a love potion which was intended for the King. The potion made Tristan and Isolde fall madly in love.

Isolde wed Mark, but the lovers continued to meet, and they were able to fool Mark for a time. The stories of how they met their end are as varied as the many tales about them.

IN MAGICK AND RITUAL — Call on Tristan in couple and sex magick, in making love magick, finding the skills of a warrior, or in working music magick.

Tuan MacCarell (Irish)

IN MYTH — [Toon Mc CARE-el] Also MacCairill. This nephew of Partholan was a hero who was created a God of animals and the woodlands by the mother Goddess Dana. The Irish deer herds are sacred to him, and because of this association he is occasionally seen as another form of the Great Horned God, or as a male counterpart of Flidais.

In *The Book of the Dun Cow* he has several incarnations, many of them human, but he is also seen as a stag, a boar, a bird, and a salmon. These are metaphors for reincarnation, and his archetype is similar to that of Edain. He also functions as a sacrificial God.

IN MAGICK AND RITUAL — Ask Tuan to aid you in learning about past-lives and shapeshifting. Invoke him when working spells for animals, for eco-magick, or evoke at Samhain as a sacrificial deity.

CORRESPONDENCES — Antlers.

Tuirrean (Irish)

Also Tuirenn and Turreann. A son of Oghma and Etan, who had three sons by Brid. The tale surrounding these young men make up one of the "Four Sorrows of Erin." This is also the name of the sister of Fionn MacCumhal, and the two should not be confused.

Twrch Trwyth (Welsh)

IN MYTH — [Toorch TROO-wid] Also spelled Trwyd. He became involved in the myth of Cuhlwch and Olwen when he was turned into a boar who was hunted by King Arthur and his court, and by numerous deities including Mabon, Modron, and Gwyn Ap Nuad. Mabon was the one who was able to snatch a magickal blade wedged between Twrch's boar ears which Culhwch needed to fulfill the many tasks necessary to free Olwen.

He is the equivalent of Ireland's Torc Triath.

IN MAGICK AND RITUAL — Archetypally, the boar is a symbol of potency, plenty, and male power. Evoke the image of Twrch for magick related to these matters.

Uar the Cruel, The Sons of (Irish)

IN MYTH — This Formorian, Uar, was the father of a male trio who are the equivalent of the Morrigan. The boy's names mean "Destruction," "Ill-Fated," and "Want." The sons had venom oozing from their hands and feet which could poison or ruin anything they touched. They made their home in the the Otherworld realm commonly called the Underworld, a domain which became the prototype for the Christian Hell.

IN MAGICK AND RITUAL — See the Morrigan for a full discussion of their attributes.

Uath MacImoman (Irish)

IN MYTH — His name translates as "horror, son of terror." He was an expert shapeshifter who could take any form he desired, and his magickal powers were both respected and feared.

Uath was often sought out to settle disputes in which he would give the comers the chance to prove their points, often at the expense of their own lives. In one tale concerning him, Cuchulain and two others approach him to settle the question of who was the greatest warrior. Uath agreed to decide if each of them would try to cut off his head, provided he could take theirs also. Only Cuchulain accepted the terms of the test. For his bravery Uath

UATH MACIMOMAN (CONT.)

swung at him with the blunt edge of his axe, leaving the warrior alive, and proclaiming him the greatest in the land.

IN MAGICK AND RITUAL — Evoke the presence of Uath when faced with a decision, challenge, or are in need of wisdom.

UGAINY THE GREAT, KING (IRELAND)

IN MYTH — Also Ugaine and Ugony. A sixth-century B.C.E. High King married to the Goddess Cessair. He was said not only to have ruled Ireland, but other parts of the Celtic world and the European continent as well. Upon his death, Ireland was divided into provinces, and his European holdings into other countries.

The reason his great kingdom was disrupted was because the son who inherited the throne, Laery, was killed by his jealous and inept younger brother Corvac.

IN MAGICK AND RITUAL — Invoke Ugainy for the qualities of wisdom and leadership.

UIGREANN, THE SONS OF (IRISH)

Also Uirgriu. When Uigreann was killed by Fionn MacCumhal, his five sons sought vengeance, sure that they could win because they were each adept at a different art and a different weapon. However, Fionn's skill was greater, and he killed them all, establishing himself as the master warrior.

UILLIN (IRISH, MANX)

Also Ullan. A grandson of Nuada and brother-in-law of Fionn MacCumhal, who is credited with the drowning death of Manann. He entered into a romantic liaison with a Druidess who turned his wife into a dog.

URIEN (WELSH, ANGLO-CELTIC)

IN MYTH — Also Uryen. A minor sun God from southern England who was married to Modron, and was the father of Owain and Mabon. He was killed by Modron during one of her murderous rages.

IN MAGICK AND RITUAL — Archetypally, Urien is a sacrificial deity associated with Samhain.

Do I not share my protection,
a ninth part to the battling Arthur?

—Taliesin, from "Death Song of Uther"

UTHER PENDRAGON (WELSH, CORNISH)

IN MYTH — A king in southern Britain during the time of the Saxon invasions.

Under an enchantment by Merlin, Uther was transformed to have the appearance of King Gorlois of Cornwall, husband of Igraine. Uther and Igraine made love, conceiving Arthur as Merlin had prophesied. This parentage was hidden from Arthur until just prior to Uther's death.

His Cornish name means "head of the dragon."

IN MAGICK AND RITUAL — Uther's story follows a fine old tradition of older men who must die so that their sons (archetypally separate aspects of themselves) may take over.

CORRESPONDENCES — The dragon, fire, the sword.

VOTIGERN (WELSH, CORNISH)

His name means "overlord" or "high king." He was the chieftain/king who tried to build a fortress against the Anglo-Saxons high in the mountains of Wales which he was told would not stand unless he could find a fatherless child to sacrifice to local deities. Unable to find such a creature, the Anglo-Saxons overtook Wales, and Merlin, the magician/Druid/wizard, was brought to him. There in Votigern's mountain stronghold Merlin foretold of the coming of King Arthur and of Votigran's death.

WANDIL (ANGLO-CELTIC)

IN MYTH — Also Wandyl and Wandell. This great giant loved the cold and, most of all, he liked to watch humans suffer through harsh winters. So every winter he would steal spring so that the world might be plunged into perpetual wintertime.

The other deities—whose lives depended as much upon the change of seasons as did humans'—conspired to attack Wandil and steal back the spring. When they had spring back, they gave Wandil a blow so fierce that he flew up into the heavens where only his two bright eyes could be seen. These are the twin stars we know today as Castor and Pollux. Folk wisdom says that when the twin stars are clearly visible in the night sky there will be a severe frost. (Incidentally, clear nights do produce the heaviest frosts.)

Today Wandil exists in folklore as an evil faery equated with Jack Frost.

IN MAGICK AND RITUAL — Evoke Wandil at Ostara or Bealtaine before your rituals, then banish him to know that spring has truly arrived. Cultivate him for making winter weather magick.

WARRIORS AND KNIGHTS (PAN-CELTIC)

Many heroes who came to be worshipped as semi-divine beings belonged to one of the elite warrior casts. Though women were also warriors for the Celts, if they ever had an elite fighting body of their own, their names have been lost to us.

These elite fighting groups all have a historical basis, though the factual basis for many of the legends and figures involved in them is open for debate.

Among the best-known of these groups were the Fianna, the personal guardians and soldiers of the Irish High Kings; the Red Branch, the warriors of the Ultonian rulers; he Degad, the warriors of Munster; the Gamhanrhide from Connacht; the Gaesetae, whose name meant "spearmen," who were known to strip naked before battle; and the Men of Harlech, a Welsh fighting group linked to the myths surrounding Bran.

Eventually medieval romantic writers took over these tales and focused them on the Welsh/Cornish Arthurian cycles. Warriors were then called knights and operated under the medieval codes of chivalry and honor.

Where now are the bones
of Wayland the wise,
that goldsmith
so glorious of yore?

—King Alfred

WAYLAND THE SMITH (ANGLO-CELTIC, WELSH, CORNISH)

IN MYTH — Also Weland, Volund, and Weylan, indicating his Germanic origins. Wayland's
   father, Wade, was king of the Finns, and his mother was a minor sea Goddess named
   Wachilt.

Wayland is not Celtic in origin, but came into Anglo-Celtic mythology from exposure to
the Teutonic tradition where he is a major mythic figure.

Wayland was a farrier, coin maker, and artificer to the deities. Also attributed to him is
the construction of several small Bronze Age relics including the Uffington chalk drawings
in England, which are believed to honor Epona. Local legend says if you leave a horse and
payment overnight at his burial mound in Berkshire, the horse will be shod for you by
dawn. Money is still left at this site for good luck. When it was archaeologically excavated
in the 1920s, lots of old coinage and very primitive artificial limbs were found, pointing to
the antiquity of his myth.

Celtic smiths have always been known for their potent magick, and their melting vats
equated with the sacred cauldron of regeneration. Wayland was captured by a jealous Briton
King who desired to be the sole possessor of his services. In the manner of ancient kings, he
kept his magickal swordmaker isolated, so the King's children stole all Wayland's gold and
jewels to make him dependent upon them. Wayland bided his time and plotted his revenge,
then flew away on wings he fashioned himself.

He is often equated with the Roman God, Vulcan.

IN MAGICK AND RITUAL — Wayland can help you find creative ways to overcoming enemies.
   Leave money for him and ask him to add his blessing and strengthening of magickal tools.
   He can also teach us patience. He also had the power to restore lost limbs, and can be called
   upon to help strengthen arms and legs which have undergone trauma.

CORRESPONDENCES — The forge, coins, lava.

WIZARD OF REAY, THE (SCOTTISH)

IN MYTH — The Wizard of Reay, whose real name was Donald MacKay, lived near the town of
   Sutherland. His great talent was the power he exerted over the local faeries. Unlike other
   humans who had to go through all sorts of pains to retrieve lost persons from faeryland, the
   Wizard could but stand before a burgh and chant a magick incantation known only to him,
   and the missing person would come out of their own accord.

One day he asked his apprentice to deliver his secret grimoire to another wizard with
the entreaty not to look inside for any reason whatsoever. As expected, the young man, overcome with curiosity, broke his vow not to look. He peeked inside and, when he read an
incantation at random, a horde of faeries appeared demanding that he give them a task to
do. The young man obliged them over and over, but still they came back for more until the
apprentice was running out of ideas. Then, in an effort to put them to task long enough for
him to get away, he began entreating them to do the nearly impossible. So worn out were

the faeries when they did these tasks designed by the apprentice to buy him time to puzzle himself out of the situation, that they left vowing never to obey the master Wizard again.

This story of the "Sorcerers Apprentice" is an old and well-known one told in story and song in many cultures. However, we only hear of what the student loses, not the teacher, as is told in this tale.

IN MAGICK AND RITUAL — Warning for teachers: teach only when student is ready, and learn to guard secrets carefully when need be.

> *Thus shall memory often, in dreams sublime,*
> *Catch a glimpse of days that are over....*
>
> —Thomas Moore

YSBADADDEN (WELSH)

IN MYTH — [EES-bahd-awth-un] Also Ifan Gruffudd and Yspaddaden Pencawr. His name has been said to mean both "chief giant" and "giant hawthorn tree," and he was the king of the Giants and the father of Olwen, a personification of the May Queen. The giant was physically strong, but possessed no inner-magick. He was forced to find a Druid to tell him how to rescue his daughter when she was once captured by faeries.

Archetypally, Ysbadadden is a sacrificial God who was fated to die if and when his daughter married his successor. Though he struggled against this end by hiding her, he was, of course, unable to prevent the inevitable. His successor, Culhwch, killed him with a spear through the eye and claimed his great love, Ysbadadden's daughter Olwen.

IN MAGICK AND RITUAL — Use Ysbadadden to help you know when to step aside, and that strength and size are not everything and cannot gain one everything. He can also play a role in seasonal rites when it is time for the old God to die.

✠ ✠ ✠ ✠

This dictionary of Gods and heroes is in no way intended to be the final word on Celtic mythology. Your own tradition may have a unique view of the masculine mythic figures and tailor its rituals accordingly. This is as it should be. Likewise, your own individual viewpoints and mythic experiences are important to your spiritual practices. The following blank pages are provided for you to jot down these feelings and insights so that you can conveniently keep in one place as much information about the Celtic Gods as possible.

NOTES

Notes

NOTES

NOTES

NOTES

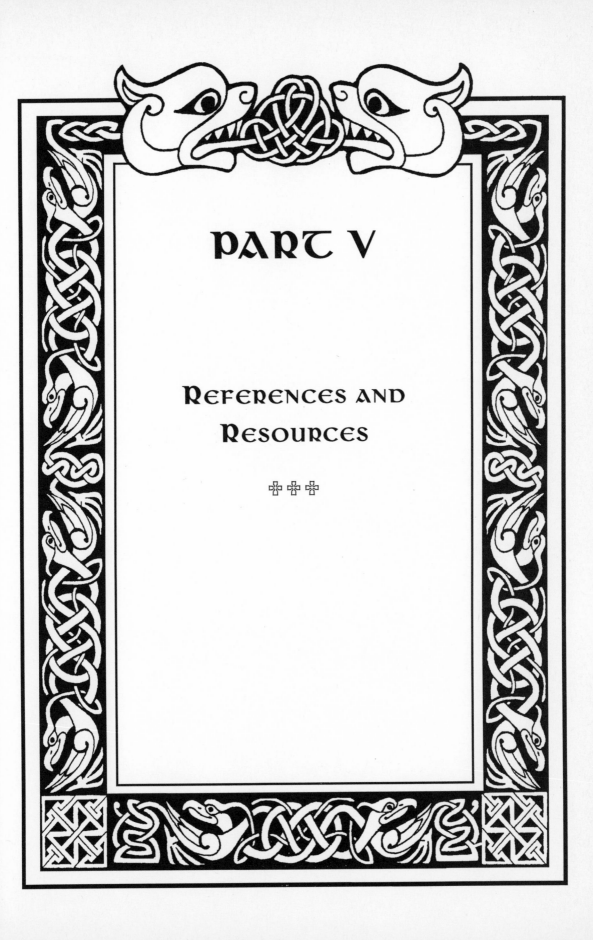

PART V

REFERENCES AND RESOURCES

✠ ✠ ✠

ELEMENTS OF RITUAL CONSTRUCTION

The writers against religion,
whilst they oppose every system,
are wisely careful
never to set up any of their own.
—Edmund Burke

BELOW IS A step-by-step guide for creating Pagan rituals which can be adapted to almost any need, and can work for either covens or solitaries.

1 Have firmly in mind the *exact purpose* of your ritual. It need not be a lofty goal, but you must know why you want to do a ritual in order for it to be coherent, meaningful, and/or successful.

2 If you wish to use an altar, have it set with items of the season: acorns, apples and gourds in fall; flowers in spring; herbs, fruits, or greenery in summer; holly and evergreen in winter, etc. The direction your altar faces is up to you. Every coven and solitary has their own views on this. Many change directions with the seasons. If you are undecided, place the altar in the center of your circle facing north until you work out your own system. West is the direction of the crone's cauldron wherein all things begin and end and begin again.

3 Cast a circle of protective energy with an athame, your creative mind, your forefinger, or with any other ritual tool you feel comfortable using. See it clearly in your mind as a perimeter of protective blue-white light.

4 Invite, but never command, friendly spirits, faeries or elementals to join you as you wish. In the Celtic traditions it is common to invite ancestors to join you, especially during the dark days from Samhain to Imbolg when it is believed that the portal between our dimensions is at its thinnest.

5 Call on the directional quarters or other sentient energies if you wish, and light a candle to honor them. This is often done by ringing a bell in each direction and asking that the spirits of that quarter join you. However, remember that bells frighten away faery beings. If you want faeries at your ritual, forgo the bell. Be sure to walk clockwise as you call the quarters. The direction with which you choose to begin is a personal one, though some traditions will dictate one for you.

6 If you adhere to the Celtic practice of feeding beings called from the Otherworld, do so now, before embarking on any other ritual or magickal efforts.

7 State out loud the purpose of your ritual: Sabbat observance, personal enrichment, rite of passage, honor of a deity, magick, or whatever. This will help you fully align all levels of yourself with the purpose.

8 Evoke or Invoke any energies or deities you wish at this time. Offer food or honors to them as befits your tradition and personal practice.

9   It is nice to use a candle or some other symbol to honor each deity whom you invite into your circle. Goddess candles are traditionally white and God candles are orange or red. Or, you can use a white, red, and black candle for the Triple Goddess. Once again, this is a matter only you can decide. If you only have plain white candles available, then use them for both the God and Goddess, marking them with male and female symbols for distinction.

10 Begin with the body of your ritual work, performing first any set procedures you or tradition deem necessary.

11 Sing, dance, chant, meditate, and/or offer praise and thanks to your deities. Let the words come from your heart. Singing (feel free to make up your own words and melodies as you go) can quickly tap your inner-state of consciousness, and dancing can raise your personal power and energies. You can write out and memorize your rituals or you can speak spontaneously as would have been customary in many ancient rituals. You can have certain set phrases you use, but be creative and celebrate with feeling. You will get more out of your ritual by being somewhat spontaneous than you will by always relying on prepared speeches. And if you find you have done something you really liked, then by all means, write it down after you have closed the circle.

12 If you choose to work magick in your ritual, have with you whatever materials you need for your spell. Once a circle is cast it is unwise to break it until it is grounded. Making a "hole" in the protective energies allows the energy you've worked to raise seep out, and can allow who-knows-what to enter. When I began my path in witchcraft I tended to ignore the sanctity of the circle, feeling myself too rational to believe some nasty entity was just waiting to get in. I had a few surprising and unpleasant experiences. Don't learn the hard way. The energy you raise will attract things you don't want around. With your circle properly cast they can't get in, and they will go when the energy they are attracted to is grounded. Always respect your circle.

13 If your ritual purpose is a rite of passage, then you should have already worked out with the family of those involved just what words, gestures, or materials will be used. Keep these as simple as possible without losing the meaning of the event.

14 Raise and send your "cone of power" if you wish. If you have no magickal need for it you might send it out to heal the polluted and ailing Mother Earth. If you have just celebrated a rite of passage then you can send loving energy to the persons or spirit involved.

15 If you are celebrating a Sabbat, enact whatever drama you wish to honor the holiday, and use whatever seasonal rituals seem appropriate. The Great Rite is appropriate at all spring Sabbats, but can be done at any and/or all of them if you wish. At Samhain many circles enact the death of the God and mourn for him. At Yule we celebrate the rebirth of the God. Adapt seasonal songs for these holidays, and thank the Goddess for the bounty of the earth at all seasons.

16 Release any evoked or invoked energy.

17 There is no rush to close the circle once you have finished your ritual. You may sit inside it and sing, meditate, feast, scry, or just feel in communion and at peace with nature and your deities. Don't dismiss the circle until you feel ready. Just being in this sacred space has a positive and healing effect on both the mind and the body.

18 When you are ready to close the circle thank the elementals and spirits who have joined you, and thank your deities especially. If you have called the quarters then dismiss them in a counterclockwise movement beginning again with the west. Dismiss all the elementals, etc., you have called upon with the traditional phrase, "Merry meet, merry part, and merry meet again."

19 Ground the energy from your circle—always! See it dissipate and return to the earth.

ELEMENTS OF SPELL CONSTRUCTION

If you be too talkative, you will not be heeded;
If you be too silent, you will not be regarded....
—from *The Book of Acaill*

THIS IS BY no means an all-inclusive guide, but the many intricacies of spellwork lie beyond the scope of this book. In an earth religion, such as Celtic Paganism, a spell can utilize anything which comes from nature. Remember that the power is not as much in the object as within the deep mind of the witch, intimately connected to his/her deep needs and desires. Remember too that elemental representations are less a concern than the will and force of the magician who draws on them.

Though, by tradition, no work—magick included—is done on the Sabbats (the word literally means "to rest"), in times of emergency or extreme circumstances, there may be a need for magickal aid on these days.

Once you decide to create a spell for any need, begin constructing it by following the basic steps listed below and on the next page.

1 Clearly understand and define your magickal goal. Write it down or state it out loud to help it form solidly in your mind. By doing this you begin to invest the spell and the desired outcome with your emotions and energy.

2 If you wish to use a specific element as a focus, then decide which one is most appropriate and collect items to represent that energy.

3 Plan how you will visualize your goal. This is the essence of the magick and very important to your outcome. The moment you start visualizing the resolution of a magickal need is the moment you begin to create the changes in your deep mind necessary for the magick to manifest. Don't skimp on visualization. Enjoy it!

4 Gather candles, stones, or whatever else you intend to use as a catalyst to send the energy you will raise. Empower those items with your personal energy as you focus upon your goal. Remember: *Clear visualization* is the key to *all* successful magic!

5 Decide upon your words of power, the words or chant you will use to focus and raise energy. You may write them out, or simply remember the key phrases you wish to use as you improvise.

6 If you wish to use a special deity or mythic figure in your magick, decide on which one or ones, and on how you will evoke, invoke, and/or honor them. You may wish to write out special prayers or blessings and memorize them.

7 If you adhere to the Celtic practice of feeding beings called from the Otherworld, do so now, before embarking on any other ritual or magickal efforts.

8 Decide when and where you want to do the spell. Where will depend largely upon your own resources and preferences. When can be anytime you like or need the magick, or you may wish to take into consideration moon phases and/or other astrological influences. This is especially true of times which correspond to the peak power times of any deities, etc., whom you wish to work with.

9 At the appropriate time gather what you will use and go to the place where you will perform the spell. This can be at your altar, outdoors, or anywhere else that feels comfortable.

10 Cast your protective circle or utilize some other form of protection which you can count on.

11 Your ritual is now beginning in earnest. Invite whatever elementals, faeries, spirits you wish to have present as you work. They should always be welcome, but they are not necessary for spell work. If you wish to use them for spellwork, then have ready a speech or words of honor and welcome which tell them what you'd like from them.

12 Make a clear statement of your purpose.

13 Clear your mind and begin clearly visualizing your goal.

14 Evoke or invoke any deities you may wish to work with. Offer them food or honors as befits your tradition or personal practice.

15 Raise energy within yourself and pour it into the magickal object(s), or have your deity help you.

16 Use your words of power, light your candles, charge your stones, dance or sing, align yourself with a deity. Do whatever you have decided to do to focus your attention and raise energy. If you are working with other beings, encourage them to raise energy with you. Get them to dance and infuse the area just outside of your circle with as much energy as possible.

17 Take advantage of natural phenomena which can help you raise energy. A storm, for instance, is an excellent source of energy which any witch can draw on to help feed a spell. Just feel yourself becoming a part of the storm, and feel yourself psychically drawing on the storm's vast stores of energy as you seek to raise your own energies or cone of power.

18 When you feel you have put as much energy into the spell as you can, send the energy out to do your will. Relax, throw up your arms, raise a tool, kneel, send out a cone of power, or do whatever else makes you feel the energy being sent. Be sure to direct it out from you visually as well. Also send out any energy raised for you by other entities at your circle side.

19 You should finish your spell with words such as "So Mote It Be." Mote is an obsolete word for "must." These words are synonymous with "Amen," "So It Is," and "It is Done." It is a statement of completion and an affirmation that you know your magick is successful. All magick is worked from the point of view that the desired goal is already manifest—it will not *come* to be, but it *is*. Always phrase your magickal desires in the present tense such as, "I have love in my life now," or, "My bills are now paid in full." Talking of magick happening in the future will keep it forever in the future, always just out of reach.

20 Meditate briefly on your goal. Visualize it as manifest. Smile, and know the magick is at work.

21 Release the energy of any evoked or invoked deities.

22 Thank and dismiss all faeries, spirits, and deities who have come to witness or aid your magick.

23 Ground your excess energy and open your circle.

24 Record your spell in your Magickal Diary or Book of Shadows with the date, time, weather conditions and any astrological data you wish to include. This will be useful later when you have done enough spells to look for patterns. For example, you may see that your most efficacious spells were done on Sundays or when it was cloudy or snowing or when you had Gnomes present, worked with a particular deity, when you burned green candles, or when the moon was full. Everyone has different affinities. These patterns will help pick the best times for your own spell work.

25 Until you achieve your magickal goal you should spend some time each day focusing on it by clearly visualizing it as a *fait accompli*. These added boosts of daily energy can often mean the difference between success and failure.

THE STEPS OF PATHWORKING

Golden slumbers kiss your eyes,
Smiles awake you when you rise....
—Thomas Dekker

FOR USING PATHS ALREADY WRITTEN

1 Choose a path that appeals to you or represents a need you feel or a goal you currently have.

2 If you are unfamiliar with meditation, or are out of practice, you may wish to begin working with some meditation exercises whose purpose is to help train your mind to focus in accordance with your will.

3 Wear loose, comfortable clothing, or go nude.

4 Use incense or music as you desire to help set the mood and aid your concentration.

5 Find a quiet and warm spot in which to work and stick to it whenever possible. Make sure you will *not* be disturbed.

6 Place yourself in an altered state of consciousness. Rhythmic breathing and steadily focusing your mind for several minutes will usually do it for you.

7 Use the "Beginning the Journey" reading, or a method of your own liking, to induce a meditative or altered state, or use a method of your own choosing if that is what you are used to.

8 Read, or have read, or have played back to you, the text of your chosen pathworking.

9 Unless there is an emergency to deal with, always finish a path once you have begun.

10 Read the "Coming Home" reading, or one of your own liking, to return to your normal consciousness, or return by whatever method you are used to. It is a wise practice to use the same route both in and out of the inner-world.

11 Make a loud noise, ring a bell, clap, recite words such as "The rite is done," or do something else to signal both your conscious and sub-conscious mind that the pathworking is at an end, and you are functioning in your normal waking consciousness.

12 Write down in your magickal journal or Book of Shadows whatever information from the working you wish to record for later study.

13 If you wish to discuss your pathworking experience with a friend who did not journey with you, do it only after you have had time to contemplate all its meanings for yourself.

14 If you prefer pathworking with a group you should all take a few moments to make some personal notes before you begin comparing experiences. This is so that someone's vision will not cloud your own encounter.

STEPS FOR WRITING/USING YOUR OWN PATHS

1 Form in your own mind exactly what you wish the pathworking to accomplish, e.g.; meeting a deity, helping with basic visualization, doing an inner-plane ritual, etc.

2 If you wish to work from myths, read through as many as you can find which are pertinent to your goal(s).

3 If you are creating a path from mythical sources you should read, re-read, and thoroughly familiarize yourself with it beforehand.

4 If you are creating a path from scratch without the aid of myths, you need to spend several days mulling over exactly what you wish the path to "feel" like. Know what ambience, tone, or atmosphere you wish to achieve before you put pen to paper.

5 Sketch out a broad rough draft which outlines the major highlights of the journey. This is so that you can take yourself from high point to high point without getting snagged in a story or with symbolism which is irrelevant to your goal.

6 Go back through your rough draft and begin filling in details, including as much symbolism as you can use. Consult books on dream interpretations, archetypes, and occult symbolism to aid you if necessary.

7 When you are satisfied that you have the pathworking you want written out in perfect detail, you should record it for yourself, or have a friend prepared to read it to you.

8 Follow steps three through fourteen in the previous section, "For Using Paths Already Written."

9 If, after your initial journey, you discover things about your pathworking that you wish to change you should feel free to do so. There is probably no pathworking in print which did not go through numerous revisions and testing before being printed.

10 The paths you write should evolve as you do or else they are worthless. Look over not only your own, but also other, pathworking texts periodically to ascertain if any changes need to be made to reflect your ever-changing spiritual needs.

RESOURCES AND MERCHANTS GUIDE

Ah, how remote, forlorn
Sounded the sad, sweet horn
In forest gloom enchanted!
—"Broceliande," a Breton poem

THE FOLLOWING BUSINESSES stock and sell items of interest to Pagans or operate organizations of interest to Celtic/Pagan people. When contacting any of them by mail be sure to enclose a self-addressed stamped envelope (SASE), or an International Reply Coupon (IRC) when addressing mail to a foreign country (that's for *any* country other than the one in which you live).

At the time of this writing all of the following organizations are active and all of the merchants are in business, and most of them are very reputable and on a very solid footing. But keep in mind that groups and businesses can move, and even the best of them can occasionally fail. Call directory assistance or the Better Business Bureau in the cities listed if you need further assistance.

HERBS, OILS, AND INCENSES

American Herb Association
P.O. Box 353
Rescue, CA 95672

This umbrella body does not sell herbs, but instead seeks to promote knowledge of and use of herbs. They can recommend reliable herb dealers throughout the United States.

Balefire
6504 Vista Ave.
Wauwatosa, WI 53213

This mail order company carries a large stock of brews, oils, and incenses designed for specific Pagan needs such as scrying, spirit contact, and spellwork. Write for free catalog.

Capriland's Herb Farm
Silver Street
Coventry, CT 06238

Write for free price list of dried herbs and herbal books. Capriland also holds special classes on herb use and has herbal lunches at various times throughout the year. Reservations are a must!

Companion Plants
7247 N. Coolville Ridge Rd.
Athens, OH 45701

Catalog $2.00.

Dreaming Spirit
P.O. Box 4263
Danbury, CT 06813-4263

Natural, homemade incenses and resins, oils, and tools for using them. Dreaming Spirit welcomes queries about custom blends of incenses or oils. The $2.00 for their catalog is refundable with your first order.

Halcyon Herb Company
Box 7153 L
Halcyon, CA 93421

Sells not only magickal herbs, but also staffs, brooms, cloaks, drums, and other items of interest to Pagan folk. Current catalog $5.00.

Herbal Endeavors
3618 S. Emmons Ave.
Rochester Hills, MI 48063

Catalog $2.50.

Indiana Botanical Gardens
P.O. Box 5
Hammond, IN 46325

Sellers of herbs, teas, charcoal blocks, herbal medicines and some books on alternative health care. Request free catalog.

Marah
Box 948
Madison, NJ 07940

Sellers of herbs, incenses, oil blends and other tools. Catalog, $1.00.

Mountain Butterfly Herbs
106 Roosevelt Lane
Hamilton, MT 59840

Write for current information and prices.

Leydet Oils
P.O. Box 2354
Fair Oaks, CA 95628

Sellers of fine essential oils. Catalog and price list is $2.00.

Sandy Mush Herb Nursery
Rt. 2, Surrett Cove
Lancaster, NC 28748

Has over 800 in-stock herbs, dye plants, and other foliage. Catalog contains helpful herbal tips as well as recipes. Catalog $4.00, refundable with your first order.

Wildwood Fragrances
717 Spruce St.
Boulder, CO 80306

Creates and sells oils, perfumes, potpourris, incenses, oils, etc., many constructed to align with the energies of deities or festivals. Also offers a mail-order course in blending ritual oils, incenses, etc. Catalog is $2.00, refundable with your first order.

STONES AND STONE INFORMATION

Lapidary Journal
P.O. Box 80937
San Diego, CA 92138

This is a publication for rock collectors which contains information on stone origins and their lore. It also has ads from companies which sell stones, tumblers, jewelry mountings, etc. Write for subscription information.

MUSIC

Circle Sanctuary
P.O. Box 219
Mt. Horeb, WI 53572

Circle sells printed and recorded music written by and for Pagans. Request a sample copy of their excellent periodical for more information. Sample copy $4.50.

Green Linnet Records
70 Turner Hill
New Canaan, CT 06840

Sells recorded Celtic music. Request free catalog.

Postings
Dept. 654
P.O. Box 8001
Hilliard, OH 43026-8001

Send $3.00 for a year of video and audio catalogs. They are sellers of videos and off-beat audio tapes and CD's. Their audio catalog usually includes a good selection of folk and ethnic music.

Southern Music Company
1100 Broadway
San Antonio, TX 78212

(210) 226-8167. Publishers and sellers of printed music, including folk and ethnic music. They publish no catalog, but stock virtually everything which is in print. Contact by phone for information on placing orders.

Rego Irish Records and Tapes
64 New Hyde Park Rd.
Garden City, NY 11530-3909

Sellers of Irish and Scottish music and videos. Music also available in CD format. Fascinating quarterly catalog, $2.00 for most recent issue.

Robin Williamson Productions
BCM 4797
London, England
WC1N 3XX

Producer of Celtic books and musical recordings.

Winners!
Valley of the Sun Publishing
Box 683
Ashland, OR 97520-0023

Publishers and sellers of New Age music and of mind/body video and audio tapes, including tapes to aid meditation, past-life recall and astral projection. First copy of their mag-a-log is free upon request, and will continue to be sent free for up to a year if you order from them.

BOOKS

Dover Books
31 East 2nd Street
Mineola, NY 11501

Dover will send a free catalog upon request. Titles cover a broad range of subject matter including mythology, needlecraft, art, celebrations, nature crafts, music, etc. Also in stock are reprints of

works of Pagan historical interest such as the *Malleus Maleficarum*.

Llewellyn's New Worlds of Mind and Spirit
(Formerly *New Times*)
P.O. Box 64383
Dept. 269
St. Paul, MN 55164-0383

This informative catalog is produced by one of the world's largest and oldest sellers and publishers of books on metaphysics, magick, Paganism, astrology, and alternative spirituality. This mag-a-log contains book reviews, articles, interviews, and a list of upcoming events, as well as order forms for their large line of excellent publications. One year's subscription $10.00.

Pyramid Books
P.O. Box 3333, Altid Park
Chelmsford, MA 01824-0933

Sellers of metaphysical, Pagan, magick books, and beautiful Pagan jewelry and statuettes. Catalog $2.00.

MAGICKAL, RITUAL, PAGAN SUPPLIES, JEWELRY, AND ODDS AND ENDS

Abyss
RR #1, Box 213 F
Chester, MA 01011

(413) 623-2155. Request this free catalog of magickal supplies. Carries many books and jewelry with a Celtic flavor.

Aphrodite's Emporium
628 N. 4th Ave.
Tucson, AZ 85705

Sells books, jewelry, oils, candles, and gifts with a Pagan focus. Catalog $3.50.

Compass Grove
Box 100
Hartland Four Corners, VT 05049

The full-color catalog is worth the $5.00 asking price. Offers a wide range of Pagan products.

DEA Mail Order Company
2968 West Ina Rd., Suite 282
Tucson, AZ 85741

DEA sells cast-iron cauldrons, chalices, crowns, swords, drums, and custom-made robes and cloaks—things of particular interest to Celtic Pagans. Write for catalog.

The Flame
P.O. Box 117
Korbel, CA 95550

The Flame bills its catalog as "complete." They carry all manner of ritual and magickal items. Catalog $2.00.

Gypsy Heaven
115 S. Main St.
New Hope, PA 18938

(215) 862-5251. Bills itself as "The Witch Shop of New Hope." Request catalog of magickal supplies, oils, jewelry, statues, cards, etc.

Isis Metaphysical
5701 E. Colfax
Denver, CO 80220

(303) 321-0867. Write for information, catalog price varies. Isis carries jewelry, incense, oils, herbs, books, and periodicals. They carry a wide stock of books on all metaphysical topics, and what they don't carry they will gladly order for you. It is also a pleasant gathering center for local Pagans and other "New Age" thinkers. They sponsor workshops, lectures, and classes. (A few years ago Isis was the target of arson by an unknown party. As Isis continues to grow as a gathering place for those seeking alternative spirituality, the threat of repeat violence is likely. Any protective energy you can send their way would no doubt be greatly appreciated.)

The Magic Door
P.O. Box 8349
Salem, MA 01971

All manner of magickal and ritual supplies. Request free catalog and ordering information.

Moon Scents and Magickal Blends, Inc.
P.O. Box 1588-C
Cambridge, MA 02238

Sells all manner of magickal paraphernalia and books. Request free catalog.

Mythic Force
92-734 Nenelea St.
Ewa Beach, HI 96707

(808) 672-3988. Jewelry, art, T-shirts, glassware, and notecards copied from Pagan designs and ancient museum pieces—many of them Celtic in origin. Catalog is $1.00, and will be credited against your first order.

Nature's Jewelry
27 Industrial Ave.
Chelmsford, MA 01824-3692

Sellers of seasonal and nature-oriented jewelry at very reasonable prices. Certain items come and go seasonally, and new items are always being added to the basic stock. Very environmentally aware. Designs include moons, suns, autumn leaves, faeries, snowflakes, cornucopia, jack o'lanterns, dolphins, snakes, and holly. A recent catalog included a set of dangling pewter earrings shaped like brooms, and a silver "father of the wind" ring. Also an excellent source for gift exchange items for Pagans gatherings and festivals. Write to request a free catalog.

POTO
11002 Massachusetts Ave.
Westwood, CA 90025-3510

(310) 575-3717. POTO is short for "Procurer of the Obscure." Their mail order catalog features services, and rare books and herbs for those in the magickal life. Special orders and requests always welcome. Send $5.00 for current catalog and ordering information.

Sacred Spirit Products
P.O. Box 8163
Salem, MA 01971-8163

Sellers of books, magickal tools, herbs, incense, and other occult items. Catalog $3.00.

Sidda
1430 Willamette #119
Eugene, OR 97401

Crafters of ritual blades and magick mirrors. Send $1.00 for brochure.

PAGAN PERIODICALS

Circle Network News
P.O. Box 219
Mt. Horeb, WI 53572

This quarterly Pagan publication is nothing less than excellent. It is full of well written articles and contacts. Circle sponsors Pagan gatherings throughout the year and helps Pagans all over the world connect with each other. At this writing a one year subscription is $15 by bulk mail to USA addresses, $20 first class to USA, Canada, and Mexico, and $27 elsewhere. Payment must be in US funds. Write for other subscription information, or request a sample copy currently priced at $4.50.

The Cauldron
Caemorgan Cottage
Caemorgan Rd.
Cardigan, Dyfed
SA43 1QU
Wales

Send one IRC for updated subscription information. This quarterly covers many nature spirituality paths.

The Green Egg
P.O. Box 1542
Ukiah, CA 95482

This was the reigning queen of Pagan periodicals in the early 1970s, and has been successfully revived. Contains beautiful artwork and well-researched articles. Subscriptions to this quarterly are $15 in the USA and $21 in Canada. Write for other subscription information. Sample copy, $4.95.

Hecate's Loom
Box 5206, Station B
Victoria, BC
Canada V8R 6N4

A quality journal of Paganism. Yearly rate for US subscriptions $13. Write for full information.

Llewellyn's New Worlds of Mind and Spirit (Formerly *New Times*)
P.O. Box 64383
Dept. 269
St. Paul, MN 55164-0383

See preceding write-up under heading of "Books."

International Wiccan/Pagan Press Alliance
P.O. Box 1392
Mechanicsburg, PA 17055

An umbrella organization for an international group of press operators, writers, and others interested in Pagan publication and information. Because they are in contact with presses and writers all over the world, they are an excellent place to begin networking efforts. Write with a SASE for information about their services and member publications. Annual dues are currently $18 a year.

PERIODICALS, ORGANIZATIONS, AND PRODUCTS OF INTEREST TO CELTIC PAGANS

Ar nDraiocht Fein
P.O. Box 72
Dumont, NJ 07628

This is both the newsletter and name of a well-respected Druidic society founded by Isaac Bonewitz. Those interested in this aspect of Celtic Paganism should contact them with a SASE for more information.

Blarney
373D Route 46 West
Fairfield, NJ 07004-9880

Blarney (cont.)

(201) 882-1269. Importers of fine Irish goods including Waterford Crystal, Belleek China, coats of arms, Claddagh jewelry, and woolen clothing. Some items are costly, but worth their price. Catalog $4.00.

Circle of the Dragon
10 rue R. Mirassou
Bordeau 33800
France

Though this networking newsletter emphasises Frankish/Germanic traditions, it can also be a valuable source for information on Pagan traditions in Celtic Brittany. Write with an IRC for more information.

Dun Na Beatha
2 Brathwic Place
Brodick, Isle of Arran
Scotland KA27 8BN

An organization of one of the Scottish Pagan traditions dedicated to preserving and studying Celtic Paganism, especially as it pertains to Scotland. Write for information about their quarterly publication.

Emania
Department of Archaeology
Queen's University
Belfast,
Northern Ireland BT7 1NN

This is the journal of the Navan Fort Research Group which studies Celtic pre-history. Write for information.

Irish Castle Gift and Mail Order
537 Geary
San Francisco, CA 94115

(415) 474-7432. Sells a large variety of items imported from Ireland. Call for information.

Irish Imports Limited, Corp.
1735 Massachusetts Ave.
Cambridge, MA

1-800-244-2511 (for orders). (617) 354-2511 (for information).This large and reputable company sells Irish imports. Call for information.

International Red Garters
P.O. Box 162046
Sacramento, CA 95816

An eight-times-a-year publication and umbrella organization for followers of the various English traditions. Prints much controversial material. Annual subscriptions in United States are $13, outside $25—US funds only.

The Irish Texts Society
c/o The Royal Bank of Scotland
22 Whitehall
London, SW1
England

Published translations of the old Irish myths and provides supporting texts such as notes, glossaries, and commentaries. Write for information and price list. Another Irish Texts society is located in Dublin at Trinity University and is attached to the Institute for Advanced Studies. Either address can provide you with, or direct you to, modern copies of original text (read Irish language) or translation texts of the Irish myths.

Keltic Fringe
Box 251 RD #1
Uniondale, PA 18470

This fledgling quarterly shows great promise. It approaches Celtic studies—which they spell "Keltic"— from many angles. Focus is not only on mythology and culture, but on present-day issues facing the Celtic nations and their people. Sample copy $3. Subscription $10 per year.

Keltria
P.O. Box 33284-C
Minneapolis, MN 55433

This popular magazine focuses on Druidism and Celtic magick. Write for current subscription information.

McNamara's Green
P.O. 15822
Seattle, WA 98115

This catalog carries art, jewelry, stickers, sun-catchers, and jewelry with a Celtic flair. Most of it is rather inexpensive. I have ordered from them for years and have always been happy with their products. Catalog and annual supplements $2.00.

Ninnau
11 Post Terrace
Basking Ridge, NJ 07920

This ethnic periodical covers news of interest to Welsh persons in North America. Also deals with history and culture. Write for subscription information.

Secretary, OBOD
P.O. Box 1333
Lewes, E. Surrey
England BN7 3ZG

The Order of Bards, Ovates and Druids currently has a correspondence course available. Write with SASE or IRC for more information.

Really Wild 'n Mild Celts
P.O. Box 280114
Dallas, TX 75228-1014

Send $1.00 plus and SASE for information on RWMC's God and Goddess art, divinations, etc.

Reformed Druids of North America
Box 6775
San Jose, CA 95150

Send an SASE for information on this modern Druidic group, organized in Minnesota in 1963.

Revue D'Etudes Druidiques
Bothuan, Commana
29237 Sizun
Bretagne
France

A journal of the studies of Breton Celtic times, particularly the study of Breton Druidism. Publication is written in French. Write for information.

Shadow
School of Scottish Studies
27 George Square
Edinburgh,
Scotland EH8 9LD

This is the journal of the Traditional Cosmology Society. Write for information.

Shenchas
Celtic Research and Folklore Society
Isle of Arran,
Scotland

This journal studies all aspects of Celtic folklore, particularly the oral traditions. Write for information.

OTHER CELTIC SHOPS AND BOOK SELLERS

MOST LARGE AMERICAN and Canadian cities have at least one import shop from a Celtic country (usually Ireland because of the large number of Irish people who emigrated to North America). The following shops are some of the better known. As of this writing they do not do mail-order, but would be more than willing to help you find items if you were to drop in. If you live in or near a major city, or are planning a trip to one, check telephone listings for import shops (look under "Gifts" or "Books") which carry goods from Celtic countries.

Books International, Inc. (Book Imports)
2015-F W. Gray
Houston, TX

British Antiques
5415 Magazine
New Orleans, LA

Celtic Currents
O'Hare International Airport
Chicago, IL

Emerald Isle Express
50 Billings Rd.
Quincy, MA

The English Shop
5360 Peachtree
Atlanta, GA

Grandma O'Donnell's
6681 N. Northwest Hwy.
Chicago, IL

House of Ireland
238 O'Farrell
San Francisco, CA

The Irish Conoisseur
1232 Wakegun Rd.
Glenview, IL

The Irish Cottage
18828 Sloane Ave.
Cleveland, OH

The Irish Shop
723 Toulouse
New Orleans, LA

La Cite Des Livres (French/Breton Books)
2306 Westwood Blvd.
West Los Angeles, CA

Scottish Tartan Shop, Inc.
840 Post
San Francisco, CA

The Scottish Connection, Inc.
At Marina Bay
North Quincy, MA

The Shannon Shop
13426 Clayton Rd.
St. Louis, MO

Teahan Irish Imports
2505 N. Harlem Ave.
Chicago, IL

ETHNIC CULTURAL SOCIETIES

THESE ORGANIZATIONS CAN be found in virtually every city and town in the United States and Canada, and they can be a great help to you in finding out more about the folklore and folkways of your Celtic heritage. Many of them run language classes, cultural literacy classes, and teach native dance and music. At these gatherings there are often items of interest to Celtic Pagans for sale such as dance music tapes, inexpensive reproduction jewelry, and walking staffs. To find these organizations, first look in your phone book or the phone book of a nearby city for a contact number. More often though, you will have to keep an eye on the local newspaper for news about where and when the local ethnic organizations meet. If you have no luck there, go to your library and ask a librarian to help you locate them.

MEADE

American Meade Association
P.O. 206
Ostrander, OH 43061

This organizations promotes and keeps alive the art and lore of meade. Also provides access to various recipes and meade making supplies. Membership is $10 a year.

SEASONAL/RITUAL ART AND POETRY

Circle Network News
P.O. Box 219
Mt. Horeb, WI 53572

See write-up under Pagan Periodicals.

Ideals Magazine
P.O. Box 148000
Nashville, TN 37214-8000

Ideals has been publishing beautiful seasonal material since just after World War II. They publish eight standard issues a year plus some specialty issues. Current copies can be found in most bookstores, and back issues in many second hand bookstores.

NATIONAL/INTERNATIONAL PAGAN ORGANIZATIONS

ASIDE FROM THE large organizations listed below, many regions have smaller organizations which provide support, networking, and a sense of community to solitary Pagans. Please look in the pages of Pagan publications for these addresses.

The Fellowship of Isis
Clonegal Castle
Enniscorthy
County Wexford, Ireland

This is an international organization of Goddess worshipers with a membership of around 10,000. Send one IRC for response to inquiries.

Lady Liberty League
c/o Circle Sanctuary
Box 219
Mt. Horeb, WI 53572

LLL involves itself in aiding Pagans who face legal difficulties due to their religion.

The Pagan Federation
BM Box 7097
London WC1N 3XX
England

Founded in 1971, this British-based organization seeks to make itself a forum for all European Pagan traditions, and to promote understanding, networking, and exchange of ideas between these diverse groups. Send one SASE or two IRCs for membership information.

Pagan Spirit Alliance
c/o Circle Sanctuary
Box 219
Mt. Horeb, WI 53572

For membership application to PSA, send SASE to Circle.

Witches' Anti-Defamation League
c/o Black Forest Publishing
P.O. Box 1392
Mechanicsburg, Pa 17055

Modeled on the very effective Jewish Anti-Defamation League, this group actively combats discrimination against persons involved in nature religions. Include SASE for response.

Witches' League for Public Awareness
P.O. Box 8736
Salem, MA 01970

Include a business-sized SASE for response. This organization seeks to educate the public about nature religions and tackles discrimination issues.

Witches Today
Box 221
Levittown, PA 19059

An organization whose goal is educating the general public about Witchcraft and Paganism, and in maintaining religious freedom for everyone. If you are interested in aiding their efforts, please write.

MYTHIC FIGURES CROSS-REFERENCE

...I hold a sovereign reign
Over the lands...and the water they contain:
Lo! the bound of the wide world around
Falleth in my domain.
—James Whitcomb Riley

THE FOLLOWING LISTS are categorized by function, need, or association, and they provide a framework for helping you choose a deity or heroic figure to aid you in achieving your magickal, ritual, and spiritual goals. These categories are general and should be used with the written entries for each figure in order to determine exactly how their power can specifically be harnessed. For example, to determine the exact type of knowledge that the Goddess Aife can help you attain, you need to know something about her myth which can be accomplished by scanning the encapsulated version in this book.

Allow this text to be your guide, a firmly planted signpost to start you on your magickal journey, but don't let your quest for knowledge about any deity or myth stop here. The best way to decide for yourself which figure(s) you should merge with or call upon for your need(s) is to read and study the Celtic myths—in all their many versions—for yourself.

ANIMALS, CONCERNS OF

Achtan
Aine
Ardwinna
Artio
Boadicea
Brid
Cadog the Wise
Cally Berry
Cernunnos
Cormac MacArt
Dagda, The
Diancecht
Eostre
Epona
Flidais
Gwyngelli
Herve the Blind
Merlin
Ossian
Saba
Tuan MacCarell
Turrean

ASTRAL PROJECTION

Balor
Beli
Bellah Postil
Coll
Ethne
Garlon
Grainne
Lavercam
Liagin
Luaths Lurgann
Manann
Sgilti

BANISHING/DESTRUCTIVE MAGICK

Aige
Aine
Badb
Cuchulain
Cythrawl
Diancecht
Elphame, Queen of

Macha
Morca
Mandred
Morrigan, The
Muireartach

BARDS

Adna
Ai
Amergin
Cairbre
Craftiny
Gwyddion
Latiaran
Laustic Le Rossignol
Lavercam
Merlin
O'Carolan
Ossian
Sion, Llewellyn
Taliesin

BEAUTY/PHYSICAL FITNESS
- Aengus MacOg
- Cliodna
- Creirwy
- Deirdre
- Edain
- Emer
- Fand
- Gebann
- Liagin
- Luaths Lurgann

BIRDS, ASSOCIATED WITH
- Aife
- Aitherne
- Arthur, King
- Badb
- Blodeuwedd
- Bran
- Cliodna
- Dechtere
- Devorgilla
- Edain
- Epona
- Fionnuala
- Garbh Ogh
- Gwion Bach
- Laustic Le Rossignol
- Liban
- Llew
- Macha
- Marcassa, Princess
- Midhir
- Morrigan, The
- Munanna
- Nemain
- Nemglan
- Ogyrvran
- Owain
- Tuan MacCarrell
- Uairebhuidhe
- Uar the Cruel

BLARNEY, GIFT OF
- Ailbe
- Baile of the Honeyed Speech
- Oghma

CHILDREN, CONCERNS OF
- Ban-Chuideachaigh Moire
- Biddy Mamionn

CHILDREN, CONCERNS OF (CONT.)
- Brid
- Caireen
- Dagda, The
- Dana
- Deae Matres
- Don
- Elffin
- Epona
- Gwyar
- Henwen
- Macha
- MacKay
- Modron

CLASSIC COUPLES
- Abelard and Heloise
- Arthur and Guinevere
- Baile and Ailinn
- Diarmuid and Grainne
- Dwyvan and Dwyvach
- Froach and Findabar
- Garient and Enid
- Gog and Magog
- Merlin and Vivienne
- Naoise and Deirdre
- Nola and Gwennolaik
- Culhwch and Olwen
- Oscar and Aidin
- Ossian and Niamh
- Tristan and Isolde

CLEAR THINKING/WISDOM
- Aeval
- Avagdu
- Baile of the Honeyed Speech
- Ban Naomha
- Blodeuwedd
- Caradoc
- Cebhfhionn
- Cerridwen
- Connla
- Dagda, The
- Feinius Farsaidh
- Fergus MacRoi
- Finegas
- Fintaan
- Fionn MacCumhal
- Gawain
- Giona MacLugha

CLEAR THINKING/WISDOM (CONT.)
- Goll MacMorna
- Gronw
- Irgalach
- Jud-Hael, King
- Llevelys
- Llewellyn
- Llud
- Lludd Llaw Ereint
- Lugh
- Mac Do Tho
- Macha
- Moingfhion
- Morann
- Muinremuir
- Odras
- Oghma
- Robin Ddu
- Uath MacImoman
- Ugainy the Great

COMPASSION/CARING, LESSONS OF
- Bealcu
- Bres
- Elen
- Finegas
- Guildeluec
- Iouenn
- Irgalach
- Luinge Fer
- Melusine
- Mervyn
- Miller of Lac de Leguer
- Neva

COMMUNICATION
- Brid
- Gadel
- Goidel
- Gwrhyr
- Oghma
- Rosmerta
- Teutates

COOPERATION, LESSONS IN
- Mac Do Tho
- Miller of Lac de Leguer
- Princess of the Sun

COUNTRY, AID IN SERVING ONE'S

Alain Barbe-Torte
Arthur, King
Bran
Brian Boru, King
Cartimandua
Caswallawn
Drem
Grainne Ni Malley
Morvan Lez-Breiz
Nomenoe
Owen Lawgoch

COURAGE, TO GAIN

Anluan
Art MacConn
Artio
Cuchulain
Cymidui Cymeinfoll
Dahud-Ahes
Froach
Goidel
Goll MacMorna
Green Knight, The
Llasar Llaesgyfnewid
Maeve, Queen
Mandred
Oscar
Ratis
Scathach

CRAFTSMANSHIP/SMITHING

Airmid
Brid
Credne
Goibniu
Govannon
Luchtain
Llud
Lugh
Miach
Partholan
Tigernmas, King
Teutates
Wayland the Smith

CREATIVE BLOCKAGES, OVERCOMING

Aerten
Aille
Amergin
Brid
Canola
Credne
Oghma
Ossian
Taliesin

CREATIVE STIMULATORS

Adna
Aengus MacOg
Amergin
Brid
Cairbre
Canola
Credne
Eadon
Emer
Fachea
Goibniu
Goidel
Laustic Le Rossignol
Lavercam
Ossian
Sion, Llewellyn
Taliesin

CRONE GODDESSES

Badb
Browach
Cailleach
Carravogue
Ess Euchen
Macha
Moingfhion
Nicevenn
Nemain
Mala Liath
Morrigan, The
Muireartach
Elphame, Queen of

DISPUTES, SETTLING

Cadog the Wise
Merlin
Morann

DIVINATION

Amerach
Arca Dubh
Badb
Ban Naomha
Bran
Caer
Caradoc
Cathbad
Cathlion
Cerridwen
Corra
Coventina
Deirdre
Drem
Epona
Fedelma
Feithline
Fionn MacCumhal
Flaithius
Idris the Giant
Gabaigline
Gwendydd
Lavercam
Mandred
Merlin
Mesgegra, King
Nemglan
Niall of the Nine Hostages
Scathach
Sithehenn

DREAM WORK

Aengus MacOg
Caer
Canola
Cartimandua
Dechtere
Drem
Epona
Epos Olloatir
Mael Duin
Marcassa, Princess
Merlin
Rhiannon
Rhonabwy
Triple Goddess, The

FAERY CONTACT (CONT.)

Llyr
Manann
O'Carolan
Olwen
Onaugh
Shoney

FATHER GODS

Arthur, King
Dagda, The
Dis Pater
Finvarra
Fisher King, The
Hu the Mighty
Lugh
Mathonwy
Owen Lawgoch
Semion

FAMILY MATTERS

Achall
Achtan
Ain
Airmid
Degad
Devorgilla
Fionnuala
Goleuddydd
Gwennolaik
Iaine
Luaths Lurgann

FEAR, OVERCOMING

Dagda, The
Ossian
Merlin
Miller of Lac de Leguer
Niamh of the Golden Hair

FEMININE POWER

Arianrhod
Biddy Early
Cartimandua
Condwiramur
Ebha Ni Murchu
Eri of the Golden Hair
Findabar
Grainne
Grainne Ni Malley

FEMININE POWER (CONT.)

Kele-De
Maeve, Queen
Nessa
Olwen
Rhiannon Rhin Branwd
Sheila-na-gig
Smirgat
Vennolandua

FERTILITY

Alisanos
Amaethaon
Anu
Arianrhod
Artio
Bebo
Becuna Cneisgel
Blathnat
Bo Find
Boann
Brid
Caolinn
Dana
Dagda, The
Damara
Deae Matres
Delbchaem
Dis Pater
Don
Epona
Ernmas
Essus
Finchoem
Fisher King, The
Green Man, The
Habondia
Henwen
Hu the Mighty
Ialonus
Idath
Inghean Bhuidhe
Mabon
Modron
MacCecht
Magog
Messbuachallo
Murna of the White Neck
Nantosuelta
Neit

FERTILITY (CONT.)

Nemglan
Partholan
Rhiannon
Semion
Taillte
Tannus
Teyrnon

FIRE DEITIES

Aibheaog
Aine
Brid
Kai
Latiaran
Len of the Many Hammers
Llew
Lugh
MacKay
MacGreine
Princess of the Sun
Sithehenn
Sul

FRIENDSHIP/LOYALTY

Abelard
Achall
Airmid
Arawen
Enid
Ferdia
Fiacha
Id
Laeg
Lavercam
Luaths Lurgann
Luduenn
Gugemar
Gwennolaik
Heloise
Laustic Le Rossignol
Mervyn
Miller of Lac de Leguer
Naoise
Nola
Pryderi
Pwyll
Rohand

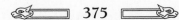

GEISE (HONOR VOW), KEEPING OF A

Airmid
Cano
Conaire
Diarmuid
Fergus MacRoi
Iouenn
Morvan Lez-Breiz
Pwyll

HARVEST/GRAIN DEITIES

Artio
Bran
Cernunnos
Cerridwen
Crom Cruaich
Deae Matres
Epona
Erce
Essus
Grannos
Habondia
Llew
Lugh
Mabon
Modron
Nantosuelta
Taillte

HEALING

Aengus MacAedh
Aengus MacOg
Aibheaog
Airmid
Argante
Biddy Mamionn
Borvo
Caolainn
Cebhfhionn
Craftiny
Diancecht
Grannos
Habetrot
Lady of the Lake
Laeg
LeFay
Liban
Marcassa, Princess
Meg the Healer

HEALING (CONT.)

Merlin
Miach
Ossian
Rosmerta
Sirona
Sul
Wayland the Smith

HERBALISM

Airmid
Cernunnos
Flidais

HUNT, DEITIES OF THE

Arawen
Cally Berry
Cernunnos
Flidais
Garbh Ogh
Gwyn Ap Nuad
Mabon

INSPIRATION (OF OTHERS)

Amergin
Canola
Coll
Credne
Dana
Don
Fachea
Miach
Veleda

INSPIRATION (OF SELF)

Amergin
Brid
Canola
Cebhfhionn
Cerridwen
Coll
Craftiny
Credne
Fachea
Merlin

JUSTICE, LESSONS OF/GOOD JUDGMENT

Ailill Olum
Cadog the Wise
Ess Euchen

JUSTICE, LESSONS OF/GOOD JUDGMENT (CONT.)

Mac Do Tho
Marcia Proba
Merlin
Morann
Prince Llewellyn
Pwyll
Uath MacImoman

KNOWLEDGE (SPECIFIC)

Aife
Ailill Dubh-Dedach
Ailill Olum
Badb
Balor
Becuma
Black Knight, The
Caolainn
Camulos
Cerridwen
Conomor, King
Cymon
Derbforgaille
Fand
Finegas
Fintaan
Fionn MacCumhal
Eliduc
Fisher King, The
Green Knight, The
Guingamor
Latis
Lavercam
Melusine
Merlin
Mervyn
Morgan LeFay
Munanna
Murigen
Odras
Ol
Percival, Sir
Rob Roy MacGregor
Robin Ddu
Scota
Sion, Llewellyn
Taliesin
Turrean
Varia

KNOWLEDGE (CONT.)

Ysbadadden

LEADERSHIP

Aeval
Ambisagrus
Anluan
Arthur, King
Banbha
Brian Boru, King
Bussumarus
Cadwallon
Caswallawn
Cessair
Cormac MacArt
Cumhal
Dealgnaid
Degad
Domnu
Elen
Fergus the Great
Giona MacLugha
Lludd Llaw Ereint
Maeve, Queen
Maon the Dumb
Milesius
Niall of the Nine Hostages
Nuada of the Silver Hand
Oscar
Owen Lawgoch
Ross the Red
Rudraidhe
Ugainy the Great
Veleda
Vennolandua

LIFE CYCLE EVENTS (SPECIFIC)

Achall
Achtland
Arianrhod
Badb
Crom Cruaich
Cyhiraeth
Dhonn
Dis Pater
Gawain, Sir
Goleuddydd
Gwyar
Gwyn Ap Nuad

LIFE CYCLE EVENTS (CONT.)

Heloise
Hu the Mighty
Isolde
Laeg
Lludd Llaw Ereint
Mathonwy
Melwas
Niamh of the Golden Hair
Odras
Oghma
Ogyrvran
Rashincoatie
Samalilaith
Taillte
Tlachtga
Vivionn

LOVE/ROMANCE

Abelard
Aengus MacOg
Aidin
Ailinn
Baile of the Honeyed Speech
Bellah Postil
Branwyn
Cano
Cian
Coll
Cred
Culhwch
Diarmuid
Enid
Eochiad
Garient
Heloise
Isolde
Gronw
Gugemar
Guildeluec
Gwennolaik
Lancelot, Sir
Laustic Le Rossignol
Naoise
Niamh of the Golden Hair
Nola
Ossian
Princess of the Sun
Taranis
Tristan

MAGICK, GENERAL AID IN

Airmid
Amaethaon
Ariadne
Arianrhod
Banbha
Biddy Early
Bov the Red
Brid
Calatin
Cernunnos
Coll
Coventina
Cymidui Cymeinfoll
Dagda, The
Dana
Don
Dis Pater
Fachtna
Feinius Farsaidh
Fer Gruadh
Figol MacMamos
Gebann
Goibniu
Gronw
Guildeluec
Gwyddion
Heloise
Llasar Llaesgyfnewid
Lugh
Maelduine
Mandred
Maol
Math Ap Mathony
Merlin
Messbuachallo
Mog Ruith
Mongan
Nemetona
Nuada
Rhiannon
Robin Ddu
Scathach
Semion
Sequana
Stine Bheag O' Tarbat
Talhariran
Taliesin
Tryphna, Princess

MASCULINE POWER

Conall
Cuchulain
Dagda, The
Fionn MacCumhal
Llew
Lugh
Semion
Somhlth
Twrch Trwyth

MAY QUEENS

Blodeuwedd
Creiddylad
Damara
Delbchaen
Elphame, Queen of
Godiva
Goewin
Guinever, Queen
Olwen
Tryphyna, Princess

MENTAL PROWESS/ MATTERS OF INTELLECT

Abelard
Ailbe
Baile of the Honeyed Speech
Brid
Cebhfhionn
Cerridwen
Dagda
Emer
Finegas
Finvarra
Gwrhyr
Gwyddion
Mandred
Merlin
Nessa
O'Carolan
Robin Ddu

MOON DEITIES

Arianrhod
Cerridwen
Dechtere
Eri of the Golden Hair
Elphame, Queen of
Rhiannon
Triple Goddess, The

MOTHER GODDESSES

Arianrhod
Brid
Caolinn
Cerridwen
Corchen
Dana
Don
Epona
Habetrot
Magog
Modron
Onaugh
Scota

MUSIC (CREATIVE OR MAGICKAL)

Aengus MacOg
Ai
Aibell
Caer
Cairbre
Canola
Craftiny
Dagda, The
Gwyddion
Hu the Mighty
Ian Og MacCrimmons
Laustic Le Rossignol
Morgan LeFay
Moriath
O'Carolan
Taliesin
Tigernmas, King

NAMINGS, GUIDANCE IN

Amergin
Arawen
Braesal
Britan
Eire
Scota
Tea and Tephi

NEW BEGINNINGS

Addanc
Cessair
Dwyfach
Dwyvan
Eostre
Llew

NEW BEGINNINGS (CONT.)

Lugh
Rudraidhe

OBSTACLES, OVERCOMING

Ailbe
Merlin
Nuada of the Silver Hand
Scathach

OTHERWORLD DEITIES/ DEATH DEITIES

Arawen
Arianrhod
Badb
Bebhionn
Beltene
Cliodna
Crom Cruiach
Cythrawl
Dagda, The
Dhonn
Essus
Gwyn Ap Nuad
Luchtain
Macha
Mael Duin
Math Ap Mathonwy
Melwas
Merlin
Morgan LeFay
Morrigan, The
Muireartach
Nemglan
Niamh of the Golden Hair
Ossian
Elphame, Queen of
Rhiannon
Pwyll
Uar the Cruel

PAST-LIFE/FUTURE-LIFE MEMORY

Amergin
Anind
Arawen
Arianrhod
Badb
Balor
Bebhionn
Beli

PAST-LIFE/FUTURE-LIFE MEMORY (CONT.)

Carravogue
Cerridwen
Connla
Corchen
Cymidui Cymeinfoll
Dhonn
Dia Griene
Edain
Gwion Bach
Llasar Llaesgyfnewid
Macha
Matholwch
Nar Thuathcaech
Ochall Ochne
Taliesin
Tuan MacCarell
Sheila-na-gig

PATIENCE

Figol MacMamos
Iouenn
Luchtain
Merlin
Miller of Lac de Leguer
Morvan Lez-Breiz
Wayland the Smith

PEACE

Aerten
Caer
Gruffddap Llywelyn
Gwalchmei
Mac Da Tho
Maon the Dumb
Nissyen
Tryphyna, Princess

PERSEVERANCE

Arthur, King
Cessair
Cormac MacArt
Cuchulain
Culhwch
Cymidui Cymeinfoll
Diancecht
Dwyvach
Dwyvan
Froach

PERSEVERANCE (CONT.)

Gwyn Ap Nuad
Llasar Llaesgyfnewid
Maeve, Queen
Merlin
Miller of Lac de Leguer
Morvan Lez-Breiz
Nuada of the Silver Hand
Owen Lawgoch

PREJUDICE AND GOSSIP, OVERCOMING

Elathan
Ess Euchen
Morann
Morgan LeFay
Ninniaw and Peibaw

PROSPERITY AND ABUNDANCE

Anu
Artio
Bebo
Bladud
Bo Find
Bran
Brigantia
Buic
Cernunnos
Dagda, The
Deae Matres
Dechtere
Diwrnach the Gael
Easal
Epona
Fisher King, The
Habondia
Henwen
Liban
MacGreine
MacKay
Mark, King
Math Ap Mathonwy
Mathonwy
Midhir, King
Nair
Teutates
Sequana

PROTECTION

Aibell
Aife
Ailinn
Ain
Aine
Balor
Baile of the Honeyed Speech
Beli
Bladud
Bran
Breasal
Brian Boru, King
Brid
Brigantia
Camulos
Conall
Conchobar MacNessa
Credne
Dagda, The
Dylan
Eoghan
Fionn MacCumhal
Gawain
Glewlwyd
Goibniu
Goidel
Goll MacMorna
Govannon
Grannos
Iaine
Llew
Llud
Luchtain
Lugh
MacCecht
Mael Duin
Manann
Mandred
Merlin
Morfan
Mullo
Nemetona
Oscar
Owain
Princess of the Sun
Ratis
Ross the Red
Sandda

PROTECTION (CONT.)
Scathach
Sin
Tamara
Tea and Tephi
Teutates
Tryphyna, Princess
Uathach

PURIFICATION
Adsullata
Beli
Boann
Brid
Grannos
Lady of the Lake
Mandred
Nechtan
Nomenoe
Sequana

RESPONSIBILITY, LESSONS OF
Amaethaon
Blodeuwedd
Carravogue
Cred
Dahud-Ahes
Drutwas
Evnissyen
Iuchar, Iucharba, and Brian
Liban
Merlin
Nynniaw and Peibaw
N'Oun Doare
Partholan

SACRED SPACE
Arianrhod
Cred
Dunatis
Llud
Merlin
Moccus
Nat Thuathcaech
Nemetona
Ochall Ochne
Ratis
Tea and Tephi
Teyrnon

SACRIFICIAL GODS
Aedan
Arthur, King
Balor
Brian Boru, King
Cernunnos
Cuchulain
Cromm Cruiach
Ferdia
Fionn MacCumhal
Holly King/Oak King
Mabon
Merlin
Owen Lawgoch
Uther Pendragon
Ysbadadden

SEASONAL RITES
Accasbel
Aibheaog
Aine
Anind
Arca Dubh
Arianrhod
Badb
Bedwyr
Beli
Beltene
Bran
Brid
Cailleach
Carman
Carravogue
Cebha of the White Skin
Cernunnos
Cerridwen
Conomor, King
Cromm Cruiach
Ebhlinne
Efflam
Eostre
Feargal
Fiongalla
Fionn MacCumhal
Galahad, Sir
Garbh Ogh
Godiva
Gronw
Guinevere, Queen
Gwyn Ap Nuad

SEASONAL RITES (CONT.)
Gwyrthur Ap Greidawl
Habetrot
Habondia
Holly King and Oak King
Igraine
Inghean Bhuidhe
Kai
Lady of the Lake
Lassair
Latiaran
Llew
Lugh
Mabon
Marcassa, Princess
Modred
Moingfhion
Nair
Nicevenn
Olwen
Plur na mBan
Sul
Taillte
Tannus
Teyrnon
Tlachtga
Tuan MacCarell
Urien
Wandil
Ysbadadden

SELF-ESTEEM
Aengus MacLamh Gabuid
Creirwy
Dagda, The
Emer
Epona
Lugh
Maeve, Queen
Mandred
Merlin

SEX MAGICK
Abelard
Achtland
Adammair
Aeval
Arianrhod
Bebo
Branwyn

SEX MAGICK (CONT.)

Cernunnos
Dahud-Ahes
Dwyvach
Enid
Eostre
Epona
Fachtna
Fergus
Findabar
Froach
Garient
Gawain, Sir
Heloise
Isolde
Kele-De
Lady of the Lake
Maeve, Queen
Naoise
Teyrnon
Tristan

SLEEPING OR UNDYING RULERS/DEITIES

Arthur, King
Bo Find
Cadwallon
Dahud-Ahes
Dechtere
Fionn MacCumhal
Merlin
Morvan Lez-Breiz
Owen Lawgoch
Triple Goddess, The

SOVEREIGNTY

Anu
Becuma
Brid
Condwiramur
Creiddylad
Dana
Don
Epona
Flaithius
Goewin
Grainne Ni Malley
Guinevere, Queen
Lady of the Lake
Maeve, Queen

SOVEREIGNTY (CONT.)

Morgan LeFay
Nessa

SPIRIT CONTACT, AID IN

Arawen
Arianrhod
Badb
Bebhionn
Beltene
Breasal
Cliodna
Coinchend
Conn
Cred
Dhonn
Essus
Feithline
Gwennolaik
Gwyar
Gwyn Ap Nuad
Lludd Llaw Ereint
Luchtain
Melwas
Merlin
Nair
Nemglan
Niamh of the Golden Hair
Nola
Oghma
Ogyvran
Ossian
Pwyll
Rhiannon

STRENGTH AND STAMINA

Art
Artio
Cuchulain
Cymidui Cymeinfoll
Hu the Mighty
Lavercam
Llasar Llaesgyfnewid
Maeve, Queen
Scathach
Sin
Taillte
Twrch Trwyth
Uathach
Wayland the Smith

SUN DEITIES

Adsullata
Aine
Anind
Balor
Beli
Grian
Gwyrthur Ap Greidawl
Len of the Many Hammers
Llew
Lugh
MacGreine
Olwen
Princess of the Sun
Rosmerta
Sul

TEACHERS/STUDENTS, MATTERS OF

Abelard
Aife
Finegas
Gwyddion
Heloise
Irgalach
Luaths Lurgann
Math Ap Mathonwy
Merlin
Scathach
Vivienne
Wizard of Reay

TIME MANIPULATION

Amercah
Amergin
Aridane
Mandred
Taliesin

TOOLS, MAGICKAL AND RITUAL

Ailinn
Baile of the Honeyed Speech
Brid
Bwlch
Credne
Fiacha
Goibniu
Luchtain
Lugh
Mog Ruith

TOOLS, MAGICKAL AND RITUAL (CONT.)

N'Oun Doare
Sithehenn
Wayland the Smith

TRIPLICITIES

Aedh/Cimbaeth/Dithorba
Anu/Dana/Badb
Bo Find/Bo Dhu/Bo Ruadh
Brid
Bwlch/Cyfwlch/Syfwlch
Deae Matres
Dechtere
Edain (three incarnations)
Eire/Fodhla/Banbha
Eponae, The (see Epona)
Fiongalla
Guinevere (Arthur's three wives)
Irnan
Latiaran/Inghean Bhuidhe/Lesair
Lugaid Riab nDerg
Melusine/Melior/Palatina
Morrigan, The
Naoise/Ardan/Ainle
Olwen
Uar the Cruel

VENGEANCE, LESSONS ABOUT

Aife
Emer
Ess Euchen

WAR DEITIES

Badb
Gwyn Ap Nuad
Luchtain
MacBeth
Macha
Morrigan, The
Neit
Nuada of the Silver Hand
Uar the Cruel

WARRIORS/WARRIORESSES

Aife
Alain Barbe-Torte
Andraste

WARRIORS/WARRIORESSES (CONT.)

Anluan
Baile of the Honeyed Speech
Boadicea
Brian Boru, King
Caswallawn
Catnenn
Conall
Cuchulain
Culhwch
Cumhal
Dagda, The
Ebha Ni Murchu
Fionn MacCumhal
Finvarra
Giona MacLugha
Gugemar
Gwyddion
Irgalach
Llew
Luaths Lurgann
Lugh
Luchtain
Maeve, Queen
Nessa
Nomenoe
Oghma
Owain
Owen Lawgoch
Pryderi
Scathach
Tristan
Veleda
Uathach

WATER DEITIES

Boann
Branwyn
Cliodna
Cessair
Cliodna
Clota
Condatis
Cyhiraeth
Dahud-Ahes
Dylan
Dyonas
Gwyddno
Lady of the Lake

WATER DEITIES (CONT.)

LeFay
Liban
Llyr
Morgan LeFay
MacCuill
Manann
Mongan
Morgan LeFay
Murigan
Nantosuelta
Nechtan
Nudons
Rosmerta
Sequana
Shoney
Sul
Tethra

WEATHER MAGICK

Ambisagrus
Bussumarus
Cailleach
Cally Berry
Fuamnach
Leucetios
Manann
Merlin
Stine Bheag O' Tarbat
Tannus
Tethra
Wandil

WOODLAND DEITIES

Ardwinna
Cernunnos
Fergus
Flidais
Garbh Ogh
Saba
Tuan MacCarell

SAMPLES OF CELTIC MUSIC

Loving voices of old companions,
stealing out of the past once more,
And the sound of the dear old music,
soft and sweet as in days of yore.

—James Lyman Molloy

CELTIC MUSIC IS available both in printed and in audio form. First of all, check your local library for books and recordings you can borrow. Next, look for sources where you can purchase music either written or recorded. Some artists to look for include Enya, Boys of the Lough, The Clancy Brothers, The Chieftains, and the Battlefield Band.

The music of Brittany is harder to locate. It seems to be overlooked in books on French folk music, and yet is rarely, if ever, included where it belongs—with Celtic music. One noted exception is The Chieftains' *Celtic Wedding*, an entire album of Breton music expertly rendered. Breton Celtic music does have a slightly different sound than that of the islands. Celtic musicologist Avigail MacPhee describes the sound of Breton music as having something of the "troubadour sound."

For serious students, books on Celtic music are available which analyze the scores and provide a historical framework for study.

Begin your search for musical resources by first checking in Appendix D for businesses which sell Celtic music and books.

All Through The Night (Welsh)

Baloo Baleerie (Scottish)

Eilir Tydain (Breton)

Llwyn On (Welsh)

Londonderry Aire (Irish)

Nós na Ronne (Irish)

O Waly, Waly (Anglo-Welsh)

Skye Boat Song (Scottish)

The Star of the County Down (Irish)

Trip to the Cottage (Irish)

RECIPES FROM THE CELTIC LANDS

Blessed be the beasts of the field
who daily lay down their lives for us.
—Rebecca Worrell,
from "The Animal's Song."

THE FOLLOWING RECIPES are not necessarily ones which were made and eaten by our Celtic ancestors, but they are ones which have come to be recognized as national dishes of their country of origin. These traditional recipes can help provide a Celtic atmosphere in your home or in your spiritual life when brought into the circle, offered as a libation, or shared with friends.

This appendix is intended only as a brief sampler of traditional Celtic fare, and is by no means inclusive. No doubt many of you familiar with Celtic cookery can name dozens of well-known recipes which have been omitted whose names immediately conjure up vivid images of their homeland. The recipes included here were selected because they are fairly easy to make, and they can be readily incorporated into the normal home eating routine, or into festival occasions.

For more cooking ideas, check your bookstore or library for cookbook titles focusing on recipes of the Celtic lands.

BOXTY (Irish)

Boxty are potato pancakes traditionally served at Samhain in northwestern Ireland.

1 lb. grated potatoes

3-3/4 cups flour

1 cup milk

2 tablespoons warm water

1 teaspoon baking soda

2 tablespoons butter or margarine

1 cup mashed potatoes, cooked

salt and pepper to taste

Soak potatoes overnight in cool water to remove the starch. Mix all ingredients and shape into flat, round cakes. Add extra milk if mixture seems too stiff. Lightly grease and preheat griddle. Drop the mixture, one heaping tablespoonful at a time, onto the hot griddle. Cook until golden brown. Turn boxty and brown other side. Boxty are either served with butter, or sprinkled with sugar.

COLCANNON (Irish)

Colcannon is traditionally served at Samhain and is used as a divination device. The person who gets the thimble in their portion will be a spinster or laborer, the button is for a bachelor, the ring foretells a marriage, and the coin indicates prosperity.

4 cups mashed potatoes (boil them yourself and mash them, don't use artificial potato flakes)

2-1/2 cups cabbage, cooked and chopped fine

1/2 cup butter (avoid corn oil margarines as they will not add the needed body and flavor)

1/2 cup evaporated milk or cream

3/4 cup onion, chopped very fine and sauteed

(traditionalists saute in lard or bacon grease, but butter is acceptable)

1/4 teaspoon salt

1/8 teaspoon white pepper

A thimble

A button

A ring

A coin

In a large cooking pan place all of the ingredients except the cabbage, thimble, button, ring, and coin, and cook over low heat while blending them together. Turn the heat to medium and add the chopped cabbage. The mixture will have a pale green cast. Stir occasionally until the mixture is warm enough to eat. Lastly drop in the thimble, button, ring, and coin. Stir well and serve. Serves eight.

CREPES (Breton)

These flat, thin pancakes, which we think of as being quintessentially French, originated in Brittany.

1/4 cup buckwheat flour

1/4 cup plus two tablespoons white flour

1/2 cup rich milk or cream

1 egg

1 tablespoon lightly salted butter, melted

filling of your choice

In a mixing bowl, combine all ingredients and mix well. Lightly butter a roomy skillet pre-heated to approximately 300°. Take the batter by the heaping teaspoonful and drop onto the hot surface. Allow the crepes to cook no more than 30 seconds per side. They should be a pale golden bronze. In the center of the finished crepe, spoon on whatever filling you have selected (unless you like them plain). Crepe stuffings can be as diverse as fruits, ice cream, fish and sea food, and whipped cream and chocolate. A simple marmalade also makes an excellent filling. Roll up the crepe and serve. Makes about 15 crepes.

EGG NOG (Pan-Celtic)

12 pasteurized eggs, separated

1 lb. confectioner's sugar

1-1/2 cups whiskey, ale, or dark rum

2 quarts whipping cream

3/4 teaspoon ground nutmeg

1/4 teaspoon salt

1 teaspoon vanilla

1 cup water

1 cup rich milk

Mix the egg yolks, sugar, alcohol, and salt together and let stand in the refrigerator overnight so that their flavors can "marry." Next day, beat the egg whites until they are just stiff, and mix them and all the rest of the ingredients together until slightly thick. Serve chilled.

FARLS (Scottish)

3 cups mashed potatoes

2 cups dry oats (not the instant variety)

2 tablespoons margarine or butter

1/2 teaspoon cornstarch

1/2 teaspoon baking powder

1/8 teaspoon salt

pinch of pepper

pinch of rosemary (optional)

Soak the oats in warm water for fifteen to twenty minutes until they are soft and slightly swollen. Mix them with all other ingredients in a large mixing bowl. Knead thoroughly even though your hands may get tired—the mixture will be like a very thick dough. When ingredients are thoroughly mixed, form small amounts into round patties which are called farls. Place the farls in a small skillet with hot vegetable oil and lightly fry. Serve immediately. Serves eight.

PASTIES (Cornish)

Pasties are meat-filled pies similar to the frozen pocket sandwiches sold in groceries today. They were, and still are, a popular Cornish dish.

FOR PASTRY SHELL:

4 cups flour

1-1/2 cups shortening

1/4 cup ice-cold water

FOR FILLING:

1/2 cup chopped turnips

2 cups chopped beef or mutton, browned

1/2 cup chopped onions (or more if your taste runs to them)

1 cup diced potatoes, slightly cooked

1 egg, beaten

1/4 teaspoon salt

1 teaspoon pepper

Coat a baking sheet liberally with butter and pre-heat oven to 400°. Combine pastry ingredients. Dough must be very dry, but not crumbly. When mixed, rub it with flour, wrap in waxed paper, and refrigerate overnight. On a floured surface roll the dough into a circle not more than 1/4 inch thick. Cut dough into five-inch rounds. Next, mix together all the ingredients for the filling. Place a scant 1/4 cup of the filling mixture in the center of each dough circle. Fold the dough in half over the mixture and, by moistening the edge with cold water, seal the pasty shut. Place pasties on baking sheet and make several small slits in the surface as you would when baking a pie. Brush the surface with a mixture of beaten egg and butter for even browning and bake for ten minutes. Reduce heat to 325° and bake for an additional 30–40 minutes. Serve piping hot. Makes about ten pasties.

SCONES (English)

This is the tea-time treat which we all think of as being very English—however, the Irish and the Scots each have their own versions of this biscuit.

2-3/4 cups flour

1 cup buttermilk

1-1/2 teaspoons baking powder

pinch of salt

Mix all ingredients to make a soft dough. On a floured surface, roll the dough out to a height of about 1/2 to 3/4 of an inch. Cut the individual scones with a round two-inch cookie cutter. Place these on a lightly greased baking sheet and bake in a 400° oven for about 15 minutes. Scones are traditionally served with jam or marmalade.

SHORT-CUT MEADE (Pan-Celtic)

The rich ale known as meade is a very old Celtic creation which was used for sacred rituals. It was thought to be a gift of the deities and was used to honor them, especially at Bealtaine. Many recipes exist, and most are jealously guarded. This short-cut method ignores the lengthy fermentation process. For more ideas on making meade write to the American Meade Association whose address can be founded in the Resources Appendix.

1/2 gallon water

1-1/2 cups raw honey

1/4 cup lemon juice

1/8 teaspoon nutmeg

1/8 teaspoon allspice, rounded

1/2 cup Everclear®

Slowly heat all ingredients together—except the alcohol—in a large stock pot. As the honey melts, an oily crust will form on the top of the meade. You can leave it there, for some feel this adds to the full-bodied texture of the meade, while others will tell you to skim it off. Do not allow the meade to come to a roiling boil. When it is well blended, remove from the heat, stirring occasionally until it settles. When it has cooled, add the Everclear® and serve.

SODA BREAD (Irish)

We think of breads as being part of the Lughnasadh or Cakes and Ale celebration, but today's soda breads are most likely to be found in bakeries outside of Ireland around St. Patrick's Day. Sometimes a cup or two of raisins are added to the dough before baking.

3 cups all-purpose flour

3 cups whole wheat flour

1-1/4 teaspoons cream of tartar

1-1/4 teaspoons baking soda

1/2 teaspoon salt

1 teaspoon sugar (raw sugar is best)

2 cups sour milk (milk can be soured with a teaspoon of vinegar or orange juice, or set out at room temperature for three days)

Mix all ingredients together except the milk, making sure they are well blended. Add the milk 1/4 cup at a time, blending well after each addition. Dough should be tacky, but not crumbly, and should hold together well. If not, add another tablespoon of milk. Continue to knead for at least fifteen minutes. Work the dough into a ball, place it in the center of a greased and lightly floured baking sheet and flatten slightly. Cut three straight, deep slash marks across the top with a sharp knife. (I'm not sure if that has any real value in the cooking process, but it is a great way to utilize the sacred number of the Celts.) If you like, you can brush a little melted butter on top, but traditionalists use cream. Bake at 375° for 45–50 minutes, then turn the loaf over and bake another 5–7 minutes or until it has a hollow sound when tapped with the blunt edge of a knife.

WASSAIL (Welsh, Anglo-Celtic)

Wassail was once a Samhain delicacy, now mostly served at Yule. Wassailing was a ritual which honored the apple tree in autumn. This recipe is only one of many variations.

1-1/2 cups water
1/2 cup heavy cream
6 baked apples, cut into small pieces
5 pasteurized egg whites
1-1/4 cups granulated sugar
1/2 teaspoon nutmeg
2 teaspoons allspice
1 teaspoon cinnamon
1/2 teaspoon ginger
8 whole cloves
1 quart ale
1 cup cooking sherry
1 cup Irish whiskey

Bring the water and cream to a slow boil, then remove from heat. Beat the egg whites until they are very well-beaten. Thoroughly mix in all the ingredients—except the alcohol—together in the cream mixture. Allow this mixture to cool slightly—enough so that the heat from it will not crack your punch bowl. Blend in the alcohol just before serving, and be sure to offer the traditional toast to the old apple tree and to the health of your company before drinking. Makes one large punch bowl full.

WELSH RABBIT (Welsh)

Though we often refer to this cheese dish as Welsh Rarebit, the word "Rabbit" is correct. The name goes back to a time when the Welsh were a poor and conquered people, and often times, their own homemade breads and cheeses were all they had to eat. It is believed now that the name of this dish began as a self-imposed joke in those times of want.

4 slices white bread
2 cups grated sharp cheddar cheese
1 tablespoon cornstarch
1/2 cup ale
1/2 teaspoon worchestershire sauce
1/4 teaspoon dried mustard
1 egg, well beaten
optional: a pinch of cayenne or parsley

Cut the crusts from the bread and set them aside. In a saucepan, combine all ingredients except the ale and egg, and allow them to melt and heat without permitting them to come to a boil. Remove from heat and stir in the egg and ale. Toast the bread. Pour the cheese mixture over the toasted bread slices. Place under a broiler for a minute or two to slightly brown the cheese.

YELLOWMAN (Irish, Scottish)

This simple taffy has been a featured item at the Ballycastle, Ireland, Lughnasadh Fair for close to four hundred years. If you are part of a coven or Pagan group, an old-fashioned taffy pull can be a nice addition to your Sabbat festivities.

> 1 cup brown sugar
>
> 1/4 cup butter (not margarine)
>
> 1 one-pound jar dark corn syrup
>
> 1 teaspoon baking soda
>
> 2 tablespoons apple cider vinegar

Melt butter in a deep saucepan. Add the sugar, syrup and vinegar. Stir constantly until all ingredients are blended and melted. Then, without further stirring, allow it to come to a boil. Continue boiling until taffy is hard and brittle when placed in icy water. Remove from heat and add baking powder (mixture will foam up). Stir well. Pour out onto a greased or waxed paper-lined plate. When it has cooled enough to handle, begin pulling and stretching until it becomes a pale yellow. Cut into squares and enjoy.

PAGAN TERMS AND COMMON CELTIC WORDS

In the culture lives the language of the people.
When the words are gone, so is the
memory of those who have come before.
—Rebecca Worrell

A NOTE ON CELTIC LANGUAGES AND PRONUNCIATIONS

THE CELTIC LANGUAGES are divided into two categories, the Brythonic group which includes Welsh, Old English, Brezonek (or Breiz), and the now extinct language of Cornwall (the Cornish language still exists on paper but, like Latin, it is no longer used in everyday contexts and is considered a "dead" language); and the Goidelic group, often called "Gaelic," which is shared by speakers of Irish, Manx, and Scots Gaelic.

The rules of pronunciation for Celtic languages are extremely complex and include broad and slender consonants, vocative forms of words, a case system, and initial consonants which change in accordance with the last letter of the preceding word. These rules are made even more confusing because of vast variations in regional dialect still at work where these languages continue to be spoken. Sometimes the differences in certain words are so striking that they appear to constitute a second language. The pronunciations given here for Celtic words are only approximations, as these languages contain many sounds unfamiliar to speakers of English.

All the Celtic countries have attempted to put their native languages back into operation and these efforts have met with some success, particularly in Wales. But, in nearly all cases, English has replaced the native tongue as the first language in most households of these countries. The exception to this is, of course, Brittany, where, though French is the official language, nearly a million Bretons still use a form of their old Celtic language for a good portion of their daily communication.

ABERFFRAW (AW-ber-froo)
The ancient royal seat of Wales on the isle of Ynys Mon (Anglesey). Today, some Celtic witches like to use the name as a synonym for the Otherworld.

ADBERTOS
Literally means "sacrifice" and was part of the Celtic religious and community world-view. Rather than the negative connotation given to its English counterpart, *adbertos* was a positive idea denoting the giving to others, to the clan, and to the larger community as well as the deities. The Celts saw the giving or receiving of sacrifice as being inherent in every living moment. This is a very old word which came to the British Isles and Brittany from Celtic Gaul.

AILEACH (AW-loch or EE-loch)
A ruined fortress in Ulster which is said to have been built by the Tuatha De Danann.

ALBA
A name once used for Scotland.

ALBION

An old Greco-Celtic name for Britain, one which is still used poetically. It is believed to be derived from the Latin word *albus* meaning "white," referring to the famous white cliffs of Dover. The Latin word "Britannia" replaced Albion in common usage.

ALL-POWER

One of the many creative names which is used to refer to the one great power, or life source, of which the Goddess and God are both a part.

AMULET

A natural object which is reputed to give protection to the carrier. Amulets are such things as stones or fossils and are not to be confused with person-made *talismans*. Stones with natural holes in them were popular Celtic amulets.

ANGLESEY

An island off the north coast of Wales which was a major Druidic center at the peak of Celtic domination in Britain.

ANNWFN (AWN-noon)

Another name for the Welsh Otherworld, sometimes called Avalon in English.

ARCHETYPE

Archetypes are universal symbols defined by Funk and Wagnalls as a "standard pattern" or a "prototype." Archetypal symbols speak to all of us in the ecumenical language of the sub-conscious. They are the images which cloud our dreams, they are the inherent power of our deities, and they are the machinery which makes all forms of divination possible. Archetypal images are used heavily throughout pathworking, for this is the only language our sub-conscious (sometimes called our super-conscious or deep mind) can understand, utilize, and with which it can communicate back to our conscious minds.

ARD-RI

An Irish or Scottish High King. Also spelled *Ard-Righ* and *Ard-Ridh*.

ARMOR

The original Celtic name for Brittany which means "on the sea."

ARMORICA

The Latin name for Brittany.

ASPECT

The particular principle or part of the Creative Life Force being worked with or acknowledged at any one time. For example, Brid is a Mother aspect of the one Goddess, Lugh is one aspect of the God, and both are merely single aspects of the Creative Life Force.

ASTROLOGY

The study of and belief in the effects the movements and placements of planets and other heavenly bodies have on the lives and behavior of human beings.

ATHAME (ATH-aah-may)

The ritual knife often associated with the element of air and the direction of the east, though some traditions attribute it to fire and the south. The knife was traditionally black-handled, but many modern Pagans now seek handles of natural wood. In some Celtic circles the athame is called the "Dagger" or "Dirk." In Ireland it is known as the *scian*.

AUTUMN EQUINOX

See "Mabon."

AVALON

See "Annfwn."

BALEFIRE

The traditional communal bonfire of the Sabbats. The name is derived from the Anglo-Saxon word *boon* meaning a "gift" or "something extra." The modern word "Bonfire" is synonymous with balefire, though it often has no religious significance.

BARDS

The bards (*bardoi*) were a class of Druids who were the poets and singers who kept alive valuable oral traditions through song. These songs (called *cetel* in Ireland and *lay* in Brittany) could also be used as magickal spells to curse or bless.

B.C.E.

"Before Common Era." This is a designation scholars often use to denote dates synonymous with B.C., but without the biased religious impli-

cations. It is also sometimes abbreviated BCE, without the periods.

BEALTAINE (BEEL-teen or BALL-tayn'eh)
Also called "Beltane" (BELL-tayn). This Sabbat, celebrated on May 1, is rife with fertility rituals and symbolism, and is a celebration of the sacred marriage of the Goddess and the God.

BESOM (BEE-sum)
The witch's broomstick. European folklore has witches riding their brooms through the sky, which many feel is an uninformed explanation of astral projection. As a tool, the broom is used to sweep a sacred area, ground a circle, or to brush away negative influences. Besoms were often mounted and "ridden" over crops in fertility rites. Though this word is Old English, Gaelic speakers sometimes pronounced it in a Gaelic-ized manner, BAYSH-um.

BODHRAN (BAOW-rahn)
The traditional goat skin drum used in Celtic music.

BOOK OF SHADOWS
(Also called "Book of Lights and Shadows.") Book of Shadows is the spell book, diary, and ritual guide used by an individual witch or coven. Some say the name came from having to hide the workings from church authorities, and others say it means that an unworked spell or ritual is a mere shadow, not taking form until performed by a witch.

BREHON
Called *Breithamhain* in Old Irish, these were the judges of the old Celtic world whose decisions were held in high regard.

BREHON LAWS, THE
This was the law code which governed old Ireland. Even in retrospect the Brehon Laws are very fair, indicate a well-educated and thoughtful people, and its equitable system of land division based on clans helped prevent the installation of the English feudal land system after their invasion. Also see "Laws of Hywel Dda."

BREIZ (Braise)
The native name of the Bretons' Celtic language, also called "Brezonek."

BRETAGNE (Bra-TAhG-na)
The French name for Brittany.

BRETON
The name for a person from Brittany, that Celtic part of France where the population has always considered itself more Celtic than French.

BREZONEK
Also spelled Brezhonek. The Celtic/Brythonic language of Brittany still spoken today as a first or second language by more than a million Bretons. Modern Brezonek is peppered with French words and phrases since all Breton natives are also conversant in that official language of their country.

BRITAIN THE GREATER
A Celtic term used to refer to Ireland and the other British Isles.

BRITAIN THE LESSER
A Celtic term used to refer to Brittany.

BROACH
An ornamental pin which was often fastened at the shoulder of a Celtic cloak, sash, or mantle. Its design and material often denoted the wearer's status in society. The most famous Celtic broach is the gold and bejeweled Tara Broach found near Tara Hill which now resides in the museum of Dublin's Trinity University. The Irish word for broach is *delg* and the Welsh is *tlws*.

BROWNIE
A very well-known, dwarf-type house faery from rural Scotland. This likable fellow will often do kind deeds for his host family and help protect the dwelling.

BRYTHONIC
One of the Celtic language groups; also a name used to refer to the Pagan traditions of Wales, Cornwall, and England.

BURGH (Broo or Burr)
The grassy hillocks of Ireland, Scotland, and Man under which the faeries live.

BURNING TIMES, THE

The time from the Spanish Inquisition through the last outbursts of persecution and witch killings in the mid-nineteenth century (though murderous persecutions began as early as the twelfth century). The last known capital sentence for witchcraft in the West took place in Scotland in the early 1800s. Figures vary on how many were killed during this hysteria, estimates range anywhere from fifty thousand to as many as nine million.

CAILLEACH (CAWL-y'ahc)

In Scots and Irish Gaelic this literally means "old woman." At one time it was a term most likely used reverently to refer to the Crone Goddess. Today it is most likely to be used derogatorily except in Pagan circles.

CAIRN

The stone burial mounds used by the Celts. They were honored at Mabon. So sacred were these mounds that a breed of dog, the Cairn Terrier (Toto in the movie, *The Wizard of Oz,* was of this breed), was developed to protect them.

CALEDONIA

The old Roman name for Scotland, still used poetically today.

CARMINA GADELICA (Car-MEEN-ah Gaw-DEL-ee-cah)

A collection of Gaelic lyric poetry and lore with a Pagan emphasis, collected from oral sources in the late nineteenth century by musicologist and folklorist Alexander Carmichael. It is also a primary source for knowledge about Celtic folk magick. This work compares with the famous *Carmina Burana* in scope and worth.

CAULDRON

Linked to witchcraft in the popular mind, this is a primal Goddess image used like a chalice or cup. This was a common magickal instrument in the Celtic traditions because it was a practical object as well, one which could be used for cooking or washing as well as making brews and magick potions. In many of the mythological stories from Ireland and Britain the cauldron is symbolic of the womb of the Mother Goddess in which all life

begins, ends, and regenerates. The Irish word for cauldron is *coire* and the Welsh word is *pair.*

C.E.

"Common Era." This term is often used by scholars to denote time which is synonymous with A.D., but without the religious implication. It is also abbreviated as CE, without the periods in between.

CEILIDH (KAY-lee)

A Scottish or Irish dance. The word literally means "visit." In the southern part of Ireland the final "dh" is usually dropped from the word. Another variant spelling is *ceiligh.*

CELTIC GAMES

Friendly, if rough, competition was always a part of Celtic gatherings, and most of the games are still played today. In some of the myths, games of skill were entered into for very high stakes, often with kingdoms or lovers on the line. Among the best-known of the games are the board games chess and brandubh, and the field games of hurling and curling which were the prototypes of several modern field games including hockey.

CELTIC LANDS

The areas of the world which are still populated by the descendents of the Celts are well-known to most: England, Ireland, Scotland, Wales, and Brittany. Before and during their scattered migration to these places the Celts had flourishing kingdoms in numerous places in Europe and the Middle East. Gaul, in western coastal Europe, is the best-known of these. Other strongholds included Galatia in central Turkey, Galacia in northwestern Spain, Gallia Cisalpina nestled between the Alps and the Appennine mountains in central Europe, and numerous smaller settlements in what are today the countries of Germany, Switzerland, Austria, and southern France.

CEOL (Kyole)

Scottish and Irish Gaelic world for "music."

CHALICE

The chalice or cup as a ritual tool represents water and the west, and it is also representative of the feminine principle of creation.

CHAPLET

A crown for the head usually made of flowers and worn at Bealtaine. Chaplets can also be made of vines and other natural material.

CHARGING

The act of empowering an herb, stone, or other magickal object with one's own energies directed towards a magickal goal. Charging is synonymous with enchanting or empowering.

CIRCLE

The sacred space wherein all magick is to be worked and all ritual contained. The circle both contains raised energy and provides protection for the witch, and is created and banished with her/his own energy. Many books on magick give in-depth explanations of circle lore and practice. It is recommended that students of Paganism study these carefully.

CIRCLES OF BEING

In Druidic philosophy both the macrocosm and microcosm are divided into three circles of being. The inner circle is *abred,* the middle is *gweynfyd,* and the outer-most one is *ceugant.* The inner-most circle is often represented by the magick circle wherein all magick and ritual is performed.

CLAN

The extended family system of the Celts. Originally clans were united by being descended from a single female ancestor, but by the third century C.E. that had been largely supplanted by a male ancestor. The clan raised children, built cities, provided for education, had an internal justice system connected to the larger political region in which they lived, and formed armies for mutual protection. So strong were these identifications that they became a target for invading forces. In Welsh the word for clan is plant. Both words mean "offspring of" or "children of."

CLAS MYRDDIN

This ancient name for Britain literally means "Merlin's Enclosure."

COIBCHE

An Irish word for dowry, or marriage portion.

COLLECTIVE UNCONSCIOUS, THE

A term used to describe the sentient connection of all living things, past and present. It is synonymous with the terms "deep mind" and "higher self." This is believed to be the all-knowing energy source that contains the entire sum of human knowledge and experience which is tapped during divination.

COMING OF AGE RITUAL

At age thirteen for boys, and at the time of a girl's first menses, Pagan children are considered to be spiritual adults. They join with other Pagans to celebrate their new maturity with rituals and parties and are permitted full membership in covens. This is also the time when ritual tools are given to them as gifts, or else they are allowed to choose their own.

CONE OF POWER

The ritual raising of a cone of energy within the circle by an individual or by a coven. When the energy reaches its peak, it is released to do its work. Dancing deosil while chanting or singing is the most common method for raising the cone.

CONSCIOUS MIND

That part of the brain which we have access to in the course of a normal, waking day. It is the part of the mind which holds retrievable memory and other easy to recall information.

CORPUS CALLOSUM

The connecting tissues which join the right and left hemispheres of the human brain.

COSMOLOGY

A philosophy about the nature and origin of the universe and of creation. Each culture/religion has its own.

COVEN

A group of witches who worship and work together. A coven may contain any number of witches, both male and female, but the traditional number of members is thirteen, which reflects the thirteen moons in the solar year, or three persons for each season plus a priest/ess.

Examples of cup and ring markings.

CROMACH (CROW-mawk)
A Scottish walking stick with a crooked handle similar to an Irish shillelagh.

CRONE
That aspect of the Goddess that is represented by the old woman. She is symbolized by the waning moon, the carrion crow, the cauldron, and the color black. Her Sabbats are Mabon and Samhain.

CROSS-QUARTER DAYS
A name sometimes given to the Sabbats not falling on the solstices or equinoxes.

CROSSROADS
The natural X formed by a crossroad figures heavily in the lore of Ireland and Britain. The Celtic Goddess Epona (envisioned as half human and half white horse) was said to appear there for those who would come to invoke her aid. The Mother Goose rhyme, "Banbury Cross," keeps this story alive.

CRUACHAN, CAVE OF (CREW-hahn)
The Irish/Manx name of the entrance to the Otherworld. In the Christian mythology of the islands this became disparagingly known as the "Gateway to Hell."

CUMDACH
A lavishly ornamented shrine, usually used as a resting place for sacred or illuminated books.

CUP AND RING MARKINGS
These very ancient carvings or chalk-on-stone drawings, consisting of meandering lines and circles intersected by lines, found all over the Celtic world (particularly in Scotland) have never been adequately explained. Various Celtic magickal traditions have devised explanations and uses for them, but they still largely remain a mystery.

CURRAGH
The animal skin-covered skiffs mentioned in myths and which are still used today in rural Ireland and Scotland.

CYFARWYDD
The Welsh word for "storyteller." The traveling cyfarwydd was an integral part of the social structure of the Celtic world, and was largely responsible for the survival of the oral traditions. Also see "Seanachai."

CYMRAEG

The Welsh word for their language. It comes from the word *Cymru* which means "Wales."

CYWYDD

(K'EE-oo'eth) A difficult-to-master form of native Welsh poetry which came into fashion around the fifth century and dominated Welsh writing until the eighteenth century. It was an artform studied in the bardic schools.

DEITY

An inclusive name for a Goddess or God.

DEOSIL (JES-l)

The act of moving, working, or dancing in a clockwise motion. This is the traditional direction one works with for creative magick. Deosil is also called "Sunwise."

DIRK

The ritual knife of the Scottish tradition.

DIVINATION

The act of divining the future by reading potentials currently in motion. Divination can be done through meditation, scrying, astral projection, with cards, stones, or any one of a myriad of means. The most popular forms of divination today are "Tarot," "Runes," "Pendulums," "Scrying," and the controversial "Ouija Board®."

DOLMEN

The standing stones of the Celtic countries which are shaped like altars with one large capstone being upheld by two endstones. Another Gaelic word for dolmen is *cromlech*.

DRAWING DOWN THE MOON

Ancient Pagan ritual enacted at the Esbats to draw the powers of the full moon, in her aspect as Great Mother Goddess, into the body of a female witch. Esbats and Sabbats can co-exist, but these conjunctions are rare.

DRAWING DOWN THE SUN

This is a lesser-known and lesser-used companion ritual to "Drawing Down the Moon," in which the essence of the Sun God is drawn into the body of a male witch.

DRUIDS

Much speculation still continues on the role of the Druids. They were the priestly class of Celtic society, the magicians and writers, poets and royal advisors. Their power flourished from the second century B.C.E. to the second century C.E. They are credited with creating the Celtic Tree Calendar, communicating with faeries, and possessing powerful divination skills which required living sacrifices. Their eventual insistence on the superiority of males as religious leaders and teachers helped pave the way for the Roman church's victory over the British Isles. The word Druid is sometimes thought to come from the Greek *drus* which means "oak," but most likely comes from the old Indo-European root word *dru* which means "steadfast" or "forthright."

DUALITY

Duality, when used as a religious term, separates two opposites such as good and evil and places those characteristics into two separate God-forms.

DUN (doon)

This Gaelic word literally means "enclosure" or "shut in," and was used in mythology when referring to a home or stronghold of a deity or heroic figure. Today, remains of these stone dwellings can be found all over Ireland and Scotland, and they are now thought to be occupied by faery folk.

EARTH PLANE

A metaphor for your normal waking consciousness, or for the everyday, solid world we live in.

ELEMENTS, THE

The four alchemical elements once thought to make up the entire universe. These are Earth, Air, Fire, and Water plus the fifth element of pure spirit in, of, and outside them all. Each Pagan tradition has their own directions, tools, and correspondences for each of these.

ELEMENTALS

Archetypal spirit beings associated with one of the four elements.

ELLAN VANNIN

The Manx name for the Isle of Man.

ERIC

A quest of honor similar to the honor vow known as the geise.

ESBAT

The monthly Pagan holy time which coincides with the full moon. The word is from the French *esbattre* meaning to "gambol or frolic."

EVOCATION

The act of summoning the presence of deities, friendly spirits, or elementals to your circle or home.

FAMILIAR

A witch's co-worker that is of a non-human existence. Animals are the most common familiars, thus the popularity of the witch's cat. But familiars can also be discarnate spirits, spirit guides, or elementals. The choice of having a familiar or not is a singular one, but must also respect the conscious choice of the being involved.

FAERY

See "Sith" and "Sidhe."

FEIS (faysh or fesh)

Once meant a gathering for Brehon judgment, but today means a dance contest or, less often, a Celtic games competition. A feis was often an excuse for holding a fair.

FILI (FEE-l'eah)

This Old Irish word translates literally as "poet" or "bard," and is often erroneously used in place of the word "Druid." However, the word means a specific division or specialization of Druidic practice.

FIR FER (FEAR-fair)

The rules which governed Celtic battle. The Gaelic words mean "fair play."

FLEADH AISE (FLEE-ah Awsh)

Literally the "Feast of Age," an annual celebratory feast of the Tuatha De Danann sometimes commemorated by Irish Pagans at Lughnasadh.

FOLKLORE

The traditional sayings, cures, fairy tales, and folk wisdom of a particular locale which is separate from their mythology.

FOUR CITIES OF THE TUATHA, THE

In Irish mythology these were the four cities of the Tuatha De Danann: Gorias, Falias, Findias, and Murias. While these have mystic significance, they have been the subject of many irresponsible and uninformed interpretations over the centuries by systems not related to any native Celtic magickal tradition. Study of them should be approached with a firm knowledge of Celtic history and mythology.

FOUR SORROWS OF ERIN, THE

Four famous stories in Irish mythology: "The Fate of the Sons of Tuirenn," "The Fate of the Children of Llyr," "The Fate of the Sons of Usnach," and "The Fate of Deirdre."

GAELTACHT (GAUL-toch)

A modern term denoting an area of the Celtic world where the language and customs of the Celtic people is preserved and used on a regular basis.

GEIMHREADH (G'yim-ray-ah)

Means "winter" in Irish which is one of the two recognized Celtic seasons. It begins at Samhain.

GEISE (gaysh, singular; gaysh-uh, plural)

Also spelled *geis*. In the Irish myths this was an obligation which bound someone to do or to not do something. The word is often equated with the more familiar Polynesian "taboo," but geise also implied a sacred bond with magickal, divine ties. To break it brought horrible misfortunes and even death, usually inflicted by the deity in whose name the vow was made. A geise is often the point on which hang the conflicts in Celtic mythic stories.

GOD

The masculine aspect of deity.

GODDESS

The feminine aspect of deity.

GOLDEN STATUTE, THE

The first known law declaring universal freedom of religion, enacted in Ireland in late Celtic times.

Great Rite, The

The symbolic sexual union (also sacred marriage) of the Goddess and God which is enacted at Bealtaine in most traditions, and at other Sabbats in many others. It symbolizes the primal act of creation from which all life comes. The sexual union is symbolized by ritually placing the athame, a phallic symbol, inside the chalice or cauldron, a womb symbol.

Grimoire (Greem-WARR)

A book of magickal spells and rituals.

Grounding

To disperse excess energy generated during any magickal or occult rite by sending it into the earth. It can also mean the process of centering one's self in the physical world both before and after any ritual or astral experience.

Gwlad Yr Haf

This is one of the names for the Welsh Otherworld, or Land of the Dead. It translates as "The Land of Summer" and is the origin of the Wiccan Land of the Dead known as the "Summerland."

Handfasting

Pagan marriage, traditionally contracted for a specific period of time depending on one's tradition. It is renewed only if both parties agree. In Old Irish the word for handfasting is *lanamnas,* and a newlywed couple is called a *lanamain.*

Hera

A feminine form of the Greek *hero,* synonymous with heroine, and preferred by some over the latter word.

Herbalism

The art of using herbs to facilitate human needs both magickally and medically.

Hibernia/Ivernia

The old Roman name for Ireland, still used poetically today.

Hywel Dda, Laws of

Welsh legal system equivilent to the "Brehon Laws" of Ireland, named for the tenth century king who united Wales.

Imbolg (Em-bowl/g)

Also known as "Candlemas," "Imbolc," or "Oimelc." Imbolg, observed on February 2, is a day which honors the Virgin Goddess as the youthful bride of the returning Sun God.

Imminent Deity

A God or Goddess who is seen as living within humanity rather than outside of it.

Invisibility Spells

This type of magick has been widely misunderstood. Though the Celtic Druids did purport to have spells called *fith fath* which rendered them invisible, most of the magic relates to working magick backwards in time to change present situations. The idea of this kind of magick gained popularity during the Burning Times when witches did not want to be seen going to meet their covens by night. This is also probably a metaphor for astral projection.

Invocation

The act of drawing the aspect of a particular deity into one's physical self. The rite of Drawing Down the Moon is an example.

Iona, Isle of

A center of Druid teaching and gathering in the Hebrides Islands off the west coast of Scotland. In the sixth century, St. Columba turned the island into a large center for Christian worship and study. Today many Catholics make pilgrimages to Iona to pray to St. Columba.

Kabbalah

The body of mystical teachings from the Jewish-Gnostic tradition upon which both Ceremonial Magick and the Alexandrian Pagan traditions base their practice. While the principles of Kabbalah are ancient, its codification as a system of religious study dates only to the medieval period. Also transliterated from the Hebrew as "Qabala" and "Caballa." Ceremonial Magick has greatly influenced modern Paganism, especially in remote areas such as the west of Ireland where numerous persons came in the late sixteenth century when fleeing the Spanish Inquisition.

KELTOI

The Greek name for the ancient Celts. Greek writings give us our first glimpse into the culture of the Celtic people dating from around 700 B.C.E.

KERNEWEK

The native name for the Cornish language.

KERNOW

The Cornish name for Cornwall.

KERSEY

See "Mantle."

KORRIGANS

A well-known sea faery from Brittany and Cornwall. They usually appear as blonde females and enjoy luring human mates into their watery realm.

LAMMAS

See "Lughnasadh."

LAW OF RESPONSIBILITY, THE

This is an often repeated corollary to the other laws of Paganism. It simply means that if you inadvertently violate someone's free will or harm them in any way, you will accept responsibility for your action and seek to make restitution. This, of course, does not apply in cases where you have used magick to protect yourself from someone seeking to harm you. Also see "Pagan Rede" and "Threefold Law."

LEPRECHAUN (LEP-ri-cawn)

The most well-known faery in the world is this treasure-hoarding, hard-drinking, Irish dwarf. The word Leprechaun is from the Irish *lu,* meaning "small," and *chorpan,* meaning "body."

LIA FAIL (Lia-ah FAWL)

"The Stone of Destiny" which was used in the crowning of the High Kings of Ireland. Many regard it as the Irish equivalent of Excalibur in the Arthurian myths.

LIBATION

A portion of food or drink ritually given to a deity, nature spirit, or discarnate.

LUGHNASADH (LOO-nas-sah)

Also known as "Lammas" and "August Eve." This Sabbat celebrates the first harvest. The date is August 1 or 2 depending upon your tradition.

MABON (MAY-bone)

Sabbat named for a Welsh God associated with the Arthurian myth cycles. This is the Sabbat observed at the Autumn Equinox and celebrates the second harvest, wine, and balance.

MAGICK

Spelled with a "k" to differentiate it from the magic of stage illusions. The best definition of magick was probably invented by infamous ceremonial magician Aleister Crowley: "Magick is the science and art of causing change to occur in conformity to will." Magick is work, and work is forbidden at the Sabbats.

MANTLE

A cloak worn by the Celts whose color, fabric, and condition was often an outward sign of the wearer's rank in society. Also a vestment of power, hence the Celtic-expression "inheriting the mantle." A mantle is often referred to as a "kersey" in Scotland.

MEGALITHS

The large standing stones of the Celtic countries which were probably erected as holy sites and/or astronomical observation points. Stonehenge, on England's Salisbury Plain, is the best known example of a surviving megalith.

MENHIRS

The standing stones from Celtic countries which are made of single stones or a circular series of stones. Menhir literally means "long stone," and surviving ones range in height from a few feet to as high as 64 feet. Brittany is famed for its many menhir circles.

MIDSUMMER

The Sabbat observed at the Summer Solstice which honors the Sun God at the height of his power, and the Goddess as the pregnant mother-to-be. This was not a Sabbat celebrated by the old Celts until they were influenced by the Norse.

MILESIANS

A cousin-race of the Celts who came to Ireland from Spain, via Scotland, as early as 1500 B.C.E.

MONOTHEISM

The belief in one supreme deity who has no other forms and/or displays no other aspects. Judaism and Islam are both monotheistic.

MUSIC MAGICK

Also called a Song Spell. This is a spell created in song, a popular Celtic method of spell casting seen used in the myths of many bards.

MYTH CYCLES

The body of lore about any land or people which makes up their mythology. The word myth does not mean something false, but rather it means a "theme" or "a traditional story." We should always keep in mind that virtually all of our Celtic myths and myth fragments come from secondary sources, perhaps most are even more removed from their original oral texts than that.

MYTHOGRAPHER

One who collects and records myths.

MYTHOLOGIST

One who studies myths and seeks their interpretation against a larger cultural or historical background.

MYTHOLOGY

The formal study of myth.

NEMED

The names of one of the invader races of Ireland; also an old Irish word meaning "sacred space." The word was derived from the better-known Gaulish word *nemeton*.

NEMETON

A Celtic-Gaulish word meaning "sacred space."

NEO-PAGAN

Name applied to the various Pagan movements after the repeal of the British anti-witchcraft laws in the early 1950s. Neo is a prefix meaning "new" or "re-formed."

NEW RELIGION, THE

A Pagan term used in reference to Christianity, but it can also be applied to all other non-Pagan religions. These New Religions are sometimes referred to as the "Patriarchal Religions" because of their exclusive, or nearly exclusive, focus on a male deity.

NIAM-LANN (NEEM-lawn)

A metallic headpiece worn like a thin crown or headband around the forehead. Often the front-piece, which rested just above and between the eyes, carried some emblem of religious or mystical significance.

NINE

A Celtic sacred number which represents the beginning and ending of all things. The square root of nine is three, the basic sacred number of the Celts.

NORSE TRADITION

The Pagan traditions from Scandinavia, also sometimes called the "Nordic Tradition," and includes the beliefs and practices of the early Vikings and Lapps. Nordic invaders had a strong influence on the Pagan practices of Ireland and Scotland.

OGHAM

This was the ancient alphabet of the Celtic people which consists of series of marks in relationship to a center line. It is used today for both sacred writings and for divination.

OIMELC

See "Imbolg."

OLD RELIGION

A name for Paganism, particularly as practiced in Britain and Ireland.

OSTARA (O-star-ah)

Also Eostra (YO-stra). The Sabbat observed at the Vernal Equinox, and often referred to simply as the "Spring Equinox." This Sabbat celebrates balance and life renewed, but it was not a Sabbat for the old Celts until the Saxons brought it to their attention around C.E. 600. Ostara is named for the Teutonic Goddess Eostre and is symbolized by the egg.

OTHERWORLD

A generic term for the Celtic Land of the Dead. Each Celtic culture had its own euphemisms for this place. A list of the best-known of these are given in the Passing Over Ritual in Chapter Seven.

PAGAN

Generic term for anyone who practices an earth or nature religion.

PAGAN REDE, THE

This is the basic tenet of witchcraft. "As ye harm none, do what thou will." The Rede prohibits Pagans from harming any other living thing, or from violating any one's free will. Exactly when this tenet became a conscious part of Paganism is unknown. Also see "Threefold Law" and "Law of Responsibility."

PANTHEISM

The belief in many deities who are really one because they are all merely aspects of the single creative life source. Celtic Paganism is pantheistic.

PANTHEON

The major deities in any religious system which make up the "whole" deity, or the complete power source.

PASSING OVER RITUAL

A ritual observed when a loved one has died. Depending upon one's tradition this ceremony includes keening and candle lighting, feasting and revelry, sitting up with the body, ritualized farewell speeches, drinking, and storytelling. Also see "Wake."

PENTACLE

A pentagram surrounded by a circle and carved on a circlet of wood or other natural object. The pentacle is used in some covens to represent the earth element, and is also called a "Disk" or "Shield." It can be, and often is, embellished with other carvings of significance to the witch or coven which owns it.

PENTAGRAM

The five-pointed star which has come to symbolize western Paganism. It is an ancient symbol with multiple meanings. It is always seen with its apex up. It can represent the four elements headed by the fifth element of spirit, or it can represent a human with its arms and legs spread to represent mind over matter. It can also represent the creative principle over all creation. Sometimes it is encased in a circle and then it is properly called a Pentacle. Satanic cults often take the pentagram and invert it to signify matter over spirit in much the same way that they pervert the meaning of the Christian cross. "Pentegram" is an alternative spelling.

PICTS

A small, dark people who came to Scotland and northern Ireland before 2000 B.C.E. Their artwork and metalsmithing was the basis for these crafts among the Celts.

POBEL VEAN

The Cornish name for the faery folk. The words literally mean "small people."

POLARITY

Polarity means that everything has two sides or two forces within it that are not wholly separate. For example, we can draw power from our Gods for either good or evil as these diverse powers are not contained in two separate entities, but in one.

POLYTHEISM

The belief in the existence of many unrelated deities each with their own dominion and interests who may have no spiritual or familial relationships to one another. Paganism is often erroneously characterized as polytheistic. But polytheism does not acknowledge a single source or force of creation, as most Pagans do.

PRE-CELTIC

Generally regarded, in the Celtic lands, as the time before 800 B.C.E.

RATH

A circular earthen fortress sometimes outlined with rocks. These ancient sites, found all over the Celtic lands, are sacred to the faeries and, even today, most natives of the region will not disturb them. When Shannon's huge international airport sought to expand their runways, the original plans called for destroying a neighboring rath. The workers all quit, refusing to disturb the site—no small matter in a country with thirty percent unemployment. The airport authories couldn't fight the old beliefs, and altered their plans.

REINCARNATION

A basic tenet of Paganism. The belief that the souls of human beings return to the earth plane in another human body, or even in another life-form, after death. Celtic Paganism embraces portions of this belief, only without the ideas of karma (divine justice) operating in most other cultures.

RITUAL

A systematic, formal or informal, prescribed set of rites whose purpose is to imprint a lasting change on the life and psyche of the participant. See Appendix A in this book for an outline which will help you create your own rituals.

RITUAL TOOLS

A general name for magickal or ritual tools used by a witch or magician, also sometimes called by their Kabbalistic name, Elemental Weapons.

SABBAT

Any of the eight solar festivals or observances of the Pagan year. The word is derived from the Greek word *sabatu* meaning "to rest." All Sabbats begin at sundown on the eve before the dates given for them.

SACRA

A name used for Ireland by Phoenician explorers of the sixth century.

SAMHAIN (SOW-een, SOW-in, or SAV-awn)

This is the Sabbat celebrated at what is now called Halloween, October 31. Samhain marked the beginning of winter for the Celts and was also their New Year's Day. It is a day to honor the Crone Goddess and the dying God who will be reborn at Yule. Samhain also marks the end of the harvest season.

SAMHRADH (SAV-rah or SOW-rah)

Means "summer" in Irish Gaelic, one of the two recognized Celtic seasons. It begins at Bealtaine.

SASSENACH

A Scottish and Irish word which literally means "outlander." It is used to describe anyone not familiar with the culture and customs of a particular area. Often used diversely. Over the last few centuries it has come to especially mean those from Sasana (England).

SAXON TRADITION

A Germanic tradition practiced by the people of Saxony. The Saxon path also shares some common elements with the Celtic traditions, including a veneration of trees. Their invasion of southern England brought their Pagan influence in contact with the Celts.

SCOTIA

An old name for Ireland taken from the name Scota, a Mother Goddess of the Milesians.

SCOURGE

This is a small device made from leather or hemp which resembles a whip and is used in flagellation rites within some Celtic traditions.

SEANACHAI (SHAN-uhk-ee)

Scottish and Irish word meaning "storyteller." The traveling seanachai was an integral part of the social structure of old Ireland, and was largely responsible for the survival of the oral traditions. Also see "Cyfarwydd."

SEAN GHALLS (SHAWN gawls)

Literally the "old Gaels." This is a term given by the Irish to invading peoples who remained in Ireland and whole-heartedly embraced the culture and life-style of the Celts. The term mostly applied to the Normans who came after the eleventh century. Americans might be interested to note that among the most prominent of the *sean ghall* families were the Geraldines, who later changed their name to Fitzgerald, and were the ancestors of President John Fitzgerald Kennedy.

SEPT

A term which can loosely describe either one's clan or the clan's holdings.

SHAMAN (SHAY-men)

The word Shaman comes from an extinct Ural-Altaic language called Tungus. They are the priests and medicine men of old tribal societies worldwide. Shamans (or Shamankas to use the feminine form) practiced in every known culture,

SHAMAN (cont.)

and many are still active today. In many vernaculars the native word for Shaman roughly translates into "walker between the worlds." In Celtic terms, Shamanic traditions are thought to relate to the stellar, or heavenly/planetary deities, as opposed to the deities of the earth and her functions.

SHAMROCK

Seamrog in Irish. A green, trifoliate clover which has long been one of the principal symbols of Ireland. It has been associated with the Triple Goddess. In its rare form with four leaves it represents the four elements, and is considered an extremely lucky find.

SHILLELAGH (Shuh-LAY-lee)

The magickal tool corresponding to the staff in other traditions. They are traditionally made from blackthorn wood.

SITH AND SIDHE (Shee)

Literally, "faery." Also *Daoine Sidhe* and *sidh*. This label/name is generically applied to all the faery races of Ireland and Scotland. Common names for them include The Little People, The Wee Folk, The Gentry, and Them That Prowl. The original word "sidhe" meant "peace," and Celtic faeries are sometimes euphemistically called "The People of Peace."

SKYCLAD

Ritual nudity, probably not originally a part of Celtic practice.

SNAKES

Symbols of reincarnation and renewal adopted by the Celts and featured in their traditional artwork.

SOLITARY

A Pagan who works and worships alone without the aid of a coven.

SPELL

A specific magickal ritual designed for the purpose of obtaining, banishing, or changing one particular thing or condition. See Appendix B in this book for a complete outline for constructing spells. Synonyms for making spells are Spell Weaving, Spellcraft, Casting, and Spell Spinning.

SPRING EQUINOX

See "Ostara."

STAFF

Ritual tool which corresponds to the wand or athame. A staff is usually used in many traditions from the mountainous Celtic regions because it was first a practical device for everyday living. The Welsh word for staff is *ffon* and the Scottish word is *lorg*.

SUB-CONSCIOUS MIND

That part of the mind which functions below the levels we are able to access in the course of a normal, waking day. This area stores symbolic knowledge, dreams, and the most minute details of every experience ever had by a person. This is sometimes referred to as the "Super-conscious Mind."

TALISMAN

An object which is reputed to offer protection or other magickal service to the carrier. It differs from an amulet by being constructed and charged by the witch rather than being found in nature.

TANAISTE (Taw-NAWS-tu)

A successor to an Irish king who was elected during the lifetime of his predecessor, and whose duty it was to protect the throne and its holdings.

TARA

The palace and hill named Tara in County Meath was the home of the High Kings of Ireland. A gathering place for the Druids. A spiritual center, and the seat of old Irish law. The name Tara comes from the Irish *Tea-Mur* meaning the "burial place of Tea," one of the Goddesses who co-founded Tara.

THEURGY

A word meaning the magick of union of a human being with a divine force. Invocation is an example.

THISTLE

The principal symbol of Scotland, used in much the same way as the shamrock is in Ireland.

THREE

The basic sacred number of the Celts.

THREEFOLD BLESSING, THE

A Celtic custom in which the Triple Goddess blesses the feet, womb/genital area, and head. See Chapters Six and Seven for details of the ritual.

THREEFOLD LAW, THE

The only karmic principle of Celtic Paganism. It states that any energy released by the witch or magician (or anyone else for that matter), either positive or negative, will return to the sender three times over. Also see "Pagan Rede" and "Law of Responsibility."

TIRN AILL (TEERN Eel)

Literally "Other Land." Another name for *Tir-na-nOg*.

TIR NA NOG (TEER-nah-nohk)

"Land of the Forever Young." This is the Irish Land of the Dead or, as it is usually called, The Otherworld. *Tir-na-nOg* is presided over by the crone and her cauldron to which all life returns to await rebirth.

TOCHER

A Scottish word for dowry, or marriage portion.

TORQUE (Tork)

A neck piece worn by Celts of high rank. Several have been excavated and have been found to be made of precious metals and embellished with jewels and/or intricate Celtic designs. The Irish word for torque is spelled *muince,* and the Welsh word is spelled *mwnci*—they are pronounced virtually the same.

TOUTA

A clan which was in fact a small chiefdom. This word is used in some Druidic circles in place of the term coven. It differs from a clan because those who meet regularly in a touta do not have to be related in any way.

TRADITION

The branch of Paganism followed by any individual witch or coven. There are hundreds of these traditions, most drawn along ethnic or cultural lines, but several are modern amalgamations. The word is synonymous with "Path." Example: Witta is but one tradition of Paganism.

TRANSCENDENT DEITY

A God or Goddess who is seen as dwelling outside, rather than inside, humanity. A non-invocable deity.

TRANSMIGRATION

A Druidic belief that the life essence of a living thing would pass immediately from their old vessel into a new lifeform after their physical death.

TREE CALENDAR, THE CELTIC

The system of reckoning the thirteen lunar months of the year by assigning each a sacred tree which represents the character of the month.

TRIPLE GODDESS

The one Goddess in all of her three aspects: Maiden, Mother, and Crone. This triple theme of feminine deity has been found in nearly every known culture on the planet. She is represented by the three phases of the moon; waxing, full, and waning.

TRIPLICITY

Sometimes also called a triad, trio, triune, or triple, this is a word used to indicate a divine threesome which is really one being with three faces. The primary example of such a triplicity is the Triple Goddess. Triple deities are known world wide, but the Celts have a special fondness for these triplicities and their myths contain examples of them—female and male.

TRISCALE

A Celtic symbol which was used by the Druids to represent the sacred number of three. It was a circle with three equal-spaced divisions separated with swirling lines which radiate out from the center. Also spelled "Triskele."

TUATHA DE DANANN (TOO-ah day THAY-nann, or DAWN-un, or DAY-nun)

Literally, "The People of the Goddess Dana," a divine race of people who are now some of Ireland's faery folk. They were one of the invader races of Ireland in the Irish myth cycles. The Cauldron of Abundance which holds the secrets of life and death was one of their many sacred treasures.

TUMULUS

A particular type of burial cairn which contains an underground chamber and ritual space where death rituals took place. A tumulus is also referred to as a barrow.

VIRGIN

The youngest aspect of the Triple Goddess also known as the "Maiden." She is represented by the waxing moon, and the colors white and blue. Her Sabbats are Imbolg and Ostara.

WAKE

A quintessentially Irish Passing Over ritual still used among the Irish regardless of their religious affiliations. It is believed the wake grew out of an older Irish ceremony called *fled cro-lighe,* "the feast of the death bed." Also see "Passing Over."

WAND

Another ritual tool brought in to the craft through Ceremonial Magick. A wand can symbolize either the element of air and the direction of east, or of south and fire. A wand is called a *slat* in Ireland and a *hudlath* in Wales.

WARLOCK

An antiquated term often misused in reference to a male witch. Warlock is a modern word akin to the word "sorcerer" and is generally not used in modern Paganism. Some male Pagans even find the term offensive.

WHEEL OF THE YEAR, THE

A conceptualization of the eternal cycle of time. In Pagan mythology the Goddess turns the Wheel of the Year bringing everything to its season. The Wheel of the Year is symbolized by either a wreath, a ring, a snake holding its tail in its mouth, or an eight-spoked wheel.

WIDDERSHINS

This word is from the Teutonic Tradition. It means to go backwards, and is the act of moving, working, or dancing counter-clockwise in order to banish, diminish or counter some negative force.

WITCH

Usually a label reserved for Pagans of the Anglo-Celtic, Celtic, and Southern Teutonic traditions.

YULE

Sabbat celebrated at the Winter Solstice. Most of its traditions come from the Roman Pagan holiday, Saturnalia. The Norse and Teutonic traditions held this as one of their most important Sabbats, and it was their New Year's Day, a celebration of the return of the Sun God to the earth. It was not a Sabbat in Celtic lands until the Norse invasion.

AND RECOMMENDED READING

*Books are not absolutely dead things, but do contain a potency of life
in them to be as active as that soul whose progeny they are; nay they
do preserve as in a vial the purest efficacy and extraction
of that living intellect that bred them.*

—John Milton

Adler, Margot. *Drawing Down the Moon* (Revised and expanded edition). Boston: Beacon Press, 1986.

Ashe, Geoffrey. *The Discovery of King Arthur.* New York: H. Holt, 1987.

_____. *Mythology of the British Isles.* North Pomfret, VT: Trafalgar Square Publishers, 1990.

Bain, Robert. *The Clans and Tartans of Scotland.* Glasgow: Collins Press, 1976.

Baxter, Sylvester. *The Legend of the Holy Grail.* Boston: Curtis and Cameron, 1904.

Bettelheim, Bruno. *The Uses of Enchantment: The Meaning and Importance of Fairy Tales.* New York: Vintage Books, 1977.

Blamries, Steve. *The Irish Celtic Magical Tradition.* London: The Aquarian Press, 1992.

Bonwick, James. *Irish Druids and Old Irish Religions.* New York: Dorset Press, 1986 (originally published in 1894).

Brennan, J. H. *Astral Doorways.* Bungay, Suffolk, England: The Aquarian Press, 1986.

Brooke, Stopford A. and T. W. Rolleston, eds. *A Treasury of Irish Poetry.* New York: The Macmillan Co., 1932.

Buchanan, Norman. *101 Scottish Songs.* Glasgow: Collins Press, 1967.

Buckland, Raymond. *Scottish Witchcraft.* St. Paul, MN: Llewellyn Publications, 1991.

Burchenal, Elizabeth. *Folk-Dances From Old Homelands.* New York: G. Schirmer, 1922.

_____. *Rinnce na Eirann (National Dances of Ireland).* New York: A.S. Barnes and Co., 1924.

Burt, Kathleen. *Archetypes of the Zodiac.* St. Paul, MN: Llewellyn Publications, 1988.

Caldecott, Moyra. *Women in Celtic Myth.* London: Arrow Books, 1988.

Campanelli, Pauline. *Ancient Ways.* St. Paul, MN: Llewellyn Publications, 1991.

_____. *Wheel of the Year.* St. Paul, MN: Llewellyn Publications, 1989.

Campbell, Joseph. *The Flight of the Wild Gander: Explorations in the Mythological Dimensions of Fairy Tales, Legends, and Symbols.* San Francisco: HarperCollins, 1990 (first published in 1951).

_____. *The Hero With A Thousand Faces.* Princeton, NJ: Princeton University Press, 1973.

_____. *The Masks of God: Primitive Mythology.* New York: Viking Press, 1959.

_____. *The Mythic Image.* Princeton, NJ: Princeton University Press, 1974.

Campbell, Joseph F. *Popular Tales of the West Highlands.* Aldershot, England: Wildwood House Press, 1983.

Carmichael, Alexander. *Carmina Gadelica (Vols. I and II).* Edinburgh: Oliver and Boyd, 1928.

Clifton, Chas S. *Witchcraft Today, Book Two.* St. Paul, MN: Llewellyn Publications, 1993.

Cole, William, ed. *Folk Songs of England, Ireland, Scotland and Wales.* New York: Cornerstone Library, 1969.

Colum, Padriac, ed. *An Anthology of Irish Verse.* New York: Liveright Publishing Corp. (second edition), 1948.

_____. *A Treasury of Irish Folklore.* New York: Bonanza Books (a division of Crown Publishers, Inc), 1967.

Condren, Mary. *The Serpent and the Goddess: Women, Religion and Power in Celtic Ireland.* San Francisco: Harper and Row, 1989.

Cowan, Tom. *Fire in the Head: Shamanism and the Celtic Spirit.* San Francisco: HarperCollins, 1992.

Crossley-Holland, Kevin, ed. *Folk Tales of the British Isles.* New York: Pantheon Books, 1985.

Crowley, Aleister. *777.* York Beach, ME: Samuel Weiser (revised edition), 1986.

Curtain, Jeremiah. *Myths and Folk-lore of Ireland.* New York: Weathervane Books, 1965 (originally published in 1890).

Cunningham, Scott. *The Complete Book of Incense, Oils, and Brews.* St. Paul, MN: Llewellyn Publications, 1989.

_____. *Crystal, Gem and Metal Magic.* St. Paul, MN: Llewellyn Publications, 1988.

_____. *Cunningham's Encyclopedia of Magical Herbs.* St. Paul, MN: Llewellyn Publications, 1986.

_____. *Living Wicca: A Further Guide For the Solitary Practitioner.* St. Paul, MN: Llewellyn Publications, 1993.

_____. *Wicca: A Guide For the Solitary Practitioner.* St. Paul, MN: Llewellyn Publications, 1988.

Davidson, H. R. Ellis. *Myths and Symbols in Pagan Europe.* Syracuse, NY: Syracuse University Press, 1988.

Davis, Courtney. *Celtic Designs and Motifs.* New York: Dover Publications, Inc., 1991.

Delaney, Frank. *Legends of the Celts.* New York: Sterling Publishing Co., 1991.

Dillon, Myles. *Cycles of the Irish Kings.* Oxford: Oxford University Press, 1946.

_____. *Early Irish Literature.* Chicago: The University of Chicago Press, 1972.

Dillon, Myles and N. Chadwick. *The Celtic Realms.* New York: Weidenfeld and Nicolson, 1976.

DuMaurier, Daphne. *Vanishing Cornwall.* Garden City, NY: Doubleday, 1967.

Ellis, Peter Berresford. *Dictionary of Celtic Mythology.* Santa Barbara, CA: ABC-CLIO, Inc., 1992.

Ericson, Lois. *Ethnic Costumes.* New York: Van Nostrand Publications, 1979.

Evans-Wentz, W. Y. *The Fairy Faith in Celtic Countries.* New York: University Books, 1966 (first published in 1911).

Farrar, Janet and Stewart. *Eight Sabbats for Witches.* Custer, WA: Phoenix Publishing, Inc., 1981.

_____. *The Witches' God.* Custer, WA: Phoenix Publishing, Inc., 1989.

_____. *The Witches' Goddess.* Custer, WA: Phoenix Publishing, Inc., 1987.

Finneran, Richard J., ed. *The Poems of William Butler Yeats.* New York: Macmillan Publishing Co., 1983.

Flower, Robin. *The Irish Tradition.* Oxford and New York: Oxford University Press, 1947.

Fox, Lady Aileen M. H. *Southwest England.* New York Praeger, 1964.

Frazer, Sir James. *The Golden Bough (abridged edition).* New York: Macmillian, 1956 (first published in 1890 in twelve volumes).

Gimbutas, Marija. *Goddesses and Gods of Old Europe.* Berkeley: University of California Press, 1982.

Glass-Koentop, Pattalee. *Year of Moons, Season of Trees.* St. Paul, MN: Llewellyn Publications, 1991.

Glassie, Henry, ed. *Irish Folk Tales.* New York: Pantheon Books, 1985.

Graves, Robert. *The White Goddess.* New York: Farrar, Straus and Giroux, 1973 (first published 1953).

Gray, William G. *Evoking the Primal Goddess.* St. Paul, MN: Llewellyn Publications, 1989.

Green, Miranda J. *Dictionary of Celtic Myth and Legend.* London: Thames and Hudson, Ltd., 1992.

Greenwich House Press. *Irish Blessings.* New York: Arlington House, Inc., 1983.

Guest, Lady Charlotte. *The Mabinogion.* London: Alfred Nutt, 1904.

Haire, Francis H. *The Folk Costume Book.* New York: A.S. Barnes and Co., 1934.

Harrold, Robert. *Folk Costumes of the World in Colour.* London: Blandford Press, 1978.

Hazlitt, W. Carew. *Faiths and Folklore of the British Isles (Volumes I and II).* New York: Benjamin Blom, 1965.

Henry, Mellinger Edward. *Folk-Songs From the Southern Highlands.* New York: J.J. Augustin, 1938.

Herm, Gerhard. *The Celts.* New York: St. Martin's Press, 1975.

Hoagland, Kathleen. *1000 Years of Irish Verse.* New York: The Devin-Adair Company, 1947.

Hubert, Henri. *The Rise of the Celts.* New York: Bilbo and Tannen, 1966 (originally published in France in 1934).

Hughes, Russell M. *Total Education in Ethnic Dance.* New York: M. Dekker, 1977 (originally published 1928).

Hull, R. F. C., ed. *The Portable Jung.* (Selections from his works with notes and other material added by mythologist Joseph Campbell.) New York: The Viking Press, 1971.

Hunt, Robert. *Cornish Folk-Lore.* Penryn, Cornwall: Tor Mark Press, 1988.

_____. *Cornish Legends.* Penryn, Cornwall: Tor Mark Press, 1990.

Jung, Carl G. *Man and His Symbols.* New York: Doubleday, 1964.

K'Eogh, John. *An Irish Herbal.* Suffolk, England: Aquarian Press, 1986.

Kinsella, Thomas. *The Tain*. Oxford: Oxford University Press, 1986.

Larmine, William. *West Irish Folk-Tales and Romances*. Totowa, NJ: Rowman and Littlefield, 1973 (originally published in London, 1893).

Larrington, Carolyne, ed. *The Feminist Companion to Mythology*. Hammersmith, London: Pandora Press, 1992.

Lehner, Ernst and Johanna. *Picture Book of Devils, Demons and Witchcraft*. New York: Dover Publications, Inc., 1971.

Leodhas, Sorche. *A Scottish Songbook*. New York: Holt, Rinehart, and Winston, 1969.

Lewis, Ralph M. *Behold the Sign: Ancient Symbolism*. San Jose, CA: Publishing Department of the Supreme Grand Lodge of AMORC (12th edition, 2nd printing), 1987 (originally published in 1944).

Lincoln, Bruce. *Priests, Warriors, Cattle*. Berkeley, CA: The University of California Press, 1981.

Lindsay, Joyce and Maurice. *The Scottish Quotation Book*. New York: Barnes and Noble, 1991.

Littleton, Scott C. *The New Comparative Mythology*. Berkeley, CA: The University of California Press, 1982.

Longstaff, John M. *Hi! Ho! The Rattlin' Bog and Other Folk Songs of Britain*. New York: Harcourt, Brace, and World, 1969.

Loomis, Roger Sherman. *The Grail: From Celtic Myth to Christian Symbol*. Princeton, NJ: Princeton University Press, 1991.

Ludzia, Leo F. *The Space/Time Connection*. St. Paul, MN: Llewellyn Publications, 1989.

MacCrossan, Tadhg. *The Sacred Cauldron: Secrets of the Druids*. St. Paul, MN: Llewellyn Publications, 1991.

MacCulloch, John A. *The Celtic and Scandinavian Religions*. London/New York: Hutchinson's University Library, 1948.

MacKenzie, D.A. *Scottish Folk Lore and Folk Life*. Edinburgh: Blackie and Sons, 1935.

MacLean, Adam. *The Triple Goddess*. Grand Rapids, MI: Phanes Press, 1989.

MacManus, Seumas. *The Story of the Irish Race*. (44th printing) Old Greenwich, CT: The Devin-Adair Company, 1992 (originally published in 1921).

Malory, Sir Thomas. *Le Morte D'Arthur*. New York: Collier Books, 1982.

Markale, Jean. *Celtic Civilization* (translation of *Les Celtes et la Civilisation Celtique*). London: Gordon and Cremonesi, 1978 .

_____. *Women of the Celts* (translation of *La Femme Celts*). Rochester, VT: Inner Traditions International, Ltd., 1972.

Matthews, Caitlin. *Arthur and the Sovereignty of Britain*. London: Arkana, 1989.

_____. *The Elements of the Celtic Tradition*. Longmeade, Shaftsbury, Dorset: Element Books, 1989.

_____. *The Elements of the Goddess*. Longmeade, Shaftsbury, Dorset: Element Books, 1989.

_____. *Mabon and the Mysteries of Britain*. London: Arkana, 1987.

Matthews, Caitlin, and Prudence Jones, eds. *Voices From the Circle: The Heritage of Western Paganism*. Wellingtonborough, Northamptonshire: The Aquarian Press, 1990.

Matthews, John. *The Elements of the Arthurian Tradition.* Longmeade, Shaftsbury, Dorset: Element Books, 1989.

_____. *The Glastonbury Reader: Selections From the Myths, Legends and Stories of Ancient Avalon.* Hammersmith, London: The Aquarian Press, 1991.

_____. *Hallowquest.* Longmeade, Shaftsbury, Dorset: Element Books, 1990.

_____. *Taliesin: Shamanism and the Bardic Mysteries in Britain and Ireland.* London: The Aquarian Press, 1991.

Matthews, John and Caitlin. *Ladies of the Lake.* Hammersmith, London: The Aquarian Press, 1992.

McAnally, D. R. *Irish Wonders.* New York: Sterling Publishing Co., Inc., 1993 (originally published in 1888).

McCoy, Edain. *The Sabbats: A New Approach to Living the Old Ways.* St. Paul, MN: Llewellyn Publications, 1995.

_____. *A Witch's Guide to Faery Folk.* St. Paul, MN: Llewellyn Publications, 1994.

_____. *Witta: An Irish Pagan Tradition.* St. Paul, MN: Llewellyn Publications, 1993.

Monaghan, Patricia. *The Book of Goddesses and Heroines.* St. Paul, MN: Llewellyn Publications, 1990.

Monroe, Douglas. *The 21 Lessons of Merlyn.* St. Paul, MN: Llewellyn Publications, 1992.

O'Faolain, Eileen. *Irish Sagas and Folk Tales.* Dublin: Poolbeg Press, Ltd., 1993.

O'Suilleabhain, Michael, ed. *The Roche Collection of Traditional Irish Music.* Cork, Ireland: Ossian Publications, 1982. (Distributed in the United States by Music Sales Corporation of New York.)

Parry-Jones, D. Welsh *Legends and Fairy Lore.* New York: Barnes and Noble Books, 1992.

Pearce, Mallory. *Celtic Borders.* New York: Dover Publications, Inc., 1990.

_____. *Decorative Celtic Alphabets.* New York: Dover Publications, Inc., 1992.

Porter, Jane. *The Scottish Chiefs.* New York: Charles Scribner's and Sons, 1956 (originally published 1921).

Price, Christine. *Widdecome Fair (Folk Songs of Britain).* New York: F. Warne, Co., 1968.

Rees, Alwyn and Brinley Rees. *Celtic Heritage: Ancient Tradition in Ireland and Wales.* New York: Thames and Hudson, 1961.

Reilly, Robert T. *Irish Saints.* New York: Avenel Books, 1964.

Rhys, Grace Little. *A Celtic Anthology.* New York: Thomas Y. Crowell Co., 1927.

Rhys, Sir John. *Celtic Folklore: Welsh and Manx (Volume 2).* Oxford: Clarendon Press, 1901.

Richardson, Alan. *Earth God Rising: The Return of the Male Mysteries.* St. Paul, MN: Llewellyn Publications, 1992.

Ritchie, James N. Graham. *Scotland: Archaeology and Early History.* London: Thames and Hudson, 1981.

Rolleston. T. W. *Celtic Myths and Legends.* New York: Avenel Books, 1986.

Ross, Anne. *Everyday Life of the Pagan Celts.* New York: G.P. Putman's Sons, 1970.

Rutherford, Ward. *Celtic Lore: A History of the Druids and Their Timeless Traditions.* Hammersmith, London: Thorson/Aquarian, 1993.

Sabrina, Lady. *Reclaiming the Power.* St. Paul, MN: Llewellyn Publications, 1992.

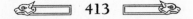

Sargent, Helen Child and Geroge Lyman Kettredge, eds. *English and Scottish Popular Ballads.* Boston: Houghton Mifflin Co., 1932 (originally published in 1904).

Sheppard-Jones, Elisabeth. *Scottish Legendary Tales.* Edinburgh: Thomas Nelson and Sons, Ltd., 1962.

_____. *Welsh Legendary Tales.* Edinburgh: Thomas Nelson and Sons, Ltd., 1959.

Sibbett, Ed, Jr. *Celtic Design.* New York: Dover Publications, Inc., 1979.

Spence, Lewis. *Legends and Romances of Brittany.* London: Frederick A. Stokes Co., 1917.

_____. *The Magic Arts in Celtic Britain.* New York: Dorset Press, 1992 (reprint of an earlier edition, original publication date not given).

Squire, Charles. *Celtic Myth and Legend, Poetry and Romance.* New York: Bell Publishing Co., 1979 (originally published in 1905 as *The Mythology of the British Islands*).

Stewart, Mary. *The Crystal Cave.* Boston: G.K. Hall, 1982.

_____. *The Hollow Hills.* New York: Ballantine Books, 1983.

Stewart, R. J. *Celtic Gods, Celtic Goddesses.* London: Blandford, 1990.

_____. *The Underworld Initiation.* Wellingtonborough: The Aquarian Press, 1988.

Sutton, Ann. *Tartans: Their Art and History.* New York: Arco Publishing, 1984.

Swinson, Cyril. *Twenty Scottish Tales and Legends.* London: Adam and Charles Black, 1940.

Thorsson, Edred. *The Book of Ogham.* St. Paul, MN: Llewellyn Publications, 1992.

Tyson, Donald. *Ritual Magic.* St. Paul, MN: Llewellyn Publications, 1992.

Walker, Barbara G. *The Crone: Woman of Age, Wisdom, and Power.* San Francisco: HarperCollins, 1985.

Weston, John C., ed. *Robert Burns Selections.* New York: The Bobbs-Merrill Company, Inc., 1967.

White, T. H. *The Once and Future King.* New York: Berkley Publishing Corp. (seventeenth printing), 1966.

Whitmont, Edward C. *The Symbolic Quest.* New York: G.P. Putnam's Sons (for the C.G. Jung Foundation for Analytical Psychology), 1969.

Wilcox, Ruth Turner. *Folk and Festival Costume.* New York: Charles Scribner and Sons, 1965 (reprint of much older edition, date not given).

Wilde, Lady. *Ancient Cures, Charms and Usages of Ireland.* Detroit: Singing Tree Press, 1970 (first published in 1890 by Ward and Downey Ltd. of London).

Williams, Gwyn, ed. *Presenting Welsh Poetry.* Miami, FL: Granger Books, 1976.

Wilson, Barbara Ker. *Scottish Folk-Tales and Legends.* London: Oxford University Press, 1954.

Wilson, Eva. *Early Medieval Designs From Britain.* New York: Dover Publications, Inc., 1983.

Winston, Henry L. *Old English Melodies.* London: Boosey and Hawkes, 1899.

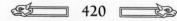

☽ REACH FOR THE MOON

Llewellyn publishes hundreds of books on your favorite subjects! To get these exciting books, including the ones on the following pages, check your local bookstore or order them directly from Llewellyn.

ORDER BY PHONE

- Call toll-free within the U.S. and Canada, 1-800-THE MOON
- In Minnesota, call (651) 291-1970
- We accept VISA, MasterCard, and American Express

ORDER BY MAIL

- Send the full price of your order (MN residents add 7% sales tax) in U.S. funds, plus postage & handling to:

  Llewellyn Worldwide
  P.O. Box 64383, Dept. K661-0
  St. Paul, MN 55164–0383, U.S.A.

POSTAGE & HANDLING

(For the U.S., Canada, and Mexico)

- $4.00 for orders $15.00 and under
- $5.00 for orders over $15.00
- No charge for orders over $100.00

We ship UPS in the continental United States. We ship standard mail to P.O. boxes. Orders shipped to Alaska, Hawaii, The Virgin Islands, and Puerto Rico are sent first-class mail. Orders shipped to Canada and Mexico are sent surface mail.

International orders: Airmail—add freight equal to price of each book to the total price of order, plus $5.00 for each non-book item (audio tapes, etc.).

Surface mail—Add $1.00 per item.

Allow 2 weeks for delivery on all orders.
Postage and handling rates subject to change.

DISCOUNTS

We offer a 20% discount to group leaders or agents. You must order a minimum of 5 copies of the same book to get our special quantity price.

FREE CATALOG

Get a free copy of our color catalog, *New Worlds of Mind and Spirit*. Subscribe for just $10.00 in the United States and Canada ($30.00 overseas, airmail). Many bookstores carry *New Worlds*—ask for it!

Visit our web site at www.llewellyn.com for more information.

MOON MAGICK

Myth & Magic, Crafts & Recipes,
Rituals & Spells
D.J. Conway

No creature on this planet is unaffected by the power of the Moon. Its effects range from making us feel energetic or adventurous to tense and despondent. By putting excess Moon energy to work for you, you can learn to plan projects, work and travel at the optimum times.

Moon Magick explains how each of the 13 lunar months is directly connected with a different type of seasonal energy flow and provides modern rituals and spells for tapping this energy and celebrating the Moon phases. Each chapter describes new Pagan rituals—79 in all— related to that particular Moon, plus related Moon lore, ancient holidays, spells, meditations and suggestions for foods, drinks and decorations to accompany your Moon rituals. This book includes two thorough dictionaries of Moon deities and symbols.

By moving through the year according to the 13 lunar months, you can become more attuned to the seasons, the Earth and your inner self. *Moon Magick* will show you how to let your life flow with the power and rhythms of the Moon to benefit your physical, emotional and spiritual well-being.

1-56718-167-8, 320 pp., 7 x 10, illus., softcover. $14.95

ANCIENT WAYS

Reclaiming the Pagan Tradition
Pauline Campanelli,
illus. by Dan Campanelli

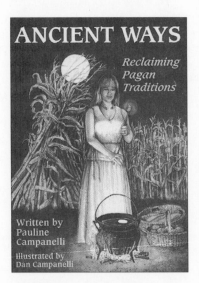

Ancient Ways is filled with magick and ritual that you can perform every day to capture the spirit of the seasons. It focuses on the celebration of the Sabbats of the Old Religion by giving you practical things to do while anticipating the sabbat rites, and helping you harness the magical energy for weeks afterward. The wealth of seasonal rituals and charms are drawn from ancient sources but are easily performed with available materials.

Learn how to look into previous lives at Yule…at Beltane, discover the places where you are most likely to see faeries…make special jewelry to wear for Lammas Celebra-tions…paint a charm of protection at Mid-summer for special animals in your life.

0-87542-090-7, 256 pp., 7 x 10, illus., softcover $14.95

CELTIC FOLKLORE COOKING

Joanne Asala

Celtic cooking is simple and tasty, reflecting the quality of its ingredients: fresh meat and seafood, rich milk and cream, fruit, vegetables, and wholesome bread. Much of the folklore, proverbs, songs and legends of the Celtic nations revolve around this wonderful variety of food and drink. Now you can feast upon these delectable stories as you sample more than 200 tempting dishes with *Celtic Folklore Cooking*.

In her travels to Ireland, Wales and Scotland, Joanne Asala found that many people still cook in the traditional manner, passing recipes from generation to generation. Now you can serve the same dishes discovered in hotels, bed and breakfasts, restaurants and family kitchens. At the same time, you can relish in the colorful proverbs, songs and stories that are still heard at pubs and local festivals and that complement each recipe.

1-56718-044-2, 264 pp., 7 x 10, illus., softcover **$16.95**

BY OAK, ASH & THORN

Modern Celtic Shamanism

D. J. Conway

Many spiritual seekers are interested in shamanism because it is a spiritual path that can be followed in conjunction with any religion or other spiritual belief without conflict. Shamanism has not only been practiced by Native American and African cultures—for centuries, it was practiced by the Europeans, including the Celts.

By Oak, Ash and Thorn presents a workable, modern form of Celtic shamanism that will help anyone raise his or her spiritual awareness. Here, in simple, practical terms, you will learn to follow specific exercises and apply techniques that will develop your spiritual awareness and ties with the natural world: shape-shifting, divination by the Celtic Ogham alphabet, Celtic shamanic tools, traveling to and using magick in the three realms of the Celtic otherworlds, empowering the self, journeying through meditation and more.

Shamanism begins as a personal revelation and inner healing, then evolves into a striving to bring balance and healing into the Earth itself. This book will ensure that Celtic shamanism will take its place among the spiritual practices that help us lead fuller lives.

1-56718-166-X, 320 pp., 6 x 9, illus., softcover **$14.95**

CELTIC MAGIC

D. J. Conway

Many people, not all of Irish descent, have a great interest in the ancient Celts and the Celtic pantheon, and *Celtic Magic* is the map they need for exploring this ancient and fascinating magical culture.

 Celtic Magic is for the reader who is either a beginner or intermediate in the field of magic. It provides an extensive "how-to" of practical spell-working. There are many books on the market dealing with the Celts and their beliefs, but none guide the reader to a practical application of magical knowledge for use in everyday life. There is also an in-depth discussion of Celtic deities and the Celtic way of life and worship, so that an intermediate practitioner can expand upon the spellwork to build a series of magical rituals. Presented in an easy-to-understand format, Celtic Magic is for anyone searching for new spells that can be worked immediately, without elaborate or rare materials, and with minimal time and preparation.

0-87542-136-9, 240 pp., mass market, illus., softcover **$4.99**

THE HANDBOOK OF CELTIC ASTROLOGY

The 13-Sign Lunar Zodiac of the Ancient Druids
Helena Paterson

Discover your lunar self with *The Handbook of Celtic Astrology!* Solar-oriented astrology has dominated Western astrological thought for centuries, but lunar-based Celtic astrology provides the "Yin" principle that has been neglected in the West—and author Helena Paterson presents new concepts based on ancient Druidic observations, lore and traditions that will redefine Western astrology.

 This reference work will take you through the Celtic lunar zodiac, where each lunar month is associated with one of the thirteen trees sacred to the Druids: birch, rowan, ash, alder, willow, hawthorn, oak, holly, hazel, vine, ivy, reed, and elder. Chapters on each "tree sign" provide comprehensive text on Celtic mythology and gods and goddesses associated with the sign's ruling tree and planet; general characteristics of natives of the sign; and interpretive notes on the locations of the planets, the Moon, the ascendant and Midheaven as they are placed in any of the three decans of each tree sign. A thorough introduction on chart construction, sign division and the importance of solstices, equinoxes, eclipses and aspects to the Moon guarantees this book will become the definitive work on Celtic astrology.

1-56718-509-6, 288 pp., 7 x 10, illus., softcover **$15.00**

CELTIC WOMEN'S SPIRITUALITY

Accessing the Cauldron of Life
Edain McCoy

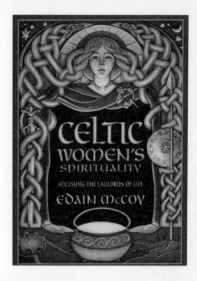

Every year, more and more women turn away from orthodox religions, searching for an image of the divine that is more like themselves—feminine, strong and compelling. Likewise, each year the ranks of the Pagan religions swell, with a great many of these newcomers attracted to Celtic traditions.

The Celts provide some of the strongest, most archetypally accessible images of strong women onto which you can focus your spiritual impulses. Warriors and queens, mothers and crones, sovereigns and shapeshifters all have important lessons to teach us about ourselves and the universe.

This book shows how you can successfully create a personalized pathway linking two important aspects of the self—the feminine and the hereditary (or adopted) Celtic—and as a result become a whole, powerful woman, awake to the new realities previously untapped by your subconscious mind.

1-56718-672-6, 7 x 10, 352 pp., illus. $16.95

LIVING WICCA

A Further Guide for the Solitary Practitioner
Scott Cunningham

Living Wicca is the long-awaited sequel to Scott Cunningham's wildly successful *Wicca: a Guide for the Solitary Practitioner*. This new book is for those who have made the conscious decision to bring their Wiccan spirituality into their everyday lives. It provides solitary practitioners with the tools and added insights that will enable them to blaze their own spiritual paths—to become their own high priests and priestesses.

Living Wicca takes a philosophical look at the questions, practices, and differences within Witchcraft. It covers the various tools of learning available to the practitioner, the importance of secrecy in one's practice, guidelines to performing ritual when ill, magical names, initiation, and the Mysteries. It discusses the benefits of daily prayer and meditation, making offerings to the gods, how to develop a prayerful attitude, and how to perform Wiccan rites when away from home or in emergency situations.

Unlike any other book on the subject, *Living Wicca* is a step-by-step guide to creating your own Wiccan tradition and personal vision of the gods, designing your personal ritual and symbols, developing your own book of shadows, and truly living your Craft.

0-87542-184-9, 208 pp., 6 x 9, illus., softcover. $12.95

To order, call 1–800–THE MOON
Prices subject to change without notice

THE SABBATS

A New Approach to Living the Old Ways
Edain McCoy

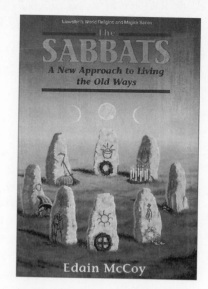

The Sabbats offers many fresh, exciting ways to deepen your connection to the turning of the Wheel of the Year. This tremendously practical guide to Pagan solar festivals does more than teach you about the "old ways"—you will learn workable ideas for combining old customs with new expressions of those beliefs that will be congruent with your lifestyle and tradition.

The Sabbats begins with background on Paganism (tenets, teachings, and tools) and origins of the eight Sabbats, followed by comprehensive chapters on each Sabbat. These pages are full of ideas for inexpensive seasonal parties in which Pagans and non-Pagans alike can participate, as well as numerous craft ideas and recipes to enrich your celebrations. The last section provides 16 complete texts of Sabbat rituals—for both covens and solitaries—with detailed guidelines for adapting rituals to specific traditions or individual tastes. Includes an extensive reference section with a resources guide, bibliography, musical scores for rituals, and more.

1-56718-663-7, 320 pp., 7 x 10, illus., photos, softcover **$17.95**

THE COMPLETE BOOK OF INCENSE, OILS AND BREWS

Scott Cunningham

For centuries the composition of incenses, the blending of oils, and the mixing of herbs have been used by people to create positive changes in their lives. With this book, the curtains of secrecy have been drawn back, providing you with practical, easy-to-understand information that will allow you to practice these methods of magical cookery.

Scott Cunningham, world-famous expert on magical herbalism, first published *The Magic of Incense, Oils and Brews* in 1986. *The Complete Book of Incense, Oils and Brews* is a revised and expanded version of that book. Scott took readers' suggestions from the first edition and added more than 100 new formulas. Every page has been clarified and rewritten, and new chapters have been added.

There is no special, costly equipment to buy, and ingredients are usually easy to find. The book includes detailed information on a wide variety of herbs, sources for purchasing ingredients, substitutions for hard-to-find herbs, a glossary, and a chapter on creating your own magical recipes.

0-87542-128-8, 288 pp., 6 x 9, illus., softcover **$12.95**

To order, call 1–800–THE MOON
Prices subject to change without notice

A WITCH'S GUIDE TO FAERY FOLK

Reclaiming Our Working Relationship
with Invisible Helpers
Edain McCoy

All over the world, from time immemorial, people have reported encounters with a race of tiny people who are neither human nor deity, who live both inside and outside of the solid human world. Now, for the first time, a book reclaims that lost, rich heritage of working with faery folk that our Pagan ancestors took as a matter of course. Learn to work with and worship with faeries in a mutually beneficial way. Practice rituals and spells in which faeries can participate, and discover tips to help facilitate faery contact.

Even among believers in faeries, the active role of these astral-world creatures in ritual and magical workings has been virtually eliminated. This book discusses the existence of the astral plane, the personality of various faery types and faery mythology. It even teaches you how to create your own thought-form faery beings.

Whether you are a Pagan or simply wish to venerate nature and commune with these creatures of the wild, *A Witch's Guide to Faery Folk* is an invaluable aid in this exciting exploration.

0-87542-733-2, 336 pp., 6 x 9, 60 illus., 17 photos, softcover. \$14.95

WITTA

An Irish Pagan Tradition
Edain McCoy

The beauty and simplicity which is paganism may never be more evident than in *Witta*. The Old Religion of Ireland was born of simplicity, of a people who loved their rugged, green Earth Mother and sought to worship her through the resources she provided. *Witta* prescribes no elaborate tools, ritual dress, or rigid and intimidating initiation rites. The magick and the ritual words come, as they did thousands of years ago, from within the heart of the practitioner.

Until now, no practical guide has presented Irish paganism as a religious system within the framework of its history. In *Witta*, you will learn who and what influenced the Wittan religion as we know it today. You will discover the mythology that shaped their deities and learn about the Sabbats which honor them. See how the Druids bridged the gap between the old ways and the new, and understand the inherent power of homespun spellcrafting. Learn about the Celtic Tree system and how the trees relate to magickal practice. Plus, learn how to construct your own rituals in accordance with Wittan tradition.

0-87542-732-4, 288 pp., 6 x 9, illus., softcover. \$12.95

To order, call 1–800–THE MOON
Prices subject to change without notice